MASTERING™
WORD 97

MASTERING
WORD 97
FOURTH EDITION

Ron Mansfield

SYBEX

San Francisco • Paris • Düsseldorf • Soest

Associate Publisher: Amy Romanoff
Acquisitions Manager: Kristine Plachy
Acquisitions & Developmental Editor: Sherry Schmitt
Editor: Pat Coleman
Project Editor: Lee Ann Pickrell
Technical Editor: Elizabeth Shannon
Book Designers: Patrick Dintino, Catalin Dulfu
Graphic Illustrator: Inbar Berman
Desktop Publisher: Susan Glinert Stevens
Production Coordinator: Alexa Riggs
Indexer: Matthew Spence
Cover Designer: Design Site
Cover Photographer: Mark Johann

Screen reproductions produced with Collage Plus and
Collage Complete.

Collage Plus and Collage Complete are trademarks of
Inner Media Inc.

SYBEX is a registered trademark of SYBEX Inc.
Mastering is a trademark of SYBEX Inc.

TRADEMARKS: SYBEX has attempted throughout this book to
distinguish proprietary trademarks from descriptive terms by
following the capitalization style used by the manufacturer.

The author and publisher have made their best efforts to prepare
this book, and the content is based upon final release software
whenever possible. Portions of the manuscript may be based
upon pre-release versions supplied by software manufacturer(s).
The author and the publisher make no representation or warran-
ties of any kind with regard to the completeness or accuracy of
the contents herein and accept no liability of any kind including
but not limited to performance, merchantability, fitness for any
particular purpose, or any losses or damages of any kind caused
or alleged to be caused directly or indirectly from this book.

Library of Congress Card Number: 96-70745
ISBN: 0-7821-1926-3

Manufactured in the United States of America

10 9 8 7 6 5 4 3 2 1

To John and Shannon Tullius, founders of the Maui Writers Conference A portion of the royalties from this book will be donated to the Maui Writers Foundation.

ACKNOWLEDGMENTS

It has been fun to watch this book evolve over the years. The best part has been getting to work with so many talented people. In this edition, more people than ever contributed improvements. I'd like to especially thank Kristine Plachy and Sherry Schmitt for guiding us all through the "developmental" phase of this major rewrite, along with Robin Merrin for her work on Part I, Claudia Willen for her revisions of Parts II and III, Alan Neibauer and Tarin Towers for help with Part VI, Asha Dornfest for that all new Part VII about Word and the Web, and Sheila Dienes for revising the Master's Reference. Thanks to one and all.

Getting a book on the store shelf at about the same time as the software ships requires either a time machine or a truly dedicated staff of editorial and production folk. At Sybex, it's *people* who make the impossible happen, not a machine. There are far too many folks to list here, but you all know who you are. Take a break. You've earned it.

Finally, I want to thank the many book distributors and booksellers who continue to stock my books. I know the shelves are crowded, and I appreciate the space. But most of all, I want to thank all of you readers who keep coming back for edition after edition. Thanks also for telling your friends, and please keep in touch!

Ron Mansfield
rmansfield@aol.com

Contents at a Glance

Table of Contents

INTRODUCTION

Word 97 is a significant upgrade to an already massive program. More and better templates and Wizards have been added, along with great features, such as improved online help (including little animated "help agents" who pop up on your screen with tips and suggestions) and truly amazing, on-the-fly grammar checking. Tables are easier to create and edit now. The Internet is almost fully integrated. (For example, if you type a URL, such as http//www.sybex.com, in a Word document, Word automatically formats it and converts it into a hyperlink!) You can even use Word 97 to create and edit your own Web pages. Graphics tools are now better integrated and easier to use.

Whether you are a seasoned Word user or a first-timer, this book is for you. If you're already familiar with Word's functionality, you'll find plenty of tips to help you streamline your work. We've highlighted features new to Word 97 so you can quickly see what has changed and how. New Word users will appreciate the many tutorials, each carefully designed to illustrate a particular feature or skill in Word. In addition, there are tips to turn you into a competent Word wonk quickly and warnings to keep you from making "rookie" mistakes.

Any product with so many features can be a little intimidating at first. But mastering Word is a bit like playing chess or the piano—you can spend the rest of your life learning new tricks and techniques.

What You Need for the Practice Exercises

If you haven't already installed Word 97, see the Appendix, *Installing Word*.

I'm assuming that you have used Windows at least briefly and that you know how to click, drag, select text, and make menu choices. The first part of the book *reviews* these concepts, but you might want to keep your Windows manuals within reach if you are just getting started.

If you want to practice saving work to floppies, find a spare diskette before you settle down to work. Let's do it!

Where to Go from Here

The book's organization is fairly straightforward, except for a detour to the appendix. Here's an overview of each section.

Part I: Getting Started

Part I helps you dive right in. Sit at a computer when you read it. You'll soon be creating, saving, and printing impressive documents, beginner or not. Word offers a number of ways to view and move through your documents. Part I will introduce you to these time-saving techniques. Chapter 1 shows you how to create and save documents; so you might want to use it as a jumping-off point to other sections of the book.

Part I also covers Word's graphics features, both new and old. You'll learn to create, import, position, and size graphic elements. The process of flowing text around graphics is illustrated. We'll also try to make some sense out of the growing collection of graphics and font standards (GIF, TIFF, PICT, EPS, TrueType, and so on) and show how they relate to Word 97.

You'll explore printing issues and see how your choice of printer and printing options affects the final look of your documents. You will even learn how Word makes envelope and label printing a snap.

Word 97's robust Find File command and Properties features are also demonstrated in Part I. You'll see how they work together to help you organize your hard disk and find misplaced files.

Part II: Formatting Fundamentals

Part II shows you how to look great in print. It is organized to help you quickly find illustrated answers to specific questions. You'll learn the fundamentals of formatting characters, lines, paragraphs, and sections. Tabs, tables, styles, style sheets, headers, footers, hyphenation, and page numbering are also covered here. Those of you who need to create footnotes will find out how in Part II.

There are numerous step-by-step "recipes" for getting the results you desire. You'll also see plenty of illustrations of the techniques at work.

Part III: Productivity Tools

As you might expect, Part III is filled with tips and techniques. Here you will learn how to find and replace text or styles. Word 97 also offers an incredible variety of templates and Wizards. You'll see how to use them to create all these and more:

Agendas
Awards
Brochures
Calendars
Directories
Faxes
Invoices
Letters
Manuals
Memos
Newsletters
Pleadings
Press Releases
Purchase Orders
Reports
Résumés
Tables
Theses
Weekly Time Sheets

We'll also demystify Word's AutoText feature and show how to create templates for repetitive tasks. Then you'll learn how to improve your documents' contents with Word's built-in thesaurus and its Spelling and Grammar checker. If you write or work on long, complex documents, be sure to read about Word's outlining features in Part III, as well.

Part IV: Desktop Publishing

Word's table of contents and indexing features are explored in Part IV. If you and others collaborate on big jobs, you'll want to check out Part IV. It shows you how to give documents a uniform look and feel, even when they have multiple authors.

You will learn how to create bookmarks, captions for your graphics, and cross-references that update automatically as you edit your documents. A new chapter on advanced graphics techniques explores features such as Microsoft's nifty Photo Editor. Chapter 18,

The Document Shop, provides step-by-step instructions on how to prepare all kinds of useful documents.

Part V: Large Documents and Team Projects

Because some desktop publishing projects can be quite complex, particularly if you work with collaborators, you'll see how to work with Word's Master Documents feature in Part V. You will learn how to share files with others and see ways to include text and graphics created by non-Word programs, such as WordPerfect.

Part VI: Power Tools

Part VI deals with topics of interest to advanced users of Word. It will show you how to use ActiveX technology to link document elements, create intelligent forms, and more. Part VI also contains chapters describing Word's print-merge feature for personalized mailings and similar documents. You'll actually set up a simple, personalized mailing project and create some mailing labels, envelopes, and postcards. Charts and graphs are explored here too. And you will learn how to personalize Word—adding toolbar buttons, changing menus, modifying default settings, and more.

Part VII: Word and the Web

After briefly reviewing the basics of the Internet, Part VII jumps right into ways to use Word with the Net. You'll see how to create Web pages, save and open HTML files via Word, and use Word to explore the Internet.

Master's Reference

The Master's Reference is a quick way to find the steps for a particular task. It is organized alphabetically and in straightforward, clear steps tells you exactly what you to need to do.

Book Conventions

We've used some standard conventions and typographer's tricks to make the book easier to read. Although most of them will be obvious, scan the next few paragraphs just in case.

About the Examples and Exercises

The book contains a number of exercises and lists of steps that you may want to try as you read along. Whenever you need to hold down one key and then press another, you'll see the keys separated by a plus sign. For instance, *Ctrl+S* tells you to hold down the *Ctrl* key while pressing the *S* key. Boldface text indicates things you are expected to type.

Menu Commands

As a shortcut and an eye-catcher, we've used a special convention to indicate menu commands. When we want you to choose a menu command, it will follow this pattern: *menu name* ➤ *command* (for example, File ➤ Open).

Tips, Warnings, Notes, and New

Throughout the book you'll find tips, warnings, notes, and discussions of new features. The new features are marked so they're easy to spot.

Because there is so much neat new stuff in Word 97 that we don't want you to miss, we've added this New icon in the margin to help experienced Word users spot differences. If you are a longtime Word user, it might be a good idea to skim each chapter looking for these easy-to-spot items.

Troubleshooting and Opportunities Sidebars

Mastering Word 97 includes a couple of new elements that both longtime and new users will find helpful. Troubleshooting sidebars are set off graphically and contain information that can help you avoid or recover from potential missteps. Opportunities sidebars are also set off graphically; they contain suggestions about how you can really use Word to improve the way you work.

Let's Get Started!

Enough, already. There's a lot to cover, so let's get started...

PART I

Getting Started

- *Create and save your first document*

- *View and navigate in Word's document windows*

- *Print documents, envelopes, and labels*

- *Enhance documents with graphics*

- *Use text boxes to frame and position text*

Chapter

1

Creating and Saving Your First Document

Creating and Saving Your First Document

I n this chapter we'll explore Word's basic text-editing features, using default settings and a Mark Twain quote. You'll type, edit, save, close, and reopen your first Word project. It's a long chapter, but worth the effort. The next chapter, along with the two chapters that follow it, will give you the foundation you need to master Word.

Document Setup

Although we'll use Word's standard settings for this first exercise, it is worth noting that many experienced users start each new project by thinking about the document's overall design and final appearance. Word gives you on-screen clues about how your document will look on paper. It can show you line endings, page endings, the relative size and placement of text, graphics, margins, and so on. In order to do this, Word needs some information from you—such as the paper size you plan to use and the kind of printer you will be using. You may also have strong feelings about how much white space you want around the edges of your pages. Once you give Word this information, it changes the on-screen appearance of margins, the ruler, and other settings to accommodate and reflect your design.

Thus, it is always a good idea to input (at least preliminary) printer, paper, margin, and other document-design decisions before you start typing. In Part Two, you will learn how to do this by using Page Setup and other tools. Word also provides *templates* that contain settings for particular kinds of jobs, making setup quick and easy.

If you are lucky enough to have a simple life with only one printer, one paper size, and similar projects, you may be able to make your setup decisions once and forget about them or even use Word's default settings and perhaps a few standard templates for every project. If you do complex tasks, if you have a variety of projects, or if you're a perfectionist, though, you'll frequently change printer and document settings.

TIP

Get in the habit of thinking about which printer and paper size you plan to use, the orientation of pages, and other design elements right when you start a new project. Check out the Page Setup dialog box before you start typing (choose File ➤ Page Setup).

Typing Habits to Break

If you learned to type on a typewriter or even an old word processor, chances are you have established habits that will be counterproductive in your use of Word. Here are a few habits you should try to break:

- Do not use the Tab key or the spacebar to indent paragraphs. Instead, use the indent control in Word's ruler (the top "handle" at the left side of the ruler). You'll learn more about this in Chapter 8, *Formatting Paragraphs*.
- Never use the spacebar to center or otherwise position text. Use the Center button on the Formatting toolbar instead. You'll learn about toolbars later in this chapter.
- Don't use the spacebar to make columns. Instead use tabs, Word's multicolumn features, or tables.
- Do not manually space paragraphs with carriage returns. Use Word's paragraph spacing instead, as explained in Chapter 8, *Formatting Paragraphs*.
- Do not press Enter repeatedly to start a new page. Instead, use Word's Insert Page Break command.

Your First Word Project

With those preliminaries out of the way, you're ready to roll. We'll use Word's default settings for this first example in order to simplify things.

Starting Microsoft Word

There are almost too many ways to start Microsoft Word. You can use the Windows 95 Start menu, the Office Shortcut bar, document icons, and more. Let's look at my favorites. Incidentally, the exact location and appearance of some of the features described in the next few paragraphs might be a little different on your machine depending upon which installation options were used. Don't panic if you can't immediately find something that's described here. You are not losing your mind.

MASTERING THE OPPORTUNITIES

Creating a Word 97 Shortcut

Windows 95 has a nifty feature called *shortcuts*. A shortcut is an icon that points to a file, a folder, or an application, but does not contain any of its data. What makes shortcuts useful is that you can place them anywhere, usually in easy-to-find places (such as on your Windows 95 desktop or in the Favorites folder), while leaving your original file, folder, or application in whatever place makes the most sense for your file organization. Then, when you double-click the shortcut, the file or folder opens or the application starts up.

To create a shortcut, open the folder in which Word 97 is installed and right-click on the WinWord icon. (You can do this in Explorer or My Computer.) Drag this icon wherever you'd like on your desktop, and it becomes your shortcut.

Using the Windows 95 Start Menu

Here's a way to start Word that will work even if you don't have Microsoft Office installed.

Simply use the "Microsoft Word" choice found on the Windows Start menu. It is probably located on the Programs submenu, although it can be moved. Assuming the choice is in the Programs submenu, here are the steps for starting Word from the Start menu:

1. Click the Start button in the bottom-left corner of your Windows 95 desktop.
2. Click the Programs choice on the resulting Start menu.
3. Click the Microsoft Word choice in the submenu.
4. This will run Word and start a new document using your default settings.

PART

I

Getting Started

If you prefer to use the Start menu (as opposed to the Office Shortcut bar described in a moment), consider moving the Word choice to the "top level" of your Start menu. See Chapter 31 to see how this can be done.

Using the Office Shortcut Bar

This is my favorite technique. If Word is installed as a part of Microsoft Office on your machine, you will probably have access to the *Office Shortcut bar*. It provides a series of buttons designed to make it quick and easy to start new projects using any of the Microsoft Office programs, including Word, Excel, etc. If you use other Office programs in addition to Word, it is a good habit to use the Office Shortcut bar for starting Word and other projects. Take a look at the right edge of Figure 1.1.

> **NOTE**
>
> There are many options available for the Shortcut bar, so its physical appearance and location might be different on your machine. In fact, the bar can be ordered to disappear automatically when not in use, so you might need to go poking around to find it. Try sliding your mouse pointer to the left, right, and top edges of your Windows 95 desktop.

Once you've found the Shortcut bar, clicking the New Office Document button will open the big dialog box you see in Figure 1.1. All of those tabs contain collections of icons designed to help you quickly start new projects (letters, reports, budgets, databases, and so on). We will learn about some of those possibilities later. For now, concentrate on the Blank Document icon in the General tab.

Click the General tab to bring it foremost if it isn't already. The General tab contains a Word document icon called *Blank Document*. Do you see it? Double-clicking on this icon will start Word and let you use your *default* or "everyday" Word settings. Try it.

Other Ways to Start Word

- You can also start Word by double-clicking the icons for Word document files. For example, if you or someone else has created and saved a memo as a Word file, simply double-clicking on the icon for that memo will run Word if it is not already running, and will display the document on screen making it available for editing, printing, etc. The *AK's Notes* icon in Figure 1.1 is an example of a Word icon.
- Your Windows 95 Start Menu might have a *New Office Document* choice. It will do the same thing as clicking the New Office Document button on the Office Shortcut bar.

FIGURE 1.1

Some of the many ways to run Word and start a Word project

Click to open the New Office Document dialog box, then double-click Word icons to start Word and/or begin new projects.

The Office Shortcut bar

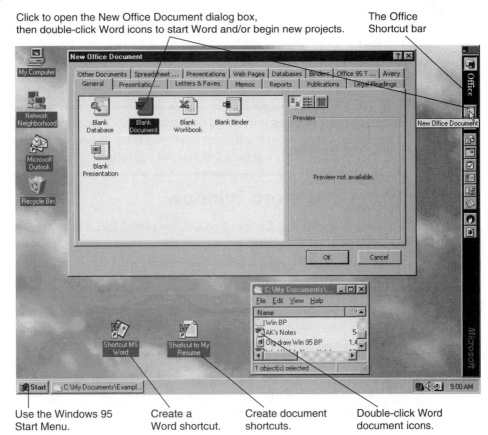

Use the Windows 95 Start Menu.

Create a Word shortcut.

Create document shortcuts.

Double-click Word document icons.

- The *Documents* choice on your Windows 95 Start menu might list Word files you've recently used. If it does, picking a Word file from that list will run Word if it is not already running and let you work with the file.

- You can place a *shortcut* to the Word program on your Windows 95 desktop and double-click it to start Word. You can see an example of this in Figure 1.1. Check out Chapter 31 or your Windows 95 online help to learn how to create shortcuts.

- You can put shortcuts to Word documents on your Windows 95 desktop, and double-click them to start Word. You can see an example of a shortcut to a résumé in Figure 1.1.

- Some non-Word document files (like ASCII text files) can be *associated* with Microsoft Word so that when you double-click on their icons, they will also run Word and let you edit them with Word. (See your Windows online help to learn more about associating files with Word.)

Getting Started

NOTE

The Office Assistant is available from the toolbar or (optionally) ever-present. This feature is extremely valuable, since it watches your every move and helps you find the best ways to accomplish tasks. See "The Assistant" section later in this chapter for more information.

TIP

There is a great shortcut for adding programs, folders, documents, or whatever to the Start menu. Simply drag the icon of what you want to add (or a shortcut of it) to the Start button, and it will be added to the Start menu. See Chapter 32 for details.

The Parts of a Word Window

An active Word window has standard Windows scroll bars, a title bar, zoom boxes, a menu bar, and so on. (If you are unfamiliar with these terms and concepts, take a moment to review your Windows manuals or online help.)

NOTE

It is good to distinguish between the *document* window and the *application* window. The document window is where individual Word files appear, and the application window will be open even if no files are open, as long as Word is running. You can see both windows in Figure 1.2. Some of the items I talk about below are specific to the document or to the application window, but it is not crucial to know what belongs where. The important thing is to know which items are which.

In addition to the usual Windows tools, you should see a ruler, toolbars, a flashing insertion point, and possibly a few other things. Word now has 18 toolbars, and you can display any of them at one time on-screen (although two at a time—Standard and Formatting—is most common). You may see more or fewer buttons on the toolbar than those illustrated in Figure 1.2. This is normal. The exact size and shape of your Word workspace will vary with your screen size and other factors. Let's look at a few of Word's window parts in a little more detail.

The Menu Bar and Commands

Normally, the top of your screen will contain traditional Windows-style menus in a menu bar. When you point to a menu title with the mouse and click once, the menu drops. Clicking on the desired command in a menu tells Word to execute that command. Commands with ellipses (...) after their names will ask you for additional information

FIGURE 1.2

A new document window appears each time you start Word.

Menu bar   Standard toolbar   Formatting toolbar   Ruler   Close box

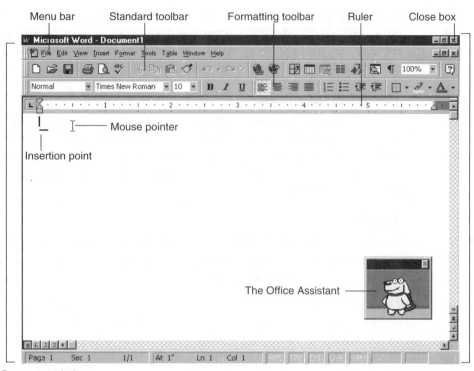

Mouse pointer

Insertion point

The Office Assistant

Document window

Application window

before they go to work. Dimmed commands are not currently available and require you to do something else first.

TIP

If you highlight a command and then change your mind before releasing the mouse button, simply slide the pointer off the menu to make the command list disappear; alternately, slide the highlight up or down the menu list without releasing the mouse button to select a different command.

You can also execute many commands by pressing specific key combinations (often called *hot keys*). These keyboard shortcuts are usually listed next to command names in menus. For instance, holding down the Ctrl key and pressing the P key is the same as choosing File ➤ Print. You'll learn more about this later.

The Mouse Pointer

Your mouse pointer should look like an I-beam and move freely about the screen. The pointer will change shape when it passes over certain parts of the Word workplace. For instance, it turns into a large arrow at the edges of Word windows. You'll soon learn how these changes in the pointer's appearance tell you what you can do next.

The Insertion Point

The *insertion point* or cursor denotes where text, graphics, and other items will be placed when you type or insert them. The insertion point is a tall, skinny, blinking vertical stick. Don't confuse it with the mouse pointer. The I-beam mouse pointer and insertion point are two different devices. Take a moment to locate them both in Figure 1.2 and on your own screen.

Toolbars

Word provides 18 toolbars, although you'll normally display only two or three at any one time. Microsoft's "factory settings" display only the Standard and Formatting toolbars. Here are the names of all 18:

- Standard
- Formatting
- Tables and Borders
- Database
- Drawing
- Forms
- Visual Basic
- Microsoft
- AutoText
- Web
- WordArt
- 3-D Settings
- Shadow Settings
- Picture
- Reviewing
- Control Toolbox
- Menu Bar
- Shortcut Menus

You won't see the names of all 18 toolbars on the Toolbars flyout menu, but you will see them on the Toolbars tab of the Customize dialog box. Choose View ➤ Toolbars ➤ Customize to see the complete list.

Toolbars contain buttons, drop-down menus, and other controls that help you quickly alter the appearance and arrangement of documents by executing a variety of Word commands.

For example, you can use the Formatting toolbar's Bold button to make text bold, or you can use its drop-down font menus to select a font and size. Point to the buttons containing arrows (next to the font and type-size menus) to see drop-down lists of choices. You can also type font names or sizes directly into the font and size boxes.

The button containing the paragraph mark (¶) alternately shows and hides paragraph marks, tab marks, space marks (the little dots), and other nonprinting items.

Word's Standard toolbar includes three new tools. The Insert Hyperlink tool is handy if you're creating a Web page, as is the Web tool—it toggles the display of the Web toolbar. I'll go into detail about all the new Web features in the last section of this book. The Document Map tool outlines your document based on the styles you've used and shows this outline on the left side of the window. Document Map is covered in Chapter 2, *Viewing and Navigating*.

We'll explore toolbar buttons in depth throughout the book. To display or hide toolbars, choose View ➤ Toolbars and check those you'd like to display.

The Rulers

You can use the rulers to quickly change margins and indents. They serve additional roles when working in columns and tables. You can use rulers to alter the appearance of multiple paragraphs or only the paragraph containing the insertion point. You'll learn more about rulers later in this chapter.

To display or hide the rulers, choose View ➤ Ruler.

NOTE

Word offers many formatting capabilities not found on the ruler or any of the toolbars. For instance, although the toolbar provides only one underline choice, you can specify one of the old standbys (Single, Words only, Double, or Dotted) or one of the five new types (Thick, Dash, Dot dash, Dot dot dash, or Wave) by choosing Format ➤ Font. Think of the toolbars and ruler as mini-formatting features. If you want to master Word, you should get to know the more powerful menu commands, as well.

Status Area

The bottom of your Word window gives additional information about your work in a place called the *status area*. It's always present unless you choose the Full Screen view (or unless you've turned it off by choosing Tools ➤ Options ➤ View ➤ Status Bar).

TIP

As you work on your documents, you might notice an animated icon in the status area (it looks like a book whose leaves are turning over). This is the automatic spell-checking tool, which checks your spelling and grammar as you write! You'll learn more about these features in Chapter 15, *Author's Tools*.

As you'll see later, on occasions you might be asked to type or click in the status area. Right now, let's start a document and put some of this horsepower to work. If it's not already running, start Word now.

Typing Text

Type the following quotation (intentionally type **The the** rather than simply *The* at the beginning). Don't worry if you also make other typing mistakes; you'll learn how to fix them in a moment.

```
The the difference between the right word and the almost right word is the
difference between lightning and the lightning bug.
```

Watch the screen as you type. Notice that Word automatically moves text down to the next line when it runs out of room near the right edge of the screen. This is called automatic word wrap, a common and useful word-processing feature. For this exercise, do not press Enter until you've typed the period after the word *bug*.

You might notice that Word has marked the second *the* in your document with a red wavy underscore. This marking indicates that Word believes the second *the* to be redundant.

Finish by typing Mark Twain's name, and then press Enter again. When you are done, your screen should look something like Figure 1.3.

Since Word checks your grammar as you type, you might find some of your text underlined in green. Don't panic. Ignore the green underline for now (it won't print), or right-click anywhere on the underlined text to see the Grammar checker choices. See Chapter 15, *Authors Tools*, to learn more.

FIGURE 1.3

Type Mark Twain's unembellished quote.

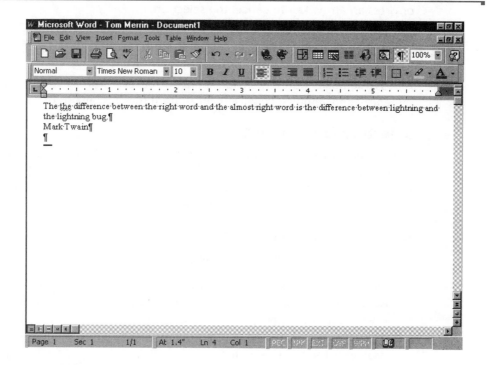

Selecting Text

Word lets you do a lot with text after you've typed it. You can change its appearance, move it around, delete it, and copy it. The first step is *always* to tell Word which text you want to work with. This is done by *selecting* it. You can select text in many, many ways in Word. For instance, you can drag your mouse pointer over the text while holding down the primary mouse button. There are shortcuts for selecting individual words, lines, sentences, and paragraphs, which you will read about in a moment.

Depending on your system configuration, selected text will either change color or be surrounded by a gray or black background. That's how you know what you have selected, as you can see here.

The the difference between the lightning bug. ¶

TIP

If you select text and change your mind, click anywhere outside the selected area or press an arrow key to cancel the selection.

Selecting Specific Blocks of Text with a Mouse

Here is a summary of text selection shortcuts for specific units of text, such as words, sentences, and graphics. Practice them all until they become second nature.

Selecting Entire Words

Double-click anywhere on a word to select the entire word and the space that follows it. To select adjacent words, drag after double-clicking on the first word. Entire words are selected when you drag this way. (With the default Automatic Word Selection turned on, you can single-click and drag to get this effect.)

Selecting Entire Lines

To select entire lines, follow these steps:

1. Move the mouse pointer to the *selection bar* (an invisible strip running down the extreme left edge of the document window). The mouse pointer will change from the I-beam to an arrow.
2. Click the primary mouse button only once. The entire *line* to the right of where you've clicked will be selected.

   Continue dragging down to select additional lines.

Selecting Entire Sentences

Hold down the Ctrl key while you click anywhere in a sentence. This also selects the sentence's punctuation mark (period, question mark, and so on) and the space following the sentence, if there is one. Dragging after you click this way selects additional sentences.

Selecting Entire Paragraphs

The quickest way to select a paragraph with your mouse is to *triple-click* anywhere in a paragraph. That is to say, point anywhere in the paragraph and quickly press and release the mouse button three times in succession. You can also select paragraphs using the selection bar by following these steps:

1. Move the mouse pointer to the selection bar (the invisible strip running down the extreme left edge of the document window). The pointer will become an arrow.

2. Double-click. The adjacent paragraph will be selected.

Selecting Your Entire Document

To select the entire document, follow these steps:

1. Move the mouse pointer to the selection bar at the left edge of the document and the pointer will become an arrow.

2. Hold down the Ctrl key and click. The entire document will be selected. Alternately, you can triple-click to select the whole document.

Selecting Graphics and Other Objects

Click anywhere within a graphic or other object. You'll see a border—usually with *handles* (small black boxes)—surrounding the selected object.

Selecting Variable Units of Text

Sometimes you'll want to select only a single character or parts of a text string. Here are some techniques to use.

Automatic Word Selection

Word features an option called Automatic Word Selection to help in selecting text. You select as many or as few characters of the first word you want to change. Then, when you drag over to the next word, the *entire* second word is selected. You must hold down Alt to select partial words when Automatic Word Select is on (as it is by default). You can turn this often frustrating option off in the Edit tab in the Options dialog box.

Dragging to Select

To select adjacent bits of text, follow these steps:

1. Point to the place where you want selection to begin.

2. Hold down the primary mouse button and drag in any direction.

3. When the pointer hits a screen boundary (top, bottom, or side) the document will scroll as highlighting continues.

4. Release the mouse button when you've selected the desired area.

Shift-Clicking to Select Large Areas

To select large blocks of continuous text, follow these steps:

1. Point to the place where you want selection to begin.

2. Click to place the insertion point there.

3. Point to the end of the desired area (scroll if necessary) and hold down the Shift key while you click.

4. Release the mouse button.

Selecting Rectangular Areas

To select rectangular areas (such as columns in a tabbed list), hold down the Alt key while you drag the mouse.

Deleting Text

There are several ways to delete unwanted text such as that extra *the* you typed in the sample Twain quote. If you had spotted your mistake right after typing it, pressing the Backspace key four times would have removed the unwanted characters and space.

Even if you did not make the correction earlier, it is easy to go back now, select the undesired text, and remove it. Follow these steps:

1. Double-click on the word to be deleted (*the* in this example). The entire word and the space following it become highlighted.

2. Press the Delete key once.

3. You can use Undo Clear (discussed in a moment) if you accidentally delete something of value.

TIP

In this case, since the unwanted text is also a spelling mistake (*redundancy* is considered a spelling error by Word), you can delete it by *right*-clicking (using your "secondary" mouse button) on the word with the red underline and choosing Delete Repeated Word from the Shortcut menu that appears.

Later, you will learn other ways to delete text and numerous strategies to reuse deleted text (move it) elsewhere. If you haven't already done so, delete that unwanted *the*.

Undo, Redo, and Repeat

Do you know what a damnosecond is? It's that fleeting instant when you realize you've done something really stupid on your computer—such as accidentally deleting or reformatting 20 pages of text.

Everyone makes choices they wish they could undo. Like few other things in life, Word often lets you rewrite history. You can even undo an Undo by *redoing* it.

And, for tasks that are repetitive and complex, it is nice to have your computer handle some of the drudgery. That's where Word's Repeat command can help. The combination of Undo, Redo, and Repeat can be both powerful and perplexing. Let's begin by looking at Undo.

Undo

Word watches as you work. With surprising attention to detail, it remembers which steps you last took. When asked, it can frequently undo your errors. The exact name of the Undo choice on the Edit menu changes as you work. Sometimes it says Undo Typing. At other times it says Undo Formatting or Undo Sort, or some such.

Here are some examples of what Word can undo if you ask soon after you discover a problem:

- Editing changes (typing, cutting, pasting, and so on)
- Most formatting actions (changing styles, fonts, and so on)
- Most projects done with tools (for example, replacing Bill with Bob)
- Most drawing actions (dragging, filling, and so on)

You can undo in three ways:

- Choose Edit ➤ Undo to reverse only your last action.
- Press Ctrl+Z repeatedly to reverse previous actions.
- Click on the Undo button and its associated drop-down list menu to undo multiple actions in sequence.

TIP

Word lets you undo more than one previous action. To see a list of your prior actions, click on the arrow next to the Standard toolbar's Undo button. You can undo one or more selected actions by selecting them from the list.

Using Undo

To undo your last action only, choose Edit ➤ Undo or press Ctrl+Z. Clicking on the Undo button on the toolbar will also work.

To undo multiple actions or selected actions, use the drop-down list by clicking on the arrow button next to the toolbar's Undo button.

Follow these steps:

1. Display the list by pointing to the Undo list arrow. Your last action will be at the top of the list.
2. Click on an item to undo it and any subsequent actions.
3. If you accidentally undo the wrong actions, use the Redo list to the right of the Undo list to "undo your Undo."

Word 97 now offers "unlimited" Undos. You can keep executing undo many, many times to get back almost to where you started. This can save you a trip to the Undo menu choice.

Redo

Yes, it *is* possible to undo an Undo. To redo only your last action, choose Edit ➤ Redo, press the keyboard shortcut (F4), or click on the Redo button on the Standard toolbar.

To redo multiple actions or selected actions, use the drop-down list reached with the arrow button next to the toolbar's Redo button.

Getting Started

Follow these steps:

1. Display the list by pointing to the Redo list arrow. Your last action will be at the top of the list.

2. Click on an item to redo (undo the Undo) it and any subsequent actions.

3. If you accidentally redo the wrong things, use the Undo list to the right of the Redo list to "undo your Redo."

Whaddaya Mean I Can't Undo?

Occasionally, you will see a "Can't Undo" message, indicating that your most recent action cannot be undone. That's why it is a good idea to save your work early and often. Then, when such a message appears, you can either close the messed-up document by saving it under a different name (with File ➤ Save As) or close it without saving the changes (that is, without saving your mistakes). Then open the earlier version that is (we hope!) in better shape. Sometimes you can save time by cutting and pasting between the earlier version and portions of the new (messed-up) work if you've saved it under a different filename.

TIP

The best approach is to stop and think immediately after you notice a big, potentially time-consuming mistake. Get help. Sometimes more experienced Word users or Microsoft's telephone support staff can talk you through time-saving repair techniques. The less you fiddle after noticing a big mistake, the better your chances of salvation. If you are a new user, don't be embarrassed to ask for help right away when you notice a problem!

Repeat

Sometimes, after you've done something repeatable (such as formatting or typing), you will find a *Repeat* command on Word's Edit menu. The shortcut is the F4 function key. Repeat watches you work and attempts to remember and recreate your actions on demand. Suppose, for instance, you change the width of a paragraph. If you have several other paragraphs scattered around your document that also need to be reformatted the same way, you could select each paragraph and use the Repeat feature to reformat them.

Like Undo, Repeat's name changes based on what you have last done, and it works with most Word actions immediately after you take them. Experiment.

Inserting Text

Word offers several ways to insert new text into an existing document. The most straightforward approach is to move the insertion point to the desired location and start typing. Word accommodates the new text by pushing the existing text to the right and down as necessary.

Suppose you wanted to add the word *obviously* between *the* and *right* in the first line of Mark Twain's quote. You would start by placing the mouse pointer (the I-beam) where you want to begin inserting text—between the space and the *r* in *right* for this example. Next, you'd press and release the mouse button to move the insertion point to the desired position.

> **WARNING**
> Beginners sometimes forget to press the mouse button after pointing with the I-beam. Don't confuse the I-beam with the insertion point! First you use the I-beam to point to where you want the insertion point placed. Then you must press and release the mouse button to move the insertion point.

Try it. Position the insertion point and type the word **obviously**, including the space that follows it. Your screen should look something like Figure 1.4.

Replacing Text

Word also makes it easy to replace text. It combines the steps of deleting unwanted text, positioning the insertion point, and inserting replacement text. Simply highlight the unwanted text and start typing. The old text disappears, and the new text snakes across the screen as you type it.

For example, watch the screen while you highlight the word *almost* (double-click on it) and type **nearly**. See how easily you can turn great prose into drivel? Because we'll be using this text for some future exercises, take a moment now to restore Mark Twain's actual words using the text-editing tricks you've learned so far.

Simple Formatting Tricks

Let's take a quick look at a few of Word's most often used ways to modify the appearance of text. They include toolbars, menus, and keyboard shortcuts.

FIGURE 1.4

You must position the I-beam and then insert the text.

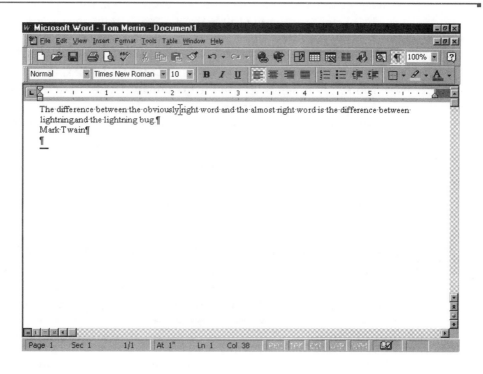

Toolbars

Word's *Formatting toolbar* is shown here.

Other toolbars also contain formatting buttons, as you'll see later. Among other things, toolbars let you make style changes by clicking on buttons or pulling down single-level menus, rather than going to the more crowded menu bar.

NOTE

The Formatting toolbar in Word 97 looks almost the same as in previous versions, with one exception—the new Font Color button. Clicking on this button gives you fast access to the feature.

As always, you must select text before working with it. For this exercise, select all the text by dragging, by choosing Edit ➤ Select All, or by using the keyboard shortcut Ctrl+A.

TIP

Get in the habit of using the Ctrl+A shortcut (or triple-clicking in the selection bar) when you want to select your entire document. These shortcuts can save you a lot of scrolling in large documents.

10
8
9
10
11
12
14
16
18
20
22
24
26

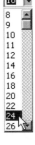

Let's start by increasing all the type from 12 to 24 points. The third arrow in the upper left corner of the toolbar reveals a list of type sizes, as shown here.

To display the type sizes, point at the triangle, and then press and hold the mouse button. Slide the pointer down to highlight *24* and release the mouse button. Your screen should look something like Figure 1.5.

TIP

You can also *type* font names or sizes directly into their respective toolbar boxes. Simply click in the box to highlight the old size (10 in our example) and type the desired size (24 in our exercise). When you're finished typing, press Enter to change the size.

Regardless of which technique you use to change the size of text, you can change as much or as little as you like. For instance, you could highlight only the first letter *T* in the quote and make it 48-point type, creating a large initial cap effect.

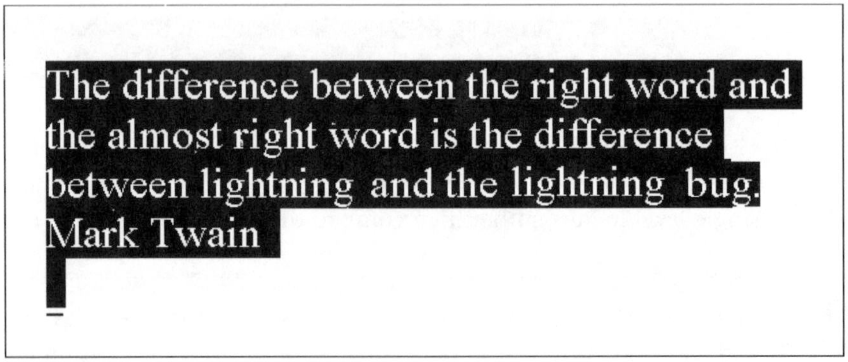
The difference between the right word and
the almost right word is the difference
between lightning and the lightning bug.
Mark Twain

FIGURE 1.5

The type size has been enlarged to 24 points.

You can accomplish better-looking versions of this and other "drop cap" effects automatically using Word's Drop Cap feature. Read about it in Chapter 7, *Characters and Fonts*.

To change the appearance of characters (making them bold or italicized, for instance), first select them, and then click on the appropriate button on the Formatting toolbar. Try italicizing the word *almost* in your Twain quote now. Here's how:

1. Point and click to select the word *almost*.

2. Click on the Italic button in the toolbar, as illustrated in Figure 1.6. Word will italicize the selected text.

Next, use the same basic techniques to make Mark Twain's name appear in boldface. First, select his first and last names by double-clicking or dragging, and then click on the Bold button on the Formatting toolbar (the uppercase B).

As you know, the button to the right of the Bold button italicizes text. The Underline button is next to the Italic button.

FIGURE 1.6

Select words you want to format and click on the desired button (Italic in this example).

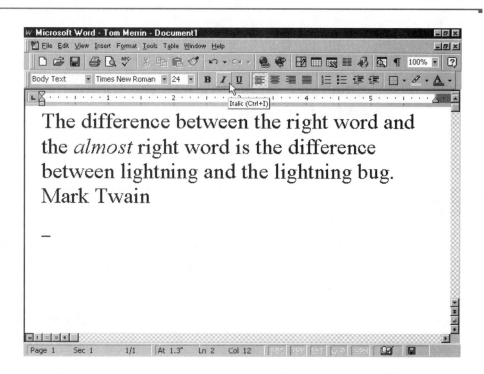

Aligning Text with the Formatting Toolbar

Notice the group of four buttons to the right of the Underline button in the Formatting toolbar. They contain horizontal lines. These let you specify left-aligned, centered, right-aligned, or fully justified text.

These "paragraph formatting" buttons and similar formatting tools work on entire paragraphs. They can be used on a single paragraph by simply placing the insertion point in the paragraph to be affected before clicking on the button. For instance, to right-align Mark Twain's name, follow these steps:

1. Place the insertion point anywhere in Mark Twain's name (point and click), as shown in Figure 1.7.
2. Click on the Align-Right button. The text will move to the right, as illustrated in Figure 1.8.

FIGURE 1.7

Click anywhere on text to be right-aligned.

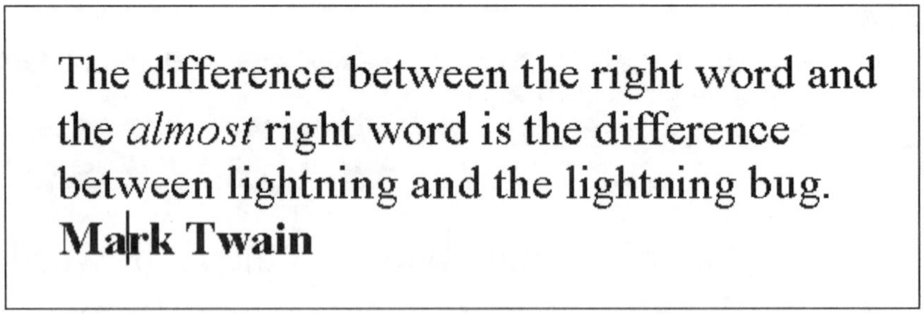

> The difference between the right word and the *almost* right word is the difference between lightning and the lightning bug.
> **Mark Twain**

FIGURE 1.8

The finished Twain quote

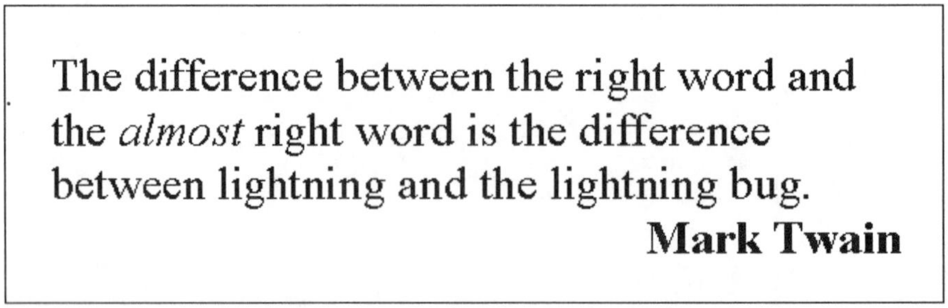

> The difference between the right word and the *almost* right word is the difference between lightning and the lightning bug.
> **Mark Twain**

To change multiple paragraphs simultaneously, select them first. Remember how plain the initial document looked? With a few mouse clicks you've changed its appearance considerably.

There's much more to learn about formatting, as you'll see throughout this book. You are probably itching to print by now, and you will in a few moments, but it would be a good idea to save your work first. That way if you have a printer or system problem, you won't need to redo the entire exercise.

Saving Documents the First Time [The Basics]

The words that you have typed and stylized so far exist only on your screen and in your computer's volatile RAM (random-access memory). If you were to switch off the computer or experience a power failure or other malfunction, your work would be forever lost. By saving your work to disk as you go, you can pick up where you have left off without losing your changes.

TIP

Many experienced computer users save every 15 minutes or whenever they are interrupted by phone calls or visitors. That's a good habit to establish. Word will even do the saving for you automatically, if you wish, as described later in this chapter.

Once you are happy with the appearance of the Mark Twain quote, choose File ➤ Save. Word displays the Save As dialog box, illustrated in Figure 1.9.

TIP

The Ctrl+S keyboard shortcut is a convenient way to save without accessing the File menu. Some folks use it exclusively. The Standard toolbar includes a button that looks like a floppy disk, which will also start the Save process.

The Save As dialog box tells you where Word plans to store your work and requests a name for the file. It also gives you many other Save options, which are discussed later in this chapter.

Let's keep things simple for now and use Word's default save options. Start by noticing where Word proposes to put your document. This is a very important habit to establish.

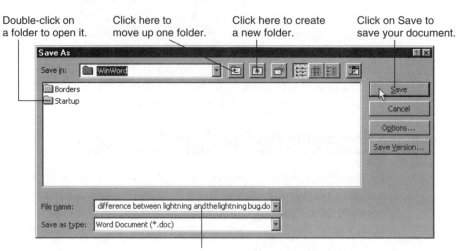

FIGURE 1.9

Word displays the Save As dialog box the first time you save a file.

Double-click on a folder to open it.

Click here to move up one folder.

Click here to create a new folder.

Click on Save to save your document.

Type your document's name here.

WARNING

If you do not get in the habit of thinking about where you and Word save documents, you will misplace them. When saving to a floppy disk or your own small, uncluttered hard disk, this can be a minor annoyance. If you work on a far-flung network with multiple servers and gigabytes of storage space, it can take hours or days to locate lost files.

In Figure 1.9, Word is proposing to store our new document in the folder containing Word itself—called WinWord. You can tell this from the picture of a folder next to its name (WinWord) near the top of the dialog box.

TIP

It's not a good idea to clutter up your Word folder with a lot of documents. It is a good idea to create some folders specifically for Word documents. If you are an experienced Windows user, you might want to do that now.

Look at your screen. Take a moment to see where Word plans to save your work. Chances are you will see something slightly different from the folder location shown in Figure 1.9.

Telling Word Where to Save Your Document

Word allows you to specify save locations. You do this by double-clicking on folders and disks to open them. You can also click on the Up One Level or Create New Folder icons (noted in Figure 1.9) to help you get around and get organized. See your Windows documentation for tips on maneuvering through your disk's or network's drives and folders. (For more information, see "Organizing Your Files" later in this chapter.)

Naming Word Documents

Type a name for your document in the File Name box and then click on the Save button. Names can be a maximum of 255 characters. This allows you to be very specific about names, dates, and subjects; you'll find that this flexibility will greatly enhance the organization of your files. Note that if you want to use older Word documents, Word 97 still supports them and their eight-character names. In fact, Windows 95 keeps track of all files by means of long and short names; so you never have to worry about backward compatibility.

Notice that back in Figure 1.9 Word proposed naming the document *difference between lightning and the lightning bug.doc.* (Actually, it's proposing a longer name than that, you just can't see the whole thing.) Word is using the first paragraph of the document as the proposed filename. This works great if you always start projects with a short meaningful title for the first line in your document—Ron's Résumé, or whatever. Often, however, you will need to select and delete or type over the proposed filename if it is as long and silly as this one.

One way or the other, Word will save your document, and if the Properties feature is turned on, you will see a Properties dialog box similar to the one shown here:

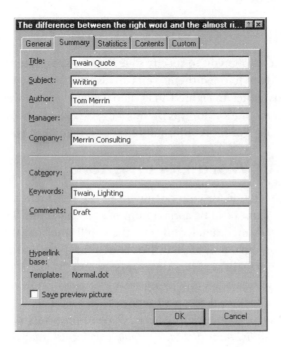

Don't be alarmed if you don't see the Properties dialog box right now. The information it collects is optional and can be added later, if you like.

Instead of clicking on the Save button, press Enter. This will have the same effect as clicking on Save. With Word, like most Windows programs, pressing Enter executes the button with the bold border in the active dialog box.

Properties

You needn't type anything in the Properties dialog box, and by default it will not appear when you save documents. But if you plan to keep many documents on your hard disk, and particularly if you will be storing files on a crowded network server, it is a good idea to use this handy feature. It will help you quickly locate projects with the File ➤ Open command when you want to round them up for later use.

Because we'll be using this document to explore the File ➤ Open feature later, take a moment to enter the information. Here are the steps:

1. If you didn't see the Properties dialog box when you saved the Twain quote, open it now by choosing File ➤ Properties.
2. Type **Twain Quote** as the title. Do not press Enter yet though.
3. Press the Tab key or point with the I-beam and click to move the insertion point to the next blank.
4. Type **Writing** as the subject.
5. Tab or point and click again and enter your name if it is not already in the Author box.
6. Tab again and fill in the Manager, Company, and Category boxes as you choose. You may leave boxes blank.
7. Tab once more and enter some keywords (such as *Twain* or *lightning*).
8. Tab again and type **Draft**.
9. If you would like to be able to preview this document when you are scrolling in the Open dialog box, click to place a check in the Save Preview Picture box.
10. When you are satisfied with your entries, click on OK or press Enter, the shortcut!

Once you have saved a document's Properties information, you will not be asked for it again when you save your work. You can modify the entries by simply following the above steps.

 TIP

To prevent the Properties dialog box from appearing when you initially save a new document, turn it off via the Save category of the dialog box opened by choosing Tools ➤ Options and unchecking Prompt for Document Properties.

Save Often As You Work

Once you've named a document and specified a place to save it, you won't see the Save As dialog box when you save unless you request it. A quick trip to File ➤ Save or, better still, pressing Ctrl+S will save your work whenever you desire. So will clicking on the Save button on the Standard toolbar. Save early, save often, and *always* save before you print or make major changes.

If you need help remembering to save regularly, Word can even save automatically at time intervals you specify. This feature is described in the "Save Options" section later in this chapter.

Organizing Your Files

Your hard disk can contain hundreds or even thousands of files. If you work in a large, networked organization, you may have access to ten times this many documents. If you've ever misplaced a file, you know how frustrating and time-consuming trying to find it can be.

Word provides two features to help you organize and locate files. They are the Search utility of the Open command and the Summary tab of the Properties command, both found on the File menu. For those of you new to Windows 95, I'll start with a quick review of the methods for managing files and folders and for navigating paths.

Files, Folders, and Paths

Your computer lets you arrange your files in a hierarchical structure. Files (Word documents, for instance) can be stored in *folders*. Folders can also be stored within folders. Figure 1.10 shows an example of this.

In the example, there is a folder called Clients. It contains all the client-related folders and files for this computer. Within the Clients folder are three client subfolders, one for each client (B&N, CNN, and Xerox, which is out of view). Each of these client folders contains additional subfolders and files relating to the particular client. For instance, the B&N folder contains the B&N Progress folder, in which project-related

FIGURE 1.10

A hierarchical arrangement contains folders within folders.

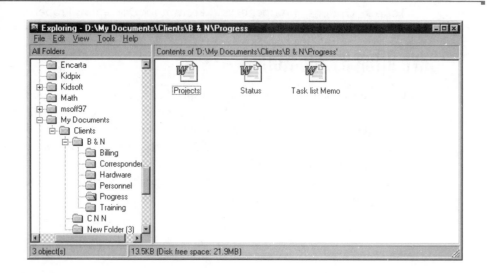

memos, lists, and reports are stored. The B&N subfolder also contains other folders with billing and contract information, hardware information, and so on. If you were to open the Xerox subfolder, you might find a similar arrangement of Xerox-specific files.

This hierarchy makes it easy to store and find things. It also provides good hiding places for lost files. For instance, you'd need to open three folders to find the Projects file.

The steps that you take to find a file form a *path*. To get to the Projects document or the Task List Memo, for example, you would start by choosing the hard disk containing the folders and then open the Clients folder. Next you would open the B&N folder and finally the B&N Progress subfolder. You can do this from the Windows Explorer by double-clicking on folders, or you can do it from within Word itself by choosing File ➤ Open (Ctrl+O).

You might have noticed that, both in Windows Explorer and in Word, you no longer see file extensions (.exe, .doc, and so on). Extensions are now hidden unless you specifically ask for them to be shown. (See your Windows manuals for details.) This can be a bit disconcerting, especially if you've just saved a document as *Memo.doc*, and it now appears as just *Memo*. What this means practically is that you should *not* try to type extensions for your documents once you've saved them. The first time, it's okay. You type **.doc**, it disappears, and everybody's happy. If you later explicitly add the extension, though, either in Explorer or in some other fashion, your document's real name is now *Memo.doc.doc*! Oops.

If you are worried about sharing files with people using older versions of Word or other word processors, your concerns are justified. Windows keeps track of both long and short (DOS-compatible) names, but its methods are by no means perfect. For instance, if you are a lawyer and you have 400 files that all begin *Motion to...* or some such, you're okay as long as you work in a Windows 95 environment. If you go to a pre-95 machine, though, it's gonna be an absolute nightmare trying to figure out which file is *Motion to Desist, ABC Trucking* and *Motion to Desist, ABC Bakery.* There is no single best solution to this dilemma; if you know you will often be working in non–Windows 95 environments, you might want to limit yourself to the old eight-character DOS constraints or work out a formalized folder scheme.

WARNING

Users of Word 95, Word 6.*x* and most other old word processing programs will not be able to open files created and saved using Word 97's default Save options unless they have updated software. There are several work-arounds for this including changing Word 97's save defaults. See Chapter 25 for details.

Save Options

It's worth exploring Word's save options, even though the default choices will work well for most people. Reach the save options with the Options button in the Save As dialog box or via the Save tab in the Tools ➤ Options command. It looks like Figure 1.11.

FIGURE 1.11

Word's save options can be found in the Save tab of the Options dialog box.

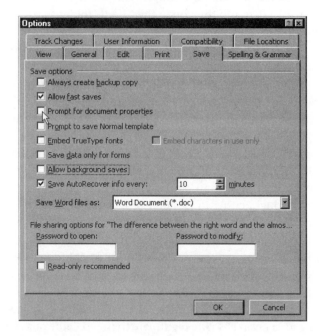

Here is a list of the options you'll see in the Save As dialog box and some information about their use, followed by examples of typical save operations. The new ones are noted as such and a few have been renamed to make their purpose more apparent.

Always Create Backup Copy

Beware the Always Create Backup Copy option! With this option selected, Word makes a copy of the most recent disk-resident version of your file (giving it the extension .BAK) before saving your current changes to the original file. This is *not* a true backup, for reasons described later in this chapter.

Allow Fast Saves

The Allow Fast Saves option instructs Word to save only your changes most of the time rather than making you wait while it rewrites your entire document to disk each time you save. Although this option can let you get back to typing and editing more quickly, it consumes extra RAM, uses more disk space, and can create real recovery problems if you have trouble with your disk while working on a big project. I recommend turning it off and leaving it off.

TIP Many experienced Word users leave Allow Fast Saves off. Always Create Backup Copies and Allow Fast Saves are mutually exclusive options; you can't select both at the same time.

Prompt for Document Properties

With this option checked, Word interrupts you the first time you save a new document and prompts for author name, document title, keywords, and other information.

Prompt to Save Normal Template

This choice displays a message when you exit Word (File ➤ Exit), asking whether you want to save changes made to default settings in the Normal Template file. If you don't display this prompt, Word automatically saves such changes, including words added to the dictionary and new macros.

Embed TrueType Fonts

This option instructs Word to save any TrueType fonts you've used with the document file so that other users can read your documents, even if they don't have the same TrueType files installed on their machines. Leave this feature off unless *all* the following are true:

- You exchange files with others.
- You use TrueType fonts.
- The users you share with do not have the fonts installed.

Embed Characters in Use Only

This option embeds only the characters you used from the True Type fonts in your document, thereby reducing the file size when you save it. The option is only available if you check Embed True Type Fonts.

Getting Started

Save Data Only for Forms

When creating forms and collecting data on forms, Word can be instructed to save the data to disk without saving the forms. See the *Creating and Using Forms and ActiveX* chapter for details.

Allow Background Saves

Word can save the data to disk without prompting you and, in general, without regard to what you are doing. For example, if you are in the middle of searching and replacing or checking spelling, you might notice some delay while Word saves. You'll also see a "pulsing disk icon" while Word is saving. However, you won't have to bother thinking about saving regularly if you let Word do it for you.

Save AutoRecover Info Every *N* Minutes

This can be a blessing or a curse. If you are one of those people who never remembers to save early and often, Word can do it for you. Place a check in the appropriate box and tell Word the desired save interval (10 minutes is the default). Thereafter, Word will save every 10 minutes or whatever without even asking.

On the other hand, if you have a slow machine, this automatic save feature can be a problem.

Save Word Files As

You can specify the default format in which Word saves documents by using the drop-down list. Most of the time, you'll be saving documents in Word Document (*.doc) format, but if you typically use Word to create documents that you share with others who don't work in Word, select the appropriate format here. Remember that the default setting of Word Document (*doc) saves in Word 97 format, which is different from Word 95 or Word 6.*x*!

You can still specify a different format for a document with the Save As command, when necessary. For example, you can save a document in Word 6/95 format to share with others who aren't using Word 97.

The File-Sharing Options

These options let you protect documents that are shared with others. If you password protect a document, you and others must use the password each time you reopen the

Getting Started

document. Document passwords can be a maximum of 30 characters. Upper- and lowercase matters, so use care when assigning and entering passwords.

Password to Open - This type of password prevents someone from opening a document without knowing its password. If you use protection passwords, don't forget them.

Password to Modify - Documents saved with only write-reservation passwords let users open them without knowing the password. Only users who know the write-reservation password can save changes though.

Read-Only Recommended - A check in this option box instructs Word to recommend that users open the document as read-only. It will *not*, however, prevent modification or deletion.

Saving under a Different Filename

Normally, once you've named a document, Word will keep saving the document under the same name. Choose the File ➤ Save As command to save a document under a different filename. Follow these steps:

1. If necessary, make the document you want to save the active document, and then choose File ➤ Save As or press F12.
2. Type a new filename in the File Name area of the dialog box. Because the cursor goes there by default, you can simply start typing.
3. Specify a new folder and disk location if you want, and then click on the Save button or simply press Enter. Future saves will use this new name and location.

Saving to Floppy and Other Disk Drives

Normally, once you've saved a document, Word will keep saving the document to the same disk and into the same folder you initially specified. Again, you use the File ➤ Save As command (or F12) to save a document to a different disk or folder. Follow these steps:

1. If you plan to save to a floppy, insert it into your computer's floppy drive. If you plan to save to a different hard drive, be sure it is turned on and available. If you plan to save on a server, be sure your network connection has been established and that the desired server drive is mounted. (See your computer manuals or contact your network manager for assistance.)
2. Make the document you want to save the active document, if it isn't already; then choose File ➤ Save As or press F12.

3. Specify the desired disk drive in the Save As dialog box by selecting a drive from the Save In drop-down list. When you've chosen the appropriate disk (or a folder on that disk), click on the OK button or press Enter. Future saves will use this new location.

Floppy disks are best used as a medium for transporting and archiving files. Do all your work in Word on files located on your hard disk or a network drive and save them there; then copy the finished files to a floppy disk as needed.

Saving in Non-Word Formats

Just as you can open non-Word files with Word, you can save your work in non-Word formats. Use the drop-down Save As Type list in Word's Save As dialog box to specify the desired file format. See Chapter 25 for details.

When Your Disk Gets Full

Occasionally, when you attempt to save, Word will tell you that there is not enough room for your project on the current disk. You may even get an "insufficient disk space" message seemingly out of the blue. This is because Word sometimes creates temporary files that need disk space of their own. There are several things you can do in this situation.

- Use the Save As command to save to a different hard drive on your computer or perhaps to a different hard drive elsewhere on your network.

- Use the Save As command to save to a floppy disk.

- Switch to the Explorer, delete old unwanted files, and then switch back to Word and attempt to save again.

Opening Previously Saved Documents

When you choose File ➤ Open, Word displays a dialog box that looks something like the one in Figure 1.12.

You show Word the path to your document by opening successive folders until the file you want is visible in the scrollable document list. To open folders, scroll through the drop-down list, double-clicking to open folders. When you have folders within folders, you will need to double-click on more than one folder.

If you open one folder too many, click on the Up One Level button.

From the Open dialog box, use the Look In drop-down menu to open the drive containing the document you need, and then choose folders and files from scrolling lists.

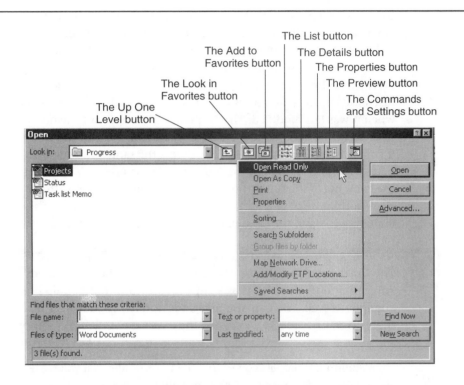

When you see the file (the document) that you want to work with, double-click on the document's name or click on it and press Enter. Your Windows manuals and online tutorials contain more information on this subject and practice exercises if you need additional help. If you choose the Open Read Only option from the Commands and Settings drop-down menu, you will not be able to save any changes to the file; rather, you will be asked to save edits to a new file.

TIP

If you are looking for non-Word documents, don't be surprised if they don't appear in the list. By default, Word shows only Word files. To see other kinds of files, select the appropriate type from the Files of Type drop-down list. If you choose All Files, Word will display any non-Word files.

Word's Open dialog box has several buttons to help you get around and organize your files (these are noted in Figure 1.12). First, there is the Up One Level button. Clicking on this button lets you see what's in the folder that contains the folder listed in the Look In box. Next to that is the Look in Favorites button. Clicking on this takes you to a folder called Favorites, found in the Windows folder. Put commonly used files in here to find them quickly. The Add to Favorites button automatically adds to the Favorites folder a *shortcut* to the selected document.

The next four buttons let you specify how you want to view files. The List button just shows a list. The Details button shows each document's name, size, type, and when it was last modified. The Properties button shows a window that tells you the revision of the document you are looking at, how many pages, words, and characters it contains, and so on. This is more or less the same information you see in the Summary and Statistics tabs of the Properties dialog box. The Preview button lets you see the contents of the file without actually opening it. Finally, the Commands and Settings button drops down a menu from which you can make a variety of selections, including to open the document as read-only or to print it.

NOTE

The Commands and Settings menu includes a couple of handy new commands. You can open a document as a copy if you want to maintain the original but make changes as well. You can also add and modify FTP locations by choosing from this menu. See Chapter 34, *Accessing the Internet with Word*, for more about this.

In addition, Word lets you restrict the types of files you will see. For instance, you can ask to see only document templates or only Rich Text Format files. You make your choice in the Files of Type drop-down list. Word also has a search utility built right into the Open dialog box.

Steps for Opening Documents from within Word

Here are the general steps for opening Word documents with Word running:

1. From within Word, choose File ➤ Open, press Ctrl+O, or click on the Open button on the Standard toolbar.
2. Use the Look In list to open the appropriate disk or scroll through the folders list.
3. Double-click on the desired filename to load the document.

Opening Non-Word Documents

Each word-processing program (Word Pro, WordPerfect, and so on) creates document files containing unique control codes for things such as character attributes, margins, and so forth. Frequently, if you use one word-processing program to open a document created by another program, you will see codes that look like unintelligible gibberish intermixed with the document's text. Margins may be different. Fonts and line spacing will often change.

There are third-party file-conversion programs that can minimize these problems (such as Word for Word, by Mastersoft). Word also has some file-conversion capabilities of its own. See Chapter 25, *Document Importing, Exporting, and Conversion.*

Don't expect perfection when moving documents from one program or computer to another. You will probably need to make some formatting changes, deal with line-ending differences, and so on. Here are the general steps for loading non-Word documents:

1. From within Word, choose File ➤ Open or press Ctrl+O.
2. Point to the Files of Type drop-down list to select the kind of files you want to view and open, or choose All Files to see a list of all files.
3. Use the Look In drop-down list to open the appropriate disk and folder (by double-clicking).
4. Double-click on the desired filename in the scrollable list.
5. Word will convert and load the document or alert you that it cannot do the necessary conversion.

TIP

If you want Word to notify you of successful conversions, select the General tab of the Options dialog box (choose Tools ➤ Options) and activate the Confirm Conversions at Open option.

6. Inspect and clean up the document.
7. Save it as a Word document if you plan to use it with Word in the future, or use the Save As command to save it in the originating program's format, if that's where you will be working on the document in the future.

Opening Documents As Read-Only

If you want to open a document as read-only to prevent yourself from accidentally making changes to the disk file, click on the Commands and Settings button and then choose the Open Read Only option from the Open dialog box.

Template documents, when opened as templates, are always opened as read-only. When you open a template document and then make changes and save them, you will be automatically prompted for a different filename. Templates are discussed in more detail in Chapter 13, *Templates, Wizards, and Sample Documents.*

WARNING

If you open a Word 95 or Word 6.*x* document with Word 97 and make any changes, Word will ask if you want to save the changes. If you say "Yes" you must decide if you want to change the format of the document from Word 95 or Word 6.*x* to Word 97. Changing to Word 97 might preclude opening it with earlier software. Consider using Save As to make a second copy of the document in Word 97 format. See Chapter 25 for details.

Finding Files

Word's file-finding utility, found in the Open dialog box, is a powerful tool that helps you locate, list, sort, examine, open, and print documents based on simple or complex search criteria. You can examine your computer's hard disk(s) or even search a server or shared drive over a network. Both Word and non-Word files can be located using this feature. You can find files by filename, creation date, and much more. For instance, if you enter document properties when saving Word documents, you can round up files based on their authors, keywords, and so on.

Let's start with a simple search. Suppose, for instance, that you've lost your Twain Quote document. Start by choosing File ➤ Open or by clicking on the Open button in the Standard toolbar.

Use the four drop-down menus at the bottom of the screen, along with the Look In box, to specify where you want Word to search. In general, you need to tell Word the following:

- Which folder or folders to search
- What to look for
- Optional, advanced criteria to narrow the search (Summary info entries, for example)

Searching by Filenames

Continuing with the case of the missing Twain Quote, let's assume you forgot where you saved it and you are at the top-level folder of your hard disk. It would be a real nuisance to open Windows Explorer and navigate through all your folders to find the missing document. Instead, let Word do the work for you! Follow these steps.

1. If it is not still open, display the Open dialog box by choosing File ➤ Open, pressing Ctrl+O, or clicking on the Open button on the Standard toolbar.

2. Type **Twain Quote** in the File Name box.

PART

I

TIP
You can still use those old-fashioned DOS wildcards (*, ?, etc.) in your searches, if you wish. For example, typing *.DOC in the File Name box will find all files that have the extension *doc*. Although this might be handy at times (for finding graphics files of a particular kind, for example), it is a bit outdated. Now that you can use longer, more meaningful filenames, searches will probably be quickest if you search for files by their names.

Getting Started

3. Click on the Commands and Settings button and choose the Search Subfolders option from the drop-down menu, as shown in Figure 1.13. This is a very important step; if you omit it, Word will search only the selected folder. Worse yet, if no folder is selected, Word will do nothing. (Well, at least nothing useful.)

4. Word starts searching for the Twain Quote file. If you want to stop the search, click on Stop. Word will then show you the results of its search, as shown in Figure 1.14. You can then do one of several things to see which file is the one you want. Click on the Details button to see where these files are on your disk, as in Figure 1.14. Alternately, click on the Preview button to get a peek at the selected file's contents.

5. In Figure 1.14, two of the three Twain Quote files are shortcuts (Word helpfully tells us this), but we want the real thing. Double-click on the correct file or preview it first if you wish, and Word will open the Twain Quote file.

FIGURE 1.13

Choose the Search Subfolders option from the Commands and Settings menu.

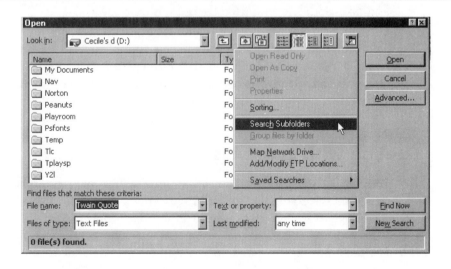

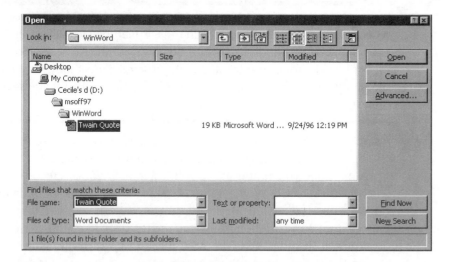

FIGURE 1.14

Word makes a list of files that match the file-name you have specified. By clicking on the Details button, you can see which is the one you want, as shown here.

TIP

With the Search Subfolders option selected, the file-finding utility is an active function; that is, you don't have to tell it to start running. It will begin searching as soon as you choose a folder in the Open dialog box or from the Look In box. This is tricky and takes some getting used to, but it is quite slick.

6. If you don't use the Search Subfolders option, you can always initiate searches by clicking on the Find Now button in the Open dialog box. Be sure that you have selected a folder to be searched, though; otherwise, nothing will happen.

7. Once Word has found the files you've requested, click on the New Search button in the Open dialog box if you want to clear the list and begin a new search.

Dealing with Large Lists

Long lists of found files can be handled in a number of ways. You can use the Sorting option on the Commands and Settings menu in the Open window to display the Sort By dialog box, which lets you sort your list (see Figure 1.15).

If you know the approximate time frame of a project, date sorts will help you narrow the list to examine. If you knew this was a big document, a sort by file size might help. Choose the appropriate setting. When you are satisfied with your criteria, click on OK or press Enter.

FIGURE 1.15

The Sort By dialog box lets you arrange lists of files in different ways.

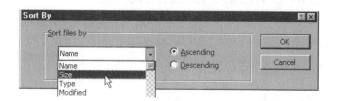

Another alternative is to redo the search with more specific criteria. Click on the Advanced button in the Open dialog box to open the Advanced Find dialog box, shown in Figure 1.16.

Three drop-down lists in this dialog box are designed to let you specify different kinds of information and limitations on your searches. Here is where you can use the information entered in the Summary tab of the Properties dialog box (discussed under the "Finding Files with Document Properties" section). You can even save search specifications for reuse.

FIGURE 1.16

Advanced search options can help shorten your hit list.

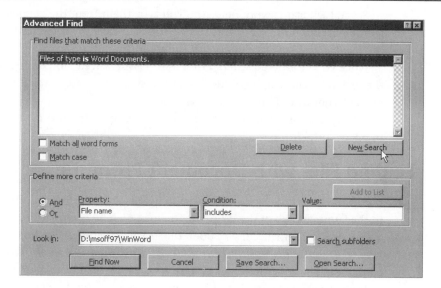

Searching inside Documents

Searches on filenames alone are the quickest and are recommended as the starting point for searches of any but the smallest disk drives. But if you cannot find a file with a filename search or if you find too many files containing the search word, it is possible to ask Word to look *inside* each file on the disk being searched and list only those files containing the word or words meeting your criteria. The file-finding utility searches entire Word documents including headers, footers, and hidden text.

First, choose the appropriate setting from the Condition drop-down menu. You might choose "includes" for this particular search. Then, in the Value box, you type what you want Word to look for. For example, you might type **Twain**. Finally, click on the Add to List button to add this criterion to the window at the top of the Advanced Find dialog box. You need to use the same care when specifying search text that you use with Word's Find and Replace commands. If you are too specific, you may miss the file you are looking for. Use too vague a search string, and you will get excessively long file lists.

Suppose, for instance, you want to round up everything you've written about DAT (Digital Audio Tape). If you use *DAT* as your search text, Word will also list files containing the words *database*, *date*, and *Datsun*. Placing a space after *DAT* in the search string or enabling the Match Case option solves that problem.

Several wildcards work here. You will type them from the keyboard. For example, *Sm?th* will find both *Smith* and *Smyth*. The wild card ^W searches for white space. See the *Finding and Replacing* chapter for more information.

Once you've entered search criteria in the Advanced Find dialog box and started the search by clicking on Find Now or pressing Enter, Word starts examining the contents of your disk. This can take a while.

Eventually a list will appear, and you can preview the hits or use the other buttons to open, sort, and so on.

Finding Files with Document Properties

If you and your colleagues have been religious about entering consistent information in the Summary tab of the Properties dialog box, you can use the file-finding feature to search for those entries. If you open the Advanced Find dialog box (from the Open dialog box), you'll notice the Property box in the lower left corner. This drop-down menu contains dozens of criteria you can use in your file searches. These properties are keyed to the entries you've made in the Properties dialog box, however; so the usefulness of this feature will depend on how assiduous you've been in recording this information.

Just remember that if you've created documents and failed to put your name in the author box when creating Summary info or if you sometimes type your whole name and at other times use your initials, you run the risk of missing documents when your search criteria include Summary info search restrictions.

Naturally, documents created with programs that do not collect Summary info (such as WordPerfect) will be ignored.

TIP

Written policies and procedures regarding file naming and summary information entries can be a big help in law firms, publishing houses, and other organizations that have networks and thousands of files.

Try It, You'll Like It

If you haven't already done so, search for your Twain Quote using some of the Summary info you entered via the Properties dialog box when you initially saved the document.

Multiple Searches

At times, you will want to do multiple searches. For instance, in our earlier example, you may discover that sometimes you referred to DAT in documents by the complete name and not the acronym. You might think you would need to search once for *DAT* and a second time for *Digital Audio Tape* to find each relevant document. Similarly, you might think that if you use multiple disk drives you will need to perform multiple searches. Fortunately, you can *combine* search criteria. This means you can do all the above in a *single* search. Read on....

Combining Searches

The classic combined search works like this. Search for the first criterion of interest (Value: = DAT for instance). Review the list.

Return to the Advanced Find dialog box and add additional search criteria. You might, for instance, type **Digital Audio Tape** in the Value box. Each time you add another limitation, click on the Add to List button to add it to the criteria list at the top of the dialog box. Then run another search by clicking on the Find Now button. The resulting list will now contain documents meeting either criterion.

You can combine the results of different types of searches. For example, you can search first by filename, then by author, and so on.

Searching Multiple Disks

If you have more than one disk drive on your computer or if you want to search both your computer's disk and other drives on a network, you can instruct Word to look in more than one place. Do this in the Look In box of the Advanced Find dialog box, as illustrated in Figure 1.17.

The Look In box of the Advanced Find dialog box

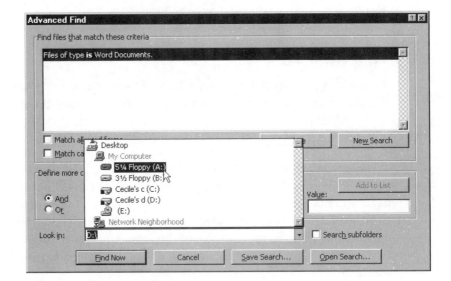

Making Backup Files for Safekeeping

It's a fact of life: Hard disks fail. Floppy disks are easily damaged. Fires, floods, winds, and earthquakes destroy computers and the files stored on their disks. Punks walk off with them. Nice people like you and me accidentally delete important files. Computers and software have a mean-spirited habit of trashing your important work-in-progress, usually when you are in a big hurry.

You need to make regular backup copies of your important Word documents, and you need to store those files far enough away from your computer so that they will survive a neighborhood disaster.

The easy way to save small, simple files is to copy them to floppies. Choose File ➤ Save As (F12) to place copies of important documents on separate disks, which should be stored away from your computer. Or you can save entire folders to floppies with the Windows Backup program.

For big Word files and large collections of documents, consider backing up to removable portable hard disks or look into tape-backup systems.

Whatever you do, don't rely on Word's automatic-backup feature as your only backup method! Backup files created with this automatic feature will almost never contain the most recent changes you've made. Many experienced users leave this automatic backup feature turned off and take active responsibility for backups themselves. (Turn it off in the Save tab of the Options dialog box, reached by choosing Tools ➤ Options.) If your organization has a computer support person or network manager, ask about backup policies and procedures.

Recovering Damaged Files

If, while you're working in Word, a power failure or other gremlin causes your computer to lock up or otherwise misbehave, you may find yourself with a damaged document that will either refuse to load when you're back in business or be missing information. Word may be able to recover most of your recent work by loading the appropriate temporary file that Word has probably created. Restart Word.

 WARNING

Never delete or rename temporary files when Word is running. Exit Word first.

Quitting and Restarting Word

You can completely quit Word in several ways. You can choose File ➤ Exit or click on the Close box in the upper right corner of the main Word window, both of which are shown in Figure 1.18. Try one or the other method now.

If you have made any changes since the last time you saved, Word will ask if you want them saved. Select Yes to save changes, No to ignore the most recent changes, or Cancel to withdraw your exit request and return to word processing.

After you have satisfied Word that you have saved everything of value, Word will quit.

 **WARNING**

Word needs to do some housekeeping when you exit. For instance, Word updates its settings files and asks if you want to save last-minute changes to your documents. When you use Word's Exit command or attempt to quit Windows, this housekeeping will proceed smoothly. But if you use the power switch on your computer (or simply unplug it) without first executing a Word Exit or Windows Shut Down command, you may damage a document file or lose valuable changes to your Word settings.

FIGURE 1.18

Quit by choosing File ➤ Exit or by clicking on the Close box in the Word application window.

Click on the close box to quit Word.

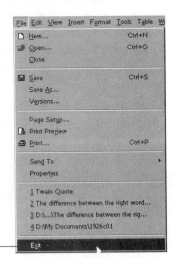

You can also choose File ➤ Exit to close Word.

Minimizing instead of Quitting

Like other Windows programs, Word can run *minimized*, which lets you get the program "out of the way" without actually exiting it. See your Windows documentation for information about multitasking between Word and other applications.

Launching Word by Double-Clicking on a Document

Once you've quit (exited) Word, you will need to restart the program before you can use it again. You could launch Word from the Start menu as you did before and then tell Word to load the document that you want to revise. But there is a shortcut. It is possible to load Word by double-clicking on a Word document icon.

Try this by double-clicking on your Twain Quote document icon in Windows Explorer. Follow these steps:

1. Click on Start in the lower left corner of your screen and slide up to Programs. From the cascading list, choose Windows Explorer.

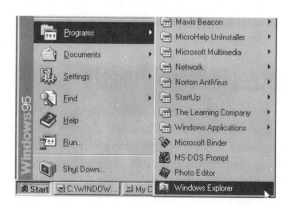

2. Find your Twain Quote (in your Winword folder), as shown in Figure 1.19.

FIGURE 1.19

Locate the Twain document.

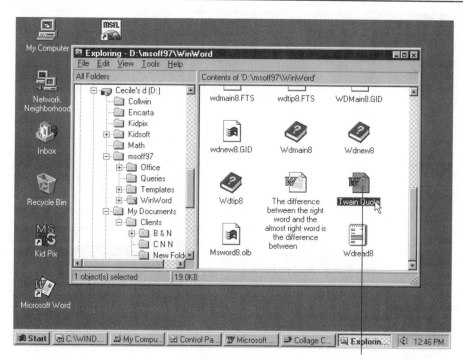

Double-click on Word files to load them and launch Word.

3. Double-click on the Twain Quote document icon.

4. After a moment, Word will appear on your screen, along with the Twain document, ready for you to edit.

It is even possible to launch Word 97 by double-clicking on documents created with earlier Word versions. Word 97 will convert them for you automatically. In addition, you can open a document by choosing Start ➤ Documents and then clicking on the document name.

Quick Access to Recent Projects

Once you have saved some Word documents, Word remembers their names and locations and lists them at the bottom of your File menu, as shown in Figure 1.20.

Choose the file of interest, and Word will attempt to locate and load it. If you have changed the document's name or moved it since your last Word session, Word may ask for help locating it.

By default, Word lists your last four documents. You can specify longer or shorter lists on the General tab of the Options dialog box (choose Tools ➤ Options). Simply check the Recently Used File List option and change the number next to Entries.

FIGURE 1.20

Word lists your four most recent projects at the bottom of the File menu.

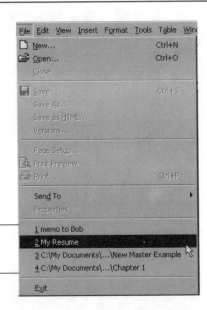

Recent projects can be loaded quickly from the File menu.

PART

1

Getting Started

Copying and Moving

Word supports all the usual Windows techniques for copying and moving information. It also provides a feature called *drag-and-drop*, a handy one-step, mouse-assisted mover.

Cut, Copy, and Paste

The traditional way to move or duplicate things in Windows programs is to select the item, cut or copy it to the Clipboard, move the insertion point to the new position, and paste in the item. For example, suppose you wanted to move the word *almost* so that it came before the first *right* in the Twain quotation. Here are the steps:

1. Start by selecting the desired text (you could simply double-click on *almost*, as shown in Figure 1.21).

FIGURE 1.21

First, select the item(s) you want to move.

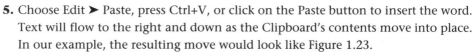

The difference between the right word and the *almost* right word is the difference between lightning and the lightning bug.
                                                    Mark Twain

2. Choose Edit ➤ Cut or press Ctrl+X. You can also click on the Cut button on the toolbar.

3. The selected text will disappear from the screen and will be placed on the Clipboard.

4. Now place the insertion point at the desired location (point and click). In this example, place it to the left of the first occurrence of the word *right*, as illustrated in Figure 1.22.

5. Choose Edit ➤ Paste, press Ctrl+V, or click on the Paste button to insert the word. Text will flow to the right and down as the Clipboard's contents move into place. In our example, the resulting move would look like Figure 1.23.

> The difference between the |right word and the right word is the difference between lightning and the lightning bug.
>
> **Mark Twain**

> The difference between the *almost* |right word and the right word is the difference between lightning and the lightning bug.
>
> **Mark Twain**

Copying from One Word Document to Another

Because you can open and work on multiple Word documents at the same time, it is easy to move things from one document to another. For example, two legal documents are open in Figure 1.24.

With a large screen, it is easy to size and position multiple windows in plain sight and quickly move back and forth simply by clicking in the window of interest. You can arrange your workspace by clicking and dragging the size boxes in the lower right corners of windows to adjust their size and shape. You can move windows around by pointing to their title bars and dragging them.

Although it is possible to have many windows in view at the same time, you can have only one active window. It is easy to tell which is the active window—it's the top one with the highlighted title bar in Figure 1.24.

FIGURE 1.24

You can open several documents simultaneously.

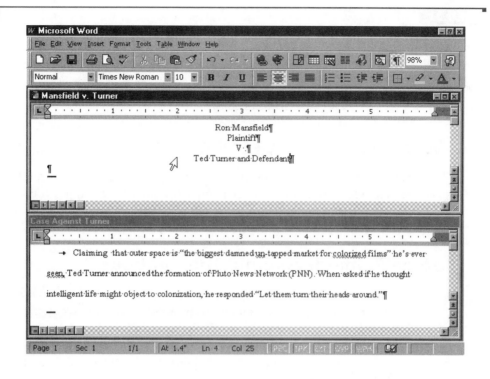

You can activate a window in several ways. The easiest is simply to click in it. Even if only a small portion of an inactive window is showing, clicking on it will activate it and bring it forward. Follow these steps:

1. Locate any portion of the desired window.
2. Click in it.
3. Resize and/or move windows if necessary to make it easier to work.

Word's Window Menu

Sometimes your screen may not be big enough to display multiple Word documents in useful sizes. Word provides the Window menu for these instances. As you can see in Figure 1.25, the Window menu lists the open documents and lets you switch between them. A checkmark indicates the active window. Using this menu, you can activate one window to copy information, go back to the Window menu to activate and display another window, and then paste.

The Window menu allows you to switch between documents.

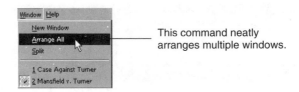

This command neatly arranges multiple windows.

What Formatting Gets Pasted?

When pasting from one document to another, sometimes you want the text being pasted to look as it did in its document of origin. At other times you want the text to take on the appearance of the document receiving it. This requires an understanding of styles, section formats, and other topics covered in Part Two of this book.

Some Reminders about the Clipboard

It is important to remember that when you cut or copy to the Clipboard, you replace whatever is stored there. If you do this by accident and spot your error immediately, Word's Undo command will restore the Clipboard's contents.

The Clipboard can store text, graphics, and even sound and animation. Although you normally don't need to see the Clipboard to use it, you can view its contents with the Windows Clipboard Viewer.

WARNING

The contents of the Clipboard disappear when you turn off your computer. If you want to save something permanently, save it in a Word document.

The contents of your Clipboard usually stay the same when you switch from document to document or from program to program, so if you're only moving small bits of text or graphics, using the Clipboard may be more efficient. If you are a Word user already, you'll find that much of what you formerly used the Clipboard for, though, has been replaced by new features in Word 97.

Getting Started

MASTERING THE OPPORTUNITIES

Copying with Document Scraps

Similar to the Clipboard is the Document Scraps feature. Like the Clipboard, a scrap can store text, graphics, sound, or animation; the difference, though, is that you can have multiple scraps, and when you create one scrap, it doesn't overwrite others. For purposes of comparison, here are the Clipboard Viewer and a document scrap.

In a sense, a scrap is like a little document and as such can be stored on disk. It is, therefore, safe, even when your computer is off. To make a scrap, you simply highlight what you want to place in the scrap file and drag it onto the desktop. To use a scrap, you simply drag it into another document or application. Note that a *copy* of what you've highlighted is placed in the scrap file. The original document is not altered; so you don't damage the original. Double-click on a scrap to view its contents.

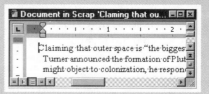

TIP

The Clipboard is probably best used now just for operations between Word documents. Windows 95 features such as document scraps and the right mouse button shortcut menu are easier ways to copy or move material between Windows applications.

If you are running several programs at once, you may find your computer will respond more quickly if you minimize one of the programs while working with the other. For instance, when copying from a spreadsheet, run Word minimized, and then minimize the spreadsheet and reactivate Word. If you are unfamiliar with this concept, consult your Windows documentation.

TIP

Advanced users will also want to explore other pasting options, including Linking and Embedding (described in Chapter 28, *Linking and Embedding to Keep Things Current*. These advanced techniques make it possible to keep multiple documents up to date when things change.

Drag-and-Drop

Word's drag-and-drop move feature lets you highlight text or other movable objects and drag them to a new location. For instance, in Figure 1.21, earlier in this chapter, the word *almost* has been highlighted with drag-and-drop enabled. With the primary mouse button pressed, the mouse pointer changes appearance slightly. Notice the small rectangle near the arrow. Notice also the pointer. The arrow, box, and pointer move as one when you move the mouse with the button held down. Once you release the mouse button, the selected items will be moved to the drag-and-drop insertion point. In Figure 1.26, the word *almost* would be inserted between *the* and *right*. If you use drag-and-drop while holding down the Ctrl key, you will move a copy of the highlighted text, leaving the original untouched.

NOTE

If you've held down your primary mouse button while selecting things (while dragging or double-clicking, for instance), you'll need to release the mouse button and press it again before you'll see the drag-and-drop pointer. Practice will make this second nature. Start by dragging and dropping the word *almost* to restore the Twain quote.

FIGURE 1.26

The pointer and insertion point change when drag-and-drop is enabled.

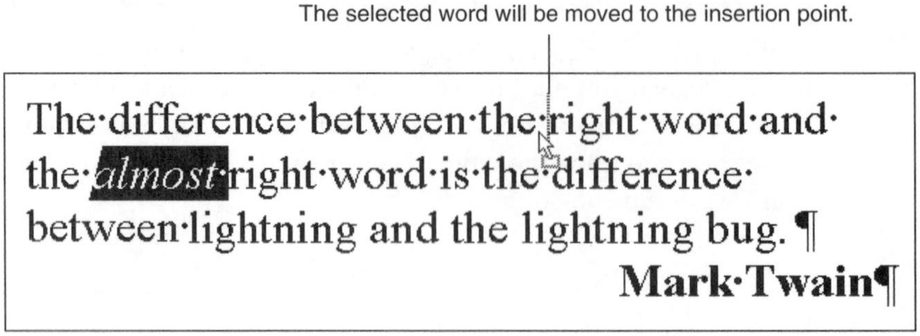

The selected word will be moved to the insertion point.

> The·difference·between·the·right·word·and·
> the·*almost*·right·word·is·the·difference·
> between·lightning and the lightning bug. ¶
> **Mark·Twain**¶

Steps for Moving with Drag-and-Drop

To move text with drag-and-drop, follow these steps:

1. Select the desired text or other item(s).
2. Release the mouse button, if necessary; then point to the selected item(s), and press and hold down the mouse button. Watch the mouse pointer.
3. When you see the pointer change to its drag-and-drop shape, drag the pointer while holding down the mouse button until the insertion point is at the desired new location.
4. Release the mouse button. The selected item(s) should move.
5. Undo immediately (Ctrl+Z) if things didn't go right.

Steps for Copying with Drag-and-Drop

Drag-and-drop copying works just like drag-and-drop moving, with one exception. You hold down the Ctrl key while you work. Follow these steps:

1. Select the desired text or other item(s).
2. Press and hold down the Ctrl key.
3. Release the mouse button, if necessary (while still holding down the Ctrl key); then point to the selected item(s), and press and hold down the mouse button. Watch the mouse pointer.
4. When you see the drag-and-drop pointer, drag the pointer while holding down the mouse button until the insertion point is at the desired new location.
5. Release the mouse button and the Ctrl key. The selected item(s) should be copied.
6. Undo immediately (Ctrl+Z) if you had a problem copying.

TIP

From time to time, you might accidentally drag and drop something when you intend to simply select by dragging. An immediate Undo (Ctrl+Z) will make things right. If you really hate drag-and-drop (and some people do), you can shut it off. See Chapter 32, *Personalizing Word*, for details.

Creating New Documents If Word Is Running

Whenever you start Word, it opens a new, untitled document so that you can begin a new project from scratch. If you want to start a new project with Word already running, simply click on the New button on the Standard toolbar or use the Ctrl+N keyboard shortcut. Word will open a new, untitled document window. Each new window opened this way in a session is sequentially numbered (Document1, Document2, and

Copying without the Ctrl Key

A new shortcut menu has been added in Word 97. It lets you copy text without holding down the Ctrl key.

To see it, drag and drop with the right mouse button instead of the left, and

you'll be able to choose Move Here or Copy Here.

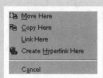

so on, and it will use your default Word settings). You'll be given a chance to use templates and Wizards (described in Part II) only when opening new document windows with the File ➤ New command. When in doubt, start with Word's default—the Normal template, shown here.

TIP

You can open a new, untitled document window by clicking on the dog-eared document icon located on the Standard toolbar.

Keyboards and Word

The first computers were like Ford's Model T—simple and utilitarian. You had no choice of keyboards. Today, manufacturers provide keyboards with a variety of layouts and features. For instance, there are international keyboards labeled with accent marks and configured with special characters for a variety of languages. Some portable computers have unique space-saving keyboard layouts and keys.

Fortunately, Word accommodates most of these differences. To use international keyboard layouts, choose Start ➤ Settings, double-click on the Keyboard icon in the Control Panel, and then select the Language tab. See your Windows documentation for details.

Keyboard Shortcuts

Touch-typists often dislike taking their hands off of the keyboard; so, as you've already seen, Word provides a variety of keyboard shortcuts, such as Ctrl+X for Cut. These shortcuts make it unnecessary to reach for the mouse. Keyboard shortcuts are mentioned throughout this book, and many are shown on Word's menus. The Customize dialog box (choose Tools ➤ Customize) will help you explore all of Word's keyboard shortcuts. It is possible to change or delete shortcuts or add your own new ones, as you will learn in Chapter 32.

Key Combinations for Special Characters

Your computer and Word can work together to display and print special characters that aren't shown on your keyboard. Examples include the copyright symbol and international characters with diacritical marks (umlauted letters, for instance). In general, you either specify these characters by using key combinations or with the Insert ➤ Symbol command. For instance, you can type the copyright symbol (©) by holding down the Alt key and pressing the Ctrl and c keys simultaneously.

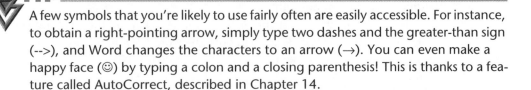

TIP

A few symbols that you're likely to use fairly often are easily accessible. For instance, to obtain a right-pointing arrow, simply type two dashes and the greater-than sign (-->), and Word changes the characters to an arrow (→). You can even make a happy face (☺) by typing a colon and a closing parenthesis! This is thanks to a feature called AutoCorrect, described in Chapter 14.

The available special characters and the procedures used to create them vary depending on which fonts you are using. That's why it's often easier to use the Insert ➤ Symbol command. Chapter 7, *Characters and Fonts,* shows you how to get the characters you need. Figure 1.27 gives you a glimpse of this feature.

Numeric Keypads and Word

Most newer keyboards have numeric keypads and cursor-movement keys (Home, Page Up, and so on). Word uses many of these keys if you have them.

Numeric keypads serve two functions in Word. With the Num Lock feature enabled, you can use the keypad to enter numbers. With Num Lock off (the default), you can use the numeric pad to navigate through your documents. Pressing 9 (Page Up) on the numeric pad scrolls the screen up, 3 (Page Down) scrolls down, and so on. If you have

FIGURE 1.27

The Insert ➤ Symbol com- mand lets you see and type special characters.

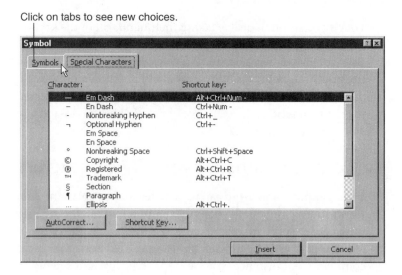

Click on tabs to see new choices.

a separate cursor-movement keypad, it's generally best to use that instead of the numeric keypad for navigating.

The key in the upper left corner of the numeric keypad toggles Num Lock on and off. Some newer keyboards contain both the word *Clear* and the abbreviation *Num Lock*. On some, it is labeled just *Clear*. Most keyboards have a light that tells you when Num Lock is enabled.

A few keyboard shortcuts are unavailable to users without numeric keypads. For example, the Unassign Keystroke command shortcut is unavailable without a numeric keypad. If you don't have a numeric keypad and you want to assign your own keyboard shortcuts to replace the ones you are missing, that is possible.

Repeating Keys

Most of the character keys and many of the navigational keys (such as arrows) will repeat if you hold them down. This is an easy way to type a series of keystrokes.

You can change the speed of this feature in the Speed tab of the Windows Keyboard Control Panel. The speed at which identical keystrokes are issued is called the Repeat Rate. A slider lets you select anything from Slow to Fast. The length of time your com- puter waits between your first key press and the rapid-fire insertion of identical key- strokes is called the *Repeat Delay* setting. See your Windows documentation for details.

Using Word's Menus without a Mouse

Beginners may want to skip this topic and revisit it at a later time. If you really hate to reach for your mouse when typing or if your mouse dies in the middle of a project, you can use Word's Keyboard Menus feature. It lets you use the right and left arrows to flip from menu to menu and the up and down arrows to make menu choices. Beginners— give yourself a week or two to get your eyes, hands, and brain working together before abandoning the mouse or trackball. If you must work sans mouse, here's how:

1. Activate the Keyboard Menu feature by pressing the Alt key.
2. Press the underlined letter of the desired menu, usually the first letter (*V* for View, *W* for Window, and so on), or you can use the left and right arrows to display the desired menu. Menus drop down and stay down as you choose them.
3. Because two of Word's menu choices start with the letter *F* (File and Format), you must remember that the shortcut for the Format menu is *O*.
4. Pressing Enter is equivalent to releasing the mouse button. Your choice will be carried out. To cancel the Keyboard Menu feature without taking any action, press the Esc (escape) key.

Keyboard Tricks in Dialog Boxes

Word supports the usual Windows navigating tricks in dialog boxes. For instance, in dialog boxes in which you are asked to type text or dimensions, you can tab from box to box. Holding down the Shift key will move you backward when you press Tab. Any time you see a button with a dark border, pressing Enter will work in place of clicking on the button. If you are unfamiliar with tricks such as these, consult your Windows manuals, or try the tutorial programs that came with Windows.

Hotspots

Even experienced users are sometimes unaware that you can display dialog boxes, windows, and other tools by double-clicking on appropriate areas (called *hotspots*) in Word. There may even be some undocumented hotspots you can discover on your own.

Beginners may want to skim this topic for now. As you gain experience with Word, you'll want to try some of these hotspot tricks and explore to find others.

Paragraph Dialog Box - Double-click on any indent marker.

Page Setup Dialog Box - If you double-click on the small square box at either end of the ruler, you'll see the Page Setup dialog box used to control header, footer, and other measurements precisely.

When in Page Layout view, if you double-click in the margins at the corners of your document, you will also see the Document dialog box.

Footnote Window - To display a footnote window, simply double-click on a footnote reference mark.

The Go To Dialog Box - To display the Go To dialog box, useful for navigating in big documents, double-click on a page or a section number in the status area at the lower left portion of the document window.

Cell Height and Width Dialog Box - Click on the space on the ruler that separates cells.

Section - Double-click on section break marks to display the Page Setup dialog box. It contains section break information.

Mouse Command Shortcuts

Word also provides a nifty mouse feature that employs the nonprimary (usually the right) mouse button. Frequently, when you point to items on the screen and press the non-primary mouse button, you'll see a list of commands that you can issue with your mouse. For instance, in Figure 1.28, Word is telling you that you can cut, paste, change fonts, change paragraph settings, and more, simply by dragging to select from the list.

FIGURE 1.28

Click the non-primary mouse button to view and select commands without using menus or toolbars.

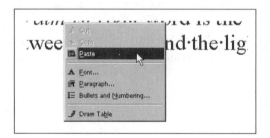

Getting Help with Word

It's a little ironic that Word has so many online help features that it takes several pages of a book to describe them. Word has four kinds of online help—Office Assistant, topic-specific help, point-and-shoot help, and (for WordPerfect users) WordPerfect help. In addition, Microsoft offers product support over the telephone, via fax, and

Getting Started

through CompuServe and the Internet. There is also TTY assistance for the hearing impaired.

Because Word's Help feature does a good job of explaining itself, we'll just touch on it here.

NOTE
The Help menu also includes a cascading Microsoft on the Web menu that helps you find Microsoft-specific information on the Internet. For more information, see the last part of this book.

The Assistant

If you are a Microsoft Word user, unless someone turned off this feature, you're already aware of the new Office Assistant, because every time you start Word, it appears—ready to assist you. (If not, press F1.) By default, the Assistant looks like a lively paper clip, but if you're not fond of dancing office supplies, you can change it into something you can live with, such as the Power Pup shown here. Click on the Assistant when you need help.

As you'd expect, clicking on Tips usually displays a tip related to what you've been doing, and clicking on Options lets you adjust the default options for Assistant (see Figure 1.29).

Changing the Assistant's persona is really easy. Click on Options to open the Office Assistant dialog box, and then click on the Gallery tab (see Figure 1.30). Use the Next and Back buttons to scroll through the available characters until you decide who you like best, and then click on OK.

FIGURE 1.29
Office Assistant offers assistance.

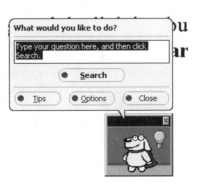

FIGURE 1.30

*Changing
Office Assistant
with the
Gallery tab*

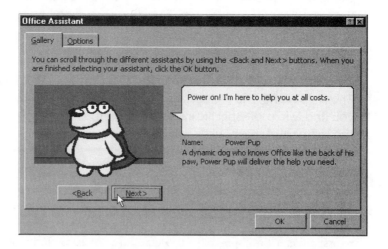

Searching for Specific Words of Wisdom

The Office Assistant lets you enter specific words and phrases that Word uses to pull up help information. For instance, to find out more about printing, you might do the following:

1. Click on Office Assistant or choose Help ➤ Microsoft Word Help. The Office Assistant asks, "What would you like to do?"
2. Type a search word or phrase (*print*, for example) and press Enter or click on Search. Word will show you a list of possible topics, as illustrated in Figure 1.31.
3. Select the one that seems closest to what you're interested in by clicking it.
4. Or, if necessary, rephrase what you searched on to locate pertinent topics.

The Help Contents Window

To see an overview of Word's online help, choose the Help ➤ Contents and Index command and select the Contents tab. Word displays a scrolling list, as shown in **Figure 1.32**.

Getting Different Kinds of Help

Double-click on an icon to see a list of subtopics. Then double-click on topics of interest to find out more about them. For example, if you double-click on What's New, you'll see a handy list of new Word features. You can then choose to find out more about Office Assistant, for instance.

PART

I

Getting Started

FIGURE 1.31

Searching Help files for specific words or phrases

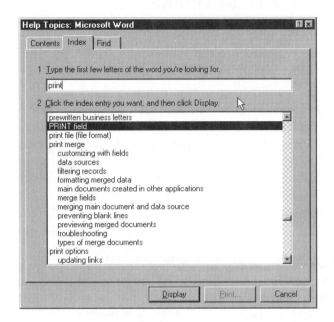

FIGURE 1.32

Use this Help window to select topics and read more about them.

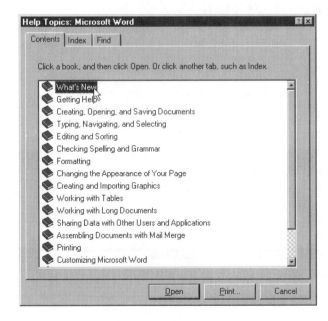

Pointing to Get Online Help

You can often use your mouse to point to things on your screen and get help by selecting Word's What's This command from the Help menu. It changes the pointer into an arrow with a question mark. When you point and click with that pointer, you get online help. Here's an example:

1. Choose Help ➤ What's This? or press Shift + F1. Your mouse pointer will become a giant question mark with an arrow. (Press Esc if this happens by mistake.)
2. Using your mouse, point to an item about which you have a question (the ruler, for instance).
3. Click on the desired item (the ruler in this case). The topic will appear in the pop-up window.
4. Read the Help text.
5. If you want, press Shift + F1 and click on another item.

> **TIP**
>
> Because most dialog boxes no longer contain Help buttons, often the quickest way to get help on an item in a dialog box is to press Shift + F1 to activate point-and-click Help; then click on the item of interest.

WordPerfect Help

WordPerfect Help is available for reformed WordPerfect users. With WordPerfect Help enabled, you'll see brief descriptions of items and their functions as you point to them. Figure 1.33 illustrates this.

To access WordPerfect Help, follow these steps:

1. Be sure that WordPerfect Help has been installed and enabled.
2. Choose Help ➤ WordPerfect Help.
3. Select a topic from the scrolling list, as illustrated in Figure 1.33.
4. Point and click on a topic to read about it.
5. Use the buttons at the bottom of the window to see demos and explore other Help options.
6. Press Esc or click on the Close button to quit.

> **TIP**
>
> Double-click on the WPH button in the status area for WordPerfect Help.

Getting Started

FIGURE 1.33

*WordPerfect
Help in action*

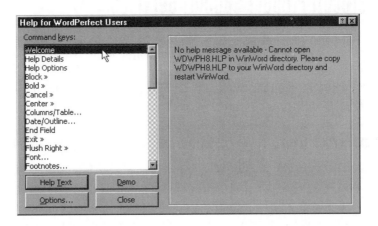

Printing Online Help

You can often print online help topics by using the Print button in a Help window. Be sure your printer is set up and ready first. For more information on printing, see Chapter 3, *Previewing and Printing*.

Quitting Online Help

Pressing Esc closes the Help window. So does clicking in the Help window's Close box, found in the upper right corner of the window.

Word Help from the Internet

Microsoft is creating an amazing collection of online help tools for all of its products, including Microsoft Word. When you visit the Microsoft on the Web tab (in Word's Help menu), you will see a list of choices like Free Stuff, Product News, Frequently Asked Questions, Online Support, and so on. If you are Internet-ready, these choices will take you to Microsoft's Web sites where you can get answers to your toughest questions, download free software updates, templates, and more. Be sure to check out the various sites, then keep going back. They are constantly updated and well worth revisiting. One of the most powerful online resources is Microsoft's Knowledge Base.

Microsoft Product Support Services

When you really get stuck, Microsoft's huge technical support staff can be a big help. Microsoft provides technical note downloading services, CompuServe forums, pre-recorded support messages, and even real live people to answer your questions. If you can't find the answers you need in Word's online help, in your manuals, or in books such as this one, it is time to call out the big guns.

To Find Out More about Tech Support Options

Microsoft is changing the way it supports users, and things that were once free are now often quite expensive. To read more about available support options, use the About Microsoft Word command on Word's Help menu and click on the Tech Support button. It will show you a list of topics something like the one in Figure 1.34. Click on topics to learn more.

WARNING

Microsoft technical support is not always free. Be sure you understand the costs before obtaining support.

FIGURE 1.34

Click on a topic to read more about Microsoft technical support operations.

Chapter

2

Viewing and Navigating

FEATURING

Chapter 2

Viewing and Navigating

You do your work in Word in *document windows*, which you can position and resize for your convenience. Word provides navigational tools that let you move quickly to the desired part of even huge documents. Several views make it easy to see what your document will look like without printing it. Other views are available to simplify and speed the creation of rough drafts and outlines. In addition, you can hide and show elements such as paragraph marks (¶) and the little dots between words that denote spaces. A new Word 97 tool called the Document Map is a big improvement over older navigational techniques. Don't overlook it.

Scrolling in a Window

Most documents are too big to be displayed in their entirety on your screen. You reveal unseen portions of your document by scrolling to bring parts of the document into view while temporarily hiding other parts. Usually, you'll scroll up and down to see long documents, but you will sometimes need to scroll left and right to see different parts of wide documents. There are many ways to scroll. Refer to Figure 2.1 while you read about scrolling.

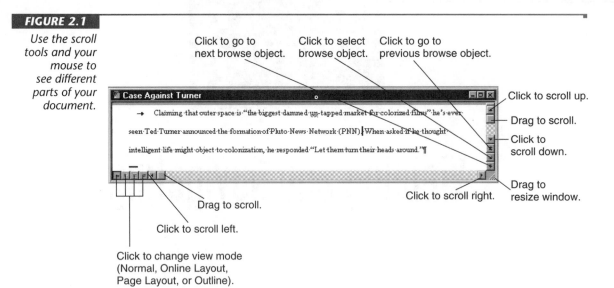

FIGURE 2.1

Use the scroll tools and your mouse to see different parts of your document.

Click to go to next browse object.

Click to select browse object.

Click to go to previous browse object.

Click to scroll up.

Drag to scroll.

Click to scroll down.

Drag to resize window.

Click to scroll right.

Drag to scroll.

Click to scroll left.

Click to change view mode (Normal, Online Layout, Page Layout, or Outline).

Scrolling with the Scroll Arrows

When you click on a scroll arrow, you will see a different part of your document. For instance, suppose you are looking at page 2 of a three-page document. If you click on the up scroll arrow (located near the top right of the active window), you will move a little nearer to the beginning of the document. Clicking on the down-pointing arrow will take you closer to the end of the document. (Typically, one click moves you up or down about one line.) The right- and left-pointing arrows let you see corresponding portions of wide documents.

TIP

If you click and hold down the mouse button while pointing to any of the four scrolling arrows, your document will scroll continuously until you reach the end of the document or release the mouse button. But there are better ways to scroll long distances. Read on.

Scrolling by Clicking in the Scroll Bars

Clicking in the shaded areas of scroll bars (as opposed to clicking on the scroll arrows themselves) scrolls approximately one screen's worth. The exact scroll distance will vary with your screen and document window size. Experiment.

Scrolling with the Scroll Boxes

The square boxes in the horizontal and vertical scroll bars can be used to move great distances quickly. For instance, if you are looking at page 1 of a 100-page document, the scroll box will be at the top of the vertical scroll bar. Dragging it with your mouse exactly half way down the scroll bar will bring page 50 into view; dragging it three-quarters of the way will take you to page 75; and so forth. Horizontal scroll boxes can be used the same way to scroll wide documents quickly.

Obviously, it is difficult to drag to the exact middle or three-quarters position on the scroll bar. Use the scroll boxes to get you in the neighborhood, and then use other scrolling tools to fine-tune, as shown in Figure 2.1.

WARNING

It's easy to forget to move the insertion point when you bounce from place to place in a document by scrolling or using the navigational tricks discussed in this chapter. Get into the habit of repositioning and then looking for the insertion point before you type, paste, or take other potentially destructive actions!

MASTERING THE OPPORTUNITIES

Speeding Screen Scrolling

If you find scrolling and other screen actions somewhat sluggish, try some of these suggestions:

- Add more RAM and try the other usual Windows speed-up tricks well-documented elsewhere. Word runs best in 8MB or more.

- Work in Normal view whenever possible.

- Close unwanted windows and applications that you are not using.

- Consider breaking one very large document into several smaller ones (books into chapters, for instance).

The Select Browse Object

 If you want to browse through your document to see all of a specific type of item, you'll find the new Select Browse Object feature handy. Basically, it lets you move around after selecting one of the pictured objects as the browse marker:

For example, if you want to move from graphic to graphic in your document, click on the Select Browse Object button near the bottom of the right vertical scroll bar, and then click on the Browse by Graphic button. The cursor moves to the next graphic.

 Clicking on the Next Graphic button (the name of this button changes based on what you selected to browse by) moves you along. Chances are you will love this feature once you remember it is available. Try it!

Navigating with Your Keyboard

Word offers many, many keyboard shortcuts for navigating. You can scroll using keyboard commands, or you can scroll and move the insertion point at the same time. Be sure you understand the difference!

Moreover, frequently if you hold the Shift key down while using keyboard shortcuts, you will select text in addition to scrolling and moving the insertion point. For example, pressing the Ctrl+→ key combination moves the insertion point to the beginning of the next word, and Ctrl+Shift+→ selects the current word starting at the insertion point and the space following it.

There should be a keyboard shortcut that lists all of Word's keyboard-navigation shortcuts, but there isn't. Table 2.1 is the next-best thing.

If your keyboard has no cursor-movement keys, use the numbers on the numeric keypad (with Num Lock off) for the tasks listed in Table 2.1. Home, End, Page Up, and Page Down keys are not available on all keyboards. If you ever memorize all of Word's keyboard shortcuts, you are spending too much time with Word. Take a very long vacation.

**WARNING**

Be careful when using the numeric keypad to navigate. For instance, if you select some text and then press the asterisk key (*) by accident when you meant to hit the Page Up key on the keypad, your text will be replaced with an asterisk! Or, if Num Lock is accidentally turned on when you press the up arrow key (or any other arrow key), the selected text will be replaced with the number corresponding to the key you've pressed. Some users avoid the numeric pad navigation shortcuts for these reasons.

Getting Started

TABLE 2.1: KEYBOARD SHORTCUTS FOR NAVIGATING AND EDITING

Scrolling

To move to...	Press...
Up	↑ or 8 (keypad)
Down	↓ or 2 (keypad)
Left	← or 4 (keypad)
Right	→ or 6 (keypad)
Previous Word	Ctrl+← or Ctrl+4 (keypad)
Next Word	Ctrl+→ or Ctrl+6 (keypad)
Beginning of line	Home or 7 (keypad)
End of line	End or 1 (keypad)
One paragraph up	Ctrl+↑ or Ctrl+8 (keypad)
One paragraph down	Ctrl+↓ or Ctrl+2 (keypad)
Next page	Ctrl+Page Down
Previous page	Ctrl+ Page Up
Top of window	Page Up
Bottom of window	Page Down
Start of document	Ctrl+Home
End of document	Ctrl+End
Scroll up one screen	Page Up or 9 (keypad)
Scroll down one screen	Page Down or 3 (keypad)

Continued ▶

TABLE 2.1: KEYBOARD SHORTCUTS FOR NAVIGATING AND EDITING (CONTINUED)

In tables or page layout view

To move to...	Press...
Next cell in table	Tab
Previous cell in table	Shift+Tab
Next page element	Ctrl+Alt+Page Down or 3
First cell in row	Alt+Home
Top cell in column	Alt+Page Up
Last cell in row	Alt+End
Last cell in column	Alt+Page Down
Up or down in row	↑, ↓, ←, →

Editing

To...	Press...
Select the entire document	Ctrl+A
Delete character to left of cursor or selected text	Backspace
Delete character after cursor or selected text	Delete
Delete previous word	Ctrl+Backspace
Delete next word	Ctrl+Delete
Copy text	Ctrl+C
Copy formats	Ctrl+Shift+C
Paste formats	Ctrl+Shift+V
Add selection to Spike	Ctrl+F3
Insert Spike contents	Ctrl+Shift+F3

The Improved Go To Command

When editing big documents, particularly when you have a marked-up paper copy in your hand, it is useful to be able to scoot quickly to a particular page or to a specific page within a certain section. If you know page (and section) numbers, Word makes this easy. Word can also take you to specified lines, bookmarks, annotations, footnotes, endnotes, fields, tables, graphics, equations, and objects.

This is all accomplished in the Go To tab of the newly reworked Find and Replace dialog box, as shown in Figure 2.2 (choose Edit ➤ Go To or press F5).

In single-section documents or documents in which page numbers do not restart in each section, simply type the page number and press Enter or click on the Go To button. Quicker than you can say *amen*, Word takes you to the requested page and places the insertion point at the beginning of the first line on the page. Here are the steps:

1. Press the F5 function key or choose Edit ➤ Go To. The dialog box opens with the Go To tab in front.

2. Type a page number in the dialog box.

3. Press Enter or click on Go To. Word will take you to the page.

4. Close the Go To dialog box with the Close button or with the Close box or press Esc.

5. Get back to work.

FIGURE 2.2

The Go To tab

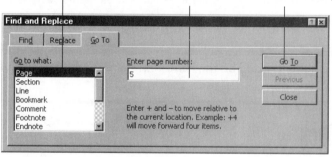

1. Select the defined item.　2. Type your choice.　3. Click here or press Enter.

Section Numbers and the Go To Command

If your document is broken into sections with page numbers that restart in new sections, you must specify section numbers in the Go To dialog box. (See Chapter 11, *Formatting Your Work with Section Breaks,* for more about sections.) To specify a section number in the Go To dialog box, type an **S**. For instance, typing **S4** would take you to the beginning of Section 4, (assuming your document has a Section 4).

To specify a particular page and section, type **P**, the page number, **S**, and the section number. Thus, **P3S5** would take you to the third page in the fifth section. **S5P3** will do the same thing.

You can also go to a particular section by selecting Section in the scrolling list and then typing the section number. Once in the section, you can use Go To again to get to the appropriate page within the section.

PART

I

Getting Started

Many Ways to Use the Go To Command

You can also use the Go To command to move forward or backward a specific number of pages. And you can use it to go to the end of a document, even if you don't know the last page number. Here's a list of some of the things you can do with the Go To dialog box and samples of typical entries:

- Move to the beginning of the document (0)
- Move to the next page (+ or leave blank)
- Move to the last page (enter any number greater than the number of pages in the document)
- Move to a specific page number (4 or P4)
- Move to a specific page within a specific section (P4S3)
- Move to the first page of a specific section (S3)
- Move forward a specified number of pages—3 for example (+3)
- Move back a specific number of pages—5 for instance (-5)
- Move to other specific document elements such as graphics, tables, bookmarks, annotations, and so on

TIP

Double-clicking on the Page Number portion of the status area will open the Go To dialog box.

Go Back

Here's a handy but often confusing gizmo. When you are editing, it is sometimes necessary to bounce from one part of a document to another part of the same document. Or, if you have two documents open, you may find yourself repeatedly moving from one document to the other.

Word remembers the last three places you have edited plus the current insertion-point location. The Go Back feature lets you quickly move to those edit points. Simply press Shift+F5 (or Ctrl+Alt+Z) repeatedly to cycle you through the last three insertion-point locations. The Go Back command is not on Word's standard menus, but you can add it or even create a toolbar button for it. See Chapter 32, *Personalizing Word*, for how to do this.

Incidentally, simply moving the insertion point somewhere in a document does not necessarily add that point to the places in the Go Back list. Generally, you need to edit something there.

Using Find to Navigate

Word's Find command is a great way to move to an area needing work. For instance, if you are looking at a printout containing a typo you want to fix, use the Find command to get to the corresponding spot on your screen. Here are the basics (see Chapter 16, *Finding and Replacing*, for details):

1. Press Ctrl+F or choose Edit ➤ Find to open the Find and Replace dialog box. The dialog box opens with the Find tab in front.
2. Enter the text you want to find and press Enter. Word searches (usually down from the insertion point) and shows you the first occurrence of the specified text.

TIP

Word has a feature in Find called Find All Word Forms, which lets you broaden the scope of your searches.

3. Click on Find Next or press Enter to move to the next occurrence, if that's not the occurrence you want. You can also click on More to see additional options you can apply.
4. If necessary, answer Yes (press Enter) when Word asks if it should search from the beginning of the document.
5. When you find what you need, close the Find and Replace dialog box or click in the document window to activate it.
6. Edit away.

There is much, much more to know about Find and its companion, the Replace command. Be sure to read Chapter 16.

MASTERING THE OPPORTUNITIES

Navigating with the New IntelliMouse

The new Microsoft IntelliMouse is the most intelligent pointing device yet—it lets you scroll and zoom on a Word document by manipulating a small "wheel" button. With it you can easily scroll, pan, or autoscroll up or down, zoom in or out, and expand or collapse the headings that display in Outline or Document Map view.

If you're lucky enough to have the state-of-the-art IntelliMouse, be sure to read Word's online help for techniques that will make you more productive. And if you are using a standard two or three-button mouse and find navigating and zooming frustratingly slow, consider upgrading to IntelliMouse.

Views New and Improved

Word can show your document with varying levels of detail to make things easier to visualize or quicker to work with. These display options are called *views*. Word provides eight views:

- Normal
- Online Layout
- Page Layout
- Outline
- Print Preview
- Split Screen
- Master Document
- Full Screen

Normal View

Unless you are very patient or have a very fast computer with a large screen, use Normal view for most of your heavy-duty text entry and editing. Word's other views respond noticeably slower to typing, editing, and scrolling.

Normal view (illustrated in Figure 2.3) keeps repagination and screen redraw delays to a minimum. It shows your text as you have typed it and displays graphics where you've inserted them (which is not necessarily where they'll print).

Normal view (the default) depicts type sizes, line spacing, indents, and so on with reasonable accuracy. It does not show side-by-side column positioning, footers, headers, or the printing position of framed items. Columns are shown at their actual width, but not side-by-side. Automatic page breaks are shown as dotted lines. Manual page breaks, if you've defined any, are shown as darker lines containing the words *Page Break*, and section breaks are double dark lines with the words *End of Section*, and so on.

NOTE If you have instructed Word to number lines, the numbers will not appear in Normal view. Use Page Layout view or Print Preview to see line numbers.

Editing in Normal View

You can create and edit text, columns, and graphics as usual in Normal view. To work on headers or footers, though, you must open Header or Footer windows from the View menu. For more detail, see Chapter 10, *Headers, Footers, Page Numbers, and Footnotes*.

Getting Started

FIGURE 2.3

Normal view is the best for ordinary editing and text entry.

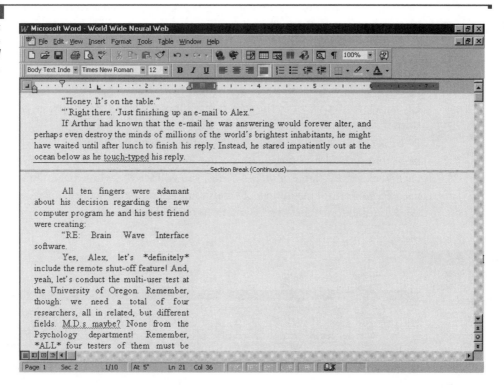

Switching Views

You use the View menu to select Normal, Online Layout, Page Layout Outline, Master Document, or Full Screen views.

Four buttons in the bottom left corner of Word's status area let you quickly switch views. They are (from left to right) Normal View, Online Layout View, Page Layout View, and Outline View.

Switch to Print Preview by choosing File ➤ Print Preview or by clicking on the Print Preview button on the Standard toolbar.

Page Layout View

Figure 2.4 shows what happens to the text from Figure 2.3 when it is displayed in Page Layout view. In this view, the screen resembles a white sheet of paper, or at least a portion of a sheet.

Look closely at the top and left edges of the screen in Figure 2.4. You will see a dark background that Word places behind the "paper." With the Zoom Control set to Whole Page View (or on a large enough screen), you will see the whole page. On smaller screens, with Zoom Control magnified, or when using a large paper setting in Page Setup, you may need to scroll to see these representations of the paper's edges.

FIGURE 2.4

In Page Layout view, you can see text as it will print.

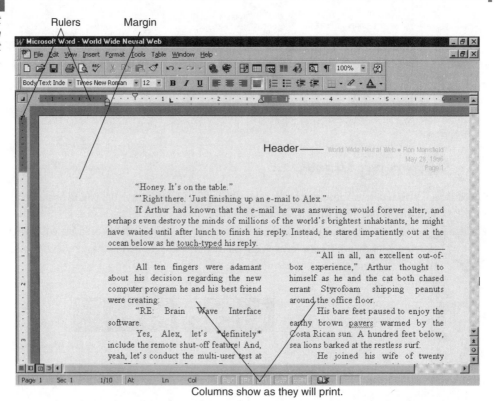

PART
I

Editing in Page Layout View

Generally, you edit as usual in Page Layout view. Text and graphics are positioned where they will print. Headers and footers can be both seen and edited. Click in a header, footer, or body text to position the insertion point. Page breaks, be they automatic or forced, are represented by new pages on the screen rather than by dashed lines in the text. You can scroll from page to page, as you'd expect.

Hidden Text in Page Layout View

If you have hidden text in your document and you reveal it, Page Layout view will display line and page endings adjusted to include the hidden text. This may not correspond to pages that you print if the Print dialog box's Print Hidden Text box is unchecked. To see what your pages will look like without the hidden text, you must hide the text by unchecking the Show Hidden Text box in the Preferences dialog box.

Headers and Footers in Page Layout View

You can see headers and footers in Page Layout view. To edit, double-click anywhere in a header or footer. It will "undim" and be surrounded by a dashed line, as shown in Figure 2.5. The Header and Footer toolbar will also appear if it's not already on your screen.

FIGURE 2.5

Click in a header or a footer to edit it.

Double-click to activate a header or a footer.

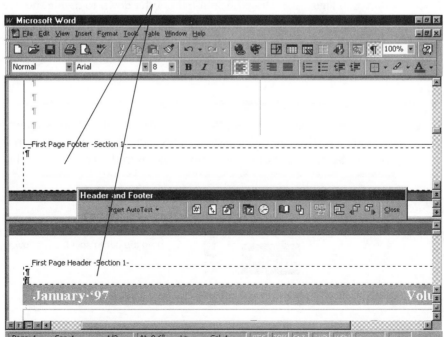

Getting Started

To add date or time entries and page numbering to headers and footers, use the buttons on the Header and Footer toolbar. You can format text in headers just as you would anywhere else in a Word document. For instance, to right-align header text, place the insertion point in the text (or select multiple lines in the header) and click on the Formatting toolbar's Right-align button.

Line Numbers Show in Page Layout View

If you have requested numbered lines, the numbers will appear in Page Layout view as shown here:

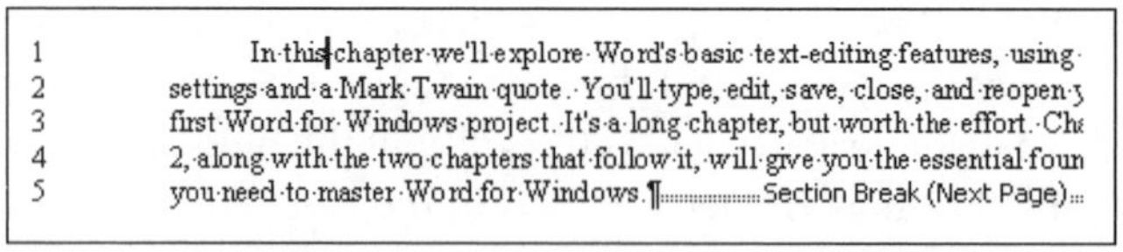

> 1   In·this·chapter·we'll·explore·Word's·basic·text-editing·features,·using·
> 2   settings·and·a·Mark·Twain·quote.·You'll·type,·edit,·save,·close,·and·reopen·{
> 3   first·Word·for·Windows·project.·It's·a·long·chapter,·but·worth·the·effort.·Cha
> 4   2,·along·with·the·two·chapters·that·follow·it,·will·give·you·the·essential·foun
> 5   you·need·to·master·Word·for·Windows.¶·············Section Break (Next Page)···

Split-Screen View

Regardless of which view you prefer, you can profit from using Word's split-screen feature. You can use the split-screen to keep two widely separated portions of a document in view at the same time. To split the screen, simply point to the small horizontal bar above the top scroll bar arrow. The pointer will change to the Split-bar pointer, as shown in Figure 2.6. Drag the Split-bar pointer down to divide the screen.

When you release the mouse button, your screen will split into two independent windows, each with its own scroll bar. To return to a single screen, double-click on the Split bar or drag it to just below the title bar. This takes some practice. Alternately, you can use the keyboard shortcut Alt+Ctrl+S.

TIP

When you unsplit the screen, the portion that the insertion point was in becomes the only screen. This can be a nuisance if you actually wanted to be in the other portion of text! So be sure that the insertion point is in the correct pane before you unsplit.

FIGURE 2.6

The pointer will change shape.

When the pointer changes shape, drag the bar to split the window.

Why Split Screens?

With the screen split you can see two parts of your document at once. Use this feature to refer to different portions of a document as you write or to speed copying, cutting, and pasting. But there's another powerful reason to use split screens.

Split Screen and Different Views

You can use a different view in each portion of the split screen. For instance, you might want to speed scrolling and editing by working in a window pane set to Normal view while watching the effects of your changes in a Page Layout view pane, as shown in Figure 2.7.

PART
I

Getting Started

FIGURE 2.7

You can arrange the document with Normal view in the top pane and Page Layout view in the bottom.

Normal view

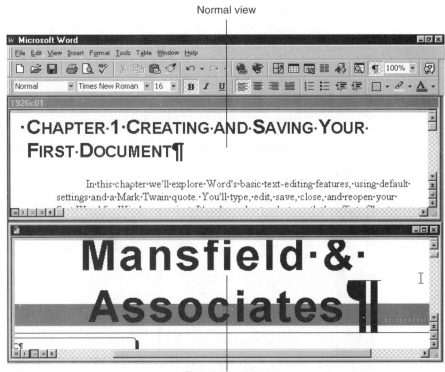

Page Layout view

Print Preview

Print Preview is more than just another way to view documents. Choose File ➤Print Preview, press Ctrl+Alt+I, press Ctrl+F2, or click on the Print Preview button.

Depending on your screen size and settings, you will see either an unreadable bird's-eye view of a page or two (like the one in Figure 2.8) or a full, readable page. You can even click on your document to see a close-up view when the cursor looks like a magnifying glass.

FIGURE 2.8

Print Preview gives you a bird's-eye view of one or two pages at once.

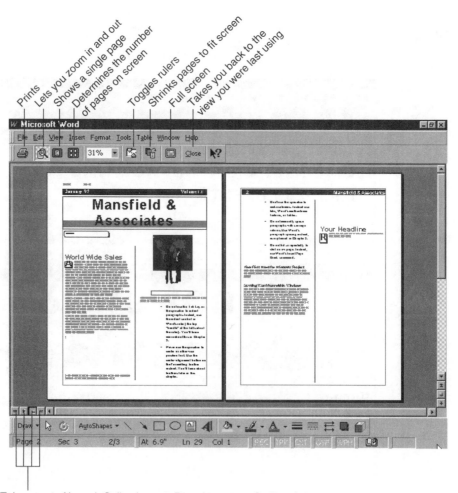

Takes you to Normal, Online Layout, Page Layout, or Outline view

In either case, you will be able to reposition margins in Print Preview. You cannot edit text or headers and footers in Print Preview. You also will not be able to see certain Page Setup printer tricks, such as image flips.

> **TIP**
>
> Click on the Close button in Print Preview to bring you back to whatever view you were in previously.

The New Online Layout View

When you switch to the Online Layout view, Word applies a series of default settings to instantly make your document easier to read on screen, without affecting its formatting. Word optimizes readability by increasing the font size and space between lines, shortening the lines and hiding some distractions such as the header and footer. This view is great for reading and reviewing the content of documents—especially those you receive from others who like to write in eight-point fonts and single-spaced lines.

> **TIP**
>
> You can set the minimum font size in this view by choosing Tools ➤ Options ➤ View and then entering the minimum font size in the Enlarge Fonts Less Than box.

The Document Map view, described next, also displays whenever you choose Online Layout view.

The New Document Map View

The Document Map view displays a pane to the left of the document window (see Figure 2.9). Think of it as an interactive table of contents based on the document's heading styles.

The document map helps you browse through a long document—click on a heading in the left to move to that section in the document window. It also helps you quickly see the structure of a long document.

Outline View

A complete description of Word's Outline feature can be found in Chapter 17, *Get Organized with Outline View*. For now, it is enough to know that if your document is properly formatted, switching to Outline view lets you quickly navigate and reorganize even large,

FIGURE 2.9

Document Map view lets you see a document's structure and contents simultaneously.

Document Map

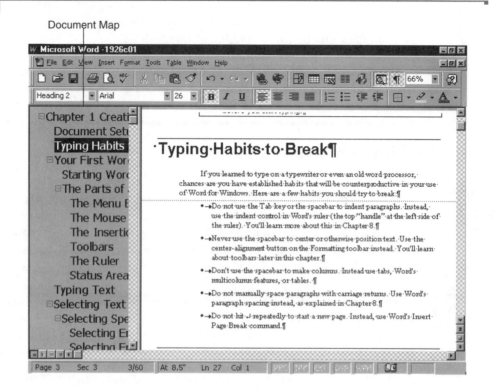

complex documents. In Outline view, you can see the entire contents of the document, only chapter headings, only section headings, and so on. For instance, Figure 2.10 shows part of a book outline down to paragraph headings, but does not include the text of the book itself.

If you wanted to move all Typing Habits to Break information to after the Typing Text section, you might ordinarily use Normal or Page Layout view to scroll through and select the complete text of Typing Habits to Break ; then you would cut and paste it into the new position. But by using Outline view, you could simply "collapse" the view, as shown in Figure 2.10, and drag the +*Typing Habits to Break* heading down. All its associated text would follow.

You need not begin projects by creating an in-depth outline, as you will see later when you read about styles and outlines. But by creating and applying appropriate styles for various heading levels, you can quickly create a document that can be expanded or compressed for viewing and editing with Outline tools. And of course, creating an outline is a good way to organize your thoughts before you begin writing.

PART

I

Getting Started

FIGURE 2.10

Part of a book outline view at paragraph-heading level

Dragging in Outline view moves headings and all associated text.

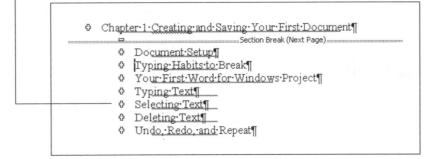

Master Document View

This view is used when working on large documents. Master Document view lets you group multiple Word documents together into one large document (like this book) while keeping the common elements such as the table of contents and index in sync See Chapter 23, *Working with Master Documents.*

View Defaults

Normal view is the default for new documents. Word will, however, remember the view you were using when you last saved a document and open the document in that view. If you opened a new document in Normal view, did some work, switched to Page Layout view, saved, and exited, the next time you opened the document it would appear in Page Layout view.

Showing Paragraph Marks, Spaces, and Other Nonprinting Characters

Word can display helpful nonprinting characters to let you see what's going on. Examples include:

- Paragraph marks (¶)
- Dots denoting spaces

- Arrows denoting tab characters
- Dashed lines for page, section, and column breaks
- Text and graphic boundaries

I like to leave these on, although turning them off can sometimes help you better visualize the final appearance of a document. To toggle the display of these items, click on the Show/Hide ¶ button on the Standard toolbar.

Zooming

The little drop-down list near the right end of the Formatting toolbar is called the Zoom Control. It lets you zoom in and out to see bigger or smaller on-screen representations. It does not affect printing size. Figure 2.11 shows it in use, magnifying the text.

The View ➤ Zoom command gives you even more control over on-screen character size.

FIGURE 2.11

Use the Zoom Control to increase or decrease the size of on-screen images.

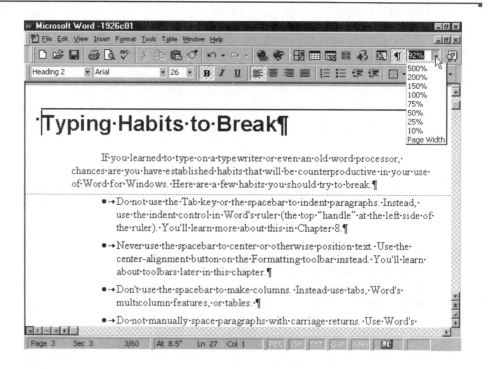

Full Screen—Seeing Only Your Work

Choosing View ➤ Full Screen or clicking on the corresponding button in Print Preview removes all the usual workspace clutter and fills your screen with your current document. You'll also see a very small window containing a button, as shown in Figure 2.12.

Edit as usual. Navigate with Page Up, Page Down, and the rest of the keyboard tools. To return to the prior view, click on the little Full Screen button, press Esc, or use the Alt+V+U keyboard shortcut. Incidentally, the Full Screen button's window can be dragged out of the way.

TIP

If you accidentally close the Full Screen button's window, don't panic. Simply press the Esc button to restore all your toolbars, menus, and other controls.

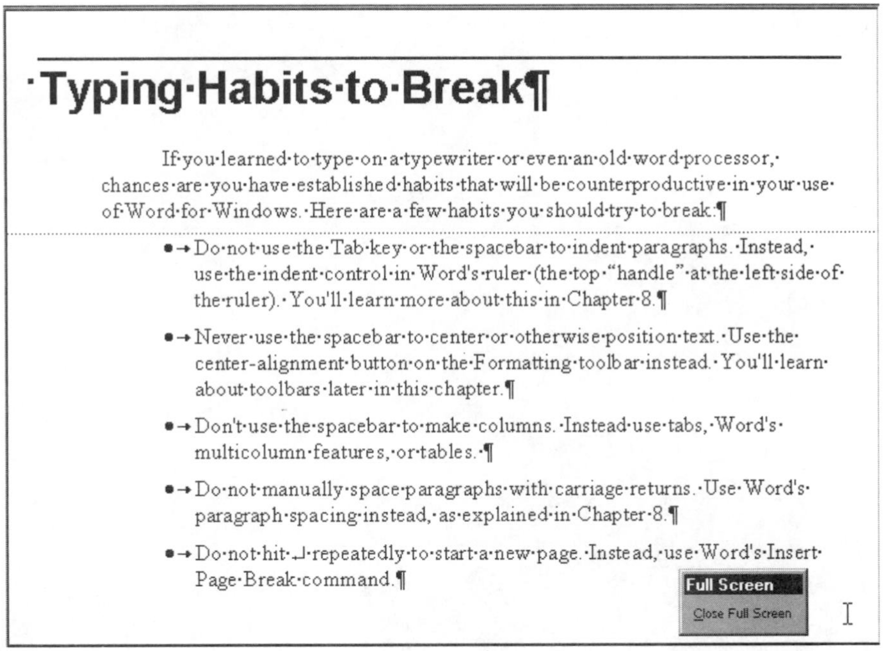

FIGURE 2.12

Full Screen removes everything but your work and a small button window.

·Typing·Habits·to·Break¶

If·you·learned·to·type·on·a·typewriter·or·even·an·old·word·processor,· chances·are·you·have·established·habits·that·will·be·counterproductive·in·your·use· of·Word·for·Windows.·Here·are·a·few·habits·you·should·try·to·break.¶

- •→ Do·not·use·the·Tab·key·or·the·spacebar·to·indent·paragraphs.·Instead,· use·the·indent·control·in·Word's·ruler·(the·top·"handle"·at·the·left·side·of· the·ruler).·You'll·learn·more·about·this·in·Chapter·8.¶

- •→ Never·use·the·spacebar·to·center·or·otherwise·position·text.·Use·the· center-alignment·button·on·the·Formatting·toolbar·instead.·You'll·learn· about·toolbars·later·in·this·chapter.¶

- •→ Don't·use·the·spacebar·to·make·columns.·Instead·use·tabs,·Word's· multicolumn·features,·or·tables.·¶

- •→ Do·not·manually·space·paragraphs·with·carriage·returns.·Use·Word's· paragraph·spacing·instead,·as·explained·in·Chapter·8.¶

- •→ Do·not·hit·↵·repeatedly·to·start·a·new·page.·Instead,·use·Word's·Insert· Page·Break·command.¶

Full Screen
Close Full Screen

Chapter

3

Previewing and Printing

Previewing and Printing

Printing can be quite simple or relatively involved, depending on what
you're trying to do. First, be certain
that the printer is cabled properly and that it is set up in Windows (see your Windows
documentation for details). Then, be sure that it is turned on, loaded with supplies
(paper, toner, and so on), and warmed up, if necessary, and that the ready light is on.

  TIP

It is always a good idea to *save before you print!* Occasionally, printing problems
can lock up your computer, and you might lose any unsaved changes if you are
forced to reboot or power-down. Get in the habit of clicking on the Save button on
the Standard toolbar or using the Ctrl+S keyboard shortcut before you print.

Simple Printing

If you want to print only a single copy of the current document and if your one printer
is properly installed and ready to go, simply click on the Print button on the Standard
toolbar. Try this now with your Twain Quote.

The status area will chart Word's progress as it prints. Page numbers and a little animated printer icon will tell you how many pages have been sent to the printer or to the Windows background printing feature.

Printing as an Interactive Process

Although printing can be as simple as previously described, it is a good idea to get into the habit of using the Page Setup dialog box, and possibly the Print dialog box, whenever you begin to create a new document—particularly if you work with a variety of printers, paper sizes, and document designs. If you wait until you have finished working on your document before choosing a printer, your page and line endings may change considerably from those you initially saw on your screen. This can be a minor annoyance or a major disaster.

For example, if you write a long document, create a table of contents, and then change printer models or choose different printing features, you will find that line and page endings may change. You'll need to redo the table of contents, or it will not agree with the printed pages. The following printer decisions affect pagination and should be selected or determined when you begin a project:

- Page Setup options (such as paper source)
- Printer model
- Paper size
- Reduction/enlargement (scaling)
- Page orientation
- Margins
- Gutters
- Larger print area
- Printing/not printing hidden text
- Printing/not printing footnotes and endnotes
- Font substitution options

Other changes affect the appearance of printed pages but have little impact on pagination.

If you have only one printer and it works properly, you can skip ahead to the section "Choosing Print Dialog Box Options" later in this chapter.

Choosing a Printer

To choose a printer, follow these steps:

1. Choose File ➤ Print or use the Ctrl+P shortcut. Word displays a dialog box like the one in Figure 3.1.
2. Notice the scroll box of printers in the Printer region. Click on the triangle to see a list of printers, and choose the one you want to use, as illustrated in Figure 3.2.
3. If the printer you've chosen has options (letter quality vs. draft, lighter/darker, and so on), you can usually reach these by clicking on the Properties button.
4. When you are finished checking the printer's settings, click on OK (or press Enter). You may have to click on OK more than once to get back to the Print dialog box. If you click on OK there, your document will print.

FIGURE 3.1

The Print dialog box

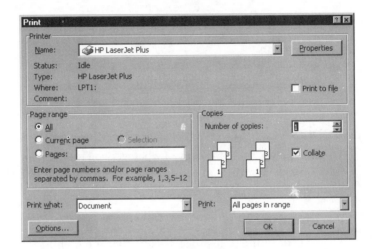

Choosing Print Dialog Box Options

The Print dialog box will show you which printer is selected. Use this dialog box to make decisions, such as how many copies of which pages you need.

What to Print

Normally, you'll want to print all or part of your document. But sometimes you'll want to print other things, such as the document's annotations or other settings information. Use the drop-down list to select any of the following options:

- Document
- Document Properties

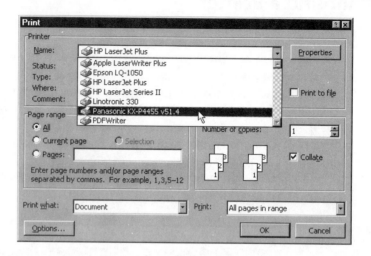

- Comments
- Styles
- AutoText entries (typing shortcuts)
- Key assignments (keyboard shortcuts)

Copies

To specify more than one copy of whatever you intend to print, either type a number in the Copies box or click on the up or down arrows next to the box to scroll and choose a number.

Page Range

To print the entire page range, be sure that the All button is darkened (the default). Click on the little button next to All, if necessary.

To print only the page in your document currently containing the insertion point, click on the Current Page button.

To print selected text, first select it, and then open the Print dialog box. Click on the Selection button in the Page Range area. This choice will be dimmed unless you've selected something in your document.

To print a range of pages (pages 6–10 in a 50-page document, for instance), type the first and last page number in the Pages text box. Separate the numbers with hyphens (*6-10*, for instance).

To print specific pages, list them separated by commas (*3,5,8* for example). Ranges and single pages can be combined, so *6-10,13,19,83* will work as well.

Print All, Odd, or Even

Normally, Word prints all pages in order, but if you are planning to do "manual" two-sided printing or if you have other reasons to separate odd and even pages, use the drop-down Print list at the bottom of the Print dialog box to specify Odd Pages or Even Pages. For example, you might first print all odd-numbered pages and then put those pages back in the printer to print the even-numbered pages on the other side.

Print to File

It's possible to print to disk files instead of to a printer. This technique is sometimes used when you want to take a document to a service bureau for typesetting or other special services. A print file contains all the information needed to allow printing even if the other computer does not have exactly the same fonts used in creating the file. It is a very good idea to do a test run before trying this technique for rush work, as there are many land mines. Consider providing your service bureau with copies of the actual Word document files instead of (or in addition to) print files and a hardcopy. Here are the steps for printing to a file:

1. Edit and polish your document as usual.
2. Consider creating a paper copy by printing normally.
3. Choose File ➤ Print or press Ctrl+P to open the Print dialog box.
4. Place a check in the Print to File box in the Printer area of the Print dialog box.
5. Click on OK. You'll see the Print to File dialog box, illustrated in Figure 3.3.
6. Use any of the Windows 95 techniques to specify where you want to save the file.

FIGURE 3.3

Enter a file-name for your print file.

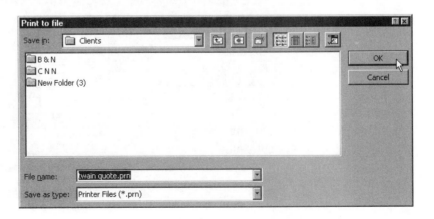

Print files can get rather big, particularly if they contain graphics. Consider printing small ranges of pages to multiple files if you need to transport print files on floppies. You'll need to experiment, since the actual number of bytes per page can vary widely, even among several pages in the same document.

Collate Copies

If you request multiple copies (five copies of a ten-page document, for instance) and don't choose the Collate Copies option, Word will print all five page 1's, then all five page 2's, and so on. You'll need to hand-collate them to make orderly sets.

The Collate Copies option prints five "books," each one complete and in order. This may or may not increase overall printing time depending on your printer and a number of other factors. Experiment.

Letterheads, Second Sheets, and Two-Tray Printers

If your printer has two paper sources (two trays or a tray and a "pass-through," for instance), Word can switch sources as needed. Use the First Page, Other Pages, and perhaps Apply To choices found under the Paper Source tab in the Page Setup dialog box, as shown in Figure 3.4.

FIGURE 3.4

The Page Setup dialog box

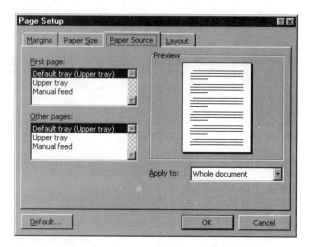

Other Printing Options

Other printer options are available. They can be reached by choosing the Print tab in Word's Options dialog box, shown in Figure 3.5, and are discussed in the following section.

You can display the Options dialog box either by choosing Tools ➤ Options or by clicking on the Options button in the Print dialog box. Most of these settings remain in place once you choose them and are used for each new printing job until you change them.

FIGURE 3.5

The Print tab in the Options dialog box

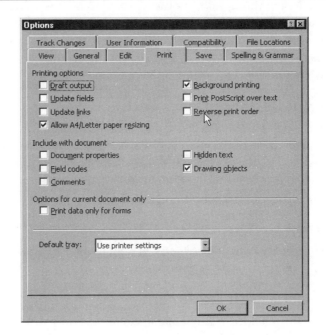

Draft Output

This option can speed printing. Its effect varies from printer to printer. Usually everything is printed in a single font, as efficiently as possible, and at the expense of appearance.

Update Fields and Update Links

As you'll see when you learn about linking and fields in Part Three, this is how you determine when and if things get updated before printing.

Allow A4/Letter Paper Resizing

Check this option if you want Word to automatically adjust the printout of your document to fit on a different size paper. For example, you'd use this option if you work in the U.S. and are exchanging documents with someone in a country where A4 is the standard paper size. Only the printout is affected when you enable this option; the formatted document is not.

Background Printing

A check in this option box causes Word to use the Windows Background printing feature. Theoretically, it lets you work on other things while your document prints in the background. In real life, it often makes your computer so sluggish that you'll end up taking a break anyway. If you keep getting printing errors or low memory messages while printing, try turning off background printing.

Print PostScript over Text

This option is only needed when you are printing a converted Word for Macintosh document—it causes Word to print PostScript code over text instead of under it, useful if a graphic has been included in encapsulated PostScript form. The option applies when the document contains a PRINT field. (See Chapter 29, *Creating and Using Fields*, for information on document fields.)

Reverse Print Order

Use Reverse Print Order when you want pages to come out last-to-first. This is handy for printers that "stack" pages in the wrong order.

Include with Document

The Include with Document choices in the Print tab of the Options dialog box are self-explanatory. A check causes the item (summary info, annotations, and so on) to be delivered with the printed pages. Click on a checkmark to remove it and prevent the item from printing. It's a good idea to keep the update options enabled.

Options for Current Document Only

The options that will appear here vary with the contents of your document. For instance, you may be given the option to print data without printing forms. See Chapter 30 for more about forms.

Default Tray

Use this choice to force something other than the standard tray choice for special print-ing jobs (for example, a cover letter on your business letterhead). Obviously, the selected printer must have more than one paper source for this to be useful. You might need to press a button or two to feed paper from some auxiliary tray. Consult your printer documentation.

Print Preview

You can bypass Print Preview and print immediately to hardcopy, but previewing is advised. It lets you see a screen representation of one or more entire pages before you print them, often saving paper and time.

If you didn't try Print Preview on the Twain quote when you read about it earlier, this would be a good time to experiment. Choose File ➤ Print Preview (or use the key-board shortcut Ctrl+Alt+I or Ctrl+F2).

TIP

Pressing Esc is a quick way to get back to the previous view.

This will give you an excellent idea of where the text will print on the paper. You can also edit this text. You will be able to see margins as well. If your document con-tains headers, footers, line numbers, and other embellishments, you will see them too, as illustrated in Figure 3.6.

Notice the buttons along the top of the screen. You use them to control many of Print Preview's functions. As always, if you forget a button's function, simply pointing to it without clicking will display button help. Here is a general description of each button.

Print Preview's Print Button

The leftmost button prints a single copy of the document without opening the Print dialog box. (If you really want to open the Print dialog box, choose File ➤ Print or press Ctrl+P.)

Magnifier

The Magnifier button lets you zoom in to better read small portions of the page and zoom out to get a bird's-eye view of one or more pages. It also toggles you in and out of the edit mode, as you will see momentarily.

FIGURE 3.6

Use Print Preview to get an overview, adjust margins, and even edit before printing.

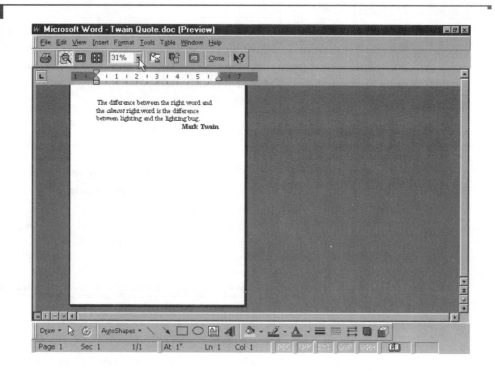

One Page

The next button (called One Page) displays a single page even if you are working with a multiple-page document.

Multiple Pages

The Multiple Pages button looks like four little pages. It lets you specify the number of miniaturized pages you'll see on-screen. Pressing this button reveals a matrix that you drag across to design your screen display. Choices range from a single page to 3 x 6 (18) pages, as shown in Figure 3.7.

Zoom Control

The Percentage text box and related zoom list are called the *Zoom controls*. They tell you the current zoom percentage and let you select a variety of zoom options from a drop-down list.

FIGURE 3.7

The Multiple Pages choices

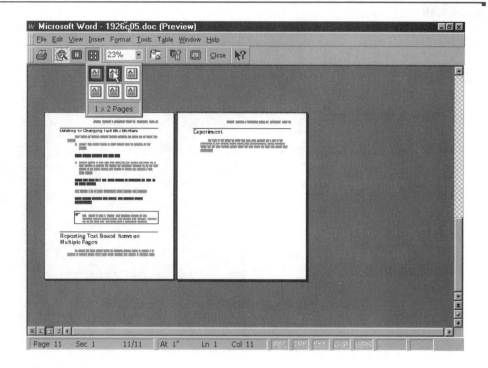

View Rulers

Next, you'll see a View Rulers button. Click on it to toggle the rulers that you use to see and change margin settings.

Shrink to Fit

When you press the Shrink to Fit button (to the right of the View Rulers button), Word attempts to tighten up documents that end with a mostly white page. For example, Figure 3.8 shows how Word proposes to tighten up the two pages shown in Figure 3.7.

To undo proposed changes, use the Ctrl+Z shortcut or choose Edit ➤ Undo Shrink to Fit. Occasionally, Word can't shrink your document and will tell you so.

Full Screen

The Full Screen button removes most of the Print Preview clutter (menu bar, status line, and so on) so that you can see a bigger version of your document. Pressing the Full Screen button a second time returns the hidden controls.

FIGURE 3.8

Word's Shrink to Fit button can often remove those ugly short last pages.

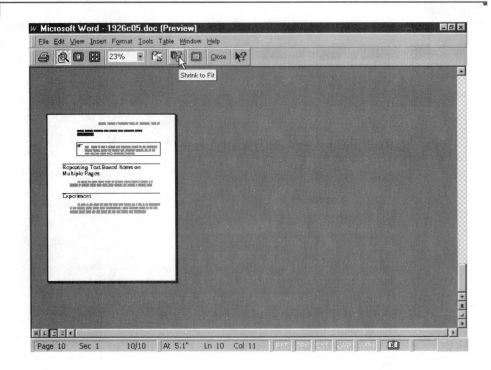

Close Button

The Close button takes you back to the previous view.

Help Button

The Help button will turn your pointer into a question mark. Point to the item of interest (the vertical ruler, for instance) to read any available help. Double-click on the Help window's Close box to quit help.

Leaving Print Preview

Click on the Close button to leave Print Preview and return to your previous view. The four standard view buttons (Normal, Online Layout, Page Layout, and Outline) are also available in the lower left corner of the status area of Print Preview.

Moving Margins in Print Preview

Although a complete explanation of margins will have to wait until Chapter 6, *Margins and Page Breaks*, here is a quick trick you can try on your Twain quote in Print Preview:

1. Display the rulers if they are not already on-screen by clicking on the View Ruler button.

2. Point to the vertical ruler on the left edge of your screen. Notice how the pointer gets smaller and has an up-and-down-pointing head if you point to the exact line where the margin setting is, as shown in Figure 3.9.

3. Hold down the primary (usually the left) mouse button and notice the dashed margin line.

4. While holding down the mouse button, drag up or down to specify a new top margin while watching the dashed line.

5. Release the mouse button, and Word will adjust the margin, moving the text up or down, as illustrated in Figure 3.10.

FIGURE 3.9

Drag the margin handle to adjust the margins.

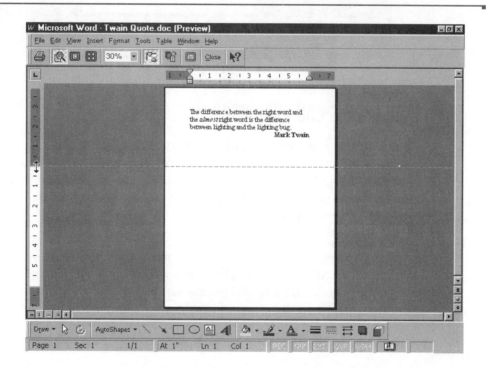

FIGURE 3.10

The Twain quote after dragging to increase the top margin

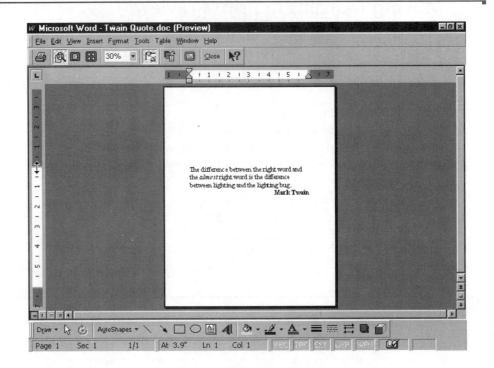

Printing Labels and Envelopes

It's ironic that expensive computers make the simple task of envelope and label printing more difficult. Many offices keep typewriters around just for this reason. Sound familiar? Computerized envelope printing is not so bad once you get the hang of it, and you can set up documents that remember the recipe for you. Word has envelope, label, mail, and list-management features that you'll find quite useful. Before we get into the details, here are some general tips:

- Use window envelopes whenever possible to avoid envelope printing altogether. Set up letterheads, invoices, and similar documents with the inside address properly positioned for standard window envelopes.
- Ask your letterhead designer to take your computer printer into consideration when choosing paper stocks and envelope designs.

- Choose envelopes designed for your printer. These supplies are easier to find now, and many office-supply stores and mail-order paper sellers stock them. (Try Paper Direct, for instance: 800-272-7377.) Laser-friendly envelopes have special flaps and flap glue that minimize jamming. Ink-jet–savvy envelopes are made of paper stock that won't fuzz up your characters.
- Purchase an envelope tray or feeder for your envelopes if you print a lot of them.

Printing Envelopes

Word can print addresses on envelopes by looking for the addresses in your documents (the inside address of a letter for instance), or you can type an address in the Envelopes and Labels dialog box, as illustrated in Figure 3.11.

To open the Envelopes and Labels dialog box, choose Tools ➤ Envelopes and Labels. In this dialog box you can:

- Print envelopes containing one-time addresses that you type into the dialog box itself.
- Copy an address from your document for envelope printing.
- Type envelope addresses and then insert them into your letters or other Word documents.

FIGURE 3.11

Word can find addresses in your document, or you can type them in.

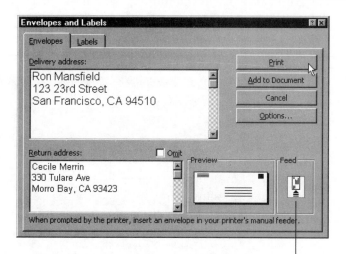

Click to choose a different orientation or position.

Setting Up a Return Address

If your envelopes have preprinted return addresses, you can skip this task. But if you want to use plain envelopes and have Word print your return address in the upper left corner of envelopes, follow these steps:

1. Choose the printer you plan to use if you have more than one.

2. Open the Envelopes and Labels dialog box by choosing Tools ➤ Envelopes and Labels.

3. Click on the Envelopes tab if it is not foremost. Word displays the dialog box shown in Figure 3.11.

4. If Word finds an address in the current open Word document, you will see it in the Delivery Address portion of the dialog box.

5. Type your return address in the large box labeled Return Address. (Part of the address may be already filled out automatically, based on your Word User Info.)

6. When you are happy with the spelling and appearance of your return address, try test printing on a plain #10 (4.125" x 8.5") envelope. Word assumes that you can center-feed envelopes in your printer. If that's not possible, click on the envelope in the Feed section of the dialog box to display the Envelope Options dialog box, shown in Figure 3.12.

7. Select a combination that will work with your printer; then click on OK. Word is rather smart about knowing the options for your specific printer, though, so they should be okay.

8. Place an envelope in your printer. Back in the Envelopes tab of the Envelopes and Labels dialog box, click on Print.

FIGURE 3.12

You can change the envelope printing options in the Envelope Options dialog box.

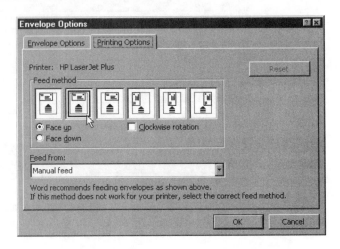

TIP Word will make a guess as to what the delivery address is, and usually it hits it. If, however, you have several addresses in your document, Word might get confused. One way around this is to select the correct delivery address before you choose the Tools ➤ Envelopes and Labels command.

Suppressing Return Addresses

If you always plan to use envelopes that contain preprinted return addresses, you can make sure that nothing prints by making the Return Address area blank. Or you can have a return address typed there and suppress its printing by clicking to place a check in the Omit box.

Printing Envelopes with New Addresses

Type an envelope address directly into the Envelopes and Labels dialog box, or select an address in your letter or other Word document and then open the Envelopes and Labels dialog box. Here are the general steps for envelope printing:

1. Select the address in your document if there is one.
2. Choose Tools ➤ Envelopes and Labels to open the Envelopes and Labels dialog box.
3. If you selected an address in step 1, you'll see it in the dialog box; if not, type an address in the Delivery Address box.
4. Insert an envelope in your printer.
5. Click on the Print button.

Adding an Envelope Page to Documents

Clicking on the Add to Document button in the Envelopes and Labels dialog box adds an envelope page to the beginning of your document. Word takes care of all the details. You can see what it does by switching to Print Preview with two pages showing, as illustrated here in Figure 3.13.

Changing Addresses

Once you've inserted an envelope page in your document, you can change the envelope and inside address at any time. Here's how:

1. Open the document.
2. Make the address change in the inside address.

FIGURE 3.13

Word will add an envelope to your document file if you so desire.

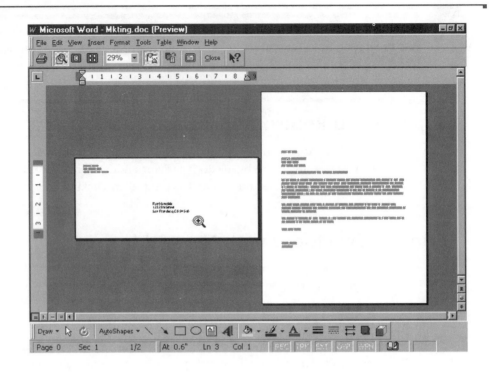

Or you can

3. Open the Envelopes and Labels dialog box (choose Tools ➤ Envelopes and Labels). Make the address change in the inside address.

4. Click on the Change Document button. The envelope will be changed.

WARNING

If you change the Delivery Address in the Envelopes and Labels dialog box and then click on the Change Document button, Word will update the envelope but not the inside address; so be careful. It's better to make the change in the document, not in the Envelopes and Labels dialog box.

Envelope Sizes, Fonts, and Other Options

Word lets you specify envelope sizes (both standard and custom), fonts used for delivery and return addresses, and more. The options are selected in two tabs in the Envelope Options dialog box. Let's look at the Envelope Options tab first. It is illustrated in Figure 3.14.

FIGURE 3.14

The Envelope Options tab

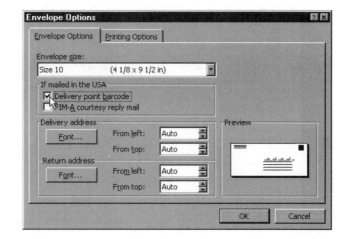

Envelope Size

Choose from any of the standard sizes listed in the drop-down list or specify a custom size by typing dimensions or selecting Custom Size in the drop-down list in the Envelope Size dialog box:

Obviously you'll need to specify dimensions that your printer can handle.

Bar Codes to Speed Postal Delivery

If you are planning to send mail within the United States, you can ask Word to print bar codes on your envelopes. These will speed automated mail sorting. Two coding techniques are provided—POSTNET for regular mail and FIM-A for "courtesy reply" mail. Both types of codes are illustrated in Figure 3.15.

Place a check in the box or boxes you desire. Word will do the rest, calculating the bar code from the mailing address.

FIGURE 3.15

Here are two types of bar codes.

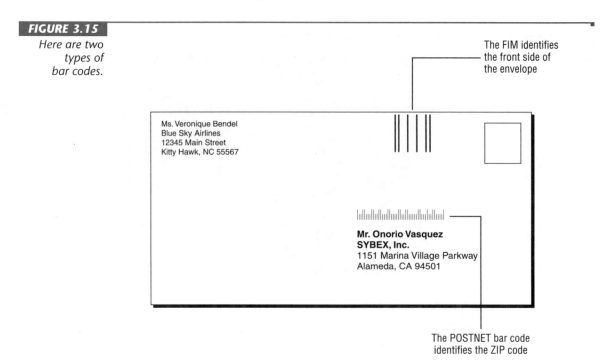

The FIM identifies the front side of the envelope

The POSTNET bar code identifies the ZIP code

Fonts and Address Positioning

Click on the Font buttons to choose the desired fonts for the delivery and return addresses. They display the Envelope Address Font tab, which lets you specify fonts, font sizes, colors, character formatting, and so on.

The dimension boxes in the Delivery Address and Return Address sections of the Envelope Options tab let you specify address spacing. Auto makes Word do all the work. You can type new dimensions or use the triangles to change dimensions. Watch the preview as you work.

The Care and Feeding of Envelopes

You've already seen the Printing Options tab in the Envelope Options dialog box, but it deserves a second look. As you can see in Figure 3.12, this is where you tell Word how you plan to feed envelopes.

The choices vary with the chosen printer. If you have multiple trays, you specify the tray containing envelopes (upper, lower, and so on). Click on Reset to return to the default settings for the chosen printer.

TIP

Many of the templates and letter wizards provided by Microsoft facilitate envelope and label printing. See Chapters 13 and 18 for details.

Labels

Label printing is a lot like envelope printing except that you have even more options. For instance, you can print single labels or sheets of labels. Word "knows" the dimensions for many industry-standard stocks from Avery and others.

Check out the Avery Wizard, which probably installed itself on your Start menu (under the program submenu). It is yet another way to create labels. You'll find Word knows how to print:

- Audio tape labels
- Business card perf stock
- Diskette labels
- File folder labels
- Mailing (address) labels
- Name tags
- Postcards

- Ready indexes
- Rotary (Rolodex) cards
- Shipping labels
- Videotape labels
- WorkSaver tabs

Printing Labels

Simple label printing is a lot like envelope printing. Here are the general steps:

1. Select the address in your document if it has one.
2. Choose Tools ➤ Envelopes and Labels to open the Envelopes and Labels dialog box.
3. Click on the Labels tab if it is not already foremost. You'll see the options illustrated in Figure 3.16.
4. If you selected an address in step 1 or if Word finds one on its own, you'll see it in the dialog box; if not, type an address in the big box.
5. Choose the desired options in the main Labels tab. To print a single label on a multi-label sheet, click on Single Label and specify the row and column location of the label. Choose to print or not print the bar code and return address.

FIGURE 3.16

The Labels tab

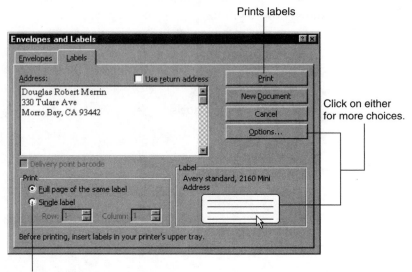

Prints labels

Click on either for more choices.

Specify the starting label position if you're not printing a full page of the same address.

PART

I

Getting Started

6. To select different label sizes, click either on the picture of a label or on the Options button. You'll see the choices illustrated in Figure 3.17.

7. Select the label maker, label product number, and printer type. For more detailed options, click on the Details button to see the choices in Figure 3.18.

8. Fine-tune Top and Side margins here if your printer prints *all* the labels of the current type too high or too far left or right. The other settings are probably correct if you selected the correct label type back in step 6. When you have made all your choices, click on OK once or twice as necessary to return to the Label tab of the Envelopes and Labels dialog box.

9. Insert a label or sheet of labels in your printer. (Be sure the label isn't too small for your printer.)

10. Click on the Print button.

TIP

Normally, you can put partially used sheets of laser labels through your printer once or twice more, but you run the risk of jamming and possibly damaging your printer. It's often better to print full sheets and file the unused labels for the next time you mail something to the same recipient.

FIGURE 3.17

The Label Options dialog box

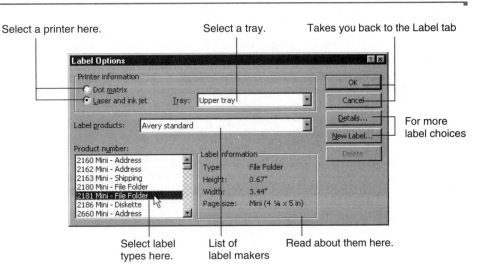

Select a printer here.   Select a tray.   Takes you back to the Label tab

For more label choices

Select label types here.   List of label makers   Read about them here.

FIGURE 3.18

Additional label details.

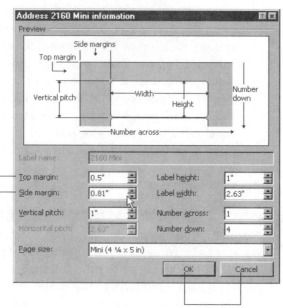

Consider adjusting these, but you'll probably leave the rest alone.

Takes you back to the Label Options dialog box

Including Graphics on Envelopes

You can print graphics on envelopes. It's a great way to add logos, special messages, business reply art, and so on. Here are the general steps:

1. Choose Tools ➤ Envelopes and Labels, and select the Envelope tab in the Envelopes and Labels dialog box.

2. Click on either the Add to Document or the Change Document button.

3. Switch to Page Layout if not already there.

4. Paste or create a graphic (using the Insert ➤ Picture command described in the next chapter), and then move it into position by dragging:

5. Make any other changes that you like (rearrange or reformat lines of text in the inside address, for instance).

At this point, the envelope is one-of-a-kind and in a separate section at the top of your current document. You can either save the document and print the envelope along with the rest of the document or save the document as a template for repeated use (see Chapter 13, *Templates, Wizards, and Sample Documents*). But there's one other possibility. If you want the artwork to appear on *all* your envelopes, you can select the art and create a special AutoText entry called EnvelopeExtra 1 or EnvelopeExtra 2. Use the techniques described in Chapter 14, *End Monotony with AutoText, AutoCorrect, and Insert*, to create AutoText entries.

Envelopes, Labels, and Long Mailing Lists

When mailing to many addresses, consider using Word's Mail Merge feature. It is described in Chapter 26, *Mail Merge—Creating Custom Documents*.

To preview labels, follow these steps:

1. In a document, type the name, address, and so forth that you want on the label.

2. Format the information, adding graphics if you wish.

3. Select the label, including the graphic.

4. Open the Envelopes and Labels dialog box.

5. Select the right label size and make any other appropriate changes.

6. Click on New Document on the Labels tab, and your labels will appear in a document, which you can preview.

It is a good idea to practice on plain white paper and hold test pages up to the light in front of a sheet of labels or an envelope to see how things will line up.

Formatting Labels

There is no easy way to insert art or change the font, size, or other elements of character appearance in the Labels tab (although you can do these things with envelopes). This means that name tags, video-spine labels, and similar specialty labels are going to look rather boring.

There is a workaround to this problem (click on the Add to Document button and then edit the individual labels in the document), but it probably isn't appropriate for big jobs.

Formatting all labels in a given document is a breeze. Select them all, make them look terrific, and then print. They won't look different from one another, but the labels for a given mailing—name badges for a conference, for example—can have a great look unique to that event.

Background Printing

Because some printing jobs can take many minutes or even hours, background printing can be a real productivity booster—at least in theory—as it supposedly lets you do other things while the printer prints "in the background." Moreover, you can use the Windows task bar to check and control the status of multiple print jobs. Simply double-click on your printer's icon in the task bar.

Your system does all this by quickly sending print jobs to a file on your hard disk rather than directly to the printer. It then spools the work to your printer in the background.

Enabling Background Printing

To turn on background printing from the Print tab in the Options dialog box, follow these steps:

1. Choose Tools ➤ Options.
2. Click on the Print tab, if necessary, to display printing options.
3. Be sure there is a check in the Background Printing box (click on it if necessary).
4. Click on OK and print as usual. Your documents will print in the background while you're working on other things.

TIP

A great Windows shortcut to know is Alt+Tab. If you press this key combination, Windows displays a dialog box with icons of all open applications. A box will appear around the active application. Repeatedly pressing Alt+Tab cycles through the icons; when you release Alt+Tab, you will switch to the selected application.

Checking the Status of a Print Job

With background printing at work, you can check and change the status of multiple print jobs. Follow these steps:

1. Double-click on the printer's icon in the Windows task bar.
2. Right-click to select the job or jobs you want to pause or cancel.
3. Click on the appropriate option (Pause or Cancel).
4. Use the menus for other options.
5. To return to Word, hold down the Alt key and press Tab as many times as necessary.

For more information about background printing with Windows, use the online help and see your Windows documentation.

Canceling a Print Job

To stop a print job before it's finished, try pressing the Esc key repeatedly until the printing-status information disappears from your screen. Even after the print-status information disappears, your printer may print a few pages that were sent before print cancellation, as many printers contain their own memory (called a *buffer*). Check your printer manual for ways to quickly clear the printer's memory if this annoys you.

If you are using background printing, you will need to double-click on the printer's icon in the task bar and cancel the job from there.

Chapter

4

Introduction to Graphics in Word

FEATURING

Introduction to Graphics in Word

Word lets you draw, place, resize, reposition, and embellish graphics. You can work with your own drawings, charts from spreadsheet packages, photos from scanners, and just about any other computer-compatible art form. In fact, Word even comes with some clip art you can use to get your graphics library started.

You can simply *paste* graphics or place them in *frames*. As you'll see in Chapter 5, *Using Text Boxes to Frame, Position, and Anchor Text*, using frames makes it easier to reposition and work with graphics.

There are plenty of graphics-related buzzwords and standards to know. In fact, another book the size of this one could be written just on those subjects. But this chapter contains all you'll need to start creating your own art and using free or low-cost clip art.

Importing Graphics

Like text, computer art can be stored in disk files. Unfortunately, different drawing packages, scanners, and other graphic tools create files in their own unique formats. Word can use some graphic formats as-is; the program comes with a number of built-in translation utilities (called *filters*) that can convert graphics from many sources, allowing you to insert them into Word documents. At a minimum, you will be able to work with the following graphic formats (their usual file extensions are listed after their names):

AutoCAD 2-D (DXF)
Computer Graphics Metafile (CGM)
CompuServe GIF (GIF)
CorelDRAW (CDR)
DrawPerfect (WPG)
Encapsulated PostScript (EPS)
HP Graphic Language (HGL)
Kodak Photo CD (PCD)
Lotus 1-2-3 (PIC)
Macintosh PICT (PCT)
Micrografx Designer 3/Draw Plus (DRW)
PC Paintbrush (PCX)
Targa (TGA)
TIFF (Tagged Image File Format—TIF)
Windows Bitmap (BMP)
Windows Metafile (WMF)

If you don't see the format you need here, contact Microsoft technical support. They may be able to provide you with new filters, give you some workaround tips, or refer you to makers of graphics-conversion programs.

Other Sources of Clip Art

If you don't have the time or inclination to draw your own art, you can purchase compatible clip art disks from mail-order firms and retail software dealers such as Egghead. Many companies and nonprofit groups also distribute low-cost or free shareware and public domain clip art. Check local computer user groups and online art libraries such as the ones provided by America Online and CompuServe. The Internet is another source of images. Chapter 21, *Advanced Graphics Techniques,* shows you how to import images using your Web browser.

It is even possible to insert graphics from your scanner directly into a Word document using the From Scanner command, also described in Chapter 21. Be sure you understand and honor any copyright restrictions when you use other people's art.

NOTE
Word 97 includes a Clip Art Gallery, with clip art, pictures, sounds, and videos you can include in your documents. Choose Insert ➤ Picture ➤ Clip Art to see a list of what is available.

Using the Insert Picture Command

The easiest way to get hooked on graphics is to import a picture or two. Let's try it.

1. Start by opening your Twain document.
2. Place the insertion point where you want the picture to appear (on a new line after Mark's name, perhaps).

3. Choose Insert ➤ Picture ➤ From File as shown in Figure 4.1. Notice that the new cascading menu lets you insert graphics from a variety of sources.
4. You'll see a dialog box something like Figure 4.2. Click on the Preview button to enable the preview option.

5. Browse by clicking on folders and files until you see something you like. You can use the Float over Text option in this dialog box to position the selected graphic over text in your document.

Use the Insert ➤ Picture cascading menu options to insert graphic files from a variety of sources.

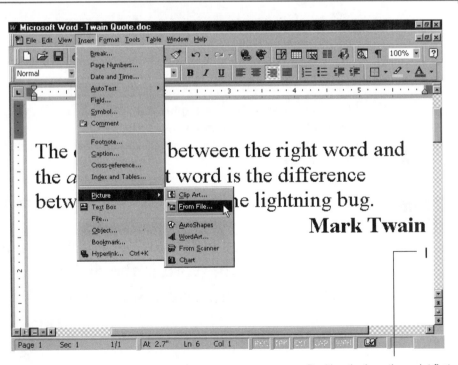

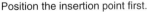

Position the insertion point first.

FIGURE 4.2

Enable the Pre-view Picture feature to browse.

Click on the Preview button to see graphics before inserting them.

Click here to insert the selected graphic into your Word document.

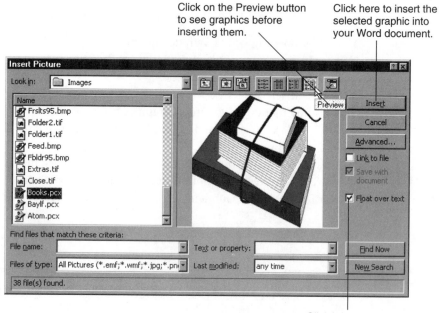

Click here to place the graphic over text.

6. When you find your favorite graphic, click on OK to insert it. (Figures 4.2 and 4.3 show Books.pcx, which comes with Word.)

7. Reposition and perhaps resize or otherwise embellish the image as described later in this chapter.

FIGURE 4.3

Graphics are placed at the insertion point.

The difference between the right word and the *almost* right word is the difference between lightning and the lightning bug.
Mark Twain

In addition to the Word Clip Art folder, chances are you have other graphic images on your hard disk. For instance, your Windows folder probably has a dozen or so bitmap files (files ending in BMP). Use the scrollable lists to find files of interest. When you see one, click on the name to highlight it, and then click on the Preview button to get an idea of what it will look like, as before.

MASTERING THE OPPORTUNITIES

Using Your Clipboard and Document Scraps to Insert Art from Other Programs

If you already have a drawing program that you use to create and edit artwork, it is possible to copy your work to the Clipboard and then paste it into a Word document. Here are the steps:

1. Switch to or run the drawing program.
2. Select the art of interest.
3. Copy it to the Clipboard (Ctrl+C).
4. Switch to or start Word (quit or minimize the drawing program if you like—this may be necessary to run Word).
5. Move the insertion point to the desired location in your Word document.

6. Choose Edit ➤ Paste or press Ctrl+V to paste the graphic.

Another way of getting graphics to Word from other applications is to use the document scraps feature of Windows 95. Simply drag the image out onto the desktop, and it will form a new file—a scrap—leaving your original untouched. Then drag it into Word. The advantage of this is that you can drag it into other documents as well, and it won't be replaced the next time you copy something, as it would with the Clipboard. The disadvantage is that when you no longer need it, you have to drag it to the recycle bin, or it just sits on your desktop like a wedge of week-old camembert.

Word 97 includes several toolbars for editing art—one of these is the Picture toolbar. Choose View ➤ Toolbar ➤ Picture to display the Picture toolbar shown in Figure 4.4. See Chapter 21 to learn about this toolbar which is used primarily to alter photographic images.

FIGURE 4.4

You can use the Picture toolbar to edit a graphic.

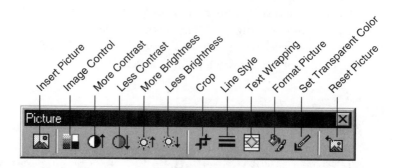

Resizing Graphics

When you click on a graphic in a Word document to select it, the picture will be surrounded by a box containing eight handles—one in each corner and one on each side of the outline box. When you position the mouse pointer on a handle, it turns into a two-headed arrow.

To increase or decrease the size of the entire graphic *proportionally*, drag a *corner* handle diagonally, releasing it when you are happy with the proposed size.

NOTE

Sizing something (a graphic, for example) *proportionally* means that as the size changes, the width and height retain the same proportions, relative to each other. That is, if the height gets three times larger, the width will get three times larger as well.

To distort a dimension, use the handles on the *edges* of the graphic outline to stretch or condense the graphic, as shown in Figure 4.5. Undo works if you act promptly.

FIGURE 4.5

Drag center handles to distort, corner handles to resize proportionally.

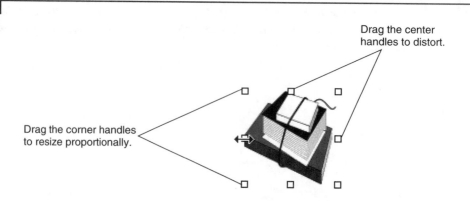

Drag the center handles to distort.

Drag the corner handles to resize proportionally.

Cropping Graphics

To crop a graphic (hide part of it), click on the Crop tool on the Picture toolbar and drag any of the handles to create the desired effect (see Figure 4.6). The mouse pointer will turn into a square with a line through it.

FIGURE 4.6

Use the Crop tool to drag to crop (hide) part of a graphic.

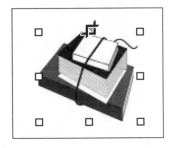

Adding White Space around Graphics

To add white space around a graphic, click on the Crop tool on the Picture toolbar and drag handles away from the graphic (see Figure 4.7). Undo can restore the original size.

FIGURE 4.7

Use the Crop tool to drag handles away from the graphic to add white space.

Sizing and Cropping Graphics with the Picture Command

Click on the Format Picture tool to open the Format Picture dialog box, shown in Figure 4.8. Its Picture tab contains information about any cropping or resizing that's been done. Click on the Size tab for information about a selected picture's original size.

FIGURE 4.8

In the Format Picture dialog box, select the Picture tab to see what you've done; you can modify or undo cropping settings here.

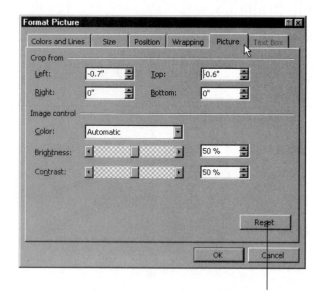

Click on Reset to return the graphic
to its original size and eliminate any cropping.

You can also use this tab to specify new cropping dimensions. The Reset button returns a graphic to its original size and uncrops it. Click on the Size tab, shown in Figure 4.9, to modify the picture's size.

Using Word's Improved Drawing Features

To create a new drawing using the Word drawing features, follow these steps:

1. Open a new or existing Word document.
2. Place the insertion point where you want your new art to be inserted.
3. Click on the Standard toolbar's Draw button. (Or, if you have a Word document containing a graphic you want to modify, double-click on the graphic.)
4. You'll see the Drawing toolbar, illustrated in Figure 4.10.

NOTE

The Drawing toolbar has been redesigned for Word 97 and includes new menus with many of the drawing functions as well as many familiar tool buttons.

FIGURE 4.9

In the Format Picture dialog box, select the Size tab to modify or undo resizing.

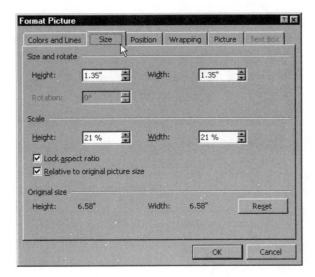

FIGURE 4.10

Use the Drawing toolbar to create new drawings and edit existing ones.

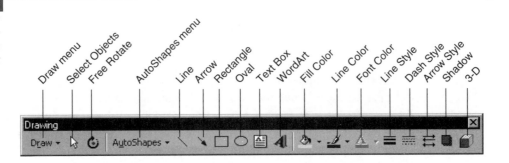

You'll use a series of buttons, menu commands, and your mouse to draw, resize, and rearrange shapes, lines, and text.

You might want to reshape the Drawing toolbar to make it easier to move around and keep out of the way. Drag an edge of the toolbar to change its shape from wide and short to tall and skinny, for instance, as shown in Figure 4.11.

Change the shape of the toolbar if you like, by dragging any side.

Drag to reshape.

Drawing Things

First, click on a shape button or a line button (line, oval, rectangle, and so on) in the Drawing toolbar; then use your mouse to create lines or shapes. For instance, to create a rectangle for an organizational chart, click on the rectangle button, click on the page to set the rectangle's upper left corner, and drag with your mouse to create a rectangle of the desired shape and size. (Holding down the Shift key while you do this creates squares.) Use the oval tool for ovals and circles. (The Shift key helps you make precise circles.)

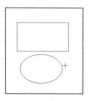

Use the AutoShapes menu on the toolbar to create more sophisticated shapes. For example, to create polygons, choose AutoShapes ➤ Lines ➤ Freeform to select the Freeform tool, and then click and drag repeatedly until you are done. For example, to make a triangle, click once to anchor the first point and drag for the first side. Click again to anchor the second point and drag again. Click to anchor the third point, and then drag back to the starting point and click one last time to complete the triangle.

However, now that you know how to draw with the Freeform tool, take a look at a set of tools that will make this easier. Simply choose AutoShapes ➤ Basic Shapes and select the triangle you need when you have to draw a triangle.

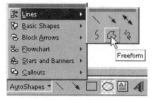

> **NOTE**
>
> To change the shape of a polygon, select it using the techniques described next, and then click on Edit Points on the Draw menu on the Drawing toolbar. Handles will appear at each intersection of the shape. Drag them as necessary to create the desired shape.

Selecting Objects

To select rectangles or other drawing elements (lines, text, and so on), click on the Select Objects button on the left side of the Drawing toolbar, and then click on the item you want to modify. This selects it.

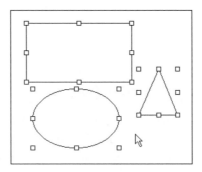

    Hold down the Shift key to select multiple objects. Choose Edit ➤ Select All to select all text and clip art, but not drawing objects. Selected objects are surrounded by small handles. Click outside any selected object to deselect all selected objects.

Text in Drawings

You can create text for drawings in *text boxes* (covered in detail in Chapter 5, *Using Text Boxes to Frame, Position, and Anchor Text*). To create a text box, use the Drawing toolbar's Text Box button. Text in boxes is automatically surrounded by black lines unless you eliminate them. Here are the steps:

1. Click on the Text Box button.
2. Drag the text box to its desired size and shape. Make it big if in doubt.

3. Type the word **Marketing** (the insertion point's already in the box, so there's no need to position it).

4. If necessary, you can increase the size of a text box by dragging, just as if it were any other graphic object.

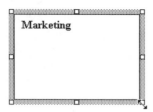

Embellishing Text in Drawings

You can embellish text (make it bold, center it, change type styles, and so on), and you can combine the effects using most of Word's formatting tools. For example, here's a box with some bold characters and a bulleted list, created with the Bullets tool on the Format toolbar.

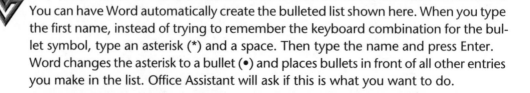

TIP
You can have Word automatically create the bulleted list shown here. When you type the first name, instead of trying to remember the keyboard combination for the bullet symbol, type an asterisk (*) and a space. Then type the name and press Enter. Word changes the asterisk to a bullet (•) and places bullets in front of all other entries you make in the list. Office Assistant will ask if this is what you want to do.

More or Less Space between Text and Box Lines

To increase or decrease the white space between the text and text box lines, follow these steps:

1. Select the text box.
2. Choose Format ➤ Text Box.
3. Select the Text Box tab. You'll see the choices illustrated in Figure 4.12.

FIGURE 4.12

Use the Text Box tab in the Format Text Box dialog box to add white space in a text box.

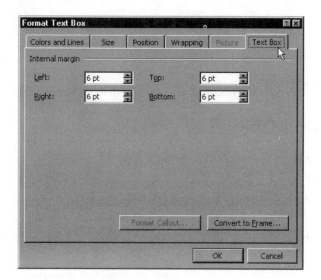

4. Specify new internal left, right, top, and bottom margins by typing new settings in the appropriate boxes or using the up and down arrow buttons. For instance, here's the marketing text box with 6 points (6pt) of internal margin on all four sides:

> **Marketing Department**
> • Sandra Lexington
> • William Johnson
> • Karen Danialson
> • Bobbie Wrightwood

Eliminating Text Box Lines

To eliminate the lines surrounding the text box, follow these steps:

1. Select the box or boxes by clicking or shift-clicking.

2. Click on the Drawing toolbar's Line Color button to display the line color palette.

3. Click on the No Line choice (at the top), as shown here:

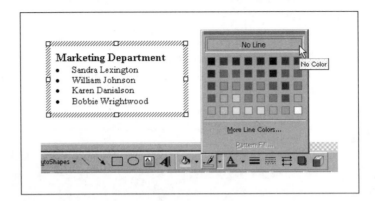

Of course, you could also use this palette to select a line color.

Moving Objects

To move objects, follow these steps:

1. Select the item or items to be moved.

2. Point to one of the selected items with your mouse pointer, avoiding the object's handles.

3. The pointer will change, now looking like an arrow with four heads:

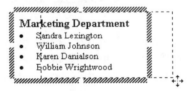

4. While the pointer has this shape, drag with your mouse and watch as an outline of the object(s) proposes a new location.

5. Releasing the mouse button completes the move.

Gridlines

Word's drawing feature now has optional *invisible gridlines* that make aligning easy. When the Snap to Grid feature is enabled, however, dragging is a little jerky. The gridlines act like magnets, and moved objects migrate to them no matter how hard you try to prevent this. For precise, smooth moves, turn off the Snap to Grid feature. You can also change the spacing and origin of grids. Do all this with the Snap to Grid dialog box. To open it, choose the Grid option on the Draw menu at the left end of the Drawing toolbar.

Choosing the Grid option opens the Snap to Grid dialog box, shown in Figure 4.13. To turn off the snap feature, remove the checkmark from the Snap to Grid box by clicking, as shown in Figure 4.13. Even if the grid is turned off, you can still use it whenever you wish by holding down the Alt key while you drag.

Use the other tools in the dialog box to change the grid's dimensions and starting point with respect to the upper left corner of the window.

FIGURE 4.13

Use the Snap to Grid dialog box to change the spacing and origin of grids.

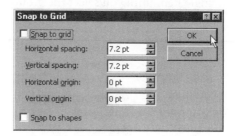

Layers

You can construct objects from multiple elements placed near, on top of, or beneath each other. For instance, the illustration in your Twain quote contains a number of separate elements.

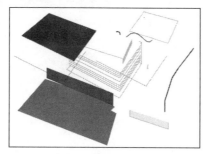

Things piled on top of each other are said to be *layered*. You can select items and arrange layers to your liking. Use the Bring to Front or Send to Back options on the Drawing toolbar's Draw menu.

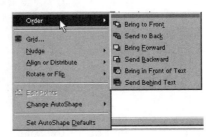

Grouping and Ungrouping

Sometimes you'll want to turn multiple drawing parts into a single object. This makes it easier to move and resize complex elements (see Figure 4.14). Simply select all the elements by Shift-clicking, and then choose Draw ➤ Group. Henceforth, all of the items will act as a single item until you select the group and choose Draw ➤ Ungroup.

FIGURE 4.14

Grouping objects makes them easy to keep together.

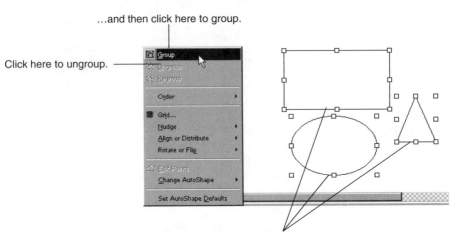

TIP

If you select multiple objects, they will move together as if grouped, but if you click on only one object, you can move it independently.

Rotating and Flipping Objects

To rotate or flip objects, select them and use the Free Rotate, Rotate Left, Rotate Right, Flip Horizontal, and Flip Vertical options available when you choose Draw ➤ Rotate or Flip.

NEW

These options won't rotate text. You'll need to use the Change Text Direction button on the Text Box toolbar to manipulate the orientation of text. Choose View ➤ Toolbar ➤ Text Box to display the Text Box toolbar shown in Figure 4.15. Then click on the Change Text Direction button until the text is in the position you want.

FIGURE 4.15

Use the Text Box toolbar to rotate text in a text box.

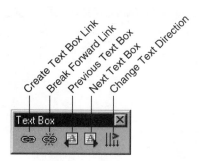

Duplicating Objects

Once you've created an object (an "org chart" box, for instance), you can select, copy, and paste it to save time. Consider grouping complex collections of lines and shapes and text before duplicating them.

Pictures vs. Drawing Objects

The two general types of graphic images are drawings, such as the ones created and discussed in this chapter, and "pictures" or "painted" images created with paint programs. Drawings are made up of individual elements—lines, circles, and so on. (These elements are sometimes known as *vectors*.) Paint images are generally treated as one large collection of dots. Files that end with the extension .BMP are bitmap "paintings." So are many Windows metafiles (.WMF). Word can use both drawings and bitmaps, but if you want to edit them, you must do so in a special window. Suppose, for instance, you want to change the contrast and brightness of the Ornamnt1.wmf file. Here are the required steps:

1. Position the insertion point where you want the graphic to appear in your Word document.
2. Choose Insert ➤ Picture ➤ From File and locate the desired file (in this case, Baylf.pcx), as shown in Figure 4.16.
3. Click on Insert to insert the graphic. It will appear in the Word document, but most of the Drawing toolbar options and buttons won't work.
4. Double-click on the graphic. You'll see the graphic and a picture boundary. The title bar shows you that a Picture window is open.

FIGURE 4.16

Find the graphic file you want to edit.

5. If necessary, right-click on the graphic and select Show Picture Toolbar from the menu.

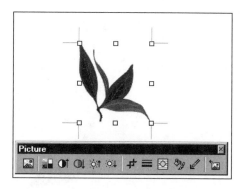

6. Edit the picture with the tools on the Picture toolbar.

7. When you're done editing, click on the Close box to close the Picture window. You'll see your edited graphic in your document.

Callouts

You can use callouts to label graphics in Word documents. Here are the steps:

1. Create or import a graphic.

2. Choose AutoShapes ➤ Callouts from the Drawing toolbar and choose the balloon shape.

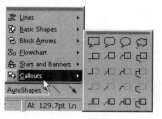

3. Click where you want the callout arrow to point.

4. Drag to where you want to position the text, and then release the mouse button. The callout will appear:

5. Type any text you want to show in the callout, and then select the text and change its appearance if you like.

6. Select the callout box and resize it if you want.

7. Drag the box and line as desired to reposition them.

8. To change the design of the callout box, choose AutoShapes ➤ Callouts ➤ Change AutoShape, and choose another style.

Filling

To fill drawn items with colors or shades of gray, follow these steps:

1. Select the desired item(s).

2. Click on the Fill Color button on the Drawing toolbar to display the fill palette.

3. Click on the desired fill color.

Line Colors and Shades of Gray

To change the color or shade of lines, follow these steps:

1. Select the desired item(s).

2. Click on the Line Color button on the Drawing toolbar to display the line color palette.

3. Click on the desired line color.

Line Sizes and Arrowheads

To change the types of lines and any arrowheads, follow these steps:

1. Select the desired line(s).
2. Click on the Arrow Style button on the Drawing toolbar to quickly add an arrow head to a line.
3. Click on the Line Style button on the Drawing toolbar to display the line style palette.
4. Click on the desired line type.
5. Choose More Lines to display the Colors and Lines tab in the Format AutoShape dialog box, illustrated in Figure 4.17.

FIGURE 4.17

The Format AutoShape dialog box gives you more control over line and shape appearance.

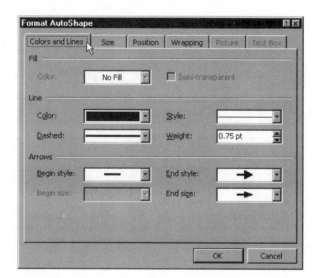

Time to Practice

If you have some free time, this would be a good place to stop and try some of your new-found skills. Type, edit, save, draw, print, and so on. At this point, you know all the basics.

But don't put away the book just yet. There's lots more to know if you plan to *master* Word.

How to Learn More

Once you have mastered the basics, check out Chapter 21, *Advanced Graphics Techniques*. It covers related topics such as creating logos with WordArt, modifying the appearance of photographs, obtaining graphics from the Internet, and so on.

Chapter 5

Using Text Boxes to Frame, Position, and Anchor Text

Using Text Boxes to Frame, Position, and Anchor Text

Sometimes it is desirable to move text around on a page free of the usual constraints of paragraphs, margins, and so on. For example, you might want to place attention-getting text in margins and/or rotate it as we've done frequently in this book. In Word, you do this by placing text in text boxes. Word 97 offers a much more robust and easy-to-use set of text box features than its predecessors.

Text boxes are very similar to frames in function; however, they also take advantage of Office Art features such as 3-D effects, fills, backgrounds, text rotation, sizing, and cropping. You can *link* text boxes, in order to flow text from one page or column in your document to another, and you can treat text boxes as a group in order to manipulate them together. Figure 5.1 shows how text boxes work.

The Text Box command appears on two Word 97 menus—the Insert menu and the Format menu. Text Box is available on the Format menu only when a Text Box is selected. What the Text Box command does depends on the menu from which it is selected.

To use text boxes, you create them, insert things into them, and then size and position them either with your mouse or with the Format Text Box dialog box. Normally, you'll want to work with text-boxed items in Page Layout view or Print Preview so that you can easily see and move them.

FIGURE 5.1

Use text boxes to contain and position text. Notice how text boxes as well as graphics "make room for themselves" in text.

Place graphics, and text will wrap around them.

CHAPTER 5

USING TEXT BOXES TO FRAME, POSITION, AND ANCHOR TEXT

All graphics have framed characteristics by default, so you no longer have to insert them in frames. This is a real advance over previous Word versions, and very elegant. However, when you open a document that you created in an earlier version of Word, any frames within it are maintained. If you select a frame, the familiar Frame command appears on the Format menu.

Word 97 expands the capabilities of text boxes for handling text in the same way as graphics, releasing you from having to frame up some graphical objects but not others, and making it only text that you must remember to turn into a graphical object in order to manipulate

it like one. Text boxes let you handle text independently of the usual text boundaries.

Text boxes are very similar to frames in function; however, they also take advantage of Office Art features such as 3-D effects, fills, backgrounds, text rotation, sizing, and cropping. You can *link* text boxes, in order to flow text from one page or column in your document to another. And, you can treat text boxes as a group in order to manipulate them together.

The Text Box command appears on two Word 97 menus—

the Insert menu and the Format menu. Text Box is available on the Format menu only when a Text Box is selected. What the Text Box command does depends on the menu from which it is selected.

To use text boxes, you create them, insert things into them, and then size and position them either with your mouse or with the Format Text Box dialog box. Normally, you'll want to work with text boxed items in Page Layout view or Print Preview so that you can easily see and move them.

It's a good idea to turn on

What About Framing Graphics?

If you've been using earlier versions of Word, you may be wondering what has happened to frames and framing graphics, which used to be very important, and whether text boxes are replacements for frames. Not exactly.

Not only are text boxes not necessary for graphics, they don't always mix well with graphics. They can obscure graphics pasted into them, you can get unintended layers of text boxes and graphics, and so on.

Place text boxes in headers and footers, and they'll print on each page.

Place text in text boxes, and it will span columns.

PART

Getting Started

What about Framing Graphics?

If you've been using earlier versions of Word, you may be wondering what has happened to frames and framing graphics, which used to be very important, and whether text boxes are replacements for frames. Not exactly.

Not only are text boxes not necessary for graphics, they don't always mix well with graphics. They can obscure graphics

pasted into them, you can get unintended layers of text boxes and graphics, and so on.

All graphics have framed characteristics by default; so you no longer have to insert them in frames. This is a real advance over previous Word versions and very elegant. However, when you open a document that you created in an earlier version of Word, any frames within it are maintained. If you select a frame, the familiar Frame command appears on the Format menu.

It's a good idea to turn on hidden paragraph marks when working with text boxes. If they are not visible, click on the Show/Hide ¶ button in the Standard toolbar. It looks like a paragraph mark (¶).

Inserting and Placing Things in Text Boxes

You can insert an empty text box and then place something in it, or you can select something and then place it in a text box. In either case, choose the Insert ➤ Text Box command *or* click on the Text Box button on the Drawing toolbar.

Inserting Empty Text Boxes

Here are the steps for creating a new, empty text box:

1. Start by switching to Page Layout view, if you are not already in it. (If you forget to do this, Word will switch views for you.)
2. Click on the Drawing toolbar's Text Box button or choose Insert ➤ Text Box.
3. Your pointer will change to a crosshair. Drag to create a text box of the approximate size and shape you desire, located about where you want it.

4. Shortly after you release the mouse button, you'll see a text box surrounded by a border. If you have the Show/Hide Paragraph feature enabled, you will see a paragraph mark within the text box and an anchor outside it, as shown in Figure 5.2.

FIGURE 5.2

The new text box will appear, surrounded by a cross-hatched border, along with a little anchor.

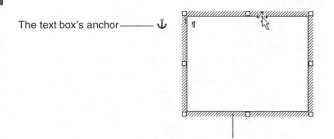

The text box's anchor

The text box looks like cross-hatched lines.

5. You can either type text in the resulting text box (you'll learn how in a moment), paste things from the Clipboard, or use one of the Insert menu commands, such as the File command.

Placing Existing Text in Text Boxes

If you already have something in your document that needs to be in a text box, follow these steps:

1. Switch to Page Layout view if you are not there already.

2. Select the text to be boxed.

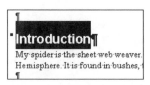

3. Either click on the Text Box button on the Drawing toolbar or choose Insert ➤ Text Box.

4. Your selected item(s) will be surrounded by a text box, and you'll see a paragraph mark and an anchor, as illustrated here, if you clicked on the Show/Hide ¶ button.

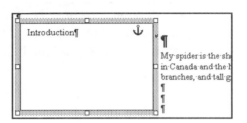

Text boxes can be resized just as you resize graphics. Drag their handles. If you accidentally box the wrong thing or too many or too few things or accidentally distort the size or shape, Undo should work.

> **TIP**
>
> If you start the process (choose Insert ➤ Text Box) and change your mind, cancel it by pressing Esc.

Try It

Try putting Mark Twain's name in a text box so that you can freely manipulate it. Follow these steps:

1. Load the Twain Quote document.
2. Switch to Page Layout View if you are not already there.
3. Select the text "Mark Twain" by clicking and dragging.
4. Choose Insert ➤ Text Box.

5. Click the Change Text Direction button on the Text Box toolbar three times (the button direction changes as the text does). Notice that the text rotates 270 degrees and doesn't fit in the text box properly yet.

6. Resize and drag the text box so that its size and shape fits the rotated text. Then drag it to the right of the quote.

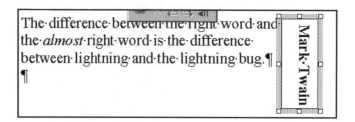

Positioning Text-Boxed Items with a Mouse

As you can see, the dirt-simple way to position text boxes is to drag them with your mouse while in Page Layout view or Print Preview. Follow these steps:

1. Place the pointer anywhere within the text box and watch the pointer.

2. The pointer will change to include a four-headed arrow.

3. Press down on the primary mouse button and drag the text box to the middle of the text.

4. Release the mouse button.

5. Soon after you release the mouse button, the text box will take up residence in its new location. Text will move out of the way for the text box, and the little anchor icon will move as well.

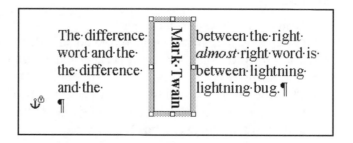

6. If the text doesn't wrap around the text box, simply change the settings. Choose Format ➤ Text Box ➤ Wrapping and select the Square and Both Sides options, as shown in Figure 5.3.

FIGURE 5.3

Wrap text around a text box in a variety of ways.

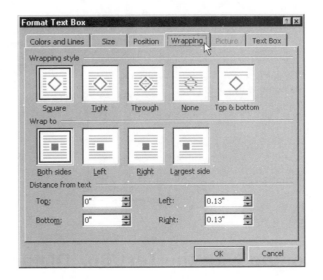

You can continue to drag the boxed text around to suit yourself. Switch to Print Preview and try moving it there too.

Remember—you'll need to click on the Magnifier button in Print Preview before you can edit the document. And once you select the Magnifier button, you'll need to click on the Select Object tool on the Drawing toolbar in order to move the text box around.

A text box is always anchored to a paragraph. When you position a text box by dragging it, it is initially anchored to its closest paragraph. To see where a text box's anchor is, select the text box. A little anchor icon like the one in Figure 5.4 will appear.

As you add or delete text in your document, the boxed item stays with its paragraph. A text box always appears on the same page with its paragraph.

This is often the desired effect. But what if you want to keep a boxed item on a particular page or a specific distance from a particular paragraph?

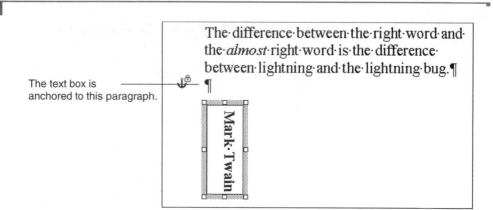

FIGURE 5.4

Normally, text boxes are anchored to nearby paragraphs.

The text box is anchored to this paragraph.

Positioning with the Text Box Dialog Box

When you want to position text boxes precisely or force a text box to position itself relative to other things that might move, select the text box and use the Position tab in the new Format Text Box dialog box (choose Format ➤ Text Box). It's shown in Figure 5.5.

FIGURE 5.5

Use the Position tab in the Format Text Box dialog box for precise text box positioning.

When you select a text box and open this dialog box, you will see its position on the Position tab. You can specify new position settings and also change the size of the text box with the Size tab, shown in Figure 5.6. Size and position settings can be specified in inches (in), centimeters (cm), points (pt), or picas (pi).

> **TIP**
>
> You change the units of measurement by using the General tab in the Options dialog box (choose Tools ➤ Options).

The Format Text Box dialog box contains four additional tabs besides Position and General:

- Colors and Lines changes the text box's fill, outline, and transparency.
- Wrapping offers methods for wrapping document text around the text box to leave white space around it and define its shape.
- Picture provides options for formatting a picture but isn't active when you're formatting text.
- Text Box defines the margin within the selected text box so that you can leave additional white space around the text.

FIGURE 5.6

Use the Size tab in the Format Text Box dialog box for precise text box sizing.

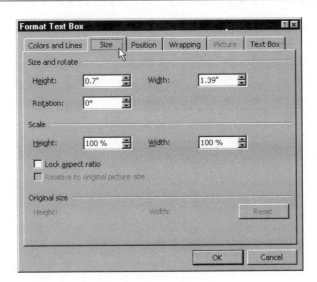

Getting Started

NOTE

The Format Text Box and Format Object dialog boxes are essentially the same, except that in the Format Text Box dialog box, the Picture tab isn't active, and in the Format Object dialog box, the Text Box tab isn't active.

MASTERING THE OPPORTUNITIES

Converting Text Boxes to Frames

If you are sharing documents with others working on an earlier version of Word, you'll want to convert text boxes in your document to frames. You can do this by selecting the text box and then choosing Format ➤ Text Box ➤ Text Box. Click on

the Convert to Frame option and then click on Yes at the confirmation prompt.

When you convert a text box to a frame, Word warns you that some of its formatting may be lost. After conversion, however, you can format the frame with the Format ➤ Frame command that you'll see when the frame is selected. The familiar Frame dialog box still looks the same.

Aligning Text Boxes with Reference Points

The Format Text Box dialog box also provides additional positioning and reference options. For instance, you can rotate a text box by a precise degree. Or, you can tell Word to keep a text box a specified distance from margins or columns. Finally, you can anchor a text box to text so that when the text moves, the text box accompanies it. Place a checkmark next to the Move Object with Text option on the Position tab to accomplish this.

Text and Text Boxes

Text boxes and text can be used together in several ways. Besides framing text, you can position text boxes relative to text or flow text around text boxes. Here are a few ways to work with text boxes and text.

Placing Text in Text Boxes

You can use text boxes as small text windows that can be moved anywhere in your document. For instance, in Figure 5.7, Adam's paragraph headings are being boxed and

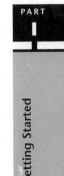

FIGURE 5.7

Text box text can be used to place headings in margins, among other things.

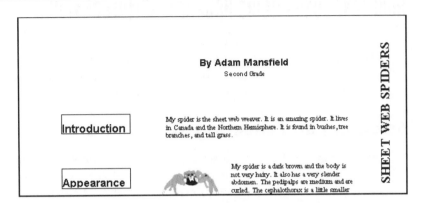

moved into his document's margin. (You may want to remove the text box borders when you do this.)

By checking the Move Object with Text option on the Position tab of the Format Text Box dialog box, you can make sure the headings will stay with their paragraphs when you edit the document.

A quick way to create a lot of marginal headings like Adam's is to create one and then *redefine the document's heading style(s)* based on the example. All your headings will be boxed and placed in the margin quicker than you can say "arachnid." (Chapter 12, *Using Paragraph Styles and AutoFormat,* shows how to work with styles.)

When framing existing *text,* Word will make the text box big enough to accommodate all the text you've selected. But if you paste text into an existing *text box,* be sure the text box is big enough to prevent "weird word wrap," a problem that arises when you specify large line indents or place long words in narrow text boxes. If the text you insert changes into a long vertical string of characters, try resizing the text box to make the text legible. Feel free to use all of Word's text formatting tools in text boxes. You can have multiple paragraphs in text boxes.

Word's Formatting toolbar and ruler work in text boxes. You can change type sizes and styles, center, justify, and otherwise fool with text in text boxes. Even Word's spelling checker peeks into them.

Inserting Text in Boxed Graphics (Captioning)

If you want to add a caption to a boxed graphic, select the text box and press Enter. You'll see a new paragraph mark in the text box. Type the caption. Stylize the text, if you like. The caption will stay with the text box when you move it.

How Text Boxed Items Appear in Different Views

You can see where boxed items will print by displaying them in Print Preview or Page Layout view. When you switch to Normal or Outline view, boxed items will appear within the page boundaries where they will print but not necessarily in their printing positions. You can easily spot boxed items in Normal and Outline views.

Selecting and Deleting Text Boxes

It's possible to delete text boxes *and their contents* by simply selecting the text box and then cutting it (Ctrl+X) or pressing the Delete key. (Select a text box by pointing and clicking with your mouse. Eight dark black handles and a black line will appear around the text box when you've selected it.)

TIP

To remove a text box, but not its text, first select the text and then use the Move option on the pop-up menu to place the text where you want it. Or simply drag and drop it. Then delete the text box as described.

Deleting or Changing Text Box Borders

Text boxes are created without printing borders, but these can be added and altered. To do so, follow these steps:

1. Select a text boxed object in Page Layout view by clicking on the object.
2. Choose Format ➤ Text Box and then click on the Colors and Lines tab to add, change, or remove the border. For instance, clicking on the No Line Option in the Color palette area shown in Figure 5.8 removes a text box's border.

See Chapter 8, *Formatting Paragraphs,* for more information about borders and shading.

TIP

There is also a Tables and Borders button on the Standard toolbar that opens the Tables and Borders toolbar. It's on the right end and looks like a four-pane window.

FIGURE 5.8

Turn off a text box's border by choosing No Line on the color palette.

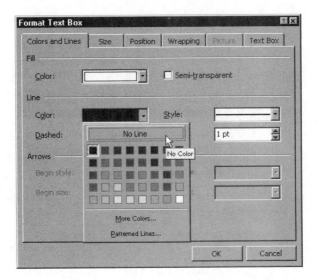

Experiment

It's time to put down the book and grab your mouse. Try a few of the techniques in this chapter. When you're done frittering—err, I mean *learning*—check out the next chapter, in which you'll see how Word can help you format your documents.

PART II

Formatting Fundamentals

LEARN TO:

- *Design your pages*

- *Create clever tables*

- *Work with fonts and symbols*

- *Add some style to your documents*

Chapter

6

Margins and
Page Breaks

Chapter 6

Margins and Page Breaks

The amount of white space around the edges of a Word page is determined primarily by margin and optional gutter settings. (Gutters add extra white space for bound documents.) One set of margin and gutter settings can be used for an entire document, or you can define different settings for different pages in your document. The paper size, paper orientation (portrait vs. landscape), margin, and gutter settings you choose work together to determine the size and shape of the text area of pages.

Larger margins and gutter settings decrease the available text area while increasing the surrounding white space on each page. Figure 6.1 shows the Word default margin and text-area dimensions for both portrait and landscape orientations when creating U.S. letter-size documents without gutters.

Get Off to a Good Start

Because margin settings (and page setup information) affect pagination, it is a good idea to define these dimensions right when you begin a new project. This will give you a better grasp of the page count and overall look of the document as you work. You can always fine-tune margin settings just before final printing.

FIGURE 6.1

Margin settings, paper size, and orientation are three of the many factors that affect the available text area.

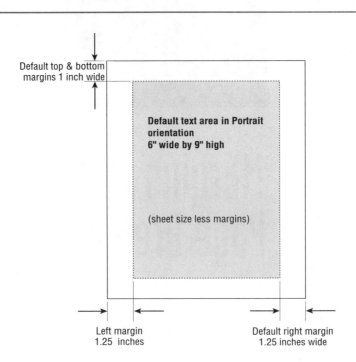

Default top & bottom margins 1 inch wide

Default text area in Portrait orientation 6" wide by 9" high

(sheet size less margins)

Left margin 1.25 inches

Default right margin 1.25 inches wide

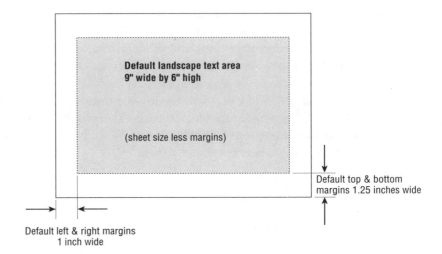

Default landscape text area 9" wide by 6" high

(sheet size less margins)

Default top & bottom margins 1.25 inches wide

Default left & right margins 1 inch wide

Margins need not all be the same width. It is possible, for instance, to have a 1.5" left margin and a 1.0" right margin, a 0.5" bottom margin and a 0.75" top margin, or just about any combination you desire.

When printing two-sided documents, you might want to use Word's Mirror Margins feature and possibly add gutters to place extra white space near the center of your book. (Note that it is conventional to have odd-numbered pages on the right and even on the left—just look at any book!) If you plan to have different left and right margins in a two-sided document (a wide left and narrow right, for instance), it is useful to think of these as *inside* and *outside* margins rather than left and right margins, because the wide margin will be on the left side of odd-numbered pages but on the right of even-numbered pages. In this chapter, you'll learn how to create such margins.

If you use headers and footers, you will want to know how they interact with margin settings. Word makes this all fairly painless.

NOTE Some printers cannot print at the extreme edges of a page. This should be a consideration when setting margins.

Document Margins vs. Indents

Don't confuse Word's margin settings with its paragraph-indention feature. A Word *page* can have only one user-specified left *margin* setting and only one user-specified right margin setting, but each *paragraph* on the page can have a different left and right *indention* setting.

Indents are *added* to margin settings. That is to say, if you specify a 1.0" left margin and a 0.5" left indent, your text will print 1.5" from the left margin. If you set a 1.0" right margin and indent the right edge of a paragraph 1.0", the text will stop 2.0" from the right edge of the page. See Chapter 8, *Formatting Paragraphs*, for more about indenting.

Changing Document Margins

You can set margins in three ways. The most straightforward method is to use the Margins portion of the Page Setup dialog box, reached with the File ➤ Page Setup command. Curiously, there is no standard keyboard shortcut for accessing this oft-visited dialog box. However, Word 97 now has a toolbar button for the Page Setup command. You can add this button or one of your own as described below. Chapter 32, *Personalizing Word*, contains more detailed information on customizing your Word 97 toolbars.

MASTERING THE OPPORTUNITIES

Add the Page Setup Button to Your Standard or Formatting Toolbar

 You can add the new Page Setup button to your favorite toolbar with the View ➤ Toolbars ➤ Customize command. This command is also useful for adding other buttons to your toolbars. Buttons provide one-click access to menu commands; so you save time by using the button instead of clicking through the menu with your mouse. You might want to add your own buttons, because the standard buttons may not be the ones you will use often.

Many menu commands in Word have corresponding toolbar buttons, but these buttons may not be in the default toolbars. As you work with Word, observe and make a list of the menu commands you use most often. For example, you might insert many tables into your documents, using commands on the Table menu (Insert Table, Delete Cells, and so on). You can add these buttons to one of the default toolbars. You can delete buttons that you don't use often to make room for buttons that you will use. You can also create an entirely new toolbar and add all the buttons you need for a particular task to that toolbar. For example, all the Table tasks in the Table menu could be added as buttons to a new "Table" toolbar. To

learn more about these toolbar options, see Chapter 32.

For now, try adding the Page Setup button to one of the existing toolbars. Here are the steps you will need to use:

1. Choose View ➤ Toolbars ➤ Customize. Word displays the Customize dialog box.
2. Highlight the Standard or Formatting toolbar under the Toolbars tab in the Customize dialog box.

 3. Select the Commands tab and highlight File in the Categories list box. In the Commands list box, scroll down to the Page Setup button, which resembles an open book.
4. Drag this button to the Standard or Formatting toolbar. An I-beam cursor will appear on the toolbar, showing you where the button will be located when you let go of the mouse button. Drop the button where you want it.
5. Your Standard or Formatting toolbar now has the Page Setup button for quick access to the Page Setup dialog box. If you decide you do not want that button or another button on the toolbar, choose View ➤ Toolbars ➤ Customize. Click on the button you want to remove and drag it into the document window. The cursor will display a small *x*. Drop the button, and it will disappear from your toolbar.

You can also drag margins using the rulers in Print Preview. Doing so lets you see the results of margin changes after a slight repagination delay.

Finally, you can drag new margins with the rulers in Page Layout view. The margin brackets are on the ruler. Let's look at all three techniques, starting with the dialog box.

> **TIP**
>
> Document margins are affected by your printer choice, page orientation, and other decisions made in the four tabs in the Page Setup dialog box (Layout, Paper Source, Paper Size, and Margins). Therefore, you should choose your printer, if you have more than one, and then use the other tabs in the Page Setup dialog box to make any necessary changes before adjusting margins. Double-clicking on a dark gray part of the ruler will display the Page Setup dialog box.

The Page Setup Dialog Box Margin Settings

Figure 6.2 shows the Margins tab in the Page Setup dialog box (File ➤ Page Setup). You can enter new Top, Bottom, Left, Right, and Gutter margins.

The From Edge settings tell Word how close to the edges of the page you want headers and footers to print. For instance, a Header setting of 0.5" places the top of a header 0.5" from the top edge of the paper; the same setting for a footer places the bottom of a footer 0.5" from the paper's bottom edge.

Settings can be uniform throughout a document or different on any and all pages. Be sure to check the setting in the Apply To drop-down list box. Choices are Whole

PART

II

Formatting
Fundamentals

FIGURE 6.2

You have complete control over margins in the Margins tab of the Page Setup dialog box.

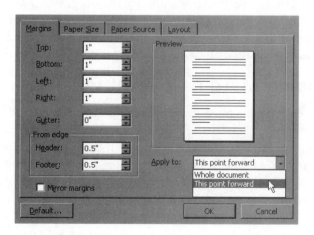

Document, This Point Forward, or (if there are section breaks) This Section. This Point Forward means from (and including) the page containing the insertion point. This Section sets new margins for the section containing the insertion point, even if this occurs in the middle of a page. If you have section breaks, This Section is the default, which requires a bit of extra attention if you want to change the margins for the whole document.

The Preview will change to show you a miniature representation of the new settings as you adjust them. After you type each new setting, press Tab to move to the next box. As with other Word dialog boxes, enter fractions as decimals; ¼" would be 0.25, for example.

Follow these general steps to change margins:

1. Place the insertion point on the page where you want margin settings to be changed (unless you plan to use the Whole Document choice).
2. Choose File ➤ Page Setup.
3. Change paper size and orientation, if required, by using the Paper Size tab.
4. Switch to the Margins tab if it is not already displayed.
5. Current settings are shown in the various margin dimension boxes.
6. Type the dimensions you desire, or click on the up and down arrows to increase and decrease settings. The Preview will change as you work.
7. When satisfied, click on OK.

TIP

Dimensional settings in most Word dialog boxes can be expressed in inches (in), points (pt), centimeters (cm), picas (pi), and, frequently, lines (li). For instance, to set a top margin's height to 12 points, you would type 12pt in the Top margin box. A 1.5"-line top margin would be 1.5li, and so on. Although you can enter dimensions in any of these units of measure, Word will convert them to the default unit of measure when you close the dialog box. You change the default measurement unit in the General tab of the Options dialog box.

Dragging Margins in Print Preview

It's easy to change a document's margins while in Print Preview. Drag on the ruler ends, as shown in Figure 6.3, and then wait a moment for your computer to redisplay the page with your new margin settings. Watch the ruler markings as you work. They will give you a good idea of the dimensions. For more precise settings, however, use the dialog box.

If you don't see the rulers in Print Preview, click on the fifth button from the right (the View Ruler button) at the top of the Print Preview window, as shown in Figure 6.4.

When displaying multiple pages in Print Preview, you will need to click in a page before adjusting margins. The ruler(s) and guidelines will move to the page where you

FIGURE 6.3

*Drag ruler ends
in Print Preview
to change
your margins.*

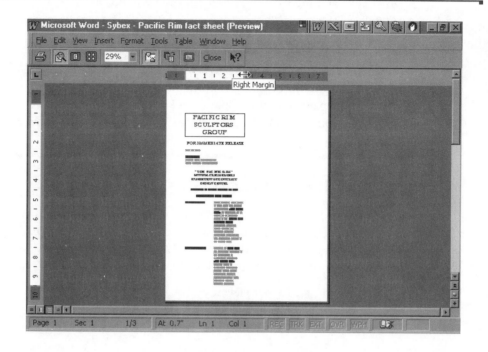

FIGURE 6.4

*Click here if
necessary to
display margin
guidelines and
handles.*

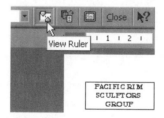

click. This lets you work with different left, right (or inside/outside), top, and bottom
margin combinations. The general steps for changing margins in Print Preview are:

1. Choose File ➤ Print Preview.
2. If the rulers are not visible, click on the View Ruler button.
3. If necessary, click in a page.
4. Point to the transition area on the ruler, where its color changes. The pointer
   will change to a two-headed arrow.

5. Drag, watching the ruler's guidelines as you do so.

6. Release the mouse button to see the effect of the margin changes.

7. Repeat steps 3 through 6 to fine-tune, if necessary.

TIP

If you've chosen Mirror Margins in the Margins tab of the Page Setup dialog box, be sure to display at least two pages in Print Preview to see the effect on facing margins as you drag. Odd pages (pages 1, 3, and so on) are always displayed on the right.

Dragging Margin Brackets on the Ruler

Word's rulers display margins as dark gray areas (this may vary, depending on your color scheme). You can drag these areas to change the document's margins. Don't confuse margin-dragging techniques with indent-dragging techniques, which are similar but have a very different effect. Follow these steps:

1. Change to Page Layout view if you're not there already.

2. If the ruler is not displayed, choose View ➤ Ruler.

3. Point to the transition area on the ruler where its color changes, as shown in Figure 6.5.

4. The mouse pointer will become a two-headed arrow.

5. Drag the margin to the desired position with your mouse. Watch the ruler's dimensions change as you drag.

FIGURE 6.5

Drag the edges where the ruler's color changes to move margins.

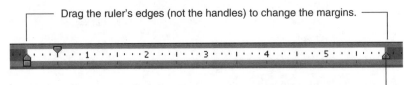

Drag the ruler's edges (not the handles) to change the margins.

Don't accidentally drag the indent handles if you want to change margins.

Alternate Facing [Mirror] Margins

Select the Mirror Margins feature in the Margins tab of the Page Setup dialog box (File ➤ Page Setup) when you want different left and right margin widths and your final output will be two-sided. Word makes inside margins of odd- and even-numbered pages the same size and does the same with the outside margins of odd and even pages, as illustrated in Figure 6.6. This is how you get white space on the appropriate side of even and odd two-sided pages.

When adjusting margins in Print Preview, be sure to display two pages if you've chosen the Mirror Margins feature. Otherwise, you won't know if you're working with an odd page or an even page.

FIGURE 6.6

Mirror Margins compensates for two-sided documents with dissimilar left and right margins.

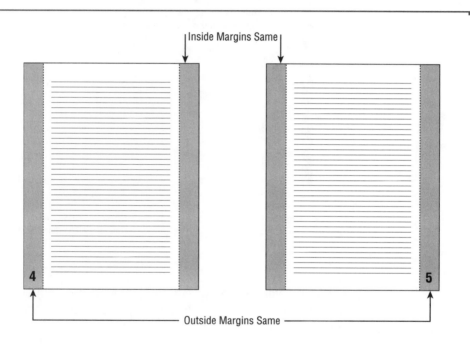

Inside Margins Same

Outside Margins Same

PART

II

Formatting
Fundamentals

Gutters Facilitate Binding

Gutter margins compensate for the paper tucked away in the binding of a two-sided book that would be unreadable. Gutters are additional white space in the inside margins. The gutter width, which you specify in the Margin tab of the Page Setup dialog box, reduces the text area, as shown in Figure 6.7.

FIGURE 6.7

Gutter space compensates for paper used in the binding process by adding space to inside margins in two-sided documents.

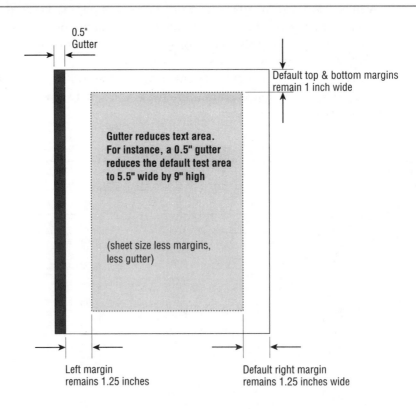

0.5"
Gutter

Default top & bottom margins remain 1 inch wide

Gutter reduces text area. For instance, a 0.5" gutter reduces the default test area to 5.5" wide by 9" high

(sheet size less margins, less gutter)

Left margin remains 1.25 inches

Default right margin remains 1.25 inches wide

In Print Preview, you can see the effect of gutter margins, but you cannot adjust them. You adjust the gutter in the Margin tab in the Page Setup dialog box (File ➤ Page Setup).

TIP

Instead of using gutters, you can simply increase the size of the inside margins to accommodate binding.

Printer Capabilities Limit Margins

Many printers, including most laser printers, are incapable of printing all the way to the edge of the paper. Keep this in mind when setting margins. If, for instance, your printer cannot print past the last half-inch of a page, any margin of less than 0.5" will result in cropped (chopped-off) text.

Some printers offer ways to increase printing area. For instance, some laser printers let you trade font memory for larger printing areas. See your printer manual for details.

Printing in the Margins

As you can see from Figure 6.8, it is possible to place text, graphics, and page numbers in margins by using indent markers. You can drag indent markers into margins, and text or graphics will follow. You can also use the Insert ➤ Text Box command to place things in margins, as described in Chapter 5, *Using Text Boxes to Frame, Position, and Anchor Text*. Page numbers can also be positioned in margins, as you will learn in Chapter 10.

PART

II

Formatting
Fundamentals

FIGURE 6.8

It's easy to print in the margins.

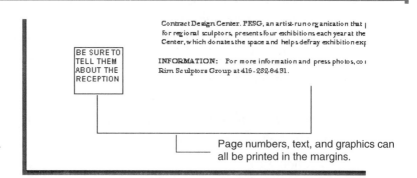

How Headers and Footers Affect Margins

Headers and footers print in the top and bottom margins. When you include headers and footers, Word automatically adjusts top and bottom margins when necessary. For instance, if you use the Margins tab of the Page Setup dialog box to specify a minimum top margin of 0.5" and then create a header that is 1.0" high, Word increases the top margin size to make room for the big header. You can override this feature by specifying exact top or bottom margins in the Margins tab of the Page Setup dialog box. Doing so forces Word to limit top and bottom margins, unless this would encroach upon headers and footers. This can create some interesting effects, desired and otherwise. Read about headers and footers in Chapter 10, *Headers, Footers, Page Numbers, and Footnotes*.

Page Breaks

Page breaks are the places in your document where one page ends and a new page begins. Several factors affect page breaks: the size of your paper, margin settings, paragraph formats, and section breaks. Word automatically computes and displays page breaks as you add and delete information. Breaks appear as dotted lines in Normal and Outline views. Because both Page Layout view and Print Preview simulate sheets of paper, page breaks are easy to see in those views as well.

You can force your own page breaks. For instance, if you always want new chapters to start on a new page, you can insert manual page breaks at the beginning of each chapter.

Repagination

To display and print page breaks properly, Word must recalculate page endings after you make changes in a document. Normally it does so in the background whenever it can steal some otherwise unused computer time. This process is called *automatic repagination*. Because page endings affect certain other features, Word always repaginates when

- You ask it to print.
- You are in Print Preview or Page Layout view.
- You compile a table of contents or an index.

To turn off automatic repagination (and speed up slower computers when working on large documents), follow these steps:

1. Choose Tools ➤ Options.
2. Click on the General tab if it's not in view.
3. Clear the Background Repagination checkbox. (You won't be able to do this if you are in Page Layout view.)
4. Close the Options dialog box.
5. Word will repaginate only when you are in a view that requires it. To force repagination, switch to Page Layout or Print Preview, or issue a Print request.

TIP

Word 97 does not have a Repaginate Now command.

Forcing Page Breaks

When you want to force a page break, you can insert manual page breaks. In Normal and Outline views, they look thicker than Word's automatic page breaks and contain the words *Page Break*.

Generally speaking, forcing a page break is not a great idea. If you must do it, wait until you have done all your other formatting, spell-checking, and so forth.

To insert a manual page break, follow these steps:

1. Move the insertion point to where you want the break.

2. Choose Insert ➤ Break. Word displays the Break dialog box:

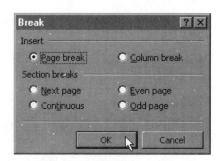

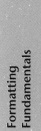

3. Be sure the Page Break button is selected (the default).

4. Click on OK or press Enter.

5. The dialog box will disappear, and you'll see a thick dotted manual page break line labeled "Page Break" on your screen. Text or graphics below the manual page break will appear on the next page of your document.

Press Ctrl+↵ to insert a manual page break without going through the dialog box.

Moving and Deleting Page Breaks

In Normal and Outline views, you can highlight and delete manual breaks just as you highlight and delete text. (You cannot delete automatic breaks placed by Word.) Select a manual break line and press Delete.

You can also use the Replace command to search for and delete manual breaks. You do this by searching for manual breaks and replacing them with nothing (see Chapter 16, *Finding and Replacing*).

Keeping Things Together on a Page

Sometimes automatic page breaks occur where they shouldn't, for example, immediately following a heading or in the middle of lists or tables. Word offers several ways to keep things together.

Keeping Lines Together

To keep lines together and prevent a page break from separating them, follow these steps:

1. Select the lines you want to keep together (this is often easiest in Normal view).
2. Choose Format ➤ Paragraph.
3. If necessary, click on the Line and Page Breaks tab to reveal the options shown here:

4. Check the Keep Lines Together checkbox, and then click on OK.

Small, black, nonprinting blocks will appear next to the lines, indicating that these lines have special formatting that may not be obvious in some views. The lines will stay together on the same page (sometimes creating very short pages).

Keeping Paragraphs or Graphics and Labels Together

To keep paragraphs together or to keep graphics and related text on the same page, follow these steps:

1. Select the paragraphs (possibly including graphics) you want to keep together.

2. Choose Format ➤ Paragraph and select the Line and Page Breaks tab if it is not visible.

3. Check the Keep with Next checkbox and click on OK.

If Show/Hide is turned on, small, black, nonprinting blocks will appear next to the lines, indicating that these lines have special formatting. The designated items will stay together on the same page (sometimes causing very short pages).

Keeping Parts of Tables Together

As you will learn when you read more about tables in Chapter 9, *Tabs, Tables, Math, and Sorting*. Word treats each row in a table as a separate paragraph. Select all the rows of a table, and in the Paragraph dialog box, check the Keep with Next checkbox to keep a table intact.

Forcing Paragraphs to Start on a New Page

To force a paragraph to start on a new page (a chapter heading, for instance), follow these steps:

1. Select the paragraph you want to place at the top of a new page.

2. Choose Format ➤ Paragraph and select the Line and Page Breaks tab.

3. Check the Page Break Before checkbox, and click on OK.

Removing Keep with Next and Similar Paragraph Options

To remove special paragraph and line options such as Keep with Next, Keep Lines Together, and Page Break Before, follow these steps:

1. Select the paragraph(s) you want to change.

2. Choose Format ➤ Paragraph and select the Line and Page Breaks tab if it's not visible.

3. Click on checkmarks to remove unwanted options, and then click on OK.

Controlling Widows and Orphans

Widows are short lines (typically a single word) at the end of paragraphs. *Orphans* are the first lines of paragraphs that print by themselves at the bottom of a page. Although both can distract readers, some editors will tell you to eliminate orphans and live with widows (pun intended). The choice is yours, unless you work somewhere with policies about such style issues.

PART

II

Formatting
Fundamentals

Word automatically eliminates both widows and orphans unless you tell it to do otherwise. You may find it helpful to turn off this feature if you are having trouble making things fit, particularly in multicolumn documents. Here's how to turn off automated widow and orphan suppression:

1. Choose Format ➤ Paragraph.
2. Remove the check from the Widow/Orphan Control checkbox in the Line and Page Breaks tab.
3. Click on OK.

Widows and orphans may occur, and you can deal with them manually or choose to ignore them.

Sometimes, Print Preview's Shrink to Fit option can help with widows.

Chapter

7

Characters and Fonts

Characters and Fonts

Specialists called typographers spend their whole lives studying and improving the appearance of printed words. It is a complex profession steeped in tradition and romance. Computers have added to the trivia and mystique surrounding typography. Word provides considerable typographic prowess. For instance, you can:

- Specify fonts (type designs)
- Specify character size (in points)
- Embellish text (bold, italics, and underline)
- Adjust spacing between characters (kerning)
- Specify colors for characters
- Change the case of text (for example, lowercase to uppercase)
- Super- or subscript characters
- Copy and repeat character formatting
- Insert international diacritical marks and special symbols
- Hide and reveal text selectively (annotations)
- Use Word's typesetting commands for equation and technical typing

For many, it may be enough to know how to print desired characters in appropriate sizes and styles. Other readers will want to know how to get just the right look. Some will need to know about various font technologies. You may need to be aware of compatibility issues when moving documents from one computer or printer to another.

This chapter progresses from simple, nontechnical techniques to fairly complex issues. Feel free to jump from topic to topic as the need arises.

TIP

If you always use the same computer and a single printer and are happy with your choice of fonts and effects, you may be able to completely ignore the technology and typesetting information found near the end of this chapter.

There are very few hard-and-fast rules where the art of typography is concerned, but there are plenty of rules where the technology of computer fonts is concerned. The best way to learn is to experiment.

Terminology

People often use the terms *font* and *typeface* synonymously. The terms are not really synonyms, but because the world seems to be treating them that way these days, I will too. With apologies to professional typographers, I'll start with some slightly oversimplified definitions.

Characters, Fonts, and Typefaces

Characters are the letters, numbers, punctuation marks, and special symbols that you type from the keyboard. For our purposes, I'll define a font or typeface as a collection of characters and symbols with a common appearance, or design. Courier is an example of a font. It will remind you of old typewriters. Times is another font (or typeface), and it will remind you of newspaper and magazine copy.

Different fonts contain different collections of characters and symbols. Some fonts are designed for specific purposes such as headings or drop caps. Sometimes these have only uppercase letters and may not even contain punctuation. Scientific and math fonts contain the necessary Greek and other symbols for technical notation. Other fonts are used for adding decorations to your document. Wingdings is an example. Instead of numbers and letters, it contains tiny pictures of airplanes, boxes, checkmarks, and so on.

Font Families

A collection of all the variations of a font is called a family. For instance, you can purchase a font family from Adobe called Lucida. This family includes Lucida Roman, Lucida Italic, Lucida Bold, and Lucida Bold Italic.

One way to add emphasis to a document is to use different fonts for headlines, paragraph headings, and body copy. Sometimes you'll decide to select different fonts from the same family; other times you'll mix fonts from different families. The headings and body type used in this book illustrate both techniques.

Character Formatting

When you use Word, you need not purchase entire font families to use effects such as bold and italics. Word has features that can often embellish the appearance of single plain fonts to create boldface, italics, shadow, and other effects. The techniques used to do this are usually referred to as character formatting. Figure 7.1 shows many of the character-formatting variations possible when using Word's character format tricks and the NewCenturySchlbk (schoolbook) font.

Don't confuse the character formatting tricks shown in Figure 7.1 with true bold, italics, and other fonts. Purists often prefer the real thing, and these character formatting effects can sometimes look downright awful when applied to certain fonts—including many of the low-cost shareware typefaces in common use.

PART

II

Formatting
Fundamentals

FIGURE 7.1

*With Word's
formatting
capabilities, you
can enhance
a font in
many ways.*

Normal (a.k.a Plain Text), **Bold,** *Italic*

Standard underline Word Underline

Double underline Dotted underline

~~Strike-through~~

all caps off, ALL CAPS ON

Small Caps Off, SMALL CAPS ON

Super Normal Subscript

Condensed character spacing Off

Condensed character spacing On

Expanded character spacing Off

Expanded character spacing On

Black Blue TurquoiseBright Green Green

Incidentally, not all font vendors provide identical-looking fonts, even when the font names are the same. The Courier installed in Windows looks slightly different from the Courier in Pacific Data's PostScript products, for instance. Occasionally (but rarely) this can cause differences in line endings. And, once in a while, you'll find different special characters in fonts from various manufacturers.

Monospaced vs. Proportionally Spaced

Some fonts are said to be monospaced or fixed-pitch; others, proportionally spaced or variable-pitch. In monospaced fonts such as Courier, characters occupy the same amount of horizontal space (*pitch*) on a line. For example, in Courier a letter *i* occupies the same amount of horizontal space as the letter *W*. Thus, if you can fit 70 *i*'s on a line, you can fit 70 *W*'s in the same space. Obviously, this is an inefficient use of space and sometimes causes sloppy-looking words. Since people such as lawyers, art directors, and publishers usually want to fit as many words as possible on a page, they turn to proportionally spaced fonts that tuck narrow letters in closer to their neighbors.

In Figure 7.2 the same word is printed first in 72-point Courier, a monospaced font, and then in 72-point Times and Helvetica, both proportionally spaced fonts. Notice the ocean of white space on either side of the letter *i* in the Courier example. A long base

FIGURE 7.2

Notice that Courier's spacing (top) is much less elegant than that of Times (middle) or Helvetica (bottom).

Wingman

Wingman

Wingman

has been added to the bottom of the *i* in an attempt to distract you from this untidiness. Compare the white space on either side of all three *i*'s in Figure 7.2.

Ironically, the monospaced Courier font uses less horizontal space on the line than either of the proportionally spaced fonts, due mainly to the much wider *W*'s and *m*'s in the proportional faces. Generally, though, proportionally spaced fonts will be more economical with space than monospaced fonts.

Point Sizes

Type is measured in points. There are 72 points to an inch. Thus, 72-point type will take 1 vertical inch of space, 36-point type will require 0.5 inch of vertical space, and so on.

Point size is measured from the lowest descender to the highest ascender in the font. For instance, in Figure 7.2 you would measure from the bottom of the *g* to the top of the *W*. Sometimes different fonts of the same point size appear taller or shorter because of the amount of space the designer has allowed for the parts of characters that go below the baseline and above the tops of caps (called descenders and ascenders) and for white space above and below the characters (called leading). Notice how the 72-point Courier looks shorter than the 72-point Helvetica in Figure 7.2.

Your choice of point size affects the amount of space between lines (the leading), as well as the height of the characters. You can have more than one point size on a line, but Word will adjust the line spacing to accommodate the largest character on the line. You can override this feature, as you will see in the next chapter.

Serif vs. Sans Serif Fonts

The horizontal cross lines on the *W*, *i*, *n*, and *m* in Figure 7.2's Courier and Times examples are called *serifs*. (The fonts themselves are called serif fonts.) Popular computer fonts with serifs include Courier, Bookman, Palatino, and Times. Fonts without these embellishments are said to be *sans serif*. Avant Garde, Modern, Arial, and Helvetica are examples of sans serif fonts.

TIP

Serif fonts, which guide the eye across the page, are traditionally used for body text. Sans serif fonts, although harder to read, are more eye-catching and so are typically used for headings, captions, and isolated bits of text.

PART

II

Formatting
Fundamentals

Character-Formatting Tools—An Overview

There are many ways to tell Word to make characters bold, italic, bigger, or smaller. Tools for character formatting include the toolbar, menu choices, dialog boxes, and keyboard shortcuts. You can change the formatting of single characters, entire words, or whole documents. Let's start with an overview of the tools that Word provides for character formatting; then we'll look at typical examples of the tools in use.

TIP

You can specify the desired appearance of characters before you type them, or you can type first, select text, and then change its appearance. Virtually all the character-formatting techniques described in this chapter can be accomplished either before or after you enter text.

Character-Formatting Choices on Word's Menus

Word's various menus contain a number of character-related formatting choices. These let you:

- Select fonts
- Select font sizes
- Select underline styles
- Highlight important text
- Add effects such as superscript, subscript, and so on
- Change the color of displayed or printed characters
- Change default characters
- Preview changes in a window
- Change character spacing
- Insert special characters and symbols
- Change case (make words all uppercase, all lowercase, and so on)
- Create drop caps and similar effects

The Font Command

Word's Format ➤ Font command opens a three-tab dialog box. The Font tab lists all the fonts installed on your computer and their standard sizes, as illustrated in Figure 7.3. (Yours may list different fonts.)

TIP

No, you are not seeing double. Word places the names of your most recently used fonts at the top of the font list in the toolbar for quick access. The font names are also available in their normal locations.

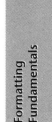

FIGURE 7.3

The Font dialog box lists and demonstrates all fonts installed on your computer.

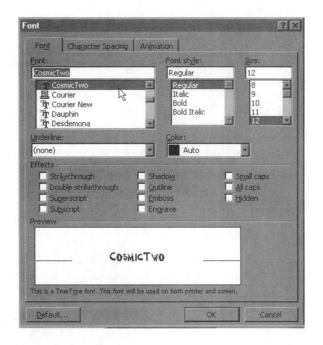

The Font tab also offers some choices for underlining and special effects and a preview area in which you can see the results of your selections. An information line at the bottom of the screen often provides other clues about how the font will look on your screen and how it will print.

Text boxes display the current font, size, and font style. The up and down arrows scroll through the standard sizes available for the selected font. You can type in the Size box to specify nonstandard font sizes not found in the list.

The Default button in the Font tab of the Font dialog box gives you the opportunity to make the current selections the new default settings used by Word.

Character Formatting with the Formatting Toolbar

The most immediately visible way to modify character appearance is to use the buttons and font menus on the Formatting toolbar, illustrated in Figure 7.4.

If the Formatting toolbar is not in view, choose the View ➤ Toolbars command. Choose the Formatting toolbar by placing a check next to the appropriate name, as illustrated in Figure 7.5.

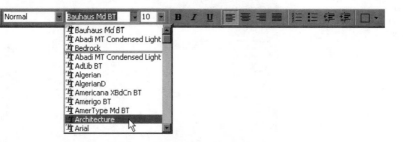

From the Formatting toolbar, you can select a font, change to a different point size, and toggle bold, italic, and simple underline. Simply click on the appropriate toolbar button or choose the desired option from the toolbar's drop-down lists. Clicking a second time on a toolbar button removes, or toggles, the effect.

The Formatting toolbar has a new drop-down button called Outside Border, which leads to all the other Border option buttons. This one button replaces the entire Borders toolbar used in earlier versions of Word and adds three new bordering options. Chapter 8, *Formatting Paragraphs,* discusses the new Outside Border button and its Bor-der button palette.

MASTERING THE OPPORTUNITIES

Light Up Your Web Page Hyperlinks with Text Animation

Word 97 has an exciting new feature in the Font dialog box (choose Format ➤ Font). A third tab, called Animation, has been added. Use this tab to liven up your online text, especially if you are creating a Web page that contains hyperlinks to sub-pages or to other Web sites.

To use this feature, select the text that will have an animated border. Choose Format ➤ Font and click on the Animation tab. You will see the animated border options, as shown below:

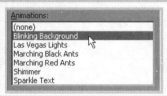

Choose one of the effects. You will see how it looks around your text in the Preview area in the lower part of the dialog box. Click on OK to apply the effect.

These effects can only be used one at a time. They will appear in online documents, but they cannot be printed out. You can combine the animations with other formatting elements, such as bold-face, text color, and different fonts.

If you start getting dizzy, turn the effects off by selecting Format ➤ Font. Select the Animation tab, and highlight (none), and then click on OK.

PART

II

Formatting
Fundamentals

Seeing Which Character Formats Are at Work

You can see most of the information regarding character formatting by selecting one or more characters and looking carefully at the Formatting toolbar. It will tell you the font name and size, and buttons will reflect the current formatting. If text is bold, for example, the toolbar's bold button will be pressed.

TIP

If all the characters you select are not identically formatted, some or all of the information areas in the toolbar will be blank or incomplete. For instance, if you select characters of different sizes, the Font size area of the toolbar will be blank. If some of your selected text is bold and some not, the Bold button will not be pressed.

Here's a great feature. Use the Help ➤ What's This command along with your mouse to see which character-formatting tools have been used on characters of interest. Follow these steps:

1. Select Help ➤ What's This. The pointer changes shape.
2. Point to a character and click the mouse button. A balloonlike box appears, containing information about the paragraph and character styling at work, as shown in Figure 7.6.
3. Press Esc when you are done reading.

Because this feature will tell you about one character at a time, it solves the mixed formatting problems mentioned earlier. Simply move your mouse pointer from character to character to learn about each one.

FIGURE 7.6

The Help ➤ What's This command will display character- and paragraph-formatting information when you point to text.

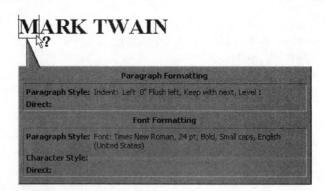

The Font Dialog Box

Choose Format ➤ Font, and Word displays the Font dialog box. It contains the most comprehensive collection of character-formatting options available in Word.

In the Font dialog box, you specify and combine a potentially gaudy array of character effects, including animation. The Font dialog box also presents yet another way to select fonts, and it lets you fiddle with inter-character spacing. Drop-down menus provide you with underline and color choices. You can even enter nonstandard font sizes in the Size box. The Font dialog box also shows which character-formatting options have been enabled from the toolbar, menu, and keyboard shortcuts. This is one busy box! Take a good look at Figure 7.7.

FIGURE 7.7

The Font dialog box gives you considerable control over character-formatting options.

Using the Font Dialog Box

Notice the Font Style section of the Font dialog box. It contains four choices—Regular, Italic, Bold, and Bold Italic. Other fonts offer more or fewer choices. For example, Lucida Sans offers only Italic and Bold Italic:

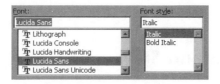

You can apply one or more of these styles to selected characters and to subsequently typed text. Simply click on the desired style. To remove effects, click on Regular.

You can often combine effects. For instance, you can usually bold, italicize, and underscore text. (Not all fonts accept all formatting options though, and occasionally you will see combinations on screen that will not print.) Click on OK after you select the desired effects.

In Figure 7.7, the chosen options are Times New Roman, Regular, 24 points.

PART

II

Formatting
Fundamentals

About Effects Boxes

If the Effects box in the Font dialog box shows gray checkmarks next to the formatting options, you have selected text with a variety of character-formatting options. For instance, some of your selected text may be Small Caps, other parts not:

This is an important concept, as you will learn when you work with the Replace dialog box in Chapter 16, *Finding and Replacing*. A black check in a character format box indicates that all the selected text exhibits that particular attribute. A completely clear box indicates that the selected text does not have the specific attribute anywhere within it. A checked gray box indicates that some of the text does and some of the text does not exhibit the character-formatting option. (This third condition must have been invented by a politician.)

Word 97 has new effects checkboxes—Shadow, Emboss, and Engrave. Try them to see how they change your text.

TIP

Many of Word's character-formatting tools have keyboard shortcuts. They are mentioned throughout this chapter.

How to Specify Everyday Character Formatting

Now that you've seen an overview of the formatting tools, let's look at some specific everyday tasks.

Choosing Fonts and Sizes

Word can use any font installed in your system. Theoretically at least, you can print any font in any size from 1 point to a whopping 1638 points. This corresponds to character heights ranging from approximately $1/72^{nd}$ of an inch to about 22 inches! In reality, you'll probably work with type sizes ranging from about 7 to 72 points most of the time, because they are easy to read and look good on traditional page sizes. For most body text, the 10–12 point range is considered the most readable.

WARNING

The type of printer you use, the fonts you've chosen, and other factors affect the final printed appearance of fonts at various sizes. More information about this is at the end of the chapter.

Word offers almost too many ways to choose fonts and sizes. Here's a summary of the various techniques (as usual, changes you make apply to currently selected text and to any following text you type):

- Use the drop-down Font and Size lists on the Formatting toolbar.
- Type the name and size of the desired font directly into the font name and size boxes on the toolbar, and then press Enter. For instance, click in the font name on the toolbar; then type the font name, such as Avant Garde. Next, click in the size box, if necessary, and type a new point size from 1 to 1638. Press Enter.
- Select fonts from within the Font dialog box (choose Format ➤ Font).
- To increase or decrease the font size one point at a time (from 10 to 11, for instance), select the text and use the keyboard shortcuts Ctrl+] and Ctrl+[.
- To increase or decrease font sizes by the standard increments listed in Word's various font size lists (10 point, 12 point, 14 point, and so on), use the keyboard shortcuts Ctrl+Shift+> and Ctrl+Shift+<.
- Assign fonts and sizes as part of styles. (See Chapter 12, *Using Paragraph Styles and AutoFormat*, for details.)

Creating Bold Characters

There are a number of ways to add bold formatting to characters you've selected or to characters you are about to type. Here are four of them:

- Click on the Bold button on the Formatting toolbar. It looks like a bold B. (A pressed button indicates that bold character formatting is enabled.)
- Use either of the two keyboard shortcuts for bold character formatting—Ctrl+B or Ctrl+Shift+B.
- Enable the Bold option in the Font Style list in Word's Font dialog box.
- Assign bold formatting as part of styles. (See Chapter 12, *Using Paragraph Styles and AutoFormat*, for details.)

Creating Italicized Characters

Create italicized characters in much the same way you create bold ones:

- Click on the Italic button on the toolbar. It looks like an italicized letter *I*. (A pressed I button indicates that italic character formatting is enabled.)

- Use either of the two keyboard shortcuts for italic character formatting—Ctrl+I or Ctrl+Shift+I.
- In the Font dialog box's Font Style menu, choose Italic.
- Assign italic formatting as part of styles. (See Chapter 12 for details.)

Highlighting Words and Passages

With Word, you can highlight text, both on the screen and on paper. You can either highlight selected words or use the highlighter as a "pen" of sorts.

TIP

If you cannot see the highlighting button on the Formatting toolbar, you can easily add it by selecting View ➤ Toolbars ➤ Customize and clicking on the Commands tab in the Customize dialog box. Highlight the Format Category, and scroll through the Commands list until you see the Highlighter pen icon. Click on this with your mouse and drag it onto the Formatting toolbar.

Here are the four ways it works:

- If text is selected when you click on the Highlight button, it becomes highlighted.
- If nothing is selected when you click on the Highlight button, your cursor turns into an animated pen, which you can use to highlight anything you wish. This tool works fairly intuitively. For instance, if you double-click on a word, it is highlighted. To turn off highlighting, simply click on the Highlight button again. You can also use it as you use its neighbors on the toolbar—Bold, Italic, and so on. Select the text you want to highlight, and click on the Highlight button. In this case, it turns itself off after use.
- If you click on the arrow part of the Highlight button, a palette drops down, allowing you to choose the color of your highlight, as shown here:

Your 15 choices include teal, bright green, turquoise, and pink. Once you choose your color, the highlight feature works as described above, doing slightly different things, depending on whether text is selected.
- To remove highlighting, select the text and then click on the Highlight button again.

Underlining

You can apply simple, single, continuous underlining with the Underline button on the Formatting toolbar or with the Ctrl+U or Ctrl+Shift+U keyboard shortcuts. If you want other underline formats, you'll need to use the Font dialog box.

The 10 choices on the Underline drop-down menu in the Font dialog box include (none), Single, Words Only, Double, and Wave. The effects of these choices are self-evident and illustrated in Figure 7.1, earlier in this chapter. Unfortunately, underline choices cannot be combined in this dialog box.

TIP

If you routinely use underline styles such as Double or Word, you can add commands for them to your menus or toolbars. See Chapter 32, *Personalizing Word*, to learn how.

Strikethrough

If you write contract drafts or work with other important documents, you might want to use Word's Strikethrough feature. It is a way to indicate proposed deletions. Choose the Strikethrough option in the Font dialog box to overlay text with a horizontal line.

TIP

Use the Strikethrough feature to format both the text and the spaces that you plan to delete in the final copy. When it comes time to delete, you can use Word's Replace command to find text containing Strikethrough and replace it with nothing, thereby deleting the text. See Chapter 16, *Finding and Replacing*, for more about the Replace command.

Expanding and Condensing Character Spacing

In Word, you can override the standard spacing between characters defined by their designers. You can move characters closer together with the Condensed character-formatting option or move them farther apart with the Expanded option. The default for expanding and condensing is 1 point.

TIP

Kerning is a typesetter's term meaning to adjust (increase or decrease) the horizontal space between two letters. Usually this is done for reasons of aesthetics, but sometimes it is necessary simply to make a word fit in the space allotted it.

Condensing can help you fit extra words on a line, and expanding can create interesting effects for headlines in newsletters, flyers, and the like. To expand or condense, follow these steps:

1. Select the text.

2. Choose Format ➤ Font.

3. Click on the Character Spacing tab.

4. Choose Expanded (or Condensed) from the Spacing list, as shown in Figure 7.8.

5. Choose a new setting by typing in the By box or by clicking on the up and down arrows. The Preview will change as you work.

6. Click on OK to save your changes, or click on Cancel to revert to the original size.

You can condense or expand characters a maximum of 1584 points. Let common sense and aesthetics be your guides in using this feature.

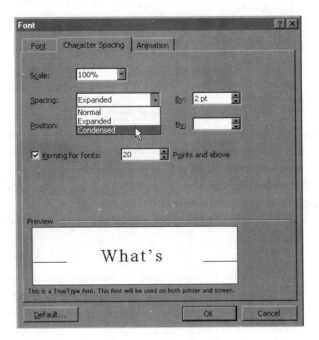

FIGURE 7.8

Expand and compress text in the Character Spacing tab of the Font dialog box.

Automatic Kerning and Manual Character Spacing

You can use the Condensed option to tuck pairs of letters closer to each other to tighten them up and improve the appearance of some awkward-looking combinations of wide and narrow letters. Simply select the letters you want to cozy up, and then choose the Condensed option in the Character Spacing tab of the Font dialog box. Or you can ask Word to automatically kern by enabling the Kerning option. Frequently, you'll want tighter spacing than the automatic feature offers, and you'll have to do it yourself.

For instance, to tighten up the *T* and *w* in Twain, follow these steps:

1. Select only the characters *T* and *w*.
2. Choose Format ➤ Font ➤ Character Spacing.
3. Select Condensed spacing.
4. Choose a point value (1.8, perhaps).
5. Watch the preview and adjust spacing if you like.
6. Click on OK to make the changes, or click on Cancel to keep the letter spacing as is.

Creating Superscripts and Subscripts

Normally, any characters that you type are placed on an invisible line called the baseline. Superscripted characters are moved above the baseline; subscripted characters are placed below the baseline. Although the obvious use for this is in equations and chemical formulas (H_2O, for instance), there are many other ways to use super- and subscripting.

If you abbreviate ordinal numbers (for example, 2nd for second), it looks really nice if the *nd* is superscripted and a bit smaller. A nice feature of Word is that it does this for you automatically. You don't even need to think about it. Simply type along, and whenever you type **1st**, **2nd**, and so on, Word makes the change for you. You can turn off this feature if you like. To do so, choose Tools ➤ AutoCorrect ➤ AutoFormat As You Type.

You can also use super- and subscripting to line up odd-sized bullets with adjacent text. As you'll soon see, it's possible to tweak the appearance of drop caps by super- or subscripting them (look ahead to the section called "Large Initial Caps, Drop Caps, and Dropped Words").

You super- and subscript in two basic ways. You can use Word's Super and Sub features, or you can raise and lower the position of characters with the Position option in the Character Spacing tab of the Font dialog box. The first method changes the size of super- and subscripted characters in addition to their position. The dialog box method can scale the size of the characters to some extent. (Typographical purists consider only the first to be "true" super- and subscripting.)

Using Superscript and Subscript

You use the Font dialog box to raise or lower characters. There are also keyboard shortcuts. Ctrl+= causes subscripting (lowering characters and reducing their size). Ctrl+Shift+= superscripts (both raising and reducing the characters). Both apply "automatic" spacing decisions.

PART

II

Formatting
Fundamentals

To gain manual control over spacing, follow these steps:

1. Select the characters you want to super- or subscript.
2. Choose Format ➤ Font.
3. If necessary, click on the Character Spacing tab.
4. Choose Raised (or Lowered) from the Position list.
5. Specify the amount by which you want characters raised or lowered in the By box or buttons.
6. To change the scale of the raised or lowered character relative to the adjoining characters, select one of the scaling options from the Scale drop-down list.
7. Click on OK to apply the changes, or click on Cancel to keep the original placement.

Figure 7.9 shows an example of characters being raised (superscripted) 3 points.

Sometimes line heights are not sufficient to display the tops and bottoms of super- or subscripted characters, making them appear cut off. Adjust the line spacing as described in Chapter 8, *Formatting Paragraphs*, if this happens.

FIGURE 7.9

These settings superscript 3 points without changing the size of the characters.

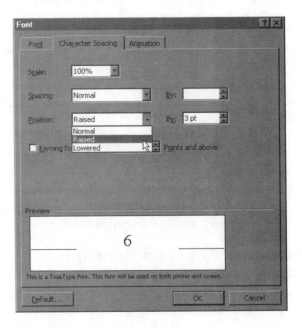

Character Color Choices

Even if you cannot display or print color, you can specify 12-character colors plus black, white, or gray. You can then take copies of your disk files to color-capable hardware for display and printing. To specify a color, follow these steps:

1. Select text or position the insertion point where you want to type colored text.
2. Choose the desired color from the drop-down Color menu in the Font tab of the Font dialog box. If your monitor supports color, you will see color characters in the Preview area. If your monitor supports shades of gray, colors will be converted to grays.
3. Click on OK to close the Font dialog box.
4. When you print, enable your printer's color or gray-scale features if it has them.

You can add a Font Color button to the Formatting toolbar. Selecting View ➤ Toolbars ➤ Customize and click on the Commands tab in the Customize dialog box. Highlight the Format Category, and scroll through the Commands list until you see the Font Color icon. Click on this with your mouse and drag it onto the Formatting toolbar. Access a drop-down font color palette with this icon, rather than going through the Font dialog box.

Remember, not all computers can display grays or colors, but you need not display color to print it. To see which color you've assigned to text when using a black-and-white monitor, select the text and choose Format ➤ Font or use the Help button "cartoon" trick to read the name of the assigned color.

WARNING

Printed colors don't always match video display colors exactly. Before starting a big color print job, test-print to see what you'll get.

Using the Change Case Command

The Format ➤ Change Case command opens a dialog box that offers five choices:

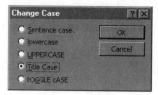

Look closely at the dialog box. The capitalization style of each option illustrates the effect it produces. For instance, UPPERCASE changes all selected characters to uppercase letters, and the choice UPPERCASE itself appears all uppercase in the dialog box. Title Case changes the first letter of each selected word to uppercase, as illustrated in the dialog box.

> **WARNING**
>
> Alas, the Title Case option is not context-sensitive; so it capitalizes prepositions and articles, including *of*, *the*, and so on. If you need to observe this distinction and you use Title Case frequently, consider creating a WordBasic macro (see Chapter 31, *Creating and Using Macros*) to search for those words and lowercase them.

To change case with this feature, follow these steps:

1. Select the text you want to change.
2. Choose Format ➤ Change Case.
3. Choose the desired case option.
4. Click on OK.

When you change case using this dialog box, the characters themselves change to the specified case. It is just as if you had retyped them using the new capitalization scheme. Undo also works here.

> **TIP**
>
> If you make a mistake in typing and accidentally capitalize several letters at the beginning of a word (for example, TWain instead of Twain), don't worry about it, because Word will correct your mistake automatically. This doesn't eliminate the need for the Change Case command, but it will make your life easier.

Using the All Caps Option

The All Caps option is found in the Font dialog box. It changes only the appearance of letters, without actually changing the letters themselves. For example, if you type the word *uppercase* and format it as All Caps, you'll see it as UPPERCASE; but a search for capital letters would not find it. Unlike the Format ➤ Change Case command, the All Caps option lets you type in lowercase and see uppercase letters as you work. Follow these steps:

1. Select the text you want to change or position the insertion point for typing.
2. Choose Format ➤ Change Case.

3. Choose the desired case option.

4. Click on OK.

Selected and/or subsequently typed text will appear in uppercase, but the underlying text will retain its actual capitalization.

Using the Small Caps Option

The Small Caps option in the Font dialog box can create some very interesting effects. Figure 7.10 shows some examples of Small Caps at work.

Remember that applying the Small Caps formatting option to text containing dingbats like those shown in Figure 7.10 will usually "capitalize" the dingbats, thereby changing the character that appears and prints. To fix this, select the dingbats and remove Small Caps formatting. Use Word's Replace command (described in Chapter 16) to do this if you need to make many changes.

Removing Font Formatting

Removing font formatting can be a simple or confusing task, depending on the situation. The six general ways to remove font formatting include:

- Toggling toolbar buttons, menu commands, and keyboard shortcuts
- Using the Remove Formats keyboard shortcut (Ctrl+spacebar)
- Changing to a different style
- Using the Font dialog box
- Using the Replace command to automate removal
- Choosing the Regular font style in the Font dialog box

Unfortunately, not all approaches work under all circumstances, and there are some land mines, particularly when styles are involved. Removing character formatting is easiest if you are not using Word styles other than Normal. See Chapter 12, *Using Paragraph Styles and Auto Format*, to learn about styles.

Toggling to Remove Character Formatting

You can use the Edit ➤ Undo command (Ctrl+Z) to undo formatting immediately after you've changed it. And you can remove most character formatting by applying it a second time. This process is called toggling (you've already encountered the toggling concept with toolbar buttons). For instance, if you select a bold word and click on the Bold button, the selected text will no longer be bold.

FIGURE 7.10

These samples of Small Caps font formatting show how easy it is to add punch and visual interest.

ASK MR. FOSTER ✠ AMERICAN INDUSTRIAL REAL ESTATE ASSN. ✠ FIRSTOURS CARLSON CORPORATION ✠ BEAR STEARNS ✠ BERGER & NORTON ✠ CABLE NEWS NETWORK (CNN) ✠ CHILDREN'S HOSPITAL LOS ANGELES ✠ SYBEX

SOUTHERN EXPOSURE

WRITTEN BY
GUY WIRE
DIRECTED BY
PHIL R. UPP
PRODUCED BY
MS. TAKE

✆	CENTRAL VALLEY	10
✆	SIERRA NEVADA	12
✆	SACRAMENTO AREA	14
✆	MARIN COUNTY	22
✆	CONTRA COSTA COUNTY	34

The Regular Font Style

The Regular font style in the Font tab of the Font dialog box will remove most character formatting. Simply select the text; then execute the choice.

Limitations of Toggling and Regular Font Style

The toggling and Regular font style techniques just described will remove formats and many combinations, such as bold or bold with underlines. In fact, toggling and the Regular font style should work with the following character-formatting features in any combination:

- Bold
- Italic
- Underline
- Double underline
- Word underline
- Dotted underline
- Strikethrough
- Outline
- Shadow
- Emboss
- Engrave
- Small caps
- All caps
- Hidden text
- Colors

However, the tricks will not tighten up characters that have been expanded, nor will they spread out characters that have been condensed. You cannot change fonts or their sizes this way either. You'll need to do so in the Font dialog box or use other specific controls.

Copying and Repeating Character Formats

The Format Painter button is a slick way to copy formatting and apply it to other characters. To apply character formatting, do this:

1. Select only the characters (but not the paragraph marker at the end of the paragraph) whose format you want to copy.

2. Double-click on the Format Painter button in the Standard toolbar. The pointer will turn into a paintbrush, and the status area will display instructions.

3. Drag across the text you want to format.

4. Release the mouse button, and the text should reformat.

Typing Special Characters

Word makes it easy to enter special characters and symbols not listed on your keycaps but available in most fonts. Let's look at the Symbol feature and then review the old reliable keyboard shortcuts.

The Symbol Command

The dialog box shown in Figure 7.11 appears whenever you choose Insert ➤ Symbol. It has two tabs, Symbols and Special Characters.

The dialog box shows you all available characters in the current font. Clicking on a symbol shows you a magnified, more readable version. Double-clicking inserts the character at the insertion point in your document. (Alternately, you can click on a character and then click on the Insert button, but that's more work.)

TIP Once you've clicked to magnify a character in the Symbol dialog box, you can see magnified views of others by moving the mouse around or navigating with the arrow keys. Doing so can eliminate the need for a lot of precision clicking. Also, once a character is highlighted, you can insert it by pressing Enter.

To see which symbols are available in which fonts, simply choose a font from the Font menu in the Formatting toolbar and choose Insert ➤ Symbol. Or, if the Symbol dialog box is already open, select a font from the Font list.

The Special Characters tab provides a scrolling list of commonly used symbols and characters. Here too, double-clicking inserts the character at the insertion point.

TIP The Special Characters tab in the Symbol window also lets you see (and change) keyboard shortcuts.

Typing Symbols from the Keyboard

If you know the key combinations, you can enter symbols right from the keyboard, bypassing the Symbol dialog box. For instance, to type the copyright symbol, hold down Alt and Ctrl and press the C key. Word also has a feature that automatically converts

FIGURE 7.11

The two tabs in the Symbol dialog box (reached by choosing Insert ➤ Symbol)

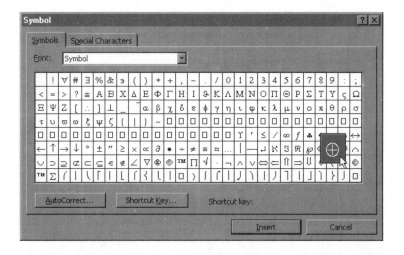

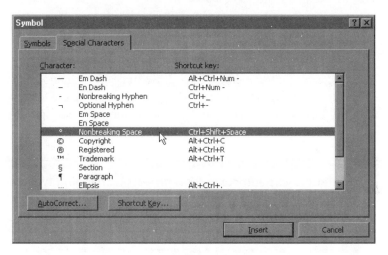

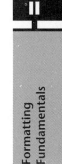

what you type into symbols. For example, if you type (c), Word inserts the copyright symbol: ©. These two might seem redundant; the first method is a bit quicker than the second because it takes a little time to make the conversion, but sometimes it's hard to remember those keyboard shortcuts for the faster way. Fiddle with them a bit to see which you prefer. Word now autoconverts a dozen or so symbols. Here is a list of some of the more useful ones.

Type this...	...to insert this
:)	☺
:(	☹
:|	☻
-->	→
<--	←
(c)	©
(r)	®
(tm)	™
==>	→
<==	←
. . .	...

Different fonts sometimes have different key combinations; so you will need to consult the documentation that comes with your fonts or use the Insert ➤ Symbol command to learn the combinations. Table 7.1 shows commonly used special characters and their keyboard shortcuts.

TIP

If AutoCorrect's autoconversion process is changing typed characters that you do not want changed, by all means turn it off! To do so, select Tools ➤ AutoCorrect. In the AutoCorrect dialog box, uncheck the Replace Text As You Type checkbox. You can also use Undo (Ctrl+Z) to get rid of autoconversions.

For all special characters, first select a font containing the symbol. To create your own key combinations, choose Insert ➤ Symbol, select the Symbols tab, highlight the desired symbol, and click on Shortcut Key. Word displays the Customize Keyboard dialog box. Press various Alt+ and Ctrl+ key combinations in the Press New Shortcut Key text box. Word will tell you whether the key combination is already assigned. When you find a satisfactory key combination that is not assigned, select Assign. That key combination will appear in the Current Keys box for that symbol. Whenever you press that key combination, the symbol will appear, as long as you have selected a font that contains that symbol.

TABLE 7.1: SOME SPECIAL CHARACTERS AND THEIR KEYBOARD SHORTCUTS

Name	Sample	Keys	Notes
Angstroms	Å	Ctrl+@+A	
Bullet	•	Create your own	
Copyright	©	Alt+Ctrl+C	
Dagger	†	Create your own	
Ellipsis	…	Alt+Ctrl+.	
Em dash	—	Alt + Ctrl + NumLock + -	Longer than hyphen. Use numeric keypad minus key.
En dash	–	Ctrl + NumLock + -	Longer than hyphen, shorter than em dash. Use numeric keypad minus key.
Function, f-stop	ƒ	Create your own	
Logical not	¬	Create your own	
Mu (lowercase)	μ	Create your own	Aka Micro
Much greater than	»	Ctrl+'',>	Also European close quote
Much less than	«	Ctrl+'',<	Also European open quote
Cents sign	¢	Ctrl+/,c	
Paragraph mark	¶	Create your own	
Plus or minus	±	Create your own	
Pound (currency)	£	Create your own	
Registered	®	Alt+Ctrl+R	
Section mark	§	Create your own	
Trademark	™	Alt+Ctrl+T	
Yen (currency)	¥	Create your own	

PART

II

Formatting
Fundamentals

International and Accented Characters

To type accented international characters (such as the ñ in La Cañada), you use three keys. First, you hold down the Ctrl key and a key to tell your computer which accent to apply; then press the character key for the character you want to accent. For example, to enter an *o* with an umlaut, follow these steps:

1. Hold down the Ctrl key and press the colon (:) key (don't forget to hold down the Shift key).

2. Release all three keys.

3. Press the o (or Shift+O) key to get a small (or capitalized) umlauted o (ö).

Incidentally, you can't accent just any old characters. Table 7.2 shows you the possibilities and their key combinations.

TIP

The keystroke combinations listed in Table 7.2 are shortcuts. If you forget them, you can always locate and insert accented characters with the Insert ➤ Symbol command.

TABLE 7.2: WORD'S ACCENTED CHARACTERS AND THEIR KEYBOARD SHORTCUTS

Name	Samples	Keys
Acute accent	áéíóú ÁÉÍÓÚ	Ctrl+' (apostrophe), letter
Circumflex	âêîôû ÂÊÎÔÛ	Ctrl+^, letter
Dieresis	äëïöü ÄËÏÖÜ	Ctrl+:, letter
Grave accent	àèìòù ÀÈÌÒÙ	Ctrl+ `, letter
Tilde	ãñõ ÃÑÕ	Ctrl+~, letter

Wingdings and Dingbats

Add some spice to your life. Use the little pictures found in the Wingdings font instead of plain old bullets. Wingdings are also great as list separators and as border decorations. You've already seen examples back in Figure 7.10, and you'll see others in later chapters. Consider purchasing and installing other "dingbat" fonts, which are often found in shareware packages at very low cost. Use the Insert ➤ Symbol command to see and insert them.

Bulleted List Command

There's a button on the Formatting toolbar that looks like a bulleted list. It places plain old bullets in front of selected paragraphs and creates hanging indents (read about hanging indents in Chapter 8, *Formatting Paragraphs*). The feature uses the current font.

If you know you want a list before you start typing, you can take advantage of a handy automatic formatting feature. All you have to do is type an asterisk (*) and then a space or a tab. When you press Enter, Word turns the asterisk into a bullet (•) and sets the spacing and other formatting. Then, all you have to do is keep adding to your list.

When you want Word to stop making bullets out of everything, press Enter or Return to insert a blank line and continue typing nonbulleted text.

Bulleting Existing Paragraphs

To bullet existing paragraphs, follow these steps:

1. Select the paragraph or paragraphs you want to format.
2. Click on the Bulleted List button. Word creates hanging indents and inserts bullets in front of each selected paragraph.

Changing Bullet Styles

Word offers an astonishing array of bulleted list options. You can even choose your own, nonstandard bullet characters. Here are the general steps. Experiment to find combinations you like. Use the Bullets and Numbering dialog box shown in Figure 7.12.

1. Select your list if you've already typed it.
2. Choose Format ➤ Bullets and Numbering.
3. Click to select a style you like.
4. Click on OK.
5. Type additional list items or a new list, as necessary.

Specifying Custom Bullets

Here's a nice way to spice up a dull list. Use Wingdings or other decorative characters instead of standard bullets:

1. Select your list if you've already typed it.
2. Choose Format ➤ Bullets and Numbering.
3. Click to select a list style you like.
4. Click on the Customize button to display the Customize Bulleted List dialog box, shown in Figure 7.13.

FIGURE 7.12

Use this dialog box to modify the appearance of bulleted lists.

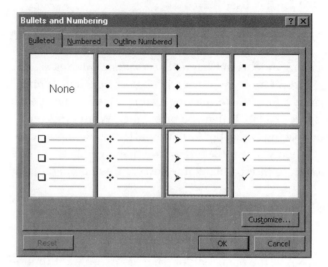

FIGURE 7.13

Use this dialog box to change spacing and choose new bullet shapes.

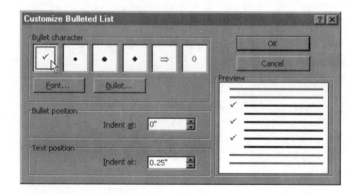

5. Change bullet positioning if you like by altering the dimensions in the Bullet Position or Text Position areas.

6. Select a different type of bullet from the Bullet Character list.

7. To use bullets not shown in the Bullet Character box, click on the Bullet button.

8. In the Symbol dialog box, choose a font that has interesting characters (Symbol or Wingdings, for instance).

9. Double-click to select the desired character to use as a bullet.

Here are some examples from the Wingdings font:

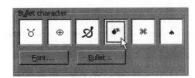

"Smart," or Typographer's, Quotes

Word can automatically place curly quotes in documents when you type straight quotes. This gives your work a typeset look. Turn the option on before typing, because Word will not automatically change quote marks you've already typed. To place Smart quotes in a document, follow these steps:

1. Choose Tools ➤ AutoCorrect. Word displays the AutoCorrect dialog box.
2. Click on the AutoFormat As You Type tab to display the AutoFormat options.
3. In the Replace As You Type area, check the Straight Quotes with Smart Quotes checkbox.

Now, when you type quotes, Word converts them to curly opening and closing quotes (assuming that your chosen font has these characters).

TIP

If you are creating a document that you plan to export (for use with different word-processing software, perhaps), turn off the Smart Quotes feature before creating documents containing quotes. Otherwise, you'll risk confusing the other folks with strange codes instead of quotation marks.

Large Initial Caps, Drop Caps, and Dropped Words

Large initial caps are just what their name implies—big letters at the beginning of paragraphs. They are used as decorative flourishes. Drop caps are large initial caps that are dropped into a paragraph or into the margin next to a paragraph. They are often placed at the beginning of chapters and major topic transitions to catch the reader's eye. Dropped words are a variation on this technique. You create drop caps or dropped words by placing large initial caps or words in text boxes and positioning them. You can also use graphics as drop caps.

TIP

You can use Word's Drop Cap command to automate the process of creating drop caps and dropped words. Read about it in the following section.

Figure 7.14 shows a few examples. Read the text in each example to get an overview of how the effect was accomplished.

FIGURE 7.14

Large initial caps and dropped words, created using text boxes and character and paragraph formatting

Word's Drop Cap feature automatically creates frames, increases the size of the initial text and switches to Print Preview. It will place drop caps in the textor in the margin as shown here.

Drop caps can be created in a number of ways. This one was made by selecting just the letter D in 12 point New Century Schoolbook text and increasing it to 48 points. The D was framed with the Format menu's Text Box ... command. The Text Box width was adjusted in the Text Box dialog box. The D was then superscripted 6 points.

Large initial caps

Create these by choosing a larger type size for the first character. Minimize the resulting extra white space between the first and second lines by setting the Space Before and Space After options to 0 points. You can use Text Boxes to create similar effects.

Graphics can be used as drop caps too. This bomb was pasted from the scrapbook, reduced in size, boxed, then dragged into place from Print Preview. The From Text option was set to 0 in the Text Box dialog box to tighten things.

Entire words can be dropped. This example was created with the Text Box command on Word's Insert menu. First the word Entire was selected.

When you can't resist the urge to be decorative, consider using specialty fonts, like Colonna MT, shown here.

Using the Drop Cap Feature

You control drop caps from the dialog box shown in Figure 7.15. Choose Format ➤ Drop Cap.

The Drop Cap command is designed to work with single-spaced text only. It won't work in tables, headers, or footers. You won't be able to see the position of drop caps or create them in Outline view. You can't place drop caps in the margins of multicolumn documents, but you can place them within text in such documents. Narrow indents sometimes screw up the automatic drop cap feature. That said, here are the general steps:

1. Format the body text the way you like it. Be sure you are happy with margins, fonts, and so on, because if you change these, you will probably have to fine-tune your drop cap all over again. Single-space the text.
2. Select the character or characters you want to drop, and choose Format ➤ Drop Cap. If you are not in Page Layout view, Word prompts you to switch. You'll see the Drop Cap dialog box illustrated in Figure 7.15.
3. If you want to use a different font for the drop cap, choose it from the drop-down Font menu.
4. The Lines to Drop box proposes the number of lines the cap will drop. For instance, 3 li indicates that the drop cap will be three lines tall and drop alongside the first three lines of text. Choose the desired number of lines from the drop-down line list, or type an exact point size for the drop cap (36 pt, for instance).
5. Choose the Dropped Position option for traditional-looking drop caps, or choose the In Margin option to place drops in the margin.
6. When you click on OK, Word places the specified text into a frame (also known as a text box) and positions the frame for you.

PART

II

Formatting Fundamentals

FIGURE 7.15

Automatic drop cap options are specified in the Drop Cap dialog box.

7. Use the font, frame (or text box), and paragraph tools, if you dare, to modify Word's settings.

TIP

You can use the Format ➤ Drop Cap command to drop graphics as well. Paste a graphic at the beginning of a line of text, drag, and, if necessary, make it reasonably small. With the graphic selected, choose Format ➤ Drop Cap.

Tips for Creating Drop Caps

When creating drop caps, keep the following in mind:

- Format text, decide on the font, and check spelling before you create drop caps.
- When using the Format ➤ Text Box command, remember to specify a text box width so that text can flow around your drop cap.
- To remove the excess space that often appears beneath a drop cap frame, use negative line spacing (space less than the point size of the type being dropped) and subscripting, as you saw in the preceding example.
- To remove excess space to the right of frames, use the Distance From Text option in the Wrapping tab of the Format Text Box dialog box.

Deleting Drop Caps

If you've just created a drop cap with the automatic Drop Cap command, Edit ➤ Undo will delete it. Otherwise, you'll need to follow these general steps:

1. Highlight the drop cap and choose Format ➤ Drop Cap.
2. Click on the None option and then click on OK.

Typing Nonbreaking Spaces

To keep multiple words on the same line (someone's title and first and last name, for instance), you use nonbreaking spaces. To do this, simply hold down the Ctrl and Shift keys when you press the spacebar.

Typing Hyphens and Dashes

To type hyphens, simply use the minus key (to the right of the zero key at the top of your keyboard). Hyphens typed this way will always print.

Typing Nonbreaking Hyphens

Nonbreaking hyphens keep hyphenated words together on the same line. Never press the minus key to enter a nonbreaking hyphen! Instead, hold down the Ctrl and Shift keys and press the hyphen on the main keyboard.

Typing Em and En Dashes

Em dashes indicate an abrupt change of thought—or did you know that already? En dashes separate numbers. People often confuse hyphens and dashes. Type the longer em dashes by holding down Alt+Ctrl+– (the minus key on the numeric pad). In some fonts, em dashes are very long and obvious. That's not always the case, though.

Word has a feature that automatically changes hyphens into dashes. When you type a hyphen, Word automatically changes it to an en dash (–). When you type two hyphens, Word changes them to an em dash (—). This is a handy way to make your documents look good without your having to do anything! Again, there are other ways to get en and em dashes; it's up to you what keyboard combos you want to try to remember.

Incidentally, em dashes get their name from their width. In most fonts an em dash is the length of a letter m. That's an easy way to remember what it's called. Shorter en dashes can be created with Ctrl+– (the minus key on the numeric pad).

TIP

Although dashes should always be longer than hyphens, in a few fonts, they are not. You are not losing your mind after all. It's a "feature."

Typing Optional Hyphens

An optional hyphen will always be displayed whenever you have the Show Paragraph feature enabled, but it will print only if the word it is in sits on the right margin. Most people use Word's automatic hyphenation feature to enter optional hyphens, but you can enter them from the keyboard. Hold down the Ctrl key and press the minus key (–) on the main keyboard (not the one on the numeric pad).

TIP

If you still have trouble remembering what's where, use the Special Characters tab in the Symbol dialog box (choose Insert ➤ Symbol).

PART

II

Formatting
Fundamentals

Automatic Optional Hyphenation

Word has an automatic feature that will work with you to place optional hyphens in words, based on certain built-in rules and a hyphenation dictionary. You can supervise the process or let Word take things into its own hands. If you use the automatic feature, there are some things you will want to do first.

WARNING

Optional hyphenation is one of the last things you want to do when preparing a document. Finish everything else that affects line endings first. Otherwise, you will need to rehyphenate repeatedly.

Preparing to Hyphenate

Be sure that your document is complete and properly organized. Do the spelling check. Polish the appearance of your text (fonts, sizes, character expansion, and so on). Remove extra spaces. Apply justification, if that's part of your plan. Break the document into sections if you need them. Set up columns. Have someone else proofread your work one last time. You may, however, want to hold off on final page-break decisions until after hyphenation.

Entering Optional Hyphens

Word will hyphenate an entire document or only selected text. When you choose Tools ➤ Language ➤ Hyphenation, Word opens a small dialog box like the one in Figure 7.16. Choose automatic or manual hyphenation.

Working from the insertion point, Word moves through your document (or selected text), looking for a possible word to hyphenate. In Figure 7.17, it has found the word *reminded*.

FIGURE 7.16

The Hyphen-ation dialog box

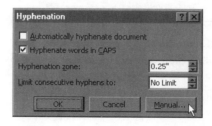

FIGURE 7.17

Word is suggesting that *reminded* be hyphenated bewteen the *e* and the *m*.

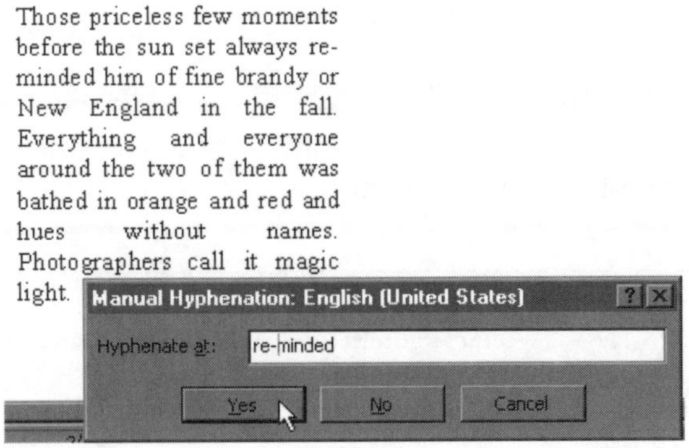

Those priceless few moments before the sun set always reminded him of fine brandy or New England in the fall. Everything and everyone around the two of them was bathed in orange and red and hues without names. Photographers call it magic light.

Manual Hyphenation: English [United States]

Hyphenate at: re-minded

Yes   No   Cancel

If you've chosen manual hyphenation, you will see a dialog box offering several alternatives. The Yes button will place an optional hyphen between the *e* and *m*. The No button tells Word not to hyphenate this word and to continue. Cancel exits the hyphenation.

Optionally, you can move the hyphenation point yourself. Use your mouse to point to where you want to place the hyphen. Press the mouse button once. A blinking pointer will appear between the characters you've chosen. Click on the Yes button to place the optional hyphen and continue the automatic search.

As you can see from Figure 7.18, Word has suggested several hyphenation points in our example. One of them is debatable. Some editors and style manuals will tell you not to hyphenate words in ways that leave only one syllable on a line, yet Word has done just that. There are few hard-and-fast hyphenation rules.

FIGURE 7.18

Word's automatic hyphenation feature may not solve all your problems.

Those priceless few moments before the sun set always reminded him of fine brandy or New England in the fall. Everything and everyone around the two of them was bathed in orange and red and hues without names. Photographers call it magic light.

Manual Hyphenation: English [United States]

Hyphenate at: Every-thing

Yes   No   Cancel

Rejecting the suggested hyphen in *Everything* creates a much nicer-looking paragraph, as you can see in Figure 7.19. The combination of manual and automatic hyphenation even found a home for the widow.

TIP

If you like tight copy, you might want to run the auto-hyphenation feature and then fine-tune a bit by hand.

FIGURE 7.19

Sometimes replacing the suggested hyphenation can improve the final appearance of the paragraph (especially in multicolumn formats).

Those priceless few moments before the sun set always re-minded him of fine brandy or New England in the fall. Everything and everyone around the two of them was bathed in orange and red and hues without names. Photo-graphers call it magic light.
Microsoft Word
Hyphenation is complete.
OK

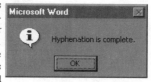

Removing Automatic Hyphens

The Edit ➤ Undo Hyphenation (Ctrl+Z) command will be available to remove optional hyphens if you use it immediately after you run the auto-hyphenation feature. You can delete hyphens as you delete any other character. Select them and cut or delete. Word's Find and Replace features will also help you delete hyphens of all sorts. See Chapter 16, *Finding and Replacing*, for details.

TIP

If you don't want any hyphenation, choose Left Alignment in the Format ➢ Paragraph dialog box. Many designers prefer the "ragged right" style for some kinds of text.

Chapter

8

Formatting Paragraphs

Formatting Paragraphs

I n this chapter, we'll explore Word's paragraph-formatting tools, which you will use for adjusting line spacing, indention, and text alignment. You'll see how to use Word's border features to create boxes and lines. Paragraph numbering, shading, and sorting are also discussed. You can save complex sets of formatting decisions as styles, as you'll see in Chapter 12, *Using Paragraph Styles and AutoFormat*.

Word's Paragraphs

¶

Your English teachers taught you that a paragraph is a collection of sentences on a related topic. Word uses a somewhat more liberal definition. A Word paragraph can be a single text character, a graphic, or even a blank line consisting only of the paragraph mark (¶), which appears in your document when you press Enter. (Click on the Show ¶ button to display this and other nonprinting characters. To display only paragraph marks, choose Tools ➤ Options, select the View tab, and check the Paragraph Marks box in the Nonprinting Characters area.) Paragraph-formatting features are an important part of Word's arsenal. Figure 8.1 contains five Word paragraphs, each ending with a paragraph mark. Can you find them all?

FIGURE 8.1

*Word para-
graphs always
end with a
paragraph
mark (¶).*

A Word Paragraph can be a single text
character, a graphic, or even a blank line.¶

Paragraphs can have different formats.¶

¶

There are five paragraphs in this example. Can
you find them all?¶

¶

Each Word paragraph in your document can be uniquely formatted and need not
contain text. For instance, the first paragraph in Figure 8.1 is single-spaced with the first
line indented about 0.5". The next paragraph is right-justified. The third paragraph is a
blank line created by pressing the Enter key. The fourth paragraph is centered. The final
paragraph is a graphic (without text), followed by a paragraph mark. Notice that this
last paragraph (the graphic) is also centered.

Creating Paragraphs

Each time you press the Enter key you create a new paragraph. It's that simple. When
you open a new document, Word applies the default paragraph settings stored as a style
called Normal. It formats each new paragraph the same way until and unless you tell it
to do otherwise.

Splitting Text into Multiple Paragraphs

If you want to split a lengthy section of text into two or more paragraphs, follow these steps:

1. Place the insertion point where you want the new paragraph to begin. (Be careful not to include unwanted spaces when splitting text.)
2. Press Enter. The text will split, and you'll see a paragraph mark if the Show ¶ feature is enabled. Note that the new paragraph will take on the characteristics of the one above. For instance, if the original big paragraph had a first-line indent, the two little ones also will.

Notice how, in Figure 8.2, the new paragraph takes on the same indention characteristics as the preceding one.

FIGURE 8.2

To split one paragraph into two or more paragraphs, position the insertion point (watching for unwanted spaces) and press Enter.

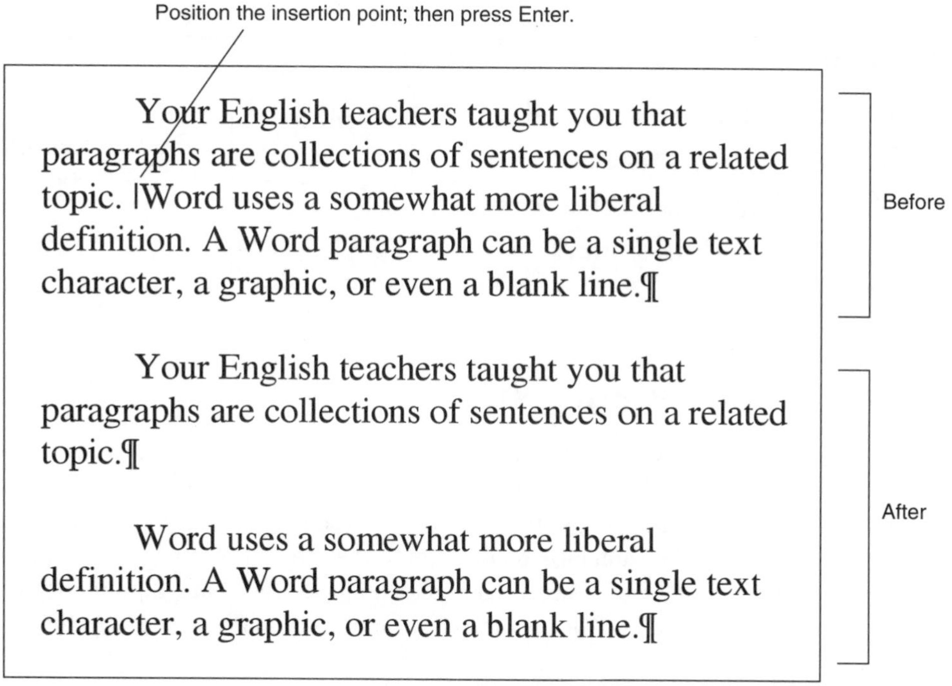

Position the insertion point; then press Enter.

Your English teachers taught you that paragraphs are collections of sentences on a related topic. |Word uses a somewhat more liberal definition. A Word paragraph can be a single text character, a graphic, or even a blank line.¶

Before

Your English teachers taught you that paragraphs are collections of sentences on a related topic.¶

Word uses a somewhat more liberal definition. A Word paragraph can be a single text character, a graphic, or even a blank line.¶

After

PART

II

Formatting Fundamentals

Joining Paragraphs

It's easy to turn two paragraphs into one. Simply delete the interceding paragraph mark and add any necessary space to separate the new neighbors. For instance, to rejoin the two short paragraphs in Figure 8.2, you'll need a space between the period after the word *topic* and the *W* in *Word*. The quick way to join these two paragraphs would be to select the unwanted paragraph mark and type a space to replace it. Follow these steps:

1. Turn on the Show ¶ feature to make things easier.
2. Delete the paragraph mark between the two paragraphs, adding space if necessary. Text above will take on the appearance of text below if the two paragraphs originally had different paragraph formatting.

Forcing New Lines without Using Paragraphs

Sometimes you'll want to force a new line without creating a new paragraph. The reasons will become more apparent as you start to use advanced Word features such as paragraph numbering and styles with Next Style options; so tuck this trivia nugget away. To force new lines without creating new paragraphs, use the Shift+↵ key combination. Instead of a paragraph symbol, you'll see arrows like the ones in Figure 8.3.

FIGURE 8.3

Use the Shift+↵ feature to force new lines without starting a new paragraph.

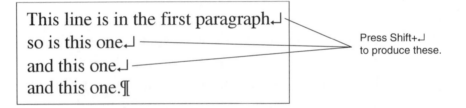

This line is in the first paragraph.↵
so is this one.↵
and this one.↵
and this one.¶

Press Shift+↵
to produce these.

Deleting Paragraphs

Think twice when deleting paragraphs. You can delete only the contents of a paragraph, or you can delete the contents and the paragraph marker. If you delete the marker, text above the old paragraph will take on the characteristics of the remaining paragraph below it. The paragraph marker contains all the formatting for its paragraph. This is by design and is not a bug. If you accidentally delete a paragraph mark and create a problem, Undo (Ctrl+Z or the drop-down list) will usually return your heart rate to normal.

Adding Blank Lines between Paragraphs

You can create blank lines, typewriter style, by just mashing on the Enter key all day. But hey, it's almost the year 2000. Instead, create white space between paragraphs. Use the Paragraph dialog box. As you'll soon see, this will give you better control over spacing between paragraphs and make it easier to keep paragraphs together. Read on.

Paragraph Formatting

You modify the appearance of paragraphs using the ruler, the Formatting toolbar, and the Paragraph dialog box. The ruler and Formatting toolbar are easy to use and readily available. When precise formatting is required, consider using the Paragraph dialog box rather than the ruler. Some formatting features have keyboard shortcuts.

> **TIP**
>
> If you want to reformat only one paragraph, simply place the insertion point anywhere within the paragraph; then make formatting changes. There is no need to select the text in a single paragraph. To alter multiple paragraphs, select them first. Your changes will affect all selected paragraphs, including any partially selected paragraphs. Double-clicking at the left edge of a paragraph selects it.

As we did in the previous chapter, let's start with a quick tour of the paragraph-formatting tools; then we'll look at some everyday paragraph-formatting tasks.

Formatting with the Formatting Toolbar

The Formatting toolbar contains a number of handy paragraph-formatting tools. If it is not showing, bring it into view with the View ➤ Toolbars command (see Figure 8.4).

PART

II

Formatting
Fundamentals

FIGURE 8.4

The Formatting toolbar places paragraph-formatting tools at your fingertips and also shows many paragraph setting options.

You must tell Word which paragraph or paragraphs you want to format before using the Formatting toolbar's tools. If you select only one paragraph or if all the selected paragraphs have identical paragraph-formatting options, activated paragraph options (such as center) will be indicated with pressed buttons. But if you select dissimilar paragraphs, these indicators will not be accurate.

Moreover, if you select two dissimilar paragraphs, you'll see subtle changes on the ruler. Indent handles will have dim outer edges, for instance. This is Word's way of saying it can't display two different settings at once.

Paragraph buttons on the Formatting toolbar include Align Left, Center, Align Right, Justify, Numbering (lists), Bullets (lists), Decrease Indent, Increase Indent, and Outside Borders. Figure 8.5 shows the buttons. You've seen some examples of these at work already.

FIGURE 8.5

Paragraph-formatting buttons on the toolbar

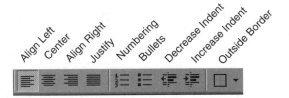

Formatting with the Paragraph Dialog Box

The Paragraph dialog box (choose Format ➤ Paragraph) is shown in Figure 8.6.

 TIP

Double-clicking on any indent marker displays the Paragraph dialog box!

The Paragraph dialog box lets you:

- Precisely specify line spacing (single, double, and so on)
- Precisely specify paragraph spacing (space before and after paragraphs)
- Dictate exact indention measurements
- Turn off line numbering for specific paragraphs
- Specify text alignment (left, centered, right, or justified)
- Specify text-flow guidelines (widows, orphans, and so on)
- Suppress hyphenation

FIGURE 8.6

Reach the para-
graph dialog
box from the
Format menu or
via hotspots.
Both tabs are
shown here.

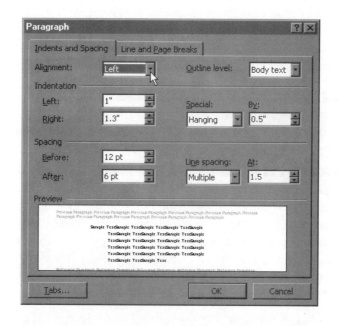

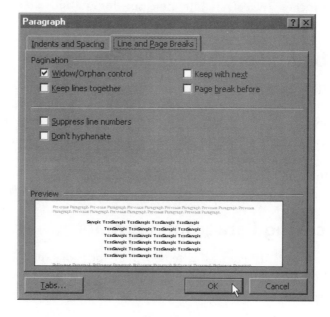

PART

II

Formatting
Fundamentals

When you enter measurements in the Paragraph dialog box, you can often use different units of measure for the same specification. For instance, you can specify line height in points (pt), lines (li), inches (in), picas (pi), or centimeters (cm). Each possible numeric entry in the Paragraph dialog box has a default unit of measure, which is shown in its entry box.

NOTE

Line Spacing shows a unit of measure when you select At Least or Exactly. When you select Multiple and enter a number, Word will assume you mean *li*.

WARNING

It is possible to make entries in the Paragraph dialog box without specifying units of measure if you know the default unit of measure for each type of entry. For instance, the default for line spacing is points. Here's the rub. If you enter **2**, Word assumes you mean 2 points, not double spacing. To specify double spacing, you'd need to enter **2 li**. When you are uncertain about the default unit of measure for a paragraph specification, always enter the abbreviation for the unit of measure, to play it safe.

In U.S. versions of Word, the default for horizontal measurements, such as indents, is inches. The default unit of measure for line and paragraph spacing is points. (There are 72 points per inch.)

Keyboard Formatting Shortcuts

There are numerous keyboard shortcuts for paragraph formatting. They are mentioned throughout this chapter. To find a list of Word shortcut keys, choose Help ➤ Contents and Index, select the Find tab, and type **shortcut keys** in the first text box. In the third list box containing help topics, scroll down to the Shortcut Keys entry and select Display.

A few keyboard shortcuts are additive. That is, instead of toggling when you press them more than once, they increase their effect. For example, pressing Ctrl+M indents a paragraph 0.5" from the left; pressing it twice indents the paragraph 1"; and so on.

Specifying Paragraph Formats

As promised, here are the steps for applying paragraph formats and everyday examples. Don't forget that it is possible to store and quickly recreate complex paragraph formats using Styles, as described in Chapter 12, *Using Paragraph Styles and AutoFormat*.

Indenting Paragraphs Automatically

You can indent paragraphs in a number of ways. Indents are *added* to margins, thereby increasing the white space and decreasing the text area for specific paragraphs. Thus, if you have a 1.0" right margin and specify a right indent of 1.0", your text will print 2.0" from the right edge of the paper.

WARNING

Don't confuse indenting with aligning. Aligning paragraphs is covered later in this chapter. Also, don't confuse indenting with margins.

The first line of each paragraph can be indented differently from other lines in the paragraph. First lines can be shorter than the others, creating regular indents, or longer than the others, creating *hanging* indents (sometimes called outdents). Once you change indents, each new paragraph you start by pressing Enter will maintain the same indention settings until you change them. Indented paragraphs can have other paragraph formatting as well. Figure 8.7 shows several indenting examples.

NOTE

Whenever you place the insertion point in a paragraph, the indent markers on the ruler move to show you the setting for the current paragraph.

PART II

Formatting Fundamentals

FIGURE 8.7

Several examples of paragraph indenting

First line indents

Indented & bulleted paragraphs

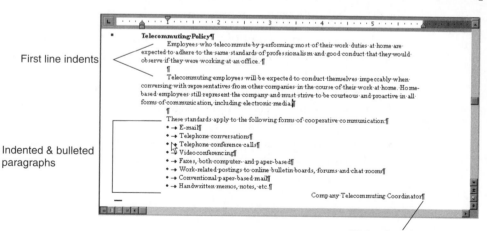

Right-aligned paragraph

Indenting with the Ruler

The quickest way to indent is to drag indent markers on the ruler. To adjust left and right paragraph indents from the ruler, follow these steps:

1. Place the insertion point in a paragraph or select multiple paragraphs.
2. Point to and then drag the appropriate triangular indent markers to the desired locations. (Drag on the bottom part of the left marker to set the overall left indention.) If you are not certain which marker is which, pause for a moment with the cursor over the marker, and a ToolTip will pop up to tell you which indent that marker controls.

3. Watch the ruler's scale as you drag. It shows the position of the indent mark in relation to its respective margin. The bottom part of the left marker is divided by a black line. Click on the upper portion of the bottom part to move it independently of the other part.
4. You will see the text move when you release the mouse button.

Indenting with the Paragraph Dialog Box

In the Paragraph dialog box, you can type specifications for right, left, first line, and hanging indents. The default dimension in the United States is inches (in). By including the appropriate unit of measurement with your entry, you can specify points (pt), picas (pi), or centimeters (cm) instead. To adjust left and right paragraph indents from the dialog box, follow these steps:

1. Place the insertion point in a paragraph or select multiple paragraphs.
2. Choose Format ➤ Paragraph or double-click on a hotspot. Word displays the Paragraph dialog box.
3. Enter specifications for right, left, and/or first-line indents.
4. You will see the effects of your changes in the Preview box. Click on OK when you are happy with the indention.
5. Once you move indent markers, each new paragraph you start by pressing Enter will maintain the same indention settings until you change them.

Indenting with Keyboard Shortcuts

You can also move the left indent marker with keyboard shortcuts. These are additive commands and can create nested paragraphs.

Command	Keystrokes
Center	Ctrl+E
Justify	Ctrl+J
Left align	Ctrl+L
Right align	Ctrl+R
Left indent	Ctrl+M
Remove left indent	Ctrl+Shift+M
Create hanging indent	Ctrl+T
Reduce hanging indent	Ctrl+Shift+T

Indenting with the Toolbar

  The Increase Indent toolbar button moves the left indent marker to the right the distance of one standard tab stop, and the Decrease Indent button moves it back the same distance. These are additive commands. Pressing Increase Indent twice indents farther than pressing it once. There are no toolbar buttons for the right indent marker.

Indents in Margins

It is possible to specify indentions that print in the right and/or left margins. Specify negative margin settings in the paragraph dialog box (**-0.5 in**, for instance) or drag indent markers into margins. Be patient. Horizontal scrolling is required when you drag indent markers into margins, and the process can sometimes be slow.

Indenting First Lines

You can indent the first line of a paragraph with the ruler, the Paragraph dialog box, or tabs. Tabs are generally the least efficient method.

First-Line Indenting with the Ruler

To set up automatic first-line indenting with the ruler, follow these steps:

1. Place the insertion point in a paragraph or select multiple paragraphs.
2. Drag the top half of the left indent marker. The text moves when you release the mouse button, and subsequently typed paragraphs will indent the same way.

First-Line Indenting with the Paragraph Dialog Box

To set up automatic first-line indenting with the Paragraph dialog box, follow these steps:

1. Place the insertion point in a paragraph or select multiple paragraphs.
2. Open the Paragraph dialog box (choose Format ➤ Paragraph or double-click on an indent marker in the ruler).
3. In the Special box, select First Line from the drop-down list and specify a first-line indent dimension in points (pt), inches (in), picas (pi), or centimeters (cm). Watch the preview to see the effect without closing the dialog box.
4. Click on OK when you are happy with the indent.

First-Line Indenting with the Tab Key

You can create first-line indents with the Tab key. But it's extra work, because you'll need to remember to tab each time you start a new paragraph. Use the ruler or dialog box instead. And as discussed in the *Using Paragraph Styles and AutoFormat* chapter, you can define a first-line indent as part of a paragraph style, available whenever you need it.

Hanging Indents

Sometimes you want the first line in each paragraph to stick out. This is particularly useful for creating bulleted lists, numbered paragraphs, bibliographies, and so forth. The first line in a hanging indent is called (cleverly) a *hanging indent*. The subsequent lines beneath are called *turnover* lines. Figure 8.8 shows some examples.

NOTE Word has a feature that automatically creates hanging indents for bullets and numbered lists. All you have to do is type (at the beginning of a new line) an asterisk and a space or a number and a space, and Word automatically bullets or numbers all other entries in your list, complete with attractive hanging indents. The effect is similar to that shown in Figure 8.8.

Hanging Indents with the Ruler

When creating hanging indents from the ruler, follow these steps:

1. Place the insertion point in the paragraph you need to format, select multiple paragraphs, or place the insertion point where you plan to begin typing hanging-indented paragraphs.

PART

II

Formatting
Fundamentals

FIGURE 8.8

*Some examples
of hanging
indents*

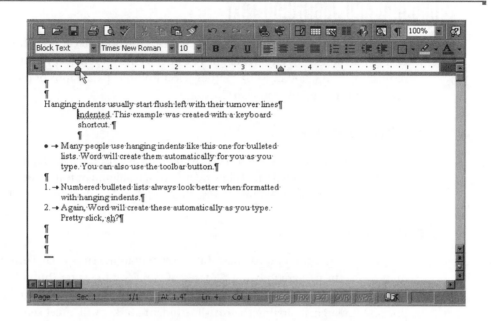

2. Set the position of the left (indented) edge of the turnover lines. To do this, with the ruler in view, drag the bottom half of the left indent marker to the right.

3. If you plan to indent the right edge of your paragraph(s), drag the right indent marker either now or later.

4. To create the hanging indent, drag the top half of the left indent marker to the left, past the turnover indent, and release the mouse button when you reach the desired point. The ruler will scroll to show you the hanging indent's position with relation to the rest of the paragraph.

Keyboard Shortcuts for Hanging Indents

There are keyboard shortcuts for moving the left indent. Press Ctrl+M to move the left tab marker to the right. Pressing Ctrl+Shift+M moves the marker to the left. Ctrl+Shift+N moves the indent back to the left margin. Movements are in the increments used for default tab settings (usually 0.5"). This is a great way to create nested indents! (Note that neither Ctrl+Shift+N nor Ctrl+Shift+M will go past the left margin.)

Aligning and Justifying Text

You can use the four Formatting toolbar buttons that look like lines of text to quickly justify, center, and right- and left-align. The lines in the buttons demonstrate the expected results. As always, you must first either select multiple paragraphs or place the insertion point in the paragraph you want to align.

Left Alignment

Left alignment is Word's default. Text sits right up against the paragraph's left indent position. If you have specified a first-line indent, the left alignment feature does not override it. Instead, it uses the specified first-line setting and then left-aligns the remaining text.

Centering

Clicking on the Center button places the text or graphics smack dab between the indent markers for the paragraph being centered. If you want to center things between document margins, be sure the left and right indent markers are sitting on their respective document margins. Moving the first-line indent marker will affect centering.

NOTE

Never use spaces to center. Always type words at the left margin and then click on the Center button.

Right Alignment

Clicking on the Align Right button places selected items flush against the right indent position for the paragraph. Use this feature for correspondence dates, inside addresses, and for added impact.

If you want to right-align something with the document's right margin, be sure the paragraph's right indent marker is sitting on the right document margin.

Justifying Text

Clicking on the Justify button causes Word to add space between words in the selected paragraphs. This results in what some people consider a typeset look.

Except for the last line in a paragraph, all the justified lines will be exactly the same length and will be flush left *and* right with the paragraph's left and right indent markers. Justified text can also have the first line indented.

If the uneven spacing and rivers of white space caused by justification annoy you, consider inserting hyphens to tighten up the text. See Chapter 7, *Characters and Fonts,* for details.

Adjusting the Space between Lines

The Indents and Spacing tab of the Paragraph dialog box provides a drop-down list for simple but effective control of the space between lines under most circumstances. The Preview area demonstrates the relative effect of single, one-and-a-half, and double line spacing. Single spacing causes 12-point line spacing, 1.5-line spacing is 18 points, and double-spaced lines will be 24 points apart. (There is little or no effect for text larger than 24 points.)

When you use these choices, Word adjusts the line spacing as needed to compensate for graphics, superscripts, and large or small type sizes. To force exact line spacing, use the At Least or Exactly choices described in a moment.

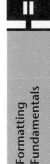

Single-Spacing Text

To single-space text, follow these steps:

1. Single spacing is Word's default. To reapply it to text spaced some other way, place the insertion point in a paragraph or select multiple paragraphs.

2. Press Ctrl+1 or choose Single in the Paragraph dialog box's Line Spacing menu.

Double-Spacing Text

To double-space text, follow these steps:

1. To apply double spacing to text spaced some other way, place the insertion point in a paragraph or select multiple paragraphs.

2. Press Ctrl+2 or choose Double in the Paragraph dialog box's Line Spacing menu.

Line-and-a-Half Spacing

To apply line-and-a-half spacing to text spaced some other way, follow these steps:

1. Place the insertion point in a paragraph or select multiple paragraphs.

2. Press Ctrl+5 or choose 1.5 lines in the Paragraph dialog box's Line Spacing menu.

Specifying Exact Line Heights

Word automatically sets the appropriate amount of white space between lines for you unless you tell it to do otherwise. It even compensates for different-size characters on the same line by setting line spacing to the largest character.

But sometimes, you'll want to specify exact line spacing for one or more paragraphs. Increasing the spacing by a nonstandard amount can help you fill unused space when your copy runs a little short. Or, specifying slightly less than normal space between lines can help keep that last lonesome line from printing on its own page.

 NOTE

You can also use the Shrink To Fit button in Print Preview to try to fit your document onto one page for printing.

You use the Paragraph dialog box to specify exact spacing. Follow these steps:

1. Place the insertion point in a paragraph or select multiple paragraphs.
2. Open the Paragraph dialog box (choose Format ➤ Paragraph or double-click on any indent marker).
3. Choose Exactly or At Least from the drop-down list.
4. Enter a specification and a unit of measure (2.5 li, 26 pt, 1.5 in, 22 cm, and so on) in the At box. Watch the preview as you work.
5. Click on OK to make the specified spacing change.

 NOTE

If the tops or bottoms of characters are cut off, you may have set a line height that is too small. In the Paragraph dialog box, increase the height.

Adjusting the Space between Paragraphs

Many people place white space between paragraphs by pressing the Enter key several times—typewriter style. Although this works, there is a more efficient method.

The Paragraph dialog box (Format ➤ Paragraph) has an area in the Indents and Spacing tab called *Spacing*. It lets you define the amount of white space Word places before and after paragraphs. You can enter spacing settings in points (pt), inches (in), centimeters (cm), or lines (li). Thus, 12 points would be entered as **12pt**, 25 centimeters would be entered as **25cm**, and so on.

Each paragraph can have unique before and after spacing. One advantage of adding space this way is that the spacing before and after paragraphs does not change when you change the point size of your text. Another advantage is that you can use different spacing combinations for different purposes.

Headings often have different spacing requirements from body text, for instance. You might want to create different Before and After paragraph spacing designs for figures and figure captions as well.

As you will learn in Chapter 12, *Using Paragraph Styles and AutoFormat*, you can save unique spacing specifications as part of a style, making it easy to keep the look of your documents consistent.

TIP

When adding space, remember that if a paragraph has space added after it, and the paragraph beneath it has space added before, the white space between them will be the *combination* of the two settings. For example, if one paragraph has 12 points of spacing after it and its successor has 6 points of spacing before, the white space between will be 18 points. Therefore, it is wiser to use either one or the other, but not both.

PART

II

Formatting
Fundamentals

Adding White Space before Paragraphs

To add a single line of white space before a paragraph, follow these steps:

1. Place the insertion point in a paragraph or select multiple paragraphs.

2. Press Ctrl+0 (zero).

To enter a specific amount of space before a paragraph, follow these steps:

1. Place the insertion point in a paragraph or select multiple paragraphs.

2. Double-click on any indent marker to open the Paragraph dialog box.

3. Enter new Before dimensions in the Spacing area in lines, inches, picas, and so on. Selected paragraphs and subsequent ones will have additional amounts of white space before them.

To remove single lines of white space (originally created with Ctrl+0), press Ctrl+0 a second time.

Fine-Tuning Paragraph Spacing

Although the ruler buttons are fine for most occasions, you might need to use the Paragraph dialog box occasionally to get just the right look. Enter appropriate specifications in the Spacing Before and After boxes to fine-tune. You can observe the effect of your changes in the Preview box. Click on OK when you are satisfied.

Space Before at Page Tops

When you print, Word ignores the Space Before setting in paragraphs that automatic pagination places at the top of a page. If you force a page or section break, however, Word retains this extra space. It also retains the additional space if you check the Page Break Before option in the Line and Page Breaks tab of the Paragraph dialog box.

Adding Borders and Shading

Word has many paragraph border and shading features. You can apply various border treatments and shading to single paragraphs or to groups of paragraphs. For instance, all the paragraphs in Figure 8.9 are surrounded by a common double-line border, and the last paragraph has a single line top border and shading.

FIGURE 8.9

You can apply borders and shading to one paragraph or multiple paragraphs.

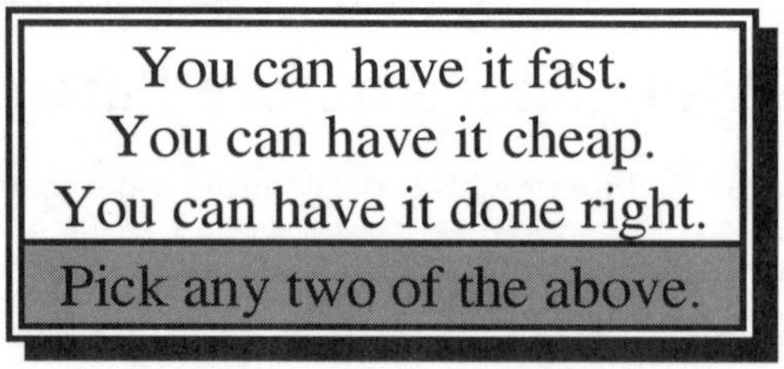

You can have it fast.
You can have it cheap.
You can have it done right.
Pick any two of the above.

Creating Lines with the Border Command

Don't be fooled by the boxy-sounding name of this command. Format ➤ Borders and Shading can be used to create lines as well. Check out the samples in Figure 8.10.

There is even a feature in Word that will automatically insert a border for you. Although this can only be used for single or double lines, it is quite a handy shortcut for creating simple borders. All you have to do is type three consecutive hyphens (---) or equal signs (= = =) on a new line and press Enter. Word converts what you've typed into a single or double line *and* sets the leading to make it look nice! Pretty nifty, eh? Well, those smart young kids at Microsoft work day and night to keep you happy. This command can do some funky things if you use it several lines in a row. Experiment.

FIGURE 8.10

By leaving off parts of borders, you can create lines.

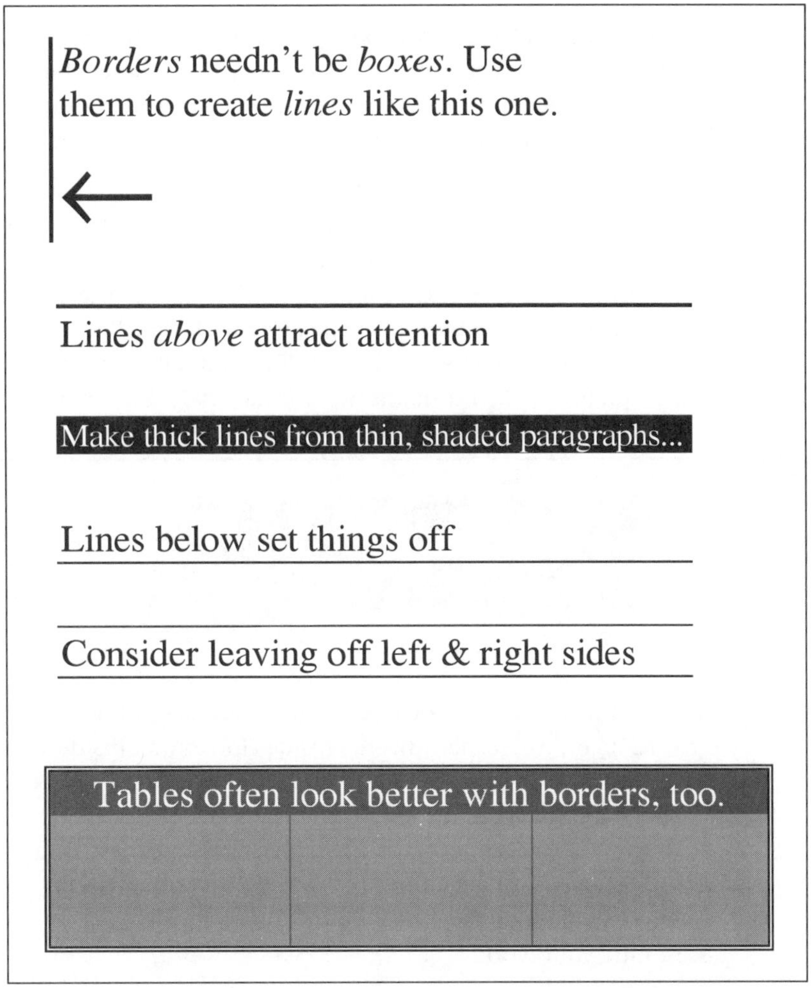

Borders needn't be *boxes*. Use them to create *lines* like this one.

←

Lines *above* attract attention

Make thick lines from thin, shaded paragraphs...

Lines below set things off

Consider leaving off left & right sides

Tables often look better with borders, too.

You adjust the horizontal *length* of borders or lines by changing a paragraph's width with indent markers or the Paragraph dialog box. It's also easy to control the distance between text and border lines. You can use borders to surround paragraphs, framed objects (such as graphics), and tables.

The Border Button Palette

Clicking on the Outside Border button on the Formatting toolbar displays a handy Borders button palette. (You can also display the Outside Border button by choosing View ➤ Toolbars and selecting Tables and Borders. The Outside Border button and its palette are on the Tables and Borders toolbar too.) You will see the changes in your document as you work. Here are general steps for using it:

1. Place the insertion point in the paragraph or select elements to be formatted—multiple paragraphs, graphics, and so on.
2. Adjust indents if necessary to define the width for the borders.
3. Display the Borders button palette (use the Outside Border button on the Formatting toolbar or select View ➤ Toolbars ➤ Tables and Borders to display the Tables and Borders toolbar, which contains the Outside Border button, too), shown in Figure 8.11.

FIGURE 8.11

The Outside Borders button palette

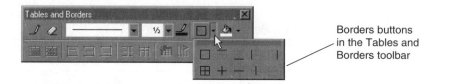

Borders buttons in the Tables and Borders toolbar

4. Click on the button corresponding to the desired border (Outside, Top, Bottom, Left, Right, All Borders, Inside, Inside Horizontal, Inside Vertical, or No Border).
5. To add fancy effects, select the bordered paragraph, and choose Format ➤ Borders and Shading. Word displays the Borders and Shading dialog box.
6. In the Borders tab, choose the desired line thickness from the Width drop-down list. Select line effects from the Style list and other effects from the Setting list.
7. Select shading, if you like, from the Shading tab.
8. Admire your work.

Custom Borders and Lines

Playing with borders and lines can be great rainy day entertainment. Just don't get carried away on busy days or with a deadline looming. Before you can effectively create custom borders, you must understand the Border sample part of the Borders and Shading dialog box, highlighted in Figure 8.12.

The border sample changes to represent the border you are creating. For instance, in Figure 8.12, the border specifications call for a double line around the entire border and a shadow effect behind the border. You specify lines (add and remove them) by clicking on border guides. They look like dotted *T*'s and *L*'s. Two of them are identified in Figure 8.12.

FIGURE 8.12

The Borders tab (top) and the Shading tab (bottom) of the Borders and Shading dialog box

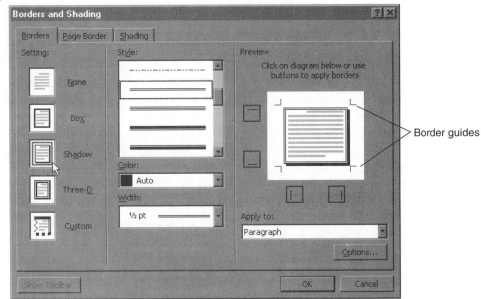

Border guides

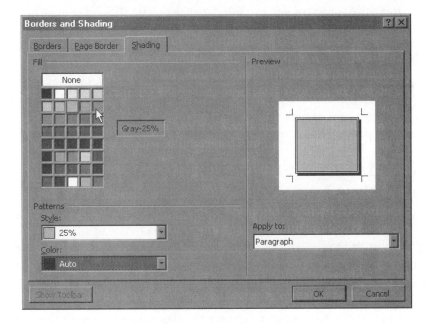

PART

II

Formatting
Fundamentals

Clicking on any of the three horizontal guides toggles horizontal lines. Clicking on vertical guides—well, you get the picture.

If you've selected multiple paragraphs (or tables) you'll be able to place lines between the paragraphs (or table rows), thanks to those center border guides. And, as you've seen in the examples, it is possible to specify the line widths used for borders. Here are the general steps for custom borders:

1. Place the insertion point in the paragraph, or select elements to be formatted— multiple paragraphs, graphics, and so on.
2. Open the Borders and Shading dialog box (shown in Figure 8.12).
3. Click on the appropriate border guides in the sample to turn them on or off.
4. Click on the line type(s) you wish. Watch your document change as you work.

Increasing the Space between Borders and Text

To add extra space between the text contained within borders and the borders themselves, select the Options button in the Borders tab of the Borders and Shading dialog box. In the Border and Shading Options dialog box, specify a measurement (in points) in the From Text portion for Top, Bottom, Left, or Right Border positions. Each border position has its own text box in which you can type the points measurements or use the up and down arrows to change the measurements. You can do this when you are designing the border, or you can select an existing border and change the spacing later in the Borders and Shading dialog box.

Controlling Border Width

A paragraph's indents (and the document's margins) control how wide the border is. On a page with standard margin formatting, the border will be as wide as the page, regardless of the dimensions of the text contained within the border. To change the border's size, select the paragraph(s) containing the border formatting and change the indents.

Using Word's New Page Border Feature

Word 97 has a new Page Border feature. You can use Page Border to place a border around the entire page or on any combination of top, bottom, and sides of the page.

NOTE

Choose Format ➤ Borders and Shading, and then choose the Page Border tab in the Borders and Shading dialog box. Select the border type from the Setting area. Choose Custom in the Setting area to specify certain sides of the page where you want the border to appear. Click on the sides where you want the border in the Preview area of the Page Border dialog box. To learn more see the "Wake Up Pages with Border Designs" sidebar later in the chapter.

Shading

Shading can be added to paragraphs with or *without* borders. Use shading to create forms or just to add decoration. Be aware, however, that shading can look pretty raggedy on many printers. Test-print some samples before spending hours shading your favorite form or résumé.

You can use the Borders and Shading dialog box to add and change shading. To add paragraph shading and color, select a shading percentage and color from the Fill palette on the Shading tab. You can further refine your selection by selecting from a list of shades lighter than your primary selection. This list appears in the Style drop-down list in the Patterns area of the Shading tab.

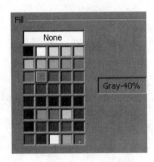
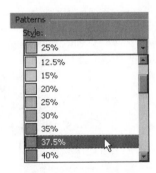

For example, to choose 40 percent shading, click on a medium gray color in the palette and press Enter. The smaller the percentage, the lighter the shading—100 percent is solid black.

Removing Borders and Shading

Although you can remove borders and shading with either the Borders button palette or the Borders and Shading dialog box, the palette's easier. Here are the general steps for using the dialog box:

1. Place the insertion point in the paragraph or select elements to be shaded—multiple paragraphs, graphics, and so on.
2. Open the Borders and Shading dialog box with the Format ➤ Borders and Shading command.
3. Click on the Shading tab.
4. Scroll through the Style list in the Patterns area and select a percentage or Clear.
5. You will see the effects of your work in the Preview box.

MASTERING THE OPPORTUNITIES

Wake Up Pages with Border Designs

For more exciting Border options, check out the Page Borders included with Word 97. Choose Format ➤ Borders and Shading, and click on the Page Border tab as shown below.

Click on the Art list box and scroll through the fantastic variety of color and black-and-white borders, which you can add around your pages.

If you select a border that encloses the entire page, you may have trouble printing the page, especially on color inkjet printers. To get around this, choose File ➤ Page Setup and then click on the Paper Size tab. Change the Paper Size to a custom size that is slightly smaller than your actual paper size. For example, enter 8.5" x10.75" dimensions for an 8.5" x 11" sheet. Select Whole Document from the Apply To drop-down list, and you are ready to print.

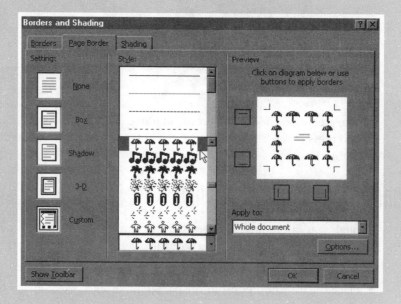

6. Click on OK.

7. Be sure to test-print new designs.

Here are the steps for removing borders or shading with the Borders toolbar:

1. Select the objects with the borders or shading you want to remove.

2. Display the Outside Border button palette (View ➤ Toolbars ➤ Tables and Borders, select the Outside Border button or use the Outside Border button on the Formatting toolbar).

3. Click on the No Border button (it's the rightmost lower button).

Chapter

9

Tabs, Tables, Math, and Sorting

Tabs, Tables, Math, and Sorting

Word novices often either under- or overuse tabs. Primarily a quick way to position text or graphics, tabs have a lot of competition in Word. Some people use the spacebar instead of tabs. Lovers of Word's table features often abandon tabs altogether in favor of tables. This is probably a mistake too. Moreover, your typing teacher may have told you to use tabs to indent the first line of each paragraph. You may prefer Word's split left indent marker. Word's first-line indent feature is probably a better choice for that task. In this chapter, you'll see some effective uses for tabs.

This chapter also shows you how to have Word do simple math calculations (a great way to compute and proof totals and subtotals in tabular typing). And you'll see how Word can sort things such as phone lists. Finally, Word comes with a separate program called Equation Editor, manufactured by Design Sciences, Inc. It will be of particular interest to scientists and academicians. Microsoft ships a customized version of the program designed specifically for use with Word. This chapter introduces you to the Equation Editor and tells you how to obtain additional information or an even more robust version of the program.

Tabs

Tabs are great for creating quick, relatively simple lists, and they do some things in Word you can't do on a typewriter. For instance, they can help you exchange Word data with spreadsheets, databases, and other programs. Each paragraph in a Word document can have the same or different tab settings. So turn off that "Gilligan's Island" rerun, and let's explore the wonderful world of tabs and tab stops!

Word offers five specialized tab-stop types. They each work with tabs to help align text and are particularly useful for making simple columnar lists like the one in Figure 9.1.

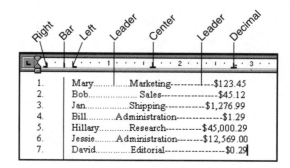

Left Tab Stops

Left tab stops are like the plain vanilla ones you find on your old Smith Corona. Text typed at these tab stops bumps up against the left edge of the stop. A left tab was used to align the peoples' names (the third tab stop) in Figure 9.1.

Center Tab Stops

A center tab stop centers your text around the tab stop. In Figure 9.1, the department names (at the fourth stop) are aligned with a center tab stop.

Right Tab Stops

Right tab stops position whatever you type to the left of the tab. As you can see in the first column of Figure 9.1, this is a great way to type long lists of numbers and have them line up.

Decimal Tab Stops

Decimal tab stops behave as you'd expect. They align columns of numbers on the decimal point and are perfect for simple financial reports.

Bar Tabs

The Bar button creates nice, thin vertical lines like the one you see separating the first and second columns in Figure 9.1. They aren't actual tab stops (that is, you cannot use them to align text), but they can be placed and moved like stops.

Tables vs. Tabs

Simple tabular columns are great if you have items that always fit on one line. But suppose that one of the departments in Figure 9.1 was the Department of Redundancy Department. If you use tabs, the title won't automatically wrap to fit the format. You would need to redesign the tab layout, shorten the department title, or cobble things up with a carriage return. Ugh. Long items such as these give tab typists fits. As you will see later in this chapter, tables make it easy to deal with this and other problems.

Serious typists will probably choose table solutions over tabs most days. The price is speed and complexity. Word's table features can be slow at times, and you may scratch your head in the beginning. Tables require an understanding of tabs too. So, for simple projects such as the example here, you might want to stick with tabs alone, at least until you've mastered them.

Setting Custom Tab Stops

In the United States, at least, Word starts out each new document with tabs set at 0.5" intervals. You can create custom tab locations to replace these.

Tab stops are always stored with the paragraph mark for each paragraph; thus, all the rules about paragraph markers apply. If, for example, you set tab stops once and type Enter at the end of each typing line, each new paragraph (line) will use the same tab stops as the preceding one until you tell Word otherwise.

Setting Tab Stops with the Ruler

You can set custom tabs as you type or use the standard tabs initially and then go back to fine-tune. Here are the general steps:

1. With the ruler in view, click on the button at the left edge of the horizontal ruler repeatedly until it shows the icon for the desired tab-stop type (Left, Right, Center, and Decimal).

2. Click on the ruler where you want to place a tab stop. If you make a mistake, drag the stop off the ruler and try again.

3. When you type, press the Tab key to move the insertion point to the new tab positions. With Show ¶ turned on, you'll see fat arrows indicating each tab character you type.

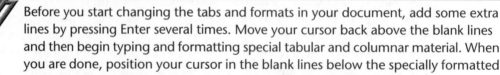

Moving Tab Stops on the Ruler

To move tab stops before you've entered text, simply point to a stop and drag away. If you have already entered text that uses the tab stops you want to move, select all the text before moving the tab stop.

For instance, if you had already typed the seven lines in Figure 9.1 and wanted to move the left tab stop for all the lines, you would need to highlight *all* seven lines before moving the tab stop. Otherwise, some lines (paragraphs) would have different stops than others. Incidentally, you'd also want to highlight the paragraph mark *beneath* the last line if you plan to enter more items. Otherwise, the last paragraph marker wouldn't know about the change, and subsequent entries would be off.

If you highlight paragraphs with different tab-stop settings, the tab stops will be dimmed. Only the stops for the top paragraph will be displayed.

TIP

Before you start changing the tabs and formats in your document, add some extra lines by pressing Enter several times. Move your cursor back above the blank lines and then begin typing and formatting special tabular and columnar material. When you are done, position your cursor in the blank lines below the specially formatted and tabbed text. Begin typing regular text here, where you do not want special formatting to apply. You have successfully avoided having to reset your tabs and other formats to what they were before you started formatting the special text!

Setting Tab Stops with the Tabs Dialog Box

Although using the ruler is easy, you may want to use the Tabs dialog box for some projects. It provides ways to set tab stops precisely and offers some additional tab-related options. Figure 9.2 shows the Tabs dialog box at work.

To open the Tabs dialog box:

- Choose Format ➤ Tabs.
- Click on the Tabs button in the Paragraph dialog box.

PART

II

Formatting
Fundamentals

FIGURE 9.2

The Tabs dialog box gives you precise control and additional table-related features.

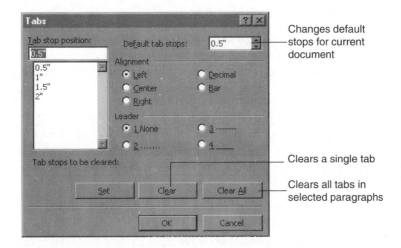

Changes default stops for current document

Clears a single tab

Clears all tabs in selected paragraphs

> **WARNING**
>
> Remember to select all affected text and paragraph markers before moving tab stops. Undo (Ctrl+Z) will save you when you forget.

Units of Measure in the Tab Dialog Box

Measurements in the Tabs dialog box are assumed to be in inches unless you type another valid abbreviation (*cm* for centimeter, *pt* for point, or *pi* for pica). For example, *5 cm* would position a tab stop five centimeters from the left margin.

You use the Alignment section of the Tabs dialog box to change current tab-stop types. This is the only way to select a bar tab.

Leading Characters for Tabs

Word *leader* characters are dots, dashes, and solid lines. These leaders precede tabbed entries, producing the effect demonstrated in Figure 9.3. You set them in the Tabs

FIGURE 9.3

Word provides tab leaders that make it easy to read lines without losing your place.

dialog box. They make it easy to read wide, sparsely populated lines without losing your place. Choose Leader 1 (the None option) if you want to remove leaders.

To create leaders, follow these steps:

1. Select the paragraphs you want to pretty up.
2. Choose Format ➤ Tabs.
3. Choose the leader style you desire from the Tabs dialog box.
4. Click on OK.

You can apply this effect when defining new tab stops or by selecting the tabbed paragraph and choosing Format ➤ Tabs to display the Tabs dialog box.

Default Tab-Stop Positions

The Word standard settings specify tabs every half-inch (0.5 in). You can change this for a single document by changing the setting in the Tabs dialog box. To change default tabs permanently, change and save stops in the Normal template, as described in Chapter 13, *Templates, Wizards, and Sample Documents*.

Clearing Tab Stops

You can drag the occasional tab off the ruler if you don't need it. The Tabs dialog box provides facilities for clearing multiple tabs at once. If you do choose a specific tab, the Clear button in the Tabs dialog box will still remove it.

When Your Tabs Don't Line Up

Select all the paragraphs that you want to conform and set identical tabs. You might also consider using the Clear All button. It removes all custom tabs. Defaults remain. This can make an absolute mess of your pride and joy. Undo should work if you accidentally clear all custom tabs, but it is always a good idea to save your work before experimenting with major changes such as these. Remember, these features work only on paragraphs you have selected.

Entering and Editing Tabular Data

Once you have set up tab stops, simply press the Tab key to reach the stop and begin typing. Word will position the text as you type. If you are typing at a center or right stop, text will flow appropriately as you type. When you type at decimal stops, the insertion point sits to the left of the decimal position until you hit the period key; then it hops to the right side. To leave an entry blank, simply tab past it by pressing the Tab key.

Tabs and Data Exchange

Tabs and carriage returns are often used by databases and spreadsheets, particularly when exchanging data with Macintosh computer users or downloading files off the Internet. Tabs usually separate fields in records, and carriage returns usually separate the records themselves, as illustrated in the database in Figure 9.4. This type of data is referred to as *tab-delimited.*

If you have a list of tab-delimited names, addresses, and phone numbers, you might be able to export the list to your favorite database or time-management program by saving it as a text-only file. Check out the importing sections of your other program manuals.

FIGURE 9.4

Many applications can use tab-delimited data created with Word.

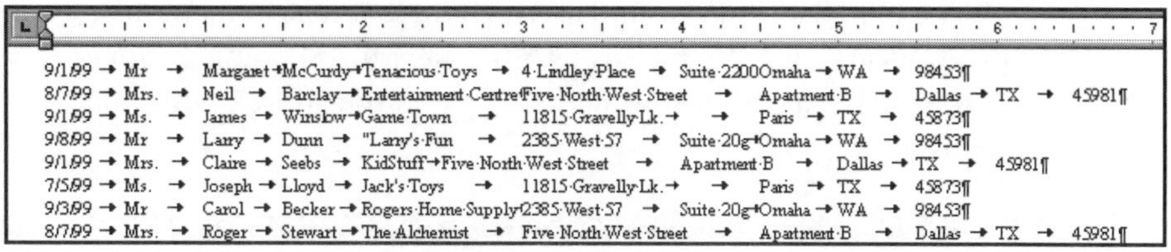
9/1/99 → Mr → Margaret → McCurdy → Tenacious·Toys → 4·Lindley·Place → Suite·2200 Omaha → WA → 98453¶
8/7/99 → Mrs. → Neil → Barclay → Entertainment·Centre Five·North·West·Street → Apartment·B → Dallas → TX → 45981¶
9/1/99 → Ms. → James → Winslow → Game·Town → 11815·Gravelly·Lk. → → Paris → TX → 45873¶
9/8/99 → Mr → Larry → Dunn → "Larry's·Fun → 2385·West·57 → Suite·20g → Omaha → WA → 98453¶
9/1/99 → Mrs. → Claire → Seebs → KidStuff → Five·North·West·Street → Apartment·B → Dallas → TX → 45981¶
7/5/99 → Ms. → Joseph → Lloyd → Jack's·Toys → 11815·Gravelly·Lk. → → Paris → TX → 45873¶
9/3/99 → Mr → Carol → Becker → Rogers·Home·Supply 2385·West·57 → Suite·20g → Omaha → WA → 98453¶
8/7/99 → Mrs. → Roger → Stewart → The·Alchemist → Five·North·West·Street → Apartment·B → Dallas → TX → 45981¶

Tables

Tables help you organize complex columnar information. Use them to create such diverse documents as forms, television scripts, financial reports, parts catalogs, and résumés. You can insert tables anywhere you need them in Word documents. Word's table feature, and the terminology used to describe it, will remind you of a spreadsheet.

Word tables consist of horizontal *rows* and vertical *columns*. You type in areas called *cells*. Cells can contain text, numbers, or graphics. Text in cells can be edited and embellished as usual with Word's Formatting toolbar and ruler.

A number of table-specific features let you control the size, shape, and appearance of cells. Border and shading features are available. It is also easy to insert and delete rows and columns.

Tables can be created from existing text without needless retyping. Or you can use the table feature to organize information and then convert your table to text. You can even import and export spreadsheet data. Figure 9.5 shows a typical Word table and its constituent parts.

FIGURE 9.5

A typical table consisting of three rows, each containing two columns, for a total of six cells. The gray cell gridlines will not print, but the default solid black table borders will print unless you turn them off.

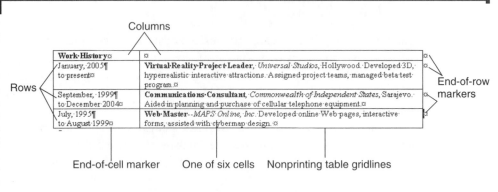

The solid gray lines around each cell represent *nonprinting table gridlines*. You can add printing borders with the Format ➤ Borders and Shading command. The larger dots are end-of-cell and end-of-row marks. Click on the Show ¶ button in the Standard toolbar to display them.

To turn off the nonprinting gridlines, select Table ➤ Show Gridlines and toggle to Hide Gridlines. To turn off the printing borders on your table, place the cursor inside one of the table cells, and then select Table ➤ Select Table to highlight the entire table. Click on the Outside Border button on the Formatting toolbar or on the Tables and Borders toolbar to display the Border buttons palette. Select the No Border button to turn off all the printing borders on the table.

Creating a Simple Table

Word has several table features that you will love almost immediately. The first is the Table button; the second is an entire Table menu. But I'll bet you'll end up using the new Draw Table feature most of the time. Let's start with the button.

If you plan to add regular (nontable) text above a table in a new document, press Enter once or twice *before* inserting a table. This will make it *much* easier to insert text above the table later. Then, if you haven't done so already, make any preliminary formatting decisions including the printer you plan to use, page orientation, margins, font, and so on. Word will consider these factors when inserting your new table. You can always change your mind later, but this step can greatly simplify things.

Using the Table Button

To create a table with the Table button, follow these steps:

1. Place the insertion point where you want to insert a table (ideally, *not* at the very beginning of a new, otherwise-empty document).
2. With the Standard toolbar in view, click on the Table button, and then drag while holding down the mouse button to highlight the desired number of rows and columns.
3. When the displayed grid represents the desired number of rows and columns, release the mouse button.
4. Word inserts an empty table.

TIP

Generally, it is best to guess at least how many columns there will be. Because Word determines the width of each column based on the number of columns and the space available, adding columns and getting them just the right width later on can be more difficult than simply adding rows.

PART

II

Formatting
Fundamentals

Don't worry if you are uncertain about the exact number of columns or rows you'll need. You can always add or delete them later. Figure 9.6 shows the grid for eight two-column rows. Try to make your own 8 x 2 table with the button.

Using the Table Menu to Create a Table

You can use the Table ➤ Insert Table command to create tables. Here's how:

1. Position the insertion point where you want the table (ideally, not at the very beginning of a new, otherwise-empty document).
2. Choose Table ➤ Insert Table.
3. Word displays the dialog box shown in Figure 9.7.
4. Enter the desired number of columns and rows for your table.
5. Click on OK.

Unless you specify a column width in the Column Width box, Word computes a column width automatically, taking into consideration the available text area in your document and the number of columns you've specified. Initially, all table columns are the same width, but you can change column widths using techniques described later in this chapter.

FIGURE 9.6

The Insert Table menu box and the resulting table it creates

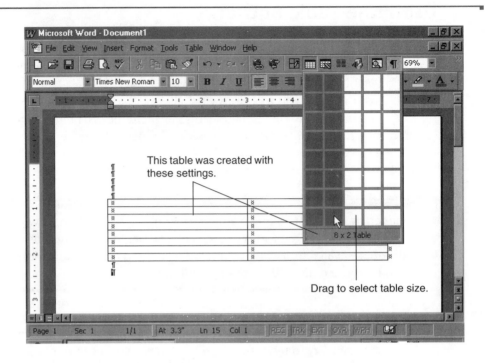

FIGURE 9.7

You use the Insert Table dialog box to define new tables.

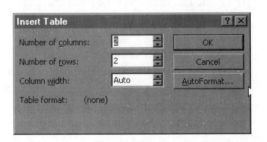

Quickly Sketching Your Table with Draw Table Features

Use Word 97's Draw Table feature to outline a basic table with columns, rows, and even color—just as if you were drawing it on paper. The following steps will get you started on your masterpiece:

1. Display the Tables and Borders toolbar by selecting the Tables and Borders button on the Standard toolbar, or choose View ➤ Toolbars ➤ Tables and Borders.

2. Select the Draw Table button on the Tables and Borders toolbar. Your cursor will turn into a pencil. Begin drawing your table by holding down the left mouse button and pulling the pencil from where you want the upper-left corner of the table across the page to where you want the lower-right corner of the table. Release the mouse button.

3. Fill in the table with horizontal and vertical lines in any arrangement, as shown here:

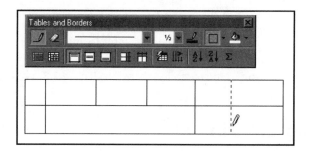

4. To add color lines, select the Border Color button in the Tables and Borders toolbar. Choose a color from the drop-down palette and begin drawing lines in that color.

5. To erase any unwanted lines, select the Eraser button in the Tables and Borders toolbar. Drag your eraser cursor over lines, and they will vanish.

6. After you finish drawing the table, use Table AutoFormat and any of the other commands in the Table menu or on the Tables and Borders toolbar to refine your table design.

Entering and Editing Text in a Table

With only the few exceptions noted in this chapter, you navigate, enter, and edit table text just as you do any other Word text. Use your mouse or arrow keys to position the insertion point, and then type normally. Think of the cell borders as margins. Word will automatically wrap text within the cell as you reach the right edge. Rows will automatically grow taller as necessary to accommodate your typing.

To move from cell to cell within a table, either use your mouse or press the Tab key to go forward and press Shift+Tab to go backward. The insertion point will move left and down to the next row when you press Tab in the last column on the right side of a table, and it will move right and up one row when you press Shift+Tab past the last column on the left. If you press Tab in the last cell of the last row, you will create a new row.

TIP

Because you use the Tab key to navigate in tables, you cannot simply press Tab to enter tab characters in cells. Instead, you need to hold down the Ctrl key while pressing Tab.

You can apply the usual character formatting to all or selected characters in a table. The familiar toolbar, ruler, and menu features all work here. Try recreating a personalized version of the to-do list shown in Figure 9.8. We'll use it for the rest of the exercises in this chapter.

Paragraphs in Cells

First-time table users are sometimes unaware of the important role that paragraphs play in tables. *A cell can contain more than one paragraph*. Create paragraphs in the usual way. While typing in a cell, press Enter. If necessary, all the cells in a row will increase in height to accommodate the extra paragraphs you create in a cell. If you haven't already done so, try adding the words *Home* and *Office* to all the cells in the second column. Create two paragraphs in the process. Copy and paste if you like:

Tuesday¤	Home¶ Office¤
Wednesday¤	Home¶ Office¤

You can apply all of Word's paragraph formats to paragraphs in cells. Because cells can contain multiple paragraphs, they can also contain multiple paragraph formats. Thus, within a single cell you can have several indent settings, tab settings, line-spacing specifications, styles, and so on. For instance, the text in this cell was selected by double-clicking and dragging, made bold with the Formatting toolbar's Bold button, and centered using the Formatting toolbar's Center button. Try it.

FIGURE 9.8

Try to add text to your first table.

	My To-Do List
Sunday	Home Office
Monday	Home Office
Tuesday	Home Office
Wednesday	Home Office
Thursday	Home Office
Friday	Home Office
Saturday	Home Office

PART

II

Formatting
Fundamentals

Selecting in Tables

As you've just seen, you can select characters, words, and other items in table cells using Word's usual mouse and keyboard features. In addition, Word also provides *table-specific* selection tools with which you can choose whole cells, entire rows, columns, or areas.

NOTE You can also use buttons in Word's new Tables and Borders toolbar for one-click access to some of the commands in the Table menu (see Figure 9.9). To display the toolbar, select View ➤ Toolbars ➤ Tables and Borders.

FIGURE 9.9

Word's new Tables and Borders toolbar

Selecting Single Cells

The area between the first character in a cell and the left edge of the cell is called the *cell selection bar*. Clicking on it selects the contents of the entire cell. You can also select an entire cell by dragging with the mouse. Just be sure you include the end-of-cell mark in your selection:

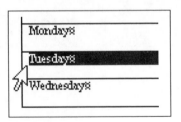

Selecting Columns

To select a column, move the mouse pointer to the area at the top of a column called the *column selection bar*. You'll know you've arrived when the pointer changes to a large down-pointing arrow.

Click to select the entire column.

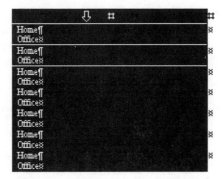

Holding down the Alt key while clicking anywhere in a column will also select the entire column. Selecting the bottom or top cell in a column and dragging up or down is somewhat tedious but will also work.

Selecting Rows

Double-clicking on any cell-selection bar will select the entire row. Selecting the leftmost or rightmost cell in a row and dragging will also work.

Selecting Adjacent Groups of Cells

To select groups of adjacent cells, either drag through the cells or click in one cell and Shift+click in the others. For instance, to select all the "weekday" cells, you could click in the Monday cell and then Shift+click in the cell to the right of Friday. The 10 weekday cells would be selected:

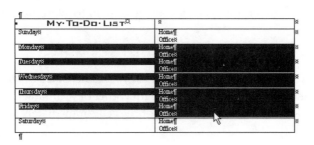

Selecting the Whole Table

To select an entire table, hold down the Alt key and double-click anywhere in the table. If your document contains multiple tables and they are not separated by paragraph marks, this technique will select all adjacent tables.

Do *not* use Word's Select All command to select a table, as this will also select paragraph marks and other things *outside* the table.

TIP

Word has a Select Table command on the Table menu.

Modifying Table Designs

Although Word's default table settings may be fine for simple typing tasks, you will eventually want to change column widths, overall table width, cell spacing, and so on. You'll want to insert, delete, and move rows and columns. As you can see from Figure 9.10, you can create professional-looking forms by modifying Word's standard tables.

Creating complex tables such as this can be a little frustrating at first. It is a good idea to save your work before you experiment with new table formats. Beginners should consider working on copies of important documents. That said, let's look at a number of ways to modify standard table designs.

Table Borders That Print

An easy way to dress up a table is to add printed borders or change the default printing borders. The form in Figure 9.10 is an example of this. Select the cell or cells you want to surround, and then use the Line Width and Style lists on the Borders tab of the Format ➤ Borders and Shading dialog box. Select the desired combination of line thicknesses, and apply the borders just as you would add them to Word paragraphs.

Adding Rows at the End of a Table

To add a new row at the end of an existing table, place the insertion point anywhere in the last cell (the one in the lower right corner of your table) and press the Tab key. Word inserts a new row using the styles of the cells immediately above.

FIGURE 9.10

Create professional-looking forms by adding borders and adjusting row and column sizes.

THE COMPASS ROSE

Finest books on Planet Earth

SALESPERSON	P.O. NUMBER	DATE SHIPPED	SHIPPED VIA	F.O.B. POINT	TERMS

QUANTITY	DESCRIPTION	UNIT PRICE	AMOUNT
			$ 0.00
			$ 0.00
			$ 0.00
			$ 0.00
			$ 0.00
			$ 0.00
			$ 0.00
		SUBTOTAL	$ 0.00
		SALES TAX	
		SHIPPING & HANDLING	
		TOTAL DUE	$ 0.00

Adding Rows in the Middle of a Table

To insert a single row in the middle of a table, follow these steps:

1. Place the insertion point in the row *below* where you want the new row.

2. Click on the Table ➤ Insert Rows command, or click on the Insert Rows button on your standard toolbar.

3. To add multiple rows, repeat the Insert Rows command, press F4 (to repeat the previous insert action) as many times as you want rows, or try the alternate approach in the next step.

4. Select as many existing rows as the number of new ones you want to insert before making the insertion. In other words, if you want to add three rows, select the three existing rows beneath the desired insertion point, and then choose the Table ➤ Insert Rows command. Word inserts three new rows.

  When you insert a table into your document, the Insert Table button on your Standard toolbar turns into the Insert Row button.

Changing Row Heights

Normally, Word sets the height of each row automatically to accommodate the cell containing the tallest entry. For instance, if one cell in a row needs 2.0" to accommodate the text or graphic it contains, all the cells in that row will be 2.0" high. All cells in a row must be the same height, but different rows can have different heights.

Dragging a Row to New Heights

To adjust the height of a row, follow these steps:

1. Click anywhere in the row you want to resize.

2. In Page Layout view or Print Preview, move the pointer to the vertical ruler at the left edge of the screen, watching the pointer as you move it.

3. When it becomes an up-and-down arrow, use it to drag the row to the desired height.

4. Release the mouse button.

Resizing Rows with Cell Height and Width

You can also overrule Word's automatic row-height (and column-width) settings via the Table ➤ Cell Height and Width command. This is one way to create forms with fixed-sized entry areas.

There is no standard keyboard shortcut for this command, but experienced table typists often create their own. Figure 9.11 shows the Cell Height and Width dialog box.

FIGURE·9.11

Specify table row heights and column widths with the Table ➤ Cell Height and Width command.

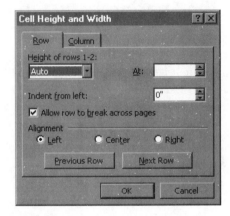

To resize cells, follow these steps:

1. Select the row whose height you want to specify. If you want multiple rows to share the same height, you can select all of them.
2. Choose the Table ➤ Cell Height and Width command.
3. Click on the Row tab, if necessary, to display its choices.
4. From the drop-down list, choose Auto, At Least, or Exactly.
5. Enter the desired dimension in points, inches, centimeters, and so on. (The default is points.)
6. To change settings for previous or next rows, click on the Previous Row or Next Row buttons.
7. Click on OK to make the change and close the dialog box.

TIP

If the exact height you specify is too small to accommodate the biggest entry in a row, the excessive text or a portion of the too-tall graphic will be cropped when printed. Simply increase the row height if this is undesirable.

Deleting Rows

To delete a row or rows of cells, select the row(s) to be deleted, choose the Table ➤ Delete Cells command, and then choose Delete Entire Row in the Delete Cells dialog

PART

II

Formatting
Fundamentals

box. This deletes both the rows themselves (the cells) and their contents (text or graphics or whatever). To delete the *contents* of cells but leave the cells intact, use Word's usual text-deletion tricks (select text or graphics and press the Delete key, for instance).

Changing the Spacing between Rows

To change the amount of white space between the contents of rows, you must change the before and after spacing of the first or last paragraphs in the cells. (Don't confuse this with changing the *height* of rows, which is something else entirely.) Use the same techniques you use to add space between nontable paragraphs (see the *Formatting Paragraphs* chapter). Select the paragraph, choose the Format ➤ Paragraph command, and specify Before and After spacing.

Inserting Columns in the Middle of a Table

To insert a single column within a table, follow these steps:

1. Select the column to the *right* of where you want the new column to appear.
2. Click on the Insert Columns button in the Standard toolbar (notice how this button replaces the Insert Rows button when columns are selected) or choose Table ➤ Insert Columns.
3. Word adds a new column but does not change the width of the earlier columns to accommodate it. To make the enlarged table fit on your page, you will probably need to adjust margins or column widths (described in a moment) or change page orientation.

TIP

To insert multiple columns, select as many existing columns to the right of the desired location of the new columns as the number of new ones you want. In other words, if you want to add three columns, select the three existing columns to the right of the desired insertion point, and then click on the Insert Columns button. Word inserts three columns.

Inserting Columns at the Right Edge of a Table

To insert a column at the right edge of a table, follow these steps:

1. Select the end-of-row markers to the right of the last column. If the markers are not visible, select the Show/Hide Nonprinting Characters button on the Standard toolbar to display them.

2. Click on the Insert Columns button in the Standard toolbar (notice how its name has changed to Insert Columns from Insert Rows), or choose Table ➤ Insert Columns. A column is inserted at the right edge of the table.

Deleting Columns

To delete columns, follow these steps:

1. Select the column or columns to be removed. The choices on the Table menu change to include column-related commands.

2. Choose Table ➤ Delete Columns.

Changing Column Widths

You can change the widths of entire columns or selected cells within columns. Most changes can be made by dragging column markers on the table scale in the ruler. But you can make precise adjustments in the Table Cells dialog box.

Changing Column and Cell Widths with the Ruler

To change the width of an entire column, follow these steps:

1. Point to a column boundary. The pointer will change shape.

2. Drag the column-width marker.

3. Watch the dotted line and ruler settings, and then release the mouse button when the column reaches the desired width. Note that if you resize the column by dragging it to the right, the column to the right of the resized column will get smaller so that the table's overall width remains unchanged.

If you hold down the Shift key while dragging, the column to the right changes size, and the table's overall width increases. If you hold down the Shift key while dragging the column to the left to make it smaller, the overall table width decreases.

Hold down Alt while dragging the column to the right or left, and you will see the exact column measurements in inches displayed on the ruler.

If you hold down Ctrl while dragging, all columns to the right change size, but the table's overall width does not.

You can also drag the column markers on the ruler to change column widths. Just don't accidentally drag the cells' indent markers instead, as illustrated in Figure 9.12.

As you can see in Figure 9.13, it is possible to change the width of one or more cells by selecting them and using the Cell Height and Width dialog box (Table ➤ Cell Height and Width). Specify a new width in the Columns tab.

TIP

When you are first learning, it's easy to mess things up while dragging cell and column borders around this way, particularly if you change individual cell widths when you meant to change column widths. If multiple undos can't fix the problem, and you don't have a better, previously saved version, perhaps the AutoFit button can help. It's described next.

FIGURE 9.12

You can also change column widths by dragging these markers.

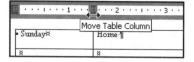

FIGURE 9.13

You can change individual cell widths or groups of cells with the Column tab in the Cell Height and Width dialog box.

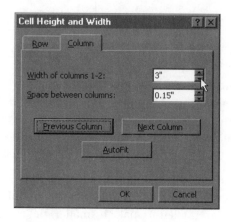

Changing Table Cell Widths with the AutoFit Button

The AutoFit button attempts to make cells snugly surround their contents. Therefore, it is best to use it after you've entered all the information in your table or after you are done adding or deleting items. Follow these steps:

1. Select the cells you want to resize or, more often, the entire table.

2. Choose Table ➤ Cell Height and Width.

3. Click on the Column tab if it is not already in view.

4. Click on the AutoFit button. Word will snug up the selected cells.

> **NOTE**
>
> To make a group of rows or cells the same height, select Table ➤ Distribute Rows Evenly, or click on the corresponding button on the Tables and Borders toolbar. To make a group of columns or cells the same height, choose Table ➤ Distribute Columns Evenly, or click on the Distribute Columns Evenly button on the Tables and Borders toolbar.

Merging Cells

Use the Merge Cells feature to combine the contents of multiple cells. This is a common way to make a heading in one cell span an entire table or selected group of columns. For example, you could merge the two cells in the top row of your To-Do list to form a heading like this that spans both columns:

As shown in Figure 9.14, you select the cells to merge, and then choose Table ➤ Merge Cells; the contents of the designated cells merge. You may need to reformat text merged this way.

Splitting Cells

To split (unmerge) cells, follow these steps:

1. Place the insertion point in a merged cell.

2. Choose Table ➤ Split Cells. You'll be asked how many cells you want after the split.

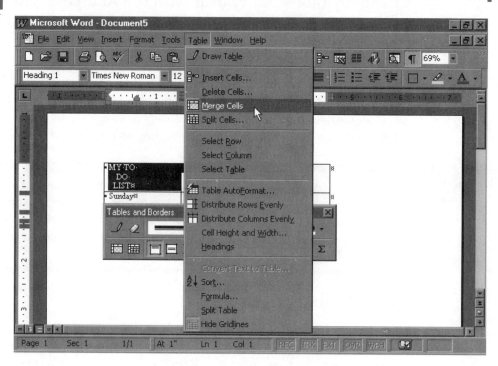

Changing the Space between Columns

Word assigns cell widths based on the available text area and the number of columns you request. In the process, it sets aside a small amount of unprintable space between (actually within) each cell. This space takes away from the usable cell space. For instance, a 0.5" column with 0.25" column spacing would have 1.25" of usable space in the middle of each cell.

To change the space between columns, follow these steps:

1. Select the columns of interest.

2. In the Cell Height and Width dialog box, click on the Columns tab.

3. Type a new specification in the Space between Columns box, or use the arrows to flip through suggested choices.

4. Click on OK.

AutoFormatting Tables

The Table ➤ Table AutoFormat command attempts to select cell settings that make a presentable table. Whether it succeeds will vary with the project and your definition of success. Personal taste plays a role too. For example, in a simple case like the one in Figure 9.15, AutoFormat successfully tightened up the table, added some nice- looking lines, and basically yupped it up.

But when the tables get big and slightly more complicated (containing merged cells, for instance), things can get a little unpredictable.

WARNING

Before using the Table AutoFormat command, save your work to disk. If you get one of those "Insufficient memory to undo" messages somewhere along the line, you'll at least have a copy of your "before" table.

Thus forewarned, here are the basic steps for using Table AutoFormat:

1. Enter, edit, spell-check, reorganize, and otherwise finish your table.

2. Save your document to disk.

3. Select the entire table (Alt+5 on the numeric keypad with Num Lock off).

4. Choose Table ➤ Table AutoFormat.

PART

II

Formatting
Fundamentals

FIGURE 9.15

*Before and after
AutoFormatting
a simple table*

Before Table AutoFormat

Work History	
January, 2005 to present	**Virtual Reality Project Leader**, *Universal Studios*, Hollywood. Developed 3D, hyperrealistic interactive attractions. Assigned project teams, managed beta test program.
September, 1999 to December 2004	**Communications Consultant**, *Commonwealth of Independent States*, Sarajevo. Aided in planning and purchase of cellular telephone equipment.
July, 1995 to August 1999	**Web Master**--*MAPS Online, Inc.* Developed online Web pages, interactive forms, assisted with cybermap design.

After Table AutoFormat

Work History	
January, 2005 to present	**Virtual Reality Project Leader**. *Universal Studios*, Hollywood. Developed 3D, hyperrealistic interactive attractions. Assigned project teams, managed beta test program.
September, 1999 to December, 2004	**Communications Consultant**. *Commonwealth of Independent States*, Sarajevo. Assisted in planning and purchase of cellular telephone equipment.
July, 1995 to August, 1999	**Web Master**—*MAPS Online, Inc.* Developed online Web pages, interactive forms, assisted with cybermap design.

5. Preview the format choices from the scrolling list, as shown in Figure 9.16, by highlighting their names one at a time. The up and down arrow keys are handy here. Pay particular attention to how Word handles row and column headings in the preview examples.

6. Select a style by highlighting it, and then click on OK.

7. Behold—then undo and try again, if necessary.

Some (but not all) styles can add special effects to last columns or rows. This is a good way to highlight grand totals. Turn these effects on and off with their corresponding checkboxes in the Apply Special Formats To area of the Table AutoFormat dialog box. You can also turn off many AutoFormat effects (borders, shading, and so on) the same way.

TIP

Word's Format ➤ AutoFormat command does not format tables. Use the Table ➤ Table AutoFormat command instead.

Graphics in Tables

Tables aren't just for bean counters. Check out Figure 9.17.

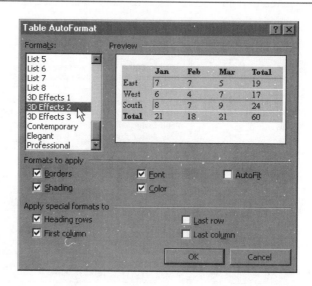

FIGURE 9.17

This is a two-column, one-row table!

☞ Nature Notebook

BIGFOOT SIGHTING CONFIRMED!

Authorities baffled by reliable accounts of swamp ape visitations

Metairie, Louisiana—Local law enforcement officials confirmed today that numerous sightings of the elusive creature known variously as 'Bigfoot,' 'Old Hairy,' 'Skunk Ape,' and 'Swamp Thing,' have been reported in the swampy bayous of central Louisiana.

The so-called 'Sportsmen's Paradise' is hosting an odd asssortment of rumors concerning the activities of the legendary hirsute, bipedal hominid that haunts desolate regions of the U.S. Bayou residents are concerned about the alarming frequency and startling nature of the Bigfoot visits. Locals want officials to do something to ensure the safety of their livestock, pets and children, but lawkeepers are at a loss about what to do.

"That skunk ape has never been tracked down in my lifetime or in the lifetimes of my father or great-grandfather," notes one prominent county sheriff. "He's smart, mean and likely to bite your head off before you even get off a shot."

Animal lovers in the area are also worried that Bigfoot hysteria will create a climate of violence that could result in the injury or death of any of the mysterious creatures if they were detected in their swamp hideaways.

"My hopes are that naturalists will be able to study them, instead of having the police or a posse gun them down,'"maintains Flora Borealis, an animal protectionist from Baton Rouge, LA.

Anyone with information on the enigmatic critters should contact the Louisiana State Game Commission at 1-800-BIGFOOT.

Travel the world tracking down strange phenomena

Earn your certificate in *cryptozoology* at **Barnes Institute of the Unexplained.**

Join dozens of *seasoned professionals* as they roam the globe in search of crop circles, extraterrestials, mindbenders and the usual assortment of bizarre events.

Listen in awe as paranormal researchers fill you in on the latest developments in the fields of parapsychology, extrasensory perception, exobiology, numerology, and metaphysics!

For more information, call 1-800-4ALIENS.

PART

II

Formatting Fundamentals

Figure 9.17 is a two-column, one-row table with graphics and a half-dozen different paragraph formats. Think of table cells as text and graphic containers; then set your imagination on turbo.

Converting Tables to Text and Vice Versa

Sometimes you'll start a project using tabs and wish you'd created a table—or a coworker will give you some tabbed text. At other times, you will want to export things you've typed using Word's table feature with database and other programs that expect tab- or comma-separated (delimited) input. Word has solutions for all these contingencies.

Word makes it quite easy to convert back and forth from tables to text. You may need to do some cleanup before or after conversion, though. Always work on copies of your documents when you do this!

Converting Text to Tables

Highlight the text in your document that you want to turn into a table. Choose Table ➤ Convert Text to Table and click on the appropriate option button in the resulting dialog box, shown in Figure 9.18.

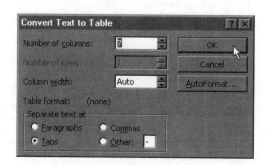

Tab-Delimited Text

Click on the Tabs button in the Convert Text to Table dialog box. Lines of text separated by paragraph marks or line breaks will become rows in your table. Tab-separated strings of text within those lines will become cell entries in the row. Word will automatically create the necessary number of columns based on the maximum number of tabs in a line.

For instance,

`Sony Corporation [Tab] 800-222-7669 [↵] SYBEX, Inc. [Tab] 415-523-8233 [Tab] Publisher [↵]`

would create two rows with three columns, even though the last cell in the first row would be empty.

Comma-Delimited Text

Click on the Commas button in the Convert Text to Table dialog box. Lines of text separated by paragraph marks or line breaks will become rows in your table. Comma-separated strings of text within those lines will become cell entries in the row. Word will automatically create the necessary number of columns based on the maximum number of commas in a line.

For instance,

`Sony Corporation [Comma] 800-222-7669 [↵] SYBEX, Inc. [Comma] 415-523-8233 [Comma] Publisher [↵]`

would create two rows with four columns, even though the last two cells in the first row will be empty.

WARNING

Notice how the comma in *SYBEX, Inc.* created an unintentional column. Although many database programs let you use quotation marks to solve this problem, Word does not.

Figure 9.19 shows part of a tab-separated text file after conversion to a table, editing, and formatting. Notice that the quotes surrounding the imported text have *not* been removed by Word's Text to Table feature. Use Replace to do this. See the *Finding and Replacing* chapter for details.

FIGURE 9.19

Once you convert text to a table, you may need to clean it up.

9/1/99	"Mr"	Margaret	McCurdy	Tenacious Toys
8/7/99	"Mr"s.	Neil	Barclay	Entertainment Centre
9/1/99	"Ms".	James	Winslow	Game Town
9/8/99	"Mr"	Larry	Dunn	"Larry's Fun"
9/1/99	"Mr"s.	Claire	Seebs	KidStuff
7/5/99	"Ms."	Joseph	Lloyd	Jack's Toys
9/3/99	"Mr"	Carol	Becker	Rogers Home Supply
8/7/99	"Mr"s.	Roger	Stewart	The Alchemist

PART

II

Formatting
Fundamentals

Converting from Paragraphs

Click on the Paragraphs button in the Convert Text to Table dialog box. If you ask Word to convert paragraphs to tables, it will propose a single column and create as many rows as you have paragraphs. Changing the number of columns will distribute paragraphs among the columns from left to right. In a two-column layout, the first paragraph would end up in the top-left cell of the new table, the second paragraph in the top-right cell, the third in the left cell of row two, and so on.

Converting Tables to Text

Select the table cells you want to convert, or use the Alt+double-click trick to select the whole table. Choose Table ➤ Convert Table to Text. Word displays a Table to Text dialog box, which asks if you want the table converted to paragraphs, tab-delimited text, or comma-delimited text. Choose one. If you select the comma or tab options, Word converts each row of your table into one line (a paragraph, actually). Cells in your old tables will become tab- or comma-separated items on the lines.

Remember that in-text commas will confuse Word. It would treat *SYBEX, Inc.* as two distinct entries. If you choose tab text, you will probably need to set new tabs after the conversion.

Choosing the paragraph option will convert each old table cell into at least one paragraph. If cells contain multiple paragraphs, the paragraph marks are retained during the conversion, so some cells will create more than one new paragraph.

Table Tips

Here are some tips to help make you a more productive table editor. They cover a variety of subjects.

Print Format Samples

Today—before you have a rush job to do—create some sample tables using the automatic formats that appeal to you *and print them* on your printer(s). Some will look great. One or two may be unreadable. Find out before you are in a hurry.

Rearrange Rows in Outline View

With a table on-screen, switch to Outline view (View ➤ Outline). Move the pointer to the left edge of your table, as shown in Figure 9.20. The pointer shape will change.

You can drag rows to new positions using Word's Outline features. See Chapter 17, *Get Organized with Outline View,* for more information.

FIGURE 9.20

Drag rows in Outline view to rearrange tables.

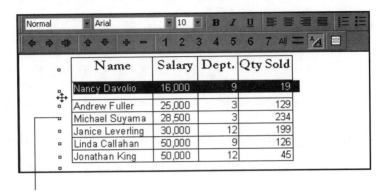

Drag rows to rearrange them.

Moving Cell Contents

To move the contents of cells, follow these steps:

1. Find or create empty destination cells in the appropriate quantity and configuration to hold the items you plan to move. For instance, if you plan to move a four-row-by-six-column collection of cells, you will need the same number of available cells in the same configuration (4 x 6) to receive the moved items.

2. Copy or cut the items by highlighting them and choosing Edit ➤ Copy or Edit ➤ Cut or the keyboard shortcuts Ctrl+C and Ctrl+X.

3. Now you can either select the same cell configuration at the destination (four rows of six columns each in our example) or try a shortcut. Simply place the insertion point in the upper left destination cell. (If you use this shortcut, do *not* select the cell.) Be sure to place the insertion point before the end-of-cell mark and then paste. All the cells will flow into their new destinations, bringing their formatting information with them.

4. Delete unused columns by choosing the Table ➤ Delete Columns command if necessary.

Styles and Tables

Word will use the current style (at the insertion point) when creating a new table. You can change the style of the whole table or apply different styles to different portions of the table.

PART

II

Formatting
Fundamentals

Consider creating multiple styles if you plan to play with table formatting. For instance, you might have a style for table headings, another for standard text, another for decimal-aligned numbers, and so on. See Chapter 12, *Using Paragraph Styles and AutoFormat,* for more detail on styles.

Apply the new style to all appropriate paragraphs in your table by selecting the paragraphs and using the Formatting toolbar's Style menu. From then on, simply changing a style will change all table text formatted with the changed style.

Repeating Headings on Multipage Tables

To repeat column headings on each page of a multipage table, tell the Wizard or follow these steps:

1. Select the row or rows you want to use as headings (typically the top one or two).
2. Choose Table ➤ Headings.

If you insert manual page breaks, the heading will *not* repeat.

Use Tables to Create Forms

When you get good at manipulating tables, you can use them to create forms like the one shown in Figure 9.21. It's simply a combination of cells, borders, shading, and paragraph formats. See Chapters 29 and 30 for more about forms and fields within forms.

FIGURE 9.21

Use tables to create forms like this one.

User Survey

Fill this out while at the user's desk			Network information (confidential)	
External Monitor?	Yes No	Screen size (diag.):	User ID	Password
Color?	Yes No	Bits (8, 24, etc.): Grays:	Mail Name	Password
Printer	Laser Dot matrix		Groups	Security Level
Please list software installed on this machine:			Interface type (Ethernet, etc.)	
			Zone & Port	
			Network user training? Yes No	Date:

Sorting in Word

Have you ever created something such as an alphabetic list of employees and their phone extensions and then needed a list of phone-extension assignments sorted by extension number? Most of us have small lists like these, and they always seem to be in the wrong order.

You could retype the old list or cut and paste, but the Table ➤ Sort command or the Sort Ascending and Sort Descending buttons on the Tables and Borders toolbar might be a better solution.

Word can sort lines of tabular text, items you've entered in tables, or even paragraphs in a document. (If you're working in Microsoft Office, however, Excel and Access provide more powerful sorting tools.) The Sort command can be helpful when preparing data files for Word's Print Merge feature, discussed in Chapter 26, *Mail Merge—Creating Custom Documents*.

WARNING

As with some other Word features, Sort can make substantial changes to your document (read: ruin your hard work), so it is best to save before you sort. Consider practicing on copies of important files.

Sorting with the Tables and Borders Toolbar

The Tables and Borders toolbar contains some sorting buttons among other things. It looks like Figure 9.22.

To sort rows of text, select them and click on either the Sort Ascending or Sort Descending button. Word will sort based on the first letter(s) at the left of each line. Remarkably, if the first row (line) of text is bold or otherwise "looks" like labels, Word will not move it.

To sort items in a table with the Tables and Borders toolbar, follow these steps:

1. Save your work, just in case.
2. Place the insertion point in the column that you want to use as the "sort by" column.
3. Click on the Ascending or Descending sort button. Word sorts the entire table (all columns), leaving labels untouched.

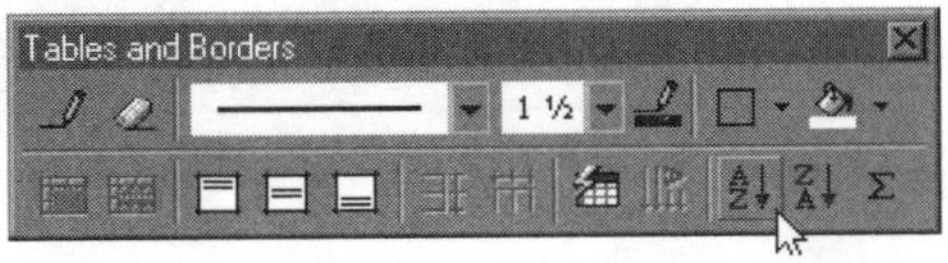

FIGURE 9.22

The Tables and Borders toolbar can help with simple sorts too.

PART II

Formatting Fundamentals

Sorting with the Sort Command

Word's Table ➤ Sort command will attempt to sort selected text alphabetically, numerically, or chronologically at your request. Sorts can be up to three levels "deep" (see Chapter 30, *Creating and Using Forms*). The Sort Text command can be used in free-form text but is much more powerful when used with a table. To sort a table with this command, follow these steps:

1. Save your work, just in case.
2. Place the insertion point in the table you want to sort.
3. Choose Table ➤ Sort
4. Word highlights (select) the entire table and displays the dialog box shown in Figure 9.23.
5. If you have labels at the top of your table, choose the My List Has Header Row option.
6. There will be up to three drop-down lists containing the column labels (if you have them) or column numbers (1, 2, and 3).
7. Specify the sort order by choosing the desired column for each sort level.
8. Choose a sort order for each column.
9. Tell Word whether the values in each column are text, numbers, or dates by choosing from the drop-down Type lists. (Word will automatically assign each value a data type, but you may not agree with what it assigns.)
10. Click on OK, and Word will sort.

If you want the sort to be case-sensitive or if you are sorting things not in a table, click on the Options button in the Sort dialog box and make the appropriate choices in the Sort Options dialog box. It is shown in Figure 9.24.

FIGURE 9.23

Word lets you sort tables up to three levels deep.

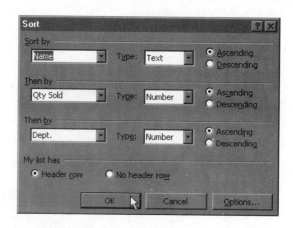

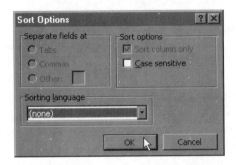

FIGURE 9.24

The Sort Options dialog box

PART

II

Formatting Fundamentals

Adding, Subtracting, Multiplying, and Dividing

Word's Table ➤ Formula command will add, subtract, multiply, and divide numbers you've typed in your documents. It is perfect for creating simple financial reports or for proofreading columns of numbers. The feature has some peculiarities, however, so if you plan to use it extensively, review the examples in this chapter and create some of your own before your next rush project.

Word's Built-in Math Capability

How often have you typed an important memo and made a math or typing error in a column of numbers? Word's Formula feature can minimize mistakes like these. In its simplest capacity, the command adds columns or rows of numbers in tables, but it can do much more. Read all about it in Chapters 29 and 30.

The Equation Editor

The Equation Editor is a more elegant way to create complex formulas. It helps you build formulas using palettes of math symbols and templates. The feature understands the rules and conventions for typesetting formulas, and it will do much of the formatting for you.

Starting the Equation Editor

The Equation Editor is a separate program that runs under Word's supervision. The program and related help file should be installed in your Commands folder. Choose Insert ➤ Object, select the Create New tab, and double-click on Microsoft Equation to start it, as shown in Figure 9.25.

You assemble equations by typing text and choosing templates and symbols from the palettes. The Equation Editor has a number of keyboard shortcuts, which are detailed in the program's context-sensitive help screens. Create equations by choosing elements from drop-down lists, as shown in Figure 9.26.

To receive online help about a particular palette or symbol, select the Equation Editor's online Help menu.

> **TIP**
>
> If you do not see the Equation Editor3 in the Object Type list in your Insert ➤ Object dialog box, you can install Equation Editor from your Office 97 CD-ROM. Put your CD-ROM in the CD-ROM drive, select Start ➤ Settings ➤ Control Panel. In the Control Panel, double-click on Add/Remove Programs. Follow the Install Wizard prompts and select Add/Remove at the Microsoft Office 97 Setup screen. Then Select Office Tools to add Equation Editor to your Office folder.

FIGURE 9.25

Starting the Equation Editor

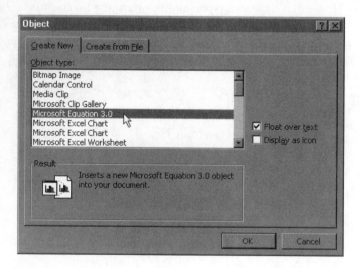

Formatting
Fundamentals

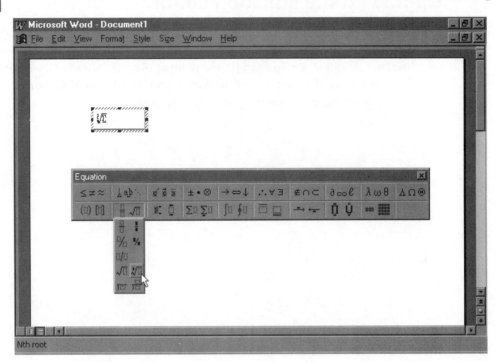

FIGURE 9.26

Choose elements for your equations from the drop-down lists.

Placing Equations in Word Documents

Closing the Equation Editor window pastes the equation you've created into your Word document at the insertion point.

Editing Equations in Word Documents

To edit equations, follow these steps:

1. Double-click on the equation in your document to open the Equation Editor window.
2. Make the changes.
3. Close the Equation Editor window to replace the old equation with the new.

Upgrading the Equation Editor

If you work a lot with equations, you might want an even more powerful version of this program available from Design Sciences, Inc. The address is 4028 Broadway, Long Beach, CA, 90803. Or you can phone them at (800) 827-0685. The e-mail address is `mtsles@mathtype.com`, and the World Wide Web URL (Universal Resource Locator) is `http://www.mathtype.com/mathtype/market/msee.html`.

Chapter

10

Headers, Footers, Page Numbers, and Footnotes

FEATURING

Headers, Footers, Page Numbers, and Footnotes

Word's *headers* and *footers* are places to put repetitive information in a document's top and bottom margins. Logically enough, headers print at the top, footers at the bottom. (Don't confuse footers with *footnotes*, which are different.)

You can use headers and footers to print something simple on each page, such as your name, or something complex, such as a graphic. Style elements such as formatted text, dates, and automatic page numbering can be included in headers and footers.

Headers and footers can be identical on all pages in your document, or you can specify different content for each section of the document. Odd and even pages can have different designs if you wish. The first page of each document or each section can be unique.

It is possible to apply virtually any paragraph or character style using the Formatting toolbar and rulers in headers and footers. You can also place text-boxed items and text-boxed anchors in headers or footers. They will repeat on all pages thereafter.

In this chapter you'll also learn about Word's footnote features, which are equally powerful and easy to use. You can enter, edit, and view footnote numbers in a variety of formats. Word simplifies inserting, deleting, and moving footnotes by automatically numbering and renumbering them as necessary.

Entering Basic Headers and Footers

In Word, you always edit headers and footers in Page Layout view. You work right in the header and footer area of your document after double-clicking to undim it or after switching from Normal view with the Header and Footer option on the View menu.

Headers and footers are also displayed in Print Preview, but when you attempt to open a header or footer in Normal view or Print Preview, Word switches you to Page Layout view and displays the Header and Footer toolbar.

To enter a header that repeats on all pages in your document, follow these steps:

1. Choose View ➤ Header and Footer. Word switches to Page Layout view if it is not already there and displays the Header and Footer toolbar.
2. Create and edit header text as you would any other. You can paste graphics, apply styles, and otherwise format your work. Figure 10.1 shows an example.

FIGURE 10.1

A header window can contain stylized text, borders, shading, and graphics.

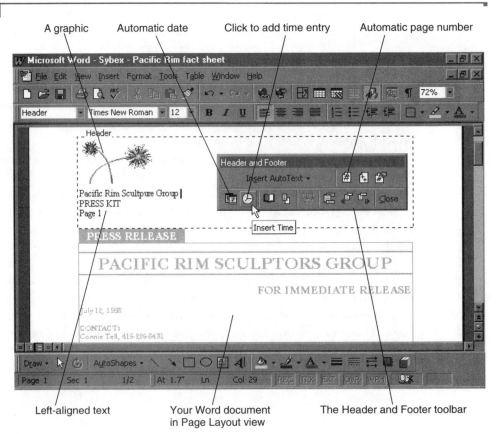

3. Use the automatic page number, time, and date features described later in this chapter.

4. Double-click in the main document to return to work there.

You enter footers the same way you enter headers, except that you work in a Footer window:

1. Choose View ➤ Header and Footer or double-click in the footer area of the first page to be modified in Page Layout or Print Preview.

2. Word switches to Page Layout view if it is not already there and displays the Header and Footer toolbar.

3. Click on the fourth button from the right on the Header and Footer toolbar to switch to the Footer window.

4. Create and edit footer text as you would any other. You can paste graphics, apply styles, and otherwise format your work.

5. Use the automatic page number, time, and date features described later in this chapter.

6. Double-click in the main document to continue working there.

Adding Dates, Times, and Simple Page Numbers

In Figure 10.2 I've inserted a page number in a footer by clicking on the page-numbering icon and centered it by clicking on the Formatting toolbar's Center button. You could use other formatting tricks as well—adding some space before the page number with the Paragraph tab's Space Before option, for instance.

> **TIP**
>
> You can place *fields* in headers or footers so that information such as authors' names, filenames, date last saved, and so on can appear automatically. See Chapter 29, *Creating and Using Fields,* for details.

PART

II

Formatting
Fundamentals

FIGURE 10.2

Use toolbars to enter and position information such as page numbers.

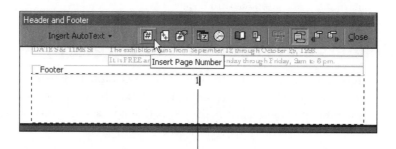

An automatic page number inserted and centered horizontally

Rulers and Toolbars in Headers and Footers

Use your regular document ruler or Formatting toolbar when working in header and footer windows. Margins, indents, tabs, and all the other tools work as you'd expect. The Header and Footer toolbar's functions are shown in Figure 10.3.

 You can now add standard header information with the new Insert AutoText button on the Header and Footer toolbar. The options available are shown in the Insert AutoText drop-down list in Figure 10.3.

FIGURE 10.3

The Header and Footer toolbar functions

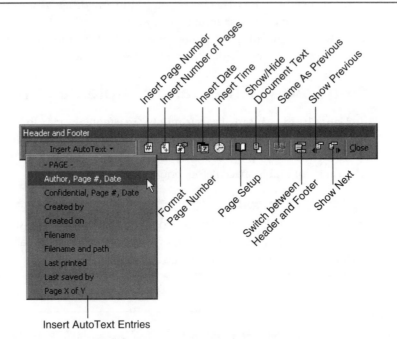

Headers and Footers in Print Preview

It is a good idea to switch to Print Preview occasionally when designing headers and footers. You can get a good approximation of how headers and footers will print and spot potential problems (such as the footer that appears only on odd pages in Figure 10.4).

FIGURE 10.4

Use Print Preview to view your work. This can help you spot potential problems and fix them before printing.

Even header

Different first page header and footer

Odd header

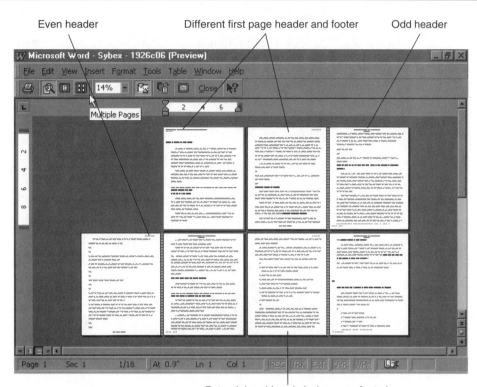

Potential problem (missing even footer)

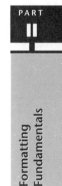

TIP

Remember that many printers cannot print at the very edges of the paper and that it is possible to position a header or footer in nonprinting areas. If you have selected the correct printer at the start of the project, Word does a good job of showing you when a header or footer will be cut off by your printer.

Take another look at Figure 10.4. Because this document will be printed on two sides and then bound, mirrored margins and odd/even headers and footers have been specified. Notice also that the first page has a different header and footer. Read on to learn how to create these effects.

PART

II

Formatting Fundamentals

Even and Odd Headers and Footers

To create different even and odd headers or footers, follow these steps:

1. Place the insertion point in the section where you want the odd/even effect to begin (read more about sections in Chapter 11, *Formatting Your Work with Section Breaks*).
2. Open the Page Setup dialog box (double-click in a blank part of a ruler or choose File ➤ Page Setup).
3. Select the Layout tab.
4. Check the Different Odd and Even choice in the Headers and Footers area.

You now have four header and footer areas in Page Layout view. Their names will change from page to page.

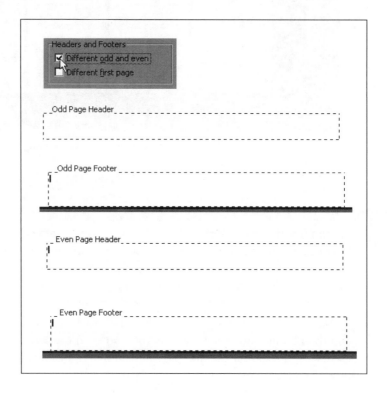

Different First Page Headers and Footers

The Layout tab in the Page Setup dialog box contains a choice called Different First Page. (Chapter 11, *Formatting Your Work with Section Breaks*, goes into more detail about sections.) To create unique headers and footers for the first page of your document, follow these steps:

1. Place the insertion point in the section where you want the different first page effect to begin.
2. Open the Page Setup dialog box (double-click in a blank part of a ruler or choose File ➤ Page Setup).
3. Choose the Layout tab.
4. Check the Different First Page option in the Headers and Footers area. You'll have different header and footer areas on the first page. Their names will be visible in Page Layout view:

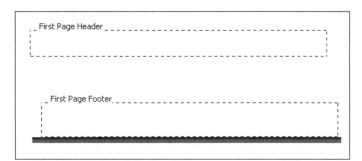

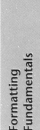

5. Create different headers and footers for the first page in Page Layout view.

Page Numbering

Word offers a variety of tools to help you automatically number pages. You are given many page-numbering format and style choices. It's possible to position page numbers nearly anywhere that pleases you. Let's explore these features and discuss the effects of document sections and pagination on page numbering.

Word provides two page-numbering techniques. Both have advantages and disadvantages. Normally, you will use only one for a particular document. Otherwise, you might end up with two or more sets of page numbers!

The Header and Footer Toolbar Method

As you've seen already, Word makes it easy to place page numbers in headers and footers. To add page numbers using the header/footer method, follow these steps:

1. Open a header or footer by double-clicking on it in Page Layout view.
2. Click on the Insert Page Number button in the Header and Footer toolbar. A number is inserted in your header or footer at the insertion point.

Like anything else placed in headers and footers, page numbers can be formatted, repositioned, surrounded with borders, accompanied by text, and otherwise embellished.

  Use the Insert Number of Pages button on Word's Header and Footer toolbar to create headings, such as Page 1 of 2. To quickly add one of these page numbering headings, follow these steps:

1. Select View ➤ Header and Footer to display the Header and Footer toolbar.
2. Click on the Insert Page Number button in the Header and Footer toolbar.
3. Type the word **of** next to the inserted page number and press the spacebar.
4. Click on the Insert Number of Pages button in the Header and Footer toolbar.

Word uses the standard header or footer style to format page numbers placed therein. You can override this by applying additional character and paragraph formats or by changing the standard header or footer style (see Chapter 12, *Using Paragraph Styles and AutoFormat*).

Headers and footers have tab stops, which you may find useful for page-number positioning.

The Page Numbers Command

The Insert ➤ Page Numbers command provides a wider variety of numbering options. It displays the Page Numbers dialog box and lets you quickly reach the Page Number Format dialog box, shown in Figure 10.5.

  You can also display the Page Number Format dialog box by clicking on the Format Page Number button on the Header and Footer toolbar.

To insert page numbers using the Page Numbers command, follow these steps:

1. Place the insertion point in the section you want to number.
2. Choose Insert ➤ Page Numbers. Word displays the Page Numbers dialog box.

FIGURE 10.5

*The Page
Number Format
dialog box*

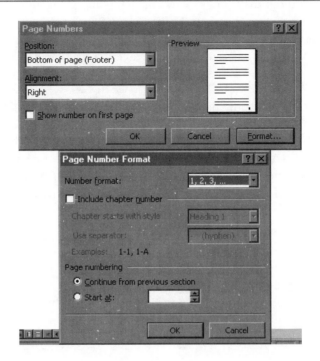

3. Word suggests page numbers in the bottom right corner of your document (0.5" from the bottom and right edges of the paper), but you can specify different positions with the Position and Alignment drop-down menus. Watch the Preview area as you work.

4. Choose whether to place a page number on the first page by clicking to add or remove the corresponding checkmark.

5. Either click on OK or click on the Format button to review other page-numbering options.

Page-Numbering Formats and Styles

Word supports five page-number formats. Standard arabic numbers (1, 2, 3, …) are the default. It is also possible to number with capital roman numerals (I, II, III, …) or with capital letters (A, B, C, …). Lowercase formats are also provided (i, ii, iii, … and a, b, c, …).

Specify number formats in the Page Number Format dialog box; click on the Format button in the Page Numbers dialog box (Insert ➤ Page Numbers), as shown in Figure 10.5. All the formats are available, regardless of which page-numbering technique you choose.

You can use Word's many character- and paragraph-embellishment features to spruce up page numbers. In the font of your choice, make numbers bold, align them, put boxes around them. Text can appear next to the numbers (*Page 1*, for instance).

After inserting page numbers, switch to Page Layout view and change their appearance.

TIP

Documents containing multiple sections can have different formats in each section. If you want all sections to have the same format, most kinds of formatting (typefaces, font sizes, styles) will be applied to the whole document as usual, but when designating formats in the Layout tab of the Page Setup dialog box, be sure to change This Section to Whole Document in the Apply To area as always when handling any aspect of multiple-section documents in this dialog box.

Chapter Numbers in Page Numbers

If you use Word's standard heading styles and if you use one of the headings for chapter titles, you can have Word include chapter numbers with your page number (*2-36*, for instance). You can specify one of five separators—hyphens, periods, colons, en dashes, or em dashes.

TIP

Don't confuse hyphens with en dashes and em dashes. Both are longer than hyphens. En dashes (–) are typically used to indicate ranges of numbers, and em dashes (—) are used to show breaks in thought.

You set up chapter page numbering in the Page Number Format box, in the section called Use Separator:

Managing Starting Page Numbers

Usually you will want Word to place the number 1 on your first printed page, but not always. For example, many people prefer their multipage letters to be printed without a 1 on the first page. They still want the second page to be numbered 2, the third 3, and so on. Let's call this *first page number suppressed*.

Or you might want to start each new section in a multisection document with 1. Let's call this *restart sections with 1*.

Sometimes you might want your first page to be printed without a number (a cover page, for instance) and then the next page to contain the number 1. Let's call this *begin second page from 1*.

Finally, you might want to use some other number for the first page, such as 25 or 100. This is helpful when you are combining your work with other documents. Let's call that *starting page other than 1*.

In all the following examples, I assume that your document does not already have page numbers.

First Page Number Suppressed

This one's easy. To suppress page numbering on the first page, follow these steps:

1. Place the insertion point in the desired section.

2. Choose Insert ➤ Page Numbers. Word displays the Page Numbers dialog box.

3. Remove the checkmark from the Show Number on First Page box:

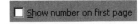

4. Click on OK.

Restart Sections with 1

To restart each section at page 1, follow these steps:

1. Select all sections that you want to start with page 1. Choose Insert ➤ Page numbers. Word displays the Page Numbers dialog box.

2. Click on the Format button. Word displays the Page Number Format dialog box.

3. Check the Start At box.

4. Specify the number with which each section will start (1 in this example).

Removing Page Numbers

Simply open the header or footer containing unwanted page numbers and delete one. The rest of the page numbers in the section will disappear. To delete all the page numbers in a multisection document, follow these steps:

1. Open a header or footer containing page numbers.

2. Choose Edit ➤ Select All or press Ctrl+A.

3. Delete a page number. The rest will disappear.

Footnotes and Endnotes

Word lets you create simple *footnotes* or *endnotes* and personalize their appearance. Although the following sections refer only to the more common footnotes, the various techniques for working with both types of notes are the same.

Easy Automatic Footnotes

Figure 10.6 shows an automatic (default) Word footnote. It should take you less than ten seconds to add your first footnote to existing text.

Follow these steps:

1. Place the insertion point where the footnote marker is needed (after the word *INFORMATION* in our example).
2. Choose Insert ➤ Footnote.
3. You can dismiss the Footnote and Endnote dialog box by clicking on OK, because Word's defaults are fine for this project.

FIGURE 10.6

Standard footnotes such as these require little effort.

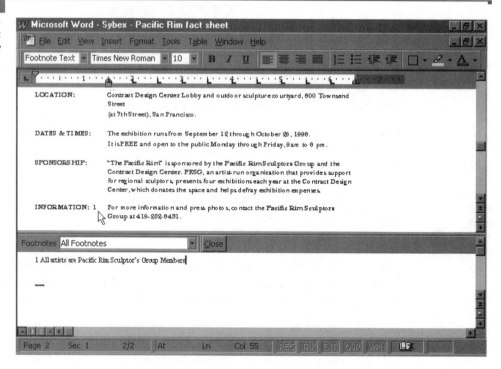

4. If you are in Normal view, a second window pane opens. Type the footnote in it:

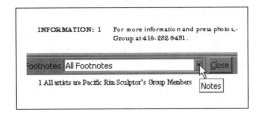

In Page Layout view, you type right where the footnote will print—usually between the text and the footer:

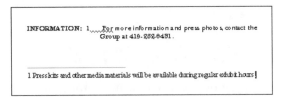

5. In either case, the insertion point automatically moves to the proper place for you to type the footnote. Type it.

6. To return to the main document, click on the Footnote window's Close button or move the insertion point with the mouse.

Viewing Footnotes

Footnotes are always displayed in Page Layout view and Print Preview. If they are not visible in Normal or Outline view, choose View ➤ Footnotes. Word opens the footnote pane.

If you are constantly entering or referring to footnotes in Normal view, you can leave the footnote window visible while you work. Scrolling in your document will cause corresponding scrolling in the footnote window. Use the footnote scroll bars if necessary to view notes. Feel free to resize the footnote window to suit your taste and screen size. Drag the bar separating the two windows the same way you resize other Word split screens (point to the Split box and drag).

To hide the footnote window, choose View ➤ Footnotes and remove the checkmark next to the command, or click on the Close button.

PART

II

Formatting
Fundamentals

TIP

Double-clicking on a footnote marker in your document displays the footnote pane and places the insertion point at the beginning of the footnote. If necessary, Word will open the footnote pane and scroll to the appropriate note. Also, clicking on a reference marker in the footnote pane causes the main document to scroll to the reference.

Inserting Footnotes ahead of Existing Ones

Whenever you insert (or delete) footnotes, Word renumbers the existing ones properly. Simply position the insertion point and choose Insert ➤ Footnote or press Alt+Ctrl+F. (This quick key combo is especially useful because it bypasses the dialog box.) Word takes it from there. To delete a footnote, simply delete its number in the text. Again, Word does the dirty work.

Editing and Personalizing Footnotes

You can copy, move, or delete entire footnotes as easily as you would a single character. To do so, follow these general steps:

1. Select the footnote marker in the document text. (This might take a steady hand, particularly if you have drag-and-drop enabled.)
2. Cut, copy, paste, or drag-and-drop the footnote mark.
3. Word does the rest. If you have used AutoNumbering, Word updates the numbers in your text and in the corresponding footnotes. If you copy and paste a mark, a corresponding new footnote will magically appear in the correct spot in your footnotes. Deletion works as you would expect.

Editing Footnote Text

You edit footnote text in the footnote pane in Normal view or in the footnote itself in Page Layout view. Cut, paste, and drag-and-drop away to your heart's content. (Note that you cannot delete a footnote in this pane; you must cut the footnote mark in the document text if you want to delete or move it.)

Footnote Text Style

You can embellish selected footnote text as you would expect. Highlight the text, and then use the ruler, Formatting toolbar, or format-related menu choices (bold, italic, and so on).

Footnote text is based on the Normal style. To change the size or font or other footnote style elements for all footnotes, you must modify the Word standard footnote text style, since manually reformatting existing footnotes will not affect new footnotes. To change the footnote-reference marks, modify the footnote-reference style.

Personalizing Footnotes

Word lets you modify many footnote parameters via the Insert ➤ Footnote command and the Note Options dialog box. Here's the general procedure:

1. Choose Insert ➤ Footnote.
2. If you want to mark each footnote with a symbol instead of a number, use the Symbol button to select a footnote symbol character. Click on OK in the Symbol dialog box when you've made your selection.
3. Click on Options to display the Note Options dialog box, shown in Figure 10.7.
4. Click to switch to the All Footnotes tab, if necessary.
5. Specify note placement, number formats, starting numbers, and starting points.
6. Click on OK.

Controlling Footnote Numbering

Footnote numbering can restart on each page if you check the Restart Each Page button in the Numbering area of the All Footnotes tab of the Note Options dialog box.

PART

II

Formatting
Fundamentals

FIGURE 10.7

Personalize footnote appearance using the Footnote choices in the All Footnotes tab of the Note Options dialog box.

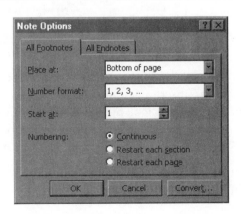

Footnote Position

You can also use the Note Options dialog box to specify where footnotes and endnotes should be placed. It has two tabs: All Footnotes and All Endnotes, each with a Place At drop-down list. Positions available for Footnote are:

- At the bottom of each page (the default)
- Directly beneath the last text on a page

Positions available for Endnote are:

- At the end of a section in multisection documents
- At the end of your document

Incidentally, in multicolumn sections, footnotes print below each column.

Footnote Separators

The little black lines that separate document text from the footnotes themselves are cleverly called *footnote separators*. Edit them as follows:

1. Switch to Normal view.
2. Choose View ➤ Footnotes to display the Footnote pane.
3. Choose Footnote Separator from the drop-down list.

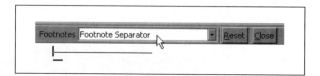

4. This is just like any other Word window. You can edit the length of the line (it's a paragraph). Insert a graphic, if you like. You can even use Word's drawing tools here. Double lines look nice. Use Word's Paragraph Border feature to create them. It is possible to use a ruler and the Formatting toolbar in the separator window.
5. Click on Close (or Reset to restore the standard separator).

When you are happy with your creation, close the separator window and view the results in Print Preview or Page Layout view.

Footnote-Reference Marks

Footnote-reference marks appear wherever you place them in your document's text area and at the beginning of each footnote in the footnote area itself.

By default, Word uses numbers for reference marks. This is the AutoNumber button in the Numbering section of the Footnotes and Endnotes dialog box. You can customize the numbering, though, by clicking on the Custom Marks button and typing your own characters or selecting them from the Symbol dialog box (display it by clicking on the Symbols button). You can use as many as ten characters as footnote reference marks. To use one of Word's default numbering styles, click on the Options button to display the Note Options dialog box. Then choose a style from the Number Format dialog box. When you click on OK, your selection becomes the default.

Footnote Continuation

Continuation separators appear whenever footnotes carry over onto the next page. These notices can be modified the same way you change regular separators as described in the previous section.

Endnotes

Endnotes are much like footnotes, except that they appear at the end of a document. Use the same basic procedures as you do for entering, editing, and moving footnotes. Select Insert ➤ Footnote and click on the Endnote button in the Footnote and Endnote dialog box. When working in the Note Options dialog box, choose the All Endnotes tab.

PART

II

Formatting
Fundamentals

Footnote Tips and Cautions

Here are some tips and caveats on using footnotes:

- Whether or not Automatic Spell Checking is turned on, spelling errors have a hard time hiding from Word. It checks your spelling even in footnotes. No need to do anything special. Simply click on the Spelling button, and Word displays any unrecognized words it finds in the footnote pane.

- Do not place index or table-of-contents entries in footnotes. They will be ignored.

- Word's Find and Replace features can help you search for and reformat footnotes.

- Save frequently used footnote entries and use AutoText to eliminate tedious retyping.

Chapter

11

Formatting Your Work with Section Breaks

FEATURING

Formatting Your Work with Section Breaks

In earlier chapters, you've seen many examples of Word's powerful formatting capabilities. In some types of documents, you'll want the same formatting decisions to apply from beginning to end; in other types, such as newsletters and the like, you may want to change page orientation or margins for some parts. You use Word's *section* feature to change major formatting in your document at places you decide.

You must start a new section whenever you need to:

- Change page orientation within a document
- Change margins in part of a document
- Turn line numbering on or off
- Change footnote appearance or numbering or suppress notes
- Change the appearance of headers and footers
- Change the format, position, or progression of page numbers

Although the exact sequence of events will vary with your project and needs, in general you will follow these steps:

1. Place the insertion point where you want a new section to begin.
2. Choose Insert ➤ Break to create the new section.
3. Make the desired formatting and other changes for that section.
4. Perhaps create other sections farther down in the document.

You'll see practical applications of sections in a moment. There are no hard and fast rules about *when* to create new sections. Experienced Word users often create 10 or 20 sections in a one-page document. Others use a single section for an entire 100-page report.

Occasionally, Word inserts section breaks for you—when creating an automatic table of contents, for instance. Mostly, you insert them yourself.

Inserting Section Breaks

To insert a section break, follow these steps:

1. Place the insertion point where you want the break. It's a good idea to press Enter before inserting a section break so that the break doesn't come between a paragraph's text and its paragraph mark.
2. Next, choose Insert ➤ Break. In the Section Breaks area of the Breaks dialog box, double-click on the text flow option you want. For instance, if you want to insert a section break and start succeeding text on a new page, double-click on Next Page. To resume text without a page break, double-click on Continuous.
3. If Show/Hide nonprinting characters is turned on or if you are in Normal view, you'll see a dotted, nonprinting line containing the words *Section Break* at the insertion point on your screen (see Figure 11.1). The status area reflects section numbers as you move the insertion point or scroll to pages in the new section.

Sections As Chapter Elements

For the largest Word projects, such as book-length manuscripts, it's usually best to make each chapter a separate document file. In medium-size documents such as reports, however, it is common to create a new section for each chapter. If you do so, you can change header and footer information such as chapter names. If you were creating an employee handbook, Chapter 1's header might contain the words *Welcome new employees*, and the headers in Chapter 2 might say *Your health plan explained*, and so forth.

Sections also make it possible to customize page numbers within chapters. Your document's front matter might be numbered in lowercase Roman numerals (i, ii, iii, and so on). Pages within chapters might contain chapter-related numbers that restart at the beginning of each chapter (1-1, 2-1, and so on). As you'll recall, you can use different page-numbering styles in each section of your document, and you can restart page numbering at the beginning of any new section.

FIGURE 11.1

Sections are marked with dotted nonprinting lines.

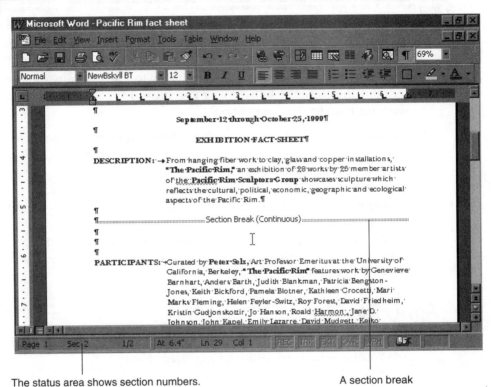

The status area shows section numbers.

A section break

The Layout Tab in Page Setup

When you double-click on the section break at the end of the section, Word displays the Layout tab of the Page Setup dialog box. You can also place the insertion point in the section being designed and choose File ➤ Page Setup; then click on the Layout tab.

Many choices in the Layout tab are covered elsewhere in this book, but the Section Start drop-down menu contains a number of section-specific items worth exploring. It is shown here:

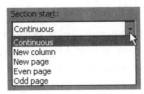

NOTE The options in the Section Start drop-down menu are the same as those in the Break dialog box (choose Insert ➤ Break).

You use the Section Start drop-down menu to tell Word where you want it to start printing the various sections of your document. You can select a different option for each section. Here are your options:

Continuous   Word's default section-printing strategy. Text from preceding sections will occupy the same page as the designated section, if there is enough room for the text from both sections.

Next Page   Word will always start new sections on new pages.

Even Page   Word starts printing the new section on an even-numbered page, even if it means leaving an odd-numbered page blank.

Odd Page   Word starts the new section on an odd-numbered page. This is a great way to ensure that new sections start on right-hand pages when designing documents for two-sided printing.

Apply To

Another area worth scrutinizing is the Apply To portion of the Layout tab. You use it to tell Word how far to go with your requested changes.

This Section   Changes affect only the section containing the insertion point.

This Point Forward   Changes are effective from the insertion point to the end of the document (or until you make other Layout tab changes at some further point).

Whole Document   Changes are applied to the entire document.

Copying Section Breaks

Section-formatting information is stored with section breaks in much the same way as paragraph formatting is stored with paragraph marks (¶). And you can copy section information by copying and pasting section breaks. It is even possible to place section breaks as AutoText items. See Chapter 14, *End Monotony with AutoText, AutoCorrect, and Insert*, for details.

Section breaks differ from paragraph marks in that a section break controls the information below it; a paragraph mark controls the information that precedes it.

Click on a break to select it. A thick insertion point will straddle the break line. You may find it easiest to do this in Normal view. Once a break is selected, you can then copy, cut, and so on.

Deleting Section Breaks

To delete a section break, select it as just described, and then press the backspace or Delete key. Text before the removed section break will take on the characteristics of the following material. It may take Word a moment to reformat and repaginate the document. Watch the status line and be patient.

Changing Page Orientation with Breaks

Using section breaks you can mix portrait and landscape page orientations in the same document. For instance, you could have a three-page memo with pages one and three in portrait mode (the text, perhaps) and the middle page in landscape mode (a wide spreadsheet, perhaps). Figure 11.2 illustrates the general concept with an article example.

NOTE Word flips headers, footers, page numbers, and other marginalia for you unless you override this. Therefore, if you've placed page numbers at the bottom of your pages, the landscape page(s) will have numbers at the right edge of the paper so that they read like the rest of the (flipped) text on the page(s).

Here are the general steps for changing orientation:

1. Position the insertion point where you want the break.
2. Choose Insert ➤ Break.
3. Choose the Next Page option.
4. Click on OK.
5. Move the insertion point to where you want the orientation to change again (if you do)—the beginning of page 3 in our example.
6. Insert another Next Page section break.
7. Position the insertion point in the section you want to change to landscape orientation.

PART

II

Formatting
Fundamentals

FIGURE 11.2

Use sections to
change page
orientation
mid-document.

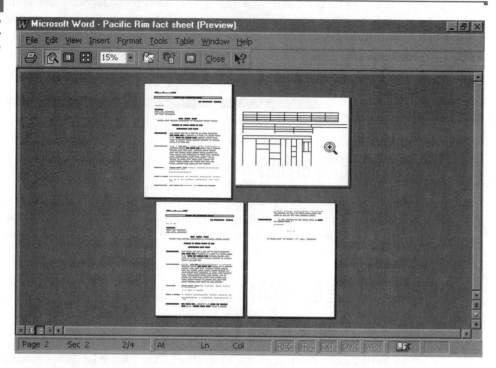

8. In the Paper Size tab in Page Setup (double-click in an unmarked part of the ruler or choose File ➤ Page Setup), mark the Landscape button in the Orientation area, first making sure that the Apply To drop-down menu says This Section.

9. Make other page layout choices in the other Page Setup tabs.

10. Preview and then print your work.

You can center a spreadsheet (or any landscape-oriented item) between the top and bottom margins of its page with the Vertical Alignment setting in the Layout tab of the Page Setup dialog box. Choose Center to create this effect.

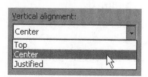

Time-Saving Section Tips

Here are some time-saving tips on using section breaks:

- Documents start out as one big section, and it is often best to wait until you are nearly finished with a document before breaking it into smaller sections. Do, however, think about the divisions in your document early on.

- Section formatting you apply when there is only one section affects the *entire* document. For instance, header and footer choices will be applied throughout.

- Set up templates and AutoText entries for complex section designs.

- One really great use of section breaks is to vary the number or formatting of columns with a document such as a newsletter, using the techniques discussed in this chapter.

PART

II

Formatting
Fundamentals

Chapter

12

Using Paragraph Styles and AutoFormat

FEATURING

Using Paragraph Styles and AutoFormat

Word's *style* features are responsible for much of its power and popularity. They also confuse and initially frustrate most new users. It is possible to plug along in Word for the rest of your life without knowing a whit about styles. That would be a shame, though. Learning about Word's standard styles, custom styles, and concepts such as Normal style and base styles can save you hundreds or even thousands of hours.

But things aren't as complicated as they seem. The two kinds of styles in Word—paragraph styles and character styles—are the equivalent of its two kinds of formatting, paragraph and font. If you understand these, you are on your way toward mastering styles. If you are not yet comfortable with font and paragraph formatting, take a look at Chapter 7, *Characters and Fonts,* and Chapter 8, *Formatting Paragraphs* before tackling styles.

When you combine your knowledge of styles with Word's AutoText, AutoCorrect, AutoFormat, and template features (covered elsewhere in this book), Word can make you a dramatically more efficient author, typist, and desktop publisher. If you work with other people on large, complex projects or if your organization wants a uniform look for all its printed documents, styles are essential.

Some styles do more than change the appearance of text. For example, heading styles make it easier to create a table of contents.

It's important to understand what styles are and how to modify them before you turn Word's AutoFormat feature loose on your documents. That way you can fine-tune things. Consume this chapter a little at a time. Try a few style experiments when you are not working on a rush project. Play with noncritical documents or use copies of important documents. If your eyes begin to glaze over or you find yourself pounding the desk with your fist, take a break. It will all make sense sooner than you think, and then all kinds of things will be easier than they ever were before. The surprising secret about styles is that once you learn to use them, they are *fun*.

What Are Styles?

Styles are collections of paragraph- and character-formatting decisions that you or others make and save using meaningful names. Styles make it easy for you to reuse complex formats without laboriously recreating them each time. "Built-in" styles are available in all Word documents, and each document can have its own collection of custom styles.

A paragraph's style is associated with its paragraph marker; so it is important to keep this marker with the paragraph. Paragraph styles can contain character-formatting information, but character formatting cannot contain information about paragraph styles.

The letter shown in Figure 12.1 illustrates nine styles. All of them are from Word's standard "gallery" of styles. In fact, the letter was created using one of the letter templates provided by Word. (*Templates* are simply collections of styles, sometimes with boilerplate text, designed to get you quickly working on everyday tasks.)

Some styles in the example are very simple. For instance, the style used for the body of the letter is called Body. It's just like the default text you use for typing except that Word adds 12 points of white space at the end of each paragraph. This "space after" separates paragraphs without your needing to type extra carriage returns. So you see, many of the formatting choices are ones you're familiar with already.

The Company Name style is more complex. It is a special Company Name heading plus 18 pt Times New Roman, all caps, condensed 1.7 pt, flush left, line spacing at least 30 pt, with a watermark...you get the idea. It's got more goodies.

As you will see later in this chapter, creating and naming your own styles like these is very easy. Developing clever style *strategies* takes much more forethought. Here's how it all works.

PART

II

Formatting
Fundamentals

FIGURE 12.1

This document uses many styles.

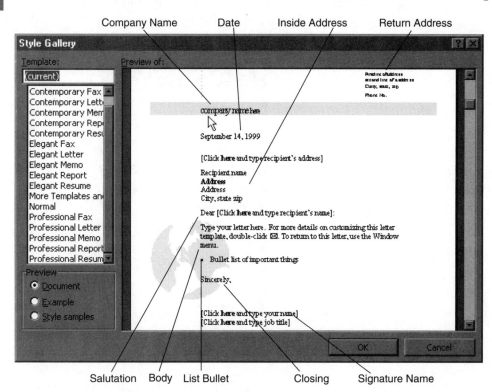

Company Name   Date   Inside Address   Return Address

Salutation   Body   List Bullet   Closing   Signature Name

Applying Styles from the Formatting Toolbar

Because Word comes with built-in styles, you can easily apply them to one or more paragraphs. Here are the general steps.

1. Either place the insertion point in a paragraph or select several paragraphs.

 NOTE

Word now shows you samples of the styles in its "improved" style list. There is no way to go back to the more compact list appearance.

2. Scroll through the drop-down style list on the Formatting toolbar to select the desired style. The items in the list will vary from document to document for reasons you'll soon understand.

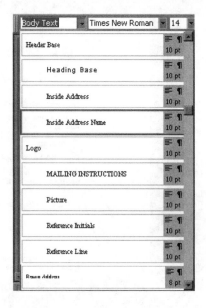

3. Click on a style name to apply it to the selected text. Your text will be reformatted using the selected style.

4. Choose Edit ➤ Undo (Ctrl+Z) if you don't like the results.

Applying Styles from the Keyboard

A few commonly used styles have keyboard shortcuts. To use them, select text or place the insertion point in the paragraph to be styled, and press one of the following key combinations:

Style	Keystrokes
Normal	Ctrl+Shift+N
Heading 1	Alt+Ctrl+1
Heading 2	Alt+Ctrl+2

Style	Keystrokes
Heading 3	Alt+Ctrl+3
List Bullet	Ctrl+Shift+L
Style shown in toolbar	Ctlr+Shift+S

TIP

The Edit ➤ Repeat keyboard shortcut (Ctrl+Y) works when applying styles. After you apply a style once, you can move the insertion point to other paragraphs and press Ctrl+Y to apply the new style where needed.

Defining Your Own Styles from the Formatting Toolbar

You can define your own styles, and many experienced users do that. But before spending hours reinventing the wheel, check out the styles already provided by Word. In fact, new styles you define are always based on existing styles. When you have satisfied yourself that what you need doesn't exist, follow these steps to create a new style:

1. Display the Formatting toolbar if it is not already in view.
2. Format at least one paragraph with all the characteristics you want in the new style.
3. Place the insertion point in the formatted paragraph that contains the style you'd like to capture. Make any last-minute changes if necessary.
4. As shown here, click *once* on the style box (the name portion of the drop-down style-name list). The style box will be highlighted, indicating that you can type a new style name.

5. Type a meaningful, unique style name and press Enter. Word saves the style information and adds the new name to the drop-down style list for the current document.

TIP

You can no longer type the first few characters of a style name to apply it as you could in earlier versions of Word.

Style Name Considerations

Style names can be a maximum of 253 characters, but shorter is often better. Names can contain any legal characters except backslashes (\), braces ({}), or semicolons (;).

WARNING

Word cares about capitalization in style names. For example, *Figure* and *figure* are two different names. Try to be consistent when naming similar styles in different documents. You'll learn why later in this chapter.

The Style Dialog Box

For styles, as is often the case with Word features, a dialog box contains powerful options not found on the Formatting toolbar. Choose Format ➤ Style, and Word displays the Style dialog box, as shown in Figure 12.2.

FIGURE 12.2

The Style dialog box

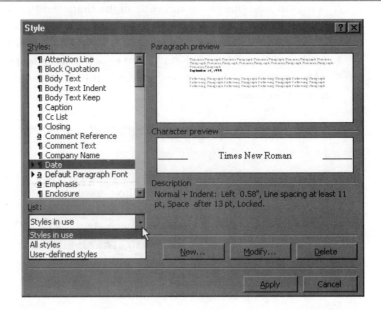

In the Style dialog box, you define new styles and rename, explore, list, or delete existing ones. It also serves other purposes, as you will soon see.

Defining Styles in the Style Dialog Box

To define a style via the Style dialog box, follow these steps:

1. Format at least one paragraph with all the characteristics you want in the new style.

2. Select (or place the insertion point in) a paragraph containing the desired format.

3. Open the Style dialog box.

4. Click on the New button.

5. Type a legal style name in the box provided.

6. Be sure the Based On box shows the appropriate base style, as discussed under "Basing One Style on Another" later in this chapter.

7. Click on OK to save the style.

Defining Keyboard Shortcuts for Styles

Word lets you assign keyboard shortcuts from the Modify Style Dialog box (click on the Modify button in the Style dialog box). You can also use the Keyboard button in the Customize dialog box (choose Tools ➤ Customize). See Chapter 32, *Personalizing Word*.

Basing One Style on Another

This time-saver is often a source of bewilderment for newcomers. It occasionally catches old pros off guard too. Word lets you build on styles or base one on another. You've seen examples of this in the sample customer letter at the beginning of the chapter. The letter's style called Body is built by starting with the Normal style and adding instructions to indent the first line of each paragraph. In other words, the style Body is based on the style Normal.

If you change the Normal style so that it uses Times New Roman instead of Arial, any paragraphs formatted with the Body style will change to Times New Roman too. That's both good news and bad news.

Word watches as you develop new styles and bases new styles on the styles you modify. For instance, if you type the last paragraph of a letter in a style that produces indented paragraphs and decide when you get to the end of the last paragraph in your letter that you want to create a new closure style, you might be tempted to press Enter to start a new paragraph and then drag the left indent marker to the left before typing *Sincerely*. If you then create a style named Closure based on the *Sincerely* line, Word bases that new style on the indented Body style, because that's the style you modified to create Closure. No problem at the moment, but wait.

If you ever change the Body style so that it indents lines differently, the Closure paragraph will change too.

Unless you are careful, you can create quite a chain reaction. Experienced users try to create one or two fairly simple base styles and tie most of the rest of their styles to those base styles, rather than basing each new style on the previous style. In our example, we could avoid the chain reaction effect by choosing Normal as the Based On style when defining the Closure style.

You use the Modify Style dialog box, shown in Figure 12.3, to force specific styles to be based on other styles of your choosing. It is important to use this box. If you don't, your new style will by default be based on the style of the paragraph the cursor is in, which may not be the right one.

To change an existing style's base, follow these steps:

1. Choose Format ➤ Style.
2. Select the style whose base you want to change.
3. Click on the Modify button.
4. In the Modify Style dialog box, choose a base style from the Based On list.
5. Make any other necessary changes in the Modify Style dialog box.
6. Click on OK when you're done.

FIGURE 12.3

Word lets you specify which style each style is based upon.

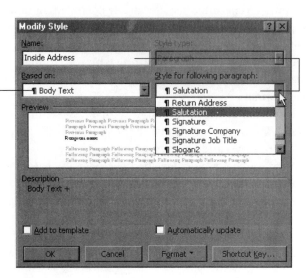

Tells which style to use as a basis for the new one

Salutation will follow Inside Address

TIP

To add a style you've *created* to the template upon which the document you are working is based, check the Add to Template option in the Modify Style dialog box. Many people find this unassuming little box easy to forget—but it is essential if you want your new or modified style to be available to future documents.

What's the appropriate base style? That will vary with your project. At first, you may find it less confusing to base all your styles on Normal. You can then experiment and observe carefully. You will soon learn from experience which combinations work best for you. Newcomers, beware. Play with *copies* of important documents, especially if it is 10 minutes before the Federal Express person is due to pick up your document.

Next Style

Frequently, you can predict the order in which styles will be used. When you type letters, for instance, you know that the To style will always be used after the From style. In reports and manuals, headings are usually followed immediately by body text, and so on.

In the Modify Style dialog box, you specify which style Word will flip to when you finish typing a paragraph and press Enter. Often, you want a paragraph in the same style as its predecessor. This is the default condition when creating styles.

But it is possible to specify different next styles. Follow these steps:

1. Choose Format ➤ Style.
2. Select the style you plan to modify.
3. Click on the Modify button.
4. In the Modify Style dialog box, choose a "next" style from the Style for Following Paragraph list, shown in Figure 12.3 earlier in this chapter.
5. Make any other necessary changes in the Modify Style dialog box.
6. Click on OK when done.

Finding Out Which Styles Have Been Used

The obvious way to sniff out styles is to place the insertion point in the text of interest and look at the Formatting toolbar indicators (the style list, which buttons are pressed, and so on). But there are several ways besides the obvious to see which styles and character formatting have been applied. The first is to print out a style list.

PART

II

Formatting
Fundamentals

Printing a Style List

It is often useful to have a printed list of styles and their descriptions. This can help you keep things consistent in a large organization, and it can help you troubleshoot formatting problems in complex documents. To print style information, follow these steps:

1. Open the document.

2. Choose File ➤ Print or press the Ctrl+P keyboard shortcut.

3. Choose Styles from the drop-down Print What list.

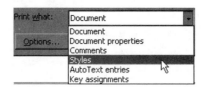

4. Click on OK.

Open a document and print a style list of your own. Take a moment to examine it. Pretty slick, eh?

The Style Gallery

This feature is a little like the Smithsonian Institution. You can spend days exploring it and learn something new each visit. It's an excellent place to see the seemingly endless collection of styles provided with Word's templates. The first figure in this chapter showed one use of the Style Gallery (previewing the effect of a template style on your document). Figure 12.4 shows another way to use the Gallery.

By clicking on the Style Samples button in the Style Gallery, shown in Figure 12.4, you can see examples of all the styles for a document or template. If you are currently working on a project, you can also see how the project would look if you applied styles from various templates. If you like what you see, you can even have Word automatically apply the styles to your current project. You need not have a project in the works to visit the Gallery, but if you think you might want to reformat something, open that document first and make it the active Word project before you begin. Here are the general steps:

1. Open a Word project if you think you might want to reformat it.

2. Open the Gallery with the Format ➤ Style Gallery command.

3. Click on the Style Samples button.

4. Choose a style from the Template list.

FIGURE 12.4

The Style Gallery showing you examples of a template's pre-defined styles

Choose templates to see their style collections.

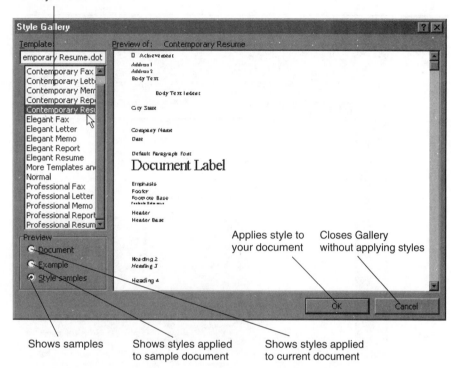

Applies style to your document

Closes Gallery without applying styles

Shows samples

Shows styles applied to sample document

Shows styles applied to current document

PART

II

Formatting Fundamentals

5. Wait a moment while Word displays the samples.
6. Choose different template names if you want to see samples of other style collections.
7. Click on the Document button if you want to see the styles automatically applied to the document you have open.
8. Click on OK to close the gallery *and apply the new styles,* or click on Cancel to close the gallery without changing your document.

Reveal Formats—the Cartoon Balloon

Another way to see style settings is to use Word's Reveal Formats command, or what I call the style "cartoon balloon." Here's how it works.

1. Choose Help ➤ What's This? (or press Shift+F1).
2. The mouse pointer gets a big question mark.

3. Point to a paragraph and click to read about formatting, as illustrated in Figure 12.5.

4. Press the Esc key to turn off the Reveal Formats display.

FIGURE 12.5

The Style "cartoon balloon" in use

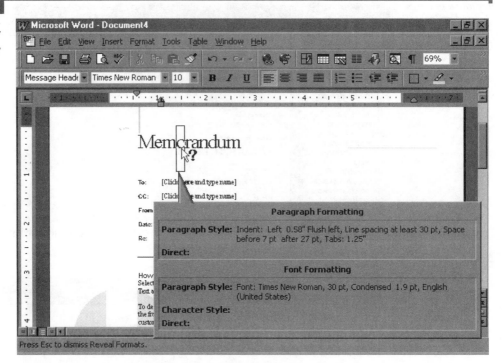

Displaying Format Names On-Screen

Here's another interesting trick. You can display style information at the left edge of the screen in something called the *style area*, illustrated in Figure 12.6.

To display the style area, follow these steps:

1. Switch to Normal or Outline view.

2. Choose Tools ➤ Options.

3. Select the View tab.

4. Choose a style-area width (1", perhaps) from the Style Area Width box in the Window section of the View tab. Figure 12.7 shows where to do this.

5. Click on OK.

6. Style names will appear at the left of the screen in Normal and Outline views.

7. To remove them, repeat steps 1 through 5, choosing 0 (zero) for the Style Area Width.

FIGURE 12.6

You can see format names in the style area if you enable it.

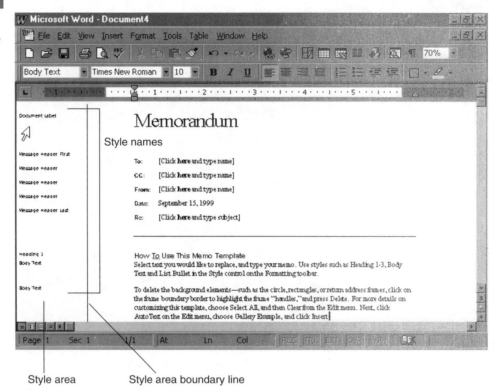

Style area   Style area boundary line

When and Where Styles Are Saved

Styles are saved with your document, and they are saved only when you save the document. This is yet another good reason to get in the habit of saving early and often. If your computer crashes after you've spent several hours setting up a complex collection of new styles or if you accidentally click on No to the "Save Changes?" prompt when you close a document, you will not be happy.

Word's Standard Styles

Word's designers have created hundreds of standard styles that are used by the footnote, outline, index, table-of-contents, page-numbering, header, and footer features.

FIGURE 12.7

Specify the width of the style area in the View tab of the Options dialog box (Tools ➤ Options).

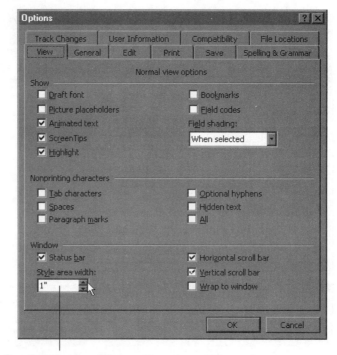

Specify style area width here (0 means no style area).

Many of the templates for letters, brochures, newsletters, and other documents have their own predefined styles. Take some time now to open a few documents based on these templates and explore their styles. As a starter, try this:

1. Choose File ➤ New.
2. Click on the Reports tab and double-click on Contemporary Report.
3. Take a few moments to look it over. Could you use this template as is? How might you modify it to make it more useful?

Styles That Word Applies Automatically

Word applies certain styles automatically, as listed here:

Style	When Word Applies
Annotation Text	Comments inserted by the Annotation command
Annotation Reference	Initials of person who inserted the comment
Caption	Captions and table and figure titles

Style	When Word Applies
Footer	Footer info
All Footnotes	Text in a footnote
All Endnotes	Text in an endnote
Footnote Reference	Numbers and characters used as reference marks
Endnote Reference	Reference marks
Header	Header info
Index l–Index 9	Index entries created with the Index and Tables
Line Number	Automatic line numbers
Macro Text	Text of a Visual Basic macro
Page Number	Automatic page numbers
TOC 1–TOC 9, Table of Contents	TOC entries
Table of Figures	Automatic figure numbering

Additional Formatting and Styles

It is possible to override or embellish styles with additional character formatting, but there are some caveats.

You already know how to make character-based changes from the Formatting tool-bar. Those changes will work in styled paragraphs, but they interact with formatting elements in your styles. Read on.

Reapply/Update or Modify Styles

If you ask Word to apply a style to a paragraph that already uses that style (applying Normal to an already Normal paragraph, for instance), Word displays this strange and powerful dialog box:

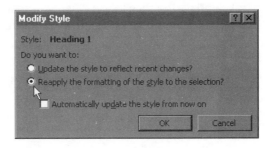

PART

II

Formatting Fundamentals

To Restore Styles

This box serves two purposes. First, it lets you reapply a style to a paragraph that you have inadvertently messed up. Suppose you accidentally dragged the first-line indent marker in a Body paragraph, and the paragraph no longer looks like the others. By choosing the Body style again from the Formatting toolbar you will get a chance to reapply your Body style and repair the errant paragraph. Follow these steps to restore a style:

1. Select the paragraph, paragraphs, or characters you want to restore.
2. Choose the desired style from the Formatting toolbar's list.
3. If asked to reapply or update, choose Reapply.
4. Click on OK.

To Redefine a Style

The second use of this dialog box is to let you quickly update a style. Suppose you hate the first-line indent you've used for body text. Change the indent in any one Body style paragraph; then select Body from the Style list. Click on the Update button and click on OK. Word updates the Body style using the new indent from your sample paragraph. All your Body paragraphs will be changed. To update a style, follow these steps:

1. Select any paragraph or character formatted with the style to be changed.
2. Make the desired appearance changes (indents, underlining, and so on).
3. From the Formatting toolbar's list, choose the style *originally* used for the formatting.
4. When you see the Update/Reapply choice, choose Update.
5. Click on OK.

Strange things sometimes happen when you redefine or reapply styles to manually embellished paragraphs, however. Although the interaction of manually applied formatting and styles may seem almost random sometimes, it is not. Read about it at the very end of this chapter.

NOTE

A new feature of the Modify Style dialog box is the Automatically Update the Style From Now On checkbox. This box is not checked by default. If you want Word to automatically update the style in use when you make changes to paragraphs formatted with a style, use this checkbox. However, automatic updates to your carefully devised styles can quickly get out of hand; so use caution in making changes when this feature is turned on.

Deleting Styles

You cannot delete Word's built-in styles (headings and Normal, for instance), but you can remove custom ones you've created and many of the fonts provided with Word's templates. To delete unwanted styles, select them in the Style dialog box and click on the Delete button, as shown in Figure 12.8.

When asked to confirm, click on Yes. All paragraphs formatted with a deleted style revert to the document's Normal style. To delete a style, follow these steps:

1. Choose Format ➤ Style to open the Style dialog box.
2. Click on the style you want to delete in the Styles list (scroll, if necessary).
3. Click on Delete.
4. Click on Yes to confirm the deletion.

TIP

You can use the Undo list from the Standard toolbar to replace accidentally deleted styles.

PART

II

Formatting
Fundamentals

FIGURE 12.8

*Deleting
unwanted styles*

Select a style…

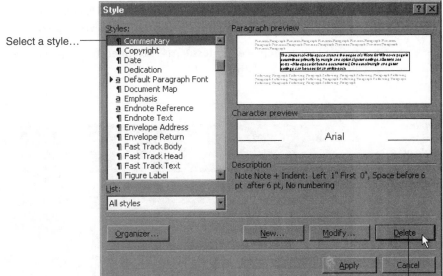

… Then click to delete.

Renaming Styles

Styles can be renamed using the Style dialog box. Follow these steps:

1. Choose Format ➤ Style to open the Style dialog box.
2. Click on the style you want to rename in the Styles list (scroll, if necessary).
3. Click on the Modify button. Word displays the Modify Style dialog box (shown earlier, in Figure 12.3).
4. Edit the name in the Name box.
5. Make any other desired changes while in the Modify Style dialog box.
6. Click on OK.

Word will not let you change a style's name to one that already exists in the document. If you try to do so, a message will appear, informing you that the name already belongs to another style. Click on OK and type another name.

Remember—Word cares about capitalization when you name styles. The names *Salutation* and *salutation* are not the same.

Finding and Replacing Styles

Style-change junkies rejoice. Word lets you search for and replace styles. Although Word's powerful Replace feature is fully described in Chapter 16, *Finding and Replacing*, here's a quick style replacement how-to. Refer to Figure 12.9 as you read through this section.

1. Choose Edit ➤ Replace or press Ctrl+H to open the Replace dialog box.
2. Click on the More button.

FIGURE 12.9

The Replace feature lets you locate or swap styles.

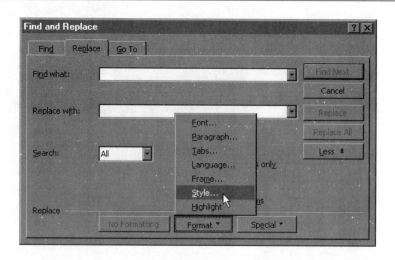

3. Place the insertion point in the Find What box.

4. Choose Style from the drop-down Format menu (see Figure 12.9). Word displays a list of possible styles in the Find Style dialog box:

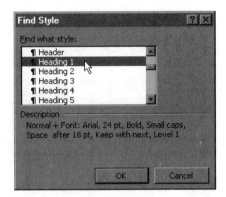

5. Select the style you want to replace (Heading 1, for instance) and click on OK. The name of the style will appear in the Format portion of the Find What area.

6. Move the insertion point to the Replace With portion of the dialog box.

7. Choose Style from the drop-down Format menu again.

8. Choose the new style from the resulting Replace Style dialog box list (Header, for example):

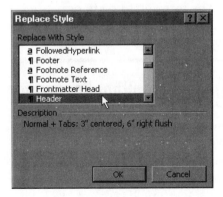

9. Click on OK.

10. Tell Word whether you want to search the whole document (All), up from the insertion point, or down from the insertion point.

PART

II

Formatting
Fundamentals

11. When you are ready, click on Find Next and Replace or on Replace All, as appropriate. For instance, to replace all Heading 1 style occurrences with Header styles, you'd select Replace All:

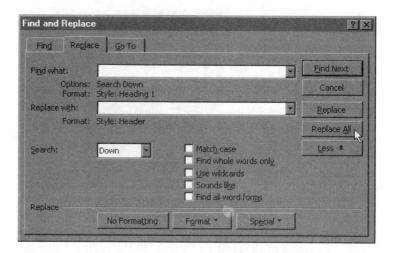

NOTE

Chapter 16, *Finding and Replacing,* covers finding and replacing in detail. If you can't wait, experiment on copies of important documents rather than the real things. And be sure you turn off format searching when you are finished. Word will continue to search only for text in the style you've specified until you click on No Formatting.

Transferring Styles to Other Documents

After you've spent time setting up complex styles, it would be nice to reuse them in new projects. Word provides several ways to do this. For repetitive tasks, consider setting up Template documents that contain styles, as described in Chapter 13, *Templates, Wizards, and Sample Documents,* and AutoText entries, as described in Chapter 14, *End Monotony with AutoText, AutoCorrect, and Insert AutoText.*

If you have only a style or two you want to copy from one document (the source) to another (the destination), follow these steps:

1. Copy some text from the source document containing the style of interest and paste it into the destination document needing the style. If it is a paragraph style, be sure to include the paragraph mark in your selection.

2. Word will bring over the style with the text.

WARNING

Remember that if the destination document has a style name identical to the style being copied from the source, the destination document will reformat the incoming text rather than take on the new style. Moreover, if you copy more than 50 styles at once, the source document's entire style sheet will be automatically copied to the destination document.

It is also possible to merge style sheets, which copies unique styles from one document to another and modifies styles with identical names.

Think of the document containing styles you want to copy as the *source* document and the document receiving the new styles as the *destination* document. Here's how to merge style sheets:

1. With styles properly named and saved, work in the source document.

2. Choose Format ➤ Style to open the Style dialog box.

3. Click on the Organizer button to open the Organizer dialog box, shown in Figure 12.10.

4. Select the Styles tab if it is not already foremost.

Formatting
Fundamentals

FIGURE 12.10

*The Organizer
dialog box*

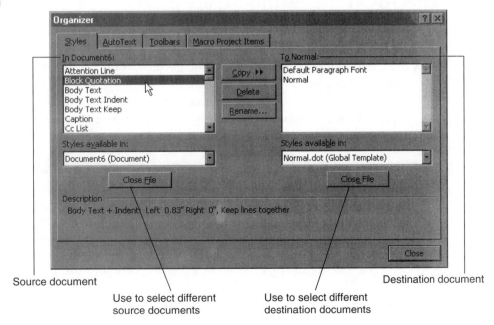

Source document   Destination document

Use to select different   Use to select different
source documents   destination documents

5. Note the two Styles Available In text boxes at the bottom of the Organizer dialog box. If the name of the destination file is not available in the Styles Available In box on the left, click on the Close File button beneath. It will change into an Open File button. Click on it again and choose the desired source file using standard Windows file-opening techniques.

6. The file Normal will probably be specified as the destination or To file on the right side of the dialog box. This is telling you that Word wants to copy new styles to the Normal template to make them available to all new documents. If you want to make the style or styles you are copying globally available, leave the To setting as Normal. If you want to add the style(s) to only a selected document or template, click on the *right* Close File button (note that there are two). It will change to an Open File button. Click on it again and choose the desired destination file using standard Windows file-opening techniques.

7. When the source and destination files have been properly identified, select the styles you want to copy in the left scrolling list. Click to choose a single style, Shift+click to select ranges, or hold down the Ctrl key while you selectively click on noncontiguous styles.

8. With the desired styles selected, click on Copy.

9. Use the Delete or Rename buttons as necessary.

10. Open other source or destination files as necessary. Click on Close when you're done.

Tips for Transferring Styles

Here are a few tips worth noting. First, save any changes to the source document before attempting to copy styles. Doing so records the current styles for the source document. Next, inspect the source and destination documents for possible style-name problems. Remember that Word styles are case-sensitive—*body* and *Body* are different style names. As you may have guessed, this can work for or against you. Consider printing out style sheets for both the source and destination documents and comparing them *before* you copy styles.

 TIP

Other Word commands that exchange style information will bring over styles as necessary. For instance, Subscribe, Link, AutoText, and Paste Special all attempt to bring styles with them.

Tips for Using Styles

- Get to know the styles provided in Word's templates before creating your own.

- Establish organization-wide style sheets and style-naming conventions. This will make it easy for groups of people to work on projects together.

- When experimenting with styles, work on document copies. This is particularly important for new users working on complex documents containing interrelated styles.

- Establish one or two base styles for complex documents. They need not be based on Word's Normal style, particularly if the look of the document is radically different from your normal work.

- Because Word's AutoFormat feature (described shortly) works only on text that has been formatted with styles, you'll want to get in the habit of using at least the Normal style when you type. Fortunately, this happens automatically unless you tell Word to do otherwise, as Word always formats typing in your new documents as Normal. If you import documents from other programs or import plain ASCII text, however, you'll probably need to select it and apply at least Normal style.

AutoFormat

AutoFormat inspects your document and suggests formatting changes that you can accept or reject. Consider this "before" glimpse at a press release that was formatted entirely in Normal:

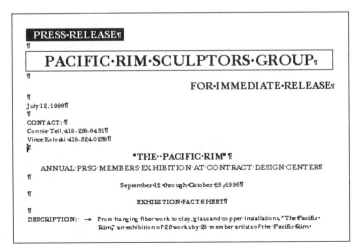

Word can locate and reformat headings, change straight quotes to curly quotes, and more. Here are the general steps and an example of AutoFormat at work:

1. Open the document you want to reformat.

2. Choose Format ➤ AutoFormat. Word displays the AutoFormat dialog box:

3. If you want to change the way AutoFormat works, click on the Options button. Click to indicate which formatting tasks you don't want it to perform. For instance, if you don't want Word to preserve any styles you've already applied, click on the Styles box to remove the checkmark.

4. Select the AutoFormat and Review Each Change button if you want to see and approve each proposed AutoFormat change.

5. When you have specified any necessary changes to Word's usual AutoFormatting habits, click on OK. Word displays the AutoFormat dialog box.

6. Click on OK.

7. Word will go to work. If you selected the review each change option, in a few moments, you'll see another AutoFormat dialog box where you can review changes:

8. To see and review each proposed change, choose Review Changes. To apply further formatting via the Style Gallery, click on the Style Gallery button; otherwise, simply accept or reject all changes.

9. Inspect your finished product carefully to be sure that you got what you wanted.

Typically, you'll want to polish Word's work. For instance, take a look at two of the pages in our sample document (see Figure 12.11).

AutoFormat removed all the highlighting in the first line and emphasized it with font changes, figuring out that it was a document title. AutoFormat was then able to emphasize additional text by converting it to special headings. AutoFormat spotted likely paragraph headings, increased their point sizes, changed their fonts, and added paragraph spacing nicely. It did not recognize the contact name list as a candidate for being emphasized, though, and therefore did not add bullets or any other formatting to these names.

So, although AutoFormat does a nice job considering that this whole document was formatted as Normal text, you can still add some polish to all but the simplest projects.

FIGURE 12.11

The effects of formatting an all-"normal" document

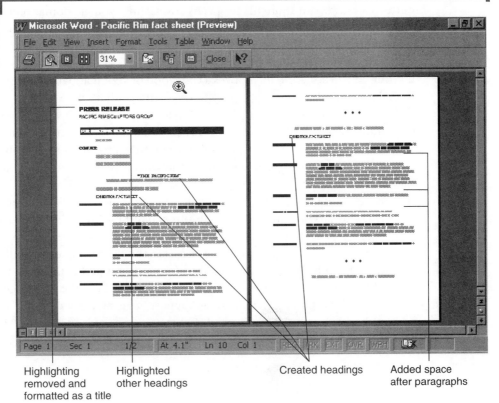

Highlighting removed and formatted as a title

Highlighted other headings

Created headings

Added space after paragraphs

Manual Formatting and Styles

As promised, here's an explanation of how styles and manual formats interact (although, perhaps *collide* is a better word). Don't feel bad if this seems confusing. It is. First, here are some important concepts to review:

- By now, you should know the difference between font and paragraph formatting. Paragraph formatting describes what happens to all the characters in a paragraph—such as indenting and line spacing. Font formatting can be applied selectively to all or to only a few characters in a paragraph. For this reason, some former versions of Word referred to font formatting as "character formatting," and this might still be the better name for it.
- You'll probably remember that some font-formatting choices toggle. Specifying bold twice, for instance, turns bold font formatting on and then off. Other font-formatting features don't toggle. Choose Helvetica twice, for example, and nothing special happens.

Now for the interesting stuff. When you use menu choices, the Formatting toolbar buttons, or keyboard shortcuts to specify formatting, you are doing something called *manual* formatting. When you use a style to format text, that's called (yep) *style* formatting. There's a difference, as you will soon see.

When you initially define a new style, Word looks at any paragraph and font formatting you've done and memorizes a collection of your manual-formatting decisions. If all the text in the sample paragraph(s) is identical, that's a no-brainer.

But what if you ask Word to a create a style from a sample paragraph or paragraphs containing inconsistent formatting? What should it do, for instance, about bold if some of the text in the sample paragraph is bold and some isn't—ignore bold formatting, make everything bold, lock up your computer? And what if some of the lines you've selected for the sample are single-spaced and others double-spaced? Or how about inconsistent spacing before and after selected paragraphs, or wacky indents? (Variety has its price.)

Word needs to come to some conclusions about these inconsistencies because when you apply styles, they must format all the specified text consistently.

Sooooo, Word looks at the first 255 characters in your sample text and decides whether to include their manually applied formatting as part of the style. If a particular manual format (bold, for instance) appears in at least half of the first 255 characters of your sample, it becomes part of the style. Suppose, for example, you have a 600-character paragraph and at least 128 of the first 255 characters are bold. The style will include bold as one of its formatting features.

Any text you subsequently apply this style to will receive bold formatting. However, if at least 128 of the first 255 characters are not bold, the style will not contain bold formatting, even if the last 300 characters in the text sample are bold. So far so good? Read on.

Once you've defined a style (1" left and right indents, plus all bold text, for instance), selecting unformatted, plain vanilla text, and applying the new style will make the text conform to the style's formatting definitions (indented, bold text, in our example).

But what if the text you apply this style to already has other manual formatting such as bold or italic—or what if you later try to apply manual formats to text you've formatted with your indented bold style? "Well," as high-ranking government officials are known to say, "that depends."

Let's take it one situation at a time—but first, a word or two about formatting *layers*, as Microsoft likes to call them.

Formatting Layers

Suppose you use a style to format otherwise plain-vanilla text. You would be applying something Microsoft refers to as the *style-formatting layer*. The once-plain text would take on the formatting characteristics defined by the style (indented, bold Times, let's say).

Then, suppose you manually format some of those same characters—italicize a word or two, increase the point size of the first character, and so on. You've added something called the *manual-formatting layer*.

Format Layers and the Replace Command

What's that? You wonder about Word's Replace command and format layers? Your concern is justified. When you run around globally replacing styles or manually applied formatting with the Replace command (described in Chapter 16), you'll need to keep in mind Word's behavior when it encounters combinations of manual formatting and styles. The Replace command causes the same toggling and other behavior problems as human intervention.

Removing Styles and Retaining Formats

Occasionally you might want to remove all the styles in a document without affecting the appearance of the document. You'll want to remove the Bold Indent style you've created, for instance, but you want the text to remain bold and indented. Some people do this before sharing Word documents with WordPerfect DOS users, for example. Here are the steps:

1. Save your document with the Rich Text Format choice in the Save As dialog box. (It's in the Save File As Type scrolling list.)
2. Word will save the document. The resulting document can be used by Word for DOS, WordPerfect for DOS, and many other DOS word-processing programs.

PART III

Productivity Tools

LEARN TO:

- *Speed editing with automated features*

- *Polish your writing with the Thesaurus, Spelling Checker, and Grammar Checker*

- *Streamline document revisions with Find and Replace*

- *Create professional results with templates, Wizards, and Outline view*

Chapter

13

Templates, Wizards, and Sample Documents

FEATURING

Chapter 13

Templates, Wizards, and Sample Documents

Word's *templates* are read-only documents containing styles and other design elements that you can use to create or restyle your own documents. *Wizards* are computerized assistants. Like you, Wizards also use templates to create documents, after asking some questions and making a few design decisions on their own.

In addition, some Word templates have pointers embedded right in their example text that explain how to personalize them to suit your own needs. These are called *sample documents,* and they are great learning tools. If you did a complete installation of Word, these files are all in their own subfolders within the folder called Templates.

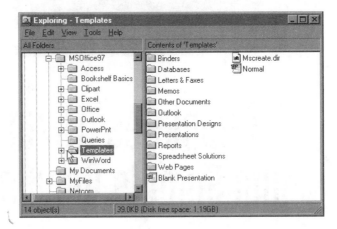

Look for the Templates subfolder in your MSOffice folder. Let's begin our tour with templates.

Templates

You can use templates in at least four ways:

- Start a new project based on a template shipped with Word
- Modify an existing project by choosing a template and completely reformatting your work in the template's styles
- Copy selected styles from templates for use in a project
- Create and save new templates of your own

NOTE

All new documents are based on Word's Normal template, unless you specify otherwise. As discussed in Chapter 14, *End Monotony with AutoText, AutoCorrect, and Insert AutoText,* Normal includes hundreds of predefined styles, and it may suit your needs just fine. To make your documents look really snazzy though, consider using Word's other templates.

To make a template for your own work, follow these steps:

1. Click on the New button on the Standard toolbar and locate the template upon which you want to base your own template.
2. Be sure the Document radio button is selected and click on OK.
3. Make any formatting, design, or other decisions you want stored in the template.
4. When you save the document, select the Word Template file type in the Save As Type list, and then click on OK. Whenever you open the document from now on, it will have the styles and design elements you've specified.

Template Types

Word's standard templates come in as many as three "flavors." Microsoft refers to these as *Template types*:

- Contemporary
- Elegant
- Professional

Each type uses fonts and effects chosen to give a document a different "mood." For instance, the Contemporary Letter template uses Times New Roman, and the Professional uses Arial. The Company Name style in the Contemporary Letter template includes shading, the Elegant type does not, and so on.

By always using templates of the same type, you can give your work a consistent look. And when creating other documents based on templates, you can copy the existing styles using the tricks you learned in Chapter 12, *Using Paragraph Styles and AutoFormat*. Many templates come in the three types discussed above, but not all templates come in all types.

TIP

No matter what kind of document you want to create (newsletter, manual, invoice, time sheet, press release, brochure, and so on), chances are Word has a template for it. Because these templates were intended to be used together, some even sharing a common design, one way to ensure some consistency within your company is to standardize the use of Word's templates.

PART

III

Productivity Tools

Using Templates

Once you know what each template looks like, you can quickly start new projects by selecting the appropriate template whenever you start. Choose File ➤ New, and click on the tab you want in the New dialog box. Then simply choose the template you want by name:

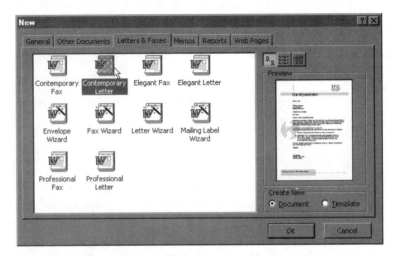

Notice that you can preview templates here. You can also start Wizards from the New dialog box. Double-click on your choice; then simply add your own text by clicking on the appropriate areas of the template and replacing the labels with your own words.

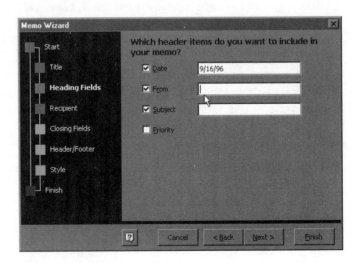

But first, it's helpful to know what the various templates look like. You could load each one and take a look, but there's an easier way.

Exploring Templates

Use the Style Gallery (choose Format ➤ Style Gallery) to preview templates. Here are the general steps.

1. Choose File ➤ New to open a new document.
2. Choose Normal (the Default template).
3. Choose Format ➤ Style Gallery. You will see a window like the one in Figure 13.1.
4. Select the template you want from the scrolling list.
5. Click on the Example button in the Preview area to see a preview of the template's appearance.
6. Scroll to make sure you see the entire template. They are often several pages long.

FIGURE 13.1

You can preview templates in the Style Gallery.

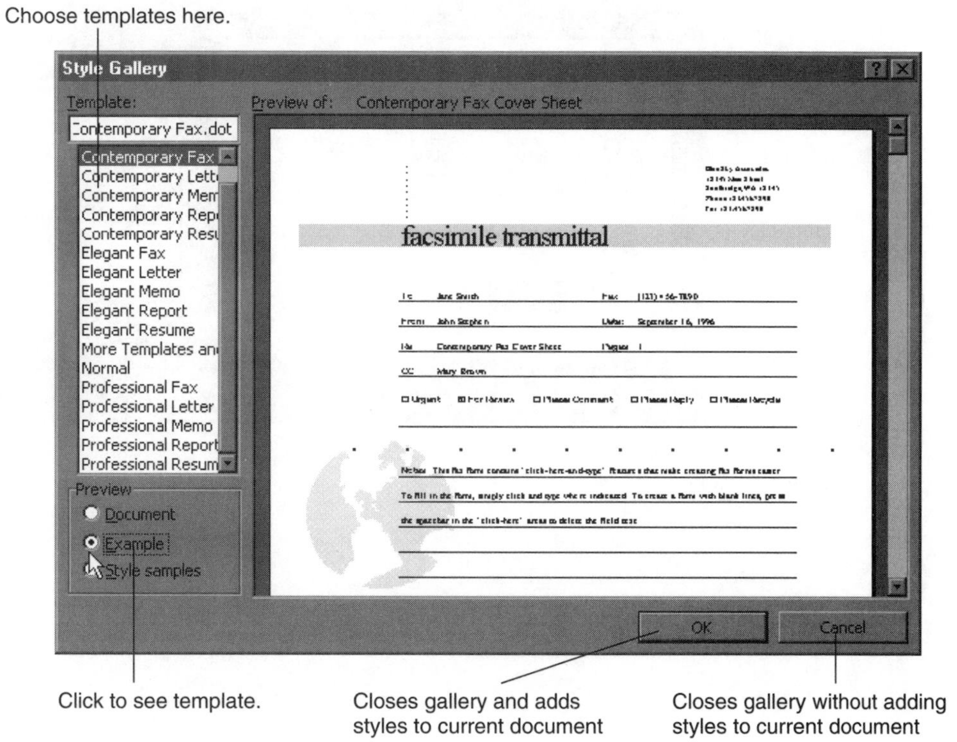

Choose templates here.

Click to see template.

Closes gallery and adds styles to current document

Closes gallery without adding styles to current document

PART

III

Productivity Tools

7. Click on Style Samples to see the names of styles displayed in the styles themselves. Unfortunately, these are often too small to read.

8. When you are done previewing, click on Cancel. (Clicking on OK copies the styles to your current document but does not load the other template elements—the boilerplate text, and so on.)

Modifying Templates

You can change templates just as you would change a Word document. The only difference is one additional step that you must take when saving your work. Suppose you want to update the Professional Letter template to include your company logo. Follow these steps:

1. Choose File ➤ New to open a new document based on the Professional Letter template:

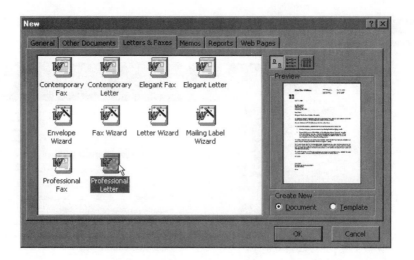

2. Make the changes, such as adding your logo and other embellishments.

September 16, 1996

[Click here and type recipient's address]

3. Print out a sample and check your work.

4. When you are satisfied, choose File ➤ Save As.

5. Type the same filename as the old template if you want to replace that template, or type a new filename to keep *both* the old and new. Be sure you choose Document Template in the Save As Type box:

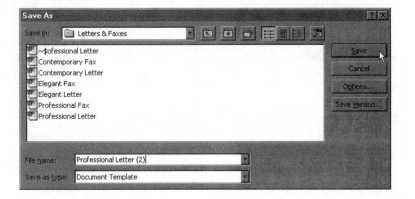

If you always save modified templates under new names, you'll have the original templates available for modifying in different ways should the need arise.

PART

III

Productivity Tools

Tips for Using Templates

- Word often gets information from the User Info tab in the Options dialog box (choose Tools ➤ Options). Be sure your info is up-to-date by selecting that tab.

- In templates that have inside addresses, signature blocks, and other multiline items, consider the Shift+↵ trick to keep lines all in the same paragraph. This eliminates unwanted "space before" in each address line, for example.

- Switching types (from Elegant to Professional, for instance) can give your documents a whole new look. And you can mix and match styles by copying selected styles from other documents.

- Some of the more complex templates (such as Manual) use a wealth of Word features, including table of contents, index entries, and so on.

- Don't forget other time-savers such as the Tools ➤ Envelopes and Labels command. They work with templates too.

- Use Find and Replace to speed the task of changing information such as product names that repeat many times in the same document.

- When experimenting with important projects, save an unmodified extra copy of your "normal" documents just in case. Sometimes converting from Normal to a different type and then back to Normal will create troublesome results.

Wizards—The Computer Wants Your Job

You've seen Wizards at work elsewhere in this book, but because they often use templates, they are worth mentioning here as well. Wizards ask you questions and then use your responses to design documents for you. Take the Web Page Wizard, for instance.

You start Wizards with the File ➤ New command. Select the Web Page Wizard from the Web Pages tab list, and it will appear:

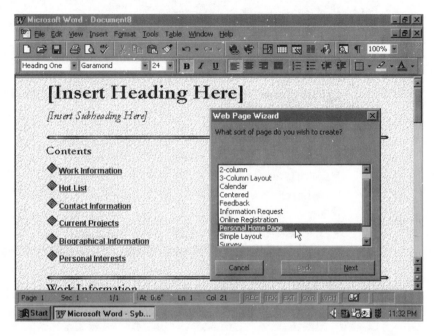

TIP

Turn off the Show ¶ feature for better-looking previews.

You'll be asked questions about your hopes and dreams for the new document. Do you want a personal Web page or an interactive online registration form? Do you want the page design to be festive, jazzy, or outdoorsy? Do you want fries with that? You get the idea.

All the while, Word shows you a preview, making changes as you answer questions. The preview is very useful because you can try several settings in each window to see which you prefer. When you click on the Finish button, the Web Page Wizard works its magic (see Figure 13.2). Simply type in the appropriate information in the Web page headings, and you're set to establish a presence on the Internet.

For more on Wizards, see Chapter 18, *The Document Shop*, and Chapter 35, *Using Word to Create a Web Page*.

PART
III

Productivity Tools

FIGURE 13.2

The Web Page Wizard's work

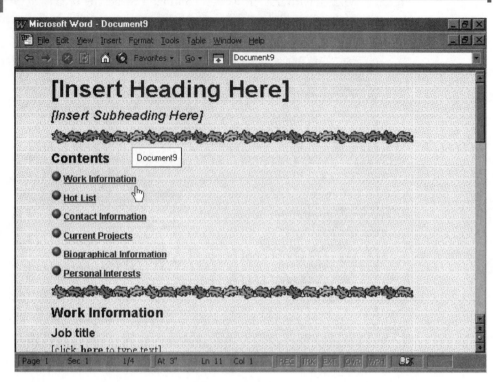

Chapter

14

End Monotony with AutoText, AutoCorrect, and Insert

FEATURING

Chapter 14

End Monotony with AutoText, AutoCorrect, and Insert

Word offers three convenient ways to store, retrieve, and insert frequently used text, graphics, and other document elements. The techniques employ Word's AutoText, AutoCorrect, and Insert commands. Each has strengths and weaknesses. Read about all three approaches before you develop a strategy and spend hours personalizing your computer.

Using AutoText

The *AutoText* feature provides an easy way to store and retrieve "boilerplate" text, graphics, addresses, letter closings, memo distribution lists, tables, logos, and just about anything else that you can create with Word.

You can store AutoText entries with the Normal template so that they are always available, or you can store them with other templates for specialty projects.

Users of older versions of Word (2 and earlier) will notice that there are no "standard" AutoText entries analogous to those in the old Glossaries. These functions (inserting dates and times, for instance) are handled in other ways, described elsewhere in this and other chapters.

Creating AutoText Entries

To create an AutoText entry, simply select whatever you want to memorialize, and choose Insert ➤ AutoText ➤ New. Word displays the Create AutoText dialog box, as shown in Figure 14.1.

If you want to store the paragraph formatting with the entry, be sure to include paragraph marks in your selection. (Even if you store an entry *with* paragraph formatting, you can later insert the entry *without* formatting if you wish.) Click on OK.

FIGURE 14.1

Name and store AutoText entries with the Insert ➤ AutoText ➤ New command.

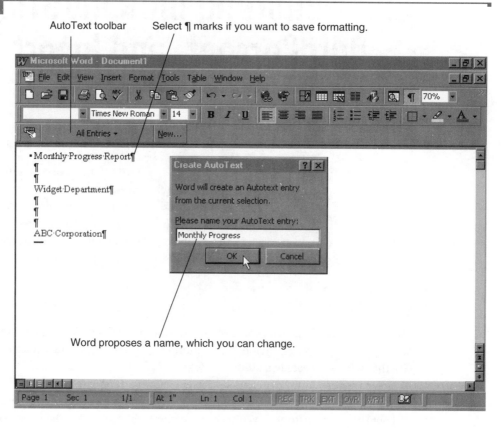

If you find that you make AutoText entries frequently, consider adding the Auto-Text button to one of your toolbars. It looks like a keyboard with a finger pointing at it. (See Chapter 32, *Personalizing Word*, for details.) You can also display the AutoText toolbar, which contains an AutoText button and a New button, by selecting View ➤ Toolbars ➤ AutoText.

Modifying AutoText Entries

To modify an AutoText entry, follow these steps:

1. Before saving an entry, you are given a chance to review and change the automatic entry name that Word assigns, as shown in Figure 14.1. To change the name, simply type a new one in the name box. Names can be a maximum of 32 characters, and spaces are permitted.

2. By default, Word stores all AutoText entries in the All Active Templates (Normal.dot) template choice in the Look In list box. If you want an entry to be available whenever you use Word, leave the default choice All Active Templates (Normal.dot) in the drop-down Look In list. To attach an entry to a different template, choose Insert ➤ AutoText ➤ AutoText and select one from the Look In drop-down list, as shown in Figure 14.2.

3. Click on the OK button.

4. If you want to change the AutoText entry in the AutoCorrect dialog box shown in Figure 14.2, delete the entry in the Enter AutoText Entries Here text box. The Preview area, which shows the phrase Word will insert, remains unchanged. For example, deleting Monthly Progress from the text box does not change the words *Monthly Progress Report* shown in the Preview area. You can, however, type a shorter entry, such as **MPR**, in the text box, which will still stand for Monthly Progress Report. Click on the Add button upon completion of your modified AutoText entry.

It is often good to select the space *after* text being memorialized when creating an AutoText entry (that is, the single space created by the spacebar, not the blank line created by the paragraph return). This will save you from typing a space each time you insert the entry later.

PART

III

Productivity Tools

FIGURE 14.2

To display the AutoText tab in the AutoCorrect dialog box, choose Insert ➤ AutoText ➤ AutoText.

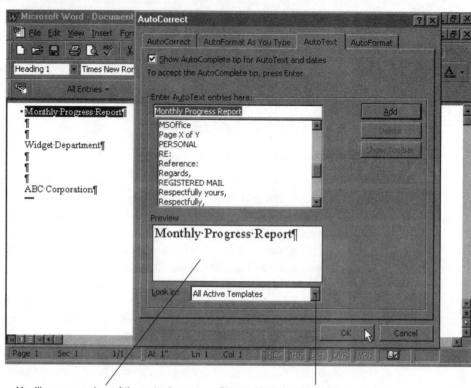

You'll see a preview of the entry here.

Choose All Active Templates or attach the entry to a particular document.

Using AutoText Entries

Once you've saved some AutoText entries, you can insert them using several techniques. Always begin by placing the insertion point where you want the entry. If you need spaces or tabs before the entry, it is easiest to type them first. When the insertion point is properly positioned, do one of the following:

- Type all or part of an AutoText entry's name; then press F3 or Enter.
- Type all or part of an AutoText entry's name; then press Alt+Ctrl+V.
- Choose Insert ➤ AutoText; then select an entry from the scrolling name list by highlighting it and releasing the mouse button.

In any event, Word inserts the entry. Edit it as you would any other text, graphic, or document element.

  NOTE

Word 97 also has an AutoComplete feature, which displays a pop-up of the entry when you begin typing the entry. Press Enter to let it complete the AutoText entry (if it guesses wrong, keep typing and ignore the pop-up until it goes away). To use this feature, check the Show AutoComplete Tip for AutoText and Dates checkbox in the AutoText tab of the AutoCorrect dialog box. This option is checked by default.

Editing AutoText Entries

To edit an entry, follow these general steps:

1. Insert the entry in a document.
2. Edit and reformat it as necessary.
3. Select the corrected entry and any necessary punctuation, paragraph marks, spaces following, and so on.
4. Choose Insert ➤ AutoText ➤ AutoText to open the AutoText dialog box.
5. Restore the entry's name in the Name box, if necessary.
6. Click on the Add button.

Deleting AutoText Entries

Deleting AutoText entries is as simple as you'd expect (and hope). Follow these general steps:

1. Choose Insert ➤ AutoText to open the AutoText dialog box.
2. Select the doomed item from the scrolling list.
3. Look in the Preview box or insert the entry and check to be *certain* that this is the entry you want to delete.
4. Click on Delete.

 WARNING

Word does not ask if you *really, really* want to delete AutoText entries, and Undo *will not work* here; so stay awake, particularly if you have a lot of similar-looking entries or entries with similar names.

PART

III

Productivity Tools

Shortcuts for Frequently Used Entries

You need not type an entire entry name when specifying it. You need type only enough characters to uniquely identify the entry. For instance, if you have an entry called *Mansfield* and another called *Manhole*, typing **Mans+F3** inserts the *Mansfield* entry, and typing **Manh+F3** gets you *Manhole*.

To use this feature, be sure to check the Show AutoComplete Tip for AutoText and Dates checkbox in the AutoText tab of the AutoCorrect dialog box. This option is checked by default.

TIP

If you like the previously described AutoText entry shortcut, keep it in mind when *naming* entries. Make the first few characters in an entry name as unique as possible.

It is also possible to assign keyboard shortcuts (hot keys) and to create toolbar buttons for your favorite AutoText entries. See Chapter 32, *Personalizing Word,* for details.

Converting Old Glossaries to AutoText

If you've upgraded from a previous Word version, your Normal template has inherited any glossary entries that were in your earlier Normal template, and they are readily available as AutoText. If you made glossary entries in other templates, they will also work with newer versions of Word. Simply open a document using the old templates.

EnvelopeExtra Entries

Word normally lets you use any names you like for AutoText entries, with two exceptions. Word reserves the names EnvelopeExtra1 and EnvelopeExtra2 for a special purpose (see Chapter 2, *Viewing and Navigating*). If you give items these names, they will appear on envelopes each time you print them. For example, you might select a logo and perhaps a return address text and then assign the name *EnvelopeExtra1*, as shown in Figure 14.3

Thereafter, whenever you use the Envelope and Labels command, Word inserts the contents of EnvelopeExtra1 and EnvelopeExtra2, if they exist. Figure 14.4 shows the results of including the EnvelopeExtra1 entry shown in Figure 14.3.

To delete these entries forever, delete them as you would any other element. To temporarily disable them, rename them. Remember, you can create different entries for different templates; so you can have multiple EnvelopeExtra1 and EnvelopeExtra2 entries for different projects. For instance, you could have one template with an entry such as *Your newsletter is enclosed* and another that says *Here is the literature you've requested* and so on.

FIGURE 14.3

Word reserves the AutoText entry names EnvelopeExtra1 and EnvelopeExtra2 for envelope printing.

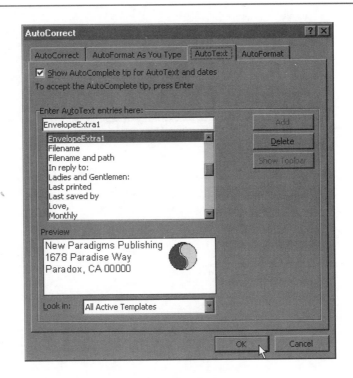

Printing Lists of AutoText Entries

To see printed examples of all AutoText entries and their full names, follow this procedure:

1. Open a new document using the template of interest (Normal, for instance).

2. Open the Print dialog box (Ctrl+P or File ➤ Print).

3. Choose AutoText Entries from the Print What list, as shown in Figure 14.5.

4. Having made sure your printer is ready, click on OK or press Enter.

Using AutoCorrect

I suspect that *AutoCorrect* started out with one purpose in life and that someone then discovered a second use for it. (I call these discoveries "hey lookits," as in "Hey look at what this can do!")

The primary reason for AutoCorrect is to fix typos such as *teh* when you meant to type *the*. Word watches you type and changes things for you.

You can create your own entries, and there are some predefined entries. For instance, if you type **(r)** or **(R)**, Word replaces those characters with the registered symbol (®).

PART

III

Productivity Tools

FIGURE 14.4

An Envelope-Extra1 entry on a letter

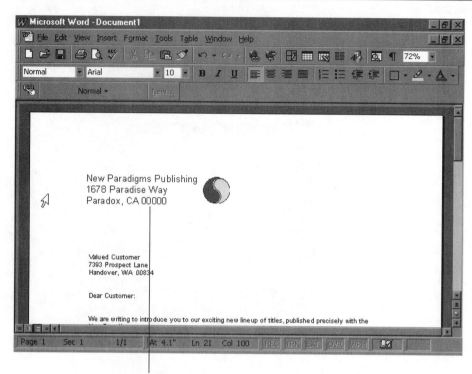

This entry was automatically inserted by the EnvelopeExtra1 AutoText command.

FIGURE 14.5

Choose AutoText entries to print out a list.

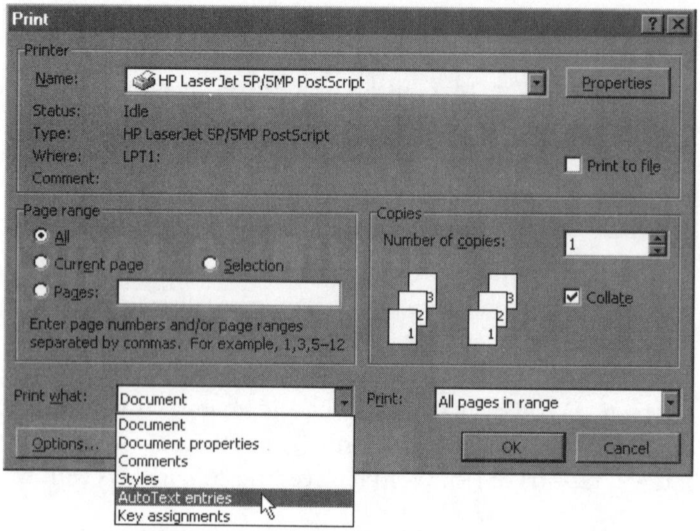

Word's AutoCorrect feature is now even more robust than before. Now Word corrects what it believes to be Caps Lock key errors, as well as inserts correct plural and possessive forms of AutoCorrect entries you have assigned. More symbols have been added that are changed automatically (such as arrows and smiley faces), and Word now formats ordinal numbers (such as *2nd*) and fractions (such as 1/2) in fancy typesetter's style. Keep in mind that AutoCorrect is different from the Automatic Spellchecking option, which doesn't correct misspelled words, but flags unfamiliar words (with red underline) as you type. If you want Word to actually correct your own personal pet-peeve typos or misspellings, AutoCorrect is the tool for the job.

To use the built-in entries, you simply type along as usual. Word makes changes when it thinks they are needed. You can see a list of the current autocorrections by scrolling in the AutoCorrect dialog box (choose Tools ➤ AutoCorrect), shown in Figure 14.6.

FIGURE 14.6

See and change AutoCorrect entries in the AutoCorrect dialog box.

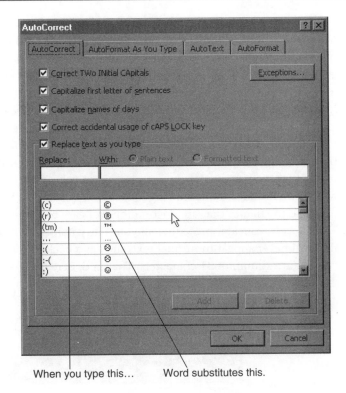

When you type this...   Word substitutes this.

PART

III

Productivity Tools

Other Uses of AutoCorrect

Here's the hey lookit. In addition to correcting typos, you can use AutoCorrect to convert "shorthand" into longer text strings. For instance, you could tell Word that you want it to replace *aka* with *also known as* or to replace *mwg* with *Mr. William Gates,* and so on. You can even insert text and graphics this way. Type *sylogo,* for instance, and insert the Sybex logo (see "Creating Your Own AutoCorrect Entries" next).

The primary difference here is that *AutoCorrect* will *always* make the replacement when you type a defined string of characters followed by a space. *AutoText* waits for you to press the F3 key before it takes over.

AutoCorrect also converts entries suspected of being URLs into hyperlinks. For example, type **www.sybex.com** and watch what happens. Microsoft calls this AutoHyperlink.

Creating Your Own AutoCorrect Entries

When creating your own AutoCorrect entries, there is one potential land mine: Auto-Correct always blindly replaces certain text strings with other text strings. For example, if you want to change each occurrence of *add* to your inside address and you assign *add* as the name for this autocorrection, things will work fine until the first time you type a sentence like *Please add my name to the carpool list.* Then you'll get your address smack in the middle of an otherwise perfectly good sentence. Because of this potential problem, it's probably safest to use AutoText for inserting boilerplate and use AutoCorrect for true corrections. If you do use AutoCorrect for insertions, take care when defining the text that AutoCorrect will react to (the name for each entry) and give some thought to whether the text string you're replacing is likely to occur in cases other than those where you'd want it replaced.

Try to use names that are uncommon, yet easy to remember. If you get hooked on AutoCorrect, consider preceding all your entry names with some unusual character that will never appear in normal text, such as a backslash (*add* for instance). Names can be a maximum of 31 characters. That said, here are the steps:

1. Choose Tools ➤ AutoCorrect to open the AutoCorrect dialog box.

2. Type the "name" (the text string you want to replace) in the Replace box.

3. Type the replacement in the With box (or see the tip that follows).

4. Click on Add.

5. Make any other entries or changes.

6. Click on OK when done.

TIP

If you select the text (or graphics and other things) you want to use as the replacement item before you open the AutoCorrect dialog box, it will appear in the With portion of the box when it opens. If the items are formatted, you'll be given the choice of pasting the items as formatted or not.

Editing AutoCorrect Entries

To modify an AutoCorrect entry, follow these steps:

1. Correct the entry in a document and select it.

2. Choose Tools ➤ AutoCorrect to open the AutoCorrect dialog box.

3. Type the old Replace name.

4. When the Replace button undims, click on it.

5. Answer Yes to the "Do you want to redefine" question.

Deleting AutoCorrect Entries

To delete an AutoCorrect entry, follow these steps:

1. Choose Tools ➤ AutoCorrect to open the AutoCorrect dialog box.

2. Select the victim.

3. Click on the Delete button.

Automatic Correction

In addition to fixing things as you type them, you can run the AutoCorrect feature at any time to inspect and clean up documents. Use the AutoCorrect dialog box to choose the options you want Word to use, as shown here:

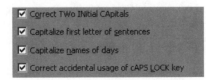

Overriding AutoCorrections

If you notice an unwanted autocorrection, try using Undo. Sometimes it will reverse the autocorrection.

PART

III

Productivity Tools

Insert Commands

Word's Insert menu has a number of useful choices that can do things similar to Auto-Text, AutoCorrect, and the now-defunct Word Glossary command. Although you'll find more about this topic in Chapter 29, *Creating and Using Fields*, let's take a quick look at a few of the commands here.

Insert ➤ Date and Time

The Insert ➤ Date and Time command gives you a wide choice of date and time formats, as shown here.

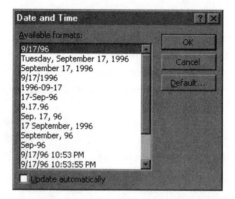

If you check the Update Automatically box, Word places a date or time field in your document. Word then updates the date and time whenever you *print* your document.

Insert ➤ File

When you choose Insert ➤ File, Word places the entire contents of any file into the open document at the insertion point. Word can insert other Word documents, documents created by many other word processors, graphic files, plain text files, and more. When in doubt, give it a try.

The Insert ➤ File command displays the File dialog box. Simply select the file and click on OK. Word inserts it. You may need to reformat it after insertion.

TIP

Save your work before inserting files, just in case.

Insert ➤ Picture

The Insert ➤ Picture command leads to another command list, including Insert ➤ Picture ➤ Clip Art. This displays the Microsoft Clip Art Gallery 3, shown in Figure 14.7.

Use the Microsoft Clip Gallery 3.0 dialog box to preview pictures, sound, and video clips. When you click on OK, a full-sized version of the selected graphic, sound, or video segment is pasted at the insertion point in your current Word document.

Crop, resize, and move the graphic if necessary using the techniques you learned in Chapter 3, *Previewing and Printing*.

NOTE

Insert ➤ Object displays the Object dialog box, which you can use to add images or files from other applications, such as Microsoft Excel and Microsoft Map.

FIGURE 14.7

Preview and choose the clip art you want to insert.

Choose categories from here.   This will place the selected graphic at the insertion point.

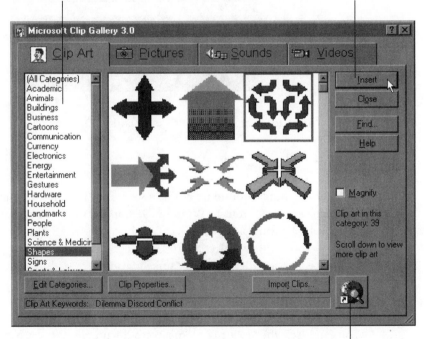

Connect to the Web for additional clips.

PART
III

Productivity Tools

Insert ➤ Field

Choose Insert ➤ Field to insert fields that can automate many aspects of document preparation. For instance, the FileName field inserts the file's name in your document. A *field* is an object in your document that inserts information. With fields turned off, you will simply see their results; however, if you turn fields on in the View tab of the Options dialog box, you will see the field instructions themselves.

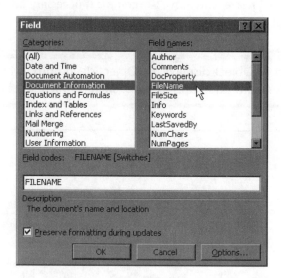

You'll learn a lot more about fields in Chapter 29, *Creating and Using Fields*.

The Spike

You can move things around in Word in several other ways. Document scraps (discussed next) are ubiquitous to Windows 95 applications. Word itself, though, has a built-in tool for cutting and pasting, called the Spike. The Spike is a special, preset Auto-Text entry. You use it to collect a series of selections into a list and then insert them all in one place, in the order that you "spiked" them.

To cut something (text or graphics) to the Spike, select it in any of the normal ways and then press Ctrl+F3. The selection will disappear. Repeat this process as often as you like to stack up a series of selections in the Spike.

You can insert the Spike's contents into a document in two ways. You can insert the contents and clear the Spike at the same time, or you can insert the contents without clearing the Spike. Use the latter method when you want to insert the Spike contents elsewhere or continue adding items to the Spike.

Insert and Clear the Spike

To insert the contents of the Spike and clear it out at the same time, place the insertion point where you want the contents to appear and then press Ctrl+Shift+F3. The contents will appear in the order that you spiked them, each as a separate paragraph (separated by paragraph marks).

Insert without Clearing the Spike

To insert the contents of the Spike without clearing it, place the insertion point at the beginning of a line or between two spaces. Then type **spike** and press F3. The contents will appear in the order you spiked them, each as a separate paragraph.

Word's Spike now features a pop-up display showing the first few words of the Spike contents. This display appears as soon as you start typing spike. Press Enter to insert the contents of the Spike without removing them from the Spike.

Spike Summary

So, just to review:

To Do This...	...Type This
Add a selection to the Spike	Ctrl+F3
Insert and clear the Spike	Ctrl+Shift+F3
Insert but don't clear the Spike	spike+F3

Document Scraps

You can place scraps of documents on the Windows desktop. Scraps are bits of text or graphics that you have copied and placed in files on the desktop. The nice part is that this feature is a no-brainer. Scraps can be pasted into other documents or programs. You can think of scrap documents as automatically saved Clipboard files. But you don't lose one scrap when you save another, unlike Clipboard entries; also, since scraps are saved to files, you can move them around and put them in folders on disk for later use.

> **NOTE**
> Only programs that support OLE (Word, Excel, Powerpoint, etc.) can make and use document scraps.

PART

III

Productivity Tools

Creating Document Scraps

Creating a document scrap couldn't be easier. All you do is select the text, graphics, or other data you want to save and then just drag it out to the desktop. Windows will then make a new file right on the desktop. You can rename, delete, or move the scrap as you see fit.

 TIP

You can view a document scrap simply by double-clicking on it. Once it is open, you can select text and edit it just as you would in any other document.

Inserting Document Scraps

Once you have a scrap or two on the desktop, inserting the contents of a scrap is quite straightforward. Simply click on the scrap and drag it to where you want it inserted. A copy of the scrap's contents will be inserted in your destination document, leaving the original scrap untouched. This is handy, because you can use a scrap over and over.

Scraps vs. the Spike

The Spike is probably best for cases in which you want to keep adding little bits of information, and scraps are better for information that you wouldn't want to lose. Experiment. Be brave!

Tips and Strategies for Using AutoText and AutoCorrect

Here are some tips for using the time-saving features discussed in this chapter:

In my humble opinion, you should use AutoText, the Insert commands, and Templates for inserting things; use Auto-Correct only for its named function—correcting typos. If you do use Auto-Correct for heavy-duty boilerplate

insertions, be certain that the names are uncommon and distinct.

- Set up keyboard shortcuts for regularly used AutoText entries.

- Consider adding buttons to the Auto-Text toolbar for the really frequent entries.

- Use the Commands tab in the Customize dialog box (Tools ➤ Customize), and scroll to the AutoText category.

Chapter

15

Author's Tools

Author's Tools

Word provides a powerful Spelling tool that lets you check the spelling of an entire document, including headers, footers, and hidden text. The Grammar tool now flags possible errors as you type, just like the Spelling tool. Word's Thesaurus and Word Count tools round out the author's tools discussed in this chapter. Let's start with the Spelling tool.

Spelling Checker

Word will spell-check your documents as you type them, flagging unfamiliar words with a red, squiggly underline. You can run a regular spelling check later to correct or ignore these words, or you can actually fix them "on the fly." Simply right-click on the word in question to see a list of possible replacements:

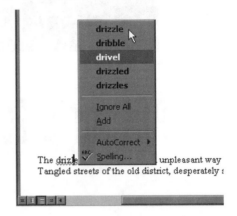

If one of the replacement words is correct, simply click on it. Otherwise, you can tell Word to ignore all future occurrences of the word or to add it to the dictionary. If you're feeling compulsive, you can even bring up the full-featured Spelling dialog box.

TIP

If you *absolutely* hate the automatic spelling checker, you can easily disengage it. Choose Tools ➤ Options, select the Spelling and Grammar tab, and remove the check from Automatic Spell Checking.

Using the automatic spelling checker is probably the safest and quickest way to ensure that your spelling is perfect, but if you prefer to do a single spelling check of your whole document at the end, you can do that instead (or also). The rest of the spell-check information in this chapter is devoted to using the full-featured Spelling dialog box to check your documents. Note that the automatic spelling checker and the Spelling dialog box both use the same dictionary.

Unlike the printed dictionary on your desk, Word's checker does not contain definitions. It does not consider words in context. Although it knows that *two*, *too*, and *to* are all proper spellings, it cannot warn you of their improper use. For instance, Word's Spelling tool would not object to the sentence, *She went two the bank too get a to-dollar bill.* (Oddly enough the new grammar checker won't catch this either.)

What it *can* do is suggest spellings with uncanny accuracy. Misspellings are usually replaced with a mouse click or two. You can add and edit your own custom dictionaries, which might contain proper nouns, technical terms, and other specialized words or numbers. You'll learn how to use all these features in this chapter.

We'll also explore the Tools ➤ Word Count command. It's a way for authors to quickly determine the number of characters, words, lines, and paragraphs in documents and footnotes.

And we'll look at the Grammar tool. It can help you spot many common writing errors and evaluate your document's readability. We'll wrap things up by examining how the Thesaurus can help you add variety to your choice of words.

Spelling Checker Setup

The first time you use the Spelling tool it's a good idea to ensure that it is set to use the proper dictionary—U.S. English. Here are the steps:

1. Choose Tools ➤ Language ➤ Set Language.
2. Scroll to the desired language—probably English (United States)—and select it by double-clicking on it or by clicking once on the name and once on OK.

3. Click on the Default button.
4. Answer Yes to the confirmation.
5. Click on OK.

WARNING
You can format certain text (foreign language or technical, for example) as "no proof" text, which means Word will skip it during spelling checks. If you don't instruct Word to use a dictionary, though, you might think Word has spell-checked your document and found nothing wrong; unlike earlier versions, Word 97 does not inform you of this.

> **TIP**
>
> You can assign different languages to different templates if you frequently use more than one language.

Checking Spelling

Start the spelling checker by pressing F7, by clicking on the toolbar button, or by choosing Tools ➤ Spelling and Grammar. Word displays the Spelling and Grammar dialog box, as shown in Figure 15.1.

Unless you've selected only a portion of your document to check, Word scans the whole thing, beginning at the insertion point, and will ask if you want to go back to the top of the document to continue checking, if necessary.

The Spelling tool looks for words that it cannot find in its open dictionaries. When it spots a word that it can't match, Word highlights the questionable characters, scrolls the document so that you can see the problem word in context, and offers you a number of choices.

> **TIP**
>
> The checker will confine itself to single words or phrases if you select items of interest before issuing the Spelling command. Of course, if you have automatic spelling enabled, right-clicking on a flagged word will offer you some choices.

FIGURE 15.1

The spelling checker lets you select suggested replacement words, type your own corrections, ignore unrecognized words, or add words to your custom dictionaries.

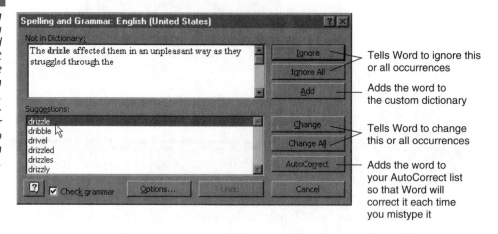

Tells Word to ignore this or all occurrences

Adds the word to the custom dictionary

Tells Word to change this or all occurrences

Adds the word to your AutoCorrect list so that Word will correct it each time you mistype it

Typing Your Own Changes

If you want to change a misspelled word only once, follow these steps:

1. Type a replacement or correct the highlighted word in the Not in Dictionary box.

2. Click on the Change button. Word replaces the problem text with the new text you have typed in the Change To box and then continues spell-checking.

To change the word throughout the document that you are checking, click on Change All instead of Change. If the new word you've typed is something you want Word to recognize in all your documents, you can add it to a custom dictionary (see the section "Custom or User Dictionaries," later in this chapter).

Word's Suggested Changes

If you have suggestions enabled (check the Always Suggest Corrections option in the Spelling and Grammar tab of the Options dialog box), Word will usually list one or more possible spellings, highlighting what it thinks is the best guess in the Suggestions box. If the default is not enabled, you can always ask for suggestions by clicking on Options and checking the Always Suggest Corrections checkbox. Other suggestions, if any, will be listed in the scrollable Suggestions box. This may take a moment. You'll know Word has finished looking for alternative suggestions when you see either (End of Suggestions) or (No Suggestions) in the Suggestions list.

If you agree with Word's best guess, simply click on the Change button to change this occurrence or click on Change All to change this and all succeeding occurrences of the word. The Spelling tool will replace the word and continue examining your document.

Word's best guess is usually, but not always, right. If one of the alternative suggestions is correct, simply click on the desired word to change it to the highlighted choice and then click on the Change or Change All button as necessary. Sometimes, however, Word's guesses will be bizarre or comical (for example, *broccoli* for *Berkeley*); so be sure you read the replacement text carefully.

Overruling Suggestions

Sometimes Word won't make correct suggestions, or you might want to correct the problem yourself without retyping the entire word or phrase. For instance, Word might spot two run-together words, such as the ones shown in Figure 15.2.

When it has no suggestions, Word moves the problem text to the Not in Dictionary box where you can edit it yourself (place a space between the two words, for instance).

PART

III

Productivity Tools

FIGURE 15.2

*Problem text
can be edited
right in the
Not in Dictio-
nary box.*

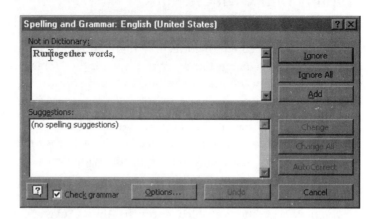

Ignoring Flagged Words

Sometimes Word will spot a word that is properly spelled, but that isn't in its open dictionaries. Proper nouns, technical jargon, HTML codes, and typesetting codes are examples.

If you want Word to ignore the text only once, click on the Ignore button. Word will leave the word or other text string as you typed it and continue spell-checking. To ignore the word throughout the document you are checking, click on Ignore All. (If the word is something you want to ignore in all your documents, you might want to add it to a custom dictionary.)

NOTE

You can set the Spelling tool to ignore Internet addresses by checking the Ignore Internet and File Addresses checkbox in the Spelling and Grammar tab of the Options dialog box (choose Tools ➤ Options).

Custom, or User, Dictionaries

Most of the words used by the Spelling tool are located in a dictionary that comes with your Word program. In the United States, Word is shipped with a dictionary called the US English Dictionary. It is kept in the Commands folder. You cannot change this dictionary.

You can, however, maintain one or more of your own *custom* dictionaries. Word checks only open dictionaries. The more dictionaries you have open, the slower spell-checking will be.

The Standard Custom Dictionary

When you install Word, the installation program places an empty Custom Dictionary in your Commands folder. The default name for the dictionary is Custom.dic. It is opened and used whenever you spell-check unless you instruct Word otherwise. This is where you will want to keep most proper nouns, trademark names, and so on.

Word places words in the Custom Dictionary whenever you click on the Add button while spell-checking. (The first time you add a word, you may be asked to create a custom dictionary.) Normally, Word places a dictionary called Custom.dic in the Proof subfolder of the Commands folder. You can overrule this default use of the Custom Dictionary by following these steps:

1. Select the Options button in the Spelling and Grammar dialog box.
2. In the Spelling and Grammar options tab, select the Dictionaries button.
3. In the Custom Dictionaries dialog box, select the Add button.
4. Navigate to the desired dictionary in the Look In box in the Add Custom Dictionary dialog box.

Custom dictionaries handle capitalization as follows. If you add a word to a dictionary as all lowercase, it will be recognized later, regardless of whether it is typed as all lowercase, all uppercase, or with an initial capital letter. If you enter a word with only the first letter capitalized, Word will recognize the word when it later appears in all caps or with a leading cap, but will question the word if it is all lowercase. Unusual capitalizations, such as *AutoCAD*, will be questioned unless they are stored in the dictionary exactly as they should be.

Creating Additional Custom Dictionaries

If you work on unusual projects that involve technical jargon, typesetting codes, and so on, you might want to create one or more additional specially named custom dictionaries, which you can turn on or off in the Custom Dictionaries dialog box, reached from the Spelling tab of the Options dialog box. To create a new custom dictionary, follow these steps:

1. Choose Tools ➤ Options or click on the Options button in the Spelling and Grammar dialog box. In the Options dialog box, select the Spelling and Grammar tab.
2. Click on the Dictionaries button to open the Custom Dictionaries dialog box, as shown in Figure 15.3.
3. Click on New to create a new dictionary. You will be prompted for a dictionary name.
4. Type a new name containing as many as 32 characters in the File Name area of the Create Custom Dictionary dialog box.
5. Open the folder where you want to store the dictionary (it is best to keep custom dictionaries with the main dictionary).
6. Click on Save.

FIGURE 15.3

You can add and edit custom dictionaries in the Custom Dictionaries dialog box.

Opening and Closing Custom Dictionaries

To be available to the Spelling tool, a dictionary must be open. Place checkmarks next to both custom dictionaries in the dialog box to make both open and available for the Spelling tool to use. Click in the box next to the desired dictionary to open or close it. A checkmark means it's open.

To open dictionaries that are not in the folder containing the main dictionary, click on the Add button. Show Word where the desired dictionary is, using standard Windows folder-navigation techniques.

Editing Custom Dictionaries

To add items to a custom dictionary, click on Add when the Spelling tool encounters a word of interest, or create a separate Word document containing all the words you want to add. Spell-check this document, adding each unrecognized word.

If you accidentally add a word to a custom dictionary, it is a good idea to delete it, because extra words mean more searching time during your spelling checks. And if you add misspelled words, they will no longer be challenged by the checker. Removing words from a custom dictionary is slightly more involved than adding them. To edit a custom dictionary, follow these steps:

1. Choose the dictionary you want to edit in the Custom Dictionaries dialog box (choose Tools ➤ Options and select the Spelling and Grammar tab).
2. Click on the Edit button.

3. If automatic spell-checking is on, Word displays the dialog box shown in Figure 15.4, offering to let you edit the dictionary as a regular Word document but warning you that automatic spell-checking will be turned off. Click on OK.

Word lets you edit custom dictionaries as Word documents.

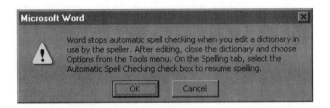

Word closes all open dialog boxes and displays the dictionary as a regular Word document.

4. Edit the dictionary.

5. Save it with the Save command (Ctrl+S).

The Spelling and Grammar tab in the Options dialog box provides other spelling options, which should be self-explanatory. Choose Help to learn more from Word's online help feature.

Speeding Up the Spelling Checker

Here are some tips for speeding up your spell-checking:

- Use that automatic checker, by golly!

- To do regular spelling checks, place the insertion point at the beginning of your document (Ctrl+Home) and spell-check in Normal view.

- If you are a good speller with a slow computer and are mostly looking for typos, either use the automatic checker or consider turning off Suggestions in the Spelling dialog box.

- Keep custom dictionaries fairly small (100 to 200 words, perhaps).

- Split larger custom dictionaries into smaller ones by categories that match different kinds of work you do (legal, technical, and so on).

- Open only the one(s) you need.

Productivity Tools

The Word Count Command

The Word Count command is found in the Tools menu. Simply choose the command to start the process. Figure 15.5 shows typical results.

TIP

There are more occasions for counting words than you might realize. If you are copy fitting and have to write a specified number of words, for example, this can be very important. And how many times have you seen on application forms the words "Write a 300–500 word essay on…"?

When you choose Tools ➤ Word Count, Word scans an entire document or selected text. It counts pages, words, characters, paragraphs, and lines. If you place a check in the appropriate box, it will include footnote and endnote text when counting. It does *not* count words in headers and footers. Also, you must display invisible text to include it in the count.

FIGURE 15.5

The Word Count feature counts characters, lines, paragraphs, and pages, both in the main text and in foot-notes, if you so desire.

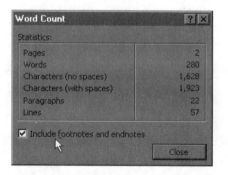

Checking Grammar and Style Checker

Word's wonderful, new Grammar tool evaluates style and points out many, but not all, grammatical errors. It can often suggest changes and even make some of them for you. Word uses collections of rules when analyzing your documents. You can turn off specific rules that annoy you or cramp your style. Word will explain and demonstrate the rules for you.

Statistics and readability indexes are created at the end of a grammar-checking session. These help you determine whether the writing style is appropriate for your audience.

Because the Grammar tool needs to work with properly spelled documents, it sometimes activates Word's Spelling tool when it encounters unfamiliar words.

Word is not a complete replacement for a human editor. For instance, it will not catch missing periods at the end of sentences. In Word 97 it does, however, catch double spaces between words.

Because Word considers parts of speech when checking grammar, you might think that it understands what you've written. This is not the case. For instance, the nonsense phrase *Eye sea sum tins knot write here* fools the grammar checker.

Nonetheless, the checker will help you spot many common problems and can help you polish your style.

Although grammar and style changes are often reversible with Undo, this is not always the case. You might want to save your document just before grammar checking, or you might want to run the check on a copy of your masterpiece. Also, be sure that you've specified a language for proofing as described at the beginning of this chapter.

To check grammar and style, follow these steps:

1. Save your work and move the insertion point to the beginning of your document.
2. Choose Tools ➤ Spelling and Grammar. Unless you select a portion of your document, Word attempts to check the whole thing.
3. Working from the insertion point, Word highlights a portion of your prose (usually a sentence) and evaluates it. There may be a slight delay. If Word spots questionable spellings, you will be given the opportunity to correct them or tell Word to ignore them.
4. Concurrently with the spell-check, Word checks grammar, pointing out questionable style and grammar issues. The text being considered is highlighted in the scrolling Sentence box. Suggestions and observations are made in the scrolling Suggestions box. For example, in Figure 15.6, the Grammar tool doesn't like the use of passive voice.

Accepting Word's Suggestions

In Figure 15.6, Word suggests rewriting the sentence to take care of the passive voice problem. Because Word is unable to make this change itself, the Change button is dim. When Word makes more specific suggestions, you can double-click on its suggestion or click on the Change button to apply the change.

PART

III

Productivity Tools

FIGURE 15.6

Word relentlessly scrutinizes documents for use of passive voice.

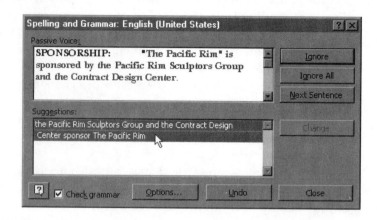

When the Grammar tool finishes checking, it will tell you so. Use the Cancel button to exit sooner. If you have the statistics option turned on, you'll see a readability report.

Making Manual Changes

Many of the problems the checker spots need your intervention. To make manual changes, type right in the Grammar window's Sentence box. Click on the Change button when done. The Grammar tool will make the change and continue checking.

Ignoring Suggestions

The Ignore button in the Grammar dialog box instructs Word to ignore the current occurrence of a problem but will not prevent the Grammar tool from pointing out similar problems in the future.

You can skip to the next sentence without making changes to the current one by clicking on the Next Sentence button.

To turn off passive-voice checking for all your projects, turn off the rule (called Sentences) in the Spelling and Grammar tab of the Options dialog box, as described next.

Changing Preferences

You can turn rules on and off by clicking on the Settings button in the Grammar Settings dialog box, reached from the Spelling and Grammar tab in the Options dialog box, as shown in Figure 15.7.

FIGURE 15.7

The Grammar
Settings
dialog box

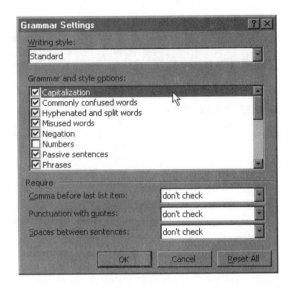

Here you can fine-tune Word's grammar pickiness. Rules are listed in one combined category called Grammar and Style Options. Checkmarks next to a rule mean the rule will be enforced. Clicking near a checkmark toggles it on and off. For more information about a rule, click on the Help button in the upper right corner of the dialog box. Your cursor will gain a question mark. Drag it to the rule list box and click there. A help tip about the list box pops up.

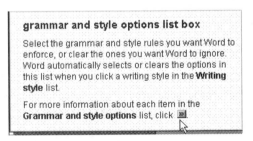

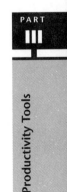

PART
III

Productivity Tools

Click on the arrow in the bottom of the tip to see more about each option.

Document Statistics

It's been said that there are liars, damned liars, and statistics. Word can provide the last named, as illustrated in Figure 15.8. Document statistics appear after the Grammar tool has finished scanning your document.

The Readability feature will count words, paragraphs, and sentences and then calculate the average number of characters per word and similar trivia. Several readability statistics are computed, including a count of passive sentences, Flesch Reading Ease, and the Flesch-Kincaid Grade Level. Click on the Help button in the Readability Statistics window and drag it over to the statistics for a brief explanation of these statistics.

The grade level measurements assign a (U.S. public school) grade level. The higher the index, the tougher the reading. Imagine how much better Shakespeare might have been, given tools like these. To write passively or not. That is the question.

Word can try to quantify your writing style.

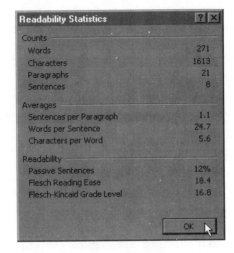

Using the Thesaurus to Find the Right Words

English is a rich language. There are many ways to say the same thing; yet we all tend to use a few words and phrases repeatedly. Word's *thesaurus* can help you add interest and texture to your prose. It gives you lists of synonyms (words that mean the same thing) and then lets you quickly replace your original word with the alternative of your choice. Sometimes Word can offer antonyms (words with opposite meanings). Word's thesaurus also contains common phrases, such as *in consideration of* and *at rest*.

The Thesaurus command lives on the Tools menu, and its keyboard shortcut is Shift+F7.

If you frequently use the thesaurus, consider adding a Thesaurus *button* to your toolbar. It's easy. Chapter 32, *Personalizing Word,* shows you how to assign any item to a toolbar button.

PART

III

Productivity Tools

Looking Up Words and Phrases

To use the thesaurus, highlight the word or phrase you want to replace, or position the insertion point in a word, and then choose Tools ➤ Language ➤ Thesaurus. Word displays a dialog box similar to the one shown in Figure 15.9.

TIP

If you don't select a word and the insertion point is not in a word, the thesaurus feature assumes you want the word closest to the insertion point.

If you haven't done so already, Word highlights the word in your document and places it in the Thesaurus dialog box next to Looked Up. This word (or phrase) is referred to as the *original* word.

If your original word has more than one meaning, the various meanings and their parts of speech will appear in the Meanings scrollable list. Clicking on a meaning in the Meanings list displays related synonyms in the Synonyms scrollable list. In Figure 15.9 the thesaurus offers three meanings for *glass*. Clicking on *drinking container* displays its synonyms.

Clicking on a particular synonym for *glass* (*beaker,* for instance) places the synonym in the editable Replace with Synonym area of the Thesaurus dialog box. If you don't like any of the choices, clicking on Cancel closes the dialog box and displays your unchanged document.

FIGURE 15.9

Word's thesaurus suggests synonyms and antonyms for highlighted words or phrases.

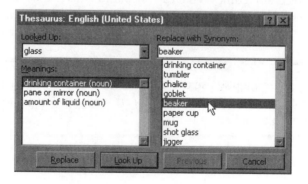

Replacing Words and Phrases

After exploring the various potential replacement words or phrases suggested by Word, you can replace your original word by following these steps:

1. Highlight the suggested replacement you like best. It will appear in the Replace with Synonym box.
2. Click on the Replace button in the Thesaurus dialog box. Word replaces the highlighted text in your document with the contents of the Replace with Synonym box and closes the dialog box.
3. If you don't like the results, the Edit ➤ Undo Thesaurus command is available, provided you act immediately.

Sometimes if you highlight a phrase, Word can suggest synonyms. Try it by highlighting the words *open to the public*, for example. Watch carefully whenever you use the thesaurus to replace highlighted phrases, because it doesn't always do what you expect:

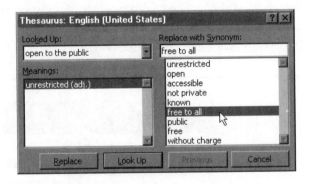

Related Words and Phrases

Frequently, Word's thesaurus will not contain an exact match for your original word. This can happen if you've misspelled a word. In that case, you will probably see an alphabetical list of words in place of the Meanings list. Select the correct word from the list, or return to your document and correct the spelling error and then try the Tools ➤ Language ➤ Thesaurus command again.

You will also have trouble matching certain tenses of words. For instance, if you attempt to replace *ambled*, Word will tell you to seek related words, as shown in Figure 15.10, because it contains the word *amble* but not *ambled*.

Clicking on a related word in the scrollable Related Word list places it in the Replace with Related Word box. For instance, double-clicking on the Related Words choice in the

PART

III

Productivity Tools

FIGURE 15.10

You may need to use a related word in the thesaurus and then edit it.

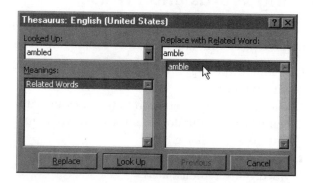

list on the left will reveal a list of related words on the right, as shown in Figure 15.11. Once you have the related word in the Replace With box, click on the Look Up button to find synonyms and antonyms.

When you find a related word (*meander*, for instance), click on it to move it to the Replace With box; then edit the word to suit your needs before clicking on Replace. For instance, you'd probably want to add *ed* to *meander* in our example.

FIGURE 15.11

With the related word moved to the Replace With box, click on Look Up to peruse a list of synonyms.

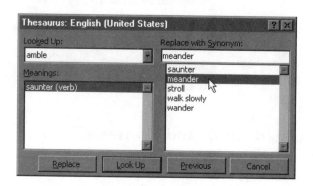

Restoring the Original Word

Clicking on the Looked Up list or on the Previous button in the Thesaurus dialog box will let you go back to earlier choices. The top of the Looked Up list contains the original word. Click to restore it. You can also use Undo to restore your original word.

Finding Antonyms

Frequently, Word can help you find antonyms. When they are available, the word *Antonyms* appears at the bottom of the scrollable Meanings list. Click on Antonyms to display a list of them on the right side of the thesaurus window. As you can see in Figure 15.12, the name of that list changes from Synonym to Antonym, and the list contains potential antonyms for the word in the Replace With box.

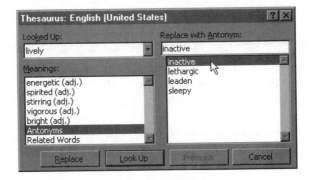

Spelling Help from the Thesaurus

Although Word's thesaurus doesn't actually contain definitions, you can sometimes use it to help choose the appropriate spelling of confusing words such as *which* and *witch* or *weather* and *whether*. Look up the words in question and compare synonyms to select the right spelling. Figure 15.13 illustrates this.

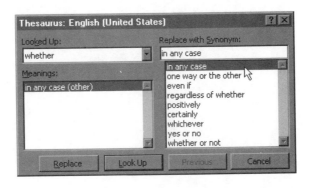

PART

III

Productivity Tools

Exploring the Thesaurus

Here are some guidelines for exploring the thesaurus:

- It is possible to really meander around in the thesaurus! A single click on any word (either in the left or right lists) places a new word in the Replace With box. You can then click on Look Up and go from there.
- Double-clicking on a synonym in the Meanings area places that word in both the Replace With and Meanings spaces.
- Double-clicking on a Meanings word places only that word in the Replace With space.

TIP

If your copy of Microsoft Office came with Microsoft Bookshelf, or if you purchased Bookshelf separately, you might want to use those tools (*The American Heritage Dictionary, Roget's Thesaurus,* etc.). Ask the Assistant for help with *Bookshelf* to learn more.

Chapter

16

Finding and Replacing

Finding and Replacing

E very contemporary word-processing product has a way to quickly locate and replace specific text strings (collections of words, numbers, and other characters). Lawyers use these features (sometimes called *global replace features*) to do things such as finding each occurrence of *Marion Morrison* in a contract and replacing it with *John Wayne*.

Some typists enter shorthand or acronyms for lengthy items when they draft. Then, while polishing the document, they replace the shorthand with the actual text. For instance, you might initially type *DRD* in the draft of a government document, and then have Word find and replace each occurrence of *DRD* with *Department of Redundancy Department*.

TIP

If you do a lot of this, consider using Word's AutoCorrect feature instead. It will replace acronyms as you type them.

Word provides two separate commands, Edit ➤ Find (Ctrl+F) and Edit ➤ Replace (Ctrl+H). Find is really just an evolutionary predecessor to Replace.

A slick feature of Word is that Find and Replace can both search for *word forms*. You can, for instance, search for all tense and person forms of verbs. Instead of searching separately for *fly*, *flew*, and *flies*, you simply search for *fly* and check the Find All Word Forms box. Replace takes this one step further. You can now replace words *with their proper forms!* This is so cool that it's positively scary. If you want to replace all occurrences of any form of the verb *to fly* with the verb *to walk*, you simply type **fly** in the Find What box, **walk** in the Replace With box, and check Find All Word Forms. Word will replace *fly* with *walk*, *flew* with *walked*, *flies* with *walks*, and so on. Now who could ask for more than that?!

With Word, you can search for and then replace or remove special characters such as paragraph marks, optional hyphens, or footnote-reference marks.

A form of wild-card searching is permitted; you can insert question marks in search requests to work around minor spelling variations. Asking Word to find **Sm?th**, for instance, would find both *Smith* and *Smyth*. You can search for ranges of numbers using a similar technique. Word's designers refer to this process as searching for *unspecified letters* and *unspecified digits*.

Occasionally, you can use Word's Find and Replace features to reformat documents. You might, for instance, search for all occurrences of two consecutive spaces and replace them with a single space. But Word can do much more than that. The Find and Replace commands can do the following:

- Help you find all or selected paragraphs formatted with a particular style and apply a different style.
- Remove items simply by telling Word to search for the item you want to delete and replace it with nothing.
- Search your entire document or selected portions. You specify the direction of the search (up or down).

The Art of Finding

The Find feature helps you quickly locate text, formats, special characters, and combinations thereof. It lets you search selected parts of your document or the whole enchilada. Simple Find requests can locate text regardless of format. It's also easy to ask Word to search for very specific items, such as occurrences of the word *Liberace* formatted in bold, blue, 24-point Playbill.

You need not limit your searches to text. You can look for section marks, graphics, paragraph marks, and more. When using the Find command (as opposed to Replace), Word finds what you've requested and then scrolls to the found item and its surrounding text without modifying anything.

You must click in the document window to work with the found item. You can leave the Find and Replace dialog box on your screen as you work, flipping between it and your document window. Figure 16.1 shows the Find and Replace dialog box.

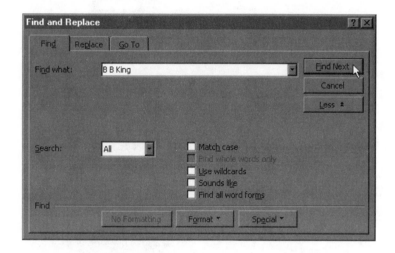

Here's a general overview of the Find and Replace dialog box. (Details will follow.) To do a search, follow these steps:

1. Choose Edit ➤ Find.

2. Specify text and special characters (if any) to find.

3. Specify formatting characteristics (if any) to find.

4. Tell Word where to search and in which direction.

5. Use the Special menu to search for section breaks, paragraph marks, and so on.

6. Check off any special search requests, such as Match Case or Find All Word Forms.

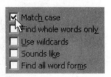

7. Click on Find Next to start the search.

8. When Word finds what you want, return to the document.

9. To find again, press Enter on the numeric keypad (if you're still in the document) or click on the Find Next button in the dialog box.

Like any good computer program, Word takes your requests quite literally, so you will need to understand each Find option fully to locate exactly what you want.

For example, if Word searches using the criteria specified in Figure 16.1, it will find *B B King* and *b b king*, but not *B.B. King*, *BB King*, or *Burger King*.

There are ways to get Word to find each of these text strings, of course. Just realize that you may need to carefully formulate and test your search strategy. In some cases, you will need to perform multiple searches to find similar but subtly different text strings.

Word automatically searches in headers and footers. For multisection documents, you may need to open and search headers and footers in each section. If your search plans include items such as paragraph marks or hidden text, the hidden text must be visible on the screen.

Consider proofing your document or at least running the spelling checker before important, major searches. If you spell *banana* correctly six times and incorrectly once, Word will find only six of your seven bananas.

Finding Text

Choose Edit ➤ Find or press Ctrl+F. Move to the text area of the Find What box and type enough text (a maximum of 255 characters) for an accurate, unambiguous search. For instance, suppose you wanted to find the word *man*. If you enter **man** in Find What, Word finds the words *man*, *Man*, *Mansfield*, *reprimand*, *manhole*, and *man* at the end of a sentence (followed by a period, question mark, and so on.).

Placing a space after **man** in your Find request would eliminate the unwanted *Mansfield*, *reprimand*, and *manhole*, but would also prevent you from finding *man* at the ends of sentences because periods, question marks, and such are not spaces.

That's the reason for the Match Whole Words Only checkbox in the Find and Replace dialog box. If you type **man** (no space) in the Find What area and check Find Whole Words Only, Word will locate only *man*, *Man*, and *man* at the end of sentences.

The Match Case checkbox instructs Word to look for exact capitalization matches. If you type **postscript** in the Find What area and check Match Case, Word will not find *POSTSCRIPT*, *PostScript*, or even *Postscript* at the beginning of sentences.

Extra spaces, nonbreaking spaces, and forced page breaks can also get in the way of searches. See the section "White Space" later in this chapter to see how to work around this.

Finding Special Characters

The Special drop-down list is a convenient way to enter certain special characters such as tab marks, nonbreaking spaces, and so on when constructing a search request. Place the insertion point in the Find What box where you want the special character to go, and choose the desired character from the drop-down list.

Find requests can combine regular text and special characters. For instance, you could ask Word to search for occurrences of *Bob* followed by two tab marks. Many of the special characters in the drop-down list are self-explanatory. Let's look more closely at the ones that are not. Some are extremely useful.

White Space

Here's one to keep you awake nights. Suppose you are searching for two words together, such as *Microsoft Corporation*. Suppose further that sometimes you used nonbreaking spaces to separate the two words. Other times you've just typed regular spaces. Occasionally, you typed two spaces between the words by mistake. Unless you use Word's White Space feature, you will not find the occurrences of *Microsoft Corporation* containing nonbreaking spaces or two spaces!

So, to do it right, insert Word's White Space special character in your search string. In our example, you'd start by typing **Microsoft** in the Find What box. Then, without touching the spacebar, choose White Space from the Special menu. The White Space code (^w) will appear next to *Microsoft*. Type **Corporation**. Your finished search string would be *Microsoft^wCorporation*. That should do it.

Any Character

You can use the Any Character character to overcome some nasty problems too. Suppose you've used accented characters sometimes but not always. *La Cañada* and *La Canada* are not the same thing to Word when it searches. A search for *La Ca^$ada* will find both. Enter the Any Letter character from the Special drop-down menu the same way you entered the White Space character. You can type these characters as well as choose them from the menu.

Any Digit

This special character will sometimes help you find numbers within ranges. It might be helpful for finding specific groups of part numbers or zip codes.

NOTE When using Any Digit once with the Replace feature, Word will find all occasions but only highlight the first two digits. So, when you use Replace, you must handle this differently. With the Find feature, it doesn't matter.

For instance, the search string **99^#** finds any number in the range 990 through 999. The specification **1^#** finds the combinations *101* and *11* in *111*. It also finds *1000*, but not *1,000*, because Word treats numbers as text, not numeric values, in searches such as these. Commas confuse things. Ah, computers.

Finding Sound-Alikes

Word can attempt to locate words that sound alike but are spelled differently (*smith*, *smyth*, *but,* and *butt*, for instance). This is an imprecise art at best, because even words that are *spelled* the same *sound* different in various parts of any country. (If you doubt this, ask a Bostonian, a New Yorker, and a Chicagoan to pronounce the word *car*.)

At any rate, the Sounds Like option can sometimes round up useful word variations and misspellings.

It is difficult to predict whether a sound-alike will match the word you're looking for, because Word is less than forthcoming about how it applies criteria. Presumably, it distinguishes consonants from vowels and then compares parts of the word in question to a table of equivalent sounds. Search for *kerection* and you'll find *correction*, but search for *cerection* and you won't. Go figure.

The real purpose of this option is to cut you some slack if you're not absolutely sure about how to spell a word. If you're searching and finding nothing, but you're sure the word is in there somewhere, check Sounds Like and try again. (Then note how to spell the word for future reference.)

Pattern Matching

To perform advanced searches for combinations of things (such as both *bet* and *bat*), you use characters called *operators*. They will remind you of wildcards. For instance, to find either *bet* or *bat*, you would place **b?t** in your Find What box and check Use Pattern Matching. If you forget to check Use Pattern Matching, the results will not be what you expect. Here's the list of operators you can use with Word and what they help you do:

Operator	Lets You Find
?	A single character: **b?t** finds *bet* and *bat*.
*	Any string of characters: **b*d** finds *bed*, *befuddled*, and *blood*.
[characters]	Any of the characters in brackets: **b[eo]d** finds *bed* and *bod* but not *bid*.

PART

III

Productivity Tools

Operator	Lets You Find
[character–character]	Any character in the range: **b[a–i]d** finds *bed* and *bid* but not *bod*.
[!character]	Any single character except the one in brackets: **b[!i]d** finds *bed* and *bod* but not *bid*.
[!characters]	Any single character except the ones in brackets: **b[!ie]d** finds *bad* and *bud* but not *bid* or *bed*.
[!character-character]	Any single character except those in the specified range: **b[!a-i]d** finds *bud* and *bod* but not *bad* or *bid*.
character{n}	Any *n* occurrences of the preceding character: **ble{2}d** finds *bleed* but not *bled* (or for that matter, *bleeeeed*). What's the purpose of this? Well it only makes sense if you're looking for a long string of a repeated character. In that case it would save you some typing. Otherwise, it seems silly: *ble{2}d* requires more typing (not to mention unusual characters) than *bleed* does!
character{n,}	At least *n* occurrences of the preceding character: **ble{1,}d** finds *bled* and *bleed*.
character{n,m}	At least *n* occurrences of the preceding character and no more than *m*: **1{1,2}5** finds both *15* and *115* but not *1115*.
character@	One or more occurrences of the preceding character (thus, @ is equivalent to {1,}): **ble@d** finds *bled* and *bleed*.
<text	The beginning of a word: **<man** finds *manhole* and *manage* but not *human*. (This works better than putting a space in front of the text, as it deals with exceptions such as the beginning of a paragraph.)
text>	The end of a word: **in>** finds *in* and *herein* but not *interfere*. (Likewise, this works much better than putting a space after the text, as it covers words that end at a period or other punctuation.)

To search for characters that are also used as operators ({, !, *, and so on), separate them with a backslash. For instance, to find the asterisk, search for *.

Notice that the ? symbol with Pattern Matching is equivalent to the ^? special character without it, just as the * symbol with Pattern Matching has the same effect as the ^* symbol without it.

You can combine all the above operators; so, for example, **<ble@d** finds *bleeding-heart*, but not *nosebleed* or *doubled*. If you combine several of these operators, you can use brackets to clarify which operations Word must evaluate first. Brackets can also go inside other brackets, though I hope for your sake that it is never necessary!

Find All Word Forms

A great feature of Word is that Find can search for *word forms*. What this means is that you can, for instance, search for all tenses and person forms of verbs. Instead of searching separately for *drink*, *drank*, and *drunk*, you simply search for *drink* and check the Find All Word Forms box. This is really uncanny the first time you see it!

It's incredibly slick too. Word seems to know most forms of most of the common verbs, as well as many irregular ones. For instance, if you enter **be** as the Find What text, Word will find all forms and tenses of the verb *to be!* That is, it will find *are, is, were, was, am*, and so on.

Find All Word Forms works with nouns too and is especially useful for nouns with irregular plurals, such as *goose* and *geese*. The only part of speech in which Word seemed overmatched was adjectives derived from proper nouns. When I tried *Shaw* and *Shavian*, Word found *Shaw* but flagged *Shavian* as a misspelling. Same with *Liverpool* and *Liverpudlian*.

The Art of Replacing

To replace, follow these general steps:

1. Save your work.
2. Choose Edit ➤ Replace or press Ctrl+H.
3. Create search criteria using the techniques discussed in the previous section.
4. Specify the desired replacement text, formats, and so on.
5. Tell Word where to search and in which direction.
6. Click on Find Next or Replace All to start the replacement.
7. Confirm the replacements.

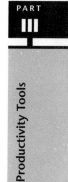

PART

III

Productivity Tools

WARNING

It is a good idea to save your work before using the Replace feature. If you are working on a complex, important project, you might want to use a copy rather than the original document because it is much easier to screw up a document with Replace than it is to repair it.

As you can see from Figure 16.2, the Replace tab in the Find and Replace dialog box looks like the Find tab with additional features. Word lets you confirm each replacement before it happens, or it will find and replace without your intervention.

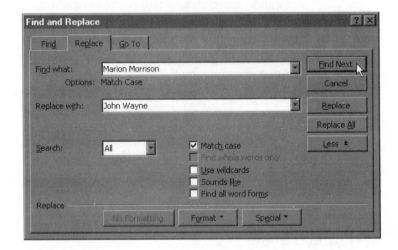

Just as you can search for text, formats, styles, and special characters, you can also replace them. For instance, you could replace *Marion Morrison* with *John Wayne*.

Or you could change each occurrence of two consecutive paragraph marks to a single end-of-line marker or change the style of certain paragraphs from chapter-heading style to appendix style. It is even possible to replace text with graphics. Here are examples of each technique.

Replacing Text with Text

To simply replace text (such as changing *Marion Morrison* to *John Wayne*) without altering formats or styles, start by entering the text to find and the desired replacement text.

For instance, you might enter *Marion Morrison* in the Find What box and *John Wayne* in the Replace With box. Follow these steps:

1. Save your work.
2. Choose Edit ➤ Replace (Ctrl+H).
3. In the Search drop-down menu, tell Word if you want it to search from the insertion point forward or backward or the entire document.
4. Use the Find What box to specify the search item and the Replace With box to specify its replacement. When your instructions are complete, click on Find Next. Word will search the document (or the selected portion) for items matching your Find criteria and propose the next replacement. The Replace button will undim, and your document screen will scroll to display the first potential replacement point.

WARNING

If any formats or styles are listed under the Find What or Replace With boxes, click on No Formatting with the insertion point in the appropriate place (Find What, Replace With, or both). This way, Word will not alter the style or format of the document. If you *do* want to replace one style or format with another, be sure that both Find What and Replace With accurately reflect your choices.

5. If you want Word to make the change it is proposing, click on Replace. To skip the change, click on Find Next. To make the change and let Word continue uninterrupted, click on Replace All. Word will make the rest of the replacements nonstop, probably too quickly for you to even see them. A message will display the number of replacements made.
6. Check your work. Undo will work here for all the replacements if you used Replace All, but only for the last replacement if you were monitoring the replacements. This is a big reason for saving your document just before running Replace.

Replacing Formatting

Suppose you have italicized words scattered throughout your text and decide to change all of them to underlined words. Start by removing any text from the Find What and Replace With boxes. (This is because you want Word to find all italicized text, not just words in the Find What box that are italicized.) Then follow these steps:

1. Specify the character attributes you want Word to find (italics, for example). You can do this in one of several ways. Always start by placing the insertion point in the Find What entry box. Then specify the Italic format from the Standard toolbar, by entering the Ctrl+I keyboard shortcut or by pulling down the Format list in the

PART

III

Productivity Tools

Find and Replace dialog box. From there, choose Font, and then click on the Italic option of the Font dialog box.

TIP

Using keyboard shortcuts or toolbar buttons is often the quickest way to specify formatting.

The word *Italic* (or whatever) will appear beneath the Find What box.

2. Next go to the Replace With box and choose a new format (Underline in this example). To prevent Word from changing italic to italic underline, double-click on the Italic button on the Formatting toolbar so that the Format information under the Replace With box reads **Not Italic, Underline.** Figure 16.3 shows how your dialog box should look after this maneuver. Note that toolbar buttons and keyboard shortcuts "cycle" through three phases; for example: italic, not italic, no formatting.

3. Let 'er rip! Either tell Word to Replace All or supervise each replacement as before.

You can also change the formatting of specific text only for that text or combine the replacement of text and formatting. To change the formatting of specific text, type the text you want to change in both the Find What and Replace With boxes. Click on the Find What format box and select the type of formatting the text has now. Then click on the Replace With format box and select the type of formatting you want to give to the text.

Changing both text and formatting at the same time is just as easy. Suppose you want to replace every instance of the italicized word *ennui* with the unitalicized word

FIGURE 16.3

This combination will change all italicized text to underlined text.

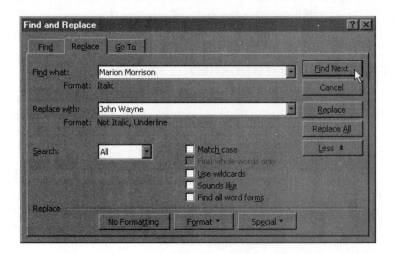

boredom. That would be simple. Simply type **ennui** in the Find What box and select Italic formatting. Then type **boredom** in the Replace With box and click on the Italic button on the Formatting toolbar twice to select Not Italic. Then proceed with Replace as normal.

Replacing Styles

If you want to change the style of certain paragraphs, the Replace command can help. Follow these steps:

1. Click on the Format button.
2. Choose Style.
3. You will see a list of your document's styles and descriptions, as shown in Figure 16.4.
4. Choose styles for both the find and replace criteria, and then proceed as usual.

In this example, paragraphs formatted with the Heading 3 style will be reformatted using the Heading 2 style. Because any custom styles you've defined will appear in the Styles list, you can use this technique to apply these styles quickly and accurately.

FIGURE 16.4

Specify styles to find and replace with the Replace Style dialog box.

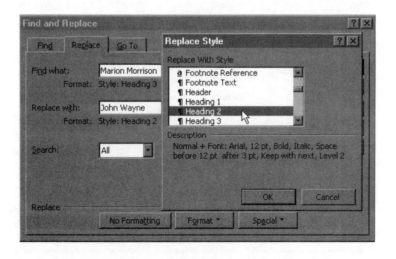

PART

III

Productivity Tools

Combining Replacement Tasks

Within reason, it is possible to combine search and replace instructions to restrict actions. For instance, assuming you had a document with appropriate styles, you could italicize all occurrences of *Gone with the Wind* in the body text of your report, while leaving the same words alone when they appear in headings, the table of contents, and the index.

You would do this by typing **Gone with the Wind** in the Find What box and specifying Body Text as its style. Then specify Italic as the format in the Replace With box. (You could type **Gone with the Wind** and specify body text style again in the Replace With box, but you don't need to.)

Again, computers are very obedient but not very clever. Undo should help you recover from most disasters, but it's a good idea to work on copies of important documents just in case.

With all the possibilities of finding text or formatting or both and replacing it with other text or formatting or both, you might sometimes find it hard to think through what exactly will change. Table 16.1 outlines how the choices interact.

TABLE 16.1: COMBINING TEXT AND FORMAT OPTIONS IN REPLACE

If you find	And replace it with	You get
text	text	all Find text replaced with Replace text
text	format	all Find text formatted
text	text and format	all Find text replaced with formatted Replace text
format	text	all formatted text replaced with Replace text in same format
format	format	all formatted text given new format
format	text and format	all formatted text replaced with Replace text in new format
text and format	text	all formatted Find text replaced with Replace text in same format
text and format	format	all formatted Find text given new format
text and format	text and format	all formatted Find text replaced with Replace text in new format

So, for example, if you type **ennui** in the Find What box, choose Underline formatting, put nothing in the Replace With box, and choose both Italic and No Underline (click on the Underline button on the Formatting toolbar twice), every underlined instance of *ennui* in your document will become italicized, but the word won't change.

Search Options

You have several choices for how Word searches your document for words you want to either find or replace. These options are found under the Search drop-down menu in the Find and Replace dialog box. Up searches back toward the beginning of the document, and Down searches toward the end. All searches the entire document, as you would expect.

If you choose Up or Down, Word searches until it gets to the beginning (or end) of the document and then tells you it has reached the end of the document and asks if you want it to continue the search. If you choose Yes, it continues in the same direction from the other end of the document until it reaches the place you started. If you choose No, it ends the search. Why would you want to end the search? Well, you may know that the word you're searching for occurs several times in the beginning of your document, and you may not want to change any of those earlier instances.

Another way to limit the range of the search is to select a portion of the document before selecting Replace. Word will search only the selection first. It will then ask if you want it to continue the search in the rest of the document. Choose No to end the search then.

If you stop in the middle of a Replace to, say, correct something else you've noticed, be sure to deselect the last found word before resuming the Replace. Otherwise, Word will begin the Replace again by searching just the selection (the last word found). This does no harm, but always having to click on Yes to continue the search gets boring.

Resume the Replace by clicking on the Find Next button.

Using the Clipboard with Find and Replace

You can use the Clipboard for several interesting Find and Replace tasks. For instance, you can copy text from your document to the Clipboard and then paste it into the Find What or Replace With boxes. This is a great way to find or replace long passages or obscure characters such as umlauted letters or math symbols. It is even possible to overcome the 255-character limitation this way.

Word also lets you replace text with graphics that you've placed on the Clipboard. Figure 16.5 illustrates how that is done.

To replace text with graphics, follow these steps:

1. Copy a graphic to the Clipboard.
2. In the Find and Replace dialog box, enter Find What criteria.
3. Click on the Replace With portion of the dialog box.
4. Choose Clipboard Contents from the Special list.
5. Replace as usual.

PART

III

Productivity Tools

FIGURE 16.5

It is possible to replace text with graphics on the Clipboard.

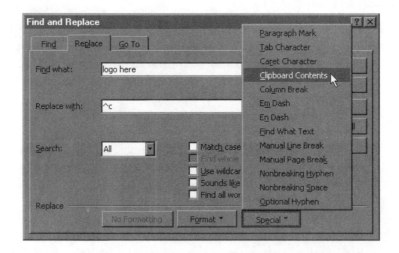

Tips for Replacing

- The Replace command uses considerable memory if you make a lot of changes. It is a good idea to perform a normal save after making sure that your replacements are satisfactory.

- Undo will undo all changes if you use Replace All, but only your last change if you have been supervising with the Find Next button.

- If you've used styles in your document, you may find it easier to make wholesale style changes by redefining or reapplying styles rather than using Replace.

- The Find All Word Forms feature works as you might hope when replacing. You can search for forms of one word, and Word will replace

them with all the correct forms of another word! For example, you can instruct Word to replace all forms of (the verbs) *drink* with *fish,* and it replaces *drink* with *fish, drank* with *fished, drunk* with *fished,* and so forth.

- You can specify any character in Find or Replace strings by typing ^**nnn**, where *nnn* is the ASCII (decimal) code for the character of interest.

- Remember to click on No Formatting when specifying new search criteria in the Find What and Replace With boxes.

- Drop-down lists in the Find What and Replace With fields show your last seven entries. You can save some typing and time by choosing from these lists.

All the special characters (paragraph markers, tabs, and so on) can be represented by caret codes that you can enter directly from the keyboard into the Find What box, the Replace With box, or both. This is often the quick way to go. Table 16.2 shows a handy reference list of special-character codes. Notice that they all require lowercase characters.

TABLE 16.2: SPECIAL CHARACTERS AND THEIR FIND AND REPLACE CODES

Character	Code	OK in Find What Box?	OK in Replace With Box?
Annotation mark	^a	Yes	No
Any single character	^?	Yes	No
Any single digit	^#	Yes	No
Any single letter	^$	Yes	No
ASCII character number *nnn*	^O*nnn*	Yes	Yes
Caret character	^^	Yes	Yes
Clipboard contents	^c	No (text only)	Yes (text or graphics)
Column break	^n	Yes	Yes
Contents of the Find What box	^&	No	Yes
Em dash (—)	^+	Yes	Yes
En dash (–)	^=	Yes	Yes
Endnote mark	^e	Yes	No
Field code	^d	Yes	No
Footnote mark	^f	Yes	No
Graphic	^g	Yes	No
Manual line break	^l	Yes	Yes
Manual page break	^m	Yes	Yes
Nonbreaking hyphen	^~	Yes	Yes
Nonbreaking space	^s	Yes	Yes
Optional hyphen (activated)	^-	Yes	Yes
Paragraph mark	^p	Yes	Yes
Section break	^b	Yes	No
Tab	^t	Yes	Yes
White space	^w	Yes	No

PART

III

Productivity Tools

How Replace Interacts with Styles

Be aware that just as manually applied formatting and styles interact when you change styles or formatting yourself, they interact when the Replace command makes changes.

As explained at the end of Chapter 12, *Using Paragraph Styles and AutoFormat*, Word distinguishes between manual formatting (formatting you apply directly from the toolbar or Font menu) and style formatting (formatting that is applied to text as part of a style definition). When you define a style based on a manually formatted selection, Word tries to include in the style any kind of formatting that is applied to the majority of the selection (actually the first 255 characters of it, to be pedantic). Any manual formatting applied intermittently is interpreted as just that—manual formatting layered on top of the style formatting.

Replace operations can include combinations of style formatting and manual formatting. Searches for boldface text, for example, will find text you've made bold manually as well as text that has been formatted with a style that includes bold. You can search for any combination of style formatting and manual formatting and replace with any other combination.

If you combine both types of formatting under the Find What box, Word finds any examples that have the style formatting and match the manual formatting. If you combine both types of formatting under the Replace With box, Word applies the style formatting first and then layers the manual formatting on top of it. Of course, you can also use different combinations of either or both in the two boxes. Table 16.3 shows how the two types of formatting interact during the Replace operation.

TABLE 16.3: COMBINING MANUAL AND STYLE FORMATTING IN REPLACE

If you find	And replace it with	You get
manual formatting	manual formatting	all formatted text given new formatting
manual formatting	style formatting	all formatted text given style formatting in addition to manual formatting
manual formatting	manual and style formatting	all formatted text given style formatting and new manual formatting layered on top
style formatting	manual formatting	all text in that style given manual formatting in addition to the style formatting
style formatting	style formatting	all text in the old style given the new style
style formatting	manual and style formatting	all text in the old style given the new style and the manual formatting layered on top

Chapter

17

Get Organized with Outline View

Chapter

17

Get Organized with Outline View

Word's *Outline view*, available from the View menu (Ctrl+Alt+O), is really more than a view. It's a collection of tools designed to help you plan, create, and reorganize long documents. It does this by letting you expand or contract the amount of detail you see on your screen. Figure 17.1 illustrates Outline view.

> **TIP**
>
> For some projects, Word's new Document Map feature might be a better choice than Outline view. For example, if you need to locate only part of a document, the map might be quicker than Outline view. If you are not familiar with the Document Map, see Chapter 2, *Viewing and Navigating,* for details.

The bottom window in Figure 17.1 shows part of a document in Normal view. The top window shows the same document in Outline view with all the body text collapsed (not displayed). Because only paragraph headings are visible in the bottom window, it's easy to see the overall organization (the outline) of the document. As you will soon see, Outline view lets you control how much detail you see. For instance, you can view the first line of text following each heading if you wish. The special split-screen view shown in Figure 17.1 is explained later in this chapter in the "Split Views" section.

FIGURE 17.1

This special split-screen view showing Outline view (top) lets you get a bird's-eye view of a large document (bottom).

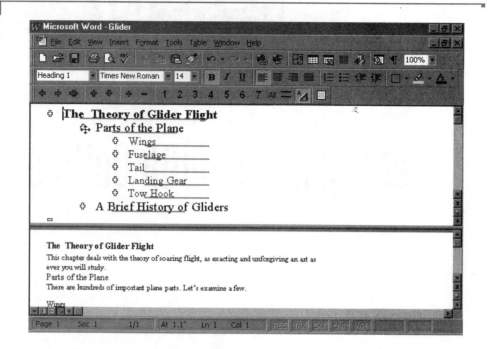

Notice also that headings in Outline view are indented, giving you a better idea of the document's organization. Each new level is indented 0.25" from the preceding one.

It's a snap to reorganize documents in Outline view. If you want to move all the paragraphs having to do with Landing Gear so that they appear before Tail, simply drag the Landing Gear heading marker using the Outline view's special pointer. This will move all corresponding paragraphs, called the heading's *subtext*.

Finally, you can quickly *promote* or *demote* portions of your document (that is, change a level 2 head to level 3, or vice versa) using the Outline view tools, found on the Outline toolbar.

Styles and Outlines

To use Outline view, you first need to format your headings using Word's standard-heading styles (Heading 1 through Heading 9). Even if you didn't use these styles when you created a document, it is easy to reformat with them. And, as you probably know, you can change the appearance of standard headings if you don't like Word's standard styles. (See Chapter 12, *Using Paragraph Styles and AutoFormat,* for more about styles.)

What You See in Outline View

Outline view presents a number of unique elements, not seen in other views. First, there is the Outline toolbar, at the top of the screen. Also, the mouse pointer changes to a compass shape when it is poised to move a heading and its text.

Another difference is that on-screen text is often underlined with an unusual line style. This does not indicate text that will be underlined when printed. Rather, it indicates collapsed subtext beneath it.

Large plus signs, boxes, and dashes appear next to many headings in Outline view. Boxes tell you that you are looking at body text; pluses indicate headings containing subtext; and minuses denote headings without subtext.

The Outline Toolbar's Tools

Figure 17.2 summarizes the Outline toolbar's unique tools. They promote and demote heading levels, hide or reveal body text, and turn formatting on and off.

The best way to understand the effect of these tools is to open a document containing standard Word headings in Outline view and experiment. If you don't have a document of your own, create one or use one of the templates by opening it as a document. The rest of this chapter describes the various Outline view tools, offering tips on how to use them.

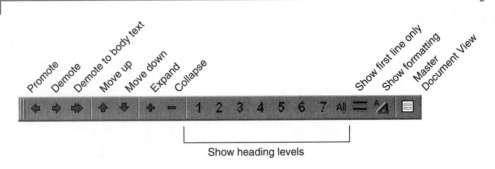

Show heading levels

Creating and Editing Outlines

When you start typing a new document in Outline view, Word assumes that you first want to type a level 1 heading. Each new paragraph you type will take on the heading level of the previous paragraph.

PART

III

Productivity Tools

One strategy is to type all your top-level headings first and then go back and insert headings in progressively lower heading levels. Another approach is to type all your document's headings in sequence, promoting and demoting as you go. It is even possible to type the entire document (all headings and text) in Outline view without doing a traditional outline first. (Of course, if you do this, you lose much of the benefit of outlining, particularly the opportunity to see all your headings in sequence and verify that they make sense.)

The outlining approach you choose is largely a matter of personal preference. In any scenario, you will need to know how to promote and demote headings and text.

Promoting and Demoting

The two arrows at the left end of the Outline toolbar are used to promote and demote headings. Place the insertion point in the heading you want to promote or demote. Click on the right arrow to demote or on the left arrow to promote. Figure 17.3 shows this at work on a new outline originally typed with everything at level 1.

Here I placed the insertion point in the *Parts of the Plane* heading and clicked on the right arrow once. I then highlighted the headings *Wings* through *Tow Hook* and clicked

FIGURE 17.3

The right arrow demotes selected headings, and the left arrow promotes them.

All headings at top level

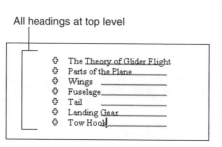

Click once to demote current heading

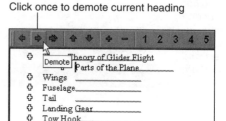

Click twice to demote two levels

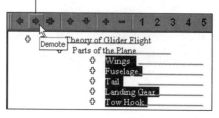

The results

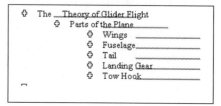

on the right arrow twice, which demoted them two levels. The results are shown at the bottom of Figure 17.3. I have left the *Theory of Glider Flight* heading at the top level; *Parts of the Plane* is now the next level down, and *Wings* through *Tow Hook* are at heading level 3. (You could confirm this by switching to Normal or Page Layout view.)

Promoting works as you'd expect. With the insertion point in a heading, click on the left arrow to turn a level 3 heading into a level 2 heading, and so on.

Outlining Existing Documents

To outline existing documents, follow these steps:

1. Open your document in Outline view.
2. Place the insertion point in each heading and promote or demote as desired.
3. Save your work.
4. Use the viewing techniques described next to view and rearrange the organization of your document.

Expanding and Collapsing Outlines

One of the main reasons to use Outline view is to get a collapsed overview of a document's contents. Do this by turning on Show First Line Only and then expanding and collapsing views with the numbers and buttons on the Outline toolbars.

For instance, Figure 17.4 shows our Glider book in a bit more detail than the view in previous figures. The first line of text beneath each heading has been revealed.

This was accomplished by clicking on the Show First Line Only button (just to the left of the Show Formatting button) on the Outline toolbar. Clicking on the All icon—just to the right of the number 8—displays all headings and text.

The document's true heading styles are apparent in Figure 17.4. The Show Formatting button at the end of the Outline toolbar turns character formatting on and off.

Clicking on the numbers 1 through 8 in Outline view hides or displays the levels of your document. For instance, in our sample document, clicking on 1 will reveal only level 1 headings (the *Theory of Glider Flight*). Clicking on the 2 would reveal both level 1 and level 2 headings (*Parts of the Plane* and *A Brief History of Gliders*).

Split Views

Figure 17.5 illustrates a strategy for working on large documents. You can split the screen and show your document in Page Layout view in one half of the window and Outline view in the other.

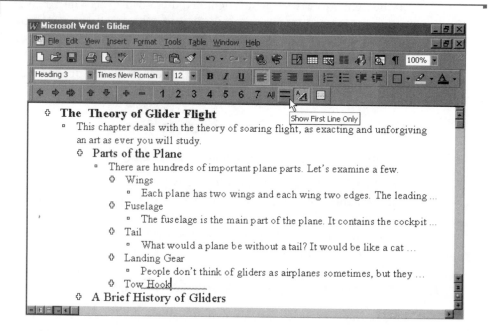

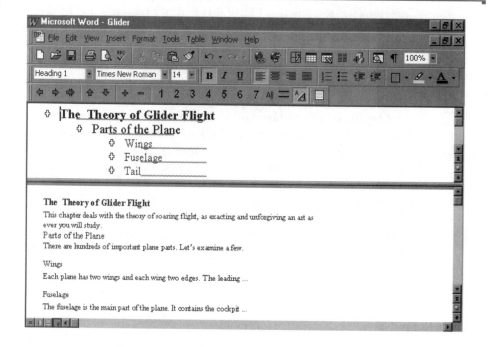

To split a window this way, double-click on the Split bar. Then drag it up or down to change the size of the two areas. Each part of the screen has its own scroll bars. Double-clicking on the Split bar (in the scroll area) or dragging the bar in the pane of a split window returns you to a single window.

> **TIP**
>
> When you double-click on the Split bar to unsplit a document divided into two panes, the pane in which you had the insertion point will become the full page. So be careful! If you are taken away from where you want to work, pressing Shift + F5 (Go Back) might help.

Moving Paragraphs

With the outline collapsed, you can move collections of paragraphs (*subtext*) by moving their associated headings. When you move a heading, *all* the lower-level heads and text below it are moved along with it. This makes it easy to move entire chapters or sections without selecting the text. Think of this feature as drag-and-drop on steroids. Figure 17.6 shows how it works.

Placing the pointer over the left edge of a heading changes the pointer's shape. It will look like a compass. Click and drag, and a large right arrow will appear along with a dotted line, like the ones shown in Figure 17.6. Drag the line and the pointer to where you want to move the text. Release the mouse button, and the document will be reorganized.

The up- and down-pointing arrows on the Outline toolbar will also move items up and down. Highlight the headings; then click on the appropriate arrow.

> **TIP**
>
> You can use Outline view to maintain alphabetic order in documents such as glossaries, membership directories, and the like. Be sure the headings to be alphabetized are all at the same level (preferably Heading 1). Collapse the outline to that level and select the headings. Then select Table ➤ Sort and click on OK with the default sorting options. You can repeat the sort after adding new entries.

PART

III

Productivity Tools

FIGURE 17.6

Drag outline headings to move them and all their related subtext.

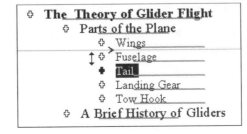

Dragging to Change Levels

You can also drag to change the indent level in Outline view. When you do, the pointer arrow changes, and you'll see a guideline that indicates the pending indent level as shown in Figure 17.7.

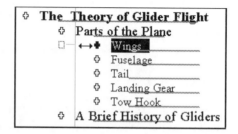

Rearrange Tables by Dragging Rows

When you view a table in Outline view, it is possible to move rows by dragging them. This is illustrated in Figure 17.8.

Numbering Headings in Outline View

You can number headings in any view, but Outline view makes it easiest to see their sequence. Figure 17.9 illustrates this.

To number headings in Outline view, follow these steps:

1. Choose Format ➤ Bullets and Numbering and then select the Outline Numbered tab.
2. Click on a sample to select a numbering format, or choose Customize for custom-numbering choices.
3. Click on OK.

FIGURE 17.9

*The Outline
Numbered tab
in the Bullets
and Numbering
dialog box*

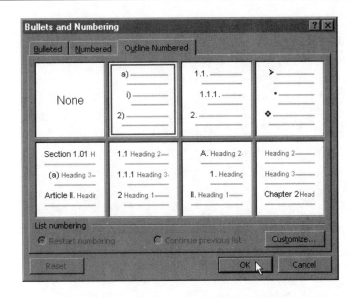

Word will renumber immediately whenever you rearrange your outline. Whenever you add a heading, it will automatically be numbered, as shown in Figure 17.10.

FIGURE 17.10

*When you add
headings, they
will be num-
bered as you
have specified.*

⊕ 1.1.4 Landing Gear
⊕ 1.1.5 Tow Hook
▭ 1.2 Thermals—Rising Hot Air

Printing Outlines

Printing in Outline view creates a document containing only the levels you see on the screen. Collapse the document to the desired level, and then choose File ➤ Print or press Ctrl+P. Even if only the first line of text appears, Word will print the whole paragraph.

PART

III

Productivity Tools

PART — IV

Desktop Publishing

LEARN TO:

- *Use templates and Wizards to create a consistent family of documents*

- *Work with multicolumn documents*

- *Create tables of contents and indexes*

- *Use Word Art and Microsoft Photo Editor*

- *Work with master documents*

- *Collaborate over a network*

- *Import, export, and convert files*

Chapter

18

The Document Shop

The Document Shop

In an earlier chapter, you read about the basics of Word templates, Wizards, and sample documents. Here, you will see examples of templates and Wizards in use. To bring some semblance of order to the many choices, I've organized the topics in this chapter to more or less mimic the tabs you'll find in Word's New dialog box—the place where you start a new project. The exact number of templates and Wizards you will find in your New dialog box might be different from the illustrations here, due to differences in installation choices. For example, if you installed Word as part of Microsoft Office, you will have a tab called Office 95 templates. (We'll cover the choices in that tab in this chapter too.) It is also possible to download additional templates and Wizards from Microsoft's Web site. That topic will also be discussed here. And, you or someone else might have added or deleted some templates.

NOTE

See Chapter 13, *Templates, Wizards, and Sample Documents*, to learn how to add your own templates and modify existing ones.

The beauty of templates is that Word does most of the busy work (setting tabs, specifying fonts, leading, borders, and other formatting options), leaving you free to create, customize, and add your own personal touch. These features are sometimes confusing, even to Word experts, but to get started, you only need to understand a few things. So as a review:

Wizards are automatic programs that run within Word. *Document Wizards* such as the ones discussed in this chapter help you set up specific types of documents: letters, memos, awards, calendars, agendas, and so forth. You use Wizards to create documents "on the fly," telling Word how you want things to look each step of the way.

Templates are partially completed documents. Usually, you fill in most of the text in templates, but some text may be filled in for you (such as the word *Fax* at the top of the Fax template). Moreover, Microsoft has provided more than a dozen templates with "canned" text, such as price increase announcements, thank-you letters, credit report requests, and many others. You fill in the specifics, but Word takes care of all the formatting and most of the wording. (These canned letters are accessed through the Letter Wizard.)

Templates contain special *styles* designed to give documents just the right look. There are *families* of styles (named Contemporary, Elegant, and Professional). You can base all your documents on templates using the same family of styles to ensure a consistent look. To learn more about styles, review the information in Chapter 12, *Using Paragraph Styles and AutoFormat*.

NOTE

Many of the templates and Wizards in this chapter will work with your Microsoft Office Address book if you've set one up. This makes it easy to enter recipients' names and addresses without retyping them. For more information about Address books, check the online documentation and owner's manual that came with Office.

Consider Differences in Families

There are obvious differences in the three style families (Contemporary, Elegant, and Professional), but there are also subtle differences worth exploring. For example, the sample document that comes as part of the Contemporary letter template has a facility for quickly adding a logo graphic. Professional and Elegant templates do not. There are often differences in the way page numbering is handled, the location and variety of header and footer material, and so forth. Take some time to explore the options in each of the template types you might use (letterheads, reports, and so on) before committing to a particular family.

Letters and Faxes

When you look in the Letters & Faxes tab of the New dialog box, you will see 10 or more choices as illustrated in Figure 18.1. There are templates for Contemporary, Professional, and Elegant letters. In addition, a Letter Wizard can lead you through the steps of creating a single letter or personalized letters for a group of recipients. This is also where you will find Wizards for creating envelopes and mailing labels.

Double-clicking on a template icon (those with names ending in .dot) opens a new document using the chosen template. Double-clicking on a Wizard icon (those with names ending in .wiz) runs the corresponding Wizard.

FIGURE 18.1

The Letters & Faxes tab

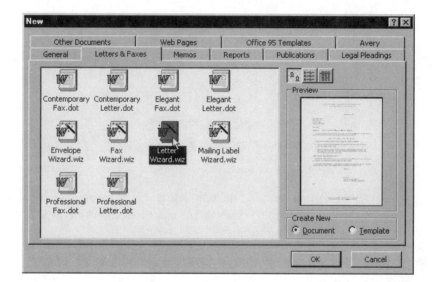

Letter Templates

Double-clicking on a letter template icon in the New dialog box opens a new letter document in the chosen style (Elegant, Contemporary, or Professional). Figure 18.2 shows a new Contemporary document.

If you plan to use the template only once or twice, simply click on the areas you want to edit (the recipient's name, for example) and then save and print the document as you would any other. If you want to create a customized template to use over and over (so that your inside address and phone information always pop up, for example) or if you

FIGURE 18.2

Beginning a Contemporary letter. (Double-click on the Envelope icon to learn more about the template.)

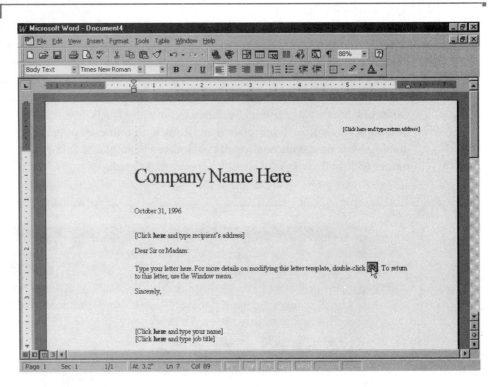

want to learn more about the template and how to modify it, double-click on the Envelope icon (as shown in Figure 18.2). Figure 18.3 shows a typical finished letter using the Contemporary letter template.

> **NOTE**
> If you don't plan to enter information in one of the Click Here boxes, select the box and delete it so that the Click Here message does not appear in your finished document(s).

The Letter Wizard

The Letter Wizard (Letter Wizard.wiz) leads you through an almost exhausting series of letter-formatting choices. Begin by clicking on its icon in the Letters & Faxes tab in the New dialog box. You will see the beginnings of a new letter and the Assistant asking if you want to send one letter or if you plan to send a letter to many folks on a mailing list, as shown in Figure 18.4.

FIGURE 18.3

A typical Contemporary letter created with the Contemporary Letter.dot template

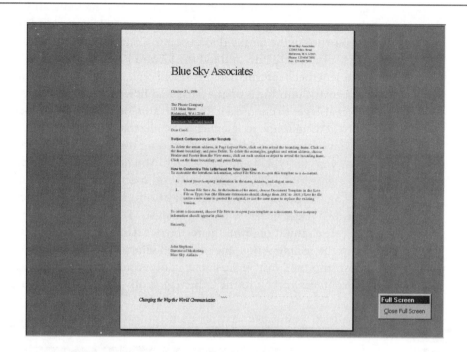

FIGURE 18.4

Getting Started with the Letter Wizard

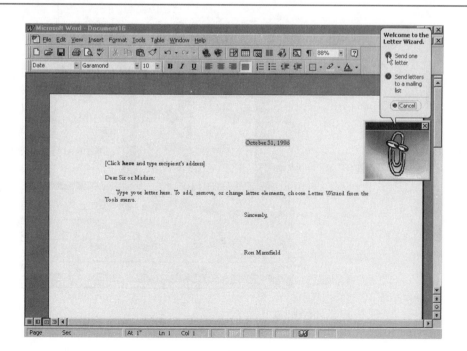

Click on the appropriate button in the Assistant's "balloon." If you are creating a single letter, you will see the progressive dialog box illustrated in Figure 18.5.

Here you choose the family (Professional, Contemporary, or Elegant.), specify the appearance of the date line, and tell the Wizard if the paper you will be feeding your printer has letterhead information preprinted on it. If the paper *is* preprinted, you tell the Wizard where the printing is on the paper and how much room is needed to accommodate it. You also get to choose a letter style (Full Block, Modified Block, or Semi-Block). Click on Next to go to the recipient choices, illustrated in Figure 18.6.

If you have set up an address book, you can use it to fill in the recipient's mailing address, or you can type it all from scratch. You do this in the Recipient's Info tab, as shown in Figure 18.6. This is also where you specify the desired standardized salutation (Dear Sir or Madam, To Whom It May Concern, and so on). Alternatively, you can type your own (Dear Buzzmunch or whatever). The Wizard is clever enough to guess how to create a salutation from the recipient's name. For example if you type **Mr. Phil DeTank** in the recipient box, the proposed salutation will be Dear Mr. DeTank. You can choose informal, formal, business, or other salutation formatting. Clicking on the Next button takes you on to the Other Elements tab, shown in Figure 18.7.

FIGURE 18.5

Letter Format choices in the Letter Wizard

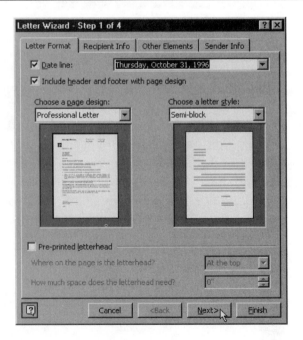

FIGURE 18.6

Recipient Info choices in the Letter Wizard

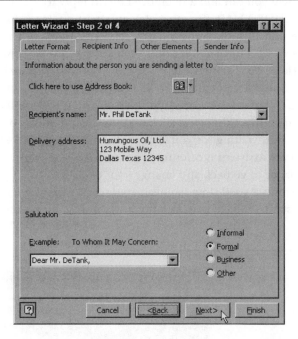

FIGURE 18.7

The Wizard's Other Elements tab

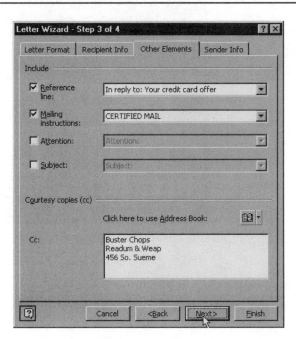

Here you can add a reference line (In reply to:, for example), mailing instructions (CERTIFIED MAIL, for example), an attention line (Attention: or ATTN:), a subject line, and a list of courtesy copy recipients. Here too you can use the address book if you've set it up. Then it's on to the Sender Info tab, illustrated in Figure 18.8.

Here you specify the letter author's name and an inside address if you are not using preprinted letterhead paper. You can also specify the other bottom matter (closing, title, initials of the writer/typist, an so on). If there will be enclosures, you can specify the quantity. When you click on the Finish button, you will see a partially completed letter just waiting for you to type the text. Figure 18.9 shows you an example. Notice that the Assistant is offering to help with an envelope or a mailing label or to give you a chance to go back and change your choices.

This is a good time to check your work. Does the return address look okay? The Assistant will take you back if you want to rethink some of your choices.

FIGURE 18.8

The Wizard's Sender Info tab

FIGURE 18.9

The Wizard's progress

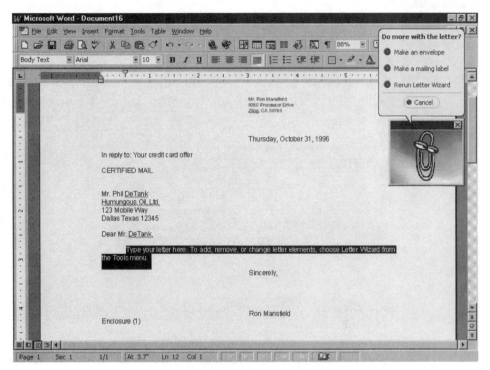

Envelopes and Mailing Labels

There are, perhaps, too many ways to create envelopes and mailing labels in Word. Chapter 3, *Previewing and Printing*, describes several options. Additionally, you can use the Envelopes and Labels Wizard found in the Letters & Faxes tab of the New dialog box, which accomplishes basically the same thing. Figure 18.10 shows the Wizard at work.

Here are the steps:

1. Choose File ➤ New to open the New dialog box.
2. Choose the Letters & Faxes tab if it is not already selected.
3. Double-click on either the Envelope Wizard.wiz icon for envelopes or the Mailing Label Wizard.wiz icon for mailing labels.
4. The assistant will ask if you want to create a single envelope (or label). The alternate choice is to use a mailing list (see Chapter 26, *Mail Merge—Creating Custom Documents*, for details). Click on the appropriate button in the Assistant's balloon.

FIGURE 18.10

The Envelopes and Labels Wizard at work

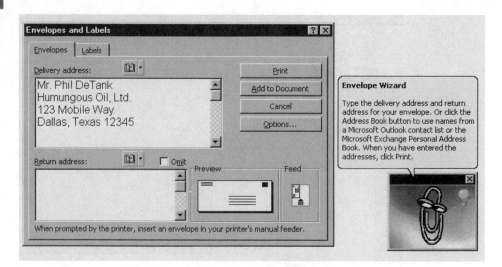

5. To choose or confirm envelope or label size and orientation settings, click on the Options button.

6. Choose a delivery address from the drop-down list or from an address book if you have one. Alternatively, you can type a delivery address in the space allotted.

7. Type a return address if it is different from what's displayed, or click on the Omit button to keep the return address from printing.

8. Click on the Preview button to see what's likely to print.

9. Click on Print, and follow the on-screen instructions.

Faxes

The Fax templates create cover sheets and come in the usual three flavors—Professional, Elegant, and Contemporary. You can use these templates alone or with the Fax Wizard. The templates and Wizard will create printed paper faxes that you can feed through a traditional fax machine, or you can use a fax-capable modem to send "paperless" fax cover sheets and Word documents. Here are the general steps for using the Fax Wizard to create a cover sheet and send a Word document:

1. If you plan to fax a document—a memo or whatever (as opposed to just sending a cover sheet with a note)—open the document you want to send.

2. Double-click on the Fax Wizard icon in the New dialog box.

3. After reading the Wizard's opening screen, click on Next.

4. Using the dialog box shown in Figure 18.11, specify the document you want to send with (or without) a cover sheet, or click on the "Just a cover sheet with a note" button if you want to send only a cover sheet containing a note. Click on Next.

5. Using the dialog box shown in Figure 18.12, choose the device and the fax software you will use to send the fax. (This can be Microsoft Fax and your modem or some other fax software and your modem, or you can print the fax on your printer and carry it to a traditional fax machine.) Click on Next.

6. Enter the name(s) and fax number(s) of the recipient(s). Use an electronic address book if you have one. Figure 18.13 shows an example of this. Click on Next when you've entered all the recipient's info.

7. Choose a fax style (Professional, Contemporary, or Elegant). Click on Next.

8. Check and edit the sender information as illustrated in Figure 18.14, and then click on Next.

9. You will see the cover sheet illustrated in Figure 18.15. Click to edit such things as the page count, subject matter, and so forth. Double click to place checkmarks in the Urgent and other boxes as necessary.

10. When you are happy with the cover page, click on the Send Fax Now button. Your fax will be sent if the Fax gods are in a good mood.

FIGURE 18.11

Specifying a Word document to fax

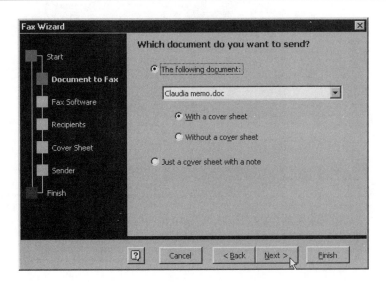

FIGURE 18.12

Choose the method of delivery (modem or printer)

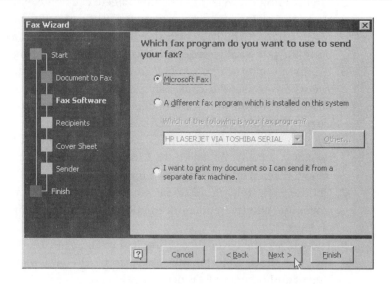

FIGURE 18.13

Entering the names and fax numbers of recipients

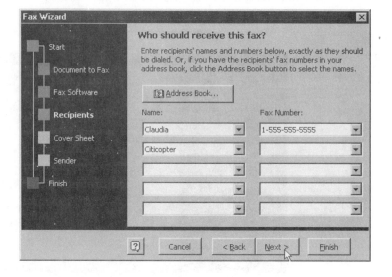

FIGURE 18.14

Editing the fax sender's information

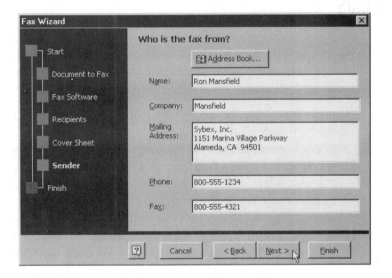

FIGURE 18.15

Previewing and editing the cover sheet

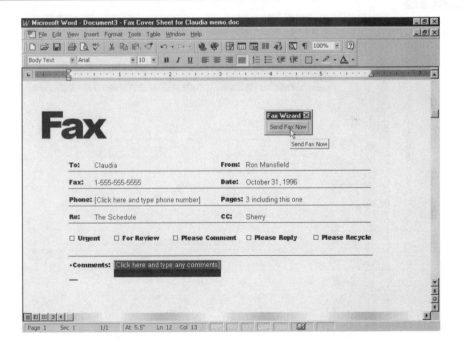

Memos

Here, as with letters and faxes, you can use the templates by themselves, or you can employ the Wizard, who will ask many questions and tailor the document to your specifications. Figure 18.16 shows a typical memo created with the Wizard.

Follow these steps:

1. Begin by double-clicking either on a memo template or on the Memo Wizard in the New dialog box.
2. Select a style (Professional, Elegant, or Contemporary) and click on Next.
3. If you want to add a title to your memo, type it in the box that appears at step 2. Click on Next.
4. In step 3 you can choose to add a date, from line, subject, and priority flag to the memo. Click on Next when you've made your choices.
5. In step 4, enter recipients' names either via the keyboard or by selecting them from your address book. Click on Next when you have all of the recipients named.

FIGURE 18.16

A typical Wizard-generated memo

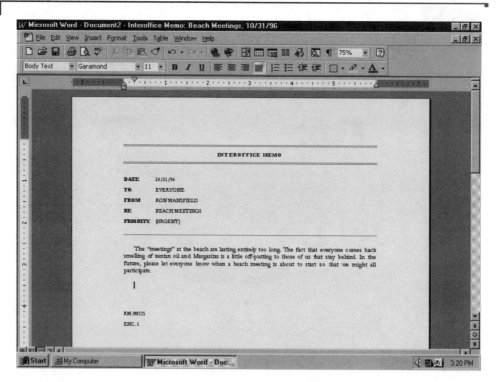

6. Now specify optional writer's initials, typist's initials, and enclosure counts. Click on Next.

7. You will be asked to specify header and footer information for pages 2+. Make your choices and click on Next.

8. Save a step here by clicking on Finish instead of Next.

9. The Wiz will display the memo and let you edit it. The Assistant will offer an opportunity to edit the headers, footers, style, recipient list, and so on.

10. Click in the body of the memo to type your words of wisdom, and then print it or electronically distribute it.

Reports

The Report templates contain gorgeous styles and carefully thought-out heading, table, header, footer, and other design elements, all capable of making you look extremely good in print, particularly when creating multipage documents.

Click on the Reports tab in the New dialog box, and then double-click on the format of your choice (Professional, Contemporary, or Elegant). Figure 18.17 shows two pages of a typical Professional report. Figure 18.18 shows the same two pages using the Contemporary template, and Figure 18.19 shows the Elegant format.

FIGURE 18.17

Two pages of a Professional report format

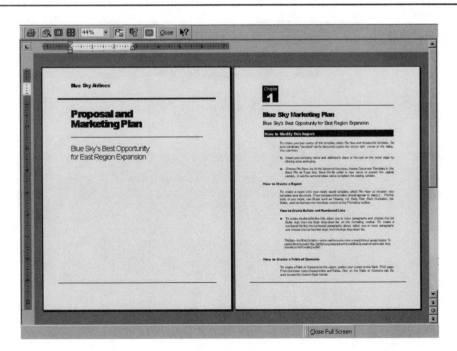

FIGURE 18.18

Two pages of a
Contemporary
report format

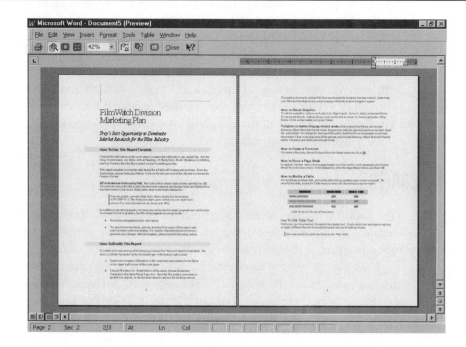

FIGURE 18.19

Two pages of an
Elegant report
format

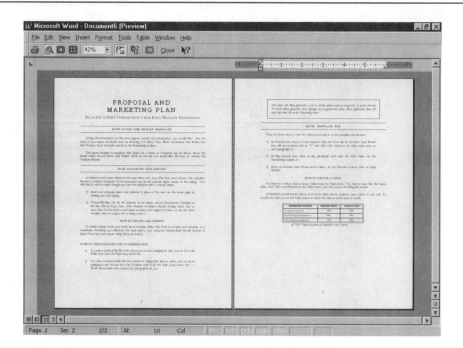

Your best bet is to start new documents using the Report template. The template itself contains "boilerplate" text that explains the elements of the template's design and how to use the template, so I'll not repeat that information here. It's a good idea to print out the sample report and read it completely; it's full of helpful tips and techniques.

Publications (Newsletters)

The Publications tab offers only one choice—the Newsletter Wizard—but it's a powerful tool. Besides making it easy to create multicolumn text and insert graphics, the Newsletter Wizard even makes room for a mailing address and a postal permit, if you like. Figures 18.20 and 18.21 show all four pages of the newsletter design. Check them out!

To create a newsletter, simply move to the Publications tab in the New dialog box, double-click on the Newsletter Wizard icon, and follow the on-screen prompts. As with the Reports template, it's a good idea to print out the sample newsletter and read it completely; it has lots of helpful tips and techniques.

FIGURE 18.20

Pages 1 and 2 of the newsletter layout

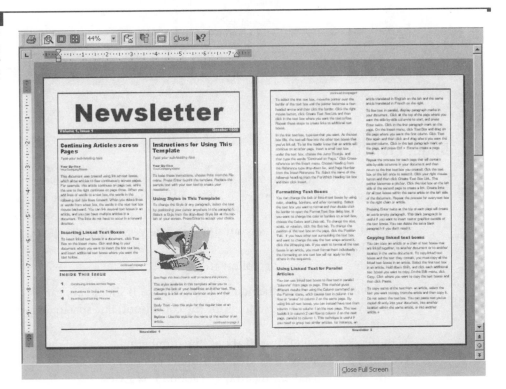

FIGURE 18.21

Pages 3 and 4 of the newsletter layout.

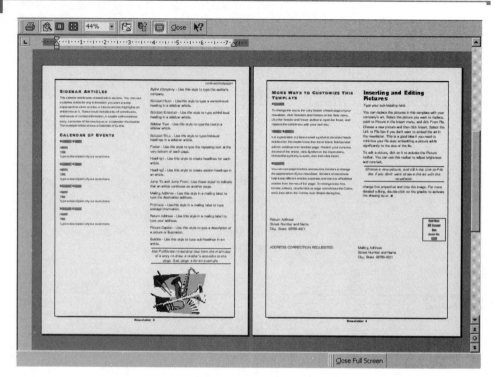

Legal Pleadings

Designed for attorneys and other legal practitioners, the Legal Pleadings Wizard walks you through the steps necessary to create a legal pleading. You are in control of many of the options, and it is up to you to determine if the end product satisfies the needs of court(s) where you plan to do your filing(s). The Wiz will not stop you from creating noncompliant documents.

To create a legal pleading, follow these steps:

1. You will be asked for the name of the court as it should appear on the pleading.
2. Next, you specify page settings for the court (font, line spacing, margins, lines per-page, and so on).
3. In step 3, you will be asked about line numbering.
4. Next, you'll specify the style and number of border lines.
5. Now, it's on to a dizzying array of caption box styles.

FIGURE 18.22

A typical Wizard-generated legal pleading

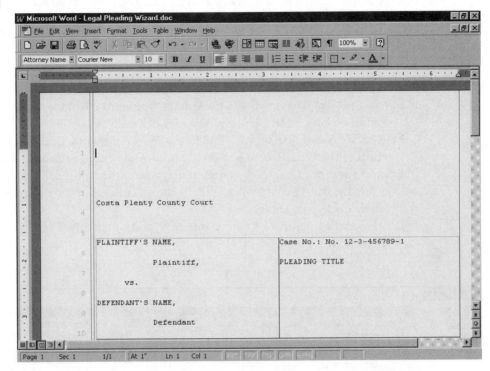

6. Next, it is time to enter the information that will appear on the beginning of the pleading (attorney and firm names, judge's name, and so on). Signature blocks are an option, and you can take them or leave them at this point in the dialog with the Wizard.

7. Once you've answered all the questions, the Wiz will save a template for you so that you can use it repeatedly (and perhaps share it with your co-workers).

Other Documents

The Other Documents tab in the New dialog box offers a résumé Wizard and templates for Professional, Contemporary, and Elegant résumés. There is also a Wizard designed to help you install additional templates (and even find more of them on the Internet). Let's take a look.

Résumés or Curriculum Vitae Templates and Wizards

You can use the résumé templates as-is to create your own résumé or vitae, but you might be better-served by the Wizard. Figure 18.23 shows one of many variations on a résumé produced with the Wizard.

To create a résumé or vitae, follow these general steps:

1. Start the Wizard by moving to the Other Documents tab in the New dialog box and double-clicking on the Resume Wizard. Click on Next.

2. Select a style (Professional, Contemporary, or Elegant). Relax. You can always return to the Wizard after you see the results and change the style. Click on Next.

3. Select the type of résumé you want (Entry-level, Chronological, Functional, or Professional). The Assistant will highlight the advantages of each. Click on Next after you've made your choice.

4. Enter your name, address, phone numbers, and e-mail info. Double-check them for accuracy, and then click on Next.

FIGURE 18.23

A typical Wizard-generated résumé

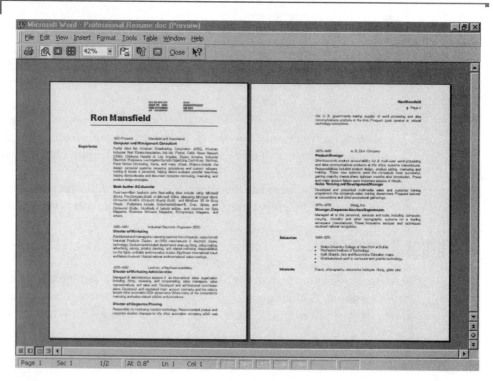

5. Begin selecting the headings you want in your résumé. (Education, Professional Experience, and so on). Click on Next.

6. Select from the second list of less-common headings (Hobbies, Security Clearance, and so forth). Click on Next.

7. You can add headings of your own if you want (Circus Experience, for example). You will see a list of headings and be given a chance to rearrange their order. Simply select a heading and click on the Move Up, Move Down, or Remove buttons. Click on Finish when done.

8. You will see the beginnings of your résumé. Click to enter and edit entries.

9. The Assistant will offer you the options of creating a cover letter or changing the style (from Professional to Elegant, or whatever), will offer to help you shrink the layout to make your résumé fit, and so on.

10. Proof carefully. This will be someone's first impression of you!

11. Save your work.

12. Print it and proof it again. Good luck!

The More Wizards and Templates Template

The More Wizards and Templates template (I know, I know) explains where to find additional templates on your installation disk or discs (see Figure 18.24). It also contains a hyperlink to Microsoft's Web site, where you might find additional useful templates. Obviously, you'll need an Internet connection to use the link. See Part VII for details.

Web Pages

Word 97 also contains a template you can use to create Web pages. For much more on how to do this, see the chapters in the last part of this book. Figure 18.25 shows an example of what you can do using this template.

Office Templates

If you purchased Word as part of Microsoft Office, you will find a tab containing additional templates. Here's a list of some of the templates you might find if you've installed them:

- Agendas
- Brochures
- Calendars

FIGURE 18.24

*The More
Wizards and
Templates
template*

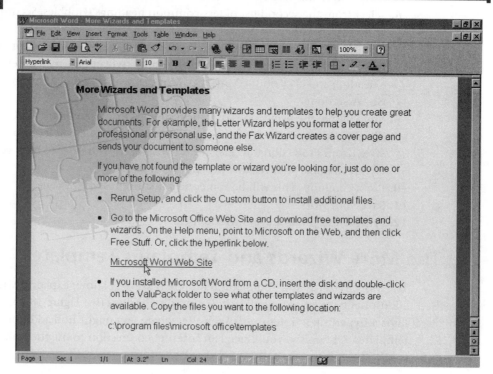

- Directories of Names and Addresses
- Press Releases
- Invoices
- Manuals
- Reports
- Purchase Orders
- Time Sheets
- Awards
- Theses
- Avery Labels

FIGURE 18.25

*A Wizard-
generated Web
page under
construction*

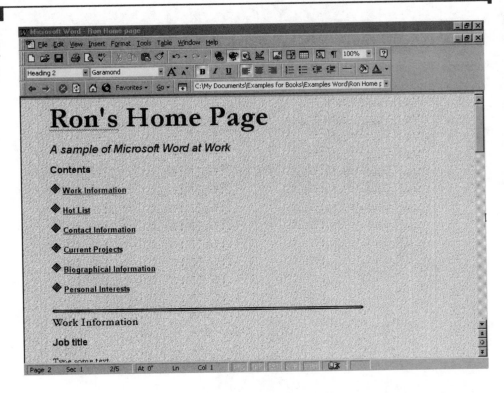

Chapter

19

Multiple Columns

FEATURING

Multiple Columns

Most people find short lines of text easier to read than long ones. That's one reason newspapers and books are frequently formatted in side-by-side snaking *columns*. Text flows from the bottom of one column to the top of the next until a page is filled; then it flows onto the next page.

Creating Multicolumn Documents

Arranging your text in columns is easy in Word. You can use the Columns button on the Standard toolbar to choose from 1 to 24 columns depending on the size and orientation of the paper (single is the default). If that's not enough, you can use the Columns dialog box (choose Format ➤ Columns) to specify as many as 45 columns (for *really* wide sheets of paper). Here are some common U.S. paper sizes and their column maximums:

Paper Size	Maximum Columns
8½ × 11 portrait	12 cols
8½ × 11 landscape	18 cols
8½ × 14 landscape	24 cols

You can also adjust the amount of white space between columns in the Columns dialog box.

When you start a new document, you can click on the Columns button to choose a maximum of six columns. Or you can use the Columns dialog box to increase the number of columns, and the Columns button will display the highest number you assigned.

In a single-section document, all pages must have the same number of columns. But, by breaking a document into multiple sections, you can have as many different column designs as you have sections. Word inserts section breaks automatically.

Word automatically adjusts column widths to accommodate your page size, orientation, and document margins. You can overrule these decisions.

It is possible to use indents within columns. You can edit columnar text just as you do any other. When you work in Page Layout view, you will see side-by-side columns as they will print. When working in Normal view, you will see text in the appropriate column width, but you will not see the columns in position next to each other. Scrolling is faster in Normal view; so Normal view is ideal for editing, and Page Layout view is better for formatting.

Word's column feature allows columns in a section to vary in width. You can drag columns or specify their widths precisely from your keyboard.

Simple Column Creation

Here's an easy way to create columns. If your document has only one section and if you want the same number of columns throughout the document, follow these steps:

1. Make any page setup, margin, and other design decisions that will affect the amount of text area on your page.
2. Click on the Columns button near the right edge of the Standard toolbar. As you can see in Figure 19.1, you *drag* across it to select the desired number of columns.
3. When you release the mouse button, Word automatically determines the appropriate width of columns and the amount of white space between them based on the page and document settings. You can see the columns as they will print in Page Layout view and Print Preview. You will see only a single column in Normal view.

Changing margins, page size, orientation, indents, and related settings will cause corresponding changes in column widths and spacing. The zero point on the ruler is always at the left edge of the column containing the insertion point. Clicking in the left column moves the zero point of the ruler to the left edge of the left column. Indents within columns work as you'd expect.

FIGURE 19.1

The Columns toolbar button puts multi-column text a click-and-drag away.

Drag to specify the number of columns.

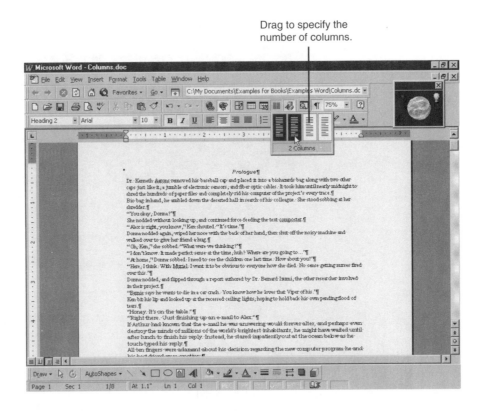

Using the Columns Dialog Box

You can create a maximum of 45 columns in either orientation if your paper is big enough, and you can specify the amount of white space between columns by using the Columns dialog box. You can also specify decorative lines between columns here, and you can create adjacent columns of different widths.

When you choose Format ➤ Columns, Word displays the Columns dialog box. Figure 19.2 shows the specifications for two columns with different widths. Notice that you can preview the results of choices made in this dialog box.

Using Different Column Designs within a Document

You can have different column designs in different parts of a document. For instance, part of a page could be a single column, and the rest, two or three columns.

FIGURE 19.2

You can pre-cisely specify the number of columns and the spacing in the columns box.

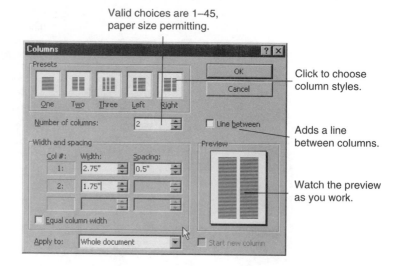

Valid choices are 1–45, paper size permitting.

Click to choose column styles.

Adds a line between columns.

Watch the preview as you work.

Word makes it easy to specify where new column settings should begin and end. Essentially, all you need to do is select text and specify a column design for it. Word formats the columns, inserts section breaks, and so on.

For example, to create the effect shown in Figure 19.3, follow these steps:

1. Select the text to be "columnized."
2. Click on the Columns button to specify column settings, or do so in the Columns dialog box (described next). Word applies the settings only to the selected text and inserts necessary breaks.

Controlling Column Width

Word initially sets the widths and spacing for you. It's possible, however, to drag columns to different widths using *margin markers*. Here's how. Follow along in Figure 19.4.

TIP

Some people find the Columns dialog box (choose Format ➤ Columns) more straightforward for adjusting column widths. The ruler method is quicker, but if you prefer, you can use the Columns dialog box to type in actual column widths.

1. Place the insertion point in any column.
2. In Page Layout view, display the rulers if they aren't already on-screen.
3. Drag any margin boundary on the ruler, and the columns will adjust to their new width.

FIGURE 19.3

Select text and then specify the column settings.

If you select text first, Word inserts the necessary breaks automatically.

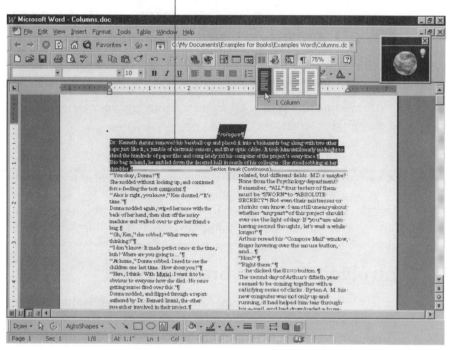

FIGURE 19.4

Drag margin markers to change column widths in Page Layout view.

Drag to change column widths and white space between columns.

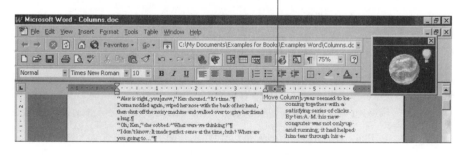

When creating columns of justified type, spacing within the lines can get a little raggedy. Consider using unjustified text or optional hyphens to tighten columns.

Adding Decorative Lines between Columns

Use the Columns dialog box if you want to add decorative lines between columns. Word provides only one line style.

1. Place the insertion point in the column you want to decorate.
2. Choose Format ➤ Columns.
3. Check the Line Between checkbox.

If you cannot see columns you've created, switch to Page Layout view. Columns are not displayed side by side in Normal view. Sometimes paragraph indenting can mess up columns. Try removing or decreasing indents.

Controlling Column Breaks

Use Word's Keep Lines Together and Keep with Next features to prevent unwanted breaks. Sometimes, you will want to force breaks. For example, the last page of a two-column document may end with uneven columns because Word will completely fill the left column before putting text in the right column.

Use Word's Insert ➤ Break command to force column breaks. Place the insertion point where you want the column break, choose Insert ➤ Break, specify Column Break, and click on OK. To remove breaks, highlight them and press Delete.

To change the position where column breaks change (to change where a page changes from single to multicolumn text, for example), simply drag the Section break while in Page Layout view.

Balancing Column Endings

Sometimes you'll have uneven column endings on the last page of a document or section. Figure 19.5 illustrates this problem (and no, you are not going blind—the text is *greeked*).

If you want to "even out" the columns, follow these steps while in Page Layout view:

1. Place the insertion point after the last character in the text.
2. Choose Insert ➤ Break.
3. In the Section Breaks area, choose Continuous.
4. Click on OK. The column bottoms will align as shown in Figure 19.6.

FIGURE 19.5

To avoid uneven columns such as this, insert a continuous break at the end of the text.

Insert a continuous break here to "even out" column lengths.

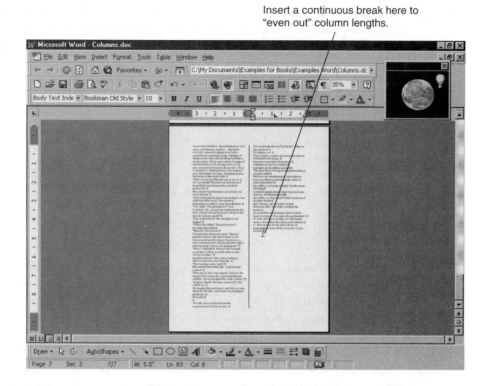

FIGURE 19.6

Flush column bottoms

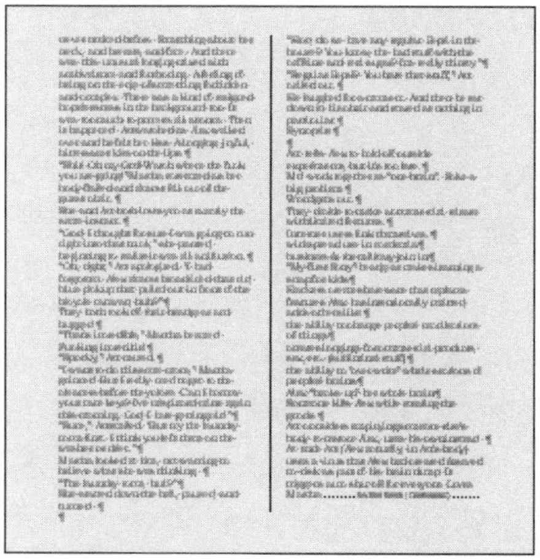

A number of things can affect column balancing. The Widow/Orphan control, Keep Lines Together, Keep with Next, and Page Break Before options can all cause you trouble. Turn them off in the paragraphs you want to balance. Use the Paragraph dialog box to do this.

Don't Forget Tables As an Alternative

Although creating and editing multiple columns is easy in Word, at times it will be easier to use tables instead of columns. This is particularly true for documents such as résumés and "television-style" scripts in which side-by-side items should always maintain the same horizontal relationship.

Removing Columns

To remove columns from an entire document, select all the text and click on the Columns button to specify a single column. To remove columns from one section in a multiple-section document, place the insertion point in the relevant section and then click on the Columns button.

If you inserted section breaks for the sole purpose of dividing areas of text with different column layouts (or if Word inserted them automatically), it is a good idea to clean up your document by deleting unwanted breaks.

Chapter

20

Creating Tables of Contents and Indexes

FEATURING

Creating Tables of Contents and Indexes

Word's slick automated features make creating a *table of contents* (TOC) for your documents a snap. If you format your headings using Word's standard heading styles or Outline feature, the Insert ➤ Index and Tables command will quickly compile (create) a simple but very usable table of contents and place it in a new section at the beginning of your document.

It is also possible to manually select items to appear in your table of contents. You do this by identifying words and phrases in your document using hidden text codes called *TOC Entry* codes. You can control the appearance of the table of contents as well. Your TOC can have one or multiple levels.

The Insert ➤ Index and Tables command and the hidden *Index Entry* codes work together to produce equally simple or distinctive *indexes* at the end of your document.

 TIP

If you plan to create an index for your document, you may want to create it before you create the table of contents so that it will show up as an entry in your TOC.

In this chapter you'll also learn how to create tables of authorities for legal documents and tables of figures for illustrated documents.

Creating a Table of Contents

Figure 20.1 shows a simple table of contents containing only paragraph headings, created using Word's standard Heading 1 through Heading 3 styles. (The appearance will vary based on the document template you use.)

Notice that Word has placed the TOC in its own new section at the beginning of the document. It has automatically inserted tabs, and page numbers. In some cases, Word will also add leading dots. This depends on which headings and document templates you use. To format and indent the new table of contents, it has used TOC styles corresponding to the standard heading styles. Thus, headings in the document formatted with standard Heading 3 will appear in the TOC formatted with a standard style called TOC 3.

To create a table of contents, follow these general steps:

1. Begin by formatting your document's headings with Word's standard heading styles.

TIP

Using the Style dialog box, you can add these styles to your Formatting toolbar's drop-down style list. See Chapter 12, *Using Paragraph Styles and AutoFormat*, for more about styles.

FIGURE 20.1

You can produce multilevel TOCs using Word's standard heading styles.

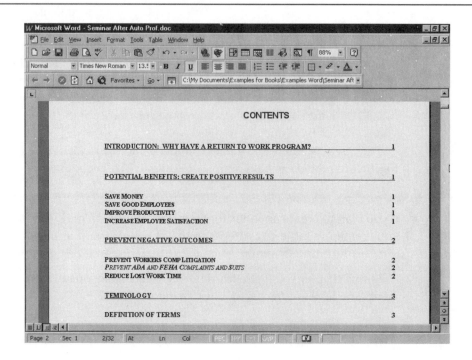

2. When you have typed and proofed your document and are happy with margins, headers, footers, and other design elements (especially those that affect page breaks), place the cursor where you want the Table of Contents and choose Insert ➤ Index and Tables. Word displays the Index and Tables dialog box, as shown in Figure 20.2.

FIGURE 20.2

The Index and Tables dialog box with the Table of Contents tab selected

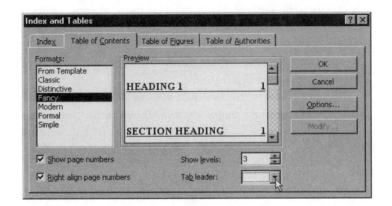

3. Choose the Table of Contents tab if it is not already selected.
4. Preview the available formats by clicking in the Formats list and watching the Preview area. Choose one.
5. Choose the number of levels you want in the TOC.
6. If you want to include a tab leader (dashes or dots, for instance), choose the style from the drop-down list.
7. Click on OK or press Enter. Word compiles the new TOC. It starts by repaginating your document, and then it inserts the TOC at the insertion point.

NOTE

If you've already created a TOC for the document, Word will ask if you want to replace it. If you choose No, you will end up with *two* TOCs at the beginning of your document. (This is a way to create two levels of content detail such as the Contents at a Glance and regular TOC at the beginning of this book.)

Including Non-Heading Styles in Your TOC

Word lets you easily include non-heading styles in your TOC. For example, suppose you create and define a style called Chapters, and you want it to be "above" Heading 1 in your TOC. You can use the TOC options to accomplish this.

1. Create and define styles for items you want to include in the TOC.
2. Format the material using these styles.
3. Open the Table of Contents tab in the Index and Tables dialog box (choose Insert ➤ Index and Tables).
4. Click on the Options button.
5. Word displays a scrolling list of all styles in the current document, as illustrated in Figure 20.3.
6. Assign "levels" to the styles you want to include in the TOC, as illustrated in Figure 20.3, where major topics will be the first level, Heading 2 topics the second, and so on.
7. Make any other formatting choices and create the TOC as usual.

A list of styles

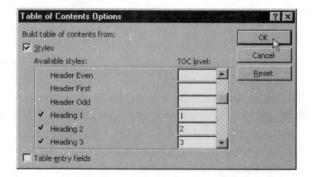

Changing a TOC's Appearance

A few styles apply formats such as all caps and small caps for different levels. Some styles include underlines. If it bothers you that, for example, some headings have both underlines and leader characters, remove one or the other format and redefine the style using standard Word techniques.

You can edit the resulting TOC as you would edit any other text in your document. Feel free to boldface characters, change line spacing, and so on. As you'd expect, changing the style definitions for styles 1 through 9 changes the appearance of your TOC. There's an easy way to do this in Word:

1. Select the Table of Contents tab in the Index and Tables dialog box (choose Insert ➤ Index and Tables).

2. Select the From Template option from the Formats list.

3. Click on the Modify button.

4. Word displays the Style dialog box, illustrated in Figure 20.4.

FIGURE 20.4

The Style dialog box

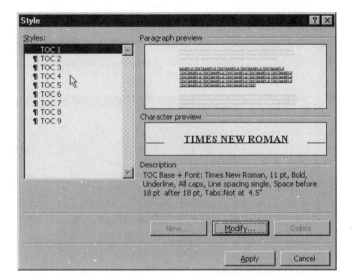

5. In the scrolling list, click on the style you want to modify.

6. Click on the Modify button. Word displays the Modify Style dialog box.

7. Make the desired changes to the style using the drop-down lists and the Format button (which takes you to familiar formatting dialog boxes).

8. Work your way back to the Index and Tables dialog box and click on OK.

Restricting Levels

If a document has numerous heading levels, you probably don't want to include all of them in your TOC. To suppress the display of all levels past a certain point (everything after 5, for instance), specify the levels you do want in the Show Levels portion of the Table of Contents tab:

You can also turn levels on and off in the Table of Contents Options dialog box. To restrict levels, follow these steps:

1. Open the Index and Tables dialog box (choose Insert ➤ Index and Tables) and select the Table of Contents tab.
2. Click on the Options button.
3. Turn off headings by removing numbers from the TOC Level box.
4. Change levels by typing in the TOC Level boxes. For instance, in this example Heading Levels 3 and 4 will not print, and headings 5 and 6 will print as levels 3 and 4.

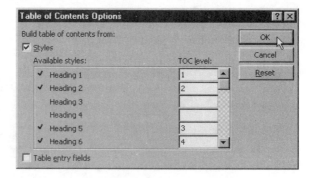

Updating a Table of Contents

You can update a TOC after you've made changes to your document. You'll be given the choice of changing only page numbers or updating the entire TOC. Here are the general steps:

1. Click in the TOC to highlight the entire TOC (it will turn gray).

2. Press F9. Word displays the Update Table of Contents dialog box.

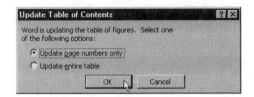

3. Choose Update Page Numbers Only or Update Entire Table.

4. Click on OK.

You can also update your TOC by clicking the right mouse button and selecting Update Field from the drop-down menu.

Creating an Index

Word compiles indexes on demand and places them at the end of your document in new sections that it creates for this purpose. You tell Word which words or phrases to include either by marking them in the document or by creating a separate list and then Automarking them. Whichever method you use, marking an index entry creates a code called an XE, or Index Entry, field.

Marking Index Entries

Word makes it easy to create an index. You can create a simple index by selecting text, issuing the Alt+Shift+X keyboard shortcut, and choosing a few options. Word then compiles and styles an index and places it at the document's end. Here are the basic steps:

1. Start by making sure that you are done proofing, fiddling with margins, page endings, and the like.

2. Select (highlight) a word or a phrase you want to use as an index entry.

3. Press Alt+Shift+X.

4. Word displays the Mark Index Entry dialog box, as illustrated in Figure 20.5.

5. Click on Mark to mark only this entry, or click on Mark All to mark all occurrences. (If you choose Mark All, Word scans the document, marking all occurrences, and the status area will tell you how many it found.) Edit the entry and add a subentry. You can also include a cross-reference at this time ("See").

FIGURE 20.5

The Mark Index Entry dialog box

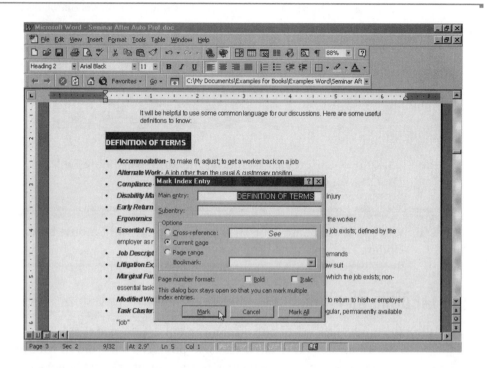

> **WARNING**
>
> The Mark All choice, while tempting, carries risks. It may include trivial as well as significant occurrences of words, which is considered bad indexing practice.

6. The Mark Index Entry dialog box remains visible so that you can scroll to other text and mark it or simply type words to be indexed into the Main Entry text box. For example, you might flag an occurrence of *garden slender salamander* and add *Amphibians* as the main entry.

7. Repeat steps 2 through 6 until you have specified all desired entries.

8. Click on the Close button to close the dialog box.

9. Place the insertion point where you want the index (typically at the end of your document).

10. Choose Insert ➤ Index and Tables.

11. Select the Index tab on the Index and Tables dialog box, as shown in Figure 20.6.

12. Select an index style using the scrolling Preview area as your guide.

FIGURE 20.6

*The Index tab
of the Index
and Tables
dialog box*

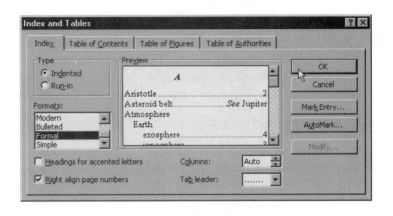

13. Double-click on the name of the desired style or click once on a style name and once on OK.

14. Word repaginates the document, creates an index, and places it at the insertion point.

Updating Indexes

Each time you close the Index tab in the Index and Tables dialog box, Word will ask if you want to replace (recompile) the selected index. Click on Yes if you do (and you probably will want to). But there's also a shortcut worth knowing:

1. Click anywhere in the index to select it.

2. Press the right mouse button to see a shortcut menu:

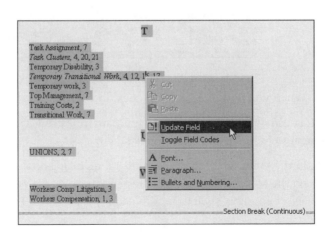

3. Choose Update Field. Word repaginates, recompiles, and updates the index.

WARNING

Generating the index should be the last thing you do with your document. Updating it can be useful, because you can reflect changes in your document, but it is time consuming; so finish editing and proofing before creating the index.

Formatting Indexes

The easy way to change the appearance of index entries is to choose a different index format choice from the scrolling Formats list in the Index tab of the Index and Tables dialog box. Watch the Preview area of the dialog box as you shop. To change the format of an index, follow these steps:

1. Click anywhere in the index to select it.

2. Choose Insert ➤ Index and Tables, and select the Index tab.

3. Click on format names and watch the preview box. (Use the down arrow to speed selection of format names if you like.)

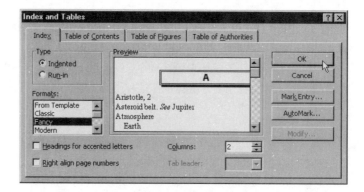

4. When you find one you like, click on OK to apply it to the index.

It is also possible to change the standard index styles (Index 1–Index 9). Here are the general steps for customizing index styles:

1. In the Index tab of the Index and Tables dialog box, select From Template and click on the Modify button. Word displays the Style dialog box.

2. Select an index style to modify from the Style list (Index 1, for instance).

3. Click on the Modify button or on the Apply button.

4. In the Modify Style dialog box, change the appearance of the style. (For instance, to apply Small Caps formatting, click on the Format button and choose Font.)

5. Work your way back to the Index tab by clicking on OK as necessary (or press Esc to cancel the dialog box and any changes you've specified so far).

6. Answer Yes to the "Replace Selected Index" question. The index will be restyled. (Undo will work if you don't like the results.)

Creating Automatic Indexes

It is possible to have Word index a document without your manual intervention. You do this by creating a list of terms you want to index (called a *concordance* list). Concordances are often best used as supplements to automatic indexes, to take care of entries that might otherwise be missed. Here are the general steps:

1. Create a new document with the New command.

2. Insert a two-column table (with the Table button, perhaps).

3. Type all index entries in the first column. They must be identical to text Word will find in the document you intend to index. (For this reason, it's often easier to simply go into the document and look up the terms.) Capitalization counts. (*Network Troubleshooting* might be a typical entry.)

4. In the second column, type all index entries as you want them to appear in the index (*Troubleshooting: network*, for instance).

5. Save the document.

6. Open the document to be indexed.

7. Choose Insert ➤ Index and Tables.

8. Select the Index tab of the Index and Tables dialog box.

9. Click on the AutoMark button.

10. In the Open dialog box, choose the concordance file.

11. Click on OK, and Word marks the entries for you.

Creating Tables of Authorities

Word can help you automatically create Tables of Authorities for legal documents. It provides commonly used categories, including:

- Cases
- Statutes
- Other Authorities
- Rules

- Treatises
- Regulations
- Constitutional Provisions

You can control the appearance of the entries and the table itself. Word will even help you seek out items to be included in your table.

Creating Entries

Always type a long citation as your first entry in a legal document—*Mansfield v. Newman, 45 Wn 2d 412 (1994)*, for instance. Subsequent entries can be short versions such as *Mansfield v. Newman*. Once you've typed all the entries, follow these steps:

1. Scroll to the first long entry and select it.
2. Press Alt+Shift+I. Word displays the Mark Citation dialog box, as shown in Figure 20.7.
3. Type your selected text in both the Selected Text and the Short Citation boxes, if necessary.
4. Edit the long citation and format it if you like. You can use the keyboard shortcuts here (Ctrl+B, Ctrl+I, and so on), because using the buttons formats the text *in the document*.
5. Select a category (Cases, for example).
6. Edit the Short Citation so that it matches the reference in your document, *Mansfield v. Newman*, for instance.
7. Click on the Mark button to mark each potential citation, or click on Mark All to mark them automatically.

FIGURE 20.7

The Mark Citation dialog box

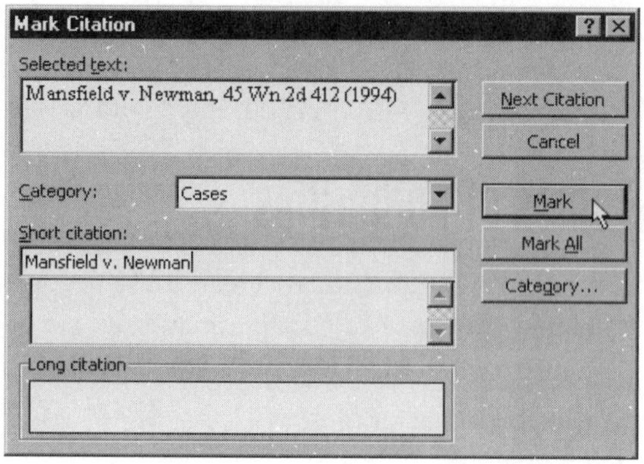

8. To find the next citation, click on Next Citation. Word searches for legalese (*v.*, *in re*, and so on) and displays possible citations. When you find one, repeat steps 2 through 7.

9. When you've marked all the citations, click on the Close button.

Generating the Table of Authorities

To format and compile the actual table, use the Table of Authorities tab in the Index and Tables dialog box. Follow these steps:

1. Choose Insert ➤ Index and Tables.
2. Click on the Table of Authorities tab. Word displays the dialog box shown in Figure 20.8.
3. Choose a format from the Format list.
4. If you want Word to replace five or more page references with *passim*, choose that option.
5. Click on OK, and Word compiles the table.

FIGURE 20.8

The Table of Authorities tab

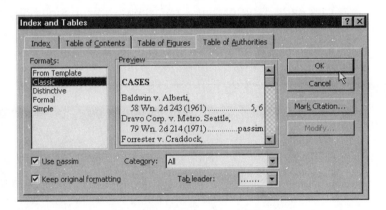

Updating a Table of Authorities

Place the insertion point anywhere in the Table of Authorities, and press F9. Word updates the table to include any recent insertions, deletions, and other changes.

Custom Styles and Categories

You can change the appearance of the styles used for Tables of Authorities, as well as create and edit category names. Consult the online help for details.

Creating Tables of Figures

Word will help you create tables of figures and other elements based on captions and bookmarks. Assuming you've captioned the figures in your document with the Insert ➤ Caption command, the process is quite simple:

1. Place the insertion point where you want the table to appear.
2. Choose Insert ➤ Index and Tables.
3. Select the Table of Figures tab if it is not in view. Word displays the dialog box shown in Figure 20.9.
4. Select the desired caption label from the scrolling list.
5. Select a format for the table.
6. To select a style that you want Word to use as the basis of the table, click on Options and choose it in the Options dialog box.
7. Back in the Table of Figures tab, choose other options (Show Page Numbers, Right Align Page Numbers, and so on).
8. Click on OK. Word compiles a table and places it at the insertion point.

FIGURE 20.9

The Table of Figures tab

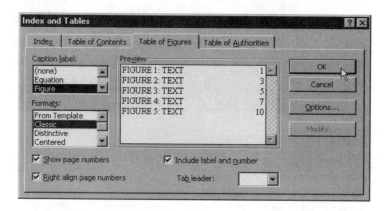

Updating a Table of Figures

Place the insertion point anywhere in the table of figures, and press F9. Word updates the table to include any recent insertions, deletions, and other changes.

Chapter

21

Advanced Graphics Techniques

Advanced Graphics Techniques

A few years back, Microsoft started shipping a little program with Word called WordArt. You can use it to create colorful, unusual-looking text objects. (Actually, these are graphic objects made from text, and you treat them more like pictures than words.) WordArt is great for creating logos, attention-getting headings, and more. For example, here are seven variations on a logo created in just a few minutes:

Using Word Art for Special Text Effects

As you can see if you've used earlier versions, in Word 97 the WordArt style choices have been significantly enhanced. WordArt has also moved to a new menu location, and there are some new effects and settings. Here's the short course:

1. Position the insertion point where you want the WordArt to be inserted. (Or skip this step since you can easily reposition WordArt objects later.)
2. Choose Insert ➤ Picture.
3. Select WordArt from the resulting submenu. Word displays the WordArt Gallery dialog box, as shown in Figure 21.1.

FIGURE 21.1

The improved WordArt feature offers many new choices.

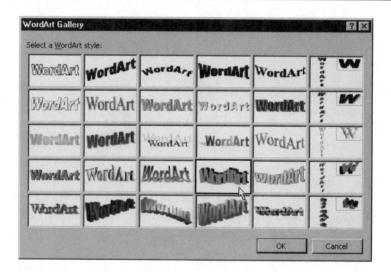

4. Double-click on the desired style to select it. Word displays the Edit WordArt Text dialog box.
5. Type new text or paste text from your Clipboard.

6. Choose a different type face and size if you desire, and perhaps opt for Bold or Italic by clicking on their corresponding buttons.

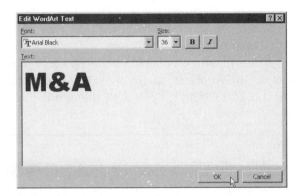

7. Click on OK, and Word places the newly created object in your Word document. You can move it around by dragging it as you would any other graphic object. (You will read about other repositioning tricks in a moment.)

8. Save your work.

Positioning and Reformatting WordArt Objects

Once you have created a WordArt object, you can drag it anywhere on the page. You can even flow text around it. For example, here I've "free rotated" some WordArt and flowed text around it:

> **Mansfield and Associates** was established in 1981 by Ron Mansfield—an innovative computerist and best-selling author. He specializes in demystifying technology. The firm provides Microsoft Windows and Apple Macintosh computer consulting, programming and technical writing services. Our current clients bring us most of our new clients. Others learn about the firm through Mr. Mansfield's national magazine articles and books. Areas of specialization include the legal, real estate, travel, and entertainment industries. Clients range from home-based businesses to multinational corporations.

After inserting a piece of WordArt, you can play with it in several ways, generally treating it as you would any other graphic as described in Chapter 4, *Introduction to*

Graphics in Word. Although space prohibits a complete explanation of all the possibilities, here is an overview and some examples to get you started.

If you click on the WordArt object, you select the object, and Word displays the WordArt toolbar, as shown in Figure 21.2. (Remember: When you hover your mouse pointer over the toolbar buttons, you will see their names and functions.)

Use the toolbar to choose a different style from the gallery, edit the text within the object, change the shape of the object, rotate the object, make the height of all letters the same within an object, change the orientation of the text to vertical, change the alignment of text within the object, or change the inter-character spacing.

FIGURE 21.2

The WordArt toolbar

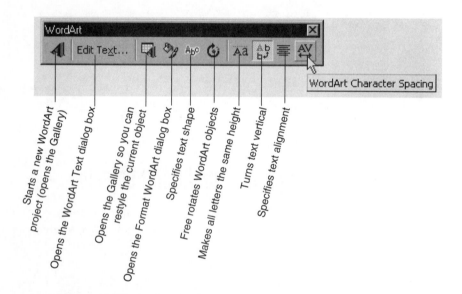

Free Rotating WordArt Objects

The preceding WordArt example (with the M&A at the upper left corner of the text) is an example of a WordArt object that was "free rotated." To free rotate a WordArt object, follow these simple steps:

1. Select the object.

2. Click on the Free Rotate button in the WordArt or Drawing toolbar.

3. When the object handles and mouse pointer change appearance, use the mouse pointer to drag any of the corner handles. The object will rotate.

4. Click anywhere to exit the Rotate feature. (Undo works if you are unhappy with the results.)

TIP

Optionally, you can specify an exact degree of rotation in the Size tab of the Format WordArt dialog box. This process is described below.

Wrapping Text around Word Art

To wrap text around WordArt (as illustrated by the M&A logo at the top left edge of the preceding example), you use the Wrapping tab in the Format Word Art dialog box. The easiest way to reach that tab is by right-clicking on the WordArt object, as described next.

Using the Format WordArt Dialog Box

A quick way to begin reformatting a WordArt object is to right-click on the object itself. When you do so, Word displays the additional shortcut menu choices shown here:

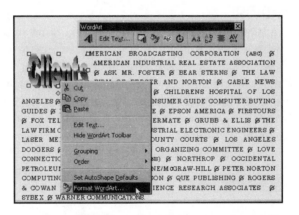

Choose Format WordArt, and Word displays the Format WordArt dialog box shown here:

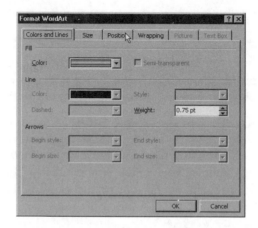

Use the various tabs to specify fill colors, how text wraps around the object, and so forth. Experiment on copies of your documents.

Wrapping

Use the Wrapping tab to define the way text flows around objects when you position them within text. For example, you can create square boxes around objects so that text makes perpendicular "edges" around objects, or you can have text butt fairly tightly against irregularly shaped WordArt objects. The effectiveness of this "tight" wrapping will vary with the size of the text, the amount of text and the relative size of the Word-Art object, and other factors. You will need to experiment. Often, for example, the combination of justified text, narrow margins, and large WordArt objects makes for acres of white space as Word struggles to both justify the text and make room for the art.

Other choices in the Wrapping tab let you run text through, over, or around Word-Art objects.

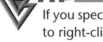

If you specify Through or None in the Wrapping tab, you will probably not be able to right-click or otherwise select the WordArt object on your screen. Choose the Wrapping tab in the Format WordArt dialog box to turn off the None or Through choices so that you can select the object for subsequent editing.

Colors and Lines

Use this tab to define the color and thickness of the lines used in WordArt objects. You can also make objects partially transparent, which is a great way to add art without overpowering your main text.

Size (and Rotate)

Use the Size tab to make an object larger or smaller and to specify an angle of rotation. You can specify exact dimensions or reduce and enlarge by a specific percentage. (Specifying 50% makes the object smaller, 150% makes it larger, and so on.) If you choose to lock the aspect ratio, any change you make in one dimension will cause a corresponding change in the other dimension. This prevents distortion of an image's shape.

You can also specify the number of degrees of rotation you want to apply to an object (45 degrees, for example). If you don't know the exact rotation setting you want, you can use Word's Free Rotate feature instead.

Position

Use the Position tab if you have a specific location in mind for your WordArt Object. (Or simply drag the object instead.) You can also "tie" an object to a specific paragraph or "lock" it to a specific location on a specific page.

MASTERING THE OPPORTUNITIES

Create a Corporate Image with WordArt

Because WordArt creates graphic objects, it is easy to paste, resize, and reposition them in just about any Windows document. Create logos using WordArt, and then add them to headers or footers of Word, Excel, and other documents.

Make business cards. Paste them into envelope and label designs. Create name badges and tent cards for meetings. Add logos to PowerPoint presentations. Stick 'em in Access report layouts. Use your imagination!

Creating Vertical Text with WordArt

WordArt is the tool to use if you want to run an occasional piece of vertical text. Here's an example of text run vertically along the edge of a paragraph:

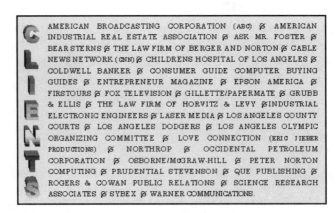

To create your own vertical text, follow these general steps:

1. Decide where you want the vertical text and what it will say.

2. Choose Insert ➤ Picture ➤ WordArt.

3. Choose a font, and make a guess at a good type size (you'll fine-tune this later).

4. Either type new text or paste text from your Clipboard.

5. Click on OK to insert the WordArt.

6. Click on the WordArt Vertical Text button on the WordArt toolbar. The text will flip.

7. Drag the text to the desired position.

8. If necessary, resize the WordArt by dragging the object's size handles.

Adding Backgrounds to Word Documents

This new Word feature lets you add colored and/or textured backgrounds that are visible when you view your Word documents on screen. You can also specify plain colored backgrounds or photographic backgrounds. None of these backgrounds will print, but the backgrounds feature can be particularly helpful when creating HTML documents for Web publications (see Part VII, *Word and the Internet*, for more about using Word to create Web pages). Figure 21.3 shows a document with the Blue Tissue Paper background texture added, along with the dialog box used to specify texture options. Let's take a look.

FIGURE 21.3

A typical back-
ground effect

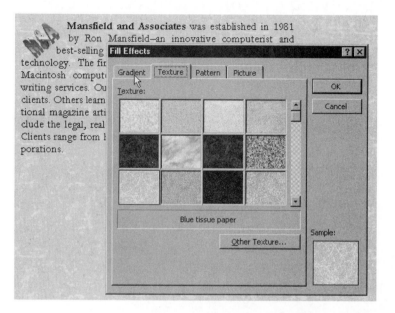

NOTE

Backgrounds added this way are only displayed and will not print! To add print-
able backgrounds, use word's Borders and Shading features.

Here are the general steps for specifying backgrounds (additional tips and techniques will follow):

1. From the Format menu, choose Background.

2. Choose one of the colors from the resulting color palette, or click on More Colors
or Fill Effects at the bottom of the palette.

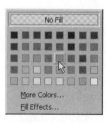

3. Word applies the selected background to all pages in the document.

Specifying Custom Background Colors

If the choices in the standard palette don't please you, choose the More Colors command to display the Colors dialog box shown here. Select the desired color either by pointing in the Standard tab or by specifying hue, saturation, and luminescence numbers in the Custom tab.

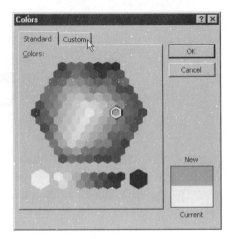

Creating Custom Background Fill Effects

It's possible to use backgrounds from other sources such as the Corel PrintHouse or Web.Gallery series. For instance, here's the Holes2 background from CorelWeb.Gallery series applied to a Word document, followed by a list of the steps necessary to create it:

> **Mansfield and Associates** was established in 1981 by Ron Mansfield—an innovative computerist and best-selling author. He specializes in demystifying technology. The firm provides Microsoft Windows and Apple Macintosh computer consulting, programming and technical writing services. Our current clients bring us most of our new clients. Others learn about the firm through Mr. Mansfield's national magazine articles and books. Areas of specialization include the legal, real estate, travel, and entertainment industries. Clients range from home-based businesses to multinational corporations.

1. Save your work in case you want to quickly revert to a document sans background.

2. Choose Format ➤ Background ➤ Fill Effects.

3. In the Fill Effects dialog box, click on the Texture tab.

4. In the Texture dialog box, click on the Other Texture button.

5. In the Other Texture dialog box, click on the Select Texture button.

6. In the Select Texture dialog box, locate the desired texture file. (This dialog box behaves just like an Open File dialog box.)

7. Double-click on the desired background file.

8. In the Fill Effects dialog box, you'll see a preview of the effect in the Sample portion. This might be a misleading, incomplete representation since you will only see a small part of the document and a miniature representation of the effect.

9. Click on OK to apply the new background. (Undo should work if you hate it.)

10. You might need to make the text larger and/or darker, or you might need to lighten the background if the text gets "lost" on the new background.

Using Photos As Background Fill Effects

You can also use photos that you have scanned (see the "Using Your Scanner with Word" section below) or photos from other sources (such as the Corel PrintHouse or Web.Gallery series) as backgrounds. For instance, here's a sunset shot I took with the text changed to bold and white to make it easier to read.

Here are the steps I used to create the effect (which, incidentally, looks much better in full size and color than it does here on the black and white printed page):

1. Save your work in case you want to quickly revert to a document sans background.

2. Choose Format ➤ Background ➤ Fill Effects.

3. In the Fill Effects dialog box, click on the Picture tab.

4. In the Picture dialog box, click on the Select Picture button.

5. In the Select Picture dialog box, locate the desired picture file. (This dialog box behaves just like an Open File dialog box.)

6. Double-click on the desired photo file.

7. In the Fill Effects dialog box, you'll see preview of the effect in the Sample portion. This might be a misleading, incomplete representation since you will only see a small part of the document and a miniature representation of the effect.

8. Click on OK to apply the new background. (Undo should work here too.)

9. You might need to make the text larger and/or a different color, or you might need to lighten the background if the text gets "lost" on the new background.

TIP

It is a good idea to keep your custom background files on your hard disk, preferably in an easy-to-find spot. I keep mine in a folder called `artwork`. That's where I keep all my logos, photos, and so on. Remember, you can add these graphic files to your Clip Gallery if you like, which makes it easy to preview them. See Chapter 2, *Viewing and Navigating*, if you've forgotten how the Clip Gallery works.

Removing Backgrounds

To remove a background, simply choose Format ➤ Background ➤ Fill Effects. In the Fill Effects dialog box, click on the No Fill button. The background should disappear.

Using Graphics from the Internet with Word

It is very easy to copy graphics from the Internet and paste them into your Word documents. This is particularly true when browsing the World Wide Web. Free graphics are often only a few mouse clicks away. Just be certain you have permission to use the graphics you pilfer. Here are the general steps:

1. Sign yourself on to the Web and locate the graphic of interest using your Web browser. In Figure 21.4, I am using Microsoft Internet Explorer 3 to grab a Sybex logo, which I will soon paste into a Word document.

2. When you locate the desired graphic (a photo, drawing, button, or whatever), right-click on the it to display the shortcut menu in Figure 21.4.

3. Choose Save Picture As to download a copy of the graphic file to your hard disk, or choose Copy to place a copy of the image on your Clipboard.

4. If the image is on your Clipboard, simply switch to the Word document window, be sure the insertion point is where you want to place the image, and choose Edit ➤ Paste

FIGURE 21.4

*Grabbing a
graphic from
the Internet*

Right-click to display
the Shortcut menu.

Turns the graphic
into a file (opens the
Save dialog box).

Places the graphic
on the Clipboard.

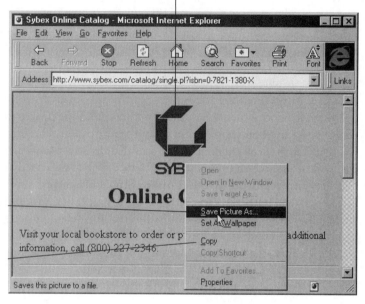

or press Ctrl+V. Use the framing, positioning, and re-sizing tips you learned in
Chapter 2, *Viewing and Navigating*, if necessary. In this example, you might want to
turn that gray background transparent too, using the Set Transparent Color button
on the Picture toolbar.

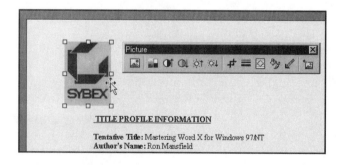

5. Caption the graphic if you wish, using the techniques described in Chapter 22,
Bookmarks, Captions, and Cross-Referencing.

Using Your Scanner with Word

If you have a graphics scanner properly hooked up to your computer, and if Windows 95 knows it is there, and if you have properly installed the necessary driver software, you might be able to import graphics directly from your scanner into a Word document. Before we review the general steps for doing that, here are some considerations worth noting.

First, it might be better and faster for you to use the graphics importing software that came with your scanner to save graphics files *directly to an artwork folder* rather than placing the images right into Word documents. If you save the graphic files in an artwork folder, they will be available for other projects and for use with other programs such as Photoshop or Excel. And you can add them to your Clip Gallery for easy previewing. You can then insert the scanned images into virtually any Microsoft document (Access, PowerPoint, and so on).

Second, many scanners come with software that will give you more control over the final appearance, color density, and other options than Microsoft Word. Your best bet might be to experiment with all the options and take notes as you work.

Scanning Directly into Word Documents

Here are the general steps for scanning graphics directly into Word documents:

1. Be sure your scanner is turned on, warmed up, and ready. (This should normally be done before you start or restart your computer.)
2. Choose Insert ➤ Picture ➤ From Scanner.

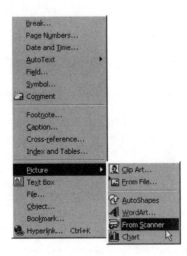

3. Follow the on-screen directions and printed documentation for your scanner.

4. Word opens a graphic object in your Word document. Manipulate it using the positioning and sizing techniques you learned in Chapter 2, *Viewing and Navigating*. Caption the graphic if you wish, using the techniques described in Chapter 22, *Bookmarks, Captions, and Cross-Referencing*.

5. If you are working with photographic images, you might want to use the Microsoft Photo Editor (described next) to adjust the appearance of the image.

Using the Microsoft Photo Editor

The Microsoft Photo Editor is a standalone program shipped with Microsoft Word. You can use it to create stunning visual effects from photo files. Figures 21.5, 21.6, 21.7, and 21.8 illustrate the possibilities.

Many, many other effects are possible, and you could fritter away an entire weekend playing with this accessory program, particularly if you have a color printer!

Here are the general steps:

1. If Photo Editor is not on your Windows 95 Start menu, look for the program itself. The file Photoed.exe is in the Microsoft Shared folder, located in the Common Files folder, buried in the Program files folder. (Phew!)

2. Double-click on the Photoed.exe icon (or drag it to the Windows 95 Start menu so that you will always have a shortcut to the program, avoiding the need to repeat step 1 ever again).

3. With the program running, choose File ➤ Open to locate a photo to modify.

4. Choose the desired effect from the Effects menu and click on Apply to see a full-size representation of it.

5. Choose Undo to restore the photo, or choose Save As to save a modified copy of the file.

Microsoft Photo Editor has its own online help, which explains the rest of the program's capabilities. Enjoy!

TIP

To see if you have Photo Editor installed on your hard disk, choose Start ➤ Find ➤ Files or Folders. Now type the filename Photoed.exe in the Named text box. Be sure that Include Subfolders is checked, and then click on the Find Now button. If you see Photoed.exe listed, drag it to the Start button to add a shortcut for the program to your Start menu. If you don't find the file, use the Word or Office installation program to add it.

FIGURE 21.5

*The original
surfer image
from Corel's
Web.Gallery*

FIGURE 21.6

*The surfer
image, using
the Chalk and
Charcoal spe-
cial effect*

FIGURE 21.7

The surfer image, using the Notepad special effect

FIGURE 21.8

The surfer image, using the Watercolor special effect

Chapter

22

Bookmarks, Captions, and Cross-Referencing

FEATURING

Bookmarks, Captions, and Cross-Referencing

Word's *bookmarks* let you name specific points or areas of your document. Use bookmarks to identify the beginning of chapters, tables, spots that need work, the place where you left off, and so on. You can mark a place, a character, ranges of characters, graphics, or almost any other Word document element. You can then tell Word to go to those specific points without a lot of scrolling and searching. You can also use bookmarks to indicate ranges of pages in indexes.

Captions are the words that appear next to a figure in your text and that identify the figure and perhaps explain what it is supposed to be illustrating. (The descriptive part of the caption is optional, but it's a good idea.)

Cross-references refer to other places in your document, and Word tracks those references when things change. For example, if you say *see Figure 3* and then add a new figure between the old Figures 2 and 3, Word automatically renumbers the figures and the in-text references to them.

Another way to cross-reference documents is to use the new hyperlink feature. It works best when your documents will be viewed electronically (as Web pages, for instance). Read about hyperlinks in Part VII, *Word and the Internet*.

Bookmarks

To use bookmarks, you simply locate things of interest, define them as bookmarks, and visit them as necessary. Here are the general steps.

Defining Bookmarks

To define a bookmark, follow these steps:

1. Either move the insertion point to the item of interest or select the item.

2. Choose Insert ➤ Bookmark (Ctrl+Shift+F5). Word displays the Bookmark dialog box, shown in Figure 22.1.

3. Give the bookmark a unique name consisting of a maximum of 40 characters. Numbers are allowed, but not as the first character of the name. Spaces are *not* allowed; so use an underscore instead, as illustrated in Figure 22.1.

4. Click on Add. (If the button is dimmed, check to see that the name is fewer than 40 characters, does not begin with a number, and contains no spaces.)

5. To create more bookmarks, you must reposition the cursor and then reopen the dialog box.

FIGURE 22.1

*The Bookmark
dialog box*

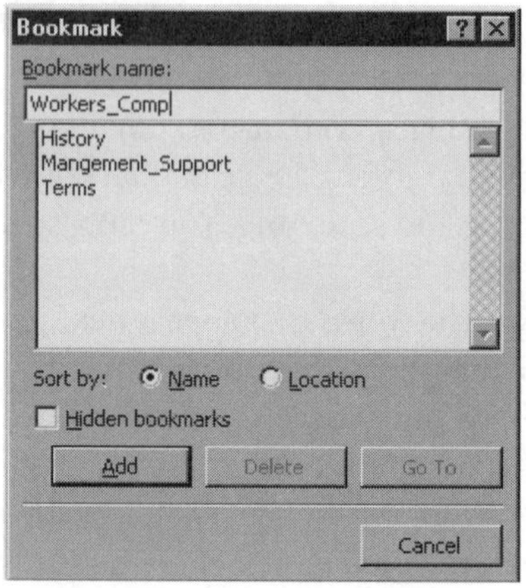

Going to a Bookmark

Once you've defined a bookmark, you can go to it in two ways. If you select Edit ➤ Go To and choose Bookmark from the Go to What list, you'll see a scrolling list of bookmarks (as illustrated in Figure 22.2). Click on a bookmark's name and click on the Go To button to go there. If you click on the Go To button in the Bookmark dialog box (Insert ➤ Bookmark), however, Word will go to the selected bookmark without displaying the Go To dialog box.

FIGURE 22.2

Double-click on a bookmark's name to go to it.

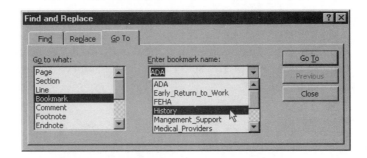

In the Bookmark dialog box, you can sort the list either by name or by the relative location of the bookmark in the document:

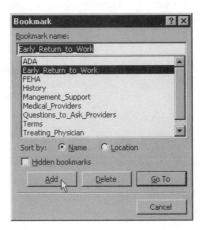

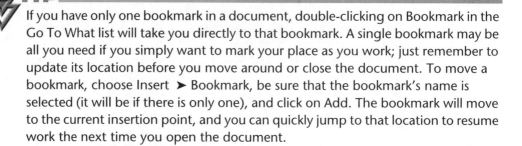

TIP

If you have only one bookmark in a document, double-clicking on Bookmark in the Go To What list will take you directly to that bookmark. A single bookmark may be all you need if you simply want to mark your place as you work; just remember to update its location before you move around or close the document. To move a bookmark, choose Insert ➤ Bookmark, be sure that the bookmark's name is selected (it will be if there is only one), and click on Add. The bookmark will move to the current insertion point, and you can quickly jump to that location to resume work the next time you open the document.

Viewing the Marks Themselves

Word also lets you display in-document markers that tip off the location of bookmarks. Choose Tools ➤ Options, select the View tab, and check the Bookmarks option in the Show area.

Large square brackets will then indicate the beginning and ending of a bookmarked area. For instance, the entire heading *Gather Historical Data* is a bookmark:

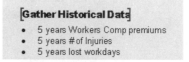

NOTE

If you select text before setting a bookmark, you'll get something that looks like [...]. If you don't select text, though, you'll get something that looks like a big *I*.

Desktop Publishing

As you can see, these markers can get in the way of the text; so you might want to turn them off and use Edit ➤ Go To when you just want to resume work at a bookmarked location, for example.

Working with Bookmarked Items

It's often easiest to work with bookmarked items and see the effect on your work if you have the markers displayed.

If you move a bookmarked item, the mark moves with it, even to another document (as long as this won't create a duplicate bookmark name in the destination document).

Deleting the entire text or other items between two bookmark markers deletes the bookmark as well. (Say that five times fast.)

To add text or objects and have them included with the bookmark, insert them within the bookmark marks. To insert text or objects and not have them included, place the insertion point to the right of the bookmark marker.

You can use bookmark names in some field operations (described in Chapter 29, *Creating and Using Fields*); so it is even possible to perform computations and do other tricks with marked items.

Deleting Bookmarks

To delete a mark *but not* the marked item(s), follow these steps:

1. In the Bookmark dialog box, choose the bookmark name, and click on Delete.

2. Click on the Close button. The bookmark disappears, and the previously marked items remain.

To delete a bookmark *and* the items it marks:

1. Choose Tools ➤ Options, and then turn on Show Bookmarks in the View tab.

2. Select the item and both bookmark markers.

3. Delete as usual (Cut, press Delete, and so on). The mark and the items(s) will disappear.

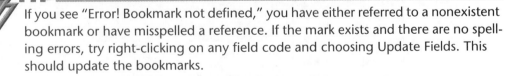

If you see "Error! Bookmark not defined," you have either referred to a nonexistent bookmark or have misspelled a reference. If the mark exists and there are no spelling errors, try right-clicking on any field code and choosing Update Fields. This should update the bookmarks.

Captions

If you write long documents with numbered figures, tables, and other elements, are you gonna love this feature! It automatically numbers items, lets you label them, and renumbers them if you move them or otherwise change their sequence in a document. There are a variety of appearance options as well.

Adding Captions

You can either manually caption the occasional item or turn on automatic captioning. To add a caption manually, follow these steps:

1. Select the item to be captioned.
2. Choose Insert ➤ Caption. Word displays the Captions dialog box, as shown in Figure 22.3.
3. Word proposes a caption label that you can accept as is or edit. For example, you can type descriptive text, as shown in Figure 22.3.

FIGURE 22.3

*Manually insert-
ing a caption*

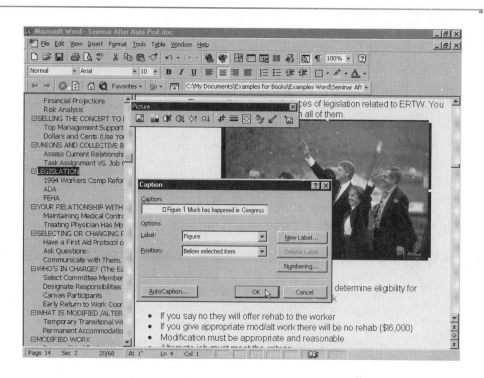

4. Change the default appearance options, if you wish, by using the Position drop-down list or by clicking on the Numbering button.

5. Click on OK to insert the caption. Be patient; it takes a moment.

To add captions automatically to items of a particular type (all Excel Charts, for instance), click on the AutoCaption button. Word displays the AutoCaption dialog box, as shown in Figure 22.4.

Word can recognize and automatically caption the following types of files:

- Most graphic files
- Windows drawings
- Windows equations
- Windows Graphs
- Microsoft WordArt
- Inserted Word documents
- Microsoft PowerPoint presentations and slides
- Paintbrush pictures
- Sounds
- Excel charts and worksheets
- Video clips
- MIDI sequences
- And much more

To automatically caption items, follow these steps:

1. Choose Insert ➤ Caption.

2. In the Caption dialog box, click on AutoCaption.

FIGURE 22.4

The AutoCaption dialog box

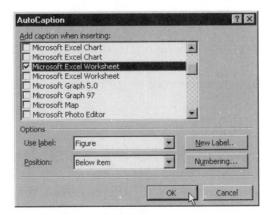

3. In the AutoCaption dialog box, select a type of item to be captioned. You can choose more than one type for the same caption label (for instance, you can choose Excel charts and PowerPoint slides to be captioned as figures). Inserting either will have the same effect.

4. Select a label type from the Use Label list, or click on the New Label button to create your own.

5. Choose a position for the label (above or below the item).

6. Change the numbering scheme if you like.

7. Repeat steps 3 through 6 for each type of caption you want.

8. Click on OK.

After you turn on AutoCaption and define the appearance options, Word automatically labels any insertion that meets the AutoCaption criteria. You can then add descriptive text to the captions.

If you move a figure and its label, Word does not immediately update the figure labels. But it *will* update figure numbers whenever you ask to print or switch to Print Preview. To force an immediate update, select all your text (Ctrl+A) and press F9.

To revise a caption, simply edit it as you would any other text. To change all the captions of a given type (*Figure* to *FIG*, for instance), select a caption in text, and in the Caption or AutoCaption dialog box, choose a different label from the Use Label List.

To create new label types (*FIG*, for example), click on the New Label button in the Caption and AutoCaption dialog boxes.

Including Chapter and Other Numbers in Captions

You can include chapter and similar numbers in automatic captions if you like. Here are the general steps:

1. Format all the main headings (chapter titles, for example) as the Heading 1 style.

2. Choose Format ➤ Bullets and Numbering. Be sure a numeric numbering style is in use (*Chapter 1*, for instance, not *Chapter One*).

3. In either the Caption or AutoCaption dialog box, click on the Numbering button.

4. In the Caption Numbering dialog box, choose Include Chapter Number.

5. Click on OK as needed to exit the dialog boxes.

Cross-References

Cross-referencing lets you say things such as *see Chapter 9 for details* and then have Word automatically update the reference if you change the chapter number. Cross-references are not limited to chapter numbers; they can refer to just about anything, including headings, footnotes, endnotes, captions, and so on. You can cross-reference items in different documents, as long as they are in the same master document (see Chapter 23, *Master Documents for Large Projects*).

Creating Cross-References

Here are the general steps for creating cross-references. Notice that the dialog box has changed slightly from earlier versions of Word. Drop-down lists replace the scrolling lists.

1. Begin by typing the in-text reference followed by a quotation mark (**see'**, for example).
2. Choose Insert ➤ Cross-reference. Word displays the Cross-reference dialog box, shown in Figure 22.5.
3. Select the Reference Type that will tie the in-text reference to the item you want to reference (Bookmark, for instance).
4. Choose the type of item to be referenced (Bookmark Text, for example) from the Insert Reference To list.
5. Choose the item you want to reference from the For Which Bookmark list.
6. With the View Fields option enabled, click on Insert. You'll see some new information at the insertion point. This is actually a field. (See Chapter 29, *Creating and Using Fields*, to learn more about fields.)
7. Click on the Close button, or add other cross-references and then click on the Close button.

Once you've created cross-references, they will be updated when you switch to Print Preview or print. To update immediately at any time, select the entire document and press F9.

If you delete an item that is referenced, Word alerts you.

FIGURE 22.5

The new Cross-reference dialog box

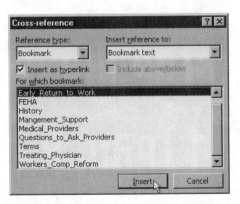

PART — V

Large Documents and Team Projects

LEARN TO:

- **Work with master documents**

- **Collaborate over a network**

- **Import, export, and convert documents**

Chapter

23

Working with
Master Documents

FEATURING

Working with Master Documents

One person's large document is another's small one. Word has the ability to create documents of virtually any length. At some point, however, you will find that Word's performance degrades as your document size increases. This is particularly true if you are running Word on an older, slower computer that has limited RAM and a slow hard disk.

Many people routinely work with documents containing hundreds of pages. But if you are disappointed by your computer's performance (scrolling speed, spell checking, autosave, and so on), you might want to split a single document into multiple documents. Another reason to split documents is so that several people can work on different parts of the project. After everyone is done, you'll probably want to print the whole body of work as if it were one document.

Sometimes people create parts of a long document at various sites and then combine them. Whether you start out with a bunch of small documents and combine them or split a big document for whatever reason, chances are you'll want to print the completed work as a whole. You *can* combine all the parts and treat the resulting large document as a single entity. Or, you can keep the document broken into multiple sections and use Word's *Master Document* feature.

Group work sometimes causes confusion, so Word offers a number of ways to annotate text and share your thoughts with other authors working on the project. You can even exchange voice notes if you have the right gear.

You need to watch for a couple of important things whenever there's more than one "cook in the kitchen"—consistency of appearance and correct page numbering across document parts. This chapter discusses both of these potential problem areas.

Planning for Large Documents

If you know you are going to create a large document, use templates, AutoText entries, and possibly a set of author's instructions to create the multiple parts.

> **TIP**
>
> Another good idea is a hardcopy stylesheet for the project and a file-routing strategy and folder structure. That way, everyone will be able to see which versions of a file are old (*foul copies*, as copyeditors used to call them), which are being revised, and which are final.

If other people will be working on parts of the document, provide them with copies of your templates and possibly copies of your custom spelling dictionaries and special fonts. The more alike your computers are, the fewer problems you will have during the crunch.

Develop a strategy. Decide how you plan to number figures, tables, and other design elements. Test these strategies on "mini" versions of your document containing a few samples of each element you plan to use (headers, footers, page numbers, tables, figures, figure captions, paragraph headings, and so forth). Work out the bugs with 20 or 30 pages before typing and formatting hundreds.

Consider making logical breaks at the beginning of chapters or sections. Use Word's standard styles and templates and the Style Gallery whenever possible. Put one person in charge of rounding everything up.

Combining Documents with Insert ➤ File

The obvious way to round up multiple files to create a long document is to use the Insert ➤ File command. It places specified files at the insertion point in your document. You are presented with the familiar file selection dialog box in which you select the next file to be inserted. If necessary, Word will attempt to convert files coming from non-Word authors.

You might be wondering why you wouldn't always use Insert ➤ File, as opposed to using the master document feature. The advantages of master documents are two:

- Because the master document doesn't actually contain the documents (only "references" to them, sort of like Windows shortcuts), you don't end up with enormous documents.
- It's much easier to move things around in a master document, because the feature is specifically designed to be a tool for organizing large documents. For example, moving an entire chapter often requires only a simple click and drag.

When you choose Insert ➤ File, how Word handles things such as headers, footers, styles, and other formatting issues will depend on the source files. Here again, it's best to test before the crunch.

WARNING

Word is likely to imitate the look of the original format, but not with styles. It is therefore advisable to attach standardized styles initially, even though it's a bit of a bother.

Master Document Features Facilitate Teamwork

You can use a *master document* and *Master Document* view to divide a long document into shorter subdocuments. This facilitates workgroup editing and makes formatting, organizing, and numbering pages easier. Master documents facilitate other tasks such as cross-referencing and creating an index or a table of contents. Master documents handle many details for you, including the automatic naming of subdocument files. Master documents are perfect for workgroups sharing a file server. When you place the master document on the server, everyone can work on the entire document or its parts without worrying about the location or names of the subfiles.

Creating a Master Document

You can create a master document at the time you start a new project, or you can turn an existing document into a master document. It's also possible to combine multiple documents to create a master.

Creating a Master Document for a New Project

Here's an easy way (but not the only way) to create a new master document at the time you begin a project:

1. Open a new document using the template you want as the starting point for your project.

2. Choose View ➤ Master Document. Your screen will look like Figure 23.1.

3. Word displays the Outline tools described in Chapter 17, *Get Organized with Outline View*, and the Master Document toolbar, nestled at the right end of the Outline toolbar. Figure 23.2 details the button names.

4. Create an outline for your master document using the techniques described in Chapter 17.

5. Assign Word's Heading 1 style *only* to the entry that you want to use as the start of each subdocument. For example, if you want each chapter to be a subdocument, apply the Word style Heading 1 to chapter heads (and to chapter heads only), as shown in Figure 23.3.

6. Select *all* the headings you want to subdivide, being sure to include the heading you want to use at the start of each subdocument (the first Heading 1 entry, for example). This heading should be the first item selected. Do not select anything you don't want to be part of the subdocument. Because this is a new outline, you don't have any text yet. Text you subsequently create will be part of the subdocument.

FIGURE 23.1

Master Document view and the Master Document toolbar

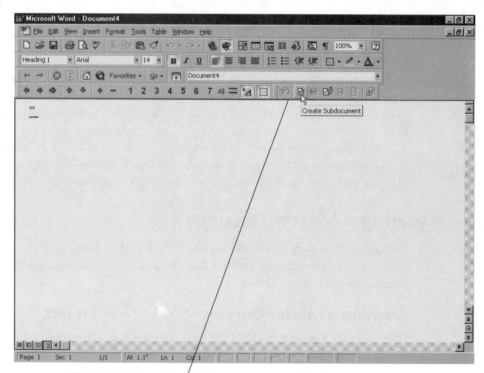

The Master Document toolbar

FIGURE 23.2

The Master Document toolbar

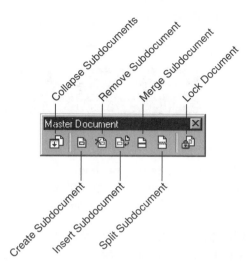

FIGURE 23.3

Assign Heading 1 only to those headings you want to start new subdocuments.

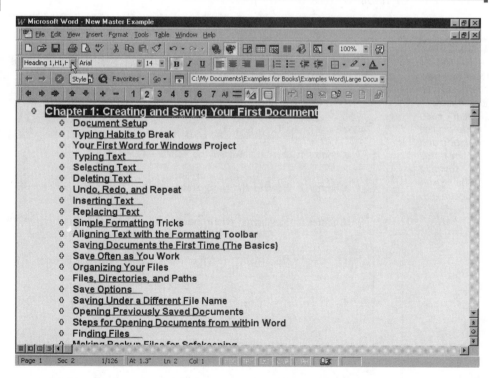

7. Collapsing the outline to the top level makes it easier to select the headings and their related text. Figure 23.4 illustrates this concept.

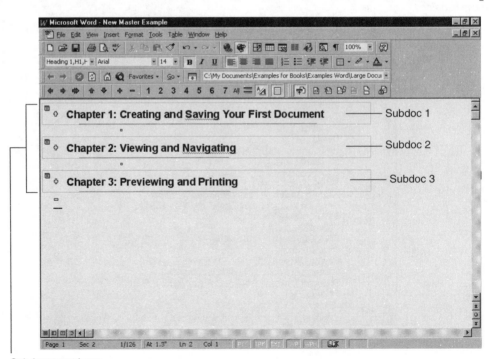

FIGURE 23.4

Select only headings you want to divide.

Chapter 1: Creating and Saving Your First Document
Chapter 2: Viewing and Navigating
Chapter 3: Previewing and Printing

8. Click on the Create Subdocument button on the Master Document toolbar.

9. Word inserts break lines and splits the entire project into subdocuments. You'll see little subdocument icons next to each subdocument break point, as shown in Figure 23.5.

NOTE

It's easy to turn an existing document into a master document. Simply open it in Master Document view, use the outlining tools to display it as an outline, and then follow steps 6 through 9.

FIGURE 23.5

The master document now contains three subdocuments— one for each chapter. The book title and author name are saved in the master document.

Subdocument icons

Turning an Existing File into a Subdocument

Once you've created a master document, it is easy to insert old Word (and many other) documents. Here are the general steps:

1. In Master Document view, position the insertion point where you want the subdocument document placed.
2. Click on the Insert Subdocument button on the Master View toolbar. It's the fourth button from the left.
3. In the Insert Subdocument dialog box, find the document of interest and click on Open.
4. Word will add the document, converting it from another format (such as Word-Perfect) if necessary.

If the incoming document and master document were based on different templates, the incoming work will take on the characteristics of the master document.

> **NOTE**
>
> If you later open an external document without using Master Document view, the document will retain its old formatting (based on its original template instead of the master document's template).

Saving Masters and Subs

When you save your master document for the first time, Word assigns filenames and locations to the subfiles as well. It does this by using characters from the first heading in each subdocument. When headings are similar, Word assigns numbers as part of the filename to differentiate the subdocuments.

For instance, in our book example, all the first headings begin with *Chapter(space)*, so Word assigns numbers at the end of each filename. In a perfect world, the subfile for Chapter 1 would be named Chapter 1, subfile 2 would be Chapter 2, and so on. But that ain't necessarily so. Read on...

A Filenaming Gotcha

If the subfolder to which you are saving already *has* files named Chapter 1, Chapter 2, and so on, Word will use different numbers for the subchapters. You can, therefore, end up with a subdocument containing Chapter 1 but named Chapter 4, and a Chapter 2 subdocument called Chapter 5, ad nauseam. Never (ever, ever) trust a computer to name your files for you without checking up on it.

To rename a subfile, follow these steps:

1. Double-click on the subfile icon of interest to open it.

2. Choose File ➤ Save As.

3. Type a more fitting name.

4. Click on Save.

5. Rename all the subdocuments this way before closing the main document.

 WARNING

Never change subdocument filenames in Windows Explorer or any other way except via the Save As command as just described. You'll confuse Word and raise your blood pressure.

Working with a Master Document

So, now what? All that work and what does it buy? Here's the deal. You can switch to Master Document view to get the big picture. Rearrange things just as you do in Outline view. Create cross-references for multiple subdocuments. You work on Chapter 1 while somebody at the other end of the network fiddles with Chapter 2. Spell-check and reformat the whole mess at once. Save a tree; print preview all 200 pages.

You can make sweeping changes by working in Master Document view or change only a subdocument or two in Normal view. Remember to switch to Master Document view before attempting project-wide changes.

Don't forget that the section breaks Word inserts for each subdocument will play a part in things such as header and footer designs. Give some thought to whether you want to design headers and footers before or after breaking a large document into subdocuments.

Incidentally, there are some things to remember when working with other people on the same project across a network. You may not be able to change subdocuments that you or others have currently opened elsewhere. Word lets you know when this will be a problem in two ways. First, you'll see a little padlock beneath certain subdocument icons as shown here:

The other sure-fire sign of trouble is an alert dialog box or an interruption from the Assistant. There are two possible reasons for this. Either you are not the original author of the subdocument, in which case it will need to be unlocked (with the appropriate password), or the subdocument is already in use by you or someone else.

If you are the culprit, close the window containing the subdocument, or start the search for your partner in crime elsewhere on the network. Be sure that your network's and Word's file protection are set to give access to those with a need to know, read, and write. Learn any necessary passwords. Contact your network manager and the subdocument author(s) for assistance.

Printing Masters and Subs

To print an entire document, follow these steps:

1. Open the master document.
2. Switch to Normal view.
3. Choose File ➤ Print Preview if you like.
4. Print.

To print the whole project's outline, switch to Master Document view, display the desired levels of detail as you would in Outline view (see Chapter 17, *Get Organized with Outline View* for details), and then print.

TIP

You can open a subdocument by double-clicking on its icon.

To print only a subdocument, open it as you would any other document and print. Be advised, however, that if you use any of Word's handy cross-referencing features, the references will probably not be properly updated, and you may see error messages unless you print from the master document.

PART

V

Large Documents and Team Projects

Chapter

24

Collaborating over Your Network

FEATURING

Chapter

24

Collaborating over Your Network

Chances are that your place of work has a network. If it does, you'll know that networks add exciting new dimensions to working with computers: Not only can *you* screw up your documents, but someone else can access them from another workstation and screw them up for you. If you guard against that, the network can strike back by crashing while you're in the middle of a project and trashing all your unsaved work.

The benefits of networks include access to files and applications that you don't have on your workstation—other people's work, applications that simply won't fit on your PC, and so on—and instant communications with others on the network. (You can also install Word on a network rather than on an individual workstation, but that's beyond the scope of this book.) In this chapter, we'll look at Word's features for sending and sharing files on a network.

When you are on a network and your organization uses Microsoft Mail or a compatible mail program for in-house electronic communications, you can use the File ➤ Send To commands to send and return copies of your Word documents to others. If you are using Microsoft Outlook or similar tools, you will also be able to distribute fax copies of your documents.

To work via e-mail, you and your recipients must have Word and Microsoft Mail (or a compatible mail program) installed on your computers. Oh, and your network has to be running, but you'd probably guessed that already.

NOTE

Word 97 makes it extremely easy to share documents over the Internet. (Certain collaborative features, such as routing slips, might or might not work over the Internet.) Moreover, Microsoft Office users will be able to use Microsoft Outlook when routing mail and documents. See Part VII to learn more about Word's Internet features, and see your Office documentation or online help for more information about Outlook.

Sending Word Documents via E-Mail

This section assumes you have a compatible e-mail program installed and an address set up. If that's not the case yet, contact your network administrator or help desk for assistance. Since there are so many variations on this theme, I'll use Microsoft's Outlook mail features for this example. Your procedures might differ considerably.

WARNING

Before we get into how easily you can propagate your Word documents all over the place, remember the importance of protecting them. You'll remember that I discussed this a bit in Chapter 1, *Creating and Saving Your First Document*; we'll look at it again briefly later in this chapter in the "Network Considerations" section.

Sending Word documents via electronic mail is simple once you have a working mail program. To do so, follow these steps:

1. Open the document you want to send.

NOTE

If the document's already open because you've just created or altered it, be sure it's saved.

2. Choose File ➤ Send To ➤ Routing Recipient. Word displays the Routing Slip dialog box, as shown in Figure 24.1.

3. Click on the Address button. In the Address Book dialog box (see Figure 24.2), select the names of the people you want to send the document to and click on the

FIGURE 24.1

The Routing
Slip dialog box

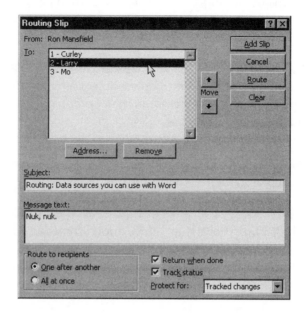

FIGURE 24.2

Choose your
victims in the
Address Book
dialog box.

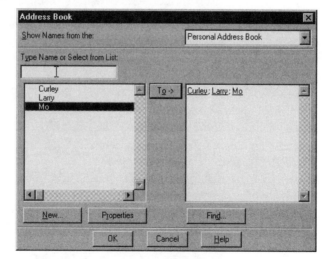

PART

V

**Large Documents and
Team Projects**

To button. Notice you can mix modes of transmission (e-mail, fax, and so on). You might have to choose a different address book from the Show Names from The drop-down list.

TIP

To route the document to one recipient after another (we'll get into this in a minute), arrange the names in the appropriate order by using the Move up- and down-arrow buttons.

4. Click on OK to return to the Routing Slip dialog box. The names you entered will appear in the To box as shown in Figure 24.3.

TIP

If the To box shows that you've added someone you shouldn't have, click on the Remove button to remove that name from the list. Click on OK again to get back to the Routing Slip dialog box.

FIGURE 24.3

The Routing Slip dialog box

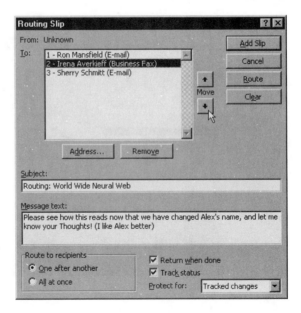

5. Type the subject of your communiqué in the Subject box and any message in the Message Text box. You can see an example of this in Figure 24.3. Each recipient will get the same subject and message, so don't get too personal.

Word automatically adds to your message instructions that tell the recipients to choose File ➤ Send To when they are finished with the document you send them; so you don't need to write that in your message.

6. In the Route to Recipients area, (shown in Figure 24.3), choose whether you want the document to be sent to the recipients One after Another or All at Once.

If you send a document to the recipients One after Another, each successive recipient will see his or her predecessors' comments. This way, you may be able to avoid duplicate comments. If you send multiple copies to All at Once, everyone's comments will be between them and you (until you put them in the ultimate document and attribute them to their maker!). You'll probably also get quicker answers this way.

7. If you're ready to send your document, click on the Route button. The document will be sent to your chosen recipients as an attached Word file.

To further edit your document before you send it, click on the Add Slip button, do your editing, and then choose File ➤ Send To to send the document. Click on Yes in the confirmation dialog box.

Let's look quickly at three further options in the Routing Slip dialog box shown in Figure 24.3: Return When Done, Track Status, and Protect For.

Return When Done Check the Return When Done box to have the document sent back to you when the last recipient finishes with the document and chooses File ➤ Send.

PART

V

Large Documents and
Team Projects

Track Status	Check the Track Status box to keep track of where your document has been routed. Word will send you a message each time the document is sent on to the next person in the To list.
Protect For	Select protection for your document from the drop-down list: Annotations allows recipients to add only annotations to the document; Revisions allows them to make changes (forcibly marked with revision marks) and add annotations; and Forms lets recipients enter information only in form fields (see Chapter 30, *Creating and Using Forms*, for more on forms).

Revising and Returning a Mailed Document

If you're the target of an e-mailed Word document, here's how you do your bit:

1. Retrieve the document from your mail program in the usual way for that program and open the document in Word.

2. Revise the document depending on how the sender has protected it:

   - If the document allows annotations only, choose Insert ➤ Annotation, type your annotation in the annotation pane, and click on Close when you're done.
   - If the document allows revisions as well as annotations, simply go ahead and make your revisions. Friendly Word will mark the revisions for you using revision marks—in fact, you won't be able to turn them off.
   - If the document is protected as a form, you're wearing a straitjacket. Fill in the fields (*all* the fields; be good) and don't try to do anything else.

3. Choose File ➤ Send To. Word displays the Send dialog box, asking if you want to use the routing slip or send the document without using the routing slip. To wing the document on its merry way, choose the Route Document option and click on OK.

   - If the original sender chose to route the document to recipients All at Once, this will return the document to the sender.
   - If the original sender chose to route the document to recipients One after Another, this will pass the document on to its next victim—unless you're the last, in which case the document will be returned to the sender.
   - If the original sender checked Track Status, Word will let the sender know when you send the document on to its next recipient. Yup, Big Brother is e-mailing about you.

There, that was painless, wasn't it?

NOTE

If you choose the Send Copy of Document without Using the Routing Slip option, all protection the original sender chose remains in effect.

The Fun Part—Merging Annotations and Revisions

So you sent out—all at once—seven copies of your latest novel, and everyone got back to you with helpful comments. Well, sort of helpful. Most of them, anyway. Bunch of cynics, the lot of them. Now you need to merge the annotations and revisions into one copy so that you can choose the best and trash the rest.

WARNING

You can't merge annotations and revisions back into the original document unless they're marked. Makes sense if you think about it. This is another good reason for protecting your document for revisions or annotations before sending it out. If you forget to protect your document, try using Tools ➤ Track Changes ➤ Compare Documents.

To merge all those pesky revision marks and annotations, follow these steps:

1. Retrieve your returned document from your mail program. Word will automatically ask you if you want to merge revisions with the original document.
2. Click on OK. Word displays the Merge Revisions dialog box.
3. Select the original file and click on Open. The original document will open, and the revisions will be merged into it.
4. Repeat as necessary with the other six copies of the report.
5. Now you have all the revisions in one place, and you can work your way through the document reviewing (accepting or rejecting) them; choose Tools ➤ Revisions.

NOTE

When you merge revisions or annotations from multiple documents into the original, Word uses a different color for each reviewer (up to eight; after that, Word cycles through the colors again).

PART
V

Large Documents and Team Projects

For Additional Help with Mail

Mail and network connections can be confusing, particularly on the complex networks that have been proliferating recently. Consult your friendly network administrator or hallway guru.

Network Considerations

As I hinted at the beginning of this chapter, networks can be a source of grief as well as of joy to the Word user. Although there's no way that you can absolutely safeguard all your work (short of sealing yourself and it in a lead-lined room), remember to take the following obvious precautions:

- Protect your documents from changes (see Chapter 1, *Creating and Saving Your First Document*).
- Save your documents frequently and back them up to a safe medium.
- If you store your documents on a network drive, be careful about who has access to them. If necessary, make your documents read-only.
- If you're sharing documents a lot, here are a few things to think about first:

  - Don't use templates that the other people in the group don't have.
  - If you share templates, keep them clean. Don't redefine built-in key combinations—you may confuse your co-workers, or worse.
  - Don't use fonts that the other people in the group don't have. But remember that you can embed TrueType fonts in shared documents so that users who don't have the fonts installed can see the fonts and print them. Choose Tools ➤ Options, click on the Save tab in the Options dialog box, and check the Embed TrueType Fonts checkbox. See Chapter 7, *Characters and Fonts*, for more information about this kind of thing.
  - Don't lose your file-protection password(s).

Chapter

25

Document Importing, Exporting, and Conversion

Document Importing, Exporting, and Conversion

Word makes it fairly easy to work with documents created in other applications. For example, if you or a colleague used WordPerfect, or most other word-processing programs to create documents, you should be able to open and work with them without experiencing major problems. Be prepared, however, to make adjustments for things such as page and line endings that might change if you open a document that expects to use fonts not found on your machine. Sometimes printer differences and other factors will cause problems as well.

If you've just upgraded to Word 97 from an earlier version of Word (including Word for Windows 95), you'll have no problem reading those files either. But, because Word 97 uses a new method of *storing* files, if you save files in the Word 97 format (the default saving method), you will probably not be able to open the new files in earlier versions of Word. (I discuss some work-arounds for this inconvenience later in this chapter.)

Opening a Document Created in Another Application

With Word 97, you can usually open documents created in many other applications. Here is a summary:

- All Microsoft Word for Windows versions
- Microsoft Word for the Macintosh versions 3.0–6.*x*

- Microsoft Word versions 3.0–6.0 for MS-DOS
- ASCII text files
- Microsoft Excel versions 2.0–8
- WordPerfect versions 6.*x* for MS-DOS and 6.*x* for Windows
- Lotus 1-2-3 versions 2.*x*–4.*x*
- Files from Microsoft Access (if Access is installed on your system)
- Files from Microsoft Excel (if Excel is installed on your system)
- A personal address book you created for use with Microsoft Exchange server
- Outlook or Schedule+ version 7 contact lists
- Compatible address lists created with a MAPI-compatible messaging system
- Files from some database programs for which you have installed an open database connectivity (ODBC) driver. (A number of these drivers are included with Microsoft Office.)

NOTE

To retrieve data from multitier database programs such as Microsoft SQL Server and Paradox, use the MailMergeOpenDataSource macro statement. For details, see Chapter 31, *Creating and Using Macros*.

Microsoft Office 97 Files Are the Easiest to Import and Export

Most files created with Microsoft Office 97 programs (Excel 97, PowerPoint 97, and so on) will open automatically in Word 97. The reverse is also true. For example, if you are running PowerPoint 97 and use it to open a Word 97 document, Power-Point 97 will attempt to convert your Word 97 document to slides. Obviously, you will need the necessary Office programs on your computer for this to work. Things get trickier when you work with Office 95, Word 6.*x*, and other word-processing programs, particularly if you need to save in Word 97 format.

Here are the general steps:

1. Choose File ➤ Open or click on the Open button on the Standard toolbar. Word displays the Open dialog box (see Figure 25.1).

FIGURE 25.1

Pop up the Files of Type list in the Open dialog box to display files other than those in Word format.

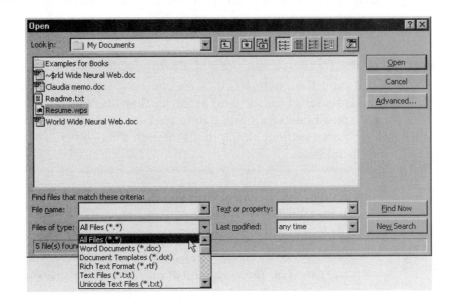

2. In the Look In box, select the drive and folder of the target document. (Hey, Ron, this is real easy! Didn't we do this in Chapter 2, *Viewing and Navigating*? Yes. Read on, MacDuff.)

WARNING

Windows 95 long filenames coupled with the default setting that *hides* file extensions opens up a huge can of worms here. Since you can no longer see the file extensions (if they are turned off), you will not be able to tell what is what in the Open dialog box. You might think that Word now compensates for this by simply finding all Word documents. But life is never that simple. If a document has an extension other than *doc*, hidden or not, Word will not consider it a Word document, even if it is one.

3. If your file is not a Word document, pull down the Files of Type list and select the appropriate option. If your target document was created in an application other than Word, you'll probably want All Files.

TIP

If you know the extension of the file you want, type it in the File Name box and press Enter for a finer sort—for example, *.lwp* for Word Pro documents or *.xls* for Excel spreadsheets (or *.lwp*; *.xls* to see both). That way, you can get the type of file you want without having to sift through all the other junk that may be cluttering the folder.

---

4. Select the file you want to open and click on OK. Word will open the file for you, with the following exceptions:

- If Word doesn't recognize the contents of the file, it will try to use the converters suggested by the file's extension. If that doesn't work, Word will probably try to treat the file as text and display garbage like that shown in Figure 25.2.

FIGURE 25.2

Word will try to treat unknown file types as text, creating a screen full of garbage. Don't make any changes; just close the file!

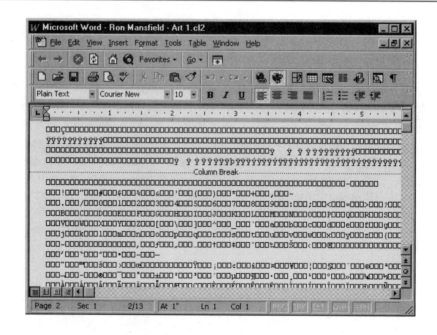

- If this happens, do not make any changes to the file. Just close it!

- Try again with another format. (Click on Help to get a complicated online explanation of what I'm about to tell you.)

> **NOTE**
>
> Remember that a file's extension may not correspond to its contents: You could take a TIFF file called Oddfaces.tif and rename it Oddfaces.doc or Whatsup.doc, but it would still be a TIFF file, not a Word document. Similarly, Idiots.ws could be a WordPerfect 6 or XyWrite file rather than the WordStar file its extension suggests. It could even be CorelDRAW! Here's a quick, free tip: Save your files with the extensions that are the default for that type of file; most applications do this automatically. If you do this, life will be more peaceful.

To make Word automatically display the Convert File dialog box when you open a file with a different format, check the Confirm Conversion at Open checkbox on the General tab of the Options dialog box.

If a document isn't converted correctly, your best bet is to close it without saving changes and try converting it again using a different converter.

> **NOTE**
>
> Exactly which files created in other applications your copy of Word can open depends on the converters you installed with your copy of Word. See the "Make Sure You've Got the Right Filters Installed" section at the end of this chapter if you know that you don't have some necessary converters installed or if Word won't open documents you suspect it should be able to open.

Saving the Converted Document

The file you converted is now stored in your computer's memory. To keep it as a Word 97 document, you need to save it as a Word file. If you select File ➤ Save, Word displays the

Save Format dialog box asking if you want to save the file in Word format or in its original format.

Note the warning in the Save Format dialog box that you may lose some formatting if you don't save the file in Word format.

To save the file in Word format and thus avoid this message, choose File ➤ Save As, select Word Document in the Save As Type drop-down list, and (optionally) give the file a new name in the Save As dialog box.

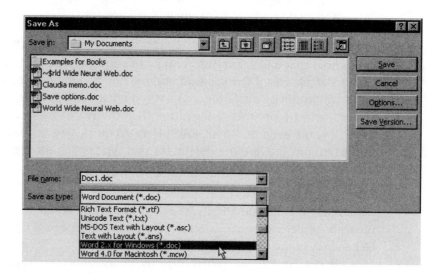

Saving a Word Document in Another Format

Suppose, for example, you need to provide a Word file for a colleague who uses Word-Perfect or an earlier version of Word. First, save your work as a Word 97 file and then save the file in the other application's file format. To do so, follow these steps:

1. Choose File ➤ Save. Save the file normally in Word 97 format.

2. Choose File ➤ Save As. Word displays the Save As dialog box.

3. Display the Save as Type list and choose the format you want. (There's quite a list to scroll through, and it's not in alphabetic order.)

4. Enter a new name for the file in the File Name box, and choose OK.

MASTERING TROUBLESHOOTING

Sharing Files with Users of Earlier Versions of Word

This is an important paragraph. It's probably a good idea to read it twice. If you are collaborating with others who do not have Word 97 (including users of earlier Word versions), either they will need to install conversion software to read the Word 97 files, or you will need to save your Word 97 documents using the Save As command and choose a non–Word 97 format. In the process, certain Word 97 document features (such as the little yellow comments) will be stripped from the document when you save it.

For this reason, if you are collaborating with non–Word 97 users, you may want to save files more than once—first for yourself in Word 97 format and then again in the non–Word 97 format(s) your colleagues need. Henceforth, you should do your editing and all other work in the Word 97 file (continuing to save it in Word 97 format). That is to say, only save in non–Word 97 formats after you have successfully saved your work in Word 97 format. Since many word processors can read and write RTF (Rich Text Format) files, this is often a good, though imperfect middle ground.

You can change the default save format so that Word automatically saves in the file format of your choice. See Chapter 32, *Personalizing Word*, for details.

PART

V

Large Documents and
Team Projects

WARNING

Don't count on a Word file's summary information (reached by choosing File ➤ Properties) being carried to any format except Word and Rich Text Format (RTF).

Exchanging Information with Applications for Which Word Has No Converter

If you need to use a Word file in an application for which Word has no converter, save the file as a plain-text file:

1. Choose File ➤ Save As. Word displays the Save As dialog box.

2. Pull down the Save as Type list and choose one of the text formats:

- You'll get similar effects with the two *text* (Text Only and MS-DOS Text) and the two *text with line breaks* options unless you're doing something very sophisticated: Your text will be saved without formatting, and all line-break characters, section breaks, and page breaks will be converted to paragraph marks.

- Rich Text Format saves all formatting, converting formatting to text instructions that other applications can read. You'll know if you want to use RTF.

3. Give your file a different name. Word will add the appropriate extension (.txt or whatever).

4. Open the file in the other application and work on it there.

NOTE

Many companies offer third-party conversion programs. For example, check out Design Software's Word for Word.

Customizing Word's Conversions

If you don't always get the results you want when you convert a document created in another application into a Word file, you can customize Word's conversions to improve compatibility with the other application. For example, differences in fonts or printer drivers in the other application might cause lines and pages to break in unsuitable places.

To customize Word's conversions, run the EditConversionsOptions macro in Convert.dot:

1. First, be sure Convert.dot is loaded and active. (See the section "Saving Time by Converting Several Files at Once" earlier in this chapter for details on how to do this.)

2. Select Tools ➤ Macro ➤ Macros. Word displays the Macros dialog box.

3. Select the EditConversionsOptions macro and click on the Run button. Word displays the Edit Converter and Filter Options dialog box, as shown in Figure 25.3.

4. Pull down the Conversion list and select the conversion you want—in the figure, I've selected Word 5.1 for Macintosh, which has a decent list of conversion options.

FIGURE 25.3

Select the conversion you want and highlight it in the Edit Converter and Filter Options dialog box (watch the area at the bottom of the dialog box for information on options).

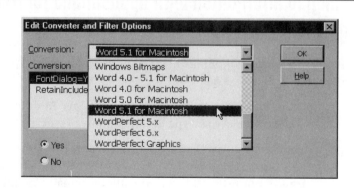

5. In the list of conversion options, highlight the one you're interested in (scroll if necessary). The area at the bottom of the dialog box will display information on that option.

6. Select Yes or No for each option you're interested in (or enter a setting in the Setting box and then click on Set); then click on OK to carry out your changes.

Improving Word's Compatibility with Other Applications

Word includes many options for improving its compatibility with the following word processors: WordPerfect, Word for Windows versions 1 and 2, Word for the Macintosh 5.*x*, and Word for MS-DOS. There's also a Custom choice for working with other word processors.

Word saves compatibility options with the document when you convert it. You can turn these compatibility options on or off at any time. These options affect only how the document behaves while you work with it in Word; it will still behave the same way in the other word processor if you convert it back to its original format.

To turn the compatibility options on or off, follow these steps:

1. Choose Tools ➤ Options. Word displays the Options dialog box.

2. Click on the Compatibility tab to bring the compatibility options to the front (see Figure 25.4).

3. Drop down the Recommended Options For list and choose the file format you want.

4. In the Options box, check or uncheck boxes to turn the options on or off.

5. To use the compatibility options you're now setting for all new documents you create using Word, choose the Default button. Word will ask whether this is really what you want to do.

6. Click on Yes if it is what you want; click on No if it isn't.

7. If the document contains any fonts that aren't available on your computer, Word will substitute some default font that may not be what you want. To apply a different substitute font, click on the Font Substitution button in the Options dialog box. In the resulting Font Substitution dialog box, the Missing Document Font box lists the fonts that could not be matched. Choose a font whose substitution you want to change and then drop down the Substituted Font list and choose a suitable font. To convert fonts permanently, click on the Convert Permanently button and choose Yes in the confirmation dialog box. When you're finished assigning substitute fonts, choose OK.

8. Click on OK to accept your choices and close the Options dialog box.

PART

V

Large Documents and
Team Projects

FIGURE 25.4

The Options dialog box with the Compatibility tab foremost.

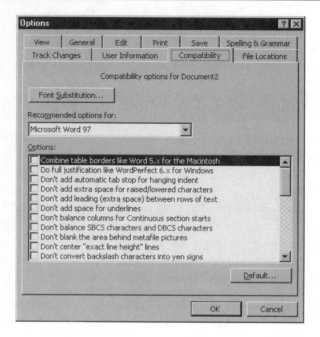

Make Sure You've Got the Right Filters Installed

As discussed earlier in this chapter, Word uses programs called converters or filters to convert documents from one file format (for example, WordPerfect, Works) to another (for example, Word itself). The converters available to you depend on which ones you installed on your computer when you installed Word.

If you chose a Complete installation of Word, all its converters and graphics filters should be available to you. But if you chose a Laptop installation, a Typical installation, or a Custom installation, you may not have all the filters you need.

To install the filters, run the Microsoft Word Setup program again by choosing Word Setup from the Start submenu. If you can't find this command, select Run from the Start menu, browse to find Setup.exe (usually in Winword\Setup), and follow the instructions to install converters and filters. Bear in mind that each converter or filter you install takes up extra space on your hard drive; so if you're pressed for space, you may want to select only the converters and filters you know you'll need. You can install other converters and filters by running Setup again at any point.

TIP

If Word came to you on CD-ROM (as part of Microsoft Office, for example) insert the CD-ROM and run Setup from the CD-ROM. If you're having a hard time finding Setup.exe on your hard disk, try using the Find command on the Windows 95 Start menu.

Give Non-97 Users the Word 97 Converter

If you or others use computers running Word for Windows 95 or Word 6.*x*, you might want to install the Microsoft Word 97 Converter on those machines, making it possible to open Word 97 documents with Word for Windows 95 or Word 6.*x*. This approach will not give non-97 users access to 97 features, and when they save, they will save in their native formats (which Word 97 can read). To learn more, ask the Help Assistant for the Word 97 Converter, and then select the resulting Obtain the Word 97 File Format Converter and Other Converters choice. The other topics offered by the Assistant are worth reviewing as well.

PART

V

Large Documents and
Team Projects

PART VI

Power Tools

LEARN TO:

- *Use mail merge and create custom documents*

- *Use charts and graphs*

- *Link and embed between Word and other applications*

- *Create and use fields*

- *Create and use forms and ActiveX controls*

Chapter

26

Mail Merge——Creating
Custom Documents

Chapter

26

Mail Merge—Creating Custom Documents

Word's Mail Merge feature lets you quickly create personalized correspondence and other documents by combining (*merging*) information from two different files. For instance, you could merge a list of names and addresses from one file (your *data source*) with a form letter in another file (your *main document*) to produce a number of personalized form letters.

Never going to do a mail merge? What about producing a catalog, a form, or an invoice—or even a whole bunch of labels or name tags? Mail Merge can help with all these tasks. You could even personalize a Christmas letter to all your relatives, tailoring the news to what would interest each one. That beats a business letter for entertainment any day; so we'll use it as an example in this chapter.

You insert special instructions (*fields*) in the main document wherever you want information from the data source to appear in your merged documents. For instance, for this Christmas letter to your friends and relatives, you could use fields to create the appropriate salutations for each recipient. Instead of writing plain old boring "Dear" to each victim, you could have a salutation field in the data source containing the personal greeting for each. You could then have a name field for the hapless recipient of the letter. And then, if you wanted, you could have another field (to appear on the same line) of further greeting. This way, you could produce such salutations as "Hi, Joe

Bob, how's it going?" and "My darling little Rosemary, how much you've grown this year!" as well as the staid "Dear Aunt Edna." How's that for variety?

Once the main document and the data source are prepared, you're ready to merge them. The main document is associated—connected to—the data source so that Word knows where to get the information to insert. Mail Merge Helper lets you send merged documents directly to your printer or save them to a file for editing and later printing.

In either case, Word will automatically take care of things such as word wrap and pagination for each new document. Figure 26.1 shows an overview of the elements in a mail-merge project.

Thanks to Word's Mail Merge Helper, merging is relatively painless, though you still need to pay plenty of attention to what you're doing. Some planning beforehand doesn't hurt either, but it's not absolutely essential. That said, let's get into it.

> **NOTE**
>
> Unfortunately, a book this size cannot cover all the variables involved in mail merges. Sometimes you'll find it easier to copy a form letter a few times and paste in the names and addresses of the recipients rather than perform an entire mail merge. Take a quick reality check before turning blindly to Mail Merge Helper.

About Data Sources and Main Documents

Data sources are organized collections of information—databases—that you can create easily as a Word table. That way you can use all the table techniques that you've already learned to add and delete rows and edit the table information. As you'll see in this chapter, the Mail Merge Helper leads you step by step through the creation of a new data source if you don't already have one.

Word can also use data from other applications, such as Microsoft Excel or Microsoft Access. All data sources, no matter where they come from, contain *records* and *fields*. For instance, a data source of information about your employees would usually contain one record for each employee. Each record would contain multiple fields—one field for the employee's first name, one for the middle initial, one for the last name, one for each part of the address, and so on.

Main documents, as mentioned above, contain the text of your merge project (the body of a letter, for instance), fields showing where to insert information from the data source, and optional instructions telling Word how to merge the information.

FIGURE 26.1

Mail-merge
projects require
a data source
(top) and a
main document
(bottom) to
produce new
documents
that contain
information
from both.

Mail Merge
Helper toolbar

The header
source (containing
field names)

Field names

Body text

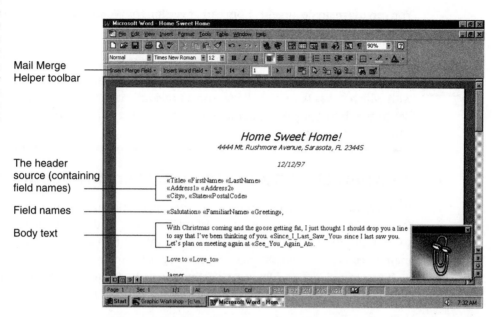

Data (fields in records)

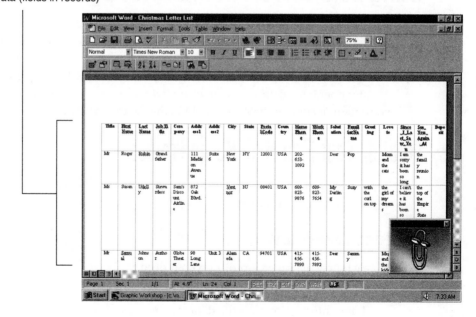

Power Tools

Using Main Documents from Earlier Versions of Word

You can use main documents from earlier versions of Word—for example, version 6.0x—with no problem. Simply open the document in Word 97 and proceed.

NOTE When you open a main document in Word, it will be associated to the data source with which it was last saved. If you use a previously created main document, remember to attach to it any new data source that you want to use. You'll see how to do that later in this chapter.

Using Main Documents from Other Applications

You can use a main document from another application by opening that document in Word and converting its contents to Word. However, field names and formatting from some applications may not translate well into Word format. Check the fields in your main document and adjust them if necessary before completing the merge.

If you experience problems, try pasting the main document into Word as plain text and then applying the formatting and entering the field names.

Using Data Sources from Other Applications

You can use data sources from other applications in your Word merges. For example, if you have data in a Microsoft Excel spreadsheet, you can insert either the whole worksheet or a range of cells. If you have Microsoft Access, you can open a database and insert records from a table or a selection of records defined by a query.

After opening a data source in another application, be sure that the merge fields in your main document match the field names in the data source.

Creating Your First Mail-Merge Project

The best way to learn how to create a merge document is to try one. Consider working along as you read the rest of this chapter.

Project Overview

For each new mail-merge project, you'll need to:

- Create or have available a data source
- Enter information into the data source

- Create and proof the text of your main document
- Insert fields into your main document
- Check for design and data-entry errors
- Merge the data source and main document and print the merge documents

For your first mail-merge project, Word's Mail Merge Helper runs you through the process of creating your data source and main document in a given order. If this feels like wearing a straitjacket, don't worry—on subsequent projects you can vary the order in which you complete the steps. For instance, you can create the main document first and then create a data source, or vice versa.

Because data sources in Word are simply documents containing tables, you can add information and edit them at any time before doing the actual merge. Once you get comfortable with merging and its possibilities, feel free to do things in any workable order that pleases you.

Although you don't need to type your main document first, it's often helpful to make a draft to get a sense of which information you will need from your data sources and where to insert it.

NOTE

If you already have a data source, simply open it or adapt it for the new project. (Adapting here usually means querying to select relevant fields and records.)

Planning Your Data Document

Designing a useful and easy-to-maintain data source is one of the most important parts of a new mail-merge project. With a little ingenuity, you can use the same data sources for a number of projects.

For instance, if you plan to use an employee data source to send letters or memos, you might want one field for the employee's full legal name and another for an informal salutation. That way, you could address mailing envelopes to Dr. Tyler Z. Gradgrinder and have the salutation of the letters or memos read *Dear Ty* or *Dear Doc*.

At first glance, it might seem a good idea to create a single field for all the address information needed for letters and labels. You could then type everything—the recipient's name, company name, street address, city, state, and zip code—in that single field, insert that field in your main documents for form letters and envelopes, and merge merrily away. The problem with this approach comes when you need to break up the information you put in that field—for example, to produce a quick list of employees (without their full addresses) who live in a particular city who might appreciate ride-sharing.

It's far better to break your data into multiple fields. Create separate fields for recipients' first and last names. You can then use Word's Sort feature to produce alphabetized lists or labels sorted by last name. Break addresses into five or six fields, as Word's Mail Merge Helper encourages you to do: street address, apartment number (if any), city, state, country (if you're international), and zip code. Putting city, state, country, and zip code in their own fields gives you enormous flexibility—you can easily find out who all your customers are in, say, Anaheim, Colorado, or Mexico.

Test your new design with small data documents containing a dozen or so representative records. Try your sample data source with a number of different main documents, or have an experienced print-merge user look over your new design before you spend hours entering data into your first data source. Consider keeping sample main documents and data sources at hand in a test folder so that you can quickly test new merge projects you put together.

Using Mail Merge Helper

Word's Mail Merge Helper guides you through the steps of merging documents. The process seems a little convoluted the first time, but it works well. Once you've tried it once or twice, you'll be merging merrily with the best of them. In the following sections, I'll discuss how to perform the different stages of a mail merge by using Mail Merge Helper, because this is the easiest way to merge.

When using the Letter Wizard, Office Assistant will ask if you want to send a single letter or letters to a mailing list. If you click the button for sending letters to a mailing list, the Mail Merge Helper dialog box opens.

To start Mail Merge Helper, select Tools ➤ Mail Merge. Word displays the Mail Merge Helper dialog box, as shown in Figure 26.2. Note the instructions in the box at the top telling you to click on the Create button to set up the mail merge. Watch these instructions as you proceed with subsequent stages of the mail merge. If you're ever confused about what to do next, consult this box.

The first step in the mail merge is to create your main document; the type of main document governs the subsequent choices you can make in the Mail Merge Helper. Because form letters, mailing labels, envelopes, and catalogs have different components, the Mail Merge Helper offers you different choices of data sources.

FIGURE 26.2

Instructions are at the top of the Mail Merge Helper dialog box.

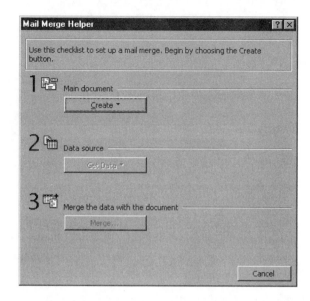

Starting Your Main Document

To start your main document, follow these steps:

1. Click on the Create button to start creating your main document. A drop-down list offers you four choices—Form Letters, Mailing Labels, Envelopes, and Catalog:

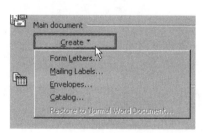

PART

VI

Power Tools

2. Select the type of main document you want. (In the example, I've chosen Form Letters.) Word displays a dialog box in which you choose the active window or a new main document:

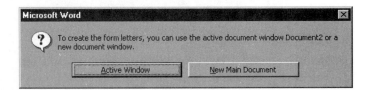

3. Select the window you want to use. If you're starting from a new document, as in the example, or if the active window contains information for your main document, choose the Active Window button. If your active window contains valuable information that has nothing to do with the mail merge, choose the New Main Document button. If you choose the New Main Document button, Word opens a new document. The previously active document stays open—Word does not save or close it.

Regardless of which button you chose, Word returns you to the Mail Merge Helper dialog box for the next stage of the mail merge, arranging the data source. You'll see that the space below the Create button now lists the type of main document you are creating and its name:

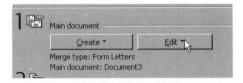

The information box at the top of the Mail Merge Helper dialog box tells you that the next step is to specify the data source. Let's do it.

Specifying the Data Source

Next, you need to create or specify the data source and arrange the fields that you want to be available to your main document for the merge.

1. Click on the Get Data button to display a list of options for your data source.

2. If you already have a data source that you want to use, select Open Data Source. If you want to create the data source, select Create Data Source. If you want to use your Address Book, choose the Use Address Book option.

If you chose Open Data Source or Use Address Book, skip ahead a section. If you chose Create Data Source, read the next section.

Creating a Data Source

The dialog box that appears when you choose Create Data Source contains a list of commonly used field names for the type of mail merge you're performing. Figure 26.3 shows the Create Data Source dialog box for form letters. You can use some or all of these suggested fields, and you can even add your own.

FIGURE 26.3

The Create Data Source dialog box offers a list of commonly used field names. Chop and change these at will.

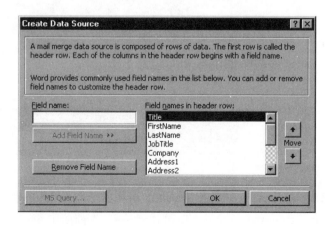

Adding a Field Name

To add field names to the list in the Field Names in Header Row box, follow these steps:

1. Type the name in the Field Name box.

NOTE

Field names can be a maximum of 40 characters and can contain letters, numbers, and underscores (_). Field names *cannot* contain spaces or hyphens and must start with a letter (not a number). For example, What_We_Discussed_At_Yesterday's_Meeting is an acceptable field name (and might be a better reminder of the field's purpose than MeetingTopic), but 1997_May_15_Meeting is not. Bear in mind that the ends of very long field names may not show in the Field Names in Header Row box; so it can be confusing to have long field names that differ only at their ends.

2. Click on the Add Field Name button. The new field name is added at the bottom of the list.
3. To move the new field name to a different position in the list, be sure that it's highlighted in the Field Names in Header Row box and click on the Move arrow buttons.

You can see the field names that I've entered for my Christmas mail merge at the bottom of the list in Figure 26.4.

FIGURE 26.4

New field names for my sample mail merge

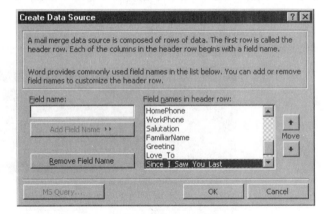

Removing or Modifying a Field Name

You may not want to use all of Mail Merge Helper's suggested fields. Why clutter up the data source table with fields that you do not plan on using? If all your clients are in the United States, for example, you can easily remove the Country field. You might also want to change a field name to make it more suitable for the types of main documents you will be creating. For example, you might want to change Address2 to Suite_Number. It's easy.

To remove or modify a field name, follow these steps:

1. In the Field Names in Header Row box, highlight the field name you want to remove by clicking on it with the mouse or by scrolling to it with the scroll bars or the down arrow. Then click on the Remove Field Name button. The field name is removed from the Field Names in Header Row list and appears in the Field Name box.
2. To modify the field name, make your changes in the Field Name box and then click on the Add Field Name button.

Rearranging Field Names

To rearrange the field names in the Field Names in Header Row box, highlight the field you want to move and click on the Move up and down arrows to move the highlighted field up or down.

Saving Your Data Source

When you've finished adding, removing, and arranging fields, click on OK to save your data source. Word displays the Save Data Source dialog box. Enter a name for your data-source file and select OK to save the file. Word saves the data-source file under the name you specify.

Editing the Data Source

Word now checks your data source to see if it contains records. If it doesn't, Word displays a dialog box informing you of this and inviting you to edit the data source or the main document, as shown below. Click on the Edit Data Source button to edit your data source, and then enter the records (the steps are discussed in a following section).

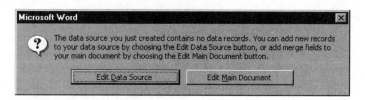

Opening a Data Source

If you already created a data source for use with a different main document, you can open it for use with another—even for labels, envelopes, or a catalog. This way, for example, you can use one data source for letters and for addressing the envelopes. To open an existing data source, select Open Data Source from the Get Data drop-down list. The Open Data Source dialog box works just like the File Open dialog box: Select the document you want to use and click on OK. Word will open the document and return you to Mail Merge Helper.

NOTE

If you want to use a data source from another application, such as Microsoft Excel or Microsoft Access, simply choose it at this point and use the application's techniques to select the data records you want to use. Dialog boxes will appear, for example, to select a table from an Access database or to select a worksheet or range of cells from an Excel workbook.

Entering Your Records

In the Data Form dialog box that Word displays (see Figure 26.5), enter the details for each of your records by typing text into the boxes. Press Tab or Enter to move from field to field. To move backward, press Shift+Tab.

TIP

It is a good idea to enter a few records at this point, if you don't have any. The following steps will be much clearer if you try out the buttons yourself.

FIGURE 26.5

Entering data in the Data Form dialog box

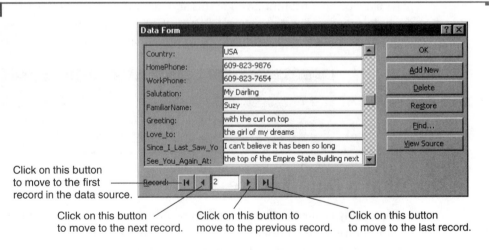

Click on this button to move to the first record in the data source.

Click on this button to move to the next record.

Click on this button to move to the previous record.

Click on this button to move to the last record.

Here's how to alter the records in the Data Form dialog box:

- To add a new record, click on the Add New button.
- To delete a record, click on the Delete button.
- If you realize you've trashed a record (by entering data in the wrong place or whatever), click on the Restore button to return its entries to their previous state. This will not, however, restore a deleted record.
- You can also use the arrows at the bottom, marked in Figure 26.5, to move around the records.

To Find a Record

Word's database functions offer great flexibility in searching. You can search for any word or part of a word in any of the fields.

To find a record, follow these steps:

1. Click on the Find Record button. Word displays the Find in Field dialog box:

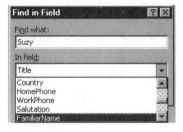

2. Type the word or words you want to find in the Find What box.
3. Click on the arrow at the right end of the In Field box to drop down the list of field names, and then select the name of the field you want to search.
4. Click on the Find First button. Word searches for the first record it finds that contains the word or words in the selected field. If you are in the data source, the record will be selected on-screen. If you are in the main document, the record's number will appear in the GoTo record box in the Mail Merge toolbar. (If you are viewing the merged data in the main document, the information from the record will appear.)
5. If this is the record you were looking for, click on Close to close the Find in Field dialog box. If not, click on the Find Next button to find the next occurrence of the text.
6. When you've finished entering or updating your records, click on OK to close the data source and save the changes. Now you're ready to edit your main document.

PART

VI

Power Tools

TIP

If the Find in Field dialog box is hovering annoyingly over the field you're trying to read, click anywhere in its title bar, and then drag it to a more convenient location on the screen.

You can also edit your data file directly as a Word table. If the Data Form dialog box is on the screen, click on the View Source button. If you've already closed the data source and main document, you can open the data-source file just as you would any document. Then simply type in the cells of the table as you would normally. (Don't worry about word wrap—or anything cosmetic for that matter. Long field names may wrap inappropriately in the cells, but that won't affect the merge process.)

You'll also notice that Word automatically includes the Database toolbar in any data-source document:

Here's what the buttons on the Database toolbar do:

Button	Name	Function
	Data Form	Displays the Data Form dialog box for adding, editing, or deleting records (the one that appeared when you first created the data source)
	Manage Fields	Lets you add, remove, or rename fields
	Add New Record	Inserts a new record (row) in the data-source table
	Delete Record	Removes the current record (row) from the data-source table
	Sort Ascending	Sorts all the records (rows) in the data source in ascending order, based on the current field (column)
	Sort Descending	Sorts all the records (rows) in the data source in descending order, based on the current field (column)
	Insert Database	Inserts records from a data source

Button	Name	Function
	Update Field	Updates the contents of selected field codes (such as links to database documents)
	Find Record	Searches for a record with specified text in a specified field
	Mail Merge Main Document	Switches you to the main document

Sorting the Data Source

If your data source grows large, you might find it useful to sort the records. This has several advantages: It makes manually searching through the data source easier, it gives you a way to keep tabs on the progress of a large print job, and it lets you take advantage of U.S. Post Office bulk mail rates that require sorting by zip code.

To sort a data source, follow these steps:

1. Put the insertion point in the field (column) on which you want to sort. It doesn't matter which record (row) you put it in.
2. Click on either the Sort Ascending or the Sort Descending button on the Database toolbar. (For normal alphabetic order, click on Sort Ascending.)

Finding a Record in the Data Source

If your data source is very large and you don't feel like sifting through it manually to find a particular record, click on the Find Record button on the Database toolbar. Word displays the Find in Field dialog box, which you can use as discussed in the "To Find a Record" section earlier in this chapter.

Inserting or Removing Fields or Records in a Data Source

If you maintain a data source long enough, you're going to have to make changes to it from time to time. The Database toolbar gives you easy shortcuts for managing your fields and records.

PART

VI

Power Tools

Inserting, Removing, or Renaming Fields

Before fooling around with your fields, back up your data source in case things go seriously awry. Then, to change the fields in your data source, click on the Manage Fields button on the Database toolbar. Word displays the Manage Fields dialog box:

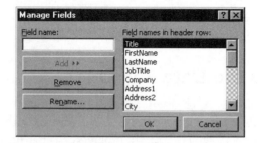

You can make all your field changes in this one dialog box.

- To insert a new field, type the field name in the Field Name box and then click on the Add >> button. (The field will be added at the end of the list—at the right side of the data table. There's no shortcut for moving a field after you've created the data source, although you can move it by selecting the entire column and dragging it to a new location in the table.)
- To remove a field and all the data in it, highlight the name in the Field Names in Header Row list box and then click on the Remove button. Then click on Yes to confirm that you really do want to do this.
- To rename a field, highlight the old name in the Field Names in Header Row list box and then click on the Rename button. Word displays the Rename Field dialog box:

Type a new field name and then click on OK.

When you are done, click on OK in the Manage Fields dialog box. If you'd like to undo your changes, click on Cancel (or press Esc) instead.

NOTE

You can also make any of these changes directly, simply by editing the table in the data source. Somehow, though, it seems easier and less risky to use the Manage Fields dialog box to do so.

Inserting or Removing Records

Data sources inevitably grow (though you occasionally need to prune them back as well) as new names are added to your mailing list or new records in general. The Database toolbar makes it easy to add or remove records when the time comes to make these changes.

TIP

You can always add a new record to the end of a data-source table simply by pressing Tab in the last field of the last record. Also, the Data Form dialog box (see Figure 26.5 earlier in this chapter) has an Add New button. Click on it to add a record to the end of the data-source table.

- To add a record to the end of the data-source table, click on the Add New Record button on the Database toolbar.

- To delete a record, first select it. Then click on the Delete Record button on the Database toolbar. To delete several records at once, select them all and then click on the Delete Record button.

Inserting Data from Another File

If you've already got the data you need for your merge in an existing file—a word-processing, database, or even a spreadsheet document—you can insert this data into your data source in two ways. You can simply insert the data directly into your data source, or you can insert field codes that link your data source to the database file. (Chapter 28, *Linking and Embedding to Keep Things Current,* explains links, and Chapter 29, *Creating and Using Fields,* explains fields.)

Power Tools

The benefit of inserting field codes is that you can update the information automatically when it changes in the original database file. If you know you'll never need to update it, you can simply insert the data directly. Either way, follow these steps:

1. Click on the Insert Database button on the Database toolbar. Word displays the Database dialog box:

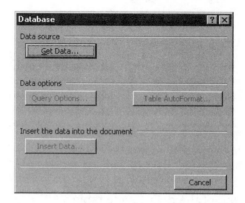

2. Click on the Get Data button. Word displays the Open Data Source dialog box, which works just like the Open File dialog box. Select the document you want to use and click on OK.

For some types of files, such as spreadsheets and databases, Word displays a dialog box in which you select only part of the data from the other file for insertion.

3. If you want to limit the data from the other file in some way, click on the Query Options button in the Database dialog box. Word displays the Query Options dialog box:

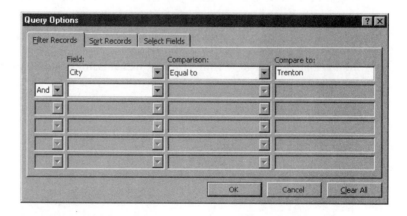

From this dialog box, you can filter the records, sort the records, and select which fields to import.

- To limit the records imported into your data source, choose a field from the Field drop-down list box (or simply type the first letter of the field you want, repeatedly if necessary). Then press Tab and choose a comparison in the Comparison box (such as Equal to, Greater than—b is greater than a—and so on). Press Tab again, and then enter a value with which to compare the field.

- If you want to add more conditions to your query, accept And as the relationship, or select Or in the little unnamed box to the left of the second row. Then repeat the process for the Field, Comparison, and Compare To boxes.

- To sort the records in the other data file before importing them, click on the Sort Records tab in the Query Options dialog box. Choose a field to sort on in the Sort By drop-down list box and then accept Ascending order or select Descending. If you want to add secondary and tertiary sort criteria, select fields and sort order in the next two boxes.

NOTE

For those of you who aren't familiar with database sorting, it simply means switching the records around into an order that you find useful, based on information in one or several of the fields. For instance, you might sort all the records by zip code if you wanted to do a mailing to only one zip code. Often records are sorted alphabetically by last name.

- To select fields to import, click on the Select Fields tab in the Query Options dialog box. Word starts you off with all the fields selected. To remove one, highlight it and click on the Remove button. To remove them all and start over, click on the Remove All button, which changes the buttons to Select and Select All. Highlight and select the fields you want. If you don't want a header row of field names in the imported data, uncheck Include Field Names.

When you are done with the Query Options dialog box, click on OK.

PART

VI

Power Tools

4. When you are ready, click on the Insert Data button at the bottom of the Database dialog box. Word displays the Insert Data dialog box, giving you one more control over the import procedure:

5. If you want to import only certain records from the data file (and you know which ones they are by number), enter the numbers of the first and last records you want in the From and To boxes of the Insert Data dialog box. (You can always remove records after importing, as explained above in the "Inserting and Removing Records" section.)

6. If you want to insert linked data into your data source instead of straight text, check Insert Data As Field.

7. When you are ready, click on OK.

8. If you already had data in your data source and the insertion point was in the table, Word will warn you that the data table will be replaced with the imported data. If you want this, click on Yes. If not, click on No and then move the insertion point past the original table (or start over with a new data document).

If you chose to insert linked data, you can update any entry by selecting it and pressing F9. To unlink the data and turn it into regular text, select the entire table and press Ctrl+Shift+F9.

Editing the Main Document

Once you've used the Helper to create the data document, you'll want to turn your attention to the Main document. Main documents contain the following:

- Text and punctuation
- Merge instructions and field names that Word uses to merge data

Figure 26.6 shows a main document for our sample mail merge. We'll discuss the various elements in detail.

FIGURE 26.6

*The main docu-
ment for the
Christmas mail-
merge letter*

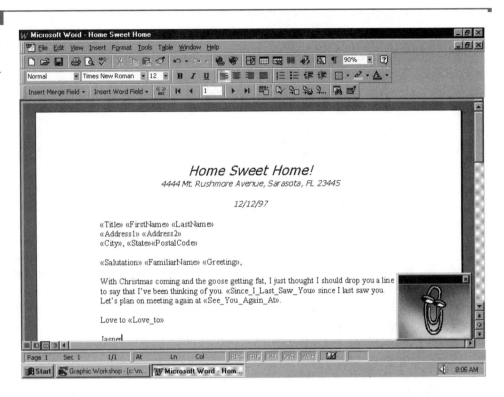

Text in Main Documents

Use Word's word-processing and graphics features to create the text and design elements for your main document. In the sample, a suitably sickly letterhead was created by typing the return address in Monotype Corsiva and centering it. (The first line was increased to 24 points, and the second to 16 points.)

The body of the letter was typed (in 10-point Times New Roman) using regular Word techniques, with data instructions containing field names and other merge devices inserted as needed, as explained below.

Inserting Data Instructions

Mail Merge Helper makes it easy to insert field names and other data instructions in your main documents. Simply place the insertion point where you want to insert a data

PART

VI

Power Tools

instruction, and then pull down the appropriate list from the Mail Merge toolbar and select the item to insert.

- Pull down the Insert Merge Field list to insert a field code that will add information from the data source.
- Pull down the Insert Word Field list to insert special instructions for performing the merge.

For example, to insert the Title field name shown in Figure 26.6, you would place the insertion point on a new line at the beginning of the document (below the header). Then click on the Insert Merge Field button on the Mail Merge toolbar to display the list of field names available in the associated data source. Next, select the appropriate field name, and Word inserts it into the document. (The guillemets « and » come free with the field name.)

When preparing the text of a main document, remember to include spaces between field names and any required punctuation following them. Running people's first and last names together will spoil the effect of your carefully personalized letters. You know the feeling if you've ever been insulted by Publishers' Clearing House.

As you'll see in a moment, you can use combinations of merge fields from the Insert Merge Field button and Word fields from the Insert Word Field button (both on the Mail Merge toolbar) with text typed from the keyboard to put together powerful merge instructions.

Try It

Take a moment to create a main document for a merge yourself. The steps below refer to the sample letter in Figure 26.6. Use these instructions for general guidance.

1. Create a letterhead for your letter by typing the return address and applying such formatting as you see fit. If you want to include the date, choose the Date and Time option from the Insert menu.
2. With the insertion point below the letterhead and at the left margin, insert the Title field by clicking on the Insert Merge Field button and selecting Title from the drop-down list. Don't press Enter yet—the Title, FirstName, and LastName fields all belong on the same line.
3. Type a space to separate the Title and FirstName fields.
4. Use the Insert Merge Field drop-down list to insert the FirstName field.
5. Add a space and insert the LastName field.
6. Now press Enter to start a new line.

7. Add the Address1, Address2, City, State, and PostalCode fields, together with whatever punctuation and spacing they need.

8. On a new line, insert the Salutation field, a space, the FamiliarName field, another space, and the Greeting field.

9. Type the body of your letter, including any merge fields that you need.

10. Save your main document.

11. If you didn't enter any data in your data source earlier, switch to it. Click on the Edit Data Source button in the Mail Merge Toolbar, or crank up Mail Merge Helper by choosing Tools ➤ Mail Merge; then choose Edit in the Data Source step:

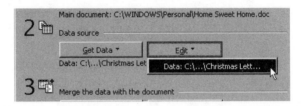

12. Add a few names and addresses. Try leaving the Address2 field blank in at least one record so that you can see how Mail Merge handles blank lines.

Sorting Merged Documents

Usually, records are merged in the order they occur in your data source, but Word's Mail Merge Helper lets you sort the records during the merge. In addition, Word lets you use filters to restrict merging to records containing certain data. (Filtering is discussed in the next section.)

To sort records before you perform a merge, follow these steps:

1. Open Mail Merge Helper and choose the Query Options button. Word displays the Query Options dialog box (see Figure 26.7).

2. Click on the Sort Records tab to enter your sorting preferences.

3. In the Sort By area, click on the down arrow; then select a field to sort by from the list that appears.

4. Select a field for one or both Then By fields if you want to refine your sort further.

5. When you've defined the sort to your satisfaction, click on OK. If you mess things up, click on the Clear All button to clear the fields and start again, or click on Cancel to escape from the dialog box.

PART

VI

Power Tools

FIGURE 26.7

FIGURE 26.7

In the Query Options dialog box, choose sorting and filters for the merge you're about to perform. I'm going to sort my relatives by FirstName and then LastName.

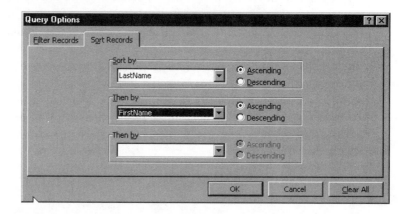

MASTERING TROUBLESHOOTING

Avoiding Merge Problems

If you create your data source and main documents using Mail Merge Helper, the process should go without a hitch. But as your merge documents become more sophisticated, errors can occur during the merge process. The most common errors occur because you have edited the data source and its field names no longer match those you've added to the main document.

Before firing up Mail Merge Helper and churning out a whole batch of letters, proofread your work. Use Word's spell checker and grammar tools (see Chapter 15, *Author's Tools*, for more information on these). Make any necessary corrections. Remember that Word will faithfully copy every error in your main document into every single copy it merges.

Next, run Mail Merge Helper's error-checking program. Choose the Check for Errors button from the Mail Merge toolbar.

Word displays the Checking and Reporting Errors dialog box:

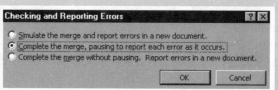

Continued

There are three options. Choose *Simulate the merge and report errors in a new document* if you don't want to actually do the merge yet (you just want to see what might go wrong if you did). Word checks your data source and main document for errors (such as missing data fields in the data source and misspelled field names in your main document). Word lists any errors in a new document so that you can correct them. If Word finds no errors, you will see a happy dialog box telling you that no mail merge errors have been found.

The second option, the default, merges the data and main documents and reports errors to you in a dialog box as they occur. The third option proceeds with the merge and lists the errors in a new document.

Whichever option you choose, correct any detected errors when the check is complete.

As a final check, consider merging some or all of your documents to a file and inspecting them, rather than printing them all at once. We'll look at how to do this in just a moment.

Filtering Merged Documents

If you're not content with sorting your records, you can *filter* them as well—that is, you can specify criteria for including or excluding certain records from the merge. Filtering gives you a lot of flexibility in removing entries from the merge that for any reason you don't want to use. For instance, if I thought that my sister would never speak to me again if I sent her a form letter for Christmas, I could exclude her record from the merge to safeguard myself.

Here's how to set up filtering:

1. Start Mail Merge Helper and click on the Query Options button. Word displays the Query Options dialog box.
2. Select the Filter Records tab.
3. In the Field column of the first row, choose the field you want to use as a filter.

PART

VI

Power Tools

4. In the Comparison column of the first row, drop down the list of filtering comparisons to choose one. This is what they do:

Comparison	Effect
Equal To	The contents of the data field you chose must match those of the Compare To box.
Not Equal To	The contents of the data field you chose must not match those of the Compare To box.
Less Than	The contents of the data field you chose must be less than those of the Compare To box.
Greater Than	The contents of the data field you chose must be greater than those of the Compare To box.
Less Than or Equal	The contents of the data field you chose must be less than or equal to those of the Compare To box.
Greater Than or Equal	The contents of the data field you chose must be greater than or equal to those of the Compare To box.
Is Blank	The merge field must be empty.
Is Not Blank	The merge field must not be empty.

5. In the second row, choose And or Or in the first column to include additional or complementary criteria for filtering.

6. Repeat steps 3, 4, and 5 for more rows as necessary to refine your criteria further.

7. When you've defined the filtering criteria to your satisfaction, select OK. If you mess things up, select Clear All to start again or Cancel to escape from the Query Options dialog box.

NOTE

When you filter a data field that contains text, Word compares the sequence of characters based on the ANSI sort order. Because *antelope* precedes *zebra* alphabetically, Word considers it "less than" zebra. So if you wanted to retrieve data records for only the second half of the alphabet, you could specify LastName Is Greater Than M. If you mix numbers with letters, Word compares the numbers as though they were a sequence of text characters.

Printing Merged Documents

When you've specified any filtering and sort-ordering that you want, you're ready to run the mail merge.

> **NOTE**
>
> We'll be using Mail Merge Helper here to merge and print the documents, but you can also use the buttons in the Mail Merge toolbar. You'll learn about this toolbar later in the chapter.

To run the Mail Merge, follow these steps:

1. Start the merge process by switching to or opening the main document.

2. Select Mail Merge from the Tools menu to start Mail Merge Helper.

3. Click on the Merge button in Mail Merge Helper to display the Merge dialog box (see Figure 26.8).

4. To merge and print the documents, select Printer in the Merge To box. To merge the documents into one long new document, choose New Document—each letter is separated by a page break in the new document.

5. Select the Records to Be Merged by choosing either All or From and To. If you choose From and To, specify the record numbers at which the merge will start and stop.

6. The default is not to print blank lines when data fields are empty. If you *do* want to do this—perhaps you have a reason, for example, to show gaps in your data source—choose the Print Blank Lines When Data Fields Are Empty option.

7. When all is set to your liking, click on Merge. The mail merge will finally take place.

When the mail merge is finished, close Mail Merge Helper. If you merged to a new document, it should be on-screen now. If you merged to a printer, the printer will be

PART

VI

Power Tools

FIGURE 26.8

The Merge dialog box—the culmination of your quest... Choose your final options here.

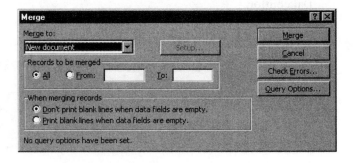

churning out your merged documents. Either way, check your output carefully before inflicting it on your victims. The law of mass mailing clearly states that you'll only notice an egregious error *after* you've mailed the whole batch.

If you have unsaved changes in your main document, Word will invite you to save them.

Specifying Header Options

The header row is the row of fields at the top of a data source that identifies each kind of information in the data source—the Title, FirstName, and LastName fields and so on.

Why would you want to reuse a header? Well, you could then use the same header row with more than one data source. If you can't change the merge fields in a data source to match the names of the merge fields in a main document (the file might be read-only), you can use a header source that contains matching merge fields.

To specify a header source, follow these steps:

1. Choose the Get Data button in the Mail Merge Helper dialog box and select Header Options. Word displays the Header Options dialog box (see Figure 26.9).
2. Choose Create to create a new header source. Or choose Open to open an existing header source; then skip ahead to step 5.
3. If you choose Create, Word displays the Create Header Source dialog box. It works just like the Create Data Source dialog box we discussed in the "Creating a Data Source" section earlier in the chapter. Add, remove, and rearrange the fields to your satisfaction; then click OK.
4. In the Save Data Source dialog box, name your header source and click on OK. Word displays the Mail Merge Helper dialog box, and the header source you created now appears under the Get Data button.
5. If you choose Open, Word displays the Open Header Source dialog box. Select the header source you want to use and click on OK. Word displays the Mail Merge Helper dialog box, and the header source you created now appears under the Get Data button.

FIGURE 26.9

In the Header Options dialog box, you can open an existing header source or create a new one.

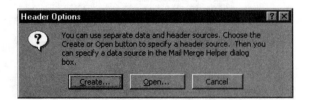

6. Word checks the header source against the data source and warns you if the data source contains too many data fields, as shown below. The Merge button in the Mail Merge Helper dialog box will be dimmed, indicating that you cannot yet run the merge.

ine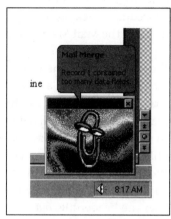

7. If the data source contains too many fields, edit the data source or header source so that they match.

Merging onto Letterhead

If you want to print your form letters on letterhead (either preprinted or created by including a header in your main document), you have to make sure that the text begins low enough on the first page to leave room for the letterhead itself. It's easy, though. Follow these steps:

1. Go to the top of your main document.
2. Choose File ➤ Page Setup.
3. Click on the Margins tab.
4. Type a new top margin, large enough to clear the letterhead contents.
5. Click on OK.
6. Go to the bottom of the first page.
7. Choose Insert ➤ Break.
8. In the Break dialog box, click on Next Page.
9. Click on OK.
10. Select File ➤ Page Setup.
11. Reenter the original top margin.
12. Click on OK.

Using Different Data Sources with a Single Main Document

You can create a master main document and merge different data sources into it. The procedure for attaching a new data source to a main document is essentially the same as the original procedure. Click on the Mail Merge Helper button on the Mail Merge toolbar. Word displays the Mail Merge Helper (shown earlier in Figure 26.2). Click on the Get Data button and select Open Data Source (or select Create Data Source if you want to create the new data document on the fly).

That's it. The new data source is attached to the main document. Check the new data source for errors right away, in case the fields don't match up perfectly. Repeat the procedure to reattach the original data source at any time.

If you need to use different database documents as data sources, you might want to attach a header file to your main document. A header file needs to contain only the field names (although it can be a complete data source in its own right and still function as a header file for another source). The new data source must have the same number of fields as the header file, *but* it does not need to have a header row of its own to identify the fields.

To attach a header file, click on the Get Data button in Mail Merge Helper and choose Header Options. Word displays the Header Options dialog box. Click on the Open button to open an existing data source as a header file or click on the Create button to create a new one.

If you click on Open, Word displays the Open Header Source dialog box (which looks uncannily like the Open Data Source dialog box). Select the file you want to use and click on OK.

If you click on Create, Word displays the Create Header Source dialog box:

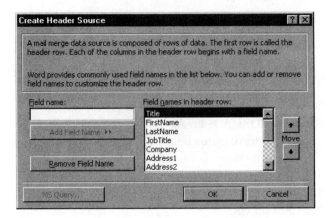

This looks about the same as the Create Data Source dialog box, and it works the same way too. Type field names and click on Add Field Name to add them to the field-name list. Highlight existing field names and click on Remove Field Name to delete them.

When you are done, click on OK. Word displays the Save Header Source dialog box (much like the Save Data Source dialog box, of course). Type a filename and click on OK.

After you attach a header source, you must still attach a data source (and it should not have a header row of its own, as it will be misinterpreted as a record).

Using Word's Merge Instructions

Word provides a number of ways to change its mail-merging behavior based on the contents of individual records in your data source. As you've just seen, it can eliminate unwanted blank lines in merged documents. It can insert special text if certain conditions are met, or it can stop during each merge to let you enter unique text from the keyboard. If you decide to use these features, be prepared to spend some time experimenting and troubleshooting.

NOTE

If you do not see the merge instructions on your screen, display field codes (select Tools ➤ Options, choose the View tab, check the Field Codes box, and click on OK).

Ask

The Ask feature causes Word to stop during the merge each time a new record is merged to prompt you for keyboard input to be printed.

Ask is normally used to include in merged documents data that has not been stored in the data document. Suppose, for example, that you were creating ten welcome letters to bungee jumpers, like the one in Figure 26.10, and that you wanted to enter a date and time for each jumper's first lesson. Suppose further that your data document does not contain a field for first lesson dates and times.

Setting Up an Ask Entry

When designing your main document, move the insertion point to where you want the information entered for the Ask field to appear. Then choose Ask from the Insert Word Field drop-down list on the Mail Merge toolbar. Word displays the Insert Word Field: Ask dialog box (see Figure 26.11).

Use this dialog box to create a new field unique to the main document (not the data source). In the Bookmark field, type a name for the bookmark. This gives you

PART

VI

Power Tools

FIGURE 26.10

This form letter (top) uses merge instructions to ask the operator for information from the keyboard, as you can see when Field Codes are displayed (bottom).

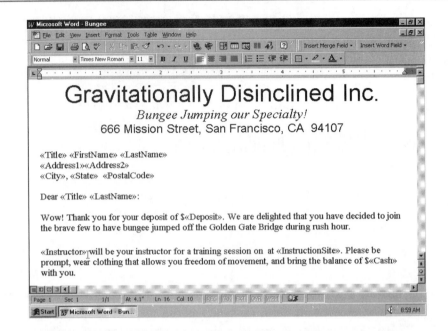

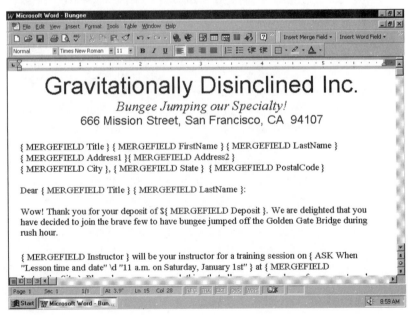

FIGURE 26.11

The Insert Word
Field: Ask dialog
box creates
prompts for
keyboard
entries when
you merge.

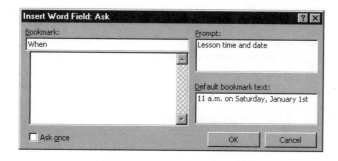

quick access to the field. In the Prompt box, enter the text that you want to appear on-screen during the merge to prompt the operator to enter appropriate information. In the Default Bookmark Text box, you can enter default text that will appear to guide the operator and which will be inserted automatically if the operator does not enter the information when prompted. If you want Word to ask for an entry with only the first merge document and then use it for all the documents, click on the Ask Once button. When you're done, click on OK.

Word gives you a preview of the dialog box that will appear:

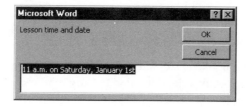

Choose OK or Cancel to close the box—both options work the same in this preview. Word inserts the Ask instruction at the insertion point.

Using Ask

When you actually merge your ten letters (to continue the bungee jumping example), you'll see a dialog box like the one shown above for each letter. In it, you enter the date and time for each bungee jumper; then click on OK or press Enter.

PART

VI

Power Tools

Set Bookmark

Set Bookmark, like Ask, inserts a field unique to the main document (that is, not in the data source). But the value you define for it is used for all documents being merged—you don't get to enter a different value for each one. For instance, you could use it to insert Winter in everyone's Semester field in winter, Summer in summer, and so on. This is the same as choosing the Ask Once option in the Insert Word Field: Ask dialog box.

Inserting a Set Field Name

When designing your main document, move the insertion point to where you want the Set information to appear. Pull down the Insert Word Field list on the Mail Merge toolbar, and choose the Set Bookmark command. Word displays the Insert Word Field: Set dialog box, as shown in Figure 26.12.

FIGURE 26.12

The Insert Word Field: Set dialog box

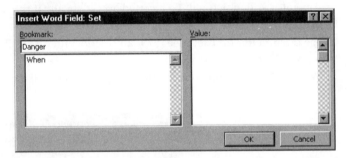

In the Bookmark box, type the name of the bookmark you want to create. If you want to specify a default value for any mail merge main document you create, enter that in the Value box. Click on OK to accept the bookmark name and value. Word inserts the Set information in your document at the insertion point.

Using Set

When you actually merge your documents (ten letters, for instance), Word automatically prints the defined Set value in each letter at the points where you've inserted the field names.

If...Then...Else...

You can use If...Then...Else... to make Word do different things based on conditions it finds in fields in your data sources. For example, you could enter a field in the bungee-jumping letter to check whether the would-be jumper had paid a deposit. If the condition was met, your Then instructions could make Word thank the jumper for the deposit and request the balance of the fee; otherwise, your Else instructions would cause Word to request the full fee.

To insert an If...Then...Else... field, click on the Insert Word Field drop-down list on the Mail Merge toolbar.

Word displays the Insert Word Field: IF dialog box:

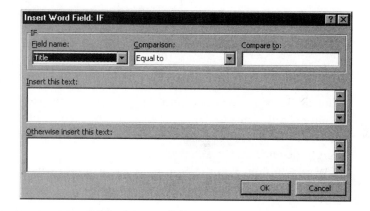

So, say you're sending out collection letters and you want to vary some of the language you use, depending on how overdue your invoices or bills are. You'd need to maintain an age field for overdue bills and then include an If...Then...Else expression that If the overdue bill's age was greater than 90 days, Then a sentence containing strong language would be included, Else a more conciliatory sentence would be included instead.

This means that in the Insert Word Field: IF dialog box, you'd select the Age field in the Field Name box, select Greater Than in the Comparison box, and enter **90** in the Compare To box. You'd then type something like "Please remit immediately to protect your credit rating!" in the Insert This Text box and something like "Did you forget?" in the Otherwise Insert This Text box. Then click on OK.

Fill-in...

Fill-in... prompts for text to be inserted at the location of the field in one document. For more than one document, use Ask instead. To insert a Fill-in... field, click on the Insert Word Field drop-down list on the Mail Merge toolbar.

PART

VI

Power Tools

Word displays the Insert Word Field: Fill-in dialog box:

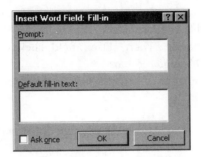

Type a prompt in the Prompt box (such as "Add a friendly message here"), and then, if you want, type a suitable example sentence in the Default Fill-in Text box (such as "Hope the weather is nice in your part of the world"). If you'll want to be prompted only once so that your answer is printed in all the merged documents, check the Ask Once box. Otherwise, you'll be able to personalize each and every merged document. Then click on OK.

Word will show you the prompt as it will appear when you merge the document:

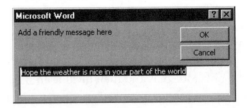

Click on OK. Word inserts a field code into your main document (field codes are explained in Chapter 29, *Creating and Using Fields*). It will appear as your default text unless you choose to view field codes in the Option dialog box (choose Tools ➤ Options, View tab). It will then look something like this:

```
{ FILLIN "Add a friendly message here" \d "Hope the weather is nice in your part of
the world" }
```

When you merge the document, you'll be prompted for a personalized message.

Merge Record # and Merge Sequence

Merge Record # inserts the merge record number in the merge document. You might use it for tracking the records you print—for example, for invoice numbers.

Merge Sequence # inserts the merge-sequence number in the merge document. This can differ from the merge-record number if only some of the records in the data source are used for a merge. For example, if you used only data records 157 to 300 for a merge, the Merge Record # for the first one would be 157, but the Merge Sequence # would be 1.

Insert these fields from the Insert Word Field drop-down list on the Mail Merge toolbar.

Next Record and Next Record If...

Next Record merges the next record into the current merge document rather than into a new merge document. Next Record If... does the same if the comparison between two expressions is true. Insert these fields from the Insert Word Field drop-down list on the Mail Merge toolbar.

Skip Record If...

Skip Record If... skips the current document and moves to the next record if the comparison between two expressions is true. Insert a Skip Record If... field from the Insert Word Field drop-down list on the Mail Merge toolbar.

Try It

Try applying some of these tricks and fields on a few practice merge documents of your own. The best way to learn how the fields work is to play around with them.

Using the Mail Merge Toolbar

As I mentioned before, Mail Merge Helper can feel like a straitjacket at first—it may seem to be pushing you all over the place, opening up this document and that, with little rhyme or reason. As you get used to it though, you'll probably find that it offers more flexibility than at first appears.

PART

VI

Power Tools

But if you don't get along with Mail Merge Helper, put together your mail merge using the Mail Merge toolbar. We've looked at it briefly along the way, but here it is in all its glory:

Here's what the buttons on the Mail Merge toolbar do:

Button	Name	Function
Insert Merge Field ▾	Insert Merge Field	Inserts a merge field at the insertion point.
Insert Word Field ▾	Insert Word Field	Inserts a Word field (for example, Ask...) at the insertion point.
《 》 ABC	View Merged Data	Toggles between viewing merge fields and the data that will appear in them.
◀	First Record	Displays the first record in the data source.
◀	Previous Record	Displays the previous record in the data source.
1	Go to Record	Enter the number of the record you want to go to in this box.
▶	Next Record	Displays the next record in the data source.
▶	Last Record	Displays the last record in the data source.
	Mail Merge Helper	Displays the Mail Merge Helper.
	Check for Errors	Displays the Check for Errors dialog box.

Button	Name	Function
	Merge to New Document	Merges the main document and the data source to a new document.
	Merge to Printer	Merges the main document and the data source to a printer.
	Mail Merge	Displays the Merge dialog box.
	Find Record	Displays the Find Record dialog box.
	Edit Data Source	Displays the Data Form dialog box.

Merge-Printing Labels and Envelopes

You can also use Word's Mail Merge Helper to merge labels of various kinds and envelopes. Because the procedures for merging labels and envelopes are similar to those for form letters, we'll discuss them only briefly here.

Printing Labels on Laser Printers

Mail Merge Helper makes merging labels on a laser printer dead simple. You use Mail Merge Helper to create a main document containing a table with fixed-size cells and cell spacing that match the size and position of your blank labels. Then insert merge instructions in each table cell. Here's how to do it:

1. Select Tools ➤ Mail Merge to fire up Mail Merge Helper.
2. Click on the Create button to drop down a list of options.
3. Select Mailing Labels from the drop-down list.
4. Arrange your data source as usual. Word will then invite you to set up your main document. In the Label Options dialog box (see Figure 26.13), make the appropriate choices for your printer and labels:

   • In the Printer Information box, select Laser and Ink Jet or Dot Matrix as appropriate. If necessary, click on the arrow to drop down the Tray list and select a different tray.

PART

VI

Power Tools

FIGURE 26.13

In the Label Options dialog box, you select the type of printer and labels you're using.

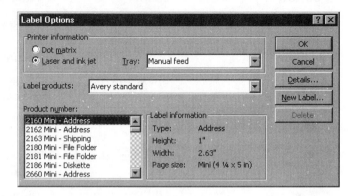

> **TIP**
>
> Consider selecting a different Tray option when printing labels on a network. That way, you might be able to avoid having someone else print a 90-page report on your precious disk labels.

- In the Label Products box, select the brand of labels you want: Avery Standard, Avery Pan European, or Other. (Other includes brands such as Inmac and RAJA.)
- From the Product Number list, select the number for the labels you're using. If you don't know the number (for Avery products it appears on the box), consult the Label Information area to find out the size of the label selected in the Product Number list. If you're still no wiser, measure your labels carefully and choose the closest match.
- For precise layout information on the labels, click on the Details button. In the dialog box that appears, make any necessary adjustments in the labels' margin, pitch, dimensions, and layout, and then click on OK.

5. When you've chosen the labels to use, choose OK to close the dialog box.
6. Word displays the Create Labels dialog box (see Figure 26.14). Enter the fields here by pulling down the Insert Merge Field list and selecting them in turn. Remember to include any necessary spaces and punctuation.

FIGURE 26.14

*Add the fields
for your labels
in the
Create Labels
dialog box.*

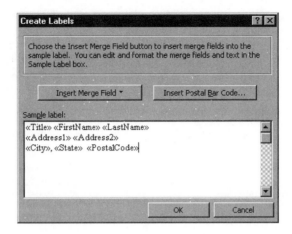

7. To include a postal bar code, click on the Insert Postal Bar Code button. In the Insert Postal Bar Code dialog box (shown here), enter the Merge Field with ZIP Code and Merge Field with Street Address in the appropriate boxes; then click OK.

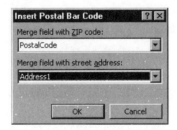

8. Click on OK when you're finished making choices in the Create Labels dialog box, to return to Mail Merge Helper, and then select to Edit the main document. Word will enter your label fields into the main document, as shown in Figure 26.15.

9. Make any necessary adjustments to your main document (for example, adding Ask or Fill-In fields).

10. Open Mail Merge Helper and choose the Merge button to merge your data source with the main document. Choose whether to merge to a new document or to the printer. (You can also use the Merge to New Document and Merge to Printer buttons on the Mail Merge toolbar here.)

PART

VI

Power Tools

FIGURE 26.15

The labels merged into the main document

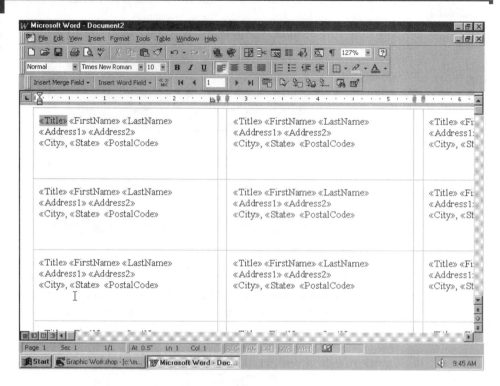

> **NOTE**
>
> The NEXT and NEXTIF fields are ones you probably won't use very often, but here's what they do. NEXT instructs Word to merge the next record's data without starting a new document. NEXTIF does the same thing, but you can enter criteria that must be met before NEXTIF will merge the next record's data without starting a new document.

11. Save your documents with meaningful names.

Making Custom Mailing Labels

If you can't find a mailing label format in the Label Options dialog box that matches the labels you have, you can always create your own. To do so, follow these steps:

1. In the Label Options dialog box, find a label format that's close to the dimensions that you need and select it.

2. Click on the New Label button. (Use the Details button to change the label's specifications.) Word displays the New Custom Laser dialog box, such as this one:

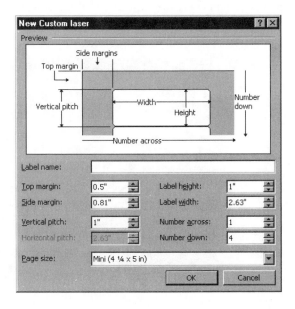

3. Type a name for the label.
4. Either type new dimensions to match your mailing labels or play with the little arrow buttons to zero in on the correct dimensions.

The diagram will change to reflect the information you enter. When you are satisfied, click on OK three times and then continue with step 6 in the previous section.

PART

VI

Power Tools

Printing a Label for a Single Piece of Mail

Labels are great for mass mailings, but you may also want to use individual labels for single pieces of mail every now and again. With your main document on the screen, select Tools ➤ Envelopes and Labels. Word displays the Envelopes and Labels dialog box:

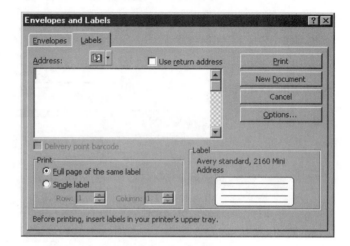

Look at the picture and description of the label in the Label panel. If the label is not the one you are using, click on Options and then select the label as explained previously.

Correct the address, if necessary, use the Insert Address button to add an address from your personal Address Book, or check Use Return Address to print a return-address label. If you want to print a single label and not a full page of the same label over and over, check Single Label.

If the upper-left label is available on your label sheet, leave Row and Column set to 1. Otherwise, type in the Row and Column of the first available label.

When you are ready, click on Print.

Printing Addresses on Envelopes

Word offers the ability to print addresses on envelopes. This can be convenient for small numbers of envelopes; but as most laser printers require you to feed envelopes in by hand, printing large numbers of envelopes can be a slow business. Take a quick reality check before you arrange to print a whole slew of envelopes and consider using mailing labels on the envelopes instead.

TIP

Before starting to prepare envelopes, be sure your return address is correct. Choose Tools ➤ Options to display the Options dialog box. Click on the User Information tab to view (and if necessary change) the name and mailing address. Click on OK when you're finished.

To print an address on an envelope, follow these steps:

1. Select Tools ➤ Mail Merge to fire up Mail Merge Helper.
2. Click on the Create button to drop down a list of options.
3. Select Envelopes from the drop-down list.
4. Create or open the data source as usual. Word will invite you to edit your main document.
5. In the Envelope Options dialog box (see Figure 26.16), make the appropriate choices for your envelopes:

   - On the Envelope Options tab, click on the Font button in the Delivery Address box or on the Font button in the Return Address box to change the font in which the addresses appear. If necessary, adjust the position of the delivery address or return address by entering From Top and From Left measurements in their boxes.
   - On the Printing Options tab, select the Feed Method and the tray to Feed From. Note that the default Feed From option is manual. For large numbers of envelopes, you'll be spending half the afternoon chez the printer.

PART

VI

Power Tools

FIGURE 26.16

Choose your envelopes in the Envelope Options dialog box.

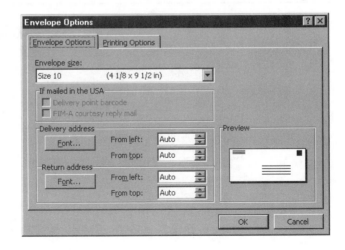

NOTE Word displays the name of your currently selected printer in the Printing Options tab of the Envelope Options dialog box. If need be, change the printer by choosing File ➤ Print, clicking on Options, and then clicking on the arrow to drop down the Default Tray list to select a different tray.

6. When you've chosen the envelope options and printing options, click on OK to close the dialog box.

7. Word displays the Envelope Address dialog box (see Figure 26.17). Enter the fields here by pulling down the Insert Merge Field list and selecting them in turn. Remember to include any necessary spaces and punctuation.

8. To include a postal bar code, click on the Insert Postal Bar Code button. In the Insert Postal Bar Code dialog box, enter the Merge Field with ZIP Code and Merge Field with Street Address in the appropriate boxes, and then click on OK.

9. Click on OK when you're finished making your choices in the Envelope Address dialog box. Word will then enter your label fields into the main document, as shown in Figure 26.18.

10. Make any necessary adjustments to your main document.

11. Open Mail Merge Helper and choose the Merge button to merge your data source with the main document. Choose whether to merge to a new document or to the printer. (You can also use the Merge to New Document and Merge to Printer buttons on the Mail Merge toolbar.)

12. Save your documents with meaningful names.

FIGURE 26.17

Enter fields for mailing labels in the Envelope Address dialog box.

Envelope address

Choose the Insert Merge Field button to insert merge fields into the sample envelope address. You can edit and format the merge fields and text in the Sample Envelope Address box.

Insert Merge Field ▾   Insert Postal Bar Code...

Sample envelope address:

«Title» «FirstName» «LastName»
«JobTitle»
«Company»
«Address1» «Address2»
«City», «State» «PostalCode»

OK   Cancel

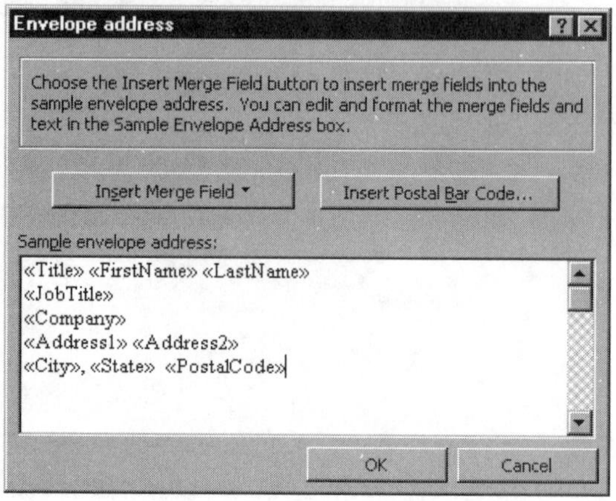

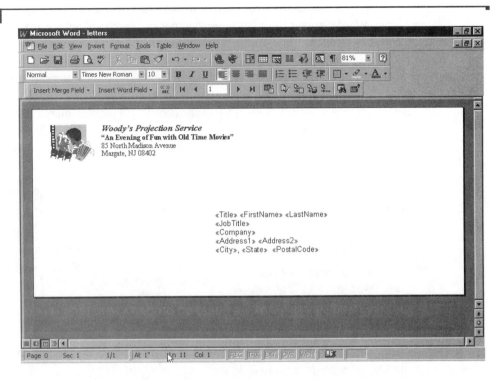

FIGURE 26.18

The envelope main document

See Chapter 3, *Previewing and Printing*, for more information on envelopes.

Creating Catalogs with Mail Merge

If you need to create a document with variations on the same information repeated throughout, you can use the Catalog option with Mail Merge. When you designate your main document as a catalog instead of a form letter, each record from the data source is merged into a single document, without a page break between them. (With form letters, each record creates a distinct resulting document.)

This enables you to create a document with a series of similar entries by only typing the basic information once. Then, as you merge the records from the data source into the catalog file, the contents of the main document will be repeated once for each record without any automatic section or page breaks between entries.

To perform a catalog merge, start with a fresh document. Select Tools ➤ Mail Merge. Word displays the Mail Merge Helper dialog box. Click on the Create button and select Catalog. Click on the Active Window button to use the new document as the main document.

Now click on the Edit button and select Catalog. Word displays the main document with the Mail Merge toolbar across the top of the screen. Type into this document any information you want to repeat for each record, and include merge fields as explained earlier in this chapter.

You can use any normal data source with a catalog document.

MASTERING THE OPPORTUNITIES

The Sky's the Limit

By combining merge fields and instructions, you can create sophisticated documents such as invoices, statements, and reports. Don't be afraid to experiment. For example, use Word's table feature to design an invoice form, and then add the merge fields to fill in the form from information in a data source.

Consider using the catalog type of merge to create lists of all types. For example, below is a client contact list created as a catalog merge.

The document was created by setting tabs at 2.5 and 5 inches and then entering the field costs like this, pressing Enter only after the final field:

The report title, date, and column headings were added after the merge.

Client Contact List
November 16, 1997

Company	Contact	Phone Number
Comuters-R-Use	Mr.John Doe	654-1098
Chandler Scientific	Miss Melanie Griffen	765-0987
Wards Computers	Mrs.Rachel Ward	654-9876
Harvenson Inc.	Mr.Paul Harvenson	765-1876

«Company» «Title»«FirstName» «LastName» «WorkPhone»

Tips, Techniques, and Troubleshooting

Here are some tips for working with Word's mail-merge feature:

- To change the appearance of merged characters—to make them bold or italic or a larger point size—format their merge instructions in the main document. Merged characters take on the formatting of their merge instructions.
- If you move your data-source files, Word will ask you to relocate them before you can merge.
- To print selected items from a longer data file, sort them and print only the range containing the desired records (from 10 to 30, for instance).

Shortcut Key Combinations for Merging Documents

The following shortcut key combinations are available when merging documents using the Tools ➤ Mail Merge command:

Key Combination	Effect
Alt+Shift+K	Checks for and reports errors
Alt+Shift+M	Prints a merge document
Alt+Shift+N	Merges the documents to a new file
Alt+Shift+E	Displays the Data Form

Restoring a Mail-Merge Document to a Normal Word Document

You can restore a mail-merge main document to a normal Word document when you've finished merging with it. This removes the association between the main document and its data source and header source (if it has one); that way, you can attach it to a different data source. The text of the main document, including merge fields and instructions, does not change.

To restore a main document to a normal Word document, follow these steps:

1. Open Mail Merge Helper by selecting Tools ➤ Mail Merge.

2. In the Main Document section, click on the Create button to display the list of options.

3. Choose the Restore to Normal Word Document option.

4. In the Restore to Normal Word Document dialog box, choose Yes. The association between the main document and its data sources will be removed.

5. Close Mail Merge Helper.

WARNING

Restoring a merge document to a normal Word document cannot be undone.

Chapter

27

Using Charts and Graphs

Using Charts and Graphs

Microsoft Graph is a supplementary application included with Word that you can use to create, import, and edit charts and graphs. These charts and graphs are *embedded* objects; not only can you insert them into any application that supports Object Linking and Embedding (more on this in the next chapter), but you can simply double-click on them to open them (and Microsoft Graph) for editing.

You can create the following using Microsoft Graph:

- Area charts
- Bar charts
- Column charts
- Line charts
- Pie charts
- Scatter charts
- Combination charts
- 3-D variations on many of the above

To give you some idea of the possibilities Microsoft Graph offers, Figure 27.1 shows a chart created with Microsoft Graph and then inserted into a Word document.

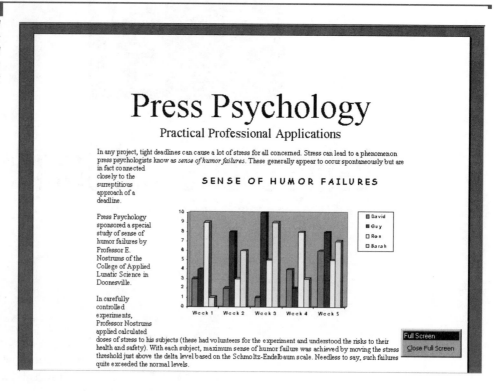

Inserting Excel Worksheets in Word Documents

Before we delve into charts and graphs, however, let's look at another type of object that you can insert into your document. If you have Microsoft Excel, you can insert a live Excel worksheet directly into a Word document without having to open Excel itself. Follow these steps:

1. Open a new Word document or place the cursor where you want the worksheet to go. Be sure the Formatting toolbar is showing.
2. Click on the Insert Microsoft Excel Worksheet button on the Formatting toolbar. A grid will drop down that looks much like the one you see when you click on the Insert Table button. It works exactly the same way.
3. Click and drag the cursor to indicate how many rows and columns you want in your worksheet (you can easily change this later).

4. When you release the mouse button, Word inserts an Excel worksheet with the specified number of rows and columns, as shown in Figure 27.2. Notice that the Standard and Formatting toolbars for Excel appear, along with the Excel Formula Bar. Very slick!

FIGURE 27.2

You can insert an Excel worksheet into your document without having to open Excel.

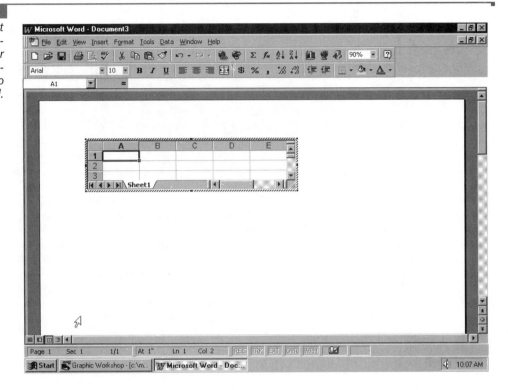

5. Then you just go about your business with the worksheet as if you were using Excel. You can use most Excel formatting and data features. Consult an Excel manual for details.

6. When you are finished editing the data, click anywhere outside the worksheet to return to your Word document with its regular Word toolbars.

If you want to modify the worksheet in some way, simply double-click within it to return to editing mode. You can then make all kinds of changes. For instance, changing the number of rows and columns is very simple. Select the worksheet, grab one of the black selection handles, and then drag the handle to add rows or columns. Notice that as you drag, the size of the grid is displayed in the Cell Location status area:

PART

VI

Power Tools

WARNING

To change the physical size of the worksheet, not the number of rows and columns, you must be in the Word document. Click anywhere outside the worksheet to return to your document. Then select the worksheet and drag the resizing handles (the black boxes).

MASTERING THE OPPORTUNITIES

Moving Excel Worksheets

When you insert an Excel worksheet, Word treats it as a block of text—moving it up and down as you insert and delete text above it and letting you drag and drop it within existing text. You can also treat the worksheet as a graphic; you can move it freely in the document and flow text around it.

To do so, right-click on the worksheet—when in Word, not when editing it—and

choose Format Object from the menu that appears. Click on the Position tab in the Format Object dialog box and choose the Float Over Text checkbox. You can now set the other options on the Position tab or select wrapping styles and other settings from the Wrapping tab.

When you click on OK to close the Format Object dialog box, you'll be able to drag the worksheet just as you would drag any other graphic object.

Making Sure Graph Is Installed

First, be sure that whoever installed Word on your PC included Graph in the installation. A Typical installation of Word includes Graph; a Minimum installation doesn't include Graph, and a Custom installation lets you choose whether to install Graph.

If Graph isn't installed on your PC, dig out that Office CD or those Word installation disks and install it. With the CD, for example, run the Setup program, and then choose the Add/Remove option. When the list of Office components appears, choose Office Tools and then click on the Change Options button. In the box that appears, choose Programs ➤ Microsoft Word ➤ Setup from the Start menu in Windows. If you are running Microsoft Office, your option will be Programs ➤ Microsoft Office ➤ Setup from the Start menu. When Setup appears, choose the Custom option and follow the instructions for installing Graph.

NOTE

For more information on installing Word on your PC, turn to the Appendix.

Getting Started with Word Graphs

The general steps for creating a graph are so simple that you can be up and running in a flash. Here they are:

1. Open a Word document and place the insertion point where you want the new graph to appear.

TIP

To create a chart from information you've already entered into a Word table, select the cells of the table that you want to chart, and then continue along here.

2. Choose Insert ➤ Object, and be sure the Create New tab is foremost; then double-click on Microsoft Graph 97 Chart in the Object Type list.

3. Graph will open with its own toolbar, displaying a *datasheet window* that looks like a small spreadsheet, together with a *chart window* (aka a *graph window*—take your pick). Enter your data and labels into the datasheet window.

4. Notice that even though Graph has some of the same menus as Word, many of the menu commands are different. We'll look at how to use these commands in the following sections. For now, just browse through them to familiarize yourself with the kinds of commands you'll be seeing.

5. Use Microsoft Graph's commands to embellish the graph with text, arrows, different typefaces and type sizes, and so on. Resize the graph by dragging the size box in the lower right corner of its window.

6. When you're ready to insert the graph into your Word document, simply click anywhere outside the graph. Your Word document will reappear, now containing the graph.

7. To resize, reposition, apply a border, control the way text wraps about the chart, and otherwise embellish the chart and its surrounding area, use the methods you would use with any other graphic object.

8. To change the content and appearance of the chart itself, double-click on it in your Word document to launch Microsoft Graph and make the necessary changes.

9. Save your Word file when you've finished editing the graph.

NOTE

If all you see in your Word document is {EMBED MSGraph Chart.5\s}, you are looking at a field code; that is, you've got field codes turned on. To turn them off, select Tools ➤ Options, click on the View tab, and uncheck the Field Codes checkbox.

PART

VI

Power Tools

TIP

Treat graph objects as you would any other embedded object. See Chapter 28, *Linking and Embedding,* for more information on object linking and embedding.

Parts of a Graph

Any Graph has three parts—the datasheet window, the chart, and the Graph object that you embed in your Word document. In the following sections, we'll look at each separately. Note that the chart no longer appears in its own window.

Figure 27.3 shows the datasheet window and the chart.

TIP

If the Datasheet window appears in an awkward position—for example, if it's blocking your view of the chart—grab the window by clicking in its title bar and drag it to somewhere more convenient.

FIGURE 27.3

Microsoft Graph's Datasheet window and its graph

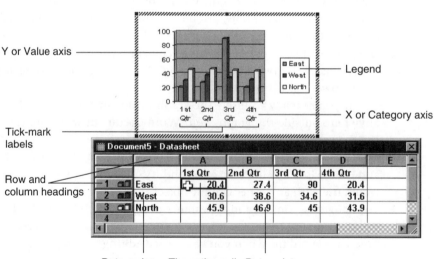

The Datasheet Window

The datasheet window, which works much like any other window, is where you enter all the numbers and much of the text that you want to graph. As you can see in Figure 27.3, it's similar to a spreadsheet. When you start Microsoft Graph, you'll see a datasheet complete with sample data.

The following sections describe the parts of the datasheet window:

Cells

The individual rectangles containing numbers and text are called *cells*, as they are in a spreadsheet. You can type and edit in cells as you'd expect. Enter each data item for your graph in a separate cell.

The Active Cell

To work in a cell, you must first make it active by clicking in it or moving to it with the arrow keys. The active cell is indicated by a dark border. In Figure 27.3, the active cell contains the number 20.4. Any data that you enter will appear in the active cell.

Rows and Columns

Cells are arranged in horizontal rows and vertical columns. A datasheet can contain a maximum of 1,024,000 cells (4000 cells by 256 columns). You can select a row or column by clicking on its heading.

Row and Column Headings

Those gray boxes at the top and along the left of the datasheet in Figure 27.3 are row and column headings. When the data in a row or column is gray (dimmed), it will not appear in your graph. Double-click on a heading to toggle its data on and off.

Data Points

Each cell containing a value is a *data point*. The datasheet in Figure 27.3 has 12 data points.

Data Series and Double Lines

A collection of related cells is called a *data series*. In Figure 27.3 there are three series—East, West, and North. Each series contains four data points.

A data series plots one line or piece of pie or one set of columns or bars in the chart.

Series Names

Series names are in the leftmost cells when a data series is plotted in horizontal rows. Series names are at the top of vertical columns when your graph will be plotted in columns. (In Figure 27.3, the series names are East, West, and North.)

Tick-Mark Labels

Tick-mark labels are the names that appear along the horizontal axes of area, column, and line charts or along a bar chart's vertical axis. In Figure 27.3, the tick-mark labels are 1st Qtr, 2nd Qtr, and so on.

The Chart

The chart object has its own terminology. Here are the basics. Everything inside the borders surrounding the chart is considered part of the chart. This includes the legend, bars, pie slices, labels, arrows, and so on.

Data Markers

Data markers come in various shapes, depending on the graph type. For example, the data markers are bars in bar charts, lines in line charts, pie slices in pie charts, and dots or symbols in line or scatter charts. Each marker represents the value of a single data point or value.

Data Series

Just as a data series in the datasheet represents a group of data points, so does a data series in the chart window. Figure 27.3 has three data series represented by three different shades of data markers.

Axis

An *axis* is a line along which data are plotted. Two-dimensional graphs such as line and bar graphs usually have a horizontal axis (or X-axis) and a vertical axis (or Y-axis). Three-dimensional charts have a third axis, called the Z-axis.

Tick Marks

Tick marks are the intersections of X and Y axes. They are usually identified with tick-mark labels.

Gridlines

Gridlines are optional vertical and horizontal lines that make it easier to judge values on a graph. Gridlines begin at tick marks and continue through the chart either horizontally or vertically.

Chart Text

Chart text comes in two flavors—*attached text*, used for things such as data and axes markers; and *unattached text*, which you can add by typing it. Use unattached text to point things out and annotate your chart. You type unattached text directly into the chart, and you can move it or size it.

NOTE

The terms *attached* and *unattached* with respect to chart text don't have anything to do with whether they're dating or not. Attached text is text that is associated with a particular element (such as an axis or a series) and as such is somewhat limited in terms of where it can go. Unattached text is free-floating text that can go anywhere.

Legends

Legends are little reference boxes that tell you which shades (or colors) are used to represent each data series. You can hide legends if they are unnecessary or get in the way. Look back to Figure 27.1 to see how useful legends can be in making things clear.

Getting Online Help

You can get online help from the Microsoft Assistant by pressing F1 at any point (the easy way) or by choosing Help ➤ Microsoft Graph Help. Type a word or topic that you want help on and then click on the Search button. You can also choose Help ➤ Contents and Index and work your way through the Help system. Figure 27.4 shows what you get by searching around a bit for information on adding a chart title.

Help in Microsoft Graph works just as it does in Microsoft Word. Use the Contents, Index, and Find tabs of the Help dialog box to find the topic you need help on, and then double-click on the topic to read about it. Often, you'll have to go through several levels of the help system to reach your topic. In Help windows, use the Help Topics and Back buttons to navigate, and use the Options button to print out help topics if you wish.

FIGURE 27.4

Press F1 to get help while working on your graph.

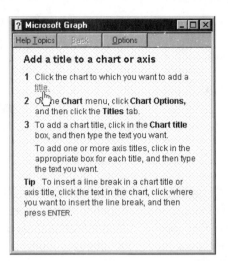

Some key words and phrases, such as the one the cursor is pointing to in Figure 27.4, lead to other topics or provide further information. Those with a solid underline contain hypertext jumps that will take you to a new help screen. Those with a dotted underline will pop up a box on the same screen explaining the word or phrase you clicked.

Working in the Datasheet Window

Use the datasheet window to enter data. It behaves so much like a Word table that we won't go into exhaustive detail here. The next section offers some pointers.

Entering and Editing Cell Data

Here are some tips for entering and editing data:

- Click in the datasheet window to activate it; then click in a cell to edit its contents.
- Always type data-series labels in the first column of a datasheet and category names in the first row.

- Changes to datasheet cell formatting (fonts, sizes, bold, and so on) are not reflected in the graph. (See the "Formatting Chart Text" section later in this chapter.) You apply formatting to all the cells in the datasheet at the same time.
- You can use the Edit ➤ Clear command in datasheets to clear the data, cell formatting, or both. Simply choose the appropriate option from the Edit ➤ Clear submenu:

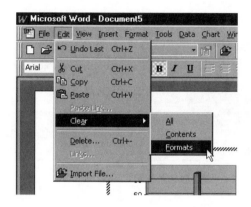

Importing Data

If you select a table in your Word document before inserting your chart, Microsoft Graph will import your selection into the datasheet when it opens.

You can import data from other places using Graph's Edit ➤ Import File command. In the Import File dialog box (see Figure 27.5), select the file you want to import.

WARNING

If you import data when you already have data in the datasheet, Microsoft Graph will warn you that you're about to lose your data and formatting. Be sure you want to do this before clicking on OK.

You can also use the Clipboard to import text. Bear in mind that incoming data must be comma-separated or tab-separated text and must not exceed the 4000-row by 256-column maximum.

NOTE

Remember that to include data in a graph, the data heading above or to the left of the data must be black (not gray). Click on these headings to toggle them.

FIGURE 27.5

Select the file from which you want to import data in the Import File dialog box.

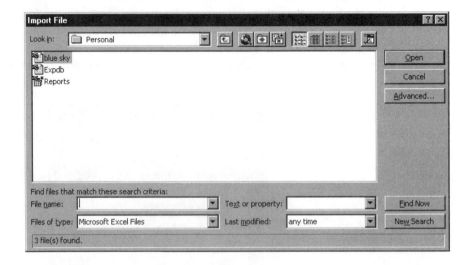

MASTERING TROUBLESHOOTING

Solving Import Problems

The Import File dialog box is set to automatically display files created with Microsoft Excel. If you want to open an Excel file, simply navigate through the system using the dialog box and double-click on the file you want to import.

To display other types of files, select an option from the Files of Type list, such as Lotus 1-2-3 Files, SYLK Files, Text Files, or All Files. Then find the file and double-click.

When you select All Files or Text Files and select a file, you may see the Text Import Wizard. Use the dialog boxes in this Wizard to specify how the data is formatted in the file. For example, you can specify either a delimited or fixed-width file, the types of delimiters or spacing, and the format of data.

If you throw Microsoft Graph a curve ball by asking it to import something it can't, it'll tell you it is "Unable to Read File." Try opening the application that created the file and using the Clipboard to transfer the data.

Navigating in Datasheets

Navigating in datasheets is so easy that you'll hardly have to read through this section. The usual navigational tricks work:

- Use the arrow keys to move from cell to cell.
- Press Tab to move from cell to cell; press Shift+Tab to move backward from cell to cell. This is one way to move around, though clicking in the target cell is quicker.
- Home takes you to the first cell in the row; End takes you to the last cell in the row.
- Ctrl+Home takes you to the first cell containing a data point in your datasheet; Ctrl+End takes you to the last cell containing a data point.
- Dragging or Shift-clicking selects multiple cells, as does holding down Shift and pressing the arrow keys.
- Clicking at the left edge of a row or at the top of a column (in the gray cells) selects the entire row or column.
- To speed data entry, select multiple cells before entering data; then tab from one to the next to move left to right or press Enter to move up and down. The active cell will never leave the selected area. For example, select a three-by-four block of cells. Make your entry in the first cell and press Enter. Graph will make the next cell down the active cell. When you reach the bottom of the block, Graph will take you to the first highlighted cell in the next column. (With Tab, you move sideways and go down a row when you reach the rightmost selected cell.)
- Minimize, maximize, and restore your datasheet window by using the familiar Windows buttons. Or click and drag the borders of the window to resize it.
- Scroll up and down your datasheet as you would in any window.

Number Formats in the Datasheet

Microsoft Graph allows you to format numbers in a variety of commonly accepted ways:

- Numbers too long to be displayed in cells will be stored as you typed them but displayed in scientific notation. For example, 1234567890 would be displayed as 1.23E+09.
- You can apply predefined number formats by selecting Format ➤ Number, choosing a number type from the Category list of the Format Number dialog box, and then selecting from the options that appear (see Figure 27.6).
- If you don't like any of the predefined formats, select Custom from the Category list. Choose from one of the sample formats shown, or select one as a victim and edit it in the Type box. Inspect the sample formats or read online help for assistance. Excel users will find the process and formats familiar. For instance, use dollar

PART

VI

Power Tools

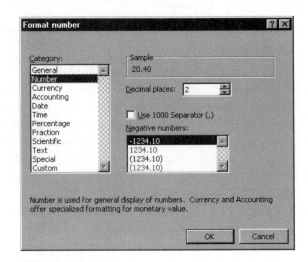

FIGURE 27.6

Choose a number format that tickles your fancy in the Format Number dialog box. If you don't like any of them, you can create your own.

signs ($), pound signs (#), commas, decimal points (.), percent signs, parentheses, and colors to specify custom formats. Thus, **$#,###.;[Red]($#,###.)** displays and prints dollars with commas and no pennies. Negative dollar amounts would be shown in parentheses and red. The custom format **0.0%** would display percentages to one decimal place.

Column Widths

Columns can be a maximum of 255 characters wide, but 9 characters is the standard column width. You can change a column's width by dragging its right edge or by using Format ➤ Column Width to specify column widths in characters.

Inserting and Deleting Rows and Columns

Inserting rows works much as it does in Word tables. Select the row beneath the point where you want to see a new one, and choose Insert ➤ Cells. If you first select multiple rows, you'll insert a like number of new ones.

To insert a column, select the column to the right of the place where you want to see a new one, and choose Edit ➤ Cells. If you first select multiple columns, you'll insert a like number of new ones.

NOTE

If you select a cell rather than a row or a column, you'll get the Insert mini-dialog box. Select to shift cells to the right or down or to insert an entire row or column, depending on what you want.

To delete rows and columns, select them and choose Edit ➤ Delete.

TIP

You can insert and delete rows and columns even more quickly by using the keyboard shortcuts. To insert rows or columns, press Ctrl++ (that's Ctrl and +); to delete rows and columns, press Ctrl+- (Ctrl and -). Again, you can first select the number of rows or columns to delete.

Working with Charts

Microsoft Graph charts are embedded into your Word document. This means that although they appear in the document, you cannot edit them directly in Word. Don't despair—there is no need to exit Word or manually start another program. Instead, simply double-click on a chart to go into "chart edit" mode. Double-clicking starts Graph, and you can specify the appearance and type of the chart or edit any of its parts.

The next few sections offer some tips for working with charts.

Select the Right Chart Type

To change the type of the chart in "chart edit mode," use the Chart ➤ Chart Type command to select the desired chart type for your projects. The right chart can convey information clearly and powerfully; the wrong chart can smother it. You can select from common standard chart types, choose a special custom format, or even create your own. Below are descriptions of the standard types of charts available and their uses.

NOTE

Most of the chart types are available in both 2-D and 3-D variations. The 3-D styles give perspective to data representations and, as discussed later in this chapter, can be rotated to change the bird's-eye view (this can sometimes emphasize or even distort relationships of related data—an effect I'll leave you to work out however you can).

Area

Area charts show changes in relative values of multiple series over time. Use area charts to emphasize differences and amount of change (for example, changes in various presidents' approval ratings at different stages of their terms). Figure 27.7 shows some of the available area formats.

Some area chart formats

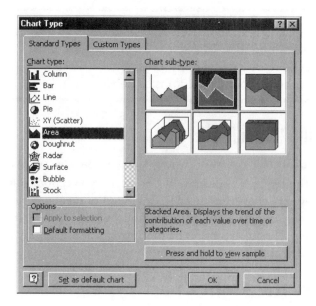

Bar

Bar charts organize categories vertically and show comparisons of items (speeds of various disk drives, for instance). You can select from six bar configurations, three two-dimensional and three three-dimensional.

Column

Column charts organize the same types of information as bar charts, but they display it with vertical bars (columns). There are seven column types, three two-dimensional and four three-dimensional.

Line

Line charts emphasize time and rate of change—such as sales growth over a 12-month period. Figure 27.8 shows some of the available line formats.

FIGURE 27.8

Some line chart formats

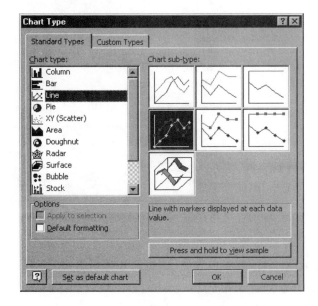

PART

VI

Power Tools

Pie

Pie charts show the relationships of parts to the whole—each department's contribution to the firm's total expense budget, for instance, or the number of arguments each member of the household causes. You can include only one data series in a pie chart; so it's not suited to a wide variety of uses.

Doughnut

Like pie charts, doughnut charts are also useful for showing the relationships of parts to the whole. Doughnut charts, however, can represent multiple series. Figure 27.9 shows some of the available doughnut formats.

FIGURE 27.9

Some doughnut chart formats

Radar

Radar charts are like area charts in that they are can be used to emphasize differences and amounts of change. Figure 27.10 shows some of the available radar formats.

X-Y (Scatter)

Scatter charts are useful for demonstrating trends and patterns. They can show dependencies or relationships between variables. Figure 27.11 shows some of the available scatter formats.

Surface

Surface charts are useful when you want to show ultimate combinations of sets of data. They appear much like topographic maps and use colors and patterns to represent values.

Bubble

The bubble chart type is a special X-Y (Scatter) chart in which the size of round data markers represent a third variable. A bubble chart can be used when another axis would be needed with other chart types.

FIGURE 27.10

Some radar chart formats

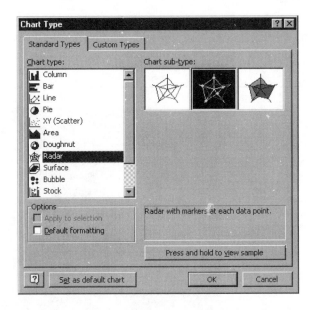

FIGURE 27.11

Some scatter chart formats

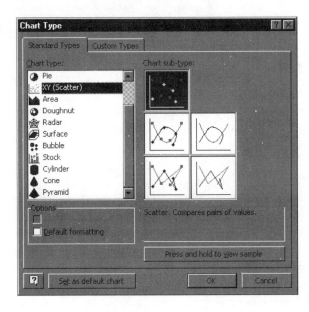

PART

VI

Power Tools

Stock

A stock chart is useful to illustrate the high, low, and close prices of stocks and other data in that format. You can also use the chart to measure volume of sales by adding another axis. Figure 27.12 shows some of the available stock formats.

Some stock chart formats

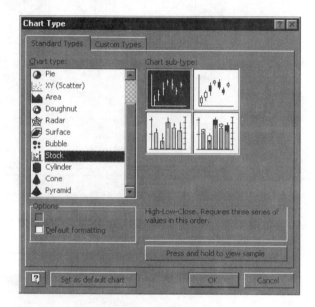

Cylinder, Cone, and Pyramid

These are actually variations of bar and column charts with three-dimensional objects representing the bars and columns. Figure 27.13 shows some of the available cone formats.

Custom Charts

The Custom Types tab of the Chart Type dialog box, shown in Figure 27.14, offers a variety of black and white, combination, and special graphic charts.

Combination charts, for example, can present data in different formats (lines and columns, for instance). They offer a great way to overlay actual versus projected data or loosely related items such as temperature and humidity. Use the black and white types when printing the chart on a monochrome printer. The other custom options offer high-impact colors and design that are perfect for on-screen presentations or for use with color printers.

FIGURE 27.13

*Some cone
chart formats*

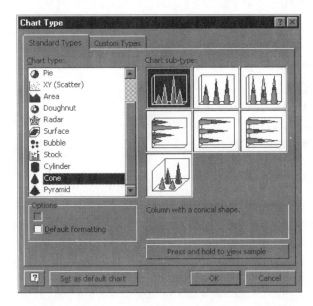

FIGURE 27.14

*Custom
chart options*

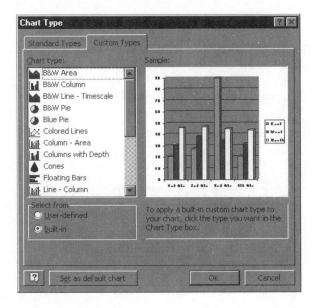

PART

VI

Power Tools

Changing the Default Chart Type

You can change the default chart type so that a chart other than the column chart greets you when you open Microsoft Graph. This can be useful when you regularly work with one type of chart. Here's how to do it:

1. Create a chart of the desired appearance (chart type, formats, and so on).
2. Choose Chart ➤ Chart Type.
3. Click on the Set As Default Chart button.
4. Click on OK.

Changing the Chart Size

You can change the size of a chart as you create it, from within the Word document, or in "chart edit" mode. If you've already embedded the chart into the document, for example, you can adjust its size without returning to Microsoft Graph.

Dragging any of the handles around the chart changes its size, and all of the text and chart parts are automatically resized to fit. To change the size of the chart in the document, click on it so that the handles appear. If you are just creating the chart or are in "chart edit" mode, move the datasheet out of the way so that you can see the chart, or click on the View Datasheet button to close it.

MASTERING TROUBLESHOOTING

Getting a Handle on Handles

Depending on what you click on, you may see two sets of handles around a chart while in Microsoft Graph, as shown here:

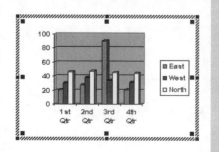

Use the handles along the border line to change the size of the chart. The handles just inside the border represent the "chart area," the background on which the chart appears. When these handles appear, you can format the background by adding a color or fill pattern as you will soon learn, but you cannot drag these handles to change the chart size.

You can also change the chart size, by the way, from within the Word document by selecting Format Object from the menu that appears when you right-click on the chart and setting options in the Size tab of the dialog box that appears.

Viewing Graphs in Different Sizes

If you want to change the size of a chart on screen without affecting its size in your Word document, select View ➤ Zoom and choose a view percentage or type one. You can also choose a zooming percentage with the Zoom Control drop-down list in the Standard toolbar. Zooming in or out changes the screen view but not the actual chart size and is useful for working on small chart elements or stepping back to get the big picture.

 NOTE

You cannot change the screen viewing size when you are in chart-editing mode. You must click outside your chart to adjust the zoom percentage from the Standard toolbar.

Editing Parts of a Chart

You can select various chart parts and then edit, move, and embellish them. In chart-edit mode, click to select a single item; Shift+click to select multiple items. Selected items are surrounded by handles. In some cases, such as with the legend, you can use the handles to move or resize the object with your mouse. In other cases, the handles only mean that the object is selected and that you can use commands to make changes. (See Figure 27.15.)

 When you point to a part of the chart in "edit mode," a tooltip appears with the part's name. When the tooltip indicates the part you want to edit, click the mouse, and then choose the "Selected" item at the top of the Format menu. When you point to a bar, a column, or other data series indicator, the tooltip will show the name of the series and the value of the item.

PART

VI

Power Tools

FIGURE 27.15

The handles around the legend mean you can move and resize it with the mouse. The handles around the bar in a chart mean you can use commands to make changes to it.

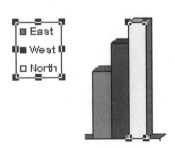

You can select and alter the following items:

- 3-D floors
- Arrows
- Axes
- Charts
- Chart area (background)
- Data series (any)
- Drop lines
- Gridlines
- Hi-lo lines
- Legends
- Plot areas
- Series lines
- Text
- Up/Down bars
- Walls

TIP

Double-clicking on an object in the chart window displays a dialog box containing the available formatting options. For instance, double-clicking on an axis displays the Axis Patterns dialog box. Double-clicking on a pie wedge displays the Area Patterns dialog box, and so on. Point to the part you want to edit, be sure the tooltip indicates the correct part, and then double-click. Explore!

Dragging to Change Data

On some kinds of two-dimensional charts (sorry, you can't do this in 3-D), you can drag data points and thereby change the appearance of a chart *and* the underlying numbers in the datasheet! Yep. Read it again. For example, you can drag a column up or down and see the changes visually in the chart and numerically in the datasheet.

Try it. Click on a bar or columns in a chart, for example, twice. That is, for once you want two separate clicks, not a double-click. This will display selection handles around the object and a larger handle indicating a draggable extremity. Drag the large handle in the appropriate direction to change the data value, as illustrated in Figure 27.16.

FIGURE 27.16

Changing data in charts is easy. Simply drag the block handle to change values both in the chart and in the datasheet.

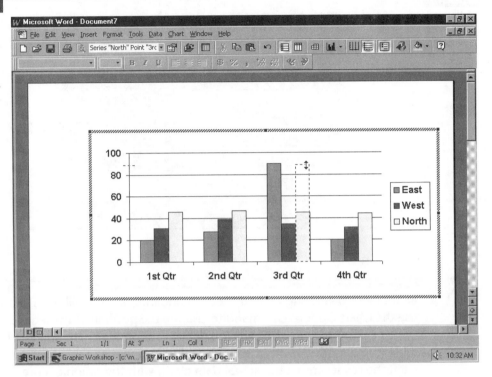

NOTE

You can't drag to change data in some chart types. In others, you can click until the cows come home, but you won't get a draggable black handle. Don't expect *too* much.

Typing Attached Title Chart Text

To type or edit attached text (titles), follow these steps:

1. Choose Chart ➤ Chart Options.
2. Click on the Titles tab to display the dialog box shown in Figure 27.17.
3. Click on the text box for the object you want to enter, such as the chart title or axis caption.
4. Type the text that you want to appear.
5. Click on OK.

PART

VI

Power Tools

FIGURE 27.17

The Titles tab
of the Chart
Options
dialog box

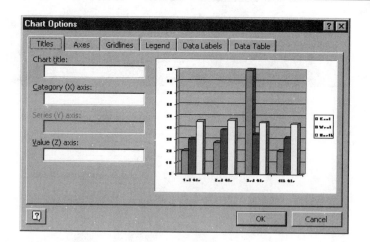

> **TIP**
>
> In addition to entering text and setting gridlines, as you will soon learn, you can use the Chart Options command to change the position of the legend, determine the type of primary axis, display the data values on the chart, and include the data table (the datasheet) with the chart. Including the data table is useful when you want the reader to see the actual data along with the graphic representation.

Typing Unattached Chart Text

If you want to add to your chart unattached text notes that you can easily move, follow these steps:

1. Simply start typing in the active chart window. The text first appears in the center of your chart window. Press Enter to force new lines without ending the entry.
2. When you've completed the entry, press Esc. A frame with handles will appear around the entry.
3. Position the text by clicking on it and dragging it to its new location.

Figure 27.18 shows a chart with a title and text added.

Editing Chart Text

To edit chart text, first click to select it. Move the pointer into the text so that it changes to an I-beam; then click and use the I-beam cursor to select and edit the desired text.

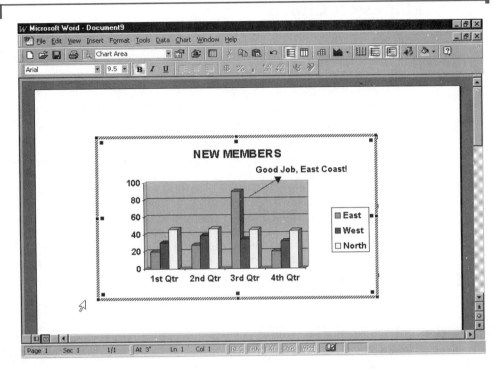

FIGURE 27.18

A chart with a title and text and other embellishments

Formatting Chart Text

To format chart text, click on it so that it is surrounded by handles. Then use the Format ➤ Font command to change the appearance of the text. If you are editing unattached text, the dialog box has one tab, which lets you choose the typeface and size, text color, and effects. You also have to drag over unattached text to select it before you can apply a format change.

If you are editing a chart title, the dialog box has three tabs:

- Font, with options for the typeface and size, text color and effects.
- Alignment, which offers you the following options:

    1. Horizontal text alignment: Left, Center, Right, and Justify
    2. Vertical text alignment: Top, Center, Bottom, and Justify
    3. Text orientation: horizontal, vertical, and angled between 90 and –90 degrees

- Patterns, which lets you add a color background behind the text and a border line around it.

PART

VI

Power Tools

Gridlines on Charts

You can turn on or off the display of horizontal and vertical gridlines by clicking on the Category Axis Gridline button (vertical lines) and Value Axis Gridline button (horizontal) in the toolbar.

For even more control of the gridlines, however, click on the Gridlines tab of the Chart Options dialog box. Here you specify gridlines for both the Category and Value axis, as well as an optional Series axis if your chart has one. You can also select to display gridlines as two-dimensional in a 3-D chart.

Double-click on gridlines to select different line patterns for them from the Line Patterns dialog box.

Rotating 3-D Charts

The benefit of 3-D charts is their visual interest and perspective. When you are creating or editing a 3-D chart, you can choose the 3-D View command from the Chart menu to customize the three-dimensional aspects. Choosing the option displays the 3-D View dialog box (see Figure 27.19).

FIGURE 27.19

You can control the orientation of 3-D charts with the Format 3-D View dialog box.

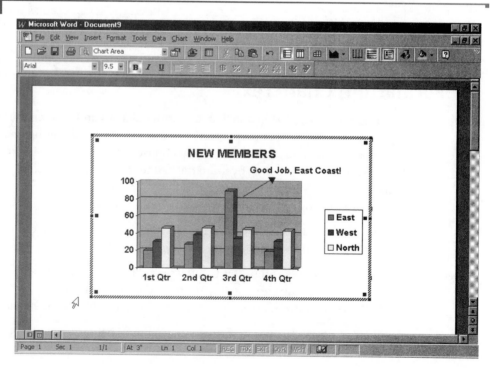

You can control elevation, perspective, rotation, axes orientation, and height by clicking on boxes that demonstrate these functions. The Right Angle Axes option forces right angles. Auto Scaling sometimes helps with converting 2-D charts to 3-D charts.

Use caution when changing a 3-D graph's orientation, particularly perspective. You can give misleading impressions of the relative size or importance of data this way. Of course, if you're doing it deliberately...

Saving Charts and Their Data

The only way to save charts and chart data is to embed them in a Word document, which is done automatically when you click anywhere outside the graph. You must then save the Word document to preserve the chart and data. Thereafter, choosing Save on the File menu, even in Graph edit mode, saves the whole Word document, including the graph.

To embed a Microsoft Graph chart in an Excel spreadsheet, select Edit ➤ Copy Chart while you're in Graph and then paste the chart into the target spreadsheet.

Positioning Graphs in Word Documents

You can use graphic formatting techniques to position embedded graphs in the document. The easiest way is to drag the chart to where you want it on the page. To set a specific or relative position, however, use the Format Object command in Word, not in Graph, as you learned for clipart and other graphics. Follow these steps:

1. Right-click on the graph.
2. Choose Format Object from the short-cut menu.
3. Click on the Position tab of the dialog box.
4. Enter a specific horizontal and vertical position, or select a horizontal position relative to the margins, page, or column and a vertical position relative to the margins, page, or paragraph.

Resizing Graphs

To change the size of a chart, follow these steps:

1. Select the embedded graph in your Word document by clicking on it. Small handles appear around the edges and in the bottom-left corner.

2. Move the mouse pointer over one of the corner handles so that it changes to a double-headed arrow, click, and drag the corner handle to resize the graph.

TIP

For more precise resizing and cropping of graphs, right-click on the graph and select Format Object. Then, set the size and scale of the graphic in the Size tab of the dialog box, or crop the graph using the options on the Picture tab. To leave white space around your graph—for example, between the graph and its border or the surrounding text—enter negative numbers in the Crop From boxes.

Editing and Updating

To update a graph, follow these steps:

1. Double-click on the graph in your Word document.

2. Make the desired changes in the graph.

3. Click anywhere outside the graph.

4. You will be returned to Word, and the updated graph will be in position.

5. Save your Word document to save the changes.

Chapter

28

Linking and Embedding to Keep Things Current

Linking and Embedding to Keep Things Current

Word is a great program, but there are lots of other great programs out there as well. Wouldn't it be nice to take advantage of the best features of every program and then simply combine your work into one document? You can.

Using Object Linking and Embedding (OLE), you can include in your Word documents information created in other applications. For example, you could create a picture in a drawing program such as CorelDRAW or Micrografx Designer and then insert it into your Word document. You could include in a Word document a table from a spreadsheet in Microsoft Excel or data from a Microsoft Access report. In each case, you could choose to have the information updated automatically whenever the source was changed, updated only when you wanted it updated, or left forever as it was when you inserted it. Choosing to update the information means that your Word document will always be current and up to date.

Big deal, I hear you say, but what does this mean to *me*? So you're a financial hotshot; you could insert in your annual report figures linked to your profit-and-loss statement in a spreadsheet or database, and then have Word update the report automatically whenever the spreadsheet or database changes. So you're a design whiz; you could keep your brochure up to date with your latest designs. As a crude example of this, Figure 28.1 shows an Excel table and chart paste-linked into a Word document with automatic updating on. Every time I change the worksheet in Excel, they'll be updated in the Word document.

Before Object Linking and Embedding, I would have had to reopen the source application, change the source data, and then copy and paste it into my Word document to bring it up to date. Believe me, this gets tedious fast.

Word implements several OLE features that are sure to interest you:

- You can display an embedded or a linked object as an icon instead of at its full size. Because the icon takes less memory to display than the full object, scrolling in your document is faster.
- You can convert an embedded or linked object to a different application. For example, say I need to update the document in Figure 28.1 on a computer that doesn't have Excel. I can convert the linked object to a similar format and then update it. Clearly this offers welcome flexibility.

FIGURE 28.1

This Excel worksheet and chart are linked to the Word document where it appears. Whenever the worksheet is changed in Excel, the table and chart will also change in the Word document.

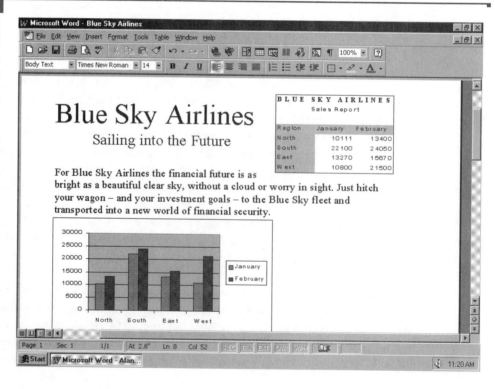

After a quick peek at the technical requirements for linking information between applications, we'll look at exactly what linking and embedding mean. Then we'll consider what each is for. Finally, we'll discuss how to link and embed.

ActiveX

OLE is a veteran in the Microsoft arsenal. There is a new kid on the block that you probably have been hearing about—ActiveX.

ActiveX and OLE are based on the same framework, something called the Component Object Model (COM) that allows programs and objects to communicate. So although they are related, OLE and ActiveX are different.

OLE lets you build compound documents using linking and embedding to share information between programs. ActiveX, on the other hand, provides controls, such as checkboxes and lists, to create interactive Web pages. For example, if you want the user to scroll a list of options in your Web page, you would embed an ActiveX list object.

OLE is rather automatic. You use the simple techniques that you will learn in this chapter to embed or link information. Your application and Windows 95 does the rest.

ActiveX requires a little more effort—at least for now. If you add an ActiveX object to your Word document, for example, you'll have to write a macro in Visual Basic for Applications that tells the object how to perform. Otherwise, it will just sit there on the Web page, looking pretty but with nothing to do.

You will learn how to insert ActiveX controls into your Word documents in Chapter 30, *Creating and Using Forms*, and you will learn how to write macros in Chapter 31, *Creating and Using Macros*.

So contrary to what some people are saying, OLE is very much alive and well.

Technical Requirements for Linking Information

To be able to link an object created in another application to a Word file, both applications must support either Object Linking and Embedding (OLE) or Dynamic Data Exchange (DDE).

If the application you used to create the object does not support OLE or DDE, you'll only be able to paste the object into your document, just as you can copy and paste text from one document to another.

You can link an object from an application that is running, as well as an object that is already stored on your disk. If the application and object are open, you use the Edit ➤ Paste or the Edit ➤ Paste Special commands, depending on whether you want to embed or link. If the application is closed and the object is already created on your disk, you link it using the Insert ➤ Object command.

What Is Linking?

Linking is one way of attaching information from another application to a Word document. When you link an object to a Word document, the Word document stores the location of the object and its source application in a *field* in the document (see Chapter 29 for more on fields). If you link an Excel worksheet into Word, the object is the worksheet, and the source application is Excel. When you double-click on the worksheet object in Word, Windows 95 will start Excel and open the worksheet file so that you can edit it.

The linked object in the Word document can then be updated at your convenience—you can choose to update it automatically whenever the source changes or manually when you want to update it. If you change the Excel worksheet file, the new information can appear in the Word document as well. You can lock the links when the document and the object it contains are finalized, and you can break the links so that objects cannot be updated any further.

If that isn't enough, you can also reconnect a lost link or change the source of a link—for example, if you update a different file in the source application.

What Is Embedding?

Embedding is an alternate way to attach information from another application to a Word document. When you embed information, it becomes part of the Word document and is stored in it.

Embedded information is connected to the source application but not with the object file. For example, suppose you embed a group of cells from an Excel worksheet into Word. If you later start Excel, open the worksheet, and change the cells, the new information will not appear in the Word document. If you double-click on the embedded object in Word, however, Windows 95 will start Excel, but it will not open the original worksheet. Instead, it transfers the information in the embedded object to Excel so that you can edit it.

NOTE

Having a touch of *déjà* viewed? As discussed in the last chapter, graphs created with Microsoft Graph are embedded in your document. When you double-click on one of them, Microsoft Graph opens with the chart and datasheet ready for editing.

You've no doubt worked out the corollary to this—embedding an object in a Word file increases the size of that file. Considerably. If you embed a whole bunch of big objects (TIFF true-gray files, for example), your Word files will grow to Brobdingnagian proportions. Time to dust off your wallet and buy a fistful more RAM. But seriously, don't embed too many objects in a file and expect your computer to run like Ricky Watters.

If you can't get around embedding masses of objects in your file (for example, if you have to give other people your files), you can do a few things to improve matters. See the section "Converting an Embedded Object to a Different Format," later in this chapter.

To Link or To Embed?

If you've read the above paragraphs, the reasons to link or embed should be rather obvious. If you link objects in documents to their sources, you can update the objects whenever the source objects change or whenever it suits you. When your document is finalized or ready for distribution, you can lock or break the links and freeze it in that state. When you embed information, you can use the best features of the source application to create, format, and edit the object, but include it in a Word document.

The major question here is which to choose—linking or embedding? To link or to embed, that is the sixty-four-million–dollar question. Which is it going to be, and why?

You'll remember from the previous sections that embedded information becomes part of the Word document (and is stored in it) and that linked information is stored in the source file in the source application. When you link, Word records the location of the information in the source file and displays a picture of the information in the Word document.

Here's the bottom line: *Link* when you will need to share information with another file. *Embed* when you know you will not need to share information with another file.

If you are still not sure which to choose, look at some of the pros and cons of each method in some more detail.

The Wonders of Linking

Linking has two major advantages over embedding. When you link, you can update the object so that it is always current, and linking keeps your documents from getting too large. No matter how large the linked information is, you only have to store it once—in the original file. The link itself increases the size of the document by only a few characters. Also, you can have one source for multiple target files.

But linking also has some disadvantages. For example, when you give someone else your Word document that's linked to other files, that user must also have the source files and the applications that those other files were created in to maintain the links.

If you've decided to link all the information you've imported into Word with its sources and have it updated automatically, do me a favor and pause for a minute to consider the dangers of automatic updating.

For example, suppose you're writing the report that's going to send your career into the stratosphere. The report's in Word, and it contains figures drawn from your company's financial database in Microsoft Access. To keep the figures in the report up to date, you link the Access object in the Word document to its source. All well and good; next stop, the head office across from Le Parc. Time for the Accounting department to chuck a wrench in the works. The day before you present your report, some fool over there runs a test program on the database to track down a ten-cent overpayment on a shipment of widgets. Like a faithful dog, Word fixes up an instant update on your figures, your report is way off target, and you find yourself reporting to the branch office in Alpha Centauri instead.

Even if you're not connected to a network, and nobody but you can change your data, I'd recommend thinking carefully before using automatic updating. If you decide to go for it, keep a backup file with manual links just to humor me.

Keep a couple of other considerations in mind:

- Linking is a complicated operation. Even if your computer's a thundering, screaming P-6 workstation with twin overhead symmetrical multiprocessors, updating large linked files will take a while. If you have a slow computer, plan a few coffee breaks.
- Linking creates a number of temp files (you know, the ones that look like they've been named by dogs—~wrf0001f.tmp and so on). Plan to have a little space available for these; more important, check your computer every now and then for stray temp files and erase them (see the note below about this). You're most likely to have them if your computer crashes while working with linked files.

Temp files (~dft064f.tmp and the like) are files created by Windows applications for temporary storage. They're supposed to be deleted automatically when you exit the application that produced them or when you quit Windows (depending on what produced them). Every now and then, check your disk for stray temp files *after* loading Windows and *before* running any Windows applications—that is, before your applications get a chance to create new temp files—by selecting Find ➤ Files and Folders from the Start menu and specifying ~*.tmp. This will round up the usual suspects ready for deletion at dawn.

The Thrill of Embedding

If you embed objects in documents, you can enjoy the quality of the originals in Word documents and the convenience of being able to edit them in the original application by double-clicking on them. No need to remember which object came from which source application—Word keeps track of that information for you. When you give the document to another user, you do not have to supply the original source file as well.

The major disadvantage of embedding is that it can make your documents enormous when they contain embedded data from bulky sources, such as graphics files. If you don't need an active link and you're concerned about the size of your document, consider simply pasting in the data or image instead of embedding it. This will require less storage space.

Another disadvantage of embedding is that it does not allow you to change a series of documents by changing the information in a single source. For instance, suppose you embed the same Excel worksheet in four Word documents. If you have to change the information, you must do so four times—in each place it is embedded—or change it once and embed it all over again four times. Changing the original source of embedded information has no effect on the document with the embedding.

How to Link

Now that you've decided to link (brave soul!), how do you go about it? You can link an object using either the Edit ➤ Paste Special command or the Insert ➤ Object command. Edit ➤ Paste Special is a little easier, but with Insert ➤ Object you don't need to open the source application. I'd recommend starting off by learning to link the easy way and then graduating to the more sophisticated way if need be.

Establishing a Link the Easy Way

With Edit ➤ Paste Special, you can choose either to link an existing object or to create a new object and then link it.

The simplest way to link an object to a Word file is as follows:

1. Fire up the source application for the object you want to link.
2. Create or open the file containing the object. If you are creating a new file, save it onto the disk.
3. Select the object and copy it to the Clipboard (select Edit ➤ Copy, or click on any Copy button the application offers).
4. Switch back to Word by clicking in the Taskbar at the bottom of your screen and selecting Microsoft Word.

PART

VI

Power Tools

5. Put the insertion point at a suitable place in your Word document and select Edit ➤ Paste Special to open the Paste Special dialog box (see Figure 28.2).

6. In the Paste Special dialog box, select the Paste Link option button to link the object to your Word file. The Paste Link option will be dimmed if it's not available—that is, if the object copied to the Clipboard is in an application that doesn't support OLE.

7. In the As box, select the form in which you want the linked object to appear. The Result box explains the effect of the option selected in the As box. In this example, I have copied a chart from Excel, and I will insert it as an object.

8. If you insert the information using the Object, Picture, or Bitmap options in the As list, you can also check the Float over Text option to insert the object in the drawing layer. This way you can position it anywhere in front or behind text and other objects. With this box unchecked, the object appears inline and is treated as regular text.

9. Click on OK. The object will be paste-linked into your Word document.

If you select the Word Hyperlink option in the As box or if you simply choose Edit ➤ Paste As Hyperlink, the object will be inserted as a hyperlink. Simply click on the object to open the linked file.

When you paste your linked object into its destination document, you might see something like

```
{LINK Excel.Chart.5 "C:\\WINDOWS\\Favorites\Chart, 1998 \a \p}
```

or something equally incomprehensible. There is nothing wrong; this is a field code, and links are inserted as fields. To see your object, choose Tools ➤ Options, click on the View tab, and uncheck the Field Codes option.

FIGURE 28.2

Select the form in which you want the linked object to appear in the Paste Special dialog box.

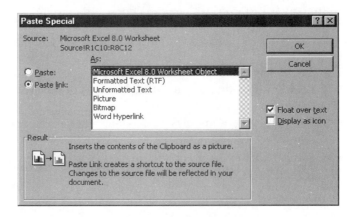

Displaying Objects As Icons

The Display As Icon option is interesting. Click on this option if you want to display the object as an icon in your Word document—not see the information itself. Use this when you want the information connected to the Word document and easily accessible, but not to actually appear. When you check this option, the standard icon for the application you chose will appear below the checkbox with a Change Icon button.

If you want to display a more exciting icon for your object—heck, you see the same boring old icons *all the time* on the Desktop—select the Change Icon button. In the Change Icon dialog box, either select one of the icons the application offers, or click on the Browse button to check out the icons from different applications. When you're done browsing, click on OK to return to the Change Icon dialog box, and then click on OK again to accept the icon you've chosen. It'll now appear in the Object dialog box.

Linking for the More Sophisticated

In case you're interested, the Insert ➤ Object command offers a slightly more complicated way of linking an object to your Word document. It lets you create and link a new object in one step or link an object that you've already created.

Linking an existing object and creating a new object to link take you down different avenues of Word, so let's look at them separately to keep the dialog boxes straight.

To Link an Existing Object with Insert ➤ Object

Here's how to use Insert ➤ Object to link an existing object to a document:

1. In your Word document, put the insertion point where you want to insert the linked object.
2. Choose Insert ➤ Object. Word displays the Object dialog box.
3. Because you're linking an existing object, choose the Create from File tab (see Figure 28.3).
4. Enter the name of the file from which you want to insert a linked object, or click on Browse to select the file from an Open-like dialog box. When you find the file you want, click on OK. In this example, the file is an Excel worksheet.
5. If you want to layer the object under or over text or other objects, check the Float over Text checkbox.
6. Check the Link to File checkbox and click on OK. The selected object is inserted and linked to your Word file.

PART

VI

Power Tools

FIGURE 28.3

You insert existing objects in the Create from File tab of the Object dialog box.

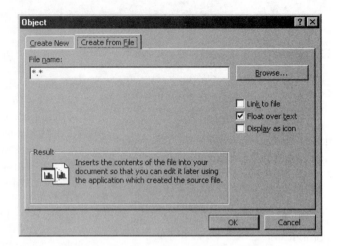

Create a New Object and Link It

To create a new object and link it to your Word document with Insert ➤ Object, follow these steps:

1. In your Word document, put the insertion point where you want to insert the linked object.
2. Choose Insert ➤ Object. Word displays the Object dialog box. The Create New tab should be displayed by default (see Figure 28.4). If it isn't, select it.
3. In the Object Type box, select the application in which you want to create the new object. Check the Display as Icon checkbox if you want the new object to appear as an icon in your Word document. Change the icon if need be (see "To Link an Existing Object," above, for details). In Figure 28.4, I've chosen to insert a Microsoft Graph 97 object.
4. Choose OK. The application you chose will open.
5. Create the object you want; then click anywhere outside the object to return to Word. For some applications, you will have to choose File ➤ Exit and Return to return to Word. The object will be inserted and linked to your document.

FIGURE 28.4

The Create
New tab of
the Object
dialog box

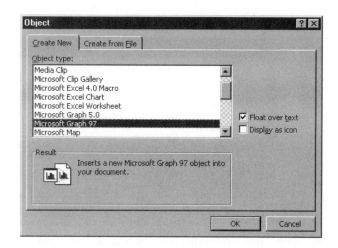

When Are Linked Documents Updated?

You can choose to have links updated in any of three ways:

- *Automatically.* This is the default. Links are created with automatic updating; so you'll have to change this option if you want something else.
- *Manually.* You update any or all links whenever you want.
- *On printing.* Whenever you print the document, all links will be updated.

Choosing How to Update a Link

Updating a link is straightforward and intuitive. Here are the steps:

1. Choose Edit ➤ Links.
2. In the Links dialog box (see Figure 28.5), select the link or links that you want to update.

TIP

To update several links, hold down Ctrl while you click on each link, or hold down Shift and click on the first and last links of the desired range to select all the links between the two.

PART

VI

Power Tools

FIGURE 28.5

*You select the
links to update,
lock, or break
in the Links
dialog box.*

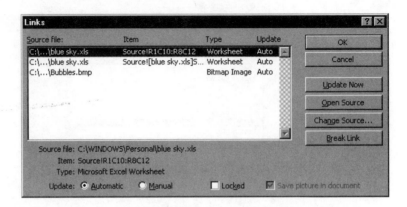

3. Choose how you want the selected links to be updated:

   - Choose the Automatic option button to update linked information every time the source file is changed.
   - Choose the Manual option button to update links only when you choose to do so.

4. Choose OK to close the Links dialog box and accept the changes you've made.

To Update a Link Manually

Update your links manually to retain the most control over your document and its linked objects. Here's how:

1. Choose Edit ➤ Links.
2. In the Links dialog box, select the link or links that you want to update.
3. Click on the Update Now button to update the links.

TIP

To update links quickly, select the links you want to update and press F9.

To Update Links Every Time You Print

To make sure your documents are up to date whenever you print them, arrange for their links to be updated whenever you print. Here's how:

1. Choose Tools ➤ Options.
2. In the Options dialog box, select the Print tab.
3. In the Printing Options area, check the Update Links checkbox (see Figure 28.6).

4. Click on the OK button to close the dialog box. Links in your documents will now be updated whenever you print.

FIGURE 28.6

Check the Update Links checkbox in the Print tab of the Options dialog box to update links whenever you print documents.

Editing Linked Information

When you need to edit the linked information, you can do it two ways. You can either run the source application from the Start button and open the file, or you can run the application directly from within Word. It is easier from within Word so let's look at that now.

To edit linked information, follow these steps:

1. Click on the linked object in your Word document.

2. Choose Edit ➤ Object (this menu item will vary depending on the kind of object you have selected—for example, Worksheet Object) and choose Edit from the mini-menu that appears. Word opens the source application and the source file for the linked information.

3. Make the edits you want in the source file.

PART

VI

Power Tools

4. Choose File ➤ Exit to get back to your Word document, which will now reflect the edits you made in the source file.

Saving your Word file at this point will also save the changes in the source file.

TIP You can often double-click on an object to display its parent application, in which you can then edit to your heart's content. Some objects, though, such as sound and video clips, you must edit using the menu commands.

Breaking Links

If you want to prevent linked information from being updated ever again, you can break a link. Once you've broken a link, though, you cannot reconnect it other than by using Undo *pronto*. If you want to *temporarily* prevent linked information from being updated, you can *lock* a link—see the next section for details.

Here's how to break a link:

1. Choose Edit ➤ Links.
2. In the Link dialog box, select the link or links that you want to break.
3. Click on the Break Link button. Word displays a dialog box asking if you are sure.
4. Choose Yes. The link or links will be broken.

Locking and Unlocking Links

You can *lock* links to temporarily prevent linked information from being updated. For example, suppose you're working on a technical manual with a number of screen illustrations. You've autoreferenced the figures in your text, and you've shot them and saved them to disk, using filenames based on the figure numbers. If you need to add or delete any, updating the autoreference fields automatically is going to make your life miserable when you try to figure out which figure is which on disk. When you want to be able to update them again, you unlock the links. Here's how to lock and unlock links:

1. Choose Edit ➤ Links.
2. In the Link dialog box, select the link or links that you want to lock or unlock.
3. To lock a link or links, check the Locked checkbox. To unlock a link or links, uncheck the Locked checkbox.
4. Choose OK to leave the Link dialog box and save your changes.

Reconnecting Lost Links

If you lose links in a document, blame yourself rather than the dog (sorry), but don't despair—you *can* reconnect lost links if there's another file you can use as the source.

How would you lose links? Well, you might delete the source file, forgetting that information in it was linked to a Word file. Someone else might even do this for you.

Here's how to reconnect lost links:

1. Choose Edit ➤ Links.
2. In the Links dialog box, choose the link you want to reconnect.
3. Choose the Change Source button.
4. In the File Name box of the Change Source dialog box, select the file to which you want to reconnect the link; then click on OK.

NOTE

If your document contains other links to the same source file, Word will ask you whether you want to change all links from the previous source file to the new source file. Choose Yes or No.

Word has the uncanny ability to track linked documents that you rename or move. Even if you change the source document's name, Word will still be able to find it. Now if you delete the file altogether, well, that's another story.

So how will you know if your links have become lost? Well, the next time you update the links in your file, any lost links will generate the notation N/A in the Update column of the Links dialog box, showing that the source file is not available. If you try to edit the linked object, by double-clicking on it for example, Word displays an error message reporting that it cannot edit the object.

If you no longer have the original source file, you can delete the linked data. If you've got a new source file, simply create a new link to the new source.

You could also lock the link to preserve the most recent data and the information in the link. Then, if you can locate or replace the source file, you can unlock the link and reconnect it to the source. (Locking and unlocking links are explained in the previous section.)

Another stopgap solution would be to break the link (as described in "Breaking Links," earlier in this chapter). This would preserve the information but sever the faulty link.

PART

VI

Power Tools

How to Embed

You can choose either to embed an existing object or to create an object and then embed it.

There's a dead simple way to embed objects, and then there's a more formal and more complicated way. Which would you like to learn first? Right. Here we go.

MASTERING TROUBLESHOOTING

Trimming File Size

A link takes up a lot less "space" than embedded data does because it stores information about where to find the data but it does not store all the data itself in the Word document. However, links do include graphical representations of the data or image linked, so the "picture" of the data will appear even if the linked file has been deleted or misplaced.

Because graphic files can be so large, for certain types of files you'll have the option of not saving the "picture" with the document, only the link information itself.

When you select the graphic file in the Links dialog box, the Save Picture in Document checkbox will become selectable. (It is usually dimmed for most linked objects.)

Deselect the checkbox to delete the graphical representation of the picture from the document. This makes your files smaller in size, but it will force Word to load the graphic representation from the file each time you open the document.

The trade-off in this situation is size versus speed. It's your call.

Embedding the Easy Way

Here's the easy way to embed objects in your documents:

1. Crank up the source application for the object you want to embed.
2. Create or open the file containing the information you want to embed.
3. Select the object and copy it to the Clipboard (choose Edit ➤ Copy, or click on any Copy button the application offers).
4. Switch back to Word using the Taskbar or Alt+tab. Do not close the source application.
5. Put the insertion point at a suitable place in your Word document.
6. Choose Edit ➤ Paste Special.
7. Be sure the Paste button—not the Paste Link button—is selected. Click on the Object type option—the first item in the As list.
8. Choose the Float over Text option, if desired.
9. Click on OK.

> **TIP**
>
> In some cases, such as when copying a drawing from the Paint application, you can embed the object by simply clicking on the Paste button or by selecting Edit ➤ Paste.

Embedding the Formal Way

If the way to embed described in the previous section is too easy for you or if you want to get a little more sophisticated with your object than simply pasting it in, use this method instead. Or combine the two.

Embedding an existing object and creating a new object to embed are a little different. Let's look at embedding an existing object first.

Embedding an Existing Object

To embed an existing object in a document, follow these steps:

1. In your Word document, put the insertion point where you want to embed the object.
2. Choose Insert ➤ Object. Word displays the Object dialog box.
3. As you're inserting an existing object, choose the Create from File tab.
4. Enter the name of the file that you want to embed.
5. If you want to display the embedded object as an icon in Word, check the Display As Icon checkbox. The standard icon for the application you chose will appear below the checkbox with a Change Icon button.
6. Choose the Float over Text option, if desired.
7. Choose OK. The selected object will be embedded in your Word file.

Creating a New Object and Embedding It

To create a new object and embed it in your Word document, follow these steps:

1. In your Word document, put the insertion point where you want to embed the object.
2. Choose Insert ➤ Object. Word displays the Object dialog box. The Create New tab should be displayed by default. (If it isn't, select it.)
3. In the Object Type box, select the application in which you want to create the new object. Check the Display as Icon checkbox if you want the new object to appear as an icon in your Word document. Change the icon if need be (see "To Embed an Existing Object," above, for details).
4. Choose OK. The application you chose will open.
5. Create the object you want, and then either click outside your object or select File ➤ Exit to return to Word. The object will be embedded in your document.

Editing Embedded Objects

You edit embedded objects just as you learned to edit graphs in Chapter 27, *Using Charts and Graphs.* Here are the steps:

1. Click on the object to select it. Selection handles and a frame will appear around it, and "Double-click to Edit" will appear in the status area.
2. You guessed it. Double-click on the object. Your computer will chug and whir for a while (quite a while if your object is something complicated, such as a Corel drawing— go get a jar of java or bug your office mate for a minute). The application in which the object was created will then open with the object ready for editing.
3. Edit the object.
4. Click outside the object or choose File ➤ Exit to quit the source application and return to Word. Word will reappear with the object updated to reflect your changes, as shown in Figure 28.7.

When you choose File ➤ Exit in the source application, Word reappears with the object updated to reflect your changes.

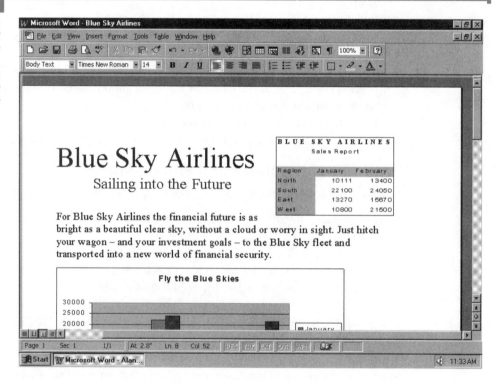

You can use a shortcut menu to carry out common commands such as Cut, Copy, and Paste on an embedded object. Right-click on the offending object, and select the command from the shortcut menu. The shortcut menu will vary depending on the source application for the embedded object.

> **NOTE**
> If the application temporarily trashes some of the Word menus and toolbars, click anywhere in the Word document to restore them. Bear in mind that embedding is even more puzzling for your computer than it is for you.

Editing Sound and Video Clips

If you've been using sound and video clips, you'll have spotted the fallacy in the preceding section. If you double-click on a sound or video clip, you'll run it. These objects object to being edited this way. They just wanna play instead.

In such cases (and in others, if you like), you must edit embedded objects using the Object command. Follow these steps:

1. Select the object you want to edit.
2. Select Edit ➤ Object, choose the name of the object you want to edit, and choose Edit.

> **NOTE**
> If Word offers you the choice of Edit or Open, choose Edit to edit the object in the Word window or choose Open to open the application to which the object belongs and edit it there.

3. When you're finished editing the object, choose File ➤ Exit and Return to get back to Word. Word will reappear with the edited object in place.

Converting an Embedded Object to a Different Format

If necessary, you can convert an embedded object to a different format. You might want to do this if you receive a file containing an embedded object created in an application you do not have or if you take a file created on your computer and containing embedded objects to a colleague's computer that does not have the relevant application.

To change an embedded object's source application, follow these steps:

1. Select the object to change.

PART

VI

Power Tools

2. Choose Edit ➤ Object, choose the object you want to convert, and select Convert from the extension menu.

3. In the Convert dialog box, specify the application to which you want to convert the file.

- Select the Convert To button to convert the embedded object permanently to the format you specify.
- Select the Activate As button to convert the embedded object temporarily to the format you specify. You can then edit the object in that format, but when you save it, it will be saved in its original format.

4. Click on OK.

Converting Graphics to Pictures

Conversion is very effective if you've been embedding graphic objects like a maniac and your file is doing a Charles Atlas and splitting its shirt. You can reduce the file's size by converting the graphics to Word's Picture format. When you then double-click on the graphic to edit it, you'll get Word's Picture editor rather than the original source application.

Before you do this, there's one little disadvantage you must know about: *You can't convert the graphic back to an embedded object. And as you'll see, it's also likely that the resolution and overall quality of the graphic will suffer. Still want to do it? Here's how:*

1. Select the object you want to convert.
2. Choose Edit ➤ Object.
3. Choose Convert.
4. In the Object Type area of the Convert dialog box, select Picture and then click on OK.

When Are Documents Containing Embedded Objects Updated?

Trick question. Answer: They are not updated—you have to edit the object yourself.

Embedded objects are not linked to a source document on the disk. When you want to change the embedded object, double-click on it to run the application that created it. Then, edit the document to update the information as needed.

Removing Embedded Objects

Removing an embedded object is easier than winking. Select it and press Delete. Alternatively, you can select it and choose Edit ➤ Cut if you want to place it somewhere else.

Editing Linked and Embedded Objects on Other People's Computers

In order to edit an embedded or linked document, the computer must have the source application installed. For instance, you might create a Word document with a linked Excel spreadsheet on your computer and take it in to show to your boss. All goes well until you double-click on the Excel object, only to find that your boss doesn't have Excel on her computer—she has Quattro Pro instead. *Bzzzzzzz!* Word won't like this.

 **WARNING**

 When you take a file containing linked and embedded objects to someone else's computer, be sure that the computer has all the necessary applications available before attempting to edit the objects.

To convert an embedded object to a different file format so that you can use it on a computer without the source application loaded, see "Converting an Embedded Object to a Different Format" earlier in this chapter.

Chapter

29

Creating and Using Fields

Creating and Using Fields

Ummm…Fields. There. Now I've said it. If you're one of the people who runs screaming into the next jurisdiction whenever anybody mentions the word *field*—and if you're still reading this—take heart. You don't actually have to use fields. Not now, not ever. You could go through your whole life without using a single Word field. It might be tough, but you *could* do it.

On the other hand, if you *do* use fields, you can save yourself a tremendous amount of work. You can keep your documents up-to-date more easily, include material from different sources with the stab of a finger, and automate your life to a large extent. As you'll see shortly, you've probably already used fields—perhaps without even knowing it.

First, let's take a squint at what fields are. Then we'll look at what you might want to use them for. Finally, we'll get into examples and check out the new fields in Word.

What Are Fields?

Fields are special codes you use to tell Word to insert information into your documents. You can insert codes to add and automatically update text, graphics, and so on. For example, you could use codes such as these:

```
{ AUTHOR \* MERGEFORMAT } {DATE \* MERGEFORMAT } {TIME \* MERGEFORMAT } {TITLE
    \* MERGEFORMAT } Page {PAGE \* MERGEFORMAT } of {NUMPAGES \* MERGEFORMAT }
```

to create a footer that looks like this:

Janice Horsefly——04/01/97 8:33 AM——The Impact of Ultraviolet Lasers on the Cerebral Cortex——Page 291 of 316

Author, date and time, title, and the page number out of the total number of pages—not bad for a few seconds' work with a half-dozen codes. If you formatted the codes, the result would look even better. But the best thing is that these fields can be updated instantly at any time, either automatically or at the punch of a key. (Yes, the page-number and number-of-pages codes update themselves automatically, adjusting for each page of your document.)

If you don't want fields to be updated, you can lock them and then unlock them when you need to update them.

As in the preceding example, Word usually displays the *result* of the field—the text or graphics the field will produce when printed. To indicate which text in your document is actually a field, you can have field results displayed shaded. You might want to do this if you find yourself choosing field codes accidentally. (See "Viewing Fields and Their Contents" later in the chapter.)

Where Do the Fields Get Their Information?

At this point, you might well be wondering where these fields get their information. Out of thin air? By psychic transmission?

Unfortunately, it ain't quite so, Joanna. And we're not talking Newtons and radio PC-to-PC communications here, either. Your copy of Word already knows a lot about you. Whatever you entered for the user name and address when you first installed Word is stored for use in your documents; you can access it by selecting Tools ➤ Options and clicking on the User Information tab in the Options dialog box. Word uses the Name field there for the Author name in the Summary tab of the Properties dialog box, the Initials for annotations, and the Mailing Address for the return address in any envelopes you print. Sure, you can change all these, but remember, Word is storing information about you.

When you save a file and fill in the Summary tab of the Properties dialog box, Word stores that information for retrieval in fields. The author information Janice Horsefly used in her footer came from this dialog box, as did the title information. The date and time information comes from the system clock that you set in Windows or DOS. The page-information fields—the page number and the number of pages—Word itself generates from your document.

There isn't space here to go into all the fields and where they get their information, but I think you get the idea: Some fields draw on permanent or semipermanent information (such as the user name), some draw on information you enter for a given document (title, keywords), and others are generated by Word (number of characters in a document, and so on).

Typical Uses of Fields

You can use fields in Word to do the following:

- Insert text, graphics, and other information in your documents
- Update information as it changes
- Perform calculations

Most people are introduced to fields in Word when they enter dates, times, and page numbers in their documents. Clicking on the buttons for these fields on the Header and Footer toolbar is an intuitive way of inserting fields. In fact, you might not even know they are fields unless you turn on field codes.

As you saw in Chapter 26, *Mail Merge—Creating Custom Documents*, Word's mail-merge features use fields extensively. As you learned in Chapter 27, *Using Charts and Graphs*, embedding charts from Microsoft Graph in Word documents also involves fields—as does Object Linking and Embedding, which I discussed in Chapter 29, *Linking and Embedding to Keep Things Current*. Boy, you can hardly get away from the little buggers! In case you're wondering, the next chapter, Chapter 30, *Creating and Using Forms and ActiveX Controls*, will feature more fields. They've got you surrounded. You might as well make the best of it.

That said, let's look at how you insert fields in your documents to produce these wonderful results.

The Types of Fields

The three types of fields are result, action, and marker.

- *Result fields* are the most common. They display information, which can come from within the document, from Word, from other documents, or from Windows.
- *Action fields* prompt the user to do something and then perform some action in response. There are only four: ASK, FILLIN, GOTOBUTTON, and MACROBUTTON.
- *Marker fields* simply indicate a location without displaying anything in the document or "doing" anything.

PART

VI

Power Tools

The Basic Parts of a Field

Unless you specifically choose to see field codes, you will only see the images or information that the result fields display, the prompts from the action fields, and no sign at all of the marker fields. If you display fields (by selecting the View tab in the Options dialog box and checking Field Codes), however, you will see neither results nor prompts. Instead you'll see the field *code*.

Field codes consist of three elements:

- Fields always begin and end with { and }, but these are not the simple curly-brace characters { and } that you can type from the keyboard. They are called *field characters*.
- The first part of a field after the opening field character is the *field name* (for example, AUTHOR or TITLE, both of which refer to entries in the Summary tab of the Properties dialog box). The field name identifies the field and the result, action, or marking it performs.
- One or more optional *field instructions* (such as * MERGEFORMAT) modify the basic field result or action in some way—supplying default text, selecting an option among several choices in a Word command, giving the filename of a linked file, and so on. (MERGEFORMAT causes the field to retain its formatting when updated, but that's getting a little ahead of ourselves.)

Field instructions come in several flavors:

- *Bookmarks*, as elsewhere, refer to locations or selections in documents. Fields with bookmark instructions can use the contents of the bookmark as well as its page number.
- *Expressions* are instructions used with the = field. They are all mathematical or logical operations, values, or references to values stored or inherent in the document.
- *Text* is enclosed in quotation marks (though this is not necessary for single words) to simply appear on screen or to supply instructions to a dialog box, prompt, or default box entry. (References to graphics are also considered text instructions, ironically enough.)
- *Switches* are instructions that further modify the result or action of a field. They all begin with the \ (backslash) character, and they tell the field what to do or how to behave. You can use *general switches* with any field or *field-specific switches* designed for that field only. A field can have a maximum of ten general switches and ten field-specific switches, though let's hope you never feel limited by this cap! (General switches are explained in nauseating detail later in this chapter in the "Adding Switches to Fields" section.)

All these types of field instructions can be represented by variables as well as by their literal names.

Inserting Fields

Some Word processes insert fields automatically. The Word commands for creating tables of contents and indices, the Page Number command on the Insert menu, many of the Mail Merge commands—all insert codes automatically.

You can insert fields manually in two ways. The easier is to use the Field command on the Insert menu, but it is also possible to type field codes directly into the document (and there are a number of keyboard shortcuts for some of the most useful fields).

Inserting Fields with Insert ➤ Field

To insert a field in a document, follow these steps:

1. Put the insertion point where you want the field to appear.

2. Choose Insert ➤ Field. Word displays the Field dialog box (see Figure 29.1).

3. In the Categories list, select the field category you want.

TIP

Select (All) to see all the fields in alphabetic order.

PART

VI

Power Tools

FIGURE 29.1

The Field dialog box

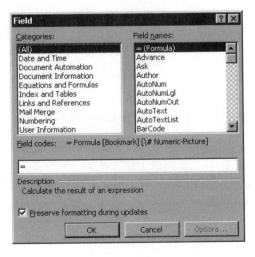

4. Select the field you want from the Field Names list.

5. Choose the Options button to add switches or formatting to the field you selected. In the Field Options dialog box (shown in Figure 29.2), select the switch or formatting you want in the box (its name varies depending on the options available for the selected field), and click on the Add to Field button. When you're finished adding formatting and switches, choose OK to return to the Field dialog box.

TIP

To remove switches or formatting from the field, click on the Undo Add button (great use of English) in the Field Options dialog box.

6. Back in the Field dialog box, click on OK to insert the selected field in your document.

FIGURE 29.2

Select switches or formatting for your fields in the Field Options dialog box.

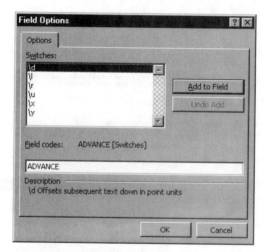

Inserting Field Codes Directly

If you know what you're doing, you can type field codes directly from the keyboard. Here's how:

1. Put the insertion point where you want to insert the new field.

2. Press Ctrl+F9. Word inserts the field characters, like so—{}—and leaves the insertion point in the middle, between the two field characters.

3. Type the field name followed by a space.

4. Type the field instructions you want, if any.

5. Press F9 to update the field immediately.

NOTE

You can also type the field name and instructions, select them, and then press Ctrl+F9.

If you have mistyped a switch, the field will display an error message, such as:

`Error! Unknown switch argument.`

If you use a nonexistent field name, you might see this message:

`Error! Bookmark not defined`

These error messages, by the way, only appear when you are viewing field results, not the codes. So if you get an error message, press Shift+F9 to display the field code again and correct your error. If the code does not appear, select the error message and press Shift+F9. Get into the habit of viewing the field results in your document to ensure that there are not errors.

Viewing Fields and Their Contents

You can view codes either as field results or as field codes. As discussed earlier, field results consist of the text or graphics that will be printed; field codes are the instructions to Word that will produce the corresponding text or graphics.

By default, Word displays field results so that you can see how your document will appear when printed. But when you are working with fields, you can display field codes instead of field results. You can display codes for a single field or for all fields at once.

To Display Field Codes for a Single Field

To display the field codes for a single field, follow these steps:

1. Place the insertion point in the field.

2. Click the right mouse button to display the pop-up shortcut menu.

3. Choose Toggle Field Codes from the shortcut menu to turn on the codes for the field.

To turn the codes off, repeat the procedure. The toggle will return the codes to their result display.

To Display Field Codes for All Fields

When inserting or adapting field codes, you may want to display all the codes in a document. Here's how:

1. Choose Tools ➤ Options.
2. In the Options dialog box, select the View tab.
3. Check the Field Codes checkbox, and then click on OK.

Your fields will now appear as codes—{TITLE * MERGEFORMAT} and so on. To return them to text, repeat steps 1 through 3 but uncheck the Field Codes box.

WARNING

Some field codes—the RD (Referenced Document), TA (Table of Authorities), TC (Table of Contents), and XE (Index Entry) fields—do not appear when other field codes are displayed; these field codes are formatted as hidden text. To display them, choose Tools ➤ Options, select the View tab, and check the Hidden Text checkbox. To hide them again, uncheck the Hidden Text box.

MASTERING TROUBLESHOOTING

Viewing Results and Codes Together

Sometimes switching back and forth between displaying the field codes and their results gets tiring. To save yourself the trouble—and cut down the wear and tear on your fingers—you may find it helpful to view both field codes and their results at the same time. In this way you can see what effect changing the field codes has on their results.

To do so, split the document window into panes. Drag the Split bar down from the top of the vertical scroll bar, or choose Window ➤ Split and drag the Split bar to an appropriate place.

Finally, set different view options for each pane. For example, click on the pane that you want to display the fields in, choose Select Tools ➤ Options, click on the View tab, and then check the Field Codes box and click on OK. Turn off the display of fields in the other pane. Voila! Two views in one.

To Display Field Results Shaded

You can choose to have field results display shaded so that you don't delete or alter them by mistake. Here's how:

1. Choose Tools ➤ Options.
2. In the Options dialog box, select the View tab.

NOTE

You can choose When Selected in the Field Shading drop-down list to have fields shaded when they are selected or choose Never (the default) to avoid having any shading at all.

3. Pull down the Field Shading list (see Figure 29.3), choose Always, and then click on OK.

NOTE

Field shading is only a convenience for working on-screen; it is never printed.

FIGURE 29.3

*The Field
Shading list*

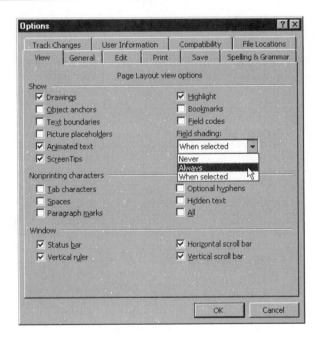

Power Tools

PART

VI

Printing Field Codes

Regardless of whether fields are shown as results (and prompts) or as field codes, they will not print as field codes unless you specifically request that they do when you print your document. It's often a good idea to print out a document with its field codes showing for reference. To do so, follow these steps:

1. Choose File ➤ Print.
2. In the Print dialog box, click on the Options button.
3. In the Print tab of the Options dialog box, check Field Codes in the Include with Document box.
4. Click on OK. Word displays the Print dialog box.
5. Click on OK again to print your document.

That's all there is to it.

Field Codes will stay selected in the Print tab of the Options dialog box until you uncheck the box; so be sure to do that before printing again (unless you want field codes to print again next time).

Formatting Fields

Fields are simple to format: You can format either the field result itself or the field code. For example, with its field codes looking like *this:*

{ AUTHOR * MERGEFORMAT } {DATE * MERGEFORMAT }{TIME * MERGEFORMAT }{ *TITLE* * *MERGEFORMAT* }
Page { PAGE * MERGEFORMAT } of { NUMPAGES * MERGEFORMAT }

the example header from the beginning of the chapter could look like *this:*

Janice Horsefly 04/01/97 8:33 AM *The Impact of Ultraviolet Light on Tuna*
Page **654** of **876**

Yes, I know that's hideous. I was just trying to make the point. OK? Good.

You can also format field results by adding switches to the field codes. This is a little esoteric and is mainly useful for very sophisticated projects. We'll take a quick look at adding switches to field codes in the next section, but I suggest you format your field results the easy ways outlined earlier unless you've got a compelling reason to use switches instead. Save this for making minor adjustments to field codes you formatted slightly incorrectly.

Adding Switches to Fields

By adding *switches* to fields, you can customize the format of a field's result or lock the result.

There are four general switches for fields, each of which has a plethora of permutations:

Switch	Effect
Format(*)	Adds formatting (for example, capitalization) to the field's result.
Numeric Picture (\#)	Controls the number of decimal places, literal characters, and so on for a numeric result.
Date-Time Picture (\@)	Formats a date or time (or both) result—to produce April 1, 1997 or 11:59 PM, for instance.
Lock Result (\!)	Prevents fields included in the result of a BOOKMARK, INCLUDE-TEXT, or REF field from being updated.

NOTE   Formatting created by switches takes precedence over manual formatting of the type demonstrated in the previous section.

Again, many field codes also have field-specific switches available in addition to the general switches. When you insert a field code with the Insert ➤ Field command, click on the Options button to see the field-specific switches available for that field code, if any.

PART

VI

Power Tools

Switches That Preserve Manual Formatting

If you can stand to learn a thing or two about switches, you can actually make it easier on yourself to format fields and keep them from reverting to other formats when updated. The two switches that preserve the manual formatting of a field after updating are:

* MERGEFORMAT

and

* CHARFORMAT

The * MERGEFORMAT switch preserves whatever manual formatting was applied to the *field result*, including both character formatting (such as boldface) and paragraph formatting (such as line spacing). If you format the result and then update the field, the formats will be applied to the new updated result. The * CHARFORMAT switch applies the character formatting of the first character of the *field name* to the entire field result. You'll see an example of this in a moment.

WARNING

The * MERGEFORMAT switch applies the formatting of the previous field result word by word to the updated field result. If the formatting is complicated and the new field result has a different number of words, the formatting may "slip" and get screwed up. If this happens, reformat the field result manually.

* MERGEFORMAT also preserves picture formatting such as scaling and cropping dimensions.

Specific Format Switches

There are two other types of * format switches—those used for case conversion and those used for numeric conversion.

Case-Conversion Switches

The case-conversion options are as follows:

Switch	What It Does
* Caps	Capitalizes the initial letter of each word in the result
* Firstcap	Capitalizes the initial letter of the first word in the result
* Lower	Makes all the letters in the result lowercase
* Upper	Capitalizes all the letters in the result

Here are some examples:

Field	Result
{ AUTHOR * Caps}	Ron Person
{ AUTHOR * Lower }	ron person
{ AUTHOR * Upper}	RON PERSON
{ AUTHOR * Lower * Firstcap * CHARFORMAT }	*Ron person*

Understanding *CHARFORMAT

Before going on, be sure you understand how the last example works—the one with the * CHARFORMAT switch. For some unknown reason, I decided to display the author name from the User Information box in bold and italic and with only the first letter in uppercase. Let's assume the name appears in that box as Ron Person.

If I had used only the * firstcap switch by itself, the field would not lowercase the first letter of the second name. I had to first make every letter lowercase with the * lower switch and then change the first letter to uppercase with the * firstcap switch.

I applied the bold and italic formats to the first letter of the field name Author. The * CHARFORMAT switch tells Word to apply the format on that first character to the entire result.

PART

VI

Power Tools

Numeric Switches

The numeric-conversion options are as follows:

Switch	What It Does
* alphabetic	Converts the resulting number to the corresponding lowercase letter of the alphabet—10 becomes j, 27 becomes aa.
* Alphabetic	Converts the resulting number to the corresponding capitalized letter of the alphabet—10 becomes J, 27 becomes AA.
* arabic	Converts the resulting number to arabic (standard) form, which is the default anyway, but it overrides any manual change to the numeric form (such as a different option in the Page Number Format dialog box).
* cardtext	Spells out the resulting number (cardtext stands for cardinal number—such as "one," as opposed to the ordinal "first"—text form) in lowercase letters.
* dollartext	Spells out the resulting number with initial letters capitalized, adds "and," and then displays the first two decimal places of the number (rounded off, if necessary) as an arabic numerator over 100, suitable for payroll checks.
* hex	Converts the resulting number to hexadecimal form.
* ordinal	Converts the resulting number to arabic ordinal form (1st, 2nd, 10th, etc.).
* ordtext	Spells out the resulting number in ordinal form (first, second, tenth, etc.).
* roman	Converts the resulting number to lowercase roman numerals.
* Roman	Converts the resulting number to uppercase roman numerals.

Here are some examples:

Field	Result
{ =2+2 * cardtext }	four
{ =7*5 * cardtext * caps }	Thirty-Five
{ =99/2 * dollartext * firstcap }	Forty-nine and 50/100
{ PAGE * ordinal * CHARFORMAT }	2nd
{ PAGE * ordtext }	second
{ PAGE * roman }	ii

NOTE

Note how you can use the = switch to perform a calculation. The field {=2+2} returns the result of the calculation (4), but the switch determines how the results appear.

Specific Numeric Picture Switches

Numeric picture switches control the appearance of the number displayed by the field code by using dummy characters to demonstrate the "picture," or pattern, that the number's display should follow. Numeric picture switches can add characters such as $ or % to the number. They can also control the number of digits displayed, the way negative numbers are displayed, whether commas are used to separate digits in the thousands place, and so on.

The numeric-picture-switch instructions (they can be combined in many ways) are as follows:

Switch Instruction	What It Does
any character	Includes that character in the number display
'multiple words'	Includes the words between apostrophes in the number display
"several numeric picture instructions"	Combines the instructions between the quotation marks and preserves spacing
#	Optional digit placeholder; displays as a space if no digit is required
0	Required digit placeholder; displays as a zero if no digit is required
x	Truncating digit placeholder, eliminates any digits to the left unless placed after a decimal point, in which case it eliminates any digits to the right
. (period)	Decimal point, holds the place of the decimal point in relation to digit placeholders
, (comma)	Thousands separator, used to group numbers by thousands to make them easier to read (compare 100000 to 100,000)
–	Uses minus sign as indicator for negative numbers

PART

VI

Power Tools

Switch Instruction	What It Does
+	Uses plus sign for positive numbers *and* minus sign for negatives (and a space for zero)
; (semi-colon)	Separates custom positive and negative numeric pictures, or positive, negative, and zero numeric pictures
'numbered-item'	Displays the number of the specified item preceding the field. For example, the switch 'table' will display the number of the table immediately before the field

Here are some examples:

Field	Result
{ =10 \# $##.00 }	$10.00
{ =10 \# "## 'dollars'" }	10 dollars
{ =(1/2)*100 \# ##% }	50%
{ =10^5 \# #,### }	100,000
{ =10 \# –## }	10
{ =-10 \# –## }	–10
{ =3255.5-10000 \# $##,###.00;($##,###.00) }	($ 6,744.50)

Specific Date-Time Picture Switches

Date-time picture switches control the appearance of the date or time displayed by the field code. The switches provide a "picture," or pattern, that the date or time should follow using simple abbreviations to represent the parts of a time or date (h for hours, m for minutes, M for month, d for day, and so on).

The date-time–picture-switch instructions (they can be combined in many ways) are as follows:

Switch Instruction	What It Does
any character	Includes that character in the date display
'multiple words'	Includes the words between apostrophes in the number display (put quotation marks around the entire instruction)
"several date-time picture instructions"	Combines the instructions between the quotation marks and preserves spacing

Switch Instruction	What It Does
h	Hours of the 12-hour clock without a leading zero for single-digit hours
hh	Hours of the 12-hour clock with a leading zero for single-digit hours
H	Hours of the 24-hour clock without a leading zero for single-digit hours
HH	Hours of the 24-hour clock with a leading zero for single-digit hours
m	Minutes without a leading zero for single-digit minutes
mm	Minutes with a leading zero for single-digit minutes
s	Seconds without a leading zero for single-digit seconds
ss	Seconds with a leading zero for single-digit seconds
AM/PM	AM or PM as appropriate
am/pm	am or pm as appropriate
A/P	A or P as appropriate
a/p	a or p as appropriate
M	Month number without a leading zero for single-digit months
MM	Month number with a leading zero for single-digit months
MMM	Three-letter abbreviation for the month
MMMM	Full name of the month
d	Day of the month without a leading zero for single-digit days
dd	Day of the month with a leading zero for single-digit days
ddd	Day of the week as a three-letter abbreviation
dddd	Full name of the day of the week
yy	Year as a two-digit number with a leading zero for years ending in 01 through 09
yyyy	Year as a four-digit number

PART

VI

Power Tools

TIP

Don't forget that the month instruction is a capital M and the minute instruction is a lowercase m.

Here are some examples:

Field	Result
{ DATE \@ "dddd, MMMM d, yyyy" }	Thursday, September 1, 1998
{ DATE \@ dd/MM/y }	01/09/98
{ DATE \@ d-M-yy }	1-9-98
{ TIME \@ h:mm:ss am/pm }	10:02:15 am

Updating Fields

As you'll have gathered by now, the whole point of inserting fields in your document rather than inserting straight information is that the fields are easy to update.

You can choose to update all fields at once or update them one at a time. Further, you can choose to update all fields whenever you print a document to ensure up-to-date information for your documents.

Updating Fields One at a Time

To update fields one at a time, place the mouse pointer in the field and press F9. You can also click the right mouse button to pop up the shortcut menu. From the shortcut menu, choose Update Field. The field will be updated and will show its most recent result.

Updating All Fields Simultaneously

To update all fields in a document at once, choose Edit ➤ Select All and then press F9, or click the right mouse button to pop up the shortcut menu. From the shortcut menu, choose Update Field. All the fields in the document will be updated to show their most recent results.

NOTE

If a document has field codes only in its headers/footers, you need to display the Header/Footer pane before choosing Select All. Otherwise, the shortcut menu will not include the Update Field option.

Updating Fields When You Print

Update fields when you print to make sure your documents, forms, and reports contain the most up to date information available. Here's how:

1. Choose Tools ➤ Options.
2. In the Options dialog box, select the Print tab.
3. In the Printing Options area, check the Update Fields checkbox and then click on OK.

All the fields in your documents will now be updated each time the documents are printed. To stop this updating, repeat steps 1, 2, and 3, but uncheck the Update Fields checkbox.

WARNING

Like other options in the Options dialog box, Update Fields is sticky—its setting will stay the same until you change it.

Undoing or Halting Updates

If you've just updated fields and want to undo the update, simply select Edit ➤ Undo Update Fields (or press Ctrl+Z). If you start updating a document and then realize that you don't want to update the whole thing or wait for it to finish, press Esc to cancel the process.

Locking the Contents of Fields

When you want to keep the result of a field from being updated and changed, you can either *lock* the field or *unlink* it. Locking a field prevents the field from being updated until the field is unlocked; unlinking a field permanently replaces the field with its current result.

To Lock a Field

To lock a field to prevent it from being updated, follow these steps:

1. Place the cursor in the field you want to lock.
2. Press Ctrl+F11 or Ctrl+3.

To Unlock a Field

To unlock a field so that it can once again be updated, follow these steps:

1. Place the cursor in the field you want to unlock.
2. Press Ctrl+Shift+F11.

PART

VI

Power Tools

To Unlink a Field

To unlink a field so that it can never again be updated, follow these steps:

WARNING

If you unlink fields and then later change your mind, you may not be able to undo your actions; so give it some thought beforehand.

1. Place the cursor in the field you want to unlink.
2. Press Ctrl+Shift+F9 or Ctrl+6.

NOTE

You can use Undo to restore fields you just unlinked, but only until *Unlink Fields* drops off the bottom of the Undo button's drop-down list.

Moving Quickly between Fields

You can move quickly between fields by using Edit ➤ Go To and selecting Field in the Go to What area on the Go To tab of the Find and Replace dialog box. You can choose to move between particular fields or between any fields, or you can simply search for the previous or next field. Here's how:

1. Choose Edit ➤ Go To.
2. In the Go to What box on the Go To tab (see Figure 29.4), select Field.
3. In the Enter Field Name box, select the name of the field or accept Any Field.
4. Click on the Next button to find the next occurrence of the field, or click on the Previous button to find the previous occurrence.
5. Click on the Close button when you get where you want.

TIP

To get to the Go To tab quickly, press F5 or double-click on some blank space in the left side of the status area.

TIP

To go to the next field, press F11; to go to the previous field, press Shift+F11.

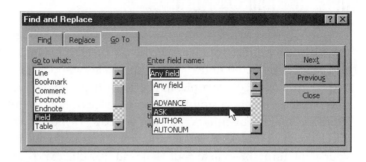

FIGURE 29.4

You can use the Go To tab to move rapidly between fields.

Shortcut Keys for Working with Fields

Word offers many shortcut keys for working with fields. Some we've touched on in this chapter; some we've met (or will meet) in other chapters. Here they all are, for your reference:

Key Combination	Effect
Alt+Shift+D	Insert a date field
Alt+Shift+P	Insert a page field
Alt+Shift+T	Insert a time field
Ctrl+F9	Insert a blank field
Ctrl+Shift+F7	Update linked information in the source document
F9	Update selected fields
Ctrl+Shift+F9	Unlink a field
Shift+F9	Toggles between field codes and results for the selected field
Alt+F9	Toggles between field codes and results for all fields in the document
Alt+Shift+F9	Perform the action in the field when the insertion point is positioned in the field
F11	Go to the next field
Shift+F11	Go to the previous field
Ctrl+F11	Lock a field
Ctrl+Shift+F11	Unlock a field

PART

VI

Power Tools

Examples of Fields at Work

The more you use Word, the more chances you'll get to use fields to enhance your documents and minimize your work. Word uses fields for many of its specialized functions, and chances are you'll find yourself using fields without having consciously made the decision to do so. For example, in previous chapters you learned how to insert graphs into Word documents using Microsoft Graph and how to link and embed objects in Word documents. In either case, choose Tools ➤ Options, select the View tab, and check the Field Codes checkbox, and you'll find that you've been using field codes—your graph turns into a field code that reads { EMBED MS Graph }, and your link to a different application turns into something a little more esoteric. Mail-merge documents use all sorts of fields—some defined by Word and some by you, the user—to produce the form letters.

Chapter 30, *Creating and Using Forms and ActiveX Controls*, further illustrates the many uses of fields in Word. In that chapter, you'll learn how to use special fields called *form fields*, and you'll learn something about ActiveX fields for use in Web pages.

Now, let's look at some ways to use fields.

Using Fields to Assign and Display Bookmarks

You can use a bookmark to indicate a location in a document that you want to move to quickly. You can also use a bookmark to supply information (text or numeric) to another field code instruction, switch, or mathematical expression.

In expressions, bookmarks play the role of variables. For example, suppose you select a section of text and give it a bookmark name using the Insert ➤ Bookmark command. You can quickly insert the contents of that bookmark—the selected text—by pressing Ctrl+F9, typing the bookmark name, and then pressing F9 to update the field. The contents of the bookmark will appear in place of the field code.

You can also use the SET field to store a value in a bookmark. The syntax is:

```
{ SET Bookmark Value }
```

For example, the field:

```
{ SET Title "Sales Coordinator" }
```

places the text Sales Coordinator into the bookmark (variable) Title. Likewise, the field

```
{ SET Age 50 }
```

inserts the value 50 into the bookmark (variable) Age.

When you want to insert the title into a document, press Ctrl+F9, type **Title**, and press F9. To insert the value of the bookmark age, just use the code {Age}.

Changing the Contents of Fields

By using the {= Formula } field, you can change field codes so that they produce the results you want. For example, suppose you work for the IRS and you create a flat-tax bookmark called TaxThemAll using the field:

```
{ SET TaxThemAll 1500 }
```

To later multiply the bookmark by 31 percent use the code:

```
{=TaxThemAll*31%}
```

If you find that 31 percent isn't giving you the revenue you need and that you need to up it to 46 percent, follow these steps:

1. Put the insertion point in the field.
2. If the field is showing its result, display the field codes by pressing Shift+F9 or by right-clicking on the field and choosing Toggle Field Codes from the shortcut menu.
3. Edit the field. Change 31 to 46:

```
{=TaxThemAll*46%}
```

4. Display the field result again by pressing Shift+F9 or by right-clicking on the field and choosing Toggle Field Codes from the shortcut menu.
5. Update the field by pressing F9 or by right-clicking on the field and choosing Update Field from the shortcut menu.

Working with Action Fields

In this section, you'll learn how to use the four action fields—ASK, FILLIN, GOTOBUTTON, and MACROBUTTON.

ASK Fields

ASK fields take the following form:

```
{ ASK bookmark "prompt text" \optional switches }
```

The field displays a dialog box that includes the prompt text and a text box. Whatever is entered in the text box is assigned to the bookmark. To display the result, you have to use the bookmark in a field as explained previously.

The field-specific switches for ASK are:

\d "*default text*"	Supplies default text (highlighted) in the text box
\o	Prompts only once during a mail merge (instead of once for each resulting document)

FILLIN Fields

FILLIN fields take the following form:

```
{ FILLIN "optional prompt text" \optional switches }
```

The field displays a dialog box that can show a prompt. Whatever text you enter in it is inserted at the insertion point (as the field result, not as regular text).

The field-specific switches for FILLIN are:

\d *"default text"*	Supplies default text (highlighted) in the text box
\o	Prompts only once during a mail merge (instead of once for each resulting document)

Note the fine difference between ASK and FILLIN. The ASK field places the result in a bookmark without displaying it until you use the bookmark name. The FILLIN field displays the result on the screen but does not insert it in a bookmark for later use.

GOTOBUTTON Fields

GOTOBUTTON fields take the following form:

```
{ GOTOBUTTON destination display-text }
```

The field shows the display text on the screen as a clickable field. Double-clicking on the result moves the insertion point to the destination, which can be any acceptable Go To destination (Go To is explained in Chapter 2, *Viewing and Navigating*) such as a bookmark, page number, table, and so on.

For example, if you enter the line:

```
Double-click on {GOTOBUTTON summary Summary} to read the results of the study
```

and then select the line and press Shift+F9, you'll see the text:

```
Double-click on Summary to read the results of the study
```

When you double-click on the word *Summary*, Word moves to the named bookmark location.

You won't be able to do much with many of these field codes unless you have field codes visible. To turn them on, choose Tools ➤ Options and, on the View tab, click to view Field Codes.

MACROBUTTON Fields

MACROBUTTON fields take the following form:

```
{ MACROBUTTON macro display-text }
```

This field works just like the GOTOBUTTON command, but double-clicking runs the named macro rather than moving to a set location.

You can format the display text and add the * MERGEFORMAT switch to preserve the formatting through subsequent updates.

> **TIP**
>
> If you insert the MACROBUTTON field with the Insert ➤ Field command, you can click on the Options button to see a list of available macros.

The field { MACROBUTTON MyMacro **Double-Click Here to Run MyMacro** } would display this text:

Double-Click Here to Run MyMacro

Note that you do not need to surround the display text with quotation marks. When you double-click on the text, Word runs the macro named Mymacro.

Nesting One Field inside Another

In addition to text, switches, and other instructions, field codes can also contain other fields. It's easier to nest a field inside a field than you might think. To do so, follow these steps:

1. Insert the first field, either with the Insert Field command (in which case, press Shift+F9 afterward to display the field code) or by pressing Ctrl+F9 and entering the code manually.
2. Move the insertion point inside the field code to where you want the nested code to appear.
3. Insert the nested field, again either with the Insert Field command or by pressing Ctrl+F9 and entering the code manually.
4. Press F9 to display the field result or prompt.

PART

VI

Power Tools

MASTERING THE OPPORTUNITIES

Automating Word with Buttons

The GOTOBUTTON and MACROBUTTON commands can really automate your work. Here are some tips.

You can use the MACROBUTTON field to perform many built-in Word functions without creating macros for them. For example, the field { MACROBUTTON File-Save **Double-Click Here to Save the File** } displays this text:

Double-Click Here to Save the File

Double-clicking there would be equivalent to selecting File ➤ Save. Other commands that you can use include FileOpen, FilePrint, FilePageSetup, FilePrintPreview, and FormatTabs.

To see a complete list of the commands that you can use, follow these steps.

1. Choose Tools ➤ Macro ➤ Macros.
2. Pull down the Macros In list in the dialog box that appears and select Word Commands. Word displays a list of commands that you can use with the MACROBUTTON command.
3. Close the dialog box and type the desired commands in the field.

You can place a border around the display-text in GOTOBUTTON and MACROBUT-TON commands to give the appearance of an actual button. For example, when entering the field {GOTOBUTTON summary Summary}, double-click on the display-text, and then click on the Outside Border button in the Formatting Toolbar. The word will be surrounded by a box in the text.

For an even more dramatic effect, you can display a graphic image as the display text by nesting the INCLUDEPICTURE field. See the "Nesting One Field inside Another" section.

Suppose you wanted to use a graphic as the display text in the GOTOBUTTON or MACROBUTTON commands, such as this:

The field would look something like this:

```
Click here {MACROBUTTON FileSave {INCLUDEPICTURE "C:\SBUTTON.BMP" \*
    MERGEFORMAT }} to save the document.
```

You would press Ctrl+F9 and then type **MACROBUTTON FileSave** and a space. Next, choose Insert ➤ Field, select the INCLUDEPICTURE field, and enter the path and name of the file. In my example, the graphic is from the file C:\SBUTTON.BMP that I created with Paint.

Getting Field Code Help

Word has extensive online help for each field code with complete syntax and switches. To see this help for a specific field code, select Help ➤ Contents and Index, and then type the field. The list of help topics will scroll to display the field—double-click on it to read complete information.

PART

VI

Power Tools

Chapter

30

Creating and Using Forms and ActiveX Controls

Chapter

30

Creating and Using Forms and ActiveX Controls

You can use the features of Word that you've learned about in the preceding chapters of this book to create your own business forms. You can create forms that you print to be filled in by hand or forms to be filled in online. Online forms are a great gift from the computer age; you can save the form on your disk and print, fax, or e-mail it as needed.

For online forms, Word has two special features—*form fields* and *form protection*. Form fields are special fields that let you create text boxes, checkboxes, and drop-down lists to make it easy for users to fill in the contents of the form. For example, do you want the user to select from a set choice of options? Create a list box that displays the options that can be chosen with a click of the mouse. You can even specify that certain fields have specific data types, formatting, or default text. You can add macros that run automatically to a form and attach help messages to fields to further assist the users.

Form protection ensures that users can only fill in information on the form—they cannot change the format or appearance of the form itself. You may be thinking that protecting a form is an extreme measure, but the way Word arranges forms, you need to protect them to be able to fill them in properly. Until you protect a form, the fancy features such as drop-down lists and help text attached to fields are set up to be edited rather than to be used.

NOTE

You won't be able to use any of the form fields in a document until you protect the form. So after you create a form, you must turn on protection. Keep this in mind as you read this chapter and create your own forms.

You can add AutoText entries to a form you save as a template. You can also add macros, customized toolbars, customized menus, and the other features associated with templates.

Designing most forms involves using Word's table features (discussed in Chapter 9, *Tabs, Tables, Math, and Sorting*) to lay out the form and then applying character, paragraph, and table formatting to give the form a satisfactory appearance. You don't have to design a form using a table, but the table structure makes it easy to position text boxes, checkboxes, and lists in specific locations on the screen and on the printed page.

TIP

When you create a form, save it as a *template* (discussed in Chapter 13, *Templates, Wizards, and Sample Documents*) rather than as a document so that you can open any number of copies based on it without altering its contents and then save them as documents. If you protect the template, that protection also applies to all new documents based on that template. (When you need to change the form, you can edit the template directly.)

Designing and Creating Forms

When designing a form, you'll probably want to start with a rough draft or sketch of what you're trying to produce. Although you *can* just type into your computer everything you think you'll need to include in the form and then hack it into shape, you may wind up with a beautifully designed form lacking one crucial component.

If you can't be bothered to make a sketch, get a similar form from somewhere and scrawl your main items in its boxes. That'll give you a head start.

Figure 30.1 shows a job log I created for Unincorporated Inc., a deconstruction firm that deals with special projects. The job log illustrates some of the main features of forms in Word. In the coming sections, we'll look at how to insert these elements, using the job log as an example.

FIGURE 30.1

Unincorporated Inc.'s Job Log form

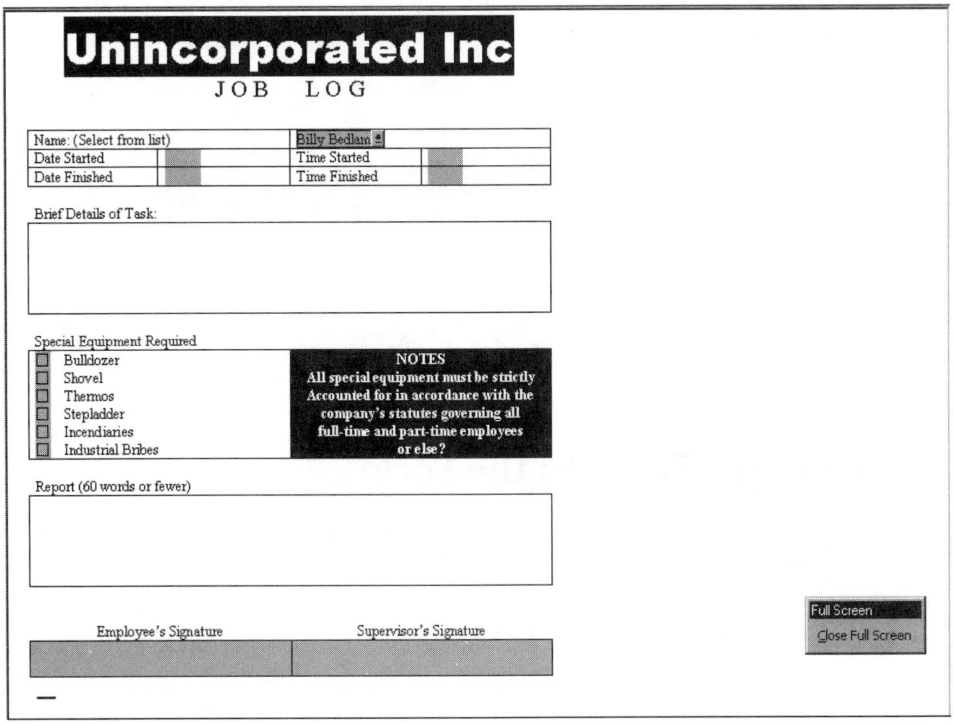

Starting a Form

To start a form, first open a new document. Because the job log will be an online form, select the Template option button rather than the Document option button in the New dialog box.

Using normal keyboard procedures, enter your new template text that doesn't need to be in a table—for example, the main headings.

Displaying the Forms Toolbar

To create forms, you need to display the Forms toolbar. Right-click on any toolbar and then click on Forms, or select View ➤ Toolbars and then click on Forms. The Forms toolbar is shown in Figure 30.2.

FIGURE 30.2

Drag the Forms toolbar wherever you want it, or double-click on it to display it at the top of the screen.

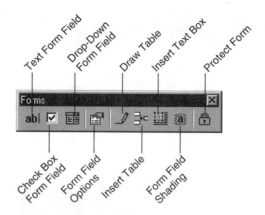

Adding a Table to the Form

Much of the Job Log form consists of tables, the cells of which contain the form fields and their descriptions. With the Forms toolbar, you can insert a table in a manner similar to the one you learned in Chapter 9.

To add a table with a specific number of rows and columns, follow these steps:

1. Place the insertion point where you want the table to start.

2. Click on the Insert Table button on either the Standard toolbar or the Forms toolbar to display the table-insertion grid.

> **TIP**
>
> You can also select Table ➤ Insert Table and specify the number of rows and columns in the Insert Table dialog box.

3. Click on the square that shows the number of rows (counting from the top) and columns (counting from the left) that you want in the table. Word inserts the table in your document.

4. Size the table by dragging its gridlines or by selecting Table ➤ Cell Height and Width and specifying measurements in the Cell Height and Width dialog box.

> **NOTE**
>
> By default, Word inserts tables as wide as your page with all cells the same width.

You can also use the Draw Table command. Click on the Draw Table button in the Forms toolbar to display the Tables and Borders toolbar; then create the table just as you learned earlier in this book.

Type text into the table cells as usual and format it in the normal ways.

MASTERING THE OPPORTUNITIES

Adding Borders and Shading to the Form

You can use all of Word's table and formatting features to spruce up the appearance of your online form so that it looks great on the screen and when printed.

To add borders or shading to a table, as in the Job Log form, for example, select the table or the cells to which you want to add the border or shading; then choose

Format ➤ Borders and Shading and specify borders and shading in the Paragraph Borders and Shading dialog box. You can also click on the Borders button in the Formatting toolbar to select a border style for selected cells.

Don't be afraid to experiment with lines and color or to add graphics, AutoShapes, or WordArt designs.

Adding a Text Box

In addition to a table, you can add a text box to the template. You use a text box to display instructions or other information for the person who is using the form, but the text box cannot be edited by the user.

To insert a text box, follow these steps:

1. Click on the Insert Text Box button on the.Forms toolbar.
2. Drag the mouse to draw a box the size you want it. When you release the mouse, the box will be surrounded by handles.
3. Type and format the text that you want in the box.
4. Drag the box to where you want it on the form.
5. Drag the handles to adjust the size of the box.
6. Click outside the box when you are done.

Inserting Form Fields into Your Form

You can automatically insert three types of form fields into your form—checkboxes, text form fields, and drop-down list boxes. The Unincorporated, Inc. form contains all three types. The following sections detail how to insert each type of box.

Adding a Checkbox to the Form

Word gives you the option of adding checkboxes to your forms, such as those in the Special Equipment Required section in Figure 30.1. Here's how to do it:

1. Place the insertion point where you want the checkbox to appear. It is usually before or after text that explains the meaning of the box, such as Bulldozer and Shovel in Figure 30.1.

2. Click on the Check Box Form Field button in the Forms toolbar.

You now have to specify how the checkbox is to work on the form by using the Check Box Form Field Options dialog box shown in Figure 30.3. Display the box using either of these techniques:

- Double-click on the checkbox.
- Click on the box to select it (it will be selected automatically after you insert it), and then click on the Form Field Options button in the Forms toolbar.

The following options are available for checkboxes:

- **Check Box Size:** Set at Auto to let Word size the box based on the current font size, or select Exactly to specify a fixed point size for the checkbox.

FIGURE 30.3

*The Check Box
Form Field
Options
dialog box*

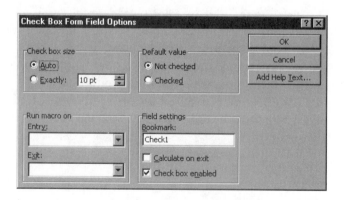

- **Default Value:** Choose Not Checked or Checked as the default value for the checkbox—that is, whether it should be checked or unchecked when the user opens the form.
- **Run Macro On:** To run a macro when the user enters or exits the form field, specify the name of the macro in the Entry or Exit box.
- **Bookmark:** Type a bookmark name to be associated with the field. You can use the bookmark name in macros to take an action based on the status of the checkbox.
- **Calculate on Exit:** Check this box to have Word recalculate any expressions that use the bookmark for this field.
- **Check Box Enabled:** Clear this checkbox to make the form field read-only for users.
- **Add Help Text:** Click on this button to display the Form Field Help Text dialog box so that you can enter help messages.

3. When you've chosen your options, click on OK to close the Check Box Form Field Options dialog box.

Adding a Text Form Field

A *text form field* allows the user to enter text. You can limit the text entry to a certain number of characters or a certain type of entry, and you can provide default text to show the user the type of text (or indeed the answer!) that you are expecting. The form shown in Figure 30.1 has four text fields—for the date and time started and the date and time finished. These have been formatted so that the user can enter only a valid date or time.

Here's how to insert a text form field:

1. Place the insertion point where you want the text form field to appear. Again, you'll need to have some text explaining what the box is all about.
2. Click on the Text Form Field button in the Forms toolbar.

3. Double-click on the form field, or click on the Form Field Options button in the Forms toolbar to display the Text Form Field Options dialog box (see Figure 30.4).
4. The following options are available in the dialog box:

- **Type:** Select the type of text form field you want—Regular Text, Number, Date, Current Date, Current Time, or Calculation.
- **Default Text:** Enter any text you want to be displayed by default when the user opens the form. (This field changes to Expression when you choose Calculation in the Type box.)

FIGURE 30.4

*The Text Form
Field Options
dialog box.*

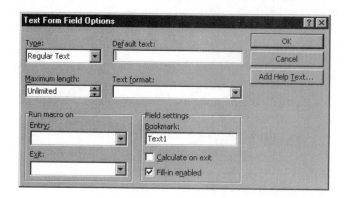

- **Maximum Length:** Enter the number of characters you want the form field to accept.
- **Text Format:** Select the format for the data in the form field.
- **Run Macro On:** To run a macro when the user enters or exits the form field, specify the macro in the Entry or Exit box.
- **Bookmark:** Type a bookmark name to be associated with the field. Macros reference bookmark names.
- **Calculate on Exit:** Check this box to have Word recalculate any expressions that use the bookmark for this field.
- **Fill-in Enabled:** Clear this to make the form field read-only for users. For example, Billy's supervisor might want to fill in the task description for each job and then disable the field before passing the form on to him.
- **Add Help Text:** Click on this button to display the Form Field Help Text dialog box so that you can enter help messages.

5. When you've chosen your options, click on OK to close the Text Form Field Options dialog box.

Your choices in the Text Format list depend on the type. For Regular Text, you can choose uppercase, lowercase, first capital, and title case. With date and time types, you

Choosing the Text Form Field Type

What are all the types for if the field is called a Text Form Field? If you select *Regular Text,* you can enter anything in the text box up to the Maximum Length setting. (Use this when you don't need to limit the type of text entry in any way.)

Choose the *Number* type when you want the user to enter only numeric values in a text box. For example, if the box is labeled Age, select the Number type so that the user cannot type **forty**.

Choose *Date* when you want only date entries in a text box.

Choose *Current Date* or *Current Time* to have the current date or time entered automatically into a text box. The user will be unable to enter any text there.

Choose *Calculation* to compute a value based on other fields or table cells, such as multiplying the bookmark Total times the bookmark TaxRate to display the tax due on the invoice. Like the Current Date and Current Time types of text boxes, a Calculation text box cannot be altered by the user.

can select a date or time format. For number and calculation types, select a numeric format in the Number Format text box, and then choose from the following examples:

Option	Display
0	123456
0.00	12345.67
#,##0	12,346
#,##0.00	12.345.67
$#,##0.00;($#,##0.00)	$12,345.67
0%	12346%
0.00%	12345.67%

PART

VI

Power Tools

Adding a Drop-down List to a Form

Word gives you the option of adding drop-down lists to your forms, which can greatly help users and speed their input. Drop-down lists can also help you by restricting the information users can enter in the fields. If you only ship by UPS or DHL, for example, you can restrict the entry to those two companies.

The Unincorporated Inc. job log contains a drop-down list of employee names:

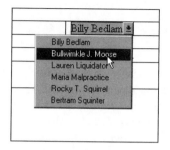

Users must select a name from the list; they cannot enter the name of a nonexistent employee to boost their own income.

To add a drop-down list to your form, follow these steps:

1. Place the insertion point where you want the drop-down list to appear.

2. Click on the Drop-Down Form Field button in the Forms toolbar.

3. Double-click on the form field, or click on the Form Field Options button in the Forms toolbar to display the Drop-Down Form Field Options dialog box (see Figure 30.5).

4. In the Drop-Down Item text box, type the items for the drop-down list to its right, clicking on the Add button to add each new item to the list.

- To remove an item from the drop-down list, select it in the Items in Drop-Down List box and click on the Remove button.
- To rearrange the items in the drop-down list, highlight the item to move and use the Move arrows to move it up or down.

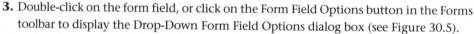

The Drop-Down Form Field Options dialog box

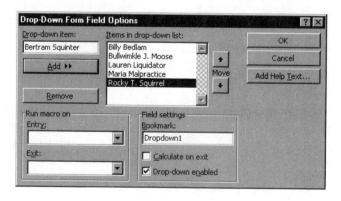

5. Choose options in the dialog box:

- **Run Macro On:** To run a macro when the user enters or exits the form field, specify the macro in the Entry or Exit box.
- **Bookmark:** Type a bookmark name to be associated with the field. Macros reference bookmark names.
- **Calculate on Exit:** Check this box to have Word recalculate any expressions that use the bookmark for this field.
- **Drop-down Enabled:** Clear this checkbox to prevent the user from selecting from the list. For example, to prevent Billy Bedlam from falsely attributing a dubious job report to Bullwinkle J. Moose, the supervisor might select Billy's name, lock the field, and forward the form to him.
- **Add Help Text:** Click on this button to display the Form Field Help Text dialog box so that you can enter help messages.

6. When you've chosen your options, click on OK to close the Drop-Down Form Field Options dialog box.

Naming Form Fields

When you insert a form field, a bookmark is automatically created that names the form field and refers to it. By default, Word chooses sequential names for your form fields—Text1, Text2, Text3; Check1, Check2; Dropdown1, Dropdown2; and so on. You can override this default, though, and give your form fields any names (any bookmarks) you want. Why would you want to do this? To make them easier to track, especially if you are referring to your bookmarks with field codes or macros.

You can name a form field as you're inserting it or at any later time.

To name a form field after you've already inserted it, double-click on the field to display the appropriate Options dialog box. You can also position the mouse pointer over the form field, click the right mouse button, and choose Properties from the menu that appears. Type a name in the Bookmark box in the Field Settings area and click on OK.

NOTE To edit a form field or to search for a form field, the form must be unprotected. See "Protecting a Form" later in this chapter.

Finding a Form Field

Suppose you need to fill in or modify a single field or a few fields in a large form. To find a form field, you must know its name (the bookmark that refers to it). If you know the name, you can find it in two ways. Here's the first way:

1. Choose Insert ➤ Bookmark. Word displays the Bookmark dialog box:

2. Select the bookmark (form field) you want.
3. Click on the Go To button.

Here's the second way:

1. Choose Edit ➤ Go To (Ctrl+G). Word displays the Go To tab of the Find and Replace dialog box:

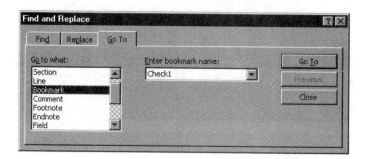

2. Select Bookmark in the Go to What list box.

3. Choose the bookmark (form field) you want from the Enter Bookmark Name drop-down list box.

4. Click on the Go To button.

Take your pick.

Formatting Form Fields

If you want the text entered or selected in a form field to be formatted, you have to format the fields yourself before protecting the document. Users will not be able to format the text they enter or select.

NOTE To format a form, the form must be unprotected. See "Protecting a Form" later in this chapter.

The best time to format a field is right after inserting it. You have all the usual methods available to you for character and paragraph formatting. Select the field, and then you can:

- Pull down the Format menu, select a formatting choice, and choose the type of formatting you want (for example, Format ➤ Font, Bold, OK).
- Click on the field with the right mouse button, select a formatting choice from the drop-down menu that pops up, and choose the type of formatting you want (for example, right mouse click, Font, Bold, OK).
- Click on a formatting button on the Formatting toolbar (for example, click on the Bold button).
- Press a keyboard shortcut (for example, Ctrl+B).

Adding Help Text to a Form

As mentioned in the previous sections, you can add help text to your form fields to assist the user. Just keep in mind that you can't actually access the help information until you've protected the form. Here's how to add help text to a form:

1. Double-click on the form field to display the Form Field Options dialog box. (Exactly *which* form field options dialog box will appear depends on the type of form field you select.)

PART

VI

Power Tools

2. Click on the Add Help Text button. Word displays the Form Field Help Text dialog box.

- To add a status bar entry, select the Status Bar tab.
- To add a help key entry, select the Help Key tab.

Figure 30.6 shows the Form Field Help Text dialog box with the Status Bar tab selected. This is perhaps the more useful option for short entries because the help text will appear in the status bar when the user encounters the field. (With Help Key entries, the user must press F1 to display the help, which appears in a message box.)

3. Choose the entry you want:

- **None:** Turns off the help text.
- **AutoText Entry:** Lets you choose an existing AutoText entry from the drop-down list.
- **Type Your Own:** Lets you do just that, to a maximum of 255 characters.

4. Click on OK to close the Form Field Help Text dialog box and then click on OK in the Form Field Options dialog box.

Protecting a Form

What's all this about protecting a form? Well, you use a form by restricting access to the form fields and other unprotected sections. This means that the user can only:

- Enter text in enabled text form field boxes.
- Click on enabled checkboxes.

- Select from an enabled list.
- Type in sections designated as unprotected.

Users cannot move the insertion point to other areas of the form, edit, format, or change it in any other way. Pressing Tab will take them from form field to form field without stopping in table cells, text boxes, or other text that they cannot modify. So, you need to protect a form before the checkboxes, text boxes, drop-down lists, and help features will work.

> **TIP**
>
> If the Forms toolbar is displayed, click on the Protect Form button in that toolbar to toggle off or on form protection.

Here's how to protect a form:

1. With the form open and in the current window, choose Tools ➤ Protect Document.

2. In the Protect Document dialog box (see Figure 30.7), select the Forms option button.

FIGURE 30.7

Choose the Forms option button in the Protect Document dialog box to protect your form. Enter a password if you like.

3. To protect some sections of the form but not others, select the Sections button (which will be dimmed if unavailable—for example, if your document doesn't have sections), and in the Section Protection dialog box that appears (see below), check the checkboxes for the sections you want to protect.

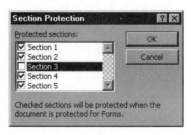

PART

VI

Power Tools

4. To assign a password to the form, type one in the Password box. Word will display asterisks (for the benefit of anyone reading over your shoulder) for each character you type, and when you select OK, Word will ask you to reenter the password in the Confirm Password dialog box.

WARNING

Passwords can be a maximum of 15 characters and can contain letters, numbers, symbols, and spaces. They're case-sensitive—you must type upper- or lowercase letters correctly in the password each time.

To unprotect your form, choose Tools ➤ Unprotect Document, or click on the Protect Form button in the Forms toolbar. If you entered a password when protecting the document, Word displays the Unprotect Document dialog box in which you must enter the password. (If you get the password wrong, Word displays a dialog box telling you that this password is incorrect, whereupon you can try again. But don't worry—Word's not like one of those ATMs that retain your card "for your security" after you miskey your PIN three times. You can keep trying to get the password right until the cows come home.)

Disabling Specific Form Fields

In addition to the document protection, which you must turn on to activate your form fields, you may also want to disable certain form fields to prevent the user from altering them. To disable a form field, follow these steps:

1. Unprotect the document if it's already protected.
2. Double-click on the form field to display its Options dialog box (or click the right mouse button and choose Properties).
3. Uncheck the Enabled (Check Box Enabled, Fill-in Enabled, Drop-Down Enabled) option in the Field Settings area.
4. Click on OK.

NOTE

Remember, even though you enable a field in the Options dialog box, the form must be protected before you can actually use the form fields.

Filling In an Online Form

When you've finished creating and editing your form, set protection as described in the earlier section "Protecting a Form," and save it as a template rather than as a document. You (or someone else) can then open copies of the form on any computer that can access the template and fill them in online.

With protection set, Word prevents the user from accessing anything but the form fields; the user can move from one form field to the next by pressing Tab.

Printing a Form's Data but Not the Form Itself

You can print the data in a form without printing the form itself. You might want to do this to fill in a preexisting paper form, such as a government form. You would set up your form template in Word to match exactly the target form and print only the data in the form. (Needless to say, this would take a *lot* of careful measuring and might not be worth the headache.) The data would then be printed in the correct areas of the target form.

To print a form's data without printing the form itself, follow these steps:

1. Choose Tools ➤ Options to display the Options dialog box.
2. Select the Print tab.
3. Check the Print Data Only for Forms checkbox in the Options for This Document Only area; then click on OK.

Printing a Form along with Its Data

To print the entire form, both its structure and contents, simply print the finished document the normal way. You can:

- Click on the Print button on the Standard toolbar.
- Choose File ➤ Print (Ctrl+P) and click on OK.

Printing a Blank Form

If you want to print out an empty form to keep a printed version of the blank form handy, simply open a new copy of the form from the template and then follow these steps:

1. Choose File ➤ New or press Ctrl+N, but don't click on the New File button on the Standard toolbar.

2. Select your form from the list in the Template dialog box.

3. Click on OK.

4. Click on the Print button on the Standard toolbar or select File ➤ Print (Ctrl+P) and click on OK.

Saving a Form's Data but Not the Form Itself

Similarly, you can save the data in a form without saving the form itself. This is useful for saving form data as a single record to use in a database. Here's how:

1. Choose Tools ➤ Options to display the Options dialog box.

2. Select the Save tab.

3. Check the Save Data Only for Forms checkbox, and then click on OK.

NOTE

Of course, to save the form with the entered data, simply save the form as you would any Word document: Click on the Save button on the Standard toolbar or select File ➤ Save (Ctrl+S).

Attaching Macros to a Form

As mentioned earlier in this chapter, you can attach both AutoText and macros to a form by making the original file a template rather than a document. We'll get into macros in the next chapter, but I should just mention here that forms are a classic place to use some of Word's autoexecuting macros:

Macro Name	Effect and Use
AutoNew	Runs whenever you open a new document based on the template to which it is attached
AutoOpen	Runs whenever you open an existing document based on the template to which it is attached
AutoClose	Runs whenever you close a document based on the template to which it is attached

You might set up an AutoNew macro to arrange the form for filling in—you could display on the screen toolbars the user might need and remove ones not needed, maximize the screen display, automatically update selected fields or the information available for them, or display a help message. You could write an AutoOpen macro that would advise users when the form was last updated and advise them to save a backup copy under a different name before they destroy your precious data. Finally, an AutoClose macro could back up the changes to the form to a different folder or drive, restore general screen preferences, display a message box advising the user to update other connected forms, and so on. You get the idea.

MASTERING THE OPPORTUNITIES

Creating a Form with Fill-in Dialog Boxes

If you are creating a form that will reuse the same information in several places, you might want to use field codes rather than form fields. This way you can enter, store, and reuse text so that the text entered in one location can be reused in all the other form fields that require the same information. Entries such as names and addresses are especially suited to this approach.

It is easy if you use the ASK field that you learned about in the last chapter. Add the field to ask for the information you want to repeat, as in:

{ ASK CustName "Type the customer's name" }

You can then reuse the bookmark value throughout the form with a field, like so:

{ CustName }

Using ActiveX Fields

If you are creating an interactive form for the World Wide Web, you should learn about ActiveX fields. As I mentioned in Chapter 28, *Linking and Embedding to Keep Things Current*, ActiveX provides controls, such as checkboxes and lists, to create interactive Web pages.

They are as easy to add as form fields, but much more difficult to use. Although you can control form fields using the Form Field Options dialog box, you have to program ActiveX controls by writing macros in Visual Basic for Applications. VBA macros are a little beyond the scope of this chapter, but here's how to add an ActiveX control to a form or to any document that you plan to publish on the Web:

1. Right-click on any toolbar, and then click on the Control Toolbox option to see the toolbar shown in Figure 30.8 You can also select View ➤ Toolbars and then click on Control Toolbox.

PART

VI

Power Tools

FIGURE 30.8

*The Control
Toolbox for
adding ActiveX
controls*

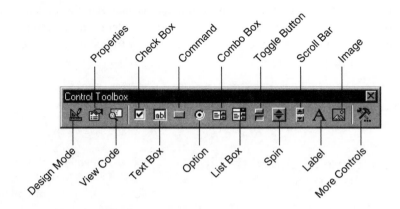

2. Click on the button for the control you want to insert. Word places the control at the location of the insertion point, surrounded by handles as shown here:

3. Drag the control to where you want it in the document.
4. Drag the handles to resize the control as desired.
5. Click outside the control.

To see even more ActiveX controls, click on the More Controls button in the Control Toolbox to see this list:

Scroll the list and click on the control that you want to enter.

To view and change the properties of a control, click on it to select it, and then click on the Properties button in the Control Toolbox. A window will appear containing a list of properties that you can adjust:

To write a Visual Basic for Applications macro that programs the control, double-click on it or click on the View Code button in the Control Toolbox. Word opens a Visual Basic window (see Figure 30.9) in which you can write the macro. Click on the window's Close box when you're done.

FIGURE 30.9

Use the Visual Basic window to write macros that program the ActiveX control.

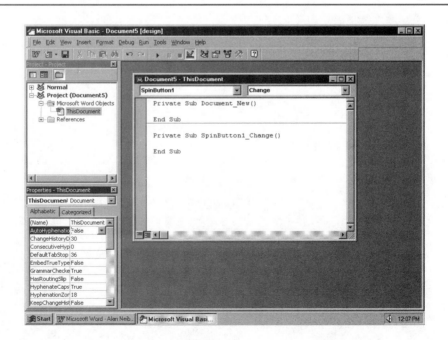

Chapter

31

Creating and Using Macros

Chapter 31

Creating and Using Macros

Most people are afraid of macros, which is a shame. Macros aren't nearly as bad as people make them out to be, and they can simplify your life considerably. All right, your work life. Macros are much more fun than having your teeth drilled. Once you get them working, they're even quicker.

First, we'll discuss what macros are and what they can do for you. Second, we'll look at Word's tools for creating, recording, editing, and running macros. Third, we'll discuss five automatic macros that every Word user should consider trying.

TIP

Macros don't have to be fancy. You can write macros that simply automate repetitive keystrokes and mouse clicks. Using such macros reduces the risk of repetitive stress disorders.

What Are Macros?

A macro is a series of Word commands grouped together as a single command to make everyday tasks easier. You can assign a macro to a toolbar, menu, or shortcut key (see Chapter 32, *Personalizing Word*, for more on this) and run it by simply clicking on a button, selecting a menu choice, or pressing a key combination. Macros can be stored either in document templates or in single Word documents. You can tailor macros to work with all your documents by keeping them in the Normal template, or you can create project-specific macros that you keep in a single Word document.

Macros are recorded as instructions in Microsoft's programming language, Visual Basic, so-called because it's the Basic language used by Word and other Microsoft programs. Don't let Visual Basic worry you; you can create macros without understanding a single word of it.

You can create a macro in two ways:

- Record a series of actions using the keyboard and mouse. This is the easiest way.
- Type a macro directly into a macro-editing window. This way you have more flexibility and can include Visual Basic instructions that you can't record using the keyboard and mouse.

If you record a macro using the keyboard and mouse, you can then open it in the macro-editing window and edit it. Often the best way to create a macro is to record as much of it as possible using the keyboard and mouse and then to edit it and add further Visual Basic instructions in the macro-editing window.

How You Might Use Macros

So what would you actually *use* a macro for? Well, several things: to perform routine editing and formatting tasks faster; to combine several commands that you always have to perform in sequence; to instantly adjust an option in a remote dialog box (for example, to change printers and set printer options with one keystroke); or to automate a complex series of tasks.

For example, say you write your reports with the body text in double-spaced Courier 12-point with 1" margins all the way around your paper. You print out drafts like that—nice and easy to read, and you don't care how typewriterish it looks—but when you print out your final report, it needs to look completely different, single-spaced 10-point Times Roman for the body text, three levels of headings in different sizes of a display font such as Braggadocio, 1.5" margins. Oh, and you always forget to run a spelling and grammar check before you print it. You could write a macro to:

- Change the body text to 10-point Times Roman.
- Apply the three heading styles to the relevant paragraphs.
- Adjust the margins and line spacing.
- Force you to check the spelling and grammar.

You gotta admit that beats dentistry any day.

Things You Can Do without Using Macros

Of course, macros are hardly the only form of automated convenience that Word offers. Before delving into the challenging process of recording a custom macro to create a shortcut, consider first whether you can achieve the effect you want with Styles, the Style Gallery, AutoFormat, AutoCorrect, AutoText, the Spike, Bookmarks, Field Codes, Form Fields, or even Find and Replace. Some of these tools can also be used in combination with macros.

- Styles help automate the formatting process, allowing you to apply multiple character and paragraph formats to separate text elements in a single step. They also allow you to change formatting consistently throughout your document. Styles are covered in Chapter 12, *Using Paragraph Styles and AutoFormat*.
- AutoFormat takes a lot of the formatting decisions out of your hands but gives you a lot of control over accepting or rejecting its suggestions. AutoFormat is also covered in Chapter 12, *Using Paragraph Styles and AutoFormat*.
- AutoCorrect is designed to fix your typos as you make them, but you can also add abbreviations to it that are automatically expanded into their full references as soon as you type them. AutoCorrect is covered in Chapter 14, *End Monotony with AutoText, AutoCorrect, and Insert AutoText*.
- AutoText is an even more sophisticated way to create abbreviations and store boilerplate text for reuse. AutoText is also covered in Chapter 14, *End Monotony with AutoText, AutoCorrect, and Insert AutoText*.
- The Spike enables you to skim through a document, pull out specific pieces of it, and then deposit them all in another location.
- Bookmarks make it easier for you to navigate through your documents and can also play the role of variables with field codes and macros. Bookmarks are covered in Chapter 22, *Bookmarks, Captions, and Cross-Referencing*.
- Field codes produce a result or start a macro somewhere in the document. They can interact with the user, taking and storing input or even producing varying results depending on the user's entry. Field codes are covered in Chapter 29, *Creating and Using Fields*.
- Form Fields can automate the process of creating a document or filling out a form. They can also be combined with field codes to take user input and reuse it throughout a document. Form Fields are covered in Chapter 30, *Creating and Using Forms and ActiveX Controls*.
- Find and Replace can automate some of your editing, particularly when you need to make identical or similar changes throughout a document. With advanced Replace features, you can carefully fine-tune what gets changed and what does not. Find and Replace are covered in Chapter 16, *Finding and Replacing*.

PART

VI

Power Tools

The Record Macro Dialog Box

The Record Macro dialog box appears whenever you start the Macro Recorder. It contains two buttons, a name box, a Store Macro In drop-down list box, and a description text box, as shown in Figure 31.1.

The name text box, as you might guess, lets you name your macro, and the description text box gives you space to describe your creation. The Toolbars and Keyboard buttons, as their names indicate, offer the option of assigning a keyboard or menu shortcut to your macro. The drop-down list box called Store Macro In lets you choose where you want your macro to live—that is, to indicate to which kinds of documents or templates your macro will be available.

FIGURE 31.1

*The Record
Macro
dialog box*

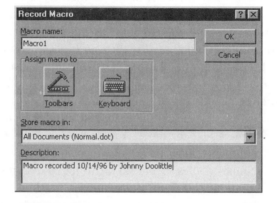

Recording Your Own Macros

To record your own macros, you start the Word Macro Recorder and record a sequence of actions. You then stop the recorder and edit the macro if need be. You can then run the macro whenever you need to perform the same sequence of actions.

Things to Do before Recording a Macro

Before you actually start recording your macro, be sure that the Word workspace is in roughly the same shape it will be in whenever you run the macro. If you end up doing some "housecleaning" while recording the macro, all those steps will be included in the macro as well and often won't make sense.

NOTE

On the other hand, you can save some tasks—such as going to the top of the document—for the beginning of the macro, if they're going to be necessary every time the macro runs.

It's good to think about what position your documents will be in when you run your new macro on them. It helps clarify the steps that will be needed when you start recording the macro. Before you begin recording a macro, follow these steps:

1. Be sure you've got open the kind of document in which you'll use your macro. If you'll want your macro available to all documents, open a document from the Normal template. (You can also choose to which documents you want to assign your macro from the Macros dialog box.)

2. Run through the procedure without recording it to notice all the steps. (It's easy to forget the details!)

3. If the macro involves selecting something, decide if you want to make the selection before the recording (in which case the macro will work properly only after you've selected something) or after.

4. Think up a good name for the macro.

5. Decide if you'll want a keyboard shortcut for it (and think of one easy to remember) or if you'll want it on a toolbar. You can do both if you wish.

Thinking Through the Steps Ahead of Time

Here's an example. Let's take a look at creating a simple macro to maximize the space available on the screen. Although the results of this macro might remind you of Word 97's Full Screen feature, it leaves those nice little view buttons at the bottom of the screen so that you can quickly switch from Outline to Normal to Full Page views and back. It's also a great way to see the many considerations you'll face when creating your own macros. You need to do the following:

- Maximize Word.
- Maximize the document window.
- Hide the horizontal ruler, the toolbars, the scroll bars, and the status bar.

To do this with the mouse or keyboard would involve a series of simple actions staggeringly tedious to repeat; so this is a great candidate for a macro.

Starting the Macro Recorder

To start the Macro Recorder, you first need to open the Record Macro dialog box. You can do so in two ways:

- Double-click on REC on the status bar. This is the quick and easy way.

PART

VI

Power Tools

- Choose Tools ➤ Macro ➤ Record New Macro.

NOTE You can also create a macro by writing it from scratch in the Microsoft Visual Basic Editor. We'll cover that later in this chapter.

Record the Macro

Let's look at the steps for recording a macro, and then let's record the one proposed above.

1. Start the Macro Recorder by double-clicking on REC on the status bar.

2. In the Record Macro dialog box (see Figure 31.1, earlier in this chapter), enter a name for the macro in the Record Macro Name text box.

- If you don't give your macro a name, Word will name it Macro1, Macro2, and so on. This is all fine and convenient for the time being or for temporary macros, but unless you rename your macros, the default names will be most uninformative after a while.

- No spaces, commas, or periods are allowed in the name.

3. Enter a description of what the macro does in the Description box. Word automatically includes your name and the current date, as in *Macro created 9/16/97 by Johnny Doolittle*. Adding other text is optional but strongly recommended, even if it's only *Second try at infernal formatting maneuver. Delete tomorrow*. This description will appear in the Customize dialog box when you add macros to toolbars or menus, so adding details other than the name and date may help you remember its purpose. You've got a maximum of 255 characters; so get typing.

4. To assign the macro to a toolbar or a keyboard shortcut, click on the Toolbars or Keyboard button. This will fire up either the Customize Keyboard dialog box or the Customize dialog box with the Commands tab selected. See Chapter 32, *Personalizing Word*, for details on assigning macros not only to the toolbars and the keyboard, but to menus as well. Or just follow your instincts. I've assigned the FixUpMyScreen macro to Shift+Ctrl+X in Figure 31.2.

NOTE If you choose to add a macro to a toolbar or to create a keyboard shortcut, clicking on Close in the Customize dialog box or Customize Keyboard dialog box will automatically start recording the macro.

FIGURE 31.2

I'm assigning the FixUpMy-Screen macro to the keyboard shortcut Shift+Ctrl+X in the Customize dialog box.

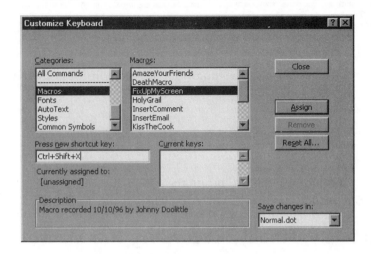

5. If your current document is attached to a template or document other than Normal, drop down the Save Changes In list box and select either that document, another template, or Normal. Selecting Normal will make the macro available at all times.

> **NOTE**
>
> If the current document is attached to Normal, Word will automatically store the macro there.

6. Click on OK. Now you can finally start recording your macro.

The Macro Recorder toolbar will appear on the screen:

It has two buttons—from left to right, a stop button and a pause button (sort of like a tape recorder, right? So where's the fast forward?). The little mini-control menu in the upper left corner of the Macro Recorder toolbar just closes the toolbar without stopping recording. If you click on it by mistake, you'll need to choose Tools ➤ Macro ➤ Stop Recording to stop the recording.

PART

VI

Power Tools

A handy trick to know is that if you accidentally close the Macro Record toolbar, you can end the macro by double-clicking on the REC button in the status area again.

Notice also that the mouse pointer gets a little cassette tape icon attached to it, to remind you that you're recording.

Notice also the REC box in the status bar becomes highlighted. This is also supposed to remind you that you're recording.

Actually, Finally, Recording the Macro

Now, perform the actions you want to record. If you stopped the Macro Recorder, start it up again! Here are the steps for recording the FixUpMyScreen macro:

1. Click on Word's maximize button to maximize Word.
2. Click on the document window's maximize button to maximize the document window.
3. Choose View ➤ Ruler to turn off the ruler. (If that turns the ruler on rather than off, don't worry—we'll fix the problem when we edit the macro.)
4. Choose Tools ➤ Options to display the Options dialog box; and then choose the View tab. Uncheck the checkboxes for Horizontal Scroll Bar, Vertical Scroll Bar, and Status Bar, and then click on OK.
5. Choose View ➤ Toolbars ➤ Standard and uncheck the Standard checkbox.
6. Choose View ➤ Toolbars ➤ Formatting and uncheck the Formatting checkbox.
7. To stop recording the macro, click on the Stop button on the Macro Recorder toolbar (or double-click on the word REC in the status bar), and the Macro Recorder toolbar disappears.

There, one macro recorded! No pain, lots of gain, and no Novocain. We'll open the macro in a moment. But first, a brief intermission.

What Gets Recorded and What Doesn't

Technically, the macro recorder does not record *actions* that you perform. It records the *commands*, the results of your actions. When you change something about your document while recording the macro, the macro remembers what you changed it to, not what it used to be.

WARNING

Some Word commands simply toggle between two possibilities, such as Show/Hide. For commands of that sort, the macro recorder will only record that the status was changed. When played back, the macro will change the status without regard to which toggle position it started in.

If you choose commands from a dialog box, you must click on OK for the result to be recorded. And clicking on OK in a dialog box records the selected state, including all defaults, of every option *in that tab* of the dialog box. To record commands in another tab of the same dialog box, you must open the dialog box again, switch to the other tab, make your selections, and click on OK again.

The Macro Recorder generally does not record mouse motions. Well, that's not exactly right. You choose commands by pulling down menus and clicking on toolbar icons with the mouse, and those results will be recorded, but you can't select (and therefore also can't drag and drop, of course) text or other elements of your document with the mouse.

NOTE

You can, of course, select text, copy it, paste it, cut it, and move it with the keyboard shortcuts. Select text by holding down Shift and pressing the arrow keys and other movement keys (or by using the Extend command—F8—and the arrow and movement keys). Press Ctrl+C to copy, Ctrl+V to paste, and Ctrl+X to cut. Use cut and paste together to move.

Because the macro recorder records results, not literal keystrokes, when you play back your macro, you won't see menus being pulled down and ghost mouse clicks like a player piano. You'll just see Word clinically and surgically executing your commands.

Taking a Break from Recording the Macro

Word allows you to suspend and resume recording a macro as you like. If you reach some impasse in the procedure that you don't want to record for posterity or if you only want to record isolated actions here and there as the fancy strikes you, here's what to do:

1. Click on the Pause button on the Macro Record toolbar to pause recording.
2. Perform the actions you don't want to record.
3. Click on the Pause button again to restart recording (just like a tape recorder!).

PART

VI

Power Tools

Solving Problems Recording a Macro

If you make a mistake while recording a macro, you can pause the macro as explained in the previous section and put the document back to the way it should be before continuing, or you can stop recording the macro and then start over from the beginning. The latter may be easier if you are near the beginning of the recording process.

NOTE

If you pause the macro recording and fool around with the document, you may still need to edit the macro when you're done to eliminate the mistake from the recording. Editing macros is covered later in this chapter.

If you choose some incorrect settings in a dialog box and can't remember what the original choices were, you can simply click the Cancel button or press Esc to close the dialog box without recording your incorrect selections. (Remember, the Macro Recorder will record your actions in a dialog box only if you click on OK when you are done.)

Another thing you can do is choose Edit ➤ Undo, press Ctrl+Z, or even click on the Undo drop-down list box on the Standard toolbar to undo your mistake. You must still check and edit the macro when you are finished, however, because the macro recorder will record both the incorrect action and the Undo. Not only is this confusing to anyone looking at the macro listing later (or watching it work), it may also give the wrong result. The Undo may only undo the last result of your previous action, if, as with some ruler, toolbar, or dialog box commands, there is more than one result.

Running a Macro

Once you have recorded a macro, you can play it back in a number of ways. You should test your macro on a saved document right away to make sure it's working correctly. If it isn't, either edit it, as explained in the next section, or record it again from scratch.

Here are the ways to run a macro:

- Choose Tools ➤ Macro ➤ Macros to open the Macros dialog box (see Figure 31.3). From this dialog box, you can choose your macro and click on the Run button.
- Click on a MACROBUTTON field code in a document (as explained in Chapter 29, *Creating and Using Fields*).
- Run another macro that itself runs this macro.
- Select the macro's menu command.
- Click on the macro's toolbar icon.
- Press the macro's keyboard shortcut.

FIGURE 31.3

In the Macros
dialog box,
you can choose
any of your
macros for
running,
editing, or
deletion.

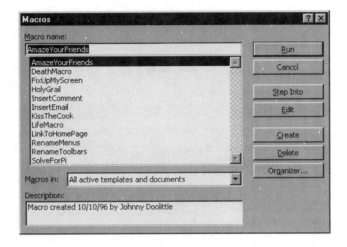

TIP

If you can't find a macro later when you try to run it, chances are you assigned the macro to a specific template or document and now have a different template or document open. Or, if you've changed global templates recently, you may not have the same selection of macros available. Go back to your old global template, and your macros may reside there.

PART

VI

Assigning a Macro to a Toolbar, Menu, or Keyboard Shortcut after the Fact

Of course, the last two options above will be available to you only if, when you first started the recording process, you assigned the macro to a toolbar or created a keyboard shortcut. If you did not do it then and wish you had, things get a little trickier.

To add a macro to a toolbar or a menu, follow these steps:

1. Choose Tools ➤ Customize to open the Customize dialog box, as seen in Figure 31.4.
2. Select the Commands tab.
3. Select Macros in the Category box.
4. Choose the macro you want to assign and highlight it by single-clicking on its name.
5. Drag the macro you want to a toolbar or menu, position it as you like, and let go. If you decide to delete it later, simply right-click on its icon. (If you don't see an icon, open the Customize dialog box before you move or delete the macro from the toolbar.)
6. If the toolbar you want to add to isn't showing, select the Toobars tab and check the checkbox in front of that toolbar's name.

Power Tools

FIGURE 31.4

In the Custom-ize dialog box, you can, among other things, add macros to menus or tool-bars or create keyboard shortcuts.

Making a keyboard shortcut for a macro is quite similar. Follow these steps:

1. Choose Tools ➤ Customize to open the Customize dialog box, as seen in Figure 31.4.

2. Click on the Keyboard button.

3. Select Macros in the Category list box.

4. Choose the macro you want to assign and highlight it by single-clicking on its name.

5. Click in the Shortcut Key text box, and press the keys you'd like for the shortcut. If the shortcut is already taken, Word will inform you.

6. Click on Assign to assign the macro to the shortcut you just chose.

Macros That Start Themselves

AutoNew, AutoOpen, AutoClose, AutoExec, and AutoExit macros (they are all explained later in this chapter) run when certain events occur. As you might imagine, they behave as follows:

- AutoNew macros start when you create a new document based on the template in which the macro is stored.
- AutoOpen macros start when you open a document containing them.
- AutoClose macros start when you close a document containing them.
- AutoExec macros run whenever you start Word.
- AutoExit macros run when you exit Word or unload the global template in which they reside.

You can also run Auto macros in all the ways that you run normal macros.

Running a Macro from the Macro Dialog Box

Whether or not you've assigned your macro to a menu, toolbar, or keyboard shortcut, you can always run any macro from the Macro dialog box. Follow these steps:

1. Choose Tools ➤ Macro ➤ Macros to open the Macros dialog box (see Figure 31.3, earlier in this chapter).
2. Select the macro you want to run. (If you don't see the macro you want, change the selection in the Macros Available In list box to the template containing the macro.)
3. Click on the Run button.

Editing Macros

Once you've recorded a macro, you can edit and run it. Often, you'll want to edit macros before running them, either to remove flaws recorded in the macro or to enhance the macro with Visual Basic commands that you cannot record.

Here's how to edit a macro:

1. Choose Tools ➤ Macro ➤ Macros to open the Macros dialog box.
2. Select the list of macros to choose from by dropping down the Macros Available In list box.
3. Choose the macro you want to edit; then click on the Edit button. Word launches a somewhat frightening-looking program called Microsoft Visual Basic (see Figure 31.5), which is used to create and edit all sorts of applications in the Microsoft universe.
4. The macros you've created have been saved to a *Module file* called NewMacros. All your macros will be displayed as one document.
5. To get to the macro you want to edit, you can scroll through the document, or you can select its name from a drop-down menu near the top right of the screen. If and when you begin to work in different macro modules, you can change modules from within the frame at the left of the Visual Basic editor window.
6. Edit the macro. It may sound a bit *too* easy, but some things will be obvious.

PART

VI

Power Tools

> **NOTE**
>
> If you turned your ruler on rather than switching it off, you can change the statement `ActiveWindow.ActivePane.DisplayRulers = True` to `ActiveWindow.ActivePane.DisplayRulers = False`. True and False, as the binary opposites they are, can be substituted for one another to change the result.

FIGURE 31.5

You can edit macros with Microsoft Visual Basic, shown here displaying the FixUpMy-Screen macro.

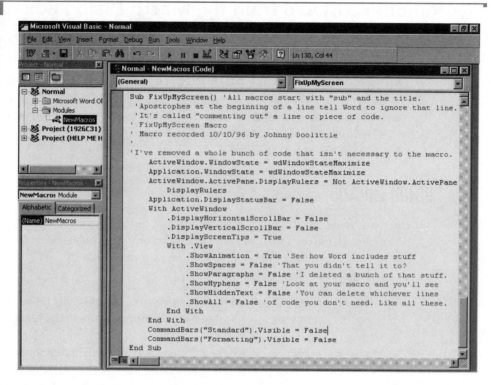

7. When you're done, close the file, and Visual Basic will save any changes to your macros.

NOTE

You'll notice that the macro appears in a window much like any normal Word document, except that it appears in the Visual Basic editing window. For your purposes, treat it as you would a Word document, and edit it as you would any document.

What is it that you'd want to edit here? Well, for instance, if you recorded some commands that you don't need, you can go ahead and delete them. Or if you accidentally turned the status bar *on* instead of switching it *off*, you can change that now. The values used in Visual Basic are mostly *binary*—that is, they're simple yes and no choices. Here you'll find them expressed as either true or false. That's easy enough to fix. If you turned on the ruler, simply change the line that reads

```
Application.DisplayStatusBar = True
```

to

```
Application.DisplayStatusBar = False
```

It's that simple.

As you look over the listing of a macro, notice what was recorded and what wasn't. Again, the macro is not so much a recording of everything you did as a recording of the *results* of everything you did. If you made a mistake and then selected Undo, there will be at least one command line for the mistaken command and then an additional line for the Undo command. (You can delete both the mistake and the Undo line.)

Also, if you made selections from a dialog box, look at the commands that were recorded. You'll see that every element of the dialog box registered some setting, whether you changed the default or not. When editing a macro, you can remove the parts of commands (the arguments) that are irrelevant to your purposes. It's not necessary to do that, but it does make the macro easier to read and interpret if you need to edit it again or see what it does later.

TIP

When you finish recording your macro, it will automatically be saved in whatever template you selected when you started recording. When you edit a macro in Visual Basic, however, you may want to save your changes periodically. You can do this just as you would save any Word document, only you're saving from the Visual Basic editor. When you close the macro document window or close Visual Basic itself, your changes will be saved automatically.

Organizing Your Macros

Word's Organizer dialog box simplifies managing your macros. You can use it to move, copy, or rename a macro. By default, macros are stored in the Global template in Normal as a Visual Basic module called NewMacros. The Normal macros are available for use with every Word document. You can, however, store them in other templates or even in single documents, if you wish. For example, if you have a macro that's only useful for annual reports, you might include it in your Annual Report template. Or if you created a macro that formatted lines in a poem, you may have saved it only in that file. (Although why you'd want to go to all the trouble of making a macro you'd only use once is beyond me.) If your spiffy macro is good enough to share with the rest of your files, the Organizer can help you move it to the Normal template or another central location.

Copying Macros from One Template to Another

Word lets you copy groups of macros easily from one template (or document) to another. For example, you can record or write a macro in an Annual Report template, then decide you want to make it available to your I'm Clever template, and transfer it across.

Macros are saved in modules, or groups. You can't transfer a single macro—only groups of macros. Here's how:

1. Choose Tools ➤ Macro ➤ Macros to open the Macros dialog box.
2. Click on the Organizer button to display the Organizer dialog box (see Figure 31.6).
3. Select the Macros Project Items tab.
4. If necessary, click on the Close File button to close documents you have open. The Close File button will then turn into an Open File button with which you can open the template or document containing the macro.
5. Select the macro group you want to copy, and then click on the Copy button.

TIP

Nearly all macro groups you'll create are called NewMacros. Before you move a group from one file to another, you might want to rename the group to prevent overwriting another set of macros. You can rename a group of macros by clicking on the Rename button in the Organizer dialog box.

FIGURE 31.6

In the Organizer dialog box, you can manage groups of macros with minimal effort.

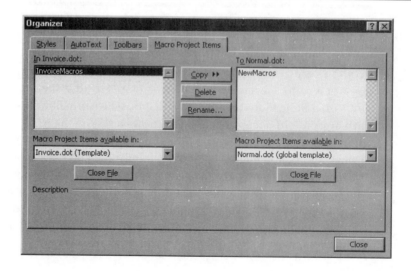

6. Click on the Close button when you've finished copying macros.

> **TIP**
>
> You can also get to the Organizer dialog box by choosing Tools ➤ Templates and Add-Ins and clicking on the Organizer button.

Renaming a Single Macro

If you give several macros in different templates the same name or if you record your macros as Macro1, Macro2, Macro3, and so on, you may want to rename macros at some point. Here's how to do it:

1. Choose Tools ➤ Macro ➤ Macros to open the Macro dialog box.

2. Click on the Edit button. Microsoft Visual Basic will open, with your group of macros ready for editing.

3. Scroll through the text area until you find the macro you want to rename. We're going to change our Spiffy Macro into a Nifty Macro.

4. Where you see the text:

```
Sub Spiffy()
'
' Spiffy Macro
' Macro created 9/16/97 by Johnny Doolittle
```

change the word *Spiffy* to the word *Nifty* by editing it as you would any other document:

```
Sub Nifty()
'
' Nifty Macro
' Macro created 9/16/97 by Johnny Doolittle
```

5. Your changes are effective immediately on leaving the Visual Basic window. If you open the Macros dialog box, you'll see that your macro has successfully been renamed Nifty.

Renaming a Group of Macros

Renaming whole batches of macros is something you might want to do if you assign groups to templates or documents other than Normal and you want to swap whole batches of macros around. This is even easier than renaming a single macro:

1. Open the document or template that contains the macro group you want to rename.

2. Choose Tools ➤ Macro ➤ Macros to open the Macro dialog box.

3. Click on the Organizer button to open the Macro Organizer dialog box.

PART

VI

Power Tools

4. Highlight the name of the macro group you want to rename. It will usually be called NewMacros by default.

5. Click on the Rename button to open the Rename dialog box:

6. Type a new name for your macro group, and click on OK.

Your macro group is now renamed, and you can move it to another template or document without overwriting another group by the same name. (See above for details.)

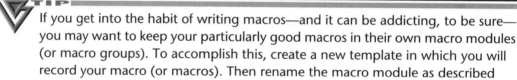

If you get into the habit of writing macros—and it can be addicting, to be sure— you may want to keep your particularly good macros in their own macro modules (or macro groups). To accomplish this, create a new template in which you will record your macro (or macros). Then rename the macro module as described above, and move it to any templates (including Normal) that you want to have access to this macro module.

Deleting a Macro

Getting rid of a macro you no longer need is easy and intuitive. Follow these steps:

1. Choose Tools ➤ Macro ➤ Macros to open the Macro dialog box.

2. Single-click on the name of the macro to delete.

3. Click on the Delete button. A dialog box will appear asking you to confirm your decision.

4. If you want to delete the macro, click on Yes. Word displays the Macro dialog box.

5. Click on the Close button to return to your document.

Sample Macros That Come with Word

Word supplies a bunch of sample macros that are built into sample templates stored in the Macros subfolder. One way to learn more about macros and get some practice editing them is to check out these sample macros.

As described in the previous section, you can copy any of these macros from the templates they are associated with to a new template using the Organizer. Once you've done that, you can run the macros, open them for editing, and change them, if you want, without harming the originals stored in the sample templates.

To access these macros, open `Microsoft Office\Office\Macros\Macros8.dot`. This template contains several macros that may be helpful to you; it also contains a Macros toolbar with easy access to these new macros. (See Chapter 32, *Personalizing Word*, for more information on adding macros to toolbars and moving toolbars between templates.)

> **NOTE**
>
> If you didn't install this template when you installed Word, you can find it on the CD in the Office\Macros folder.

The text of the template itself describes the functions of these macros, each of which is stored in an individual macro module so that you can move it from the Macros8.dot template to another template that you might want to have access to the macro. Let's take a quick look at these sample macros and what they can do for you.

The Macro	What it Does
AnsiValue	Pops up a dialog box displaying the numerical ANSI equivalent of the character or character string.
AutoCorrectUtil	Lets you move and make backups of AutoCorrect entries.
CopySpike	Customizes the Spike so that text will be copied rather than cut to it.
FindSymbol	Runs a Find dialog box that allows searching for symbols.
InsertFootnote	Launches Word's Footnote Wizard.
NormalViewHeaderFooter	Launches the Normal View HeaderFooter dialog box, which lets you create and edit a header or footer in Normal rather than Page Layout view.
SuperDocStatistics	Displays a SuperDocStatistics dialog box that contains much more information than the regular Properties dialog box, including which fonts, styles, and hyperlinks appear in the document.
TableCellHelper	Pops up a dialog box telling you how many columns and rows your table has and in which cell your cursor currently resides.

PART

VI

Power Tools

Those are the macros supplied with Word. Some of the macros listed above actually contain still more, smaller macros, the uses of which may not be apparent to you until you launch the Macros dialog box for the Macros8 template and start exploring. You might want to play with these macros within that template itself. When you're done, simply close Macros8 and tell Word that you don't want to save your changes.

NOTE

The `Microsoft Office\Office\Templates` folder contains a variety of templates to assist you in creating smart-looking letters, faxes, memos, and Web documents. Most of these templates contain a macro that automatically generates a file with detailed instructions on customizing the template. These macros might be good to look at if you want to automatically generate new files with a lot of formatting and text already in them. Some of the templates contain additional macros; dig around and see what looks useful to you.

Word's Automatic Macros

Even if you never get deeply into writing and using macros, you should look briefly at Word's five autoexecuting macros. With only a little effort, you can use these to set and restore screen preferences, open a bunch of documents, and generally make life a little more pleasant for you.

The five automatic macros are:

Macro Name	What It Does
AutoExec	Runs when you start Word
AutoNew	Runs when you open a new file
AutoOpen	Runs when you open a file you created before
AutoClose	Runs when you close a file (new or created before)
AutoExit	Runs when you exit Word

You can create automatic macros as you create any other macros—by typing the commands into the macro-editing window (reached by selecting the Edit or Create button in the Macro dialog box), by recording a series of actions, or by a judicious mixture of the two. The following sections suggest a few uses for these automatic macros; no doubt you'll quickly come up with your own uses.

Uses for an AutoExec Macro

If you don't like having Word automatically create a new document based on the Normal template whenever you start Word, you could write a brief AutoExec macro to specify a new document based on a different template, such as Special for You.

```
Sub AutoExec()
  Documents.Add Template:="C:\msoffice\Templates\Memos\Contemporary Memo.dot",
  NewTemplate:=False
End Sub
```

Or you could arrange to have Word open the same file—for example, a journal—whenever you start Word and go to either your last edit or the end:

```
Sub AutoExec()
  Documents.Open FileName:="mybig.doc"
End Sub
```

Get your imagination to work on a good AutoExec macro—it can improve your life.

Uses for an AutoOpen Macro

Although you can have only one AutoExec macro for your copy of Word, you can have a different AutoOpen macro for each template. As a result, you may want to use AutoOpen macros to customize the screen for templates, to display a message box to greet the user, or both:

```
Sub MAIN
Print "Hang on a tick while yer favorite template customizes yer screen..."
    Viewtoolbars .ColorButtons = 1, .LargeButtons = 1, .tooltips = 1
    Viewtoolbars .toolbar = "Standard", .Show
    Viewtoolbars .toolbar = "Formatting", .Show
    ViewRuler
MsgBox "Screen customized to your satisfaction—well, mine anyway.", "thank you!
  You are free to proceed!", 0 +48"
End Sub
```

Or you could use an AutoOpen macro to insert a date, refresh a field, or go to a bookmark in your Word document.

Uses for an AutoNew Macro

You can use an AutoNew macro in ways that are similar to the ways you use an AutoOpen macro to set up the screen and options for a given template. But you might also want to

PART

VI

Power Tools

ensure that the user saves the file immediately to prevent lost data and gives it the necessary summary information for you to keep track of things:

```
Sub MAIN
Dim SaveNow As FileSaveAs
Dialog(SaveNow)
Dim SumItAllUp As FileSummaryInfo
Dialog(SumItAllUp)
End Sub
```

Here (in the custom SaveNow dialog box that would be displayed by the `Dialog` [SaveNow] command) the user is automatically asked to save the document. Other possibilities include setting up the screen to suit the user or document, or initializing your Word session by filling out form fields or plugging in dates and names.

Uses for an AutoClose Macro

The AutoClose macro is the perfect choice for either restoring screen preferences for documents using other templates or, as in the example below, backing up the file being closed to a file server or backup drive:

```
Sub MAIN
    ClosingFile$ = FileName$()
    FileClose 1
    Copyfile ClosingFile$, "f:\ronstuff\worddocs\backup"
    MsgBox "Backed up your file successfully!", "Backup",
    0 + 64
End Sub
```

You can also write AutoClose macros that will check field entries or print documents when you close Word. AutoClose macros can also be written to reset custom settings, change global templates, and fax or e-mail your documents when you're done.

NOTE As you can with the AutoOpen and AutoNew macros, you can have an AutoClose macro for each template. This gives you great flexibility.

Uses for an AutoExit Macro

An AutoExit macro runs whenever you quit Word. You might want to use it to reset any environment options that your other macros and templates are liable to change. That way, when you restart Word, all the settings will be as you like them.

Here's how you might turn off the toolbars that the AutoOpen macro turned on earlier:

```
Sub MAIN
    Viewtoolbars .toolbar = "Standard", .Hide
    Viewtoolbars .toolbar = "Formatting", .Hide
MsgBox "thank you for using your own copy of Word for Windows. Please have a
    good day.", "Drive Safely and Be Nice to Your Spouse", 0 +48
End Sub
```

Debugging Your Macros

If your macro is not working properly, you can use the Step button on the Debug toolbar to debug it. *Debugging* is a programming term for finding the errors in a program. As the macro executes, you can step through it one command at a time and figure out exactly when it goes wrong. (After a macro fails, the offending command is highlighted in red; so that should help too.)

If necessary, you may have to include special commands at various places in your macro to display the current contents of variables (see "Macros That Talk Back" later in this chapter).

Macro Virus Detection, Prevention, and Eradication

One of the downsides of a flexible application such as Microsoft Word that can embed macros in a document is that it can also contain macro viruses. When these macros are activated, their virus properties can make them replicate and infect the other documents and templates that reside on your hard drive. The least harmful of the virus family, macro viruses are relatively easy to prevent and get rid of.

What's a Macro Virus?

A virus, no matter what kind, is really just another piece of software. Software can consist of only a few lines of code—macros are mini-applications, and so are viruses. The difference between viruses and the kind of software you use on purpose is that viruses are designed to be annoying, or harmful, or both. Some viruses are particularly nasty—they often replicate themselves, filling up valuable disk space and memory until none is left. The Ebola of the virus world can eat your hard drive alive.

Macro viruses, on the other hand, are generally harmless; they're more like common colds than flesh-eating monstrosities. This kind of bug tends to annoy rather than destroy—creating odd messages in documents, making it difficult to perform routine tasks. However, the increased flexibility of Visual Basic as the programming

PART

VI

Power Tools

language for macros means that the chances are greater that a macro virus could drop another virus into the hard drive—one that could delete your system files or reformat your hard drive.

One thing that both kinds of viruses do is eat up valuable memory and disk space. If a virus is running in the background while you're unaware of its presence, it may be hogging memory you need to run other applications. And, since viruses can replicate themselves and take up file space, they may make some of your hard drive inaccessible because they're filling it with their own kind. Macro viruses may make your Word documents larger than necessary, achieving the same effect.

Both macros and viruses are often hidden from the general user, becoming apparent only when some trigger, such as keystrokes, a date, or an action in an application sets them off. The other good news, besides the fact that macro viruses are rarely, if ever, actually harmful, is that they're generally quite easy to cure.

WARNING

Macro viruses may tend to spread more rampantly now that macros can be added not only to templates but to single documents. This makes having a good virus protection program that much more important.

Preventing Macro Virus Infection

Although Microsoft Word itself doesn't come with virus eradication tools, it does include a handy warning screen, as seen in Figure 31.7, when you're about to open a document that contains foreign macros. Why would you get one of these documents? Well, if you retrieve a Word document from the network at your workplace or the Internet or if a co-worker gives you a Word file on disk or via e-mail, these documents may contain macros designed to make your life easier.

FIGURE 31.7

This dialog box warns you that you are about to open a document that contains foreign macros.

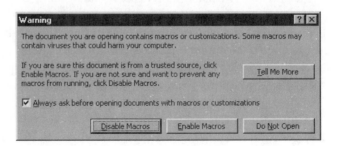

WARNING

Other applications in the Office 97 family, particularly Excel, can be affected by macro viruses as well. This is particularly true when you swap files back and forth regularly between Word and Excel. Although a Word macro virus can infect Excel documents, and vice versa, it's unlikely that the virus will be able to do much to the files of the other program other than take up space.

Unfortunately, like any other disease, your friend may not know that her hard drive is infected by a macro virus. Thus, she sends Word files to hill and dale, blissfully unaware that she's also sending viruses as stowaways.

If you get the dialog box seen in Figure 31.7, you have three options:

- **Enable Macros**   You can go ahead and open the document, macros and all. You can probably do this safely if it's a document from a trusted source, such as a knowledgeable co-worker or the tech support department of a company such as Microsoft itself.
- **Disable Macros**   You can open the document without macros. You won't be able to use these macros, obviously, but if the main goal of having the document is to read it, this is a good choice.
- **Do Not Open**   You can cancel and not open the document. This would be a good point at which to call your friend and ask about the macros she wrote (or if she knows her document has macros in it). Or you could run a virus protection program on the file before opening it again (more on that later).
- **Tell Me More**   This button will display more information about viruses, including how to download protection against them from the Internet.

Detecting Macro Virus Infections

So how do you know if you have a macro virus? Sometimes your virus sits there for quite a while, breeding happily and quietly, before it makes itself known to you. Sometimes Word begins to act strangely. Dialog boxes may appear with a strange message or no message at all. Strange phrases may show up in your document, sometimes from scratch and sometimes replacing text you've already typed. Or you may not be able to perform some normal functions, such as Save As or Close.

One way to find out if you have a macro virus (rather than elves) is to open the Macros dialog box and see if there are any strange macros you don't remember writing yourself or getting from a reliable source. This is one reason why the description field can come in handy—most macros you wrote yourself will have your name and a date in the description field, and macros from outer space usually won't.

If you aren't sure whether a macro is kosher or not, open it up in Visual Basic and scan the text to see whether it seems useful to you. If the text of the macro code contains a strange message or an odd name in comments, it may be a macro virus. You might even want to run it in a blank document to see what it does. Chances are that if you already have a macro virus, it's gone ahead and installed itself into the Normal template, and you have little to lose by running it to see what happens. If, after you either eyeball the text or run the macro, you can't tell what it does, and you don't use it anyway, go ahead and delete it.

Eliminating Infections

One way to get rid of macro viruses, as we just discussed, is to delete any unfamiliar macros that are in your macro files. This may only be a temporary fix, however. The one sure way to get rid of macro viruses—and other kinds of viruses your hard drive may have—is to get a virus protection program and run it regularly. These programs are available in stores as well as on the Internet. Try to select one, such as McAffee Virus Shield or Norton Anti-Virus, that is updated often. These two companies in particular search the world for new viruses and create software updates to get rid of these new plagues. Often, buying a virus protection program entitles the user to free updates via the Internet, but shareware programs may be a cheaper alternative.

TIP

Microsoft has various macro detectors and eradicators available for download from `http://www.microsoft.com/mswordsupport/content/macrovirus/page6.htm`.

Advanced Macros and Visual Basic

So far we have looked at how to record and edit simple macros in Word 97. Perhaps without even noticing it, you have been using the Visual Basic programming language. To enhance your macros and to add extra sophistication and elements to these little "programs," you need to know a little about Visual Basic. Don't worry about this too much. You have the advantage of being able to add new commands and utility to your macros one piece at a time. You can also learn the Visual Basic programming language a piece at a time, doing only what you need to achieve your macro's designed purpose. To write or edit a Visual Basic macro, you *do not* have to be a professional programmer. So relax, pour yourself your favorite beverage, and read on.

The Concept Virus

What a concept! The Concept Virus is the single most common macro virus. It can affect both Word and Excel documents. You get the Concept Virus from another file, which another user gave you. It consists of a series of macros, which may also change some macros you already have. When you open this file, a series of macros execute that make it do the following:

- Install the virus into the Normal template, and from the Normal template into other files, and from other files into other templates.

- Corrupt the AutoOpen, AutoExec, AutoNew, AutoClose, and AutoExit macros, if you're still running these. Many users of Word 97 will not find these macros on their system, but users who import older documents may find that they do have the Auto suite of macros.

- Affect all documents opened from the Normal template so that they cannot be saved as anything other than templates. This can be quite annoying, especially if you're trying to save your file as an RTF file or a file in an earlier version of Word.

- Install macros called PayLoad, AAAZFS, and AAAZAO.

Besides the annoying bug that affects Save As, you'll know if you have the Concept Virus if you have the PayLoad macro. Other symptoms may be a dialog box that contains only the number 1 and an OK button.

To get rid of the Concept Virus, delete all the Auto macros: AutoOpen, AutoExec, AutoNew, AutoClose, and AutoExit, as well as the macro called FileSaveAs. This will not affect normal Word usage. You should also delete the macros called AAAZFS and AAAZAO. However, *do not* delete the PayLoad macro. This macro tells the Concept Virus suite that the document or template is already infected and that it can go ahead and look for something else to infect. A rather useful tool, actually—virus protection built into a virus.

Of course, you'll still probably want to purchase anti-virus software to protect against Concept and other viruses. Now that macros are written in Visual Basic instead of WordBasic, virus programmers have that much more versatility available to them. It's hard to tell what interesting tricks they'll come up with to infect you and affect you, but you'll want to be prepared when they come for you.

PART

VI

Power Tools

Why Visual Basic?

As word-processing applications, including Word, became more complex and acquired advanced features, the demand increased for an easy, yet sophisticated way to automate a series of commands. Thus, the "macro" concept and script was born.

As the macro concept advanced and grew, the macro script began to look more and more like a programming language. Microsoft met this demand by extending the ability of the Word macro script (and now called it a "language" in the programming sense) to encompass some of the flexibility and features of the BASIC programming language and called it WordBasic. As Word advanced, the limitations of old versions of BASIC, especially when compared with current "visual" program development tools, were becoming a hindrance.

At that time, Microsoft Visual Basic was a tremendous success in programming circles and had become the most widely used programming language in the world. It, therefore, made sense to transfer the advantages of this easy-to-use programming language and design environment to Word macros. This new macro language became known as Visual Basic for Applications (VBA) and formed not only the underlying macro language for each of the Microsoft Office suite of applications, but became the "language" that enabled the various members of the Office family to interact and converse.

TIP

If you are familiar with the older WordBasic, see the entries in Online Help for Visual Basic. (To do so, you must have selected this option when you installed Word.)

With Word 97, you have at your fingertips a powerful, yet deceptively easy-to-use macro language that forms a subset of one of the all-time great Windows software development tools.

Let's see how Visual Basic operates, and let's find out how to enhance Word through Visual Basic. *Remember, you do not have to become a Visual Basic programmer.* In this chapter, I simply want to introduce you to Visual Basic as a macro programming tool and point you in the direction to learn more.

Follow along, and develop a feeling for how this works. Later, when you really need extended Word macros, you will be prepared to jump in and start using the Visual Basic components.

The Structure of Visual Basic Commands

Although originally developed as a simple-to-follow programming language for beginners, the BASIC programming language has become far more powerful and sophisticated without losing its "readability" and endearing "English-like" qualities. For now, suspend any preconception you may have had about either programming or BASIC. This is no longer the little freebie language that came on those home computers of the late '70s and early '80s. This is another beast entirely. Wait until we have explored it a little together before you pass judgment.

One of the nicest features of this new version of Visual Basic is that as you type or edit commands for your macro, Visual Basic prompts you with lists of the next possible piece of the command. This is a tremendous aid when first learning how to program macros; you don't have to remember every little detail and instruction. This assistance, if followed, will ensure that you at least get the syntax (computer "grammar") and command structure correct. Allow Visual Basic to guide you.

Before we get down to business, though, let's look at a few concepts and some terms that are important in understanding how Visual Basic works. First, Visual Basic is an *object-oriented* programming language. Its programs and macros are an assembly of application objects that you gather together, adjust their properties (characteristics), and instruct them how to interact. These objects are really tiny programs that you can use again and again.

For example, an option button is a button object. Someone in the past wrote all the programming necessary to display and operate a button object. You don't have to reinvent that wheel; you simply set the button object's parameters and use the object. When you program with Visual Basic, then, you can concentrate on writing the instructions that tell the objects how to behave. Most of the work is already done for you!

In Visual Basic, you use Windows *controls*—text boxes (or fields), list boxes, combo boxes (drop-down lists), checkboxes, option buttons, message boxes, pictures, and other "things" that you frequently see on forms and windows. You can drag these controls from a toolbox (see Figure 31.8) and drop them anywhere you want in your document and/or design form (window). By changing the characteristics (properties) of these controls, you establish the visual design of your macro or program before writing any code at all.

FIGURE 31.8

Visual Basic's toolbox of controls

The ability to "plug-in" these Windows components whenever and wherever you need them and to adjust their properties to suit your needs is referred to as *object-oriented programming*.

Besides being object oriented, Visual Basic is *event driven*. This means what it sounds like. In older programming days, the computer interpreted and acted upon lines of computer instructions ("code") in sequence. The program would be instructed to continue cycling until it received the required user input and then continue to the next line of code in order. All code was processed sequentially as the programmer intended. There was no opportunity for the program to "react" to whatever the user wanted to do next unless the user followed an expected operation.

Nowadays software needs to be event driven to work well in graphical operating environments such as Windows. Graphical environments respond to mouse movements, clicking, dragging-and-dropping, keyboard presses, and other such user-activated events. Programs that run in graphical operating systems are, in effect, dormant until the user triggers an appropriate event, thus starting the program's code for that event.

Programmers who work in Visual Basic and similar event-driven languages write their program in sections called *subroutines* (small sections of the program) that react to user and system events. The program is "packaged" into many subroutines that respond to user events, and the program runs only *the code* intended to respond to *that event*. Sequential processing of the lines of code is still relevant, but only within that subroutine.

Once the event has been processed, the program simply (unless told to do otherwise) hangs around, waiting for whatever user event it needs.

The Visual Basic interface is known as its Interactive Development Environment (IDE) and is similar to the user interface of a computer graphics or drawing program (see Figure 31.9). You can write a Word/Visual Basic macro in two ways: (1) You can simply provide the instructions to perform a task, or (2) you can use the IDE to provide visual components and an interface with which the user interacts.

Writing Macro Instructions in a Module

When you record or write a Visual Basic macro from scratch, you do so within a *module*. A module is simply a file that holds your programming instructions, whether you write them yourself or generate them by recording a series of operations within Word. A module contains only the macro program; it does not contain any visual elements. The macros that automate Word functions are of this type; they don't necessarily provide an "interface" for the user's input or interaction.

FIGURE 31.9

*The Visual Basic
Interactive
Development
Environment*

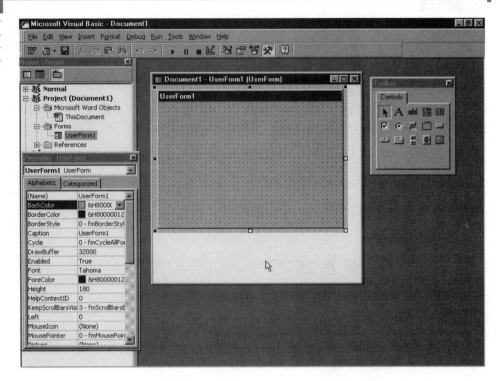

Using the IDE to Create a Macro

You can use the Visual Basic IDE to create a macro or to edit or enhance an existing one. Using the IDE allows you to incorporate the visual elements of a Windows program into a Word macro, thus providing for tremendous interaction with your user. You can even design the appearance of your macro interface first and then worry about how to write the Visual Basic commands that make it work. You'll see how to do this in detail later.

Because Visual Basic is object oriented, you can select controls or components by clicking on them in the Controls toolbox (see Figure 31.8, earlier in this chapter). You can then place them onto a window object, which represents our program's/macro's form, or you can place them directly onto the document surface by dragging out a position for them as shown in Figure 31.10. Double-clicking on the toolbox's component achieves much the same effect; double-clicking places the selected object in the default position on your form or document. Once you select and place a component, you can then move it, adjust it, and change its properties.

- You move an object by dragging it.
- You size an object by dragging any of the sizing handles that appear at the sides and corners of the object when it is selected.

PART

VI

Power Tools

FIGURE 31.10

*A button and
a text box
placed on the
surface of a
Word document*

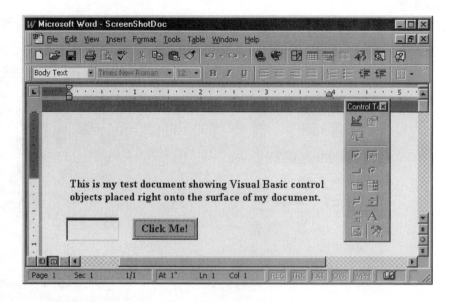

- You change an object's properties by right-clicking on it and selecting the Properties option from the pop-up menu. This menu displays a list of the object's properties that you can change at design time.

In this manner, you can "assemble" the components you want to display in your document or macro and get the "look-and-feel" aspects squared away. When you are satisfied with the design of the interface, you can then start building the *instructions* behind each object and the events to which they will respond.

As I mentioned earlier, these instructions are contained in subroutines, and each subroutine is packaged to respond to an action, or an event, from the user or the computer. A typical event is the user's clicking the mouse on a button or a checkbox. When that event occurs, the subroutine for that object runs (or executes). You could, for example, write an instruction for a button to display the text "Donuts" in a text box when a user clicks on that button. The subroutine for that button would contain an instruction to change the text property of the text box to "Donuts," and the button would do so only when clicked.

If you design visual controls (buttons, checkboxes, text boxes, and so on) into your macro, you then have to write only the instructions appropriate for performing the associated tasks. Programming in modular pieces allows you to assemble a macro intuitively by supplying the function to each component of your visual design as needed. You don't necessarily need to provide code for all the visual controls you've included.

Visual Basic executes only the code you provided and then only when the appropriate event (such as a mouse double-click) occurs.

Once you get the knack of providing code for the appropriate events of each component in a macro, you can then apply some of the more conventional programming procedures to the object. Among these procedures, the most commonly used are *conditional* and *loop*.

Conditional Procedures

Conditional procedures (called *clauses*) simply check to see if a certain condition in the program is in effect before making the next move and then process the appropriate instructions. For example, you have a checkbox on a form that is labeled "Older than 50." If a user who is older than 50 is filling out the form, he or she checks that checkbox.

The logic is:

> IF Older-than-50-checkbox is checked, THEN set the value for this user's age data to "older than 50"

where IF is a conditional clause. Visual Basic has several conditional clauses, including IF, THEN, ELSE, and SELECT CASE. You'll see more on these later.

Loop Procedures

Loops are frequently used in programming to process repetitive functions. A loop is a section of code that is repeated until a certain value or state is reached or changed as required. A loop that never reaches the condition that will cause it to stop is referred to as an *infinite loop* (it repeats the loop of code infinitely, as it cannot stop).

Here is a loop instruction:

> *From employee database record number 1, until you reach the end of the database file, read in the value of the employee salary, and if you read one that equals $34,667 per year, then stop looking; otherwise proceed to the next employee record.*

Such an instruction constitutes a loop, and one that would end if either the last record is reached or a record that has $34,667 per year is reached.

Now that we have explored the Visual Basic language a bit and have looked at how it operates, let's see which subelements we can use within subroutines and procedures.

Subelements in Visual Basic

The five subelements available within Visual Basic are statements, functions, variables, constants, and arguments. Let's look at each in detail.

PART

VI

Power Tools

A *statement* is a word that is reserved only for a command in the programming language, and it is used to perform certain actions. For example, the statement *UCase()* converts whatever text is placed within the parentheses to uppercase.

A *function* is a procedure (similar to a subroutine) that returns (produces) results. For example, a function might calculate a loan payment: The *principal amount*, the *interest rate,* and the *loan term* are passed to the function, and it returns a calculated *monthly payment.*

A *variable* is a name assigned to a value of a certain type (read about types below). A value can be a whole number, a currency amount, or a piece of text (called a *string*). A name is assigned to the variable (value-holder) so that you can refer to it in your program and can easily recognize it among the other Visual Basic instructions. The values that variables carry can be reassigned and changed. Much as you do in algebra (remember that back in high school?), you assign a name (such as X and Y, or A and B, or Customer1 and Address1) to a variable, insert that variable in the instructions, and then use it to calculate, compare, store values, and so on. Here's an example of storing a value in a variable:

```
"Customer = 'Mr. Briggs'"
```

NOTE

The variable being altered is always to the *left* of the operator (+, -, *, /, =, etc.).

A *constant* is similar to a variable in that it is a name assigned to a stored value of a specific type. Because (as their name suggests) variables "vary" and constants "stay constant," constants are given a value once when the program starts, and that value doesn't change. You can define your own constants, or you can use any of the many predefined constants provided with Visual Basic.

While you are programming, Visual Basic prompts you with a list of predefined constants when it expects a constant. In addition, if you click your right mouse button in the line of code where a constant can be used, this list of constants is available from the pop-up menu that appears. You can then choose the one that best suits your needs without having to remember them all.

An *argument* is a form of a variable that passes a value into and out of a subroutine, a procedure, or a function. In the function example above, the values for *principal*, *rate*, and *term* would have been passed using *arguments*, and the *monthly payment* returned by the function would have been also passed using an *argument*.

The FixUpMyScreen macro, shown back in Figure 31.5, consists entirely of statements, object properties, and comments.

> **NOTE**
> *Comments* are notations in the middle of the macro, for the benefit of those reading the program, and have no bearing on the instructions. A comment is any line of code that begins with a single apostrophe. If you want to remove a line of code from operation temporarily, placing an apostrophe in front of it will disable it and turn it into a comment. Visual Basic ignores all lines of code that are "commented out." Unless you specify otherwise, comments are shown in green text.

Using these elements together in the right order produces our Word macro instructions. Let's examine a line of code in Figure 31.5 to see how these instructions work.

Figure 31.5 shows the commented lines and the actual instruction lines. The instructions follow a common format. Look at the second to last line in the instructions, and follow the format. First is the name of the object you want to reference CommandBars ("Formatting"), followed by a period, the property you want to modify (Visible), an operator (=), and the new value (False). This instruction:

```
CommandBars("Formatting").Visible = False
```

is simply telling Visual Basic that you want to hide (make invisible) the Formatting Command Bar of the Command Bars object. You do so by making the Visible property false.

Makes sense, doesn't it? What do you think setting the Visible property of the CommandBars("Formatting") to True would do?

In the example, rather than repeat a separate line of instruction for each property of the ActiveWindow object (or any object for that matter) you want to adjust, you can use the With statement to group instructions. See how that section begins with With ActiveWindow? Subsequent lines simply start with a period because until the End With statement, everything starting with a period is considered a property (or a method, as explained later) of whatever object the With Statement refers to (in our example, that is ActiveWindow). So, for example, if there were a Command Button object and if the code started With CommandButton, each line thereafter starting with a period, up until the End With statement refers to a property of the CommandButton object.

As you can see, the sequence of these instructions tells Word what to do when performing your macro. All you need to do is get a feel for the statements and syntax and think in discrete sequential terms about what you want to achieve with the macro.

This particular macro has no visual elements; it doesn't refer to any of the window's components. Hang in there. You'll see more of those in a short while.

PART

VI

Power Tools

Getting Advanced Macro Help

Visual Basic comes with one of the best help files you are likely to find anywhere. You may as well avail yourself of it! To access the help file, you have to be in the Visual Basic editor, and there check out the Help menu. If you didn't install the Visual Basic help file as an option during your original installation of Word, you will have to do so. Instructions on how to do this are in Word's own help file, under "Visual Basic Help."

TIP

You might want to do something I find useful, and that is to have a Windows shortcut icon to this help file on your Windows desktop at all times. Locate the help file itself on the hard drive using Windows Explorer, create a shortcut icon for it (click on the actual file with the right mouse button, and select the Make Shortcut option), and drag it to the Windows desktop. Now it is always accessible and close at hand.

Once you have the Visual Basic help file running, then, as with any help file, typing the word of interest will display all close matches to your request. In addition, the Find function tab (shown in Figure 31.11) will do a "content search," casting a wider

FIGURE 31.11

Use the Find tab to search for Visual Basic help on the specific topic of interest. I've typed "statement" here.

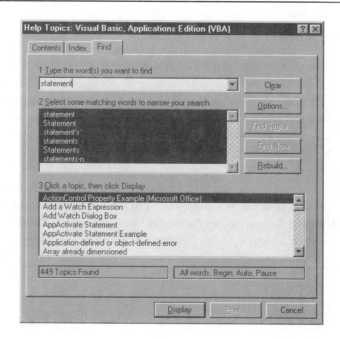

net for your search. Type the beginning of the word or anything related to it to narrow the search to something you can use. You'll be surprised at the wealth of information available here.

Furthermore, when in the thick of programming or editing a macro, click on anything in the Visual Basic IDE, or highlight any command in the code screen, and press the F1 function key. This will display the help file already open on the selected topic page (see Figure 31.12).

You can find complete syntax information for each Visual Basic command, help in making dialog boxes, and all kinds of examples and helpful explanations. Here we're looking at the help topics for the Debug menu.

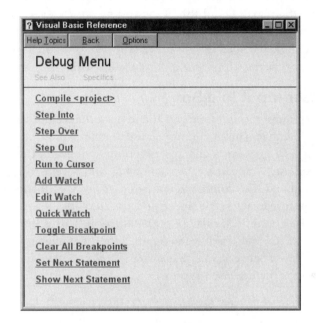

Not-Too-Hard Visual Basic Programming

So, we have seen how to create a Visual Basic macro by simply recording a sequence of operations and then look at Word's translation of that into Visual Basic instructions in the editing window. As mentioned, at some stage you will want to enhance these instructions by adding visual Windows components and by offering user interaction and perhaps additional processing power (maybe that loan payment calculation?). Displaying the results of your computation in a special way (perhaps in its own window and with a picture?) could also be of benefit.

Let's look at these sorts of features and how you can add them. Remember, you can take this one step at a time—adding only those functions you want and ignoring the rest until you have a use for them. Don't feel swamped by all this "programming stuff." Just digest it a little bite at a time.

Hello in There!—Talking to Macros

As your macros get more sophisticated, you're going to want to make them more responsive and flexible. One way to do this is to have them prompt the user for input and then do different things depending on what gets "put in." The flip side of this is that you'll want your macros to report on what they're doing—that's the output side of the coin. Recorded macros are taciturn. They do their work and disappear, but you can set up your macros to both "listen" and "talk."

User Input in a Box

To prompt the user for input and to place that value into a variable that you can process in your macro instructions, you use the standard Windows InputBox dialog box. (A dialog box represents a dialog between the system and the user—a request for input and a response.) You can create a dialog box and handle its input values with one simple command. This command is also referred to as a function because it returns a value that you store in a variable (more on that later).

First, look at the syntax of the function. This is the "skeleton" of the actual statement. You may not have to fill in all these parameters. Optional parameters are always displayed between square brackets ([]). Now look at the pieces you want to use in your macro. The InputBox syntax is:

```
Variable = InputBox(prompt [,title] [,default] [,XPos] [,Ypos] [,HelpFile]
    [,Context])
```

Remember that the variable to the left of the operator (in this case, the equals sign) is the part to be changed. In this example, we are assigning user input to our variable. Simply by placing the variable to the left of the equals sign, we are instructing Visual Basic to fill that variable with input from the InputBox, which is to the right of the equals sign.

Since the Prompt parameter is the only parameter that is required, you could, if you want, ignore the remaining parameters and have an InputBox instruction that looks like this:

```
JobTitle = InputBox("Please enter your job title")
```

This InputBox would provide the user's input in the variable *JobTitle*, and would look like Figure 31.13 when the macro is run.

If you want your InputBox to look a little more elaborate and professional, add Title and Default values. This requires the following line of Visual Basic code:

```
JobTitle = InputBox("Please enter your job title", "Request For Employment
    Information", "Manager")
```

The new, more elaborate InputBox would look like Figure 31.14. Notice the difference created by those extra parameters.

You could also add parameters for the X and Y coordinates (XPos, YPos) on the screen where you want the InputBox to appear when the macro is run, and you could associate a section of a Windows help file (the HelpFile parameter provides the actual help file name and location, and the Context parameter tells the program which page of the help file to display for this InputBox) with the InputBox so as to offer assistance to the user. This is usually more sophisticated than most Word macros need, but you never know!

After the user types input and clicks on OK or presses Enter, the value is stored in the *JobTitle* variable and can be processed as shown below:

```
JobTitle = InputBox("Please enter your job title", "Request For Employment Infor-
    mation", "Manager")
Selection.InsertAfter (JobTitle)
```

FIGURE 31.13

Our InputBox asking for a job title

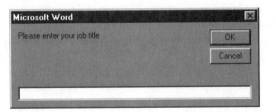

PART

VI

Power Tools

FIGURE 31.14

A more elaborate InputBox formatted with additional parameters

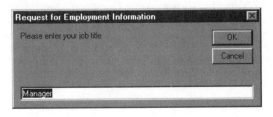

The second line of code above inserts whatever input the user gave to the Input-Box, stored in the *JobTitle* variable, directly after either the currently selected piece of text or, if no text is actually selected, the cursor position.

Can you see how this works? With a simple function such as InputBox and with a couple of parameter values, Visual Basic provides a completely formatted and prede-signed window specially for this task and sets you up for the next line in your code. Now isn't that relatively simple?

Just Yes or No, Please

If all you need from the user is an answer to your question, as opposed to an input value, you can use the MsgBox() command. Like the InputBox, the Message Box is a preformatted dialog box with which to interact with your user. Unlike the InputBox, which asks the user to enter a response, the Message Box offers a multiple-choice set of response buttons. It can present a question and provide a way for you to know the user's response. That response is always one out of as many as three options. The possible answers, such as Yes/No, Abort/Retry/Ignore, are listed in Table 31.1 and are built-in constants that you can use.

A nice feature of these constants is that their names suggest their functions when you use them with a Message Box, and you don't have to remember the numeric value to achieve the styling required of your Message Box.

The Message Box also allows you some additional flexibility in its design and style, above and beyond choosing the type of answer buttons. You can use the provided constants to show an exclamation mark (VbExclamation), a stop sign (VbCritical), and other symbols used by the Windows operating system to convey the nature of the message. Try them to see the effect of changing the sign shown on a Message Box.

The Message Box syntax is:

```
Variable = MsgBox(prompt [,buttons][,title$][,helpfile][,context])
```

where *buttons* can be the numbers, or the Visual Basic constants, shown in Table 31.1.

To implement a specific button set and a specific message icon, simply add the constants in the MsgBox function. For example, if you want a Message Box to display the Yes/No/Cancel buttons and the Question Mark icon, your code would look like this:

```
Answer = MsgBox("Do you really want to save your work before exiting the pro-
    gram?", VbYesNoCancel + VbQuestion, "Save before exiting")
```

TABLE 31.1: VISUAL BASIC CONSTANTS

Constant	Value	Result
VbOKOnly	0	Display OK button only.
VbOKCancel	1	Display OK and Cancel buttons.
VbAbortRetryIgnore	2	Display Abort, Retry, and Ignore buttons.
VbYesNoCancel	3	Display Yes, No, and Cancel buttons.
VbYesNo	4	Display Yes and No buttons.
VbRetryCancel	5	Display Retry and Cancel buttons.
VbCritical	16	Display Critical Message icon.
VbQuestion	32	Display Warning Query icon.
VbExclamation	48	Display Warning Message icon.
VbInformation	64	Display Information Message icon.

Can you see these elements of the MsgBox function in Figure 31.15?

> **NOTE**
>
> I am referring to the Message Box here as a function, because it returns a value that you keep in a variable. You can also use the Message Box to simply display a message, without any required response from the user, perhaps to inform the user that a process has been completed.

Now that you have popped a Message Box up in front of your user, he or she will click on one of the buttons (even if only to get rid of it), and you will want to know which button was selected so that you can handle that response. In the above example, it would be critical to know which button the user selected so that you could determine whether to save the file.

PART

VI

Power Tools

FIGURE 31.15

Message Box formatted with the line of code shown

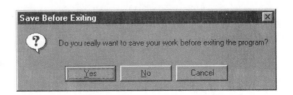

The user's response is determined by the value of the variable you assigned to the task. In the previous example, the *Answer* variable is to the left of the equals sign. The value that this variable is given when the user clicks on one of the Message Box buttons tells you which button has been selected.

These values and their buttons are shown in Table 31.2.

TABLE 31.2: VALUES AND THEIR RESULTING BUTTONS

Constant	Value	Button
VbOK	1	OK
VbCancel	2	Cancel
VbAbort	3	Abort
VbRetry	4	Retry
VbIgnore	5	Ignore
VbYes	6	Yes
VbNo	7	No

For example, if your variable now contains a value of 6, you know that the user clicked on the Yes button. You are now free to process this response as you wish.

NOTE

A Message Box (like an Input Box) returns a value for the user's response, which you must then deal with in your macro code. There is no "automatic" dealing with the answer, only a "handle" for you to use in subsequent instructions. For example, if the user clicks on the Yes or Cancel buttons, your program must figure out how to react. Without your instructions, the Message Box does nothing, and the user's response is ignored.

The following code takes our previous example a little further and "reacts" to the user's response:

```
Answer = MsgBox("Do you really want to save your work before exiting the pro-
    gram?", VbYesNoCancel + VbQuestion, "Save before exiting")
If Answer = VbYes Then

    'Process a "Yes" answer by saving the user's file at this point in the code

Else
```

```
'Process a "No" or "Cancel" response by either continuing to exit, or abort
the exit process

End if
```

Here we are using a Conditional statement, as discussed earlier, to evaluate the response. The actual code is far more elaborate than you would want to see right now, so I have substituted a commented line to indicate the process. The important point is to see the sequential logic of how to use Message Boxes.

> What is your title?

Macros That Talk Back

So now you know a couple of ways to pass information from your user (who may be you) to your macros. The second part of this equation is the feedback of information from your macro. You'll, therefore, also need to know how macros can report back to you. Two simple ways to display information are on the status bar or in a dialog box.

On the Status Bar

To display text on the status bar, use the StatusBar statement. The syntax is:

```
StatusBar = String
```

To display a message in Word's status bar, you need only to assign a piece of text to it, such as the following:

```
StatusBar = "This is my very own message in Word's Status Bar!"
```

You might want to process the information you want to display in the status bar before you show it. You can then pass a string (text) variable's contents to the status bar, like this:

```
Title = "Vice President of Marketing"
Name = "George Fallon"
StatusBar = Name & ": " & Title
```

PART

VI

Power Tools

This will display "George Fallon: Vice President of Marketing" on the status bar as shown in Figure 31.16.

NOTE

I added a colon character and a space between the two string variables. Without these characters, the status bar would have displayed "George FallonVice President of Marketing", which wouldn't look very good (and would probably offend George's boss, the actual president of marketing!).

TIP

You can print numeric values also, as long as you present them as a string. The status bar requires that messages be in string format.

FIGURE 31.16

The Word status bar displaying our message

In a Message Box

If you want your macro to really announce the information it has, you can use the simple form of MsgBox that I discussed above. Remember, this is a statement; it is not the MsgBox function we looked at earlier. Thus, you can use it to display information when you don't need the user's response. All you are doing is displaying the message until the user clicks. In this case, a simple OK button will do (which is the default setting if you don't specifically choose one of the button group styles mentioned earlier). The Msg-Box statement has the following syntax:

MsgBox *Message*

where *message* is a string variable or piece of text in quotation marks. Thus, the statement:

```
EmployeeTitle = "Director of Finance"
EmployeeNumber = "123456"
MsgBox "Your title is " & EmployeeTitle & " and your employee number is " &
   Str(EmployeeNumber)
```

displays the message in a dialog box with the title specified and an OK button.

> **NOTE**
> I used the Str() statement to convert a number (which is a numeric value) into a string (a piece of text). This may sound redundant, but think of it this way. The number in the example, 123456, has a numeric value. The text "One hundred and twenty-three thousand, four hundred and fifty-six" may seem like the same thing, but it has no numeric usable value for the computer. It is simply a collection of characters making words that form a sentence. We read them and understand the meaning of the value they represent, but to do math with the words will not make sense to the computer. It needs the actual number values, just as a calculator needs numbers, and cannot add words. Because a Message Box requires a string (textual) message to display, the numeric value of 123,456.00 has to be converted into the text "123456" so that it can be shown in the Message Box as a collection of those characters, not their represented value.

Creating Dialog Boxes

You've already seen how to display simple dialog boxes and use them to get input or display output, but those dialog boxes are limited. If you understand a little more about how dialog boxes work, you can modify existing dialog boxes or even create your own.

Understanding Dialog Boxes

As mentioned earlier, a dialog box is one of the easiest ways for a user to communicate with a macro program. With Visual Basic at your disposal, you can avail yourself of the many standard dialog boxes that are part and parcel of Windows. As a Windows user, you are familiar with these dialog boxes. When you want to open a file, your Windows application (including Word) provides a standard Open dialog box. It displays a view of your disk drives, their contents, and usually a way to display a group of a particular file type. You can select a file to open or type a filename. Figure 31.17 shows a standard Open dialog box.

You also use dialog boxes to print, change printer settings, change font parameters, select colors from a palette, save files, and more. The point is that these are standard Windows features, and Visual Basic provides an easy way to use dialog boxes. With Visual Basic, you don't need to design the window, set the buttons, display the filenames, figure out how to program the functions, or ensure that your design meets the Windows design standards.

FIGURE 31.17

The standard
Open
dialog box

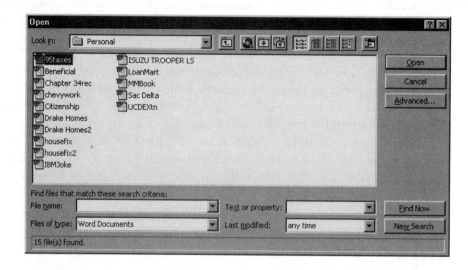

Creating Your Own Dialog Boxes

As mentioned above, dialog boxes come in many styles and types. Think of the work you would have to do to program your own from scratch! All this work is done for you, and you can display it in your macro with one simple command:

```
LoadFileName = Dialogs(wdDialogFileOpen).Show
```

In this example, the *LoadFileName* variable holds the result of the user's "dialog" with the dialog box. In this case, it is the full path and filename for the file the user wants to open. The above line of macro code displays the dialog box shown in Figure 31.17.

The Visual Basic syntax for a dialog box is:

```
Dialogs(index)
```

where *index* is a WdWordDialog constant that identifies the dialog box.

If you want the dialog box to return a response that you can then process, place a variable and an equals sign before the syntax. But be sure that you use a dialog box that returns a response, such as the Open dialog box (which returns the name of the file to open). If you omit the variable to catch the response, the dialog box will simply go about its business and do whatever you told it to do, such as open and display a document selected in the Open dialog box. The only difference is that your macro doesn't have the filename of the file loaded. This may or may not be useful to you.

By simply inserting the appropriate supplied constant within the parentheses, you can invoke the dialog box of choice. Simple, isn't it? The bulk of the work has been done for you. Now it's up to you to process the response that the dialog box transfers from the user.

Displaying a Dialog Box in Another Way

You can also display a dialog box with this code:

```
Dialogs(wdDialogHelpAbout)
.Display
```

This displays the Help/About Dialog Box, just as the Show method did, but offers another aspect. Another optional parameter tells the dialog box to disappear if it receives no user response after a predetermined time. This time is expressed in milliseconds (1000 milliseconds = 1 second). This option looks like this:

```
Dialogs(wdDialogViewZoom)
.Display TimeOut:=9000
```

This example displays the Zoom dialog box for approximately nine seconds.

Custom Dialog Boxes and Forms

You now have some information about how to use the standard Windows dialog boxes, but you may need a dialog box for which there is no standard Windows equivalent. In Visual Basic, such a dialog box is called a form, and you can think of it in its paper sense. A form is displayed for the user, and the user must fill in information on it. You can also think of a form as a window. When you design a visual macro in Visual Basic, you work in a form window that you can pop up in a Word document. This form has all the characteristics of a standard window, and on it you "paint" control objects (such as buttons, text boxes, menus, list boxes, images, and so on). This will become more apparent later.

Let's create a form on which the user will enter name, address, phone number, and Social Security number.

Building the User Interface for a Custom Form

We will first build the user interface (the form) and then create the code that will process the user's responses on the form. This form will hold the information for us until

PART

VI

Power Tools

we remove it from the screen. Therefore, we must store the information in variables so that we can process it when the form disappears.

This process is rather involved. Visual Basic provides excellent help, however, and will prompt you as you go.

You can create this example in an infinite number of ways—or at least in as many ways as there are programmers! The purpose of this example is to give you an insight into how forms are constructed and to provide a taste of the programming involved. As you work through this example, I hope that you will see that it is not as imposing as you might think.

So, let's together design and implement a custom form to request input from a user about herself and then format and place the input in our document—all automatically! Here are the steps:

1. Start Word and choose Tools ➤ Macros ➤ Visual Basic Editor. Word displays the Visual Basic IDE, ready for you to start designing or programming your new macro.

2. To display a new blank form, choose Insert ➤ UserForm or click on the Insert User-Form button.

3. To place four text boxes on this form, click on the TextBox control in the Toolbox, hold down the mouse button, and drag it to place it on your form. You should now have a beveled Text Box on your form. To resize and reposition the Text Box, select it and then adjust it with the sizing handles that appear around its edges. To change only its position, hold the mouse button down in the center of the Text Box, and drag the whole thing to where you want it to be.

Congratulations! You have just succeeded in creating the first element of functionality on your new custom form!

4. Repeat step 3 until you have four text boxes nicely arranged on your form, as shown in Figure 31.18.

It is good practice at this stage to name your text boxes so that you can recognize them in your code when you refer to them. Let's change the Name property of the text box to suit.

5. If the Properties dialog box is not displayed, select the first text box, and then press F4 or click on the Properties Window button.

6. In the Properties dialog box, locate the (Name) property and select the box to its right. Type **txtName** (to identify this box as a text box that will record the name of the user). Figure 31.19 shows the Properties window as it should look after you make this change.

FIGURE 31.18

*Our new form
with four
text boxes*

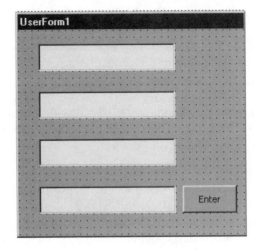

FIGURE 31.19

*The TextBox
Properties
window*

 TIP

All Visual Basic objects, including the form itself, are named in this way. Check the Visual Basic help file for object-naming conventions. You can call an object anything you please, but following the conventions makes it easier to locate the object later and revise the code.

7. Change the name properties for the other text boxes in turn, calling them txt-Address, txtPhoneNumber, and txtSocialSecurity, respectively.

> **NOTE**
>
> There are no spaces in the object names.

Now, what would text entry fields be without some indication of their purpose? Let's position Label objects above each text box in the same way that we placed the text boxes themselves on the form.

8. Select the Label control in the Toolbox and drag out a rectangle above the first text box to place and size the label. Repeat this procedure for the three other labels, positioning each above its text box.

9. To name these Label objects, follow the procedures in steps 6 and 7 for the text boxes. Name the labels lblName, lblAddress, lblPhoneNumber, and lblSocialSecurity.

10. Now, change the labels' Caption properties so that they look like the illustration. The Caption property for a control sets the text to be displayed as a caption on the control. The result should look like Figure 31.20.

Now our form is beginning to take shape and look like a real form! The next step is to add a button, somewhere below the text boxes. This button will provide the function of transferring our text box contents to our Word document. (Or whatever other

FIGURE 31.20

Our form with text boxes and labels

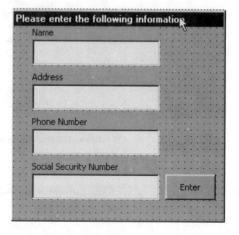

process we can dream up! We could write our program to do just about anything at that point.)

11. From the Toolbox, select the CommandButton control, drag it to an area on the form, let go of the mouse button, and *hey presto!* We have a neat beveled button on our form!

12. To change the name of the button, select it, and then enter a new name in the box next to (Name) in the Properties dialog box. Type **cmdEnter** (cmd is the naming convention for a command button).

13. As you did with labels, change the button's Caption property to **Place Data**. This text now appears on the face of the button on your form.

Writing the Code for the Custom Form

At this stage we have a sufficient design for our purpose (you can always make changes later by adjusting the objects's properties in the Properties dialog box). Now we need a program to perform our required operation! Here are the steps:

1. Double-click on any object in our design to open a new window in which you can enter the instructions for the event associated with that object.

TIP

To enter actual code for any object, simply double-click on the object, ensure that the correct event "trigger" is selected in the top right drop-down list, and begin coding!

2. To have your Visual Basic form macro insert the contents of your text boxes in your document at the cursor's current position, enter the following instructions. Do *not* enter the text shown in italics; it is already provided for you in the coding window.

```
Private Sub CommandButton1_Click()
Dim LineFeed As String
Dim InsertText As String

LineFeed = Chr(10)

InsertText = txtName.Text
InsertText = InsertText & LineFeed & txtAddress.Text
InsertText = InsertText & LineFeed & txtPhoneNumber.Text
InsertText = InsertText & LineFeed & txtSocialSecurity.Text

Selection.InsertAfter (InsertText)
End Sub
```

PART

VI

Power Tools

Here's what is happening:

1. You use the Dim statement to declare two string variables, *LineFeed* and *InsertText*.

NOTE

"Declaring" a variable is telling Visual Basic that this is the name of a new variable you intend to use and that you want it to be the type specified after the *As* part of the statement.

2. You set the value of *LineFeed* to chr(10), which is the code for a linefeed character in Visual Basic. By including the *LineFeed* variable, you instruct Visual Basic to split the text following that variable onto the next line. It's just like pressing Enter when you type.

NOTE

You could have set *LineFeed* to a constant of the same value, since it remains constant in value throughout our code. Your choice.

3. Now you are going to sequentially store the contents of each text box in the *InsertText* variable, each separated by a linefeed. Store the first TextBox text in *InsertText*, add a linefeed, store the next TextBox contents, add another linefeed, and so on until you have concatenated all the pieces of text.
4. Finally, you use the InsertAfter method to insert the contents of the *InsertText* variable after the cursor position, where Selection refers to any text selected at the time.

Now your completed macro form should look like Figure 31.21. In Word, run your macro, and take a look at the results.

As you can see, with a few simple lines of code and using visual design, you can create quite a sophisticated macro for use within Word 97.

What Other Kinds of Macros Can I Create?

You have at your command a complete software development application with which you can create programs to do almost whatever you want in Word 97 without compromise. Visual Basic is an advanced programming tool, but one that is relatively easy to follow (given a little time) and, more important, one that lets you gather information as you need it for a project. You can learn as you go; you don't have to assimilate the entire Visual Basic language before you use it. Take it one step at a time.

FIGURE 31.21

The complete
macro interface
running in Word

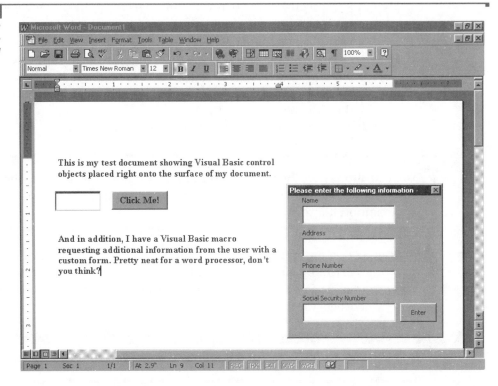

Step 1: Plan out (on paper) what you want your macro to do. Programmers often overlook this step, and yet it is so important. By knowing in advance what you want to achieve (at least in outline), you can focus on gathering the components of the puzzle that your current project needs, and you can ignore the rest.

Step 2: Here you have two options.

- Create a macro by recording the sequence of steps in Word that you want to reproduce programmatically. Use this automatically generated code as the basis for your extended macro.
- Create a visual design that meets your needs (and tastes). By designing the look and feel of your macro before adding any instructions, you not only create something tangible to work with, but you also focus on how the macro will operate for the user. You can now apply the necessary instructions in code to the actual pieces (objects) that need it. That is step 3.

Step 3: Selecting the object that you want to perform the task and under what circumstances (events), write the instructions for what you want to happen next. If you want to change the selected text to a certain set of style parameters when a button is clicked, for example, write those instructions for that button (remember, you can double-click on the button in the Visual Basic IDE to access its code window) in the appropriate event for the button (in this case the Click event).

Step 4: Save your macro with the document.

You can also export the program as a separate Visual Basic project. This is handy if you want to use the full Visual Basic programming language to modify the project and reimport it into Word.

Step 5: To use your macro, choose Tools ➤ Macros, choose Macros and select your macro by name from the list, and click on the Run button, or assign the macro to a toolbar button or keyboard combination and invoke it that way whenever you need it.

You also can assign a macro to be run whenever you start the document.

Where to Go from Here

The intent of this chapter is to give you some clues as to why a macro may be needed and how it does what it does. I want to get you going on your first steps with macros and then provide you with enough information to enable you to find out how to produce more sophisticated programming.

Probably the most important thing to remember is that Visual Basic is a forgiving development tool:

- It will prompt you as you write your instructions with what it believes to be (and what usually is) the next part of the "sentence."
- It will tell you when you make a mistake, where the mistake is, and (usually) exactly what the mistake is.
- It allows you to "paint" your design on the screen before writing a single instruction; you can, therefore, concentrate on the user interface.
- It allows you to "place" code into whatever object you want to program by simply double-clicking on it.

- It allows you to learn as you go and to pick up additional pieces of the language as you need them.
- It provides you with a comprehensive, easy-to-search-through help file that has many examples of how to apply a newly learned instruction. Help is only the press of a function key away.

PART

VI

Power Tools

Chapter

32

Personalizing Word

Personalizing Word

This chapter discusses how to customize Word. You'll learn how to change Word's standard menu settings, toolbars, and keyboard shortcuts. You'll also learn how to add, delete, and rename menus. You'll even be able to create your own custom menus and toolbars from scratch.

A Caution

Imagine living in a community where everyone made their own laws. One driver could decide that red traffic lights mean go and green lights mean speed (I know, some do this already). Your neighbor could decide to build a toxic-waste dump in his or her backyard (yes, likewise). Similarly, changing Word's look, feel, and functions carries risks and responsibilities.

Adding a couple of extra commands such as PrevWindow and NextWindow (which take you to the previous window and next window, respectively, without your having to specify which number window you'd like) to the File or View menu won't usually harm anyone. Deleting menu items that you never use might also seem reasonable—if you never use tables, you could get rid of most of the Table menu and put something more useful in its place. But what if you substitute a tricky command such as ExitWindows, which closes Word *without even giving you a chance to save changes* and then quits Windows, for File ➤ Exit? You could even give it the same hot key. Anybody who didn't know your machine wouldn't stand a chance and would probably lose unsaved work when trying to exit Word.

Moving items from menu to menu or from toolbar to toolbar (or from menu to toolbar to key combination—here's that flexibility we were talking about) may make life easier and more logical for you, but it may make life difficult for others who need to use your machine. Imagine being a temporary worker trying to figure out a completely reorganized set of Word menus or even a copy of Word with no visible menus and most of the screen obscured by toolbars that are not easy to remove (the menus have gone, remember). The training of new hires can be slowed by undocumented, department-wide changes to menus as well. Moving menu items and buttons can confuse macros, as well.

If you work in a large organization, your systems manager may have strong feelings about your changing Word's menus, toolbars, and shortcuts. Check first. With that out of the way, let's look at ways to personalize Word.

Default Settings

Word's original settings are referred to as the *defaults*. Microsoft designers have chosen settings they feel will work for the majority of people doing general typing and correspondence. For instance, they assume you will use standard letter-size (8.5" x 11") paper and have specified right, left, bottom, and top margins that should accommodate most binding, header, and footer needs. They have turned on popular Word features and turned off more esoteric ones that annoy some people. They have organized the menus for you and held back many potential menu choices.

Many of these defaults will not suit you perfectly. For instance, you probably won't want to type all your documents in Times New Roman 10 point, as Word's designers apparently would have you do. Maybe you want to use legal-size paper or print out all your documents on postcards. This is all quite natural and perfectly harmless. But rather than having to change one particular feature the same way every time you start a document, you'll probably want to change Word's default settings and save yourself time and temper.

Understanding and Changing Word's Options

Word gives you a great deal of control over its various features. For example, you can dictate default view settings, menu appearance, default font settings, and much more.

Many of these choices are made using the Tools ➤ Options command and the tabs in the Options dialog box. These choices apply to all your Word templates.

Choices made using the Tools ➤ Customize command and the tabs in the Customize dialog box are template-specific—they apply only to the template in which you arrange them. This means you could have Normal.dot and all documents based on it display the default Word menus, toolbars, and so on, but have your Clever Me and Special for You templates and their documents display customized menus and toolbars. This way, both you and your default temp can be happy.

TIP

For some of Word's default settings, you don't use the Options or Customize dialog boxes. To change the default font, for example, you change your settings in the Font dialog box (Format ➤ Font) and then click on the Defaults button. Similarly, the Page Setup dialog box (File ➤ Page Setup) also has a Defaults button for its settings.

Let's look at the Options dialog box tab by tab and see how easy it is to customize Word in this way.

View

The View tab (see Figure 32.1) lets you control what you see by default in your document. For instance, if you want to see hidden text, check the Hidden Text checkbox. If you want a 3" style area, here's where you set it up. The following sections discuss these options in more detail.

These are the default settings for the options on the View tab:

Feature	Default Setting
Show	
Draft Font	Off
Picture Placeholders	Off
Animated Text	On
Screen Tips	On
Highlight	On
Bookmarks	Off
Field Codes	Off
Field Shading	When Selected

PART

VI

Power Tools

Feature	Default Setting
Nonprinting Characters	
Tab Characters	Off
Spaces	Off
Paragraph Marks	Off
Optional Hyphens	Off
Hidden Text	Off
All	Off
Window	
Status Bar	On
Horizontal Scroll Bar	On
Vertical Scroll Bar	On
Wrap to Window	Off
Style Area Width	0"

FIGURE 32.1

You decide what you want to see in your documents in the View tab of the Options dialog box. I've decided to hide the horizontal scroll bar and display hidden text.

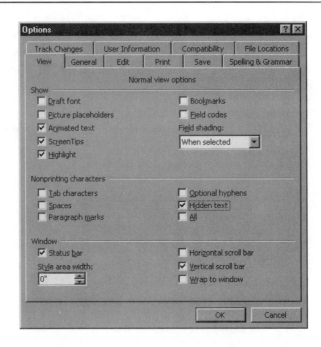

Draft Font

The Draft Font choice is for Outline and Normal views and determines whether Word displays your prose in the fonts you've chosen or in its draft font. The draft font is the font used in menus, the message boxes saying that your system is about to crash, and so on. It's faster to use than your fancy fonts; it's also uglier. Use this option when you're hacking the text in large documents on a small-brained computer and you're not worried about how things look on-screen.

Draft font displays any character formatting as underlined and bold. All for speed.

> **NOTE**
> When you're in Page Layout view, you'll get three options: Draft Font will change to Drawings. Again, this speeds up scrolling the document. You'll also get an Object Anchors option, which displays the anchor connecting an anchored object to a paragraph as a little anchor symbol. Text Boundaries displays dotted lines around page margins, text columns, objects, and formats.

Picture Placeholders

On slower PCs, Word can slow to a crawl if your document contains large graphics. To speed up work in such documents, mark the Picture Placeholders checkbox to display graphics as empty boxes. But then, if your PC is *that* slow, why the *heck* are you using Windows 95 and Word 97?

Animated Text

If you've gone to all the trouble of creating animated text in your documents, you'll be glad to know that Word defaults to show the animations. However, if a colleague is in the habit of animating the text in documents you need to review, and it annoys you, this is where you can turn off those dancing letters.

Screen Tips

The screen tips specified here are the ones in the Microsoft Word toolbar. When you run your mouse over the toolbars, a little text box shows you what the particular button does. If you don't need this extra help, you can turn off screen tips.

Highlight

It's a good idea to leave this on because it allows you to highlight text on-screen (and on printouts, if you have a color printer). Unchecking this box might speed up slower machines.

PART

VI

Power Tools

Bookmarks

Check the Bookmarks checkbox to display the bookmarks and links your document contains. Bookmarks appear in square gray brackets.

Field Codes

You'll probably want to view field codes rather than field results when you're inserting and editing fields. Simply check the checkbox. As you learned in Chapter 29, *Creating and Using Fields*, fields look like this:

```
EDITTIME \* MERGEFORMAT }
```

Field Shading

When you're working with a document that contains fields, you can choose to have their results shaded so that you can avoid changing them by mistake—remember, the results may look like regular text. Choose from When Selected (when the insertion point is in the field), Always, and Never.

Tab Characters

Check the Tab Characters checkbox to display tabs as right-pointing arrows. You may want to do this if you're aligning things and can't be bothered to use tables or if you handle a lot of documents formatted by less skillful Word users and want to distinguish tabs from first-line indents. Tabs are also displayed or hidden by the Show/Hide ¶ toolbar button.

Spaces

Check the Spaces checkbox to display spaces entered with the spacebar as dots about halfway up the height of the line. This helps you find double or triple spaces in proportional fonts. Spaces are also displayed or hidden by the Show/Hide ¶ toolbar button.

Paragraph Marks

Check the Paragraph Marks checkbox to display hard returns entered with the Enter key as ¶. This can be especially useful when you're editing a document that uses styles and deleting the wrong paragraph mark inadvertently will apply the wrong style to your text. Paragraph marks are also displayed or hidden by the Show/Hide ¶ toolbar button.

Optional Hyphens

Optional hyphens—the ones you insert to indicate where to break a word if it falls at the end of a line—are normally not displayed. To display them, check the Optional Hyphens checkbox.

Hidden Text

To view hidden text, check the Hidden Text checkbox. It will appear as text with a dotted underline. Bear in mind that viewing hidden text will change the line breaks and pagination of your document, but hidden text will not print unless you've selected Tools ➤ Options and then chosen Hidden Text in the Print tab.

All

Check this check box to display all the nonprinting characters—tabs, spaces, paragraph marks, optional hyphens, and hidden text. You can still toggle them off with the Show/Hide ¶ button, but this *unchecks* All. A little confusing until you think of them as two different ways to do the same thing.

TIP

If you don't always want nonprinting characters displayed but like to know what's there every now and then, you can get the same effect more easily by clicking on the Show/Hide ¶ button on the Standard toolbar.

Status Bar

If you find the information on the status bar confusing, or if you simply need more space on your screen for displaying your immortal words in huge point sizes, uncheck this box to remove the status bar.

Horizontal Scroll Bar

If you never use the horizontal scroll bar—and why should you, if your documents fit in the width of the screen and you don't need the three buttons to flip between views—you can remove it by unchecking the checkbox. That'll give you a little more space on the screen.

PART

VI

Power Tools

Vertical Scroll Bar

If you always use the keyboard for moving through your documents, you may want to remove the vertical scroll bar from your screen to give yourself a bit more space. Simply uncheck the box, and it'll be gone.

Wrap to Window

Wrap to Window wraps the text from one line to the next within the document window, using the window width rather than the margin width as the guide for text wrapping on your screen. Use this when you need to work with several windows visible on your desktop at the same time and you don't want your text to be wider than the window.

Instead of setting Wrap to Window, you could choose View ➤ Zoom and select a page proportion smaller than 100 percent.

Style Area Width

You'll recall that the style area is the area to the left of the text that shows the applied style names. By default, the style area width is 0"; so you don't see it. To display it, enter a positive decimal measurement, such as 0.5" (which should be enough for most of the predefined style names; if you define styles with long names, enter a larger measurement). To rid the display of the style area, enter 0 (that's an actual zero, not a capital O).

General Options

The options on the General tab (see Figure 32.2) modify Word settings such as the default units of measurement and the display of three-dimensional effects. You can also choose how many of your last-opened files Word tacks onto the bottom of the File menu, whether Word repaginates your document in the background as you work, and whether Word beeps at you when you screw up. This is a good tab to mess around with.

In the following sections, we'll look briefly at each of the settings on the General tab. But first, here's a quick summary of the default settings:

Feature	Default Setting
Background Repagination	On
Help for WordPerfect Users	Off
Navigation Keys for WordPerfect Users	Off
Blue Background, White Text	Off

Feature	Default Setting
Provide Feedback with Sound	On
Provide Feedback with Animation	On
Confirm Conversion at Open	Off
Update Automatic Links at Open	On
Mail As Attachment	On
Recently Used File List	On; 4 Entries
Macro Virus Protection	On
Measurement Units	Inches

FIGURE 32.2

You decide how many of your last-opened files Word tacks onto the bottom of the File menu in the General tab of the Options dialog box. I've gone for the max—nine.

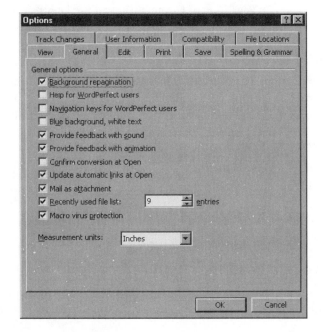

PART

VI

Power Tools

Background Repagination

With the Background Repagination checkbox checked, as it is by default, Word automatically repaginates your documents as you work, computing new lines and page endings whenever you are not typing. There's not much wrong with that except it takes a bit of your computer's horsepower; so unless you're running an immensely complex project on a very slow computer or you're typing like an extremely fast typist, I suggest you leave this checked. If you uncheck the box, Word will not repaginate until you turn it back on or print. (Background repagination is always on in Page Layout view and Print Preview. Think about it.)

Help for WordPerfect Users

The Help for WordPerfect Users checkbox will be selected only if you agreed to have it active when you installed Word. With this option selected, Word displays information or demonstrates a command when you press a WordPerfect for DOS key combination in Word. This disables many of Word's own key combinations; so you'll have to make up your mind about which to use.

Navigation Keys for WordPerfect Users

Check the Navigation Keys for WordPerfect Users checkbox to change the functions of the Page Up, Page Down, Home, End, and Esc keys to their WordPerfect equivalents. Bear in mind that this disables those keys' regular functions for Word.

Blue Background, White Text

I guess this is a techno-nerdy takeoff on that book *Blue Water, White Death*, but this command has nothing to do with sharks. Check the checkbox to display the text as white characters on a blue background. It will make some WordPerfect users feel right at home.

Provide Feedback with Sound

Word 97 comes with sounds galore. Darned near every time you do anything, Word will beep, click, zing, or make some other cute noise. To disable this charming feature, uncheck this box. This feature replaces the "Beep on Error Actions" feature in Word 95—now, instead of beeping when you make a mistake, Word seems to beep any old time it feels like it.

Provide Feedback with Animation

Some of the actions you perform in Word will be accompanied by zippy little animations. They don't really serve any purpose, so you can disable them by unchecking this box.

Confirm Conversion at Open

With this option enabled, Word will always display the Convert File dialog box when you try to open a non-Word document. In organizations where Word 95 and Word 6.*x* users share files, this feature is a useful reminder of the thin ice upon which they tread.

Update Automatic Links at Open

The Update Automatic Links at Open checkbox is one you might seriously consider unchecking. When it's checked, any information in a document that's linked to other files is updated every time you open the document. If you're linked to something fancy, such as a drawing-application figure or six, you'll be subjected to a few minutes of your hard disk grinding before you can use the document. Then again, keeping it checked will keep your documents up-to-date. Forcibly.

Mail as Attachment

Check the Mail as Attachment checkbox to attach documents to a mail message. You need to have an e-mail program installed on your computer to use this option; Office 97 comes with one.

Recently Used File List

The Recently Used File List box controls how many last-used files appear at the bottom of the File menu. Choose between 0 and 9. Most people find this feature useful, but some consider it a threat to security. (The boss can find out about all those love letters you were writing while ostensibly working on your report.) You decide. If you add any commands to the File menu and choose 9 for this list, the menu may not fit on your screen. Life's tough.

Macro Virus Protection

This option warns you when you're about to open a document containing macros. You can then open the document without macros, which will both prevent you from using them and protect against macro viruses. You can read more about macro viruses in Chapter 31, *Creating and Using Macros*. Keep this feature enabled.

Measurement Units

Pull down the Measurement Units list and choose Inches, Centimeters, Points, or Picas as the default measurement unit for Word. You may want to choose Points or Picas if you're typesetting documents.

Edit Options

The Edit tab (see Figure 32.3) is where you control a whole bunch of important options that affect the way you work. This is where you control whether what you type will replace a selection or bump it along, how Word handles drag-and-drop editing, and whether Word worries about extra spaces when you use Cut and Paste.

PART

VI

Power Tools

FIGURE 32.3

*The Edit tab of
the Options
dialog box*

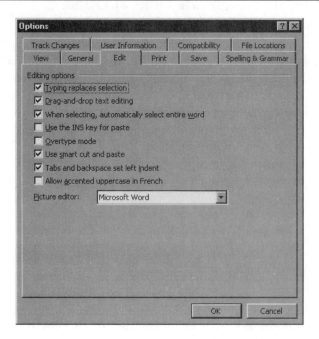

In the following sections, we'll look at each of the options on the Edit tab. But first, here are their default settings:

Feature	Default Setting
Typing Replaces Selection	On
Drag-and-Drop Text Editing	On
Automatic Word Selection	On
When Selecting, Automatically Select Entire Word	Off
Overtype Mode	Off
Use Smart Cut and Paste	On
Tabs and Backspace Set Left Indent	On
Allow Accented Uppercase in French	Off
Picture Editor	Microsoft Word

Typing Replaces Selection

With the Typing Replaces Selection checkbox checked, any text you've selected gets deleted as soon as you start typing. This saves you the step of deleting a selection when you want to replace it, but if your mind doesn't work that way and you find this option awkward, uncheck the checkbox. Then selected text will be bumped along to the right when you type something.

Drag-and-Drop Text Editing

Drag-and-drop, as you'll recall from Chapter 1, *Creating and Saving Your First Document*, lets you move or copy selected text without pasting it to the Clipboard. If you never use it, turn it off by unchecking the Drag-and-Drop Text Editing checkbox.

When Selecting, Automatically Select Entire Word

When the Automatic Word Selection checkbox is checked, Word selects the entire word (*including any trailing space at the end*) when you select any part of it by dragging the mouse pointer from the previous word. If this bugs you (it does me), uncheck the checkbox.

Use the Ins Key for Paste

Check the Use the INS Key for Paste checkbox if you get tired of pressing Shift+Ins to insert the contents of the Clipboard into your document. Needless to say, this stops you from using the Ins key to toggle between Insert and Overtype modes.

Overtype Mode

Check the Overtype Mode checkbox to have Overtype mode turned on by default when you use Word. Few people want this.

Use Smart Cut and Paste

Check the Use Smart Cut and Paste checkbox to have Word automatically remove extra spaces when you delete text or add spaces when you insert text. This isn't one hundred percent perfect, but it's pretty cool.

Allow Accented Uppercase in French

Check the Allow Accented Uppercase checkbox if you're working with text formatted as French and you want to allow the spelling and grammar checkers to suggest that Word add an accent mark to an uppercase letter. If you're not working in French, leave this checkbox unchecked, as it is by default.

PART

VI

Power Tools

Tabs and Backspace Set Left Indent

Leaving this option checked allows you to set margins using the tab key and to undo them using the backspace key. This is how many users work intuitively, but if you want to make sure you don't change your margins by accident, you may want to uncheck this.

Picture Editor

Select the application you want to use as a picture editor from the drop-down list. Your choices will depend on what's loaded on your machine, and the default is Microsoft Word (which most Microsoft Word users will undoubtedly have).

Printing Options

The Print tab (see Figure 32.4) allows you to make some vital settings; so listen up for a minute. You can decide to print backward (à la Merlin), you can make sure fields and links get updated before you print, and you can print stuff like annotations and hidden text with your document.

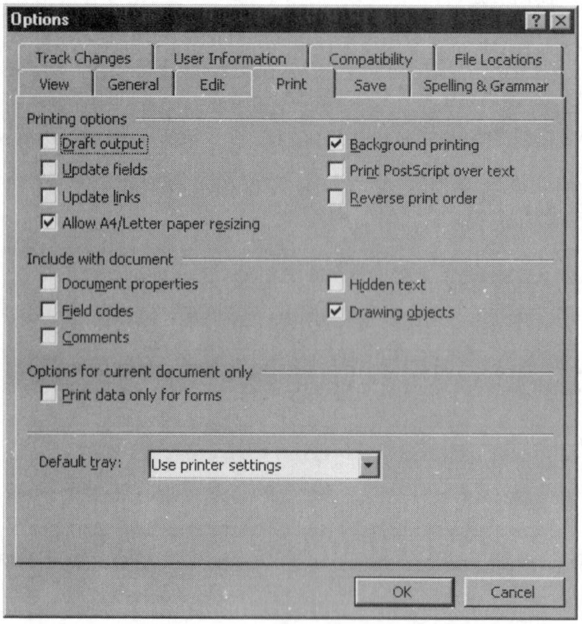

FIGURE 32.4

The Print tab of the Options dialog box

NOTE

The options you have will depend upon your printer.

In the following sections we'll look at each option in turn. Before that, let's take a quick glance at their default settings:

Feature	Default Setting
Printing Options	
Draft Output	Off
Update Fields	Off
Update Links	Off
Allow A4/Letter Paper Resizing	On
Background Printing	On
Print PostScript over Text	Off
Reverse Print Order	Off
Include with Document	
Document Properties	Off
Field Codes	Off
Comments	Off
Hidden Text	Off
Drawing Objects	On
Options for Current Document Only	
Print Data Only for Forms	Off
Default Tray	Use Printer Settings

Draft Output

Check the Draft Output checkbox to print your documents with minimal formatting. The amount of formatting that will be printed depends on the printer. As its name implies, this option is intended for fast printing of drafts of documents. Its value varies from one printer model to the next. Experiment.

PART

VI

Power Tools

Update Fields

Be sure the Update Fields checkbox is checked if you want all fields in your document (for example, date fields and page numbers) to be updated whenever you print. If you're aiming for special effects, uncheck this checkbox.

Update Links

Check the Update Links checkbox to have all links in your document updated every time you print. If the sources for your links are apt to change or be unavailable, leave this checkbox unchecked.

Allow A4/Letter Paper Resizing

If you used A4 (8.27" x 11.69") paper for one version of your Word document and you want to automatically adjust the document margins to American standard letter size, this is the box for you. Check it to automatically resize your documents to letter-sized pages.

Background Printing

Check the Background Printing checkbox if you want to be able to continue working in Word while you print a document. Bear in mind that background printing takes up memory and may slow both your work and your printing. If you have a comfortable amount of RAM and a speedy processor, you can print in the background with impunity. If background printing slows you down, you can turn it off and wait until your documents are printed to resume working.

Print PostScript over Text

This option applies to you only if you're endowed with a PostScript printer and you're embedding PostScript commands for printing graphics in your documents. If you want to invoke the power of PostScript over and above your text, check this box.

Reverse Print Order

Check the Reverse Print Order checkbox to print your documents starting at the last page. You might want to use this if you've got one of those weird copiers that reverses the order of collated copies. It's also quite handy if you're printing out large manuscripts: Print the last page first, and the rest will stack up so that page one is on the top of the heap. Don't use it when printing envelopes.

Document Properties

Check the Document Properties checkbox to have Word print file-summary information on a separate page after printing the document.

Field Codes

Check the Field Codes checkbox to have Word print the field codes rather than the field results in the document.

Comments

Check the Comments checkbox to have Word print out a document's annotations on a separate page at the end of the document. This replaces the Annotations option in Word 95.

Hidden Text

Check the Hidden Text checkbox to have Word print out any hidden text the document contains. Hidden text will look like normal text when printed; Word doesn't print the dotted underline you see for hidden text on the screen. Bear in mind that printing hidden text will affect line and page breaks in your document; if that matters to you, view hidden text on-screen before printing it and do any necessary fiddling with line and page breaks.

Drawing Objects

Check the Drawing Objects checkbox to have Word print drawing objects (for example, charts, graphics, and equations) created in Word with the document.

Print Data Only for Forms

Check the Print Data Only for Forms checkbox to print only the information entered in form fields in a form—not the form itself. You might want to use this for filling in preprinted forms. Note that this option applies only to the current document, not to all documents.

Default Tray

Choose a default paper tray from the drop-down list. The default setting is Use Printer Settings, as that's where you'll probably set printing options for all your Windows applications. However, if you want to set a paper tray to use with Word that's different from what you use with other applications, this may be a handy solution. If you want to use different paper sources for different sections of documents (for example, if you're printing an envelope and a letter), choose File ➤ Page Setup.

Save Options

The settings on the Save tab in the Options dialog box (see Figure 32.5) let you customize how and when you save your documents and choose protection for file sharing for

FIGURE 32.5

You can decide how and when to save your documents in the Save tab of the Options dialog box. I've chosen to always create a backup copy and not use the fast save option.

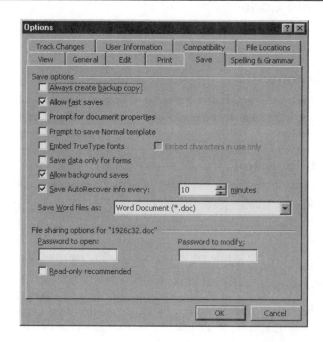

the current document. (See Chapter 1, *Creating and Saving Your First Document,* for more about saving.)

In the following sections we'll look at each of the options. But first, here's a sneak preview of their settings:

Feature	Default
Save Options	
Always Create Backup Copy	Off
Allow Fast Saves	On
Prompt for Document Properties	Off
Prompt to Save Normal Template	Off
Embed TrueType Fonts	Off
Save Data Only for Forms	Off
Allow Background Saves	On
Save AutoRecover Info Every:	On; 10 Minutes

Feature	Default
Save Word Files As	*.doc
File Sharing Options	
Password to Open	None
Password to Modify	None
Read-Only Recommended	Off

Always Create Backup Copy

Check the Always Create Backup Copy checkbox to have Word make automatic backups for you. Each time you save a document, Word saves a duplicate with a .bak extension. This is a useful option if you tend to bastardize your documents by mistake, but bear in mind that it doubles your disk-space requirements, and takes a little more housekeeping attention.

Allow Fast Saves

Check the Allow Fast Saves checkbox to speed up saving. Word then records only the changes to the document when you save it (rather than resaving the whole file).

NOTE Fast saves take up more space than regular saves. This option can also cause problems for some third-party conversion programs. If you're strapped for space, consider switching off fast saves.

Prompt for Document Properties

Back in the days of the horse and buggy, this used to be called the Prompt for Summary Info option. Now, the summary information that used to occupy its own dialog box is found as a tab in the Properties dialog box. Check the box to have Word display said Properties dialog box automatically whenever you save a new document. You can adjust the Document Properties at any time for each document by choosing File ➤ Properties.

PART

VI

Power Tools

Prompt to Save Normal Template

Check the Prompt to Save Normal Template checkbox if you want Word to consult you when you exit before saving changes you made to the default settings in your Word session. This box is unchecked by default; so Word automatically saves changes to Normal when you exit.

Embed TrueType Fonts

Check the Embed TrueType Fonts checkbox if you want others who read the document on PCs that do not have the fonts used in it to be able to view it with the right fonts. If you're not sharing documents, leave this box unchecked, since it's a real hard drive space hog. If you do use it, remember to toggle it off again when you're through embedding.

Save Data Only for Forms

Check the Save Data Only for Forms checkbox to save the data in a form as a record you can use in a database. To save the data with the form, leave this box unchecked.

Allow Background Saves

This features lets you continue working while Word saves your document (either when you tell it to or when it automatically saves for you). When Word is saving, you'll see a little disk icon pulsing on the status bar. It's probably rare that you have a document so large that it will take more than a second to save anyway, but if that is the case, ironically, you'll probably want to disable background saves, because the longer they take, the more system resources they sap.

Save AutoRecover Info Every *nn* Minutes

Check the Save AutoRecover Info Every *nn* Minutes checkbox to have Word provide a safety net for you in the event of a power failure or computer crash. This used to be called Automatic Save. With this option enabled, Word will automatically save the changes you've made to your document in, say, the last 10 minutes. When you restart Word after a power failure or a crash, Word will open all documents open at the time of the crash and display (Recovered) in the title. This gives you a chance to compare your original file with the Recovered version and choose the more recent of the two.

Set the number of minutes between 1 and 120.

Save Word Files As

The default for this option is, of course, Word Documents, or .doc files. However, you now have the option of having Word save all your files as .rtf, .txt, .html, or a number of other document formats. This is particularly useful if you work in a multi-platform intranet environment in which not all users have access to the latest (or any) version of Microsoft Word. See Chapter 25 before changing this setting.

Password to Open

Enter a password (a maximum of 15 characters: letters, spaces, symbols, and numbers are all okay) in the Password to Open text box to prevent other users from opening the current document unless they have the password.

Password to Modify

Enter a password (a maximum of 15 characters: letters, spaces, symbols, and numbers are all okay) in the Password to Modify text box to prevent other users from saving changes to the current document. You'll then need to enter the password to open the document normally, but you can open the document as read-only by choosing the Read-Only button in the Password dialog box.

Read-Only Recommended

Check the Read-Only Recommended checkbox to recommend that others open the current document as read-only. (It's only a recommendation—they can disregard it.)

Spelling & Grammar

Spelling and Grammar have been combined into a single tab in the Options dialog box. The settings on the Spelling & Grammar tab let you control the behavior of Word's spelling checker and grammar checker (both covered in Chapter 15, *Author's Tools*). You can instruct the spelling checker to ignore certain words, use as many as ten dictionaries, and use a specific language. And you can tell the grammar checker which rules to obey and which to ignore. Figure 32.6 shows the Spelling & Grammar tab of the Options dialog box.

In the following sections, we'll look at each of the options. But first, here's a preview of their default settings:

Feature	Default Setting
Spelling	
Check Spelling As You Type	On
Hide Spelling Errors in This Document	Off
Always Suggest Corrections	On
Suggest from Main Dictionary Only	Off
Ignore Words in UPPERCASE	On
Ignore Words with Numbers	On

PART

VI

Power Tools

Feature	Default Setting
Ignore Internet and File Addresses	On
Custom Dictionary	CUSTOM.DIC
Grammar	
Check Grammar As You Type	On
Hide Grammatical Errors in This Document	On
Check Grammar with Spelling	On
Show Readability Statistics	Off
Writing Style	Standard

FIGURE 32.6

The Spelling & Grammar tab of the Options dialog box

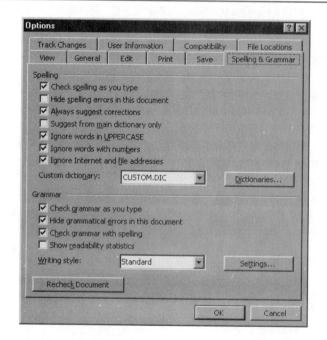

Check Spelling As You Type

This option is enabled by default, and it instructs Word to do background spell checking. This can be a real boon, because Word will automatically fix common typing errors such as "teh" (for "the") and "hda" (for "had"). If you want to know what else Word thinks of your spelling habits, you need to make sure that the next option, Hide Spelling Errors in This Document, is unchecked. When that's the case, you'll see a squiggly red line under presumably misspelled words, letting you see right away which ones may need rethinking.

Hide Spelling Errors in This Document

If you hide the spelling errors in the current document, you won't see the benefits of the squiggly red line. On the other hand, you may not *want* a squiggly red line, particularly if you're dealing with a lot of proper names or technical terms that aren't in Word's dictionaries. This option lets you disable the squiggles in the current document only, which is probably better for you than disabling automatic spell checking altogether.

 NOTE

For more on AutoText and AutoCorrect, with which you can add to Word's corrective capabilities, see Chapter 14, *End Monotony with AutoText, AutoCorrect, and Insert.*

Always Suggest Corrections

Check the Always Suggest Corrections checkbox to have Word display suggested spellings for misspelled words it finds during a spelling check. Note that this is an "official" spelling check—not the squiggly stuff we just talked about.

Suggest from Main Dictionary Only

Check the Suggest from Main Dictionary Only checkbox to have Word display suggested correct spellings from the main dictionary but not from any open custom dictionaries. If you leave this box checked, Word won't load your custom dictionaries and will ignore any words you've added to them in previous spell-checks.

Ignore Words in UPPERCASE

Check the Ignore Words in UPPERCASE 'checkbox to have Word's spelling checker ignore words in which every character is uppercase. This is useful for working with technical terms, abbreviations, and so on.

Ignore Words with Numbers

Check the Ignore Words with Numbers checkbox to have Word's spelling checker ignore any word that contains a number. This too is useful for working with technical terms and the like.

Ignore Internet and File Addresses

At last! No more squiggles under every URL! Check the Ignore Internet and File Addresses checkbox to have Word's spelling checker ignore likely candidates for path names, such as things starting with c:\ or http://.

Custom Dictionary

The default custom dictionary, in which all your "Add to Custom Dictionary" entries go during spelling checks, is called Custom.dic. For more custom dictionary options, including creating multiple custom dictionaries, click on the Dictionaries button. Word displays the Custom Dictionaries dialog box, in which you specify which dictionaries are to be loaded. Don't forget that dictionaries must be loaded in order for Word to use them in spell checks—remember which one you want to work with before you start. Figure 32.7 shows the Custom Dictionaries dialog box in all its glory.

> **TIP**
>
> The Custom Dictionaries dialog box is your friend. You can import old custom dictionaries from other computers by clicking on the Add button. You can also create new custom dictionaries for occasional use. One writer I know keeps his Land of Gylthmoor science fiction dictionary separate from his technical-writing dictionary.

FIGURE 32.7

You use the Custom Dictionaries dialog box to add or create your own dictionaries for projects with various spelling requirements. I've added custom dictionaries called History and Poetry.

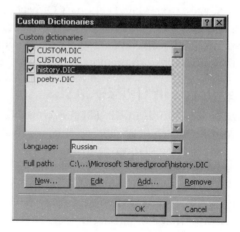

Check Grammar As You Type

With the Check Grammar As You Type checkbox checked, the grammar checker will automatically correct some common grammar errors and will indicate others with a wavy green line. What exactly it checks for depends on the grammar options you choose in the selections outlined below.

Hide Grammatical Errors in This Document

If you want to wait to check your grammar or if you'd rather take your chances and not use Word's grammar suggestions, check the Hide Grammatical Errors in This Document box.

Check Grammar with Spelling

To include grammatical queries when you run a spelling check, leave this box checked.

Show Readability Statistics

Check the Show Readability Statistics checkbox (unchecked by default) if you want to see the Readability Statistics dialog box after each completed grammar check.

Writing Style

Choose from Casual, Standard (the default), Formal, or Technical writing styles to use for checking grammar. Or choose Custom and click on the Settings button to define your own set of rules.

Grammar Settings

Adjust the set of rules used for Word's built-in grammar style guides, or define a Custom set of grammatical rules for your own uses. Click on the Settings button to adjust the rules for custom or default grammar styles. Figure 32.8 shows some of the options open to you in defining a custom grammatical style.

Recheck Document

Clicking on this button instructs Word to recheck the spelling and grammar in your document.

Track Changes

Reviewers of a document can use different-colored revision marks. Choose Tools ➤ Options, and select the Track Changes tab of the Options dialog box (see Figure 32.9) to specify the revision options you want.

PART

VI

Power Tools

FIGURE 32.8

Use the Grammar Settings dialog box to choose which rules you want to abide by.

FIGURE 32.9

The Track Changes tab of the Options dialog box

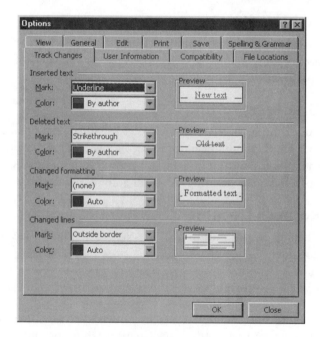

In the following sections we'll discuss each option in turn, but here are the default settings for the Track Changes tab:

Feature	Default Setting
Inserted Text	
Mark	Underline
Color	By Author
Deleted Text	
Mark	Strikethrough
Color	By Author
Changed Formatting	
Mark	None
Color	Auto
Changed Lines	
Mark	Outside Border
Color	Auto

Mark Inserted Text

Drop down the list for the Mark option and select the format with which you want to mark new text. Choose from none, Bold, Italic, Underline, and Double Underline.

Color for Inserted Text

Drop down the list for the Color for Inserted Text option and select the color with which you want to mark new text. Choose By Author for automatic choice of colors by Word for the first eight people to revise the document (after that, Word starts over with the colors), or choose one of the colors manually.

Mark Deleted Text

Use the Mark drop-down list to select how you want to display text you are deleting from the document. Choose Hidden or Strikethrough.

Color for Deleted Text

Drop down the Color list and select the color with which you want to mark deleted text. Choose By Author for automatic choice of colors by Word for the first eight people to revise the document (after that, Word starts over with the colors), or choose one of the colors manually.

PART

VI

Power Tools

Mark Changed Formatting

Use the Mark drop-down list to select how you want to display text you are reformatting. Choose from None, Bold, Italic, Underline, or Double Underline. The default is None; it may be difficult to determine which changes were made if all formatting is marked by using another kind of formatting.

Color for Changed Formatting

Drop down the Color list and select the color with which you want to mark reformatted text. Choose Auto if you're using None; choose By Author for automatic choice of colors by Word for the first eight people to revise the document (after that, Word starts over with the colors); or choose one of the colors manually.

Mark Changed Lines

Drop down the Mark list and select how to mark revised lines. Choose from None, Left Border, Right Border, or Outside Border (the default).

Color for Changed Lines

Drop down the list and select the color with which to mark revised lines. Choose By Author for automatic choice of colors by Word for the first eight people to revise the document (after that, Word starts over with the colors), or choose one of the colors manually. Consider using a different color for each group of authors when working on large projects with more than eight authors.

User Information

The User Information tab (see Figure 32.10) specifies information about the primary user of this copy of Word: the name, the return address for envelopes, and the initials for annotations.

For a little change of pace, the User Information tab doesn't have default options worth listing. It takes its information from what you entered when installing Word.

FIGURE 32.10

The User Information tab of the Options dialog box

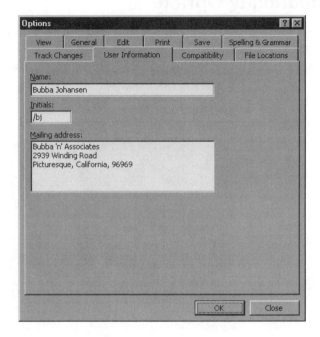

Name

Type the name for Word to use as the author in the Summary tab of the Properties dialog box (File ➤ Properties) for documents you create. The default setting is the name entered when installing.

Initials

Enter the initials you want Word to use for annotation marks. The default setting is the initials entered for the name when installing Word.

Mailing Address

The Mailing Address area displays the return address used on envelopes once you've used the Create Envelope command. Until then, the default setting is the address entered when installing Word. Any address you enter here will be displayed as the return address in the Envelopes and Labels dialog box.

Compatibility Options

The options on the Compatibility tab determine how Word displays documents created either in earlier versions of Word or in other word-processing programs. Use these settings to make such documents in Word more closely match their originals.

Figure 32.11 shows the Compatibility tab of the Options dialog box.

The Compatibility tab of the Options dialog box

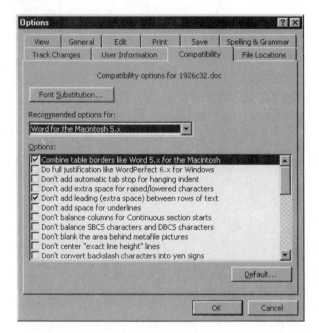

Font Substitution

If the active document has fonts that are not available on your computer, select the Font Substitution button to choose substitute fonts.

Recommended Options For

Pull down the Recommended Options For drop-down list and select the word-processing application for which to set options. Select Custom to specify options for an unlisted application. In the list of Options, check the options you want to use.

File Locations

You use the File Locations tab (see Figure 32.12) of the Options dialog box to specify where your documents, templates, and other items are stored by default.

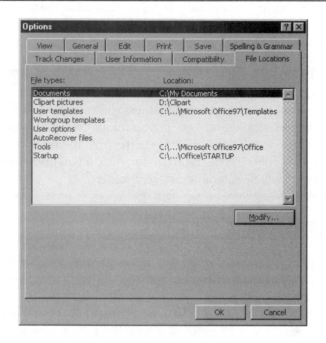

Here are the default settings for options on the File Locations tab if you are running Word by itself and on your hard drive rather than a CD-ROM. Your settings may be somewhat different if you are using Microsoft Office 97 as a suite instead of Word by itself.

File Type	Default Location
Documents	C:\MSOffice\WinWord
Clipart Pictures	C:\Clipart
User Templates	C:\MSOffice\Templates
Workgroup Templates	(Depends on workgroup selections)
User Options	C:\MSOffice\WinWord

PART
VI

Power Tools

File Type	Default Location
AutoRecover Files	(Depends on system settings)
Tools	C:\MSOffice\WinWord
Startup	C:\Winword\Startup

To set a new default location for an item, select the item and choose the Modify button. In the Modify Location dialog box, select the drive and folder for the item, and then click on OK. You can create a new subfolder by clicking on the Create New Folder button.

You may want to define a new default location for documents to keep them separate from your Word program files. You can use the C:\My Documents folder that Windows supplies for you, or you might create new folders for each project you work on. In this way, you'll be better able to find and use your files than if you let them all collect in the Word folder. Also, if you update or uninstall Word, your documents will be safer in a different folder.

Customizing Word's Toolbars

You can customize Word's toolbars to simplify the way you work. You can add and remove commands, macros, AutoText entries, and styles and move buttons from one toolbar to another. You can even create custom toolbars. You can move toolbars to different positions on the screen or have them float freely above the document. You can move and resize a floating toolbar as if it were a window. And you can plop floating toolbars onto the toolbar array at the top of the Word window to make them part of your regular platter of options. In the following sections, we'll look at what you can do with toolbars.

Figure 32.13 shows how zany you can get with toolbars by illustrating the "text porthole" concept.

Displaying Toolbars

To display toolbars, choose View ➤ Toolbars, and then select the toolbar you want to display from the menu.

Or, if you'd rather choose several at a time, choose Tools ➤ Customize, and then select the Toolbars tab (see Figure 32.14). Check the checkboxes for the toolbars you want to see, and click on OK.

FIGURE 32.13

I've arranged my toolbars for easy access.

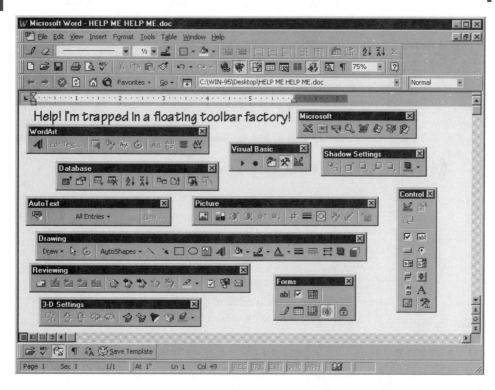

FIGURE 32.14

Check the checkboxes for the toolbars you want to see in the Toolbars tab of the Customize dialog box.

To remove a toolbar from the screen, choose View ➤ Toolbars and uncheck the checkbox of the guilty party.

TIP

To display and remove toolbars using the mouse, right-click on a displayed toolbar to display a shortcut menu and click to display an unchecked toolbar or to hide a checked toolbar. Click on Toolbars or Customize to display the Toolbars or Customize dialog box.

Moving and Resizing Toolbars

You can place toolbars anywhere on your screen and resize them to a number of shapes.

To move a toolbar displayed at the top of the screen, click on the dual lines at the left of the toolbar and drag it to where you want it. It'll change shape as soon as you drag it out of the toolbar area at the top of the screen. Alternatively, double-click on the dual lines to display a toolbar in its last floating position on the screen.

To return a now-floating toolbar to the top of the screen, click on the top of the toolbar and drag it to the top of the screen, where it'll revert to its long and wide shape. Alternatively, double-click in any blank space to flip it back up there.

To resize a floating toolbar, move the mouse pointer over one of its borders so that a double-headed arrow appears; then click and drag the border to the shape you want. Toolbar shapes adjust in jumps, not smoothly, so that they're the right size and shape for their buttons.

Changing the Predefined Toolbars

If you want, you can change Word's predefined toolbars. You might want to remove buttons that you never use or change the command that an existing button runs. Here's how:

1. Display the toolbar you want to change.
2. Choose Tools ➤ Customize to open the Customize dialog box.
3. Select the Commands tab (see Figure 32.15).
4. To add a button, select the correct category in the Categories box, and then choose a command in the Commands box.
5. Drag the button or item to where you want it on the toolbar.
6. To delete a button, drag the button off the toolbar and drop it in the dialog box (or to any other location not containing a toolbar).
7. When you're done, click on the Close button.

FIGURE 32.15

The Commands tab of the Customize dialog box contains all the menu commands. You can add any of these commands to a toolbar by dragging it there.

> **WARNING**
>
> When you delete a built-in toolbar button, it'll still be available in the Customize dialog box. But when you delete a custom toolbar button, it's gone for good. Consider creating a storage toolbar for keeping unused buttons rather than deleting them permanently.

Moving or Copying a Toolbar Button

Here's how to move or copy buttons from one toolbar to another:

1. Select Tools ➤ Customize to open the Customize dialog box.
2. Select the Commands tab.

> **TIP**
>
> To move a toolbar button quickly, without opening the Customize dialog box, hold down Alt and drag the button to where you want it. To copy a button, hold down Ctrl+Alt and drag the button to where you want it.

3. To move a button, drag it to where you want it on the same or another toolbar.

PART

VI

Power Tools

4. To copy a button, hold down Ctrl and drag the button to where you want it on the same or another toolbar. Word will automatically close the gap (when you move a button) and shift the buttons along in the new location. So if you want 15 smiley FoxPro faces on your Microsoft toolbar, go right ahead.

5. Click on the Close button.

Resetting a Built-In Toolbar

If you modify a built-in toolbar and then regret it, here's how to restore it to its original settings:

1. Select Tools ➤ Customize to open the Customize dialog box.

2. Select the Toolbars tab.

3. Highlight the toolbar you want to restore, and then click on the Reset button.

4. In the Reset Toolbar dialog box (see Figure 32.16), select the template in which to make the change, and then choose OK.

5. Click on OK to close the Reset Toolbar dialog box.

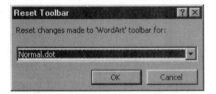

Creating a Custom Toolbar

If you find yourself using buttons on a half-dozen toolbars in the course of the day's work, you might want to create a custom toolbar that has only the buttons you need. Here's how:

1. Choose Tools ➤ Customize to open the Customize dialog box.

2. Select the Toolbars tab.

3. Click on the New button to open the New Toolbar dialog box:

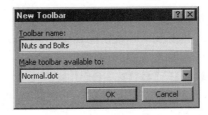

4. Type a name for the new toolbar in the Toolbar Name box.
5. Select the template in which to store the toolbar in the Make Toolbar Available To box, and then click on OK. Word displays the Customize dialog box with the Toolbars tab selected and a new toolbar without buttons in its own toolbar window.
6. Now you can customize your toolbar by dragging buttons from existing toolbars or by selecting the Commands tab and choosing from the array of options therein.
7. Drag the appropriate button to the new toolbar (see Figure 32.17).

FIGURE 32.17

*Dragging a
button to the
new toolbar*

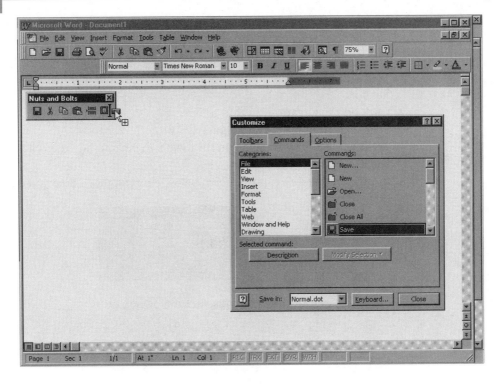

PART
VI

Power Tools

8. Add further buttons as appropriate.

9. When you finish building your new toolbar, click on the Close button.

Your new toolbar will appear in the Toolbars dialog box and in the shortcut menu produced by right-clicking on a displayed toolbar.

Deleting a Custom Toolbar

When you get sick of your custom toolbars, you can easily delete them. To do so, follow these steps:

1. Choose Tools ➤ Customize and then click on the Toolbars tab to display the Toolbars dialog box.

2. Highlight the custom toolbar you want to delete and click on the Delete button.

3. Click on Yes in the confirmation dialog box.

NOTE

Word won't let you delete the toolbars it provides; you can delete only your own custom toolbars.

Renaming a Custom Toolbar

You can rename a custom toolbar at any point. Follow these steps:

1. Choose Tools ➤ Templates and Add-Ins to open the Templates and Add-Ins dialog box.

2. Click on the Organizer button to open the Organizer dialog box.

3. Select the Toolbars tab (see Figure 32.18).

4. In the left or right box, highlight the toolbar to rename, and then click on the Rename button.

5. In the Rename dialog box (shown below), enter a new name and click on OK:

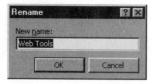

6. Click on Close to close the Organizer dialog box.

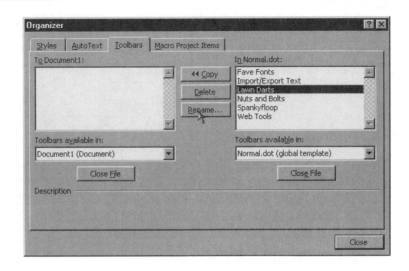

Copying a Toolbar from One Template to Another

If you create a toolbar in one template and you'd like to make it available in another,
it's easy. Here are the steps:

1. Choose Tools ➤ Templates and Add-Ins to open the Templates and Add-Ins dialog box.
2. Click on the Organizer button to open the Organizer dialog box.
3. Select the Toolbars tab.
4. Click on the Close File button on the left side of the Organizer dialog box. It turns
   into an Open File button.
5. Click on the Open File button to open the Open dialog box. Find and select the
   template you want to copy the toolbar *from*. Then click on OK.
6. Click on the Close File button on the right.
7. Click on the Open File button that appears in its place. In the Open dialog box,
   select the template you want to copy the toolbar *to* (see Figure 32.19).
8. Highlight the toolbar or toolbars to copy, and then click on the Copy >> button.
9. Click on Close to close the Organizer dialog box.

The toolbar (or toolbars) you selected will be copied to the other template.

PART

VI

Power Tools

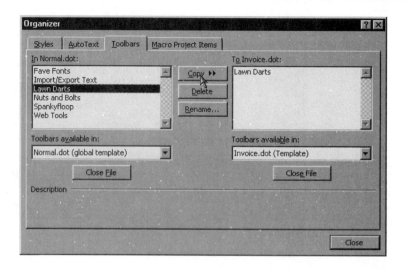

Assigning an Item to a Toolbar Button

You can assign toolbar buttons to run commands and macros, to fonts, to AutoText
entries, or to styles. You can attach toolbars to specific templates or even to specific
documents, which gives you great flexibility.

To assign an item to a toolbar button, follow these steps:

1. Open a document based on the template containing the item you want to assign—
or open the template itself.

2. Display the toolbar you want to change.

3. Choose Tools ➤ Customize to open the Customize dialog box.

4. Select the Commands tab (see Figure 32.15, earlier in this chapter).

5. In the Save In box, select the template containing the item you want to assign to
the toolbar.

6. In the Categories box, select the category containing the command to add.

7. Drag the item name from the Commands box (to the right of the Categories box)
to the toolbar.

NOTE

When you choose an item without a built-in button, you'll get a text button describing the action instead. For information about how to design an icon for this button, see the section "Creating a Custom Button," coming up in a moment.

Creating a Custom Button

If you're assigning a toolbar button to an item for which Word does not have a built-in button image, you might want to use the button editor. Getting to the button editor is a bit tricky these days. To do so, follow these steps:

1. Display the toolbar whose button image you want to edit.
2. Choose Tools ➤ Customize to open the Customize dialog box. Although you won't actually use this dialog box, you'll want to leave it open while you work.
3. Right-click on the button whose image you want to edit.
4. From the pop-up menu that appears, you have several options:

   - Paste Button Image: Use the Clipboard to paste in an image from a graphics application.
   - Edit Button Image: Open the Button Editor dialog box and modify an existing button to suit your needs.
   - Change Button Image: Choose from some cute clipart images supplied by Microsoft.

Pasting a Button Image from a Graphics Application

If you've got a good graphics program, you can have some fun creating your own image; then paste it onto a button via the Clipboard. To do so, follow these steps:

1. In the Custom Button dialog box, click on Cancel to return to the Toolbars tab of the Customize dialog box.
2. Switch to your graphics application. Create the image, and copy it to the Clipboard, preferably in bitmap or picture format.
3. Switch back to Word, where your target toolbar should still be displayed, along with the Toolbars tab.
4. Right-click on the blank toolbar button that will receive the image.
5. Choose Paste Button Image from the shortcut menu.
6. Click on the Close button.

Creating or Modifying a Button Image in the Button Editor

If you don't have a graphics program, you can use the Button Editor to create or modify a button image for the item you've just assigned. To do so, follow these steps:

1. With the Customize dialog box open, right-click on the button you want to modify.
2. From the pop-up menu that appears, choose Edit Button Image.
3. Word displays the Button Editor (see Figure 32.20) and the image you selected (if any) or a blank bitmap grid.
4. If you want to start from scratch, click on the Clear button.
5. Change the button image to your liking.
6. Click on the Close button.

You can use the Button Editor to modify any button at any time, if you feel creative. Simply display the toolbar whose button you want to modify, choose Tools ➤ Customize, click on the Toolbars tab, and then right-click on the button. From the shortcut menu, choose Edit Button Image, and Word displays the Button Editor.

FIGURE 32.20

Change or design your button with the Button Editor.

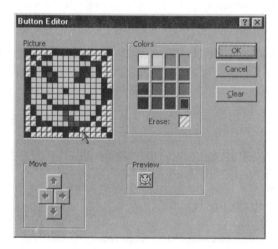

Restoring a Built-in Toolbar Button's Image

If you don't like the changes you made to the image on a button, you can easily restore it. Follow these steps:

1. Display the toolbar whose button you want to change.
2. Right-click on the button. From the pop-up menu that appears, select Customize to open the Customize dialog box.
3. Right-click on the button you want to restore.
4. Choose Reset Button Image from the shortcut menu.
5. Choose Close.

Enlarging Toolbar Buttons

If you're tired of peering at Word's toolbar buttons, unable to make out one button from another, you might want to enlarge the toolbar buttons. The only problem with doing this is that fewer buttons will fit across the width of the screen; you might want to remove unnecessary commands from the toolbars so that the necessary ones fit.

To display large toolbar buttons, follow these steps:

1. Choose Tools ➤ Customize to open the Customize dialog box.
2. Select the Options tab.
3. Check the Large Icons checkbox, and then click on OK. Your toolbars will appear with large buttons, as illustrated in Figure 32.21.

PART
VI

FIGURE 32.21

The difference between toolbars with large buttons (top) and regular buttons (bottom)

Power Tools

To restore toolbar buttons to their normal size, choose View ➤ Toolbars and uncheck the Large Buttons checkbox.

Customizing Word's Menus

Word lets you control the appearance and arrangement of its menus. You can add, delete, and reposition menu items. You can also change the keyboard shortcuts for most menu items. You can use this flexibility to make your copy of Word extremely easy to use or to deliberately restrict someone's options. For example, you could prevent a temp worker from applying any formatting to your precious documents.

Adding Menu Items

Here's how to customize Word's menus to contain the commands, macros, fonts, Auto-Text entries, and styles you need most often:

1. Open a document based on the template containing the item you want to assign—or open the template itself.
2. Choose Tools ➤ Customize to open the Customize dialog box.
3. Select the Commands tab.
4. In the Save In box, select the template in which the item is stored.
5. In the Categories box, select the category to which the item belongs.
6. Select the item you want to assign in the Commands box to the right of the Categories box, and click on it.
7. Drag the command to the menu of your choice, position it where you like it, and let go.

Removing Menu Items

Here's a quick way to remove items you don't need from menus:

1. Press Ctrl+Alt+- (that's Ctrl+Alt+minus). The mouse pointer will change to a heavy horizontal line.

If you change your mind, press Esc to return the mouse pointer to normal.

2. Click on the menu item you want to remove. It'll disappear.

To remove a menu-item separator bar, choose (Separator) in the Commands area of the Customize dialog box and click on the Remove button.

Restoring Built-in Menus to Their Original Settings

To quickly restore all built-in Word menus to their original state, follow these steps:

1. Choose Tools ➤ Customize to open the Customize dialog box.
2. Select the Commands tab.
3. Select the template to restore in the Save In box.
4. Click on the Toolbars tab and then highlight the Menu Bar listing in the list of Toolbars.
5. Click on the Reset Button
6. Click on the OK button to confirm that you want to reset the menu bar.
7. Click on the Close button.

WARNING

Think twice before restoring all menus, especially if you've made any significant changes. Consider backing up any superb pieces of customization in separate templates so that you can't trash them in an instant with the Reset button.

Adding New Menus

Word lets you add your own menus—a real boon to wonks! You can add as many menus as you want, but they might not all fit on your screen.

To add a new menu, follow these steps:

1. Choose Tools ➤ Customize to open the Customize dialog box.
2. Select the Commands tab.
3. Select the template for the new menu in the Save In box.
4. From the Categories box, highlight the New Menu entry (it's all the way at the bottom). The Commands area will be updated to reflect your choice, as shown in Figure 32.22.

PART

VI

Power Tools

FIGURE 32.22

The Customize dialog box with the New Menu option selected in the Commands tab

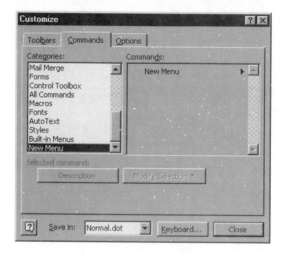

5. Drag the New Menu placeholder from the Commands area to the menu bar, position it where you like, and let go.

6. With the Customize dialog box still open, right-click on the words New Menu in the menu bar and look for the shortcut menu.

7. Here you'll see space (called Name) to type a name for your new menu.

TIP

An ampersand (&) before a letter in the name of a menu indicates a hotkey. For example, &View becomes <u>V</u>iew, and T&able becomes T<u>a</u>ble.

8. Start adding items to your menu as described earlier in this chapter.

NOTE

When you drag an item to your new menu for the first time, aim for the little blank square below the name of the menu. When the heavy cursor alights on that blank box, let go. Otherwise, you'll add the items to the menu bar itself, not to the new menu.

9. Close the Customize dialog box to finish.

Renaming Menus

You can rename a menu so that it suits your purposes better. Perhaps Fail would be more appropriate than File, or Fools than Tools? It's easy as pie. Follow these steps:

1. Choose Tools ➤ Customize to open the Customize dialog box.
2. Right-click on the menu of your choice and type the new name in the shortcut menu's white space.
3. Remember that an & in a menu name indicates a hotkey.
4. Close the Customize dialog box to finish.

Customizing Word's Keyboard Shortcuts

You can get the most use from your keyboard by customizing Word's keyboard shortcuts. You can assign shortcut keys to commands, macros, fonts, AutoText entries, styles, and special characters. You want Ctrl+A to change selected text to 40-point Kidnap? *No problemo.* You need Ctrl+Shift+T to type: "I was quite ecstatic to see you last night, darling!"? Read on!

Changing Keyboard Shortcuts

Here's how to see what your current keyboard shortcuts are and change them:

1. Choose Tools ➤ Customize to open the Customize dialog box.
2. Choose either Toolbars or Commands, and click on the Keyboard button. Word displays the Customize Keyboard dialog box (see Figure 32.23).
3. In the Categories box, select the category containing the items you want.
4. In the Commands box, select the command whose shortcut you want to view. The shortcut will appear in the Current Keys box.
5. If you would like to change this, move to the Press New Shortcut Key box and press the keyboard shortcut you want to assign. Word will display the current assignation of that keyboard shortcut, if any.
6. Click on the Assign button to assign the shortcut key to the item.
7. Click on the Close button to close the Customize Keyboard dialog box.

PART

VI

Power Tools

TIP

Here's a shortcut: Press Ctrl+Alt++ (that's three keys: Ctrl+Alt+plus). The mouse pointer changes to a command symbol (⌘). Choose a menu command or click on a toolbar button. Word displays the Customize Keyboard dialog box showing the command you select. Follow steps 5 through 7 of the preceding list.

FIGURE 32.23

The Customize Keyboard dialog box

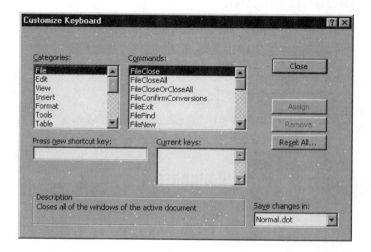

Deleting Shortcuts

By deleting shortcuts, you can prevent yourself or another user of your computer from performing unwanted actions. Here's how:

1. Choose Tools ➤ Customize to open the Customize dialog box.
2. Click on the Keyboard button.
3. Select the template containing the item whose shortcut you want to remove in the Save In box.
4. In the Categories box, select the category containing the item.
5. In the Commands box, select the item.
6. Select the shortcut key to delete in the Current Keys box.
7. Click on the Remove button.
8. Click on the Close button to close the Customize dialog box.

Reverting to Default Keyboard Shortcuts

Here's how to restore all shortcut key assignments to their original settings:

1. Choose Tools ➤ Customize to open the Customize dialog box.
2. Click on the Keyboard button.
3. Select the template containing the shortcut key assignments you want to restore in the Save In box.

4. Click on the Reset All button.

5. Choose Yes in the confirmation dialog box that Word throws at you.

6. Click on the Close button to close the Customize dialog box.

As is resetting the toolbars, this is a quick way of undoing many hours of work; so be sure you really want to abandon your custom key combinations.

Features for Physically Challenged Users

Word includes a number of features to assist physically challenged users. These are discussed in the following sections.

Microsoft's Access Pack

For people with motion or hearing disabilities, Microsoft's Access Pack provides better access to computers running Windows. With the Access Pack, you can:

- Type Shift+, Ctrl+, and Alt+key combinations with one finger.
- Instruct applications to ignore accidental keystrokes.
- Adjust the repeat rate (the rate at which a key registers multiple presses when held down) or turn off character repeating.
- Use the keyboard to control the mouse cursor.
- Use an alternate input device to control the keyboard and mouse.
- Display visually when the computer beeps or makes sounds.

Getting Access Pack

You'll find Access Pack in the file Access.exe in the Microsoft Windows Driver Library. You can also download the Microsoft Windows Driver Library from network services—CompuServe, GEnie, Microsoft Network, and Microsoft Download Service (MSDL). MSDL's number is (206) 936-MSDL (that's 936-6735).

If you don't have a modem, you can order the Access Pack by calling Microsoft Product Support Services at (206) 637-7098 or (206) 635-4948 (text telephone).

Single-Handed Keyboard Layouts

If you have difficulty using the standard QWERTY keyboard, you can get from Microsoft the Dvorak keyboard layouts that make the most frequently typed characters on a keyboard more accessible.

PART

VI

Power Tools

The three Dvorak keyboard layouts are:

- Two-handed
- Left hand only
- Right hand only

The left-handed and right-handed layouts can be used by people who type with a single finger or with a wand. You don't need any special equipment to use them.

Low Vision Aids

Users with impaired vision can customize the Word display to make it easier to see. In Chapter 2, *Viewing and Navigating*, we discussed how to zoom in and out to improve your view of Word, and in the "Enlarging Toolbar Buttons" section earlier in this chapter, we looked at how to display Word's large toolbar buttons. It's also possible to choose a large font size in the Format ➤ Font dialog box and set it as the default.

Other products available include screen-enlargement utilities and screen readers that provide output by synthesized voice or refreshable Braille displays.

Audio Documentation

You can get Microsoft software documentation on audio cassettes and floppy disks. Contact Recording for the Blind, Inc., at this address:

Recording for the Blind, Inc.
20 Roszel Road
Princeton, NJ 08540
Phone: (800) 221-4792
Phone outside the U.S.: (609) 452-0606
Fax: (609) 987-8116

TDD Product Support

Microsoft provides a text telephone (TT/TDD) service to give people who are hard of hearing access to product and support services.

Microsoft Sales and Service and Microsoft Product Support Services are open 6 A.M. to 6 P.M. Pacific time. Here are the numbers for the text telephones:

Microsoft Sales and Service: (800) 426-9400
Microsoft Product Support Services: (206) 635-4948

Microsoft will charge you for support services. You have been warned.

For More Assistance and Information

For more information on Microsoft products and services for people with disabilities, contact Microsoft Sales and Service at (800) 426-9400 (voice) or (800) 892-5234 (text telephone).

For general information on how computers can help you, consult a trained evaluator. To find one, contact the National Information System, Center for Developmental Disabilities, Benson Building, University of South Carolina, Columbia, SC 29208. Here are the numbers:

Voice/text telephone outside South Carolina: (800) 922-9234, ext. 301
Voice/text telephone in South Carolina: (800) 922-1107
Voice/text telephone outside the United States: (803) 777-6222

You can also get the *Trace ResourceBook* from the Trace R&D Center at the University of Wisconsin-Madison. The *Trace ResourceBook* describes and illustrates about 2000 products to help people with disabilities use computers. Here is the address:

Trace R&D Center
S-151 Waisman Center
1500 Highland Avenue
Madison, WI 53705-2280
Voice telephone: (608) 263-2309
Text telephone: (608) 263-5408
Fax: (608) 262-8848

PART
VI

Power Tools

PART VII

VII

Word and the Internet

- Connect to the Internet

- Open Internet documents in Word

- Use Word to create a Web page

- Enhance your Web page with exciting design effects

Chapter

33

Word and the Web

FEATURING

Chapter 33

Word and the Web

The *Internet*—a word that's in every newspaper, in many corporate meeting rooms, and on everyone's lips. Only a few years ago, PCs were isolated appliances that helped you create documents, analyze data, and (if you were a lucky member of a company LAN) send messages to other people on your network. Today, the Internet makes it possible to communicate and share information with millions of people all over the world.

The revolutionary move from the desktop into cyberspace has changed the way many of us use our computers. It's no longer enough to create sophisticated reports and publications that can be printed up and handed around the meeting table. Why not put information online for all to see?

Understanding the importance of this paradigm shift, Microsoft has made Word 97 Internet-aware. You can use Word to explore and, more important, to publish information on the World Wide Web.

What Is the Internet?

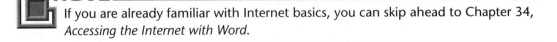

NOTE If you are already familiar with Internet basics, you can skip ahead to Chapter 34, *Accessing the Internet with Word.*

The Internet (or the *Net*) is a global network of computers connected by telephone lines and high-speed links (see Figure 33.1 for an illustration). When you use the Internet, you access information stored on these computers (called *servers*, since they serve you the information you want) by using your PC and modem to connect to an *Internet service provider* who, in turn, provides you with access to this widespread network. An Internet service provider is a company whose fast, powerful computers are connected to the Internet via special, high-speed lines. Internet service providers sell connect time and storage space to those who want to access and publish on the Internet.

FIGURE 33.1

The Internet

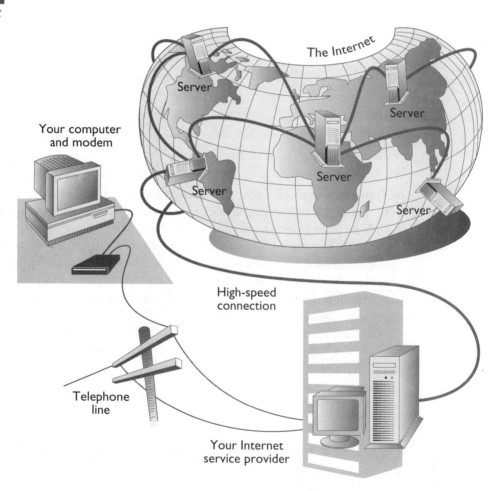

The telephone system is a good analogy. Your telephone connects you to a widespread network of telephone lines all over the world. By pressing a specific set of numbers on your telephone keypad, you can reach just about anyone else who has a phone. Same with the Internet: You access sites on the Internet by specifying their unique addresses (like dialing a phone number). Your Internet service provider is like the phone company, and the Internet is like the thousands of phone lines that crisscross the globe.

Some companies and organizations are serious enough to purchase and maintain their own servers and Internet connections, bypassing an Internet service provider altogether. This gives them greater control over many of the technical aspects of their Internet presence. They hire a *system administrator* (known to other techies as a *sysadmin*) to take care of the server and to make sure it works with the rest of the company's computer network.

What Is the World Wide Web?

The *World Wide Web* (a.k.a. the *Web*, *WWW*, and *W3*) is but one of the Internet's many identities, yet it has become so popular many people think of it as the only way to get around the Net.

The Web has revolutionized the Internet by making it easy for the average Jane or Joe to navigate. In the same way that Windows makes the DOS interface more attractive and easier to use without changing its underlying structure, the Web puts a user-friendly mantle on top of the Internet's vast array of information. The Web isn't separate and distinct from the Internet; it's an interface for exploring what is already there.

To view and navigate the Web, you need to use a piece of software called a *Web browser*. Browsers interpret the information stored on the Web, translate the information into a readable form, and present you with the colorful documents you see on your screen. You may already have ventured online with a browser such as Netscape Navigator, Microsoft Internet Explorer, or Mosaic. Word is also able to open documents from the World Wide Web (you'll find out more about this feature in the next chapter).

The Web is made up of thousands of individual *Web sites*. A Web site is a particular place you can visit on the Web. Web sites consist of one or more *Web pages*. Like pages in a book, Web pages are individual files that are linked together to make up the Web site as a whole.

When you hear people say they have a Web site or a *home page*, they have their own place on the Web to which you can direct your browser to find out more about them or their services. Their site may consist of a page (or more likely a bunch of interconnected pages) describing a product they offer, displaying their logo, and linking to other sites with related information.

NOTE

The term *home page* refers to three related (but different) things: a Web site as a whole, the opening or initial page of a Web site, and the start page from which you begin each Web browsing session.

The Web's star attraction is its use of *hyperlinks*. Hyperlinks connect Web pages and sites, creating a seamless flow of information. A hyperlink is a piece of text or an image that has been formatted to act as a springboard to another location. Clicking on the hyperlink transports you to another place in a Web page or to another location on the Web altogether.

MASTERING THE OPPORTUNITIES

The Internet: A Rich Cast of Characters

The Web's glamour tends to overshadow the Internet's other features. I'll take a minute to mention the three most popular ones here: e-mail, FTP, and Usenet newsgroups.

- Electronic mail, or *e-mail*, is the communications heart of the Internet. E-mail software lets you send messages to anyone else with an e-mail address.

- File Transfer Protocol, or *FTP*, allows you to exchange documents and files over the Internet. You use an FTP program to transfer files to other computers over the Internet or to log on to a public-access computer (called an *anonymous FTP site*) and download files from that computer to yours.

- *Usenet newsgroups* are some of the Net's more dynamic places to visit. A newsgroup is an electronic discussion group; it is devoted to a particular

topic, and anyone can join in, post opinions, and respond to other people's posts. There's a newsgroup for just about every topic you can think of, plus a few you probably would never dream of in a million years. Newsreader software lets you select the newsgroups to which you'd like to subscribe (read on an ongoing basis) and then displays the day's posts for you to read at will.

The programs I've mentioned are generally included by your Internet service provider in the software package you get when you sign up for an account. If your Internet connection comes care of a company server (and your company doesn't provide these programs), you can download them from the Internet. Advanced Web browsers, such as Microsoft Internet Explorer and Netscape Navigator, integrate some or all of these capabilities into one package.

What Is Web Publishing?

The ease with which one can browse the Web is only half the story (and not the most exciting half!). *Web publishing*, or the ability to create and post your own content, is the real fuel behind the Web phenomenon. Corporations, small businesses, and individuals are beating a path to the Web so that they can tell the world about their services, their products, and themselves.

When you publish a Web site, you do two things: You create one or several Web pages, and you make the pages publicly accessible on the Web.

A Web page is like any other computer file (say a Word document or an Excel worksheet), except it is written in a special language called *Hypertext Markup Language*, or *HTML*. HTML is nothing more than a set of plain text codes that define the structure of the page. Your Web browser interprets the codes (called *tags*) and presents you with the beautifully formatted documents you see while surfing the Web.

Word saves you from having to learn all of HTML's tags. It contains a built-in *HTML editor*, a program that simplifies Web publishing. You work with Word's familiar interface, and it cranks out the HTML for you.

Once you create a Web site, you need to make it accessible on the Web. To do this, you need to transfer your Web site files (with the help of an FTP program) to your Internet service provider's or company's Web server.

What Is an Intranet?

An *intranet* is a company network that is based on the same technology as the Internet, but it is only accessible by those within an organization or a corporation. In some cases, users of an intranet can venture out onto the Internet, but unauthorized users can't come in.

Because intranets use the same infrastructure as the Internet, you can use Word to create an internal Web site as easily as you would create a site for the World Wide Web. Although these chapters focus specifically on publishing a Web site on the Internet, they apply to publishing on an intranet site as well.

Getting an Internet Connection

To publish your site on the Web, you first need to get an Internet connection. In this section, I'll talk about how to choose and sign up with an Internet service provider. If you work with a company that has its own server or you are publishing on an intranet site, you can skip this section and, instead, discuss your options with your system administrator.

> **NOTE**
>
> I'm assuming you already have the hardware you need, that is, a computer and a modem (or other connection device). If not, read the review sections of popular computer magazines and ask your friends and co-workers for their recommendations. Then, visit your local computer merchant and pick his or her brain about the best choices for you.

A Note about Online Services

Signing up with an online service such as America Online is not the same thing as getting an Internet account. Although most of the online services offer access to the Internet, not all provide storage space on a Web server for your use. Those that do may charge a premium for the service or provide limited Web publishing capabilities.

If you currently have an account with an online service, I recommend getting a separate account with an Internet service provider for the sole purpose of Web publishing. You'll have full access to the Internet, you'll have plenty of personal storage space on a Web server, and you'll be able to use state-of-the-art Web browsers and publishing tools.

Choosing the Right Type of Internet Service

You have plenty of options when deciding upon your Internet service provider. New providers appear regularly, and each one has its own way of describing its services. Don't let the vast number of choices overwhelm you; in fact, you need to know only a few things to choose the right service.

SLIP or PPP Connection

Most providers offer two types of accounts for the average home or office user: *shell accounts* and *SLIP/PPP (Serial Line Protocol/Point-to-Point Protocol) accounts*. To use Word's Web capabilities, you need a SLIP or PPP account (preferably PPP). A SLIP/PPP account gives you full access to the Internet using the Windows interface. A shell account, while providing the same access, does so using a text-only, Unix-based interface.

Full Internet Software Package

Your Internet account should come with a full suite of Internet software and easy instructions for installing it onto your computer (or better yet, an automatic installation program). The package should include:

- *A TCP/IP stack.* Short for *Transmission Control Protocol/Internet Protocol*, this program allows your computer to exchange information over the Internet.
- *An e-mail program.*
- *A Web browser.*
- *An FTP program.*

If your software package *doesn't* include all the above programs, your Internet service provider should direct you to the location on the Web where you can download them for free.

TIP

Be sure to tell your provider that you plan to use Windows 95. You will probably be instructed to use Win 95's Bulletin Internet software.

Web Server Storage Space

In addition to Internet access and a software package, your account should include at least 10 megabytes of storage space on your provider's Web server (where you will be storing your Web site files). If your Web site includes lots of graphics, sounds, or videos, you may want 15 megabytes or more, since these file formats quickly eat up storage space.

NOTE

Organizations called *Web presence providers* offer storage space on their Web servers without giving you full access to the Internet. This is a cost-effective option for some, but if you're planning on getting involved with Web publishing, you need full Internet access.

Local Access Number

Be sure your provider has an access phone number (often called a *point of presence* or a *POP*) in your local calling area. When you connect to the Internet, you use your modem to "dial in" to your provider's servers. Essentially, your modem places a phone call to a modem connected to their computers. Once a connection is made, you can log on to the Internet. The last thing you want is for that connection to accrue long-distance phone charges. I can tell you from personal experience that this can add up to hundreds of dollars a month.

Some providers have 800 numbers that allow you to dial in toll-free from anywhere in the country (a handy feature if you travel a lot), although you usually pay a higher rate to use them.

Services for Web Publishers

Look for an Internet service provider that caters to Web publishers by providing the following services:

- *CGI Scripting*

  Certain Web-publishing features such as HTML forms must interact with a special program, stored on the Web server, to be able to function correctly. These programs, called *CGI scripts*, require programming expertise to create, and they usually must be written by your Internet service provider's staff. Many Internet service providers make *generic scripts* available to all their users, eliminating the need to write an individual script for each user that requests one.

- *Hit Logs*

  Hit logs record how many visits, or "hits," your site receives. More sophisticated logging programs include information such as the time and date of the hit and the domain from which it came. This information is invaluable if you want to track your site's usage statistics.

- *Custom Domain Names*

  The *domain name* identifies the organization that controls and maintains the Web server. Companies who maintain their own servers generally have their own domains; Microsoft's domain, for example, is microsoft.com. Companies and individuals who get their Internet connection from an Internet service provider, however, must use their provider's domain name, since their Web site files are stored on the provider's server. Some companies feel that anything other than their own domain promotes a "small-time" image, so many Internet service providers create *custom* or *virtual domain names*. They alias the real domain name to a name of the company's choice, creating the illusion of a dedicated server to the outside world.

These services may cost extra but will be useful as your Web-publishing expertise grows and your Web site becomes more sophisticated.

Network Setup

You should inquire about your provider's hardware and network setup. You should know:

- *The user-to-modem ratio*

  This gives you an indication of how busy the provider is. When you dial into your provider, an unoccupied modem needs to be on that end to answer the call and connect you to your provider's servers. If all the modems are already occupied by other users, your modem will go unanswered or will get a busy signal, and you won't be able to connect. This can be extremely annoying, especially if you have to wait a long time to log on. To avoid this, providers need to keep the user-to-modem ratio relatively low. A good baseline is one modem per twenty users.

- *Modem speeds*
  Your provider's modems must be of the same speed *or faster* than yours. If the modem speeds are different, you will connect at the slower rate. For example, if you use a 28.8 modem, but connect to a provider who only has 14.4 modems, your Internet connection will only be 14.4. (The numbers here refer to kilobytes of data transferred per second.) Most providers accommodate modem speeds of at least 14.4, with many supporting 28.8 modems as well.

- *Backup procedures*
  Internet service providers aren't immune to system crashes. For that reason, it is imperative that they have a consistent backup procedure in place. After all, you store your Web pages on their computers; the last thing you need is for your files to be wiped out by a system glitch. (This, by the way, is why you should also maintain your own backup copies of your Web site files. It is also a good reason to check your e-mail regularly.)

- *System security*
  Your provider should have someone on staff who is an expert in network security, a "hacker-guard," if you will. You should feel confident that a professional is in charge of keeping your information secure.

Responsive Customer Support

No matter how easy the Web is to use, you may find yourself in need of help from time to time. Your provider's customer service staff should be approachable, responsive, and knowledgeable. They should be reachable by phone and e-mail and should respond to problems or questions promptly.

In addition to support, customer-oriented providers make other help resources available, such as internal "members-only" newsgroups (so that users can benefit from others' experiences), online instructions for common tasks (such as uploading files to the Web server, changing your password, and so on), and an *FAQ list* (list of frequently asked questions and their answers).

Cost

The cost for the kind of Internet service I describe above varies. Some providers charge a low monthly fee, with a per-hour charge for the time that you are connected. Others charge a higher monthly fee, with no connect charges. Still others also charge a one-time setup fee when you sign up.

Word and the Internet

You should expect to pay somewhere in the neighborhood of $25 a month for 50 hours or more, with an initial setup fee of $30. You can find cheaper rates, but they may come at the expense of service and support (not necessarily, but it's something to keep in mind as you shop around).

Be sure to ask if the charges are the same if you establish a personal versus a commercial Web site. Some providers charge more if they think your site is a money-making operation or can be written off as a business expense. Also, ask if they charge higher rates for high-traffic sites. Some providers make you pay an extra fee if your Web site consistently receives a high volume of visitors. Finally, ask how much they charge per megabyte if you find you need additional server storage space.

WARNING

I caution you against working with providers that attract you with low monthly fees, only to charge you for the hours you're online. You'd be surprised how quickly those hours add up, especially as you get more involved with Web publishing. I recommend paying a little more each month for the peace of mind that comes with not having to worry about how long you've been connected. Fifty hours a month is a good place to start.

Choosing an Internet Service Provider

Now that you know what you're looking for, it's time to start shopping around. Here are a few tips on how to find out about the Internet service providers in your area:

- Ask your friends for their recommendations. Word of mouth is often the most reliable source of information.
- Read your local or regional computer magazines. These magazines, available free in many cities, include advertisements and articles about Internet service providers.
- Check with your local computer user groups for advice and recommendations. Many user groups have *SIGs* (special interest groups) devoted to Internet use and access, which are full of friendly advisors.
- If you have Internet access through your work or school (or if you can borrow a friend's account for an evening), you'll find some excellent resources on the Web. One is the ever-helpful Yahoo (http://www.yahoo.com), with links to the home pages of providers all over the world. Another is called The List (http://thelist.com), and it is single-mindedly devoted to indexing Internet service providers. The List is handy, because you can search by geographical location, by area code, by name, and more.
- When shopping around, call a selection of regional *and* national providers. National providers service the entire country, and often other countries as well.

Although regional providers serve a smaller geographical area, they often have a more personal touch, as well as a devoted community of users.

Once you establish your connection, you're ready to use Word to access the Internet.

PART

VII

Word and the Internet

Chapter

34

Accessing the Internet with Word

Accessing the Internet with Word

Fasten your seat belts, because you're about to leave the cozy comfort of your computer and enter the exciting realm of cyberspace. Word's new Net-smarts erode the boundaries between your hard drive and the Internet.

With Word 97, you open World Wide Web documents as easily as you open documents stored on your own computer. Word can also follow hyperlinks within Web pages, giving you access to the Web's vast network of linked resources.

Word does most of its Internet magic with the help of the Web toolbar (see Figure 34.1).

Here, you'll find most of the tools you need to access and navigate files on the Internet. To show the Web toolbar, click on the Web Toolbar button in the Standard toolbar, or choose View ➤ Toolbars ➤ Web.

To hide other toolbars while you're working with the Web toolbar, click on the Show Only Web Toolbar button.

FIGURE 34.1

The Web toolbar

Opening Internet Documents

Word treats the Internet as if it were an extension of your own hard drive—simply another location from which to retrieve information. As long as you have an active Internet connection, you can open documents (including Web pages) stored on servers on the other side of the world.

Opening a Document on the World Wide Web

To open a document stored on a Web server, you need its location. A *universal resource locator*, or *URL*, is the technical name for a Web address. As an example, the URL for Sybex's Web site is http://www.sybex.com. This cryptic-looking bunch of letters, dots, and slashes tells Word where to go to find the page you want, as well as how to retrieve and display the page. Every document on the Web has its own URL, and each URL follows these conventions:

- It begins with http://. An abbreviation for *hypertext transfer protocol,* this code identifies the address to the Web browser as a World Wide Web URL. URLs for other types of servers contain a different protocol notation. For example, URLs for FTP servers begin with ftp://.
- Next comes the name of the Web server upon which the page resides (for example, www.sybex.com). The www refers to the name of the Web server itself. The sybex.com is the *domain name*, which means that Sybex maintains this particular server. The .com at the end indicates that this is a commercial site. Other types of sites include educational (http://www.berkeley.edu), governmental (http://www.whitehouse.gov), and nonprofit organizations (http://www.npr.org). Although this is the standard URL formatting scheme, it isn't mandatory. Don't be surprised if you see a URL that looks a little different.

This is all some Web URLs need to be complete. Sometimes, however, URLs include additional slashes and names. This information points to specific directories and files on the Web server, similar to the *path* that describes where files are located on your hard drive. For example, the URL http://www.sybex.com/books.html bypasses Sybex's home page and takes you straight to the Sybex Online Catalog.

To open a document from the Web, follow these steps:

1. Activate your Internet connection.
2. In the Standard toolbar, click on the Open button.
3. In the File Name field, type the URL of the document you want to open, and press Enter.
4. Word connects to the server and opens the document.

If the document contains pictures, they take a bit longer to appear. The images are actually distinct files that are retrieved separately from the text of the document. Small images take a few seconds to load. Larger images can take much longer.

PART

VII

Word and the Internet

NOTE

When you use Word to open a page from the Web, it is a *read-only* version of the page, which means you are unable to edit the original file stored on the Web server. If you make changes to the document and try to save it, Word prompts you to save a copy of the page on your hard drive.

TIP

You can also open Web pages by clicking on the Address field in the Web toolbar and entering the URL or by clicking on Go in the Web toolbar, selecting Open, entering the URL in the Address field, and clicking on OK. If you have a Web browser installed on your computer, it launches automatically and displays the page. If you don't have a Web browser installed, the page opens in Word.

Accessing FTP Sites

Word can also open documents stored on *FTP servers*. *FTP* stands for *file transfer protocol*, and it is another way of transferring information over the Internet. Usually, FTP servers act as holding sites for software and files that are available for download.

Unlike Web servers, which are publicly accessible to anyone with a Web browser, you must *log on* to an FTP server in order to access its files and directories. Public FTP servers allow people to log on *anonymously*, which means that anyone can log on without identifying themselves. Other FTP servers only allow users with passwords to log on.

Adding an FTP Server to Word's Site List

To open a document stored on an FTP server, you must first add the server to Word's list of available Internet sites. To do so, follow these steps:

1. Click on the Open button.
2. Click on the Look In field, and select Add/Modify FTP Locations.
3. In the Name of FTP Site field, type the URL of the FTP server to which you want to log on. It should look something like `ftp://ftp.microsoft.com`.
4. If you're logging on to an anonymous FTP site, in the Log On As section, click on Anonymous. If you're logging on to a site that requires special user permission, click on User.

5. If you're logging on to an anonymous FTP site, type your e-mail address in the Password field. If you are logging on to a site that requires user permission, type your access password.

6. Click on Add.

7. Click on OK.

Word adds the profile to its list of FTP sites. From now on, you can simply select the profile to access information on that site. To add another FTP site profile or to modify or remove an existing profile, select Add/Modify FTP Location.

NOTE

When you log on to an anonymous FTP site, you don't need to enter a password. It is, however, accepted Internet etiquette (more commonly known as *netiquette*) to enter your e-mail address in place of a password so that the site administrators can track who has visited the site.

Opening Documents on FTP Sites

Once you add an FTP site to Word's list of Internet sites, you may access it just like you would another drive on your computer. To open a document from an FTP site, follow these steps:

1. Activate your Internet connection.

2. Click on Open.

3. In the Look In box, select the name of the FTP site to which you want to log on, and click on Open.

4. Word logs on to the site. Once the connection is established, Word displays the site's folders.

5. Find the name of the document you want to open, and double-click on it. (If you can't see it, be sure the proper file type is visible in the Files of Type field.)

NOTE

When you edit a document opened from an FTP site, Word saves the changes to the original file on the server (unlike Web documents, for which changes are saved to a copy of the document and stored on your hard drive).

Opening Your Start Page

If you consistently open the same document each time you start Word, you can specify that document as your Start page. You can also use your Start page as an entry point to the Internet.

By default, Word's Start page points to Microsoft's Web site. You can, however, specify any document you wish, either on your computer or on the Web, as your Start page.

> **NOTE**
>
> If you have a Web browser installed, Word uses the browser's Start page setting. Also, if your Start page points to a location on the Internet and you have a Web browser installed, Word launches the browser to display your Start page.

To open your Start page, do one of the following:

- On the Web toolbar, click on Start Page.
- Click on Go, and select Start Page.

To change your Start page, follow these steps:

1. Open the page you would like to specify as your Start page.
2. Click on Go, and select Set Start Page.
3. Click on Yes.

Opening Your Search Page

Is it on the Web? If you like to surf the Internet, you'll find yourself asking this question all the time. Whenever you need to do some research, find an obscure fact, or figure out what to make for dinner, chances are you'll turn to the Web for answers. As you've probably noticed, the Web is a big place, and the information you want is not necessarily at your fingertips—you have to dig for it. Luckily, several fantastic search utilities are on the Web. When you use them, you'll usually find the information you want in just a few clicks.

Word gives you quick access to Microsoft's All-in-One Search page, an entry point to the Web's most popular search utilities. Once you're there, type the words you're looking for, select the search utility you want to use, click on Go, and you're on your way. If you have a particular Internet search utility you prefer to use, you can change Word's Search page to point there instead.

> **NOTE**
>
> If you use the Internet Explorer Web browser, Word uses Internet Explorer's Search page setting. Also, if you have a Web browser installed, Word launches the browser to display your Search page.

To open your Search page, do one of the following:

- In the Web toolbar, click on the Search the Web button.
- Click on Go, and select Search the Web.

To change your Search page, follow these steps:

1. Open the page you would like to make your Search page.
2. Click on Go, and select Set Search Page.
3. Click on Yes.

Browsing Internet Documents

Word lets you do more than simply open documents from the Internet—you can browse them as well. Word knows how to follow hyperlinks. Word also lets you explore documents and jump to other Internet locations.

Following Hyperlinks

When you click on the underlined words or phrases in a Web page open in Word, you are instantly transported to a different location within the page or to a different page altogether. You can also click on a *graphic hyperlink*. A graphic hyperlink works just like a text hyperlink, except you click on pictures to move to another place.

NOTE

Hyperlinks don't necessarily point to documents on the Internet. You can create hyperlinks between regular Word documents (in fact, you can use hyperlinks in any Microsoft Office document) to move easily between locations. You don't need to be connected to the Internet to follow hyperlinks between documents stored on your computer. Learn how to place hyperlinks in your documents by reading about them in Chapters 14 and 35.

After a while, jumping between hyperlinks can leave you feeling like you are wandering in a dense forest of information. Don't worry—Word leaves a trail of bread crumbs for you to follow back home. To move back to a previous page, click on the Go Back button. You'll go back, in order, through the pages you have visited so far.

To return to your present location from a previous page, click on the Go Forward button.

You can also click on Go and select Go Back or Go Forward.

Some Web sites take several minutes to load (they may contain large, complex graphics, for example). If you want to stop a page while it's downloading, click on the Stop Current Jump in the Web toolbar to stop the download process.

If you stop the download process after the new page has begun to appear on your screen, click on the Go Back button to view the previous page you visited, or click on the Refresh Current Page button to download the page again and view it in its entirety.

Viewing Your History List

If you want to return to a page you recently visited, but you don't want to click on the Go Back button a million times, you can use your *History List* to transport yourself directly there. Your History List contains the titles and URLs of pages you've recently visited, both on your computer and on the Web.

To access your History List, in the Web toolbar, click on the down arrow next to the Address list. To jump to a location, select an item from the list.

Visiting Favorites

You'll probably find yourself opening certain documents, both on your computer and on the Internet, again and again. For quick access, include them in your list of Favorites. To add a document to your Favorites list, follow these steps:

1. Open the document.
2. From the Web toolbar, click on Favorites, and select Add to Favorites to open the Add to Favorites dialog box.
3. Word prompts you to save a shortcut to the open document. If you like, change the name of the shortcut.
4. Click on Add.

After that, open your Favorites list for a direct link to the document. To view your Favorites, click on the Favorites button.

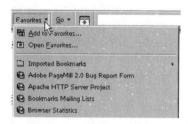

To remove an item from the Favorites folder, follow these steps:

1. Click on Favorites, and select Open Favorites.

2. Select the item you want to remove, and press Delete.

3. Word confirms that you want to delete the item. Click on Yes.

4. Click on the Cancel button in the Favorites dialog box.

Using Other Web Browsers

Word isn't a "real" Web browser; it's a word processor in browser's clothing. Although it is an excellent tool for Web publishing, its capabilities as a browser are limited. Word is a natural when it comes to writing HTML documents, because it takes advantage of an elegant word-processing interface. As a browser, however, it is clumsy.

I recommend that if you intend to do any serious Web surfing (and believe me, you will!), use a full-fledged Web browser. Not only will your ride on the Web be smoother and faster, you will be able to enjoy all its goodies and features.

The dueling leaders in the war of the Web browsers are Netscape Navigator and Microsoft Internet Explorer. One of the many reasons Web publishers prefer these two browsers is that each uses *browser-specific extensions to HTML*. Each company has created special HTML tags that produce amazing design effects—when viewed through *their* browser. The good news is that Web publishers have more ways to enhance Web pages with cutting-edge design effects. The bad news is that those effects are only visible to readers who are using the appropriate browser.

Netscape is a sophisticated browser that supports many of the Web's latest developments. You can read about all of Netscape's amazing features, and how to take advantage of them while Web publishing, in *Surfing the Internet with Netscape*, by Daniel A. Tauber and Brenda Kienan, available from Sybex.

Internet Explorer is an equally powerful browser with its own advantages. It supports several impressive HTML design effects of its own and has the added plus of fitting nicely into your Windows 95 interface. What's more, Word includes built-in support for several of Explorer's fancy effects, making it easy to create sophisticated Web pages for those of your readers who use the Explorer browser. For more information see *The ABCs of Microsoft® Internet Explorer 3* by John Ross and published by Sybex.

Visit the home pages of Microsoft (`http://www.microsoft.com/ie`) and Netscape (`http://home.netscape.com`) to download your free copy of Internet Explorer and an evaluation copy of Netscape Navigator (the evaluation copy expires in 30 days, after which you need to download a new copy or buy the program for $49). Take them for a test surf to see which one you like best. You will be amazed when you see the Web's true colors.

Enough about browsing! In the next chapter, you'll discover how to use Word to create a Web page.

Chapter

35

Using Word to
Create a Web Page

Using Word to Create a Web Page

Word's Internet savvy shines when you put it to work building a Web site. Creating a Web page is so similar to creating a regular Word document, you may decide to make Web publishing your new hobby (or maybe even your new career).

You'll find you're already familiar with most of Word's Web page authoring features, since they are similar to the options available in a Word document. Other authoring features look the same on the outside, but act somewhat differently, since Web pages are subject to the limitations of HTML and can't display all the effects a Word document can.

In this chapter, I'll show you how to use Word to build a basic Web site. You'll learn to create and format Web pages, insert pictures, and create hyperlinks, all from within Word's familiar interface. You'll also find out how to make your Web pages visible on the World Wide Web.

> **NOTE**
> Throughout this chapter, you'll use tools in the Standard and Formatting toolbars. Make them visible by choosing View ➤ Toolbars ➤ Standard and View ➤ Toolbars ➤ Formatting.

MASTERING THE OPPORTUNITIES

Some Thoughts on Web Design

Although this chapter shows you how to put Word's Web publishing capabilities to work, *Web design*—the delicate skill of balancing a site's visual appeal, navigability, and content—is beyond its scope. Web design is such a meaty topic, it merits a book of its own (such as *Mastering Web Design* by John McCoy, available from Sybex). So rather than trying to cram an intensive Web design chapter into a little sidebar, I'll simply offer a few points to keep in mind.

The best Web sites have a clear purpose. Some exist to sell products, others to spread the word about an important issue, still others to share a bit of personal history with the world. However you decide to use your Web site, be sure its purpose is clear to everyone who visits.

Once you've established a purpose, be sure your Web site is easy to navigate. Group your site's information into logical categories, and place links in locations where a prospective visitor would likely look for related information.

Your site's content should be well-written, free of grammatical and spelling errors, and easy to read.

Finally, use color, graphics, and design elements to complement your site's content rather than fill it with visual clutter.

Creating a New Web Page

Word gives you two ways to create a new Web page: You can create a blank page and fill in your own details, or you can use the Web Page Wizard, which gives you a head-start on a simple page.

To create a blank Web page, follow these steps:

1. Choose File ➤ New.
2. Select the Web Pages tab in the New dialog box.
3. Double-click on Blank Web Page, and Word creates a new Web page.

When you use Word to create and edit Web pages, the toolbars and menu items automatically change to accommodate Web Page authoring features.

WARNING

To create a new Web page, you must select File ➤ New to display the New dialog box. If you click on the New button in the Standard toolbar or if you use the keyboard shortcut Ctrl+N, Word bypasses the dialog box and creates a regular Word document.

NOTE

If you don't see the Web Pages tab when you choose File ➤ New, you may not have Word's Web Page Authoring features installed. You need to run the Word Setup program again and be sure that Web Page Authoring features are selected. For more information, refer to the Word Help system item on adding and removing components.

To create a Web page with the Web Page Wizard, follow these steps:

1. Choose File ➤ New.
2. Select the Web Pages tab.
3. Double-click on Web Page Wizard.
4. The Wizard launches and prompts you to select the style of page you want to create. Select a style, each time clicking on Next to move to the next dialog box or clicking on Back to move to a previous dialog box.

5. When prompted by the Wizard, click on Finish.
6. The Wizard creates a new Web page, complete with graphics and generic text you can replace with the text of your choice.

MASTERING THE OPPORTUNITIES

Working with Web Page Templates

Web page templates, like regular Word templates, speed the creation of pages with a standard layout or design.

To create your own Web page template, first create a new Web page using the Blank Web Page template. Add whatever standard elements (such as text or graphics) you wish. Choose File ➤ Save As. In the Save As Type field, select Document Template (*.dot). Word switches the saving location to the Templates folder. Double-click on the Web Pages folder to open it, and then click on Save.

Converting an Existing Document to HTML

Word's conversion filters make short work of turning other document formats to Web pages. Any document you can open in Word—even if it contains complex formatting such as styles, tables, and embedded graphics—can be saved as a Web page.

Word's HTML conversion filter takes care of the following tasks:

- It changes the filename extension to *.html* (so, for example, if you convert a file called *report.doc* into a Web page, Word names the resulting file *report.html*).
- It converts the document into a Web page, applying the HTML formatting effects that most closely resemble the styles used in the document.
- It converts embedded graphics and objects into GIF images and saves copies of the graphic files in the same folder as the new Web page. (You'll learn more about image conversion and the GIF format in "Adding Pictures to Your Web Page.")
- It makes Web page authoring toolbars, styles, and menu commands available.
- It saves the new page in the same directory as the original file.

WARNING

Certain features in Word have no HTML equivalents and therefore will be lost during the conversion process. For a complete listing of features that change during conversion to HTML, refer to the Word Help system.

To convert a document into a Web page, follow these steps:

1. Open the document.
2. Choose File ➤ Save As HTML.

3. In the Save As HTML dialog box, click on OK.

4. A Microsoft Word dialog box appears, warning about information and formatting that is lost when you convert a Word document to HTML. To proceed with the conversion process, click on Yes.

Using the Microsoft Word Viewer

Converting Word documents into Web pages isn't necessarily the easiest or best way to make them available over the Internet. If you regularly convert documents (a process that can be time-consuming and tedious) or if your documents contain information or formatting that can't make the transition, you may prefer to take advantage of Microsoft Word Viewer.

Word Viewer is free software that lets visitors view, print, and follow hyperlinks in fully formatted Word documents even if they don't have Word installed on their systems. Using Word Viewer, visitors can view Word documents over the Internet just as they would Web pages.

For more information on how to use Word Viewer to publish Word documents on the Internet, visit Microsoft's Word Viewer Web site at http://www.microsoft.com/msword/Internet/Viewer/default.htm.

Word Viewer is included on the Windows 95 version 7 CD-ROM. You can also download it from Microsoft's Web site, or you can obtain it by calling the Microsoft Order Desk at (800) 360-7561.

Adding a Title

Every Web page you create requires a *title*. A title is one of the most important aspects of your page, because it describes the page to the rest of the world. The title appears at the topmost portion of your visitor's browser window. It is what is displayed when you add a Web page to your Favorites list. It is also the name that appears in your History List.

You should choose a title that encapsulates the page's content; it should be brief (no more than 64 characters), descriptive, and meaningful.

TIP

Many Web search utilities index your page based on key words in the title. Make the most of this by using words in your title that someone searching for your site would likely choose.

To add a title to your page, follow these steps:

1. Choose File ➤ Properties.
2. Type your title in the Title field.
3. Click on OK.

NOTE

Unless you title your Web page, Word will suggest a title based on the first few words in the Web page. Your title will probably be better.

Enhancing Your Web Pages with Formatting and Styles

Although Web pages can't take advantage of all the formatting and layout wizardry available in a regular Word document, you still have plenty of options from which to choose.

Creating Bold, Italic, and Underlined Characters

Creating bold, italic, and underlined characters in Web pages is no different from doing so in a regular Word document. Select the text you want to format, and choose one of the following options:

- Click on the Bold, Italic, or Underline button in the Formatting toolbar.
- Press Ctrl+B for Bold, Ctrl+I for Italic, or Ctrl+U for Underline.

TIP

You can use the Format Painter to quickly apply a formatting effect to other locations in your document.

Defining Characters as Superscript, Subscript, or Strikethrough

You can use Word to create superscript and subscript characters in your Web page. You can also apply a strikethrough effect to selected text. To do so, follow these steps:

1. Select the text you want to format.
2. Choose Format ➤ Font.
3. Click on the Superscript, Subscript, or Strikethrough checkbox.
4. Click on OK.

Changing Character Size

You can shrink or enlarge your document's text. To do so, select the text you want to change, and choose one of the following options:

- Click on the Increase Font Size or Decrease Font Size button in the Formatting toolbar.
- Choose Format ➤ Font, select the desired point size from the Size list, and click on OK.

How Font Size Works in HTML

Although font sizes in regular Word documents are based on an absolute measurement such as points or picas, font size changes in Web pages are based on a relative system of *increments*. In HTML, font sizes range in increments from 1 to 7, with 1 being the smallest, and 7 the largest. In Word, the default font size (or *basefont*) is 3, which is displayed on your screen as 12-point type. When you change the font size by using the Increase Font Size command, you simply increase the basefont size by one increment, making it 4 instead of 3. In Word, this increases the size of the text to the next increment in the list of available font sizes and is displayed as 14-point type.

Even though the Format ➤ Font command uses point size as a reference, the HTML source behind it is still based on the increment system (that is, 12-point type is really size 3).

Why does all this matter? Because when a visitor views your page with a Web browser, the *browser* determines the point-size equivalent for each increment. Some display size 3 as 12-point type; some display size 3 as 14-point type. Therefore, you don't ultimately have control over the exact size of the text in your Web page— only its size relative to other text.

Choosing Your Document's Font

You can use any font stored in your font directory in your Web pages. This is great news for Web publishers, since the right choice of font lends a distinctive feel to documents. As of this writing, however, typeface variations are only visible to those of your visitors using the Microsoft Internet Explorer or Netscape Navigator (version 3 or later) Web browsers. For everyone else, the normal text in your documents will appear in whatever default font the browser displays (usually Times New Roman).

You can use as many fonts as you like in a Web page (just as in a regular Word document). The font (or fonts) you choose, however, must be present on your visitors' computers for them to be visible on their screens. If the font isn't present, the text will be displayed in their browser's default font.

To apply a font to a section of text, follow these steps:

1. Select the text you want to format.

2. Choose a font from the Font list in the Formatting toolbar.

 NOTE You can also change the font using the Format ➤ Font command.

Changing the Color of Individual Characters

You can change the character color of your document's text. To do so, follow these steps:

1. Select the text you want to format.

2. Click on the down arrow next to the Font Color button to display the Color palette.

3. Choose the color you want.

 TIP The color you select appears on the Font Color button as a thick underline. In the future, simply click on the button to apply that color to text.

Changing the Color of Your Document's Body Text

Changing text color with the Font command affects individual characters, but setting *body text* color applies to the entire document.

To set the color of your document's body text, follow these steps:

1. Choose Format ➤ Text Colors.

2. Select a color from the Body Text color list.

3. Click on OK.

 NOTE Setting the color of your document's body text does not change the color of characters already formatted with the Font Color command.

Formatting Text with Other Styles

HTML contains formatting options that don't have counterparts in Word's word-processing interface. These options are available in the Style list (see Figure 35.1).

Certain styles in the Style list duplicate the formatting effects of other, more commonly used styles (for an explanation of why these styles exist, read the sidebar "Physical vs. Logical Styles"). The Address style, for example, creates italic text. Two styles, however, have unique qualities of their own: the *Typewriter* style and the *Preformatted* style.

The Typewriter style applies a monospaced font (most browsers display Courier) to selected text. This is useful if you want to set off certain sections of text, such as quotes or technical notes.

The Preformatted style also applies a monospaced font to Selected text. Additionally, it preserves multiple character spaces and line breaks. This is handy when you want to control the exact placement of text on the page.

WARNING

The Style dialog box (accessible by choosing Format ➤ Style) contains options that allow you to modify Web page styles and create new ones. This is misleading, because new and/or modified HTML styles *only* affect how the text appears on your screen when you use Word to create Web pages and browse the Web. Modified styles will *not* change the way your Web pages appear when viewed on other computers with Word or when viewed with Web browsers.

FIGURE 35.1

*The HTML
Style list*

Physical vs. Logical Styles

HTML contains certain styles that specify less what the text actually *looks like* once it's seen through a Web browser, and more what the text *means*. In HTML lingo, this difference is called *physical* vs. *logical* styles. Physical styles (such as bold or italic) affect the physical look of the text. Logical styles (such as the Address style) indicate the meaning or content of the text or display certain types of standard text.

The Web browser is responsible for translating HTML tags into the actual style you see when you look at a Web page. Some browsers may translate the Address style into italicized text (this is most common), and others may translate it as bold text of a smaller size. For that reason, using the Address style ensures that every browser, while it may display addresses differently from other browsers, at least displays all addresses the same way.

Other logical styles in Word's Web page Style list include Cite, Code, Emphasis, Sample, Strong, and Variable. The Style list shows how each style appears in most Web browsers.

Using Headings

Headings are a group of styles that call out important text in your document, such as page banners and categories. Six levels of headings are available in the Web page Style list: Heading 1 is the boldest, and Heading 6 is the most modest. Generally, you use larger headings as page banners and for important categories, and you use smaller headings for lesser categories.

To apply a heading to a section of text, follow these steps:

1. Click inside the line of text you want to transform into a heading.
2. From the Style list, select the level of heading you want to apply (HTML headings are listed in the Style list as H1 through H6).

Creating Lists

You can insert three types of lists in your Web pages: a bulleted list, a numbered list, and a definition list.

To create a list, either apply the list style to selected text or activate the style and then type the contents of the list.

To end a list and return to regular text, press Enter twice.

Bulleted Lists

As you would do in a regular Word document, click on the Bulleted List button in the Formatting toolbar to create a bulleted list.

If plain, black bullets are too sedate for your taste, you can replace them with colorful graphics. Word comes with a lively selection of bullets you can use to spruce up your page.

To change the bullet style, follow these steps:

1. Create a bulleted list.
2. Select the list items.
3. Choose Format ➤ Bullets and Numbering, or right-click on the selection and choose Bullets and Numbering.
4. In the Bullets and Numbering dialog box, click on the bullet style that you like and click on OK. The graphic bullets replace the plain bullets in your list.

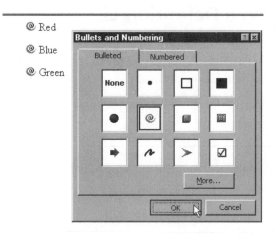

NOTE

When you use a graphic bullet, Word makes a copy of the bullet graphic file and places it in the same folder as the Web page. To understand how graphics work in Web pages, refer to the section "Adding Pictures to Your Web Page," later in this chapter.

Numbered Lists

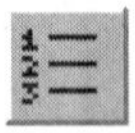

To create a numbered list, click on the Numbered List button in the Formatting toolbar.

You can change the style of the number in your list to letters or roman numerals. To do so, follow these steps:

1. Create a numbered list.
2. Select the list items.
3. Choose Format ➤ Bullets and Numbering, or right-click on the selection and choose Bullets and Numbering.
4. In the Bullets and Numbering dialog box, select the Numbered tab and double-click on the style you want.

NOTE

Use the Restart Numbering and Continue Previous List options in the Bullets and Numbering dialog box to control the order of the numbering in your list.

Creating a Definition List

A *definition list* is another way to display information in your Web pages. Definition lists are useful when you want to explain or define terms.

In a definition list, the *definition term* is aligned with the left margin, and the *definition* appears underneath, slightly indented (see Figure 35.2).

FIGURE 35.2

A definition list

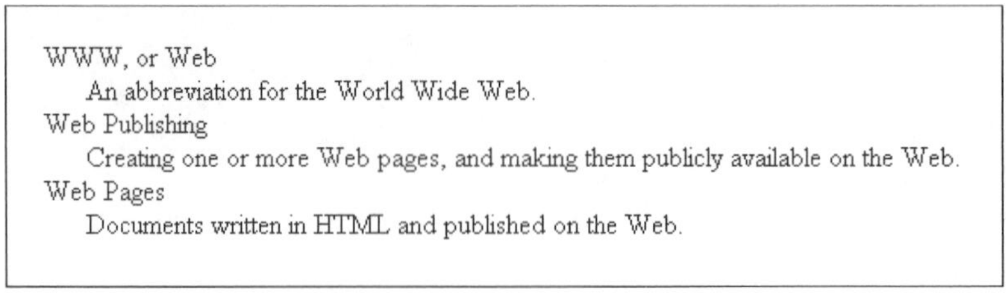

WWW, or Web
    An abbreviation for the World Wide Web.
Web Publishing
    Creating one or more Web pages, and making them publicly available on the Web.
Web Pages
    Documents written in HTML and published on the Web.

To create a definition list, follow these steps:

1. Type the first term in the list.
2. From the Style list, select Definition Term and then press Enter to create a new line.
3. The new line appears indented. Type the definition for the first term, and press Enter.
4. The new line sits next to the left margin, like the first line. Type the second term and press Enter.
5. Keep typing terms and definitions until you are done.
6. To end the list, press Enter to create a new line, and select Normal from the Style list. (Pressing Enter twice to end the list doesn't work in this case.)

WARNING

Strangely enough, the Definition style in the Style list has nothing to do with definition lists. It is an example of a *logical style* (see the sidebar "Physical vs. Logical Styles" earlier in this chapter for more information).

Previewing Your Document in a Web Browser

While you are creating a Web page, it's a good idea to view it with a Web browser or two to see what it will look like once it's "live" and available for public viewing on the Web. That way, you can modify the design as you go along to be sure that the page looks the way you want once it's online. Word's WYSIWYG ("what you see is what you get") interface approximates how your page will look on the Web, but because it can't display all the features it can create as a Web publishing tool, you are better off previewing your document in another, more powerful browser.

The Web Page Preview button on the Standard toolbar allows you to preview

your document with one click. This tool (also available in the File menu) launches whatever Web browser you have installed on your computer and displays the current Web page in a new viewing window.

Once you preview the document in the browser, you can switch back to Word to make any changes you like. To view the changes, save the page, return to the browser window, and select the browser's Reload or Refresh command. If you have access to multiple browsers, try them all. You will be amazed at the differences, and probably find a few important compatibility issues.

Changing Paragraph Alignment

  New paragraphs in Web pages are automatically left-aligned. You can easily center or right-align paragraphs by clicking on the Center or Align Right button in the Formatting toolbar.

Indenting a Paragraph

In Web pages, you don't have access to tabs. You can still create an indented paragraph, however (useful for quotes and all sorts of other things). To do so, follow these steps:

1. Select the paragraph(s) you want to indent.
2. Click on the Increase Indent button.

To return an indented paragraph to its original position, click on the Decrease Indent button.

TIP

You can also create indented paragraphs by applying the Blockquote style (available in the Style list) to selected paragraphs.

Inserting Special Characters and Symbols

On a basic level, Web pages are plain text files with special tags sprinkled throughout. If you want to use special characters and symbols in your Web pages (©, for example), you need to insert specific tags into your document. Word's Insert Symbol command does all the legwork for you.

To insert a symbol into a Web page, follow these steps:

1. Position the cursor where you want to insert the symbol.
2. Choose Insert ➤ Symbol.
3. Select the Symbols tab.
4. Select (normal text) from the Font list. (You can insert symbols from other fonts in your Web pages, but they will be visible only to visitors who have that particular font installed on their machines. See the "Changing Your Document's Font" section for details about using fonts in Web pages.)
5. Double-click on a symbol to insert it into your page.
6. Click on the Close button when you are finished.

WARNING

Many of the characters in the Special Characters section of the Symbols dialog box don't translate into HTML. Those that do (©, ®, and ™) are accessible from the Symbols section.

Adding a Horizontal Line

Typeface variation, headings, and lists are all good ways to "break up" the text on a page. Another option is to use a *horizontal line*.

A horizontal line is a solid gray line that runs the width of your Web page, similar to a border in Word. You can insert lines anywhere you would like to separate different types of information or add a visual break.

To insert a horizontal line, position the cursor where you want the line to appear, and choose one of the following options:

- Click on the Horizontal Line button in the Formatting toolbar.
- Choose Insert ➤ Horizontal Line.

If you prefer more colorful horizontal lines, choose Insert ➤ Horizontal Line, and select from one of Word's diverse collection.

NOTE

When you insert a graphical horizontal line into your page, Word places a copy of the graphic file in the same folder as the Web page. For more information on how graphics work in Web pages, see the "Adding Pictures to Your Web Page" section.

Adding Pictures to Your Web Page

The Web's popularity comes from its easy-to-access storehouse of information combined with brilliant, full-color pictures.

When you insert a picture in a Web page, you create what's called an *inline image*. An inline image is a reference within the document to the graphic file you would like to display in that location. When a Web browser encounters the inline image reference, it searches for the graphic file to which it refers and displays it as part of the Web page.

Web graphics must be in one of two file formats: *GIF* or *JPEG*. These are the only graphic file formats Web browsers know how to display. GIF (Graphics Interchange Format) is the most commonly used format and is best suited to high-contrast, flat-color images. The JPEG (Joint Photographic Experts Group) format can pack more graphic detail and color range into a small file size, which makes it the preferred format for scanned photographs and images with subtle gradations of continuous color.

You can insert graphics, clip art, or Word Drawing objects into Web pages. You can also insert other objects, such as equations and charts. When you save the page, Word automatically converts them to GIF images and saves a copy of the new graphic file in the same folder as the Web page.

WARNING

Once a picture or object is converted into a GIF image, it can no longer be edited with Word's Drawing or Object tools. You can, however, resize the picture by clicking on it and dragging its size handles.

MASTERING THE OPPORTUNITIES

Balancing Beauty and Function

Although pictures give your site personality and color, they significantly increase the time it takes for the page to load. Most Web surfers want to look at attractive, creatively designed pages, but they don't want to sit, tapping their fingers, for 30 seconds or more while the page downloads. Remember, not all of your visitors have access to lightning-fast Internet connections or state-of-the-art browsers. In fact, some of your visitors won't even see the pictures because they have turned off image loading or are using a text-based browser that doesn't display pictures at all.

Here are a few tips to help you make the most of pictures in your Web site:

- Use pictures judiciously; include only those that will add to the overall feel of your site.

- Limit the size of pictures in your Web pages; small ones take less time to load than large ones.

- Use a graphic editing program to limit the number of colors in your pictures; those with fewer colors load more quickly than those with many.

- Be sure that your page isn't dependent on pictures to make its point.

Keeping these points in mind will help you design beautiful, fast-loading pages your visitors will appreciate.

Inserting a Picture

To add a picture to your site, follow these steps:

1. Position the cursor where you want the image to appear.
2. Click on the Insert Picture button in the Standard toolbar, or choose Insert ➤ Picture ➤ From File.
3. In the Insert Picture dialog box, navigate to the folder that contains the image you want to add.
4. Double-click on the file to insert it.

NOTE

You can choose pictures from the Clip Art Gallery, from a file on your hard drive, or from Microsoft's Web site. You can also insert a Word Chart. Choose Insert ➤ Picture, and select the option you want.

MASTERING TROUBLESHOOTING

Keeping Your Web Site Files Organized

It's always a good idea to keep the documents and files on your hard drive well organized with a clear system of folders. It's even more important when you work with Web pages. Here's why.

First, your site will grow quickly as you add new pages, graphics files, and design elements such as sounds and videos. Storing all your Web site files in one folder will make it easier to track everything as the site grows larger and more complex.

Second, and most important, your file structure determines how the links between local files in your site work.

When I say "links" here, I mean any reference to another file within a Web page. This can take the form of an inline image, a hyperlink, or a link to a multimedia file (inline video clips or sounds, for example). To understand how links between local documents work and how file systems affect them, see the sidebar "Relative vs. Absolute Hyperlinks." For now, let me suggest a file strategy.

Create a main folder that contains all your Web site files. Store all your Web pages and associated graphic and multimedia files in that folder. If your site is large and comprises many documents and several categories of information, you can organize them into subfolders.

WARNING

Many Web tools (browsers, servers, etc.) expect filenames with very specific, consistent capitalization. For example, if you replace a file named BEACH.GIF with beach.GIF, problems may occur.

Formatting Pictures

Word lets you control certain aspects of the appearance and function of pictures in your Web pages. The Format Picture dialog box allows you to:

- Control how text wraps around the picture.
- Control the amount of space that separates pictures from surrounding text.
- Provide placeholder text.

To access the Format Picture dialog box, select the picture, and then choose Format ➤ Picture. For a shortcut to picture formatting options, view the Picture toolbar by choosing View ➤ Toolbars ➤ Picture. (Figure 35.3 illustrates the Picture toolbar.)

FIGURE 35.3

The Picture toolbar

Controlling Graphic Alignment and Text Wrapping

Sometimes, you will want graphics in your Web pages to appear next to text on the same line or in the same paragraph. By default, pictures inserted into Web pages are left-aligned, and no text wraps around them. You can change graphic alignment, as well as text wrapping settings.

To change picture alignment, follow these steps:

1. Click on the picture.

2. Click on the Left Align, Center, or Right Align button in the Formatting toolbar.

To control text wrapping, follow these steps:

1. Click on the picture.

2. Choose Format ➤ Picture, or click on the Format Picture button in the Picture toolbar to open the Picture dialog box.

3. Select the Position tab.

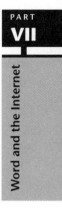

4. In the Text Wrapping section, select Left or Right (or click on None to turn off text wrapping).

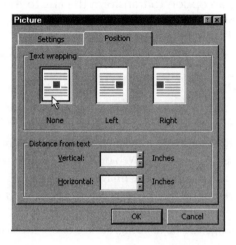

5. In the Distance from Text section, enter the amount of vertical and horizontal space you would like to place between the picture and the surrounding text.

6. Click on OK.

The Picture toolbar contains shortcuts to the text-wrapping options.

Providing Picture Placeholder Text

You can create a descriptive text placeholder for each of your Web graphics. The placeholders appear in place of the graphics when visitors view your Web page with the browser's image-loading option turned off. Placeholders also identify pictures to those of your visitors using nongraphical browsers.

To create a placeholder, follow these steps:

1. Click on the picture.

2. Choose Format ➤ Picture to open the Picture dialog box.

3. Select the Settings tab.

4. In the Picture Placeholder section, type a short label that describes the picture.

5. Click on OK.

NOTE

The Link section of the dialog box displays the name of the graphic file. It also contains an option to transform the link to the graphic file into an absolute, or fixed, link to the file's location. For more information on how links work, see the sidebar "Relative vs. Absolute Hyperlinks."

Inserting a Background Pattern

Another way to boost your site's impact is to use an image or a solid color as the background of a page.

How the picture appears when displayed as a background depends on the size of the image itself. The visitor's Web browser *tiles* the image to create a background pattern; in other words, it repeats the image over and over until it fills the screen, creating a uniform background for the text. Different browsers treat backgrounds differently too.... Experiment!

To change the page background, follow these steps:

1. Choose Format ➤ Background, or click on the Format Background button in the Formatting toolbar to display a palette of colors.
2. If you want to use a solid color as your background, click on the color you want to use. To use a background pattern, click on Fill Effects.

3. A selection of background patterns appears. Scroll down to see more patterns, and double-click on the one you want to use.

NOTE

When you use a background pattern, Word copies the background graphic file to the same folder as your Web page.

Working with Hyperlinks

Sure, you can spruce up your Web pages with text formatting and pictures. But, as we all know, the excitement of HTML lies in those little powerhouses called *hyperlinks*, the bits of text or images within each Web page that, when clicked on, transport you to another location. You can link to another spot within the document, to another document on the same computer, or to another location on the World Wide Web.

Creating Hyperlinks

The essence of the Web's appeal is the ease with which you can hop from page to page, not having to think about whether the files are down the street or across the world. You can easily create hyperlinks to documents on your own computer, on your network, or on the World Wide Web. You can even tell Word to turn network addresses such as URLs or e-mail addresses into hyperlinks as you type them.

To create a hyperlink, follow these steps:

1. Select the text or image you want to turn into a hyperlink.
2. Click on the Insert Hyperlink button in the Standard toolbar, or choose Insert ➤ Hyperlink to open the Insert Hyperlink dialog box.
3. In the Link to File or URL field, type the path to the file or the Internet URL to which you want to link. To select a file manually, click on the Browse button.

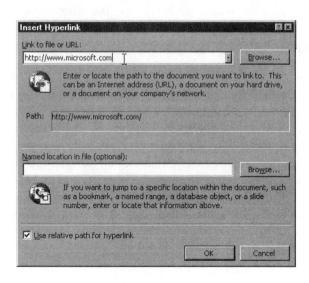

4. Navigate to the folder on your hard drive that contains the Web page to which you want to link.

5. Double-click on the document's filename to select it. The path information Word uses to create the hyperlink appears in the Path field.

6. To link to a named location in a file, such as a bookmark, enter the bookmark name in the Named Location in File field, or click on Browse to choose from a list of bookmarks in the page to which you are linking. (The next section explains how to link to bookmarks in detail.)

7. Click on OK.

8. The selected text turns blue and underlined, indicating it is now a hyperlink. (If the source of the hyperlink is an image, its appearance doesn't change.) To test it, click on the link, and the link destination document will appear.

To auotmatically turn URLs and e-mail addresses into hyperlinks as you type them, follow these steps:

1. Choose Tools ➤ AutoCorrect.

2. Select the AutoFormat As You Type tab.

3. In the Replace As You Type section, mark the Internet and network paths with hyperlinks checkbox.

4. Click on OK.

5. Type a URL or an e-mail address, and press Enter.

6. The text turns into a hyperlink to that location. If the hyperlink leads to an e-mail address, clicking on it activates the visitor's e-mail program.

Linking to Bookmarks

Bookmarks, when used in Web pages, have a slightly different function than when used in regular Word documents. Like regular bookmarks, HTML bookmarks define specific locations in the page. In Web pages, however, bookmarks exist solely to become the destinations of hyperlinks. To jump to a bookmark, you create a hyperlink to it from somewhere else in the page or from another document.

Bookmarks are especially useful for navigating long Web pages that would other-wise require lots of troublesome scrolling to get around.

Creating and linking to bookmarks is a two-step process. First, you must define the bookmark (the link destination). Second, you create the hyperlink that will jump to the bookmark.

Relative vs. Absolute Links

Links to other documents (whether they are hyperlinks or references to included files such as inline images or multimedia files) come in two flavors: *relative* and *absolute*. Although the distinction is invisible when you are Web surfing, it is important for you as a Web publisher to understand.

Relative links locate the link destination relative to the location of the source page. For example, take a look at the HTML tag for the following hyperlink:

```
<A HREF="document.html">
Hyperlink text</A>
```

Hyperlinks have an opening tag, <A>, and a closing tag, </A>, with the hyperlink text itself nestled in between. The rest of the tag consists of the *hypertext reference* (HREF for short). The hypertext reference is the place to which visitors will jump when they click on the hyperlink.

In the example above, the hyperlink destination is simply the filename document .html. When a Web browser encounters this hyperlink, it looks for the file document.html in the same folder as the page that contains the hyperlink. If document.html isn't there, the link won't work.

Here is another example of a relative link, the HTML tag for an inline image:

```
<IMG SRC="images/Image1.gif">
```

The inline image consists of the tag, <IMG>, and a reference to the graphic file itself,

called the *image source* (abbreviated SRC). The image source is the name and location of the file that is to be displayed in the document (in this case, Image1.gif, which is stored in a subfolder called images).

An absolute hyperlink contains the full URL of its destination. Look at HTML source for a hyperlink to a site on the Internet:

```
<A HREF="http://www.sybex.com/
document.html">Hyperlink text</A>
```

When a Web browser encounters this kind of hyperlink, it goes straight to the destination URL, no matter where the original file is located.

Although the difference between relative and absolute links may seem too technical to worry about, it is central to the workings of your Web site. You use relative links with documents you've created, because you control their locations and can therefore create valid links. You use absolute hyperlinks when linking to URLs on the Web.

It's crucial that you have a well-organized file system, since file locations are included in the HTML source of your relative links. When it comes time to transfer your files to your Web server, you must maintain the same file system so that the relative links will work.

Refer to the Help system for more information on relative and absolute links and how to manage your Web page file system.

To create a bookmark, follow these steps:

1. Select the text or image you want to turn into a bookmark.

2. Choose Insert ➤ Bookmark to open the Bookmark dialog box.

3. In the Name field, type a short, logical bookmark name.

4. Click on the Add button.

To create a hyperlink that jumps to a bookmark, follow these steps:

1. Select the text or image you want to turn into a hyperlink.

2. Click on the Insert Hyperlink button, or choose Insert ➤ Hyperlink.

3. To link to a bookmark in another page, enter the file location or the URL in the Link to File or URL field. To link to a bookmark in the current page, leave the field empty.

4. Enter the bookmark name in the Named Location in File field (or select it manually by clicking on Browse).

5. Click on OK.

Word creates a hyperlink to the bookmark location. To test it, click on the hyperlink, and you will jump to the location of the bookmark.

Changing Hyperlinks

You can change the text or destination of existing hyperlinks. You can also change the color of regular and followed hyperlinks.

PART
VII

Word and the Internet

Create a Table of Contents with Bookmarks

Bookmarks are often used to create tables of contents for long Web pages. Create an index list at the top of a long page, and link each list item to a bookmark in the interior of the page.

At the location of the bookmark, create another link that brings visitors back to the index at the top of the page. In this way, you make it easier for your visitors to jump around the long page quickly.

Changing Hyperlink Text

When you click on a hyperlink directly, Word thinks you want to follow the link and, therefore, transports you to the destination. To edit hyperlink text, you must position the cursor to the left or right of the hyperlink and then use the arrow keys to move the insertion point. You can add, delete, or change hyperlink text just as you would regular text.

Changing the Hyperlink Destination

It's easy to modify the destination of an existing hyperlink. Follow these steps:

1. Right-click on the hyperlink, and choose Hyperlink ➤ Edit Hyperlink.
2. Enter a new file location, URL, or bookmark.
3. Click on OK.

Changing Hyperlink Color

You can change the color of your document's hyperlinks. Hyperlinks have two states: those that haven't yet been followed, and those that have. You can define colors for each of these states to help your visitors remember which links they've already visited.

To change hyperlink color, follow these steps:

1. Choose Format ➤ Text Colors.

2. Choose a color from the Hyperlink and Followed Hyperlink color lists.

3. Click on OK.

"Unlinking" a Hyperlink

You can disable any of the links in your Web pages and turn them back into regular text. To "unlink" a hyperlink, follow these steps:

1. Right-click on the hyperlink, and choose Hyperlink ➤ Edit Hyperlink.
2. Click on Remove Link.
3. Click on OK.

Making Your Web Site Visible on the World Wide Web

To make your Web site visible on the Web, you need to transfer all your Web site files and directories—Web pages, GIF and JPEG images, and any multimedia files—to your company's or Internet service provider's Web server. Transferring, or *uploading*, your files is a simple matter of using an FTP program. As I mentioned in Chapter 33, *Word and the Web*, FTP software lets you transfer files to and from computers over the Internet. Most providers give you an FTP program as part of your Internet service. If you don't have an FTP program or if you have one, but don't know how to use it, contact your system administrator or your provider's customer service staff for recommendations.

NOTE

Although Word is able to save Web pages directly to Internet servers to which you have access, it isn't able to transfer your Web site's associated graphic and multimedia files. For that reason, I recommend using an FTP program to transfer your Web site files.

Each company and Internet service provider has its own set of instructions for how and where to upload your files. Because the steps depend on your FTP program and your provider's server setup, you need to speak to your system administrator or Webmaster for more information.

TIP

Remember, for all of your relative links to remain intact, you must duplicate the directory structure of your computer on the Web server. For example, if, while creating your Web site with Word, you stored all your Web graphics in a folder called *images*, you need to create an *images* folder on the Web server and store uploaded graphic files there. Refer to the sidebars "Keeping Your Web Site Files Organized" and "Relative vs. Absolute Hyperlinks" for more information.

Once you upload your site, be sure everything works as it should. Take a look at your Web site at its new URL with a Web browser, and give each page a final survey to be sure it's perfect. If you notice a problem, such as a hyperlink that doesn't work or a graphic that doesn't load, correct your original Web page and upload it again. To view the edited file, choose your browser's Reload or Refresh command.

Updating your Web site is easy: You simply make the changes you want on the original Web pages on your computer, save them, and upload them to the Web server. The new versions (as long as they have identical filenames) will automatically replace the old versions of the files that are already stored there.

Adding new pages to your Web site is just as simple. Create a new Web page, be sure its design is consistent with the other pages, and integrate it into the rest of your Web site by adding links to it from other pages. Once you're done, upload *all* the pages you've changed to the Web server again.

TIP

Each time you make changes to your Web site, be sure to test it to ensure that all the hyperlinks and graphics work properly.

This chapter showed you how to create a basic Web site with Word. In the next chapter, you'll find out about more exciting features you can add to your Web page.

Chapter

36

Exciting Web Page Additions

FEATURING

Chapter 36

Exciting Web Page Additions

n the previous chapter you learned how to use Word to build a basic Web page, complete with text, graphics, and hyperlinks. In this chapter, you'll discover more of Word's exciting Web publishing features.

With Word, you can:

- Create HTML tables to organize information and structure page layout.
- Build interactive forms to communicate with Web site visitors.
- Take advantage of fancy design effects, such as scrolling text, sounds, and video clips.
- View and edit the page's HTML tags.

Organizing Information with Tables

As they do in a regular Word document, *tables* help organize information in Web pages. The information in tables is divided into chunks and placed in individual *cells* that are arranged in rows and columns.

Tables in Web pages come in two flavors: those with borders, and those without. Tables with borders look like boxed grids and are perfect for presenting rows and columns of data (as in Figure 36.1).

FIGURE 36.1

*A table
with borders*

	January	February	March
Week One	$200,000	$250,000	$275,000
Week Two	$175,000	$200,000	$225,000

Tables without borders (also known as *invisible tables*) are a boon to creative Web publishers who want more layout flexibility in their Web pages. Whereas regular Web page text layout is the one-paragraph-after-another format (with the occasional list thrown in for variety), invisible tables allow you to precisely place text and graphics on the page by inserting them into table cells (as in Figure 36.2).

NOTE Although most Web browsers can display tables, a few don't. This is something to keep in mind as you design your Web pages. Some Web publishers want the majority of their visitors to enjoy creative layouts, and they accept the consequence that a few visitors won't be able to read their pages. Others create a separate set of Web pages without tables for those visitors using browsers that can't display them. The choice is yours.

FIGURE 36.2

*A two-column
invisible table
creates the
appearance of
newspaper
columns.*

**This is
Column 1**
You can use a
multi-column
invisible table
to simulate the
appearance of
newspaper
columns in your
Web pages.

**This is
Column 2**
You can use a
multi-column
invisible table
to simulate the
appearance of
newspaper
columns in your
Web pages.

Creating a Table

Creating a table in a Web page is just like creating a regular Word table. You can either insert a table grid by clicking on the Insert Table button, or you can draw a table by choosing Table ➤ Draw and using the table drawing tools. For more details, see Chapter 9, *Tabs, Tables, Math, and Sorting*.

Once you've created the table, insert information as you would in a regular Word table. Click on a cell and begin typing. To move to the next cell, click on it with the mouse or press the Tab key.

You can format text inside table cells with any of the effects discussed in Chapter 35, *Using Word to Create a Web Page*. You can also insert graphics, hyperlinks, form fields, and even other tables into table cells.

The Tables and Borders toolbar contains shortcuts to several table editing functions. To make it visible, choose View ➤ Toolbars ➤ Tables and Borders.

Adding Borders

By default, new Web page tables are invisible. If you want to create a traditional gridlike table, like the one in Figure 36.1, you need to add borders.

When you work with regular Word tables, you have lots of flexibility with the placement of borders. Web page tables, however, can only be invisible (with no defined borders) or have borders around every cell.

To add borders to your table, follow these steps:

1. Click inside the table.
2. Choose Table ➤ Borders.
3. Click on the Grid option.
4. Select a border thickness from the Border width drop-down menu.
5. Click on OK.

NOTE
Web page table borders appear raised, because that's how they appear when viewed with most Web browsers.

Aligning Cell Contents

Word allows you to control the vertical alignment of the contents of table cells. (By default, Word horizontally aligns cell contents with the left cell border.) To align cell contents, follow these steps:

1. Highlight the cells or rows you want to format.

2. From the Tables and Borders toolbar, click on the Align Top button, on the Center Vertically button, or on the Align Bottom button. Alternatively, choose Table ➤ Cell Properties, choose an alignment option, and click on OK.

Changing Row Height and Column Width

You can define the row height and column width in a table by dragging table borders or by specifying a precise measurement for each.

To resize rows and columns by dragging borders, follow these steps:

1. Pass the cursor over the table boundary you want to move. The pointer will change shape.

This is Column 1	This is Column 2
You can use a multi-column invisible table to simulate the appearance of newspaper columns in your Web pages. 	You can use a multi-column invisible table to simulate the appearance of newspaper columns in your Web pages.

2. Drag the border to the desired position, and release the mouse button.

If you prefer to specify the dimensions of each row or column, follow these steps:

1. Select the row or column you want to resize.

2. Choose Table ➤ Cell Properties.

3. If you're working with rows, enter a new height measurement in the Height field. If you're working with columns, enter a new width measurement in the Width field.

4. Click on OK.

> **WARNING**
>
> If you use this command to change row width or column height or to apply different width and height values to individual cells, you may get unpredictable results. Preview all tables in a Web browser to be sure they appear as you intend.

Adjusting the Space between Columns

You can control the amount of white space between columns in Web page tables. To do so, follow these steps:

1. Click inside the table, and choose Table ➤ Table Properties.

2. Enter a measurement in the Space between Columns field.

3. Click on OK.

Adding Background Color

Word allows you to add background color to a Web page table. You can apply color to the entire table or to selected cells.

> **NOTE**
>
> Table background color is an extension to HTML visible only in Netscape Navigator (version 2 or later) and Internet Explorer.

To apply background color, follow these steps:

1. Highlight the cells or rows you want to format. To color the entire table, click anywhere inside the table.

2. To apply a background color to selected cells, choose Table ➤ Cell Properties. To apply a background color to the entire table, choose Table ➤ Table Properties.

3. Choose a color from the Background drop-down menu.

4. Click on OK.

Controlling How Surrounding Text Wraps Around a Table

If you insert a table in the same line as regular text, you can control how the text wraps around the table. Follow these steps:

1. Click inside the table.

2. Choose Table ➤ Table Properties.

3. In the Text Wrapping section, choose None, Left, or Right.

4. In the Surrounding text section, specify the horizontal and vertical distance separating the table from surrounding text.

5. Click on OK.

Making Your Web Page Interactive with Forms

A Web site is a powerful method of communication, but it's passive; all it can do is be seen. An *interactive form* changes your Web site from an electronic bulletin board—attractive but static—into a place where visitors can submit their ideas and questions.

Interactive forms are much like regular paper forms. They collect data by prompting visitors to fill in *fields*, either by typing information or by selecting an item in a list. Once your visitors complete the form, they click on a button (usually at the bottom of the form) that sends the information to the site's administrator.

You can use forms in your Web pages for many purposes: to survey visitors, to solicit requests for further information, or to invite feedback, to name only a few.

How Forms in Web Pages Work

Before we begin, let me give you a brief introduction to how forms work. I'll dispense with the technical details, since the goal here is to give you a general idea of what happens when a Web form is filled out and submitted.

Interactive forms consist of one or more fields. Fields are the places your visitors fill in the information you request. You can include three basic types of fields in a Web page form:

- Fields in which visitors enter any information they want.
- Fields in which visitors select from a list of predefined choices.
- *Hidden fields* that are invisible to visitors but that include data of your choosing along with the information that visitors submit. (I'll explain why this is useful later in this chapter.)

You can include as many fields of as many types as you like in your form.

Once the form is complete, the visitor clicks on a button that sends the information to the Web server on which the Web site is located. The information is compiled into a list of *name/value pairs*. The *name* is a label you assign to each field in your form. The *value* is the information submitted by the visitor.

The final step is for the Web server to process the form data in some way, for example, format it and send it to you as an e-mail message, or enter the name/value pairs into a database. This is not automatic; it requires coordination with your Internet service provider. Your provider must write and activate a special program called a *CGI script* to process form submissions.

Some Internet service providers create "generic" form-processing CGI scripts that all customers can use. Other providers charge a fee to write custom CGI scripts for those users who need them. Discuss your options with your provider's system administrator before you include forms in your Web site.

Creating a Form

If you want help creating a form or if you're not sure which fields to include, let the Web Page Wizard assist you. If you have a sense for how you'd like your form to look, build it from scratch.

With the Web Page Wizard

The Web Page Wizard contains templates for three popular types of forms: a feedback form, a registration form, and a survey.

To create a form with the Web Page Wizard, follow these steps:

1. Choose File ➤ New to open the New dialog box.
2. Select the Web Pages tab, and double-click on the Web Page Wizard.
3. Select the type of form you want—Feedback, Registration, or Survey—and click on Next.
4. Select a page style, and click on Finish.

The Wizard creates a standard form based on your selections. You can modify the form (change text, add and customize fields, and so forth) as you like.

From Scratch

If you would rather build your own form, you can do so. You can insert a form into an existing Web page, or you can create a new, blank page on which you add the form.

 To begin form-building, click on the Form Design Mode button in the Standard toolbar.

Word displays the Controls toolbar, which has buttons for each of the form fields available.

To create a form, insert a form field by clicking on a button in the Controls toolbar (each type of form field is explained in the following sections). The first time you insert a field, lines appear inside the Web page that define where the form begins and ends. These form boundaries demarcate the area of the page where you can insert form fields.

Once you insert a field, you must customize it by giving it a unique name and, in some cases, a value. You can also adjust the appearance of the field. The next section explains how to customize each type of form field.

Adding Form Fields

The types of fields you use in your form depend on the types of information you want to gather. Do you want your visitors to select an option from a list of choices you define? Do you want them to fill in the blank? The answers to these questions will tell you which field is appropriate in each case.

NOTE While creating a form, use the Web Page Preview command often. Forms look different in Web browsers than they do in Word.

After you insert a field, you must customize it. To display customization options, double-click on the field, or click on the field and then click on the Properties button in the Controls toolbar. Word displays the Properties dialog box (see Figure 36.3).

You can view field properties based on category or in alphabetic order (the steps below assume alphabetic order). The left column contains the names of each property. To define a property, enter the appropriate information in the right column.

FIGURE 36.3

The Form Field Properties dialog box

Text Boxes

The most basic type of form field is called a *text box*. This type of field can hold one line of text input. Use it to collect information that's different for each person (such as a name or comments).

Name:

To insert a text box, follow these steps:

1. Place the cursor where you want the field to appear (you must place the cursor between the two form boundaries).
2. Click on the Text Box button in the Controls toolbar, or choose Insert ➤ Forms ➤ Text Box.
3. Double-click on the field to customize it.
4. Select the Alphabetic tab to display properties in alphabetic order.
5. In the HTMLName field, type a short, descriptive name for your field. Every field you create must have a name.
6. To limit the amount of text that visitors can enter into the field, enter a number of characters in the MaxLength field.
7. If you want the field to initially appear with text inside (instead of empty), enter the text in the Value field.
8. Click on the form page to continue adding and customizing fields, or close the Properties dialog box.

TIP

To adjust the length of a text box, click on the field and drag its size handles until it is the size you want.

Text Areas

Text areas work just like text boxes, except that they hold more than one line of text. Use a text area to collect information such as comments and questions, which often require additional space.

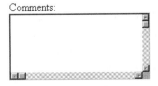

To insert a text area, follow these steps:

1. Place the cursor where you want the field to appear (it must be between the two form boundaries).
2. Click on the Text Area button in the Controls toolbar, or choose Insert ➤ Forms ➤ Text Area.
3. Double-click on the field to customize it.

4. Select the Alphabetic tab.

5. In the Columns field, enter the width of the text area in number of columns. (You can also use the size handles to adjust the width by hand.)

6. In the HTMLName field, enter the field name.

7. In the Rows field, enter the height of the text area in number of rows (or resize the field manually once you're through customizing it).

8. If you want the field to initially appear with text inside (instead of empty), enter the text in the Value field.

9. Click on the form page to continue adding and customizing fields, or close the Properties dialog box.

Password Fields

Password fields are just like text boxes, except that when a visitor types into the field, dots appear in place of characters, obscuring the information from passers-by.

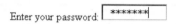

To create a password field, follow these steps:

1. Place the cursor where you want the field to appear (it must be between the two form boundaries).

2. Click on the Password button in the Controls toolbar, or choose Insert ➤ Forms ➤ Password.

3. Double-click on the field to customize it.

4. Select the Alphabetic tab.

5. In the HTMLName field, enter the field name.

6. To limit the amount of text visitors can enter into the field, enter a number of characters in the MaxLength field.

7. If you want the field to initially appear with text inside (instead of empty), enter the text in the Value field.

8. Click on the form page to continue adding and customizing fields, or close the Properties dialog box.

Checkbox Fields

Checkboxes are perfect when you want to present your visitors with a short list of options from which to choose. Your visitors click on the checkboxes to choose as many options as they like (including zero).

In text fields, the visitor's input is the field's value, but you must specify a value for each checkbox field. Because a checkbox field has only two states, marked and unmarked, you need to tell Word what a marked field signifies.

To insert a checkbox, follow these steps:

1. Place the cursor where you want the checkbox to appear.
2. Click on the Check Box button in the Controls toolbar, or choose Insert ➤ Forms ➤ Check Box.
3. Double-click on the field to customize it.
4. Select the Alphabetic tab.
5. In the Checked field, select True for the checkbox to appear automatically marked, or select False to leave the checkbox unmarked.
6. In the HTMLName field, enter the field name.
7. In the Value field, enter the field value when checked.
8. Click on the form page to continue adding and customizing fields, or close the Properties dialog box.

Option Buttons

Option buttons are similar to checkboxes: They present visitors with a visible list of options from which to choose. The difference, however, is that visitors can make only one choice. (This is much like the station buttons on your car stereo: You press one, and the one that was pressed in before pops back out.)

How old are you?

○ 10-25

◉ 26-40

○ 41-65

○ 66 or over

Unlike checkboxes, which can act independently (each checkbox in a group can be given a different name), option buttons *must* work as a team (each option button in the group must be given the same name).

To create a group of option buttons, follow these steps:

1. Place the cursor where you want the first option button to appear.
2. Click on the Option Button button in the Controls toolbar, or choose Insert ➤ Forms ➤ Option Button.
3. Double-click on the field to customize it.
4. Select the Alphabetic tab.
5. In the Checked field, select True for the option button to appear automatically marked, or select False to leave the option button unmarked.
6. In the HTMLName field, enter the group name.
7. In the Value field, enter the field value when marked.
8. Click on the form page to add another Option button.
9. Insert another Option button, and click on it to display its properties.
10. In the Checked field, select True for the option button to appear automatically marked, or select False to leave the option button unmarked.
11. In the HTMLName field, enter the same name as for the first option button.
12. In the Value field, enter the field value when marked.
13. Click on the form page to continue adding and customizing fields, or close the Properties dialog box.

NOTE

Unless you specify otherwise, the first option button in the group appears marked.

Drop-Down Boxes

You have another option. If you'd like your visitors to select from a list of choices you define, you can use a *drop-down box*. When visitors click on a drop-down box, a list of choices appears, and they can select the one they want. Drop-down boxes are useful when you have a long list of choices and would like to save space in your document by not making the entire list visible at once.

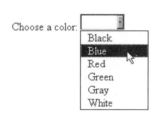

You can create drop-down boxes that allow your visitors one or more choices from the list.

To insert a drop-down box, follow these steps:

1. Place the cursor where you want the drop-down box to appear.
2. Click on the Dropdown Box button in the Controls toolbar, or choose Insert ➤ Forms ➤ Dropdown Box.
3. Double-click on the field to customize it.
4. Select the Alphabetic tab.
5. In the DisplayValues field, enter the items to appear on the list. Each item must be separated by a semicolon, with no spaces between items.
6. In the HTMLName field, enter the field name.
7. If you want visitors to be able to select more than one item from the list, select True in the MultiSelect field.
8. To specify which item in the list appears initially selected, type the item name in the Selected field. (If you leave the field empty, the first item in the list appears selected.)
9. In the Size field, enter the size of the font.
10. If you want the field values to differ from the display names, enter them in the Value field. Like DisplayValues, field values must be separated by a semicolon, with no spaces between values.
11. Click on the form page to continue adding and customizing fields, or close the Properties dialog box.

List Boxes

List boxes are just like drop-down boxes, except that all the list items are initially visible.

Choose a color:

To insert a list box, follow these steps:

1. Place the cursor where you want the list box to appear.
2. Click on the List Box button in the Controls toolbar, or choose Insert ➤ Forms ➤ List Box.
3. Double-click on the field to customize it.
4. Select the Alphabetic tab.
5. In the DisplayValues field, enter the items to appear on the list. Each item must be separated by a semicolon, with no spaces between items.
6. In the HTMLName field, enter the field name.
7. If you want visitors to be able to select more than one item from the list, select True in the MultiSelect field.
8. To specify which item in the list appears initially selected, type the name of the item in the Selected field. (If you leave the field empty, the first item in the list appears selected.)
9. In the Size field, enter the number of items initially visible.
10. If you want the field values to differ from the display names, enter them in the Value field. Like DisplayValues, field values must be separated by a semicolon, with no spaces between values.
11. Click on the form page to continue adding and customizing fields, or close the Properties dialog box.

Hidden Fields

Hidden fields allow you to attach "invisible" information to the data your visitors send when they submit the form. This can be helpful when you want to include information in the form that visitors don't need to see.

Hidden fields are generally used to pass information to the Web server's forms-processing CGI script. Talk to your system administrator or your Internet service provider's Webmaster about using hidden forms in conjunction with CGI scripts.

To create a hidden field, follow these steps:

1. Place the cursor where you want the field to appear.
2. Click on the Hidden button in the Controls toolbar, or choose Insert ➤ Forms ➤ Hidden.
3. Double-click on the field to customize it.
4. Select the Alphabetic tab.
5. In the HTMLName field, enter the field name.
6. In the Value field, enter the value.
7. Click on the form page to continue adding and customizing fields, or close the Properties dialog box.

NOTE

Hidden fields are only visible in Word when hidden text is visible. When viewed with a Web browser, the hidden field is invisible.

Adding a Submit Button

The *Submit button* is the linchpin of your form, because it tells the Web browser what to do with form information and where to send it. All forms must have a Submit button.

The Submit Button Properties dialog box (see Figure 36.4) allows you to program the Submit button to send the form's information to the right location in the right structure.

To add a Submit button to your form, follow these steps:

1. Position the cursor where you want the Submit button to appear.
2. Click on the Submit Button button in the Controls toolbar, or choose Insert ➤ Forms ➤ Submit.
3. Double-click on the button to customize it.
4. In the Action field, enter the URL of the server-based CGI script that processes the form data. Your system administrator or Webmaster will tell you the correct URL.
5. In the Caption field, specify the text label that appears on the button itself.

FIGURE 36.4

The Submit Button Properties dialog box

6. In the Encoding field, specify the format of the form's data. You don't need to change anything in this field (Word has taken care of the proper settings for you).
7. In the HTMLName field, specify an optional field name for the Submit button.
8. In the Method field, specify how you would like Word to submit the information. You have two choices here: POST and GET. Suffice it to say that for 99% of Web-based forms, the correct method is POST (despite Word's default GET setting).

If you like, you can substitute a GIF or a JPEG image for the Submit button by using an Image Submit field.

To use an image as your form's Submit button, follow these steps:

1. Position the cursor where you want the button to appear.
2. Click on the Image Submit button in the Controls toolbar, or choose Insert ➤ Forms ➤ Image Submit to open the Insert Picture dialog box.
3. Navigate your hard drive, and insert the image you want to use as your Submit button. The image appears in the page.
4. Double-click on the image field to customize it.
5. Follow steps 4 through 8 above.

Adding a Reset Button

The Submit button's partner, the *Reset button*, gives your visitors an easy way to clear the contents of the form with one click. Reset buttons aren't mandatory, but visitors appreciate them.

To add a Reset button, follow these steps:

1. Position the cursor where you want the Reset button to appear (usually, it sits next to the Submit button).

2. Click on the Reset Button button in the Controls toolbar, or choose Insert ➤ Forms ➤ Reset.

3. Double-click on the button to customize it.

4. In the HTMLName field, enter an optional field name.

5. In the Caption field, enter the button's text label.

Once you are finished building your form, click on the Form Design Mode button to exit form design mode. Preview your form in a Web browser to test it and ensure that it works properly.

Fancy Design Effects

Word gives you access to fancy design effects you can use to make your pages look snazzy. These effects are purely optional—in fact, they are more for fun than anything else—but they offer you a great way to dress up your Web site and express your creativity.

WARNING

The flip side is that these effects won't be displayed by all browsers. In fact, certain features such as scrolling text will appear *only* in Internet Explorer. For this reason, be sure that your site's design doesn't depend too heavily on the use of the following effects.

Adding a Scrolling Text Banner

If you want to highlight special announcements or other information, a *scrolling text* banner is the perfect way to do it.

NOTE

Scrolling text is an extension to HTML specific to the Internet Explorer browser (version 2 or later). When viewed in other browsers, scrolling text appears as regular text.

To insert scrolling text, follow these steps:

1. Position the cursor where you want the scrolling text to appear.
2. Choose Insert ➤ Scrolling Text to open the Scrolling Text dialog box.
3. In the Type Scrolling Text Here field, enter the text you want to scroll.
4. Choose an option from the Behavior field. Scroll creates scrolling text, Slide creates text that originates on one side of the page and stops at the other side, and Alternate creates text that bounces back and forth.
5. Choose an option from the Direction field. Left creates text that originates on the right side of the screen and moves left, and Right does the opposite.
6. To change the banner's background color, choose a color from the Background Color field.
7. Choose the number of times you want the banner to loop. You can select a number from 1 to 5, or you can select Infinite if you want the text to scroll continuously.
8. To adjust the movement speed of the text, slide the Speed control to the right or left.
9. Click on OK.

MASTERING THE OPPORTUNITIES

Bringing Your Site to Life with Java Applets

If you've surfed the Web, you may have noticed Web sites that have scrolling text banners similar to the ones Word can create. Chances are, you saw a *Java applet* in action. Whereas a Word scrolling text banner is simply another type of HTML tag, an applet (so-called because it's a mini-application) is a piece of programming code—written in the programming language Java—that is then referenced in the HTML source of a Web page. Advanced Web browsers such as Netscape and Internet Explorer can interpret Java and display the effects you see on the screen.

Java is a powerful language, requiring programming experience to write.

Adding Sound

With Word, you can insert a *background sound* that plays when the page is viewed with a Web browser. As soon as visitors access the page, they are greeted by the sound of your choice—perhaps a lively musical interlude or your voice welcoming them to the Web site.

NOTE
As of this writing, only Internet Explorer (version 2 or later) and Netscape Navigator (version 3 or later) can play background sounds.

As it does when you insert a picture, Word creates a relative link between your Web page and the sound file to create a background sound. Web sound files must be stored in the WAV, MID, AU, AIF, RMI, SND, or MP2 sound file formats.

NOTE
Adding sounds to your Web page (and inline video clips, which I'll talk about in a moment) significantly increases the page's load time. For this reason, be sure that the files you use are as small as possible.

To insert a background sound, follow these steps:

1. Choose Insert ➤ Background Sound ➤ Properties to open the Background Sound dialog box.
2. In the Sound field, enter the path to the sound file you want to insert, or click on the Browse button to navigate to and select the file manually.
3. In the Loop field, specify the number of times you want the sound to repeat when someone visits the page. You can select a number from 1 to 5, or you can select Infinite if you want the sound to play continuously until the visitor leaves the page.
4. Be sure the Use Relative Path and Copy to Document Folder options are marked.
5. Click on OK.
6. Word copies the sound file to the same location as the Web page and creates a relative link to the file.

NOTE
To review the sound again later, choose Insert ➤ Background Sound ➤ Play. To stop the sound, choose Insert ➤ Background Sound ➤ Stop.

Adding a Video Clip

Word lets you go a step beyond inline images: You can add inline *video clips* to your Web pages as well. Video clips are images that move; they can be a small section of movie footage, say, or an animated graphic. When viewed with a Web browser, a video clip, like an inline image, sits within the Web page and plays when the page is opened or when the visitor passes the cursor over the video (or both).

NOTE

Inline video clips are an extension to HTML and are only visible in Netscape Navigator (version 3 or later) and Internet Explorer (version 2 or later). Unless you specify an alternate image for the video, other browsers display an "unknown graphic" icon.

Inline video clips must be stored in the AVI file format to be visible in both Internet Explorer and Netscape.

To insert an inline video clip into your document, follow these steps:

1. Position the cursor where you want the video clip to appear.
2. Choose Insert ➤ Video to open the Video Clip dialog box.
3. In the Video field, enter the path to the AVI file you want to insert, or click on the Browse button to navigate to and select the file manually.
4. In the Alternate Image field, enter the path to the image file that appears in browsers that don't support inline video clips, or click on the Browse button to navigate to and select the file manually.
5. In the Alternate text field, enter a text label that appears in place of the graphic in browsers that don't display graphics or that appears if the visitor has turned off the browser's image-loading function.
6. The Start field allows you to specify when the video begins playing. To have the video play immediately when the visitor opens the page, select Open. To have the video play when the visitor moves the cursor over the video, select Mouse-over. To specify both, select Both.
7. In the Loop field, enter the number of times you'd like the video to automatically repeat itself. You can select a number between 1 and 5, or you can have the video play continuously by selecting Infinite.
8. Mark the Display Video Control checkbox to display control buttons in the Web page that allow visitors to stop and start the video themselves. The controls appear beneath the inline video clip.

9. Be sure the Use Relative Paths and Copy to Document Folder options are marked.
10. Click on OK.

Word inserts a link to the video clip and copies the AVI file to the location of the Web page.

Working Directly with HTML Tags

HTML is an ever-changing language, with new tags and extensions being added all the time. Microsoft understands this and built a catch-all into Word that lets you insert HTML tags yourself. That way, when a new tag comes along (or if you want to use one that exists now but that Word doesn't support), you can easily add it to your page by hand.

To insert tags, you need to know what they *are*, which means that you need to learn HTML. If this prospect scares you, remember, it's *optional*. Word includes built-in support for every HTML tag you need to build a great Web page. But if you want to expand your Web-publishing horizons, Word won't hold you back.

To view and edit HTML source, follow these steps:

1. Choose View ➤ HTML Source.
2. If you haven't saved your page recently, Word displays a dialog box prompting you to save the page. Click on Yes.
3. The page's HTML source appears. To edit the HTML tags, click anywhere in the page and type, just as with a regular Word document.
4. When you are through, click on the Exit HTML Source button to return to the regular view.

Appendix

Installing Word

Installing Word

In the good old days, I just showed you how to install Word from floppies, and that was it. Today, however, life is more complicated, because there are more options designed to make things simpler! Funny that...

Nowadays, many people are installing from CD-ROMs, which makes a lot of sense, given the size of Word and other applications. Furthermore, Microsoft is making it very tempting for people to go ahead and spring the extra money, over what it would cost to buy Word by itself, to purchase the whole office suite. You can get Microsoft Office (which includes Access, Word, Excel, PowerPoint, and Schedule+) for an incredible cost of roughly half-again the price of Word.

This appendix shows how to install Word using the Microsoft Office Setup software. I also assume you will be installing from a CD-ROM (although additional steps are included for those of you who like to spend all afternoon installing a mountain of floppies). If you are *not* installing Word as part of Office, don't worry; your installation will look similar. You just won't have as many choices.

System Requirements

You can install Word 97 on any machine that runs Windows 95 (including an 80386) that has a minimum of 8MB of RAM. Note that you probably can't realistically run Word 97 on a 386. Best to just pony up for that Pentium! You cannot use Word 97 with a system earlier than Windows 95. You'll need an EGA or better display. You really should have a mouse or trackball, though it is not a requirement. Disk-space estimates vary with your needs.

A *Minimum* installation requires 6 to 10MB of disk space. You'll get just the bare bones—the program, Spelling and Grammar checker, and Word's Readme Help file (*not* online help). Travelers, listen up. You are gonna wish you had the online help at midnight in some hotel room. Read on.

If you are installing on a laptop, Word will automatically detect this and ask if you would like a *Laptop* installation. Although this installation puts more stuff on your computer and makes certain allowances for the limitations of laptops, just think how frustrating it would be to be on the road and realize that you can't install the feature you *need* to use, because your installation disk is 6000 miles away.

A *Typical* installation requires 20MB or more. It includes the program, Spelling and Grammar checker, new online help (well worth the disk space!), and supplementary programs such as Word Art and Graph.

A full installation requires 25 to 30+ MB. If you have the room, do a full install; then go back later to remove things you never use, such as the Equation Editor. But at least try them and the many other tools provided in a full installation. After all, you paid for them, didn't you?

TIP

Because Word 97 can use your old custom dictionaries, glossaries, styles, and templates, the installer doesn't throw out these files when it deletes Word version 6 or Word 95. But just to be safe, you might want to make backup copies of these things before you run Setup. Also, back up your system files before installing the software.

Network users can choose a Workstation installation, which requires about 5MB of local hard-disk real estate. Word's installer will check to see if you have enough space, but you can save some time by making sure there is room beforehand.

Running Setup from a CD-ROM or Floppies

NOTE

Depending on the source of your Office CD-ROM, you might or might not be required to use a license disk. This floppy records the number of hard disks on which you install Word or Office. Do not lose this floppy.

The files on the installation disk, whether you are installing from a CD-ROM or from floppies, cannot simply be dragged onto your hard disk. You need to run the Setup program, which will walk you through these simple installation steps:

1. Start Windows.
2. Insert the first Setup disk in a floppy drive if you are installing from floppies (or if your CD-ROM came with a "License" disk).

3. Choose Run from the Start menu.

4. If you are installing from floppies, type the disk-drive name (**A:** or **B:**), a backslash, and **Setup**, as shown here:

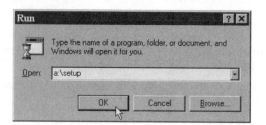

If you are installing from a CD-ROM, Word displays a splash screen offering you the option of installing or upgrading your software when you insert the disc.

5. Click on the Install (or perhaps Upgrade) icon.

6. In a moment, you will see a Setup dialog box similar, but probably not identical, to this one:

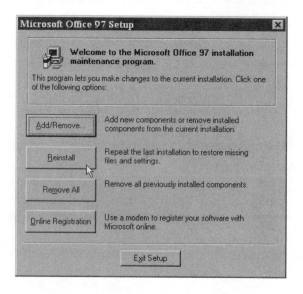

7. The choices you will be given will vary with your situation. Read each choice carefully before clicking on the Continue button.

8. When asked if you want a Typical, Minimum, Laptop, Complete, or Custom installation, opt for Complete if you have the required disk space. You can always remove unwanted elements after you've had a chance to explore them.

9. If you are installing Office, you may have to click on the Change Options button to get to the Word installation options (see "Custom Installation and Removing the Unwanted," below).

10. If you are installing from a CD-ROM, that's about it. Word (or all of Microsoft Office) will be installed straight from the CD-ROM without your intervention. If you haven't invested in a CD-ROM drive yet and are using floppies, though, go get yourself some lunch or a good book, 'cause you're going to be disk-swapping for about an hour and a half. Word will tell you which floppies it needs when. All you have to do is take the old floppy out, put the correct one in, and click on OK or press Enter. Fun, isn't it?

11. When the installation is finished, Setup will ask you to restart your computer. It is not wise to defy the will of Setup; so simply click on Restart.

12. Your computer will restart, and you will be ready to dazzle the free and other worlds with your bold and innovative faxes!

APDX

A

Installing Word

Running Setup from a Server

If your company has a network and is licensed to do so, you may be able to install Word from the server (over the network) without the need for floppy shuffling. Contact your network administrator for details.

Custom Installation and Removing the Unwanted

If you choose not to do a complete installation, you can tell Setup which items you want to install. And you can revisit the Setup program later to remove items you don't use. This is helpful if you have limited disk space or if one of your nonessential floppies is damaged.

In either case, you'll see a series of dialog boxes, each with lists of items that can be added or removed. Most of the dialog boxes also contain Change Options buttons that give you more detailed control. For example, the first dialog box lets you add or delete all Online Help, and the next level down lets you pick and choose from options such as Help for WordPerfect Users, and Help for Microsoft Word. As you add or remove checks in the various option boxes, Word revises its estimation of the required disk space and displays the statistics at the bottom of the dialog boxes.

The "top-level" dialog box looks like this:

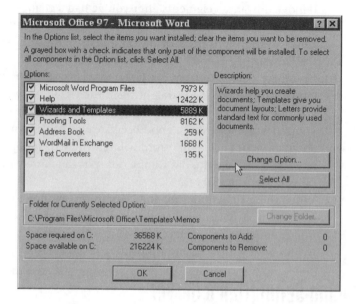

To reach the detailed choices, click the on Change Option button:

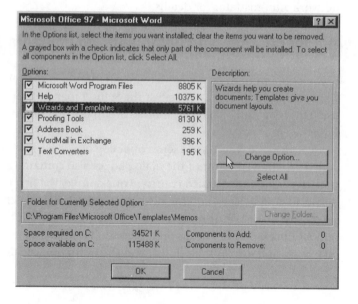

It's a good idea to install the templates and sample documents, as they contain helpful files and examples. If you choose not to install certain features, they will either not appear on your Word menus or will always be dimmed. You can always return to Setup later and install only the items you left off when you last did a custom installation.

Using Old Word Files

If you have old Word documents, custom dictionaries, and templates from Word version 6 or Word 95 scattered around your hard disk, you will be able to use them with Word 97. Word will convert them when you open them, and you can either save them as Word 97 files or save them as earlier version files. You can even use your old custom menu, toolbar, and keyboard settings, although you may be better off personalizing the Word 97 tools from scratch.

If you have modified Word's Standard styles in earlier versions, Setup tries to preserve these changes. Old macros should work as well.

It goes without saying that you should explore the effects of Setup's "automatic" conversions and accommodations before you start any large rush projects that depend on them.

APDX

A

Installing Word

Master's Reference

Master's Reference

AutoCorrect

Use Word's AutoCorrect feature to automatically correct punctuation and spelling errors in your documents. You can also use AutoCorrect when you want to replace a unique abbreviation you have defined with text or a graphic you use frequently. For example, you can abbreviate entries for a logo, a phrase, or a word you often misspell. When you type the defined abbreviation followed by a space or punctuation mark, AutoCorrect automatically inserts the text assigned to the abbreviation.

Automatically Correcting Typing Errors

AutoCorrect is designed to correct some common typing errors. Follow these steps to define which errors AutoCorrect will automatically correct:

1. Choose Tools ➤ AutoCorrect to display the AutoCorrect dialog box.

2. Select the checkbox of any of the following options on the AutoCorrect tab:

   - To have AutoCorrect change the second letter in a word from uppercase to lowercase, select the Correct TWo INitial CApitals checkbox.

   - To have AutoCorrect capitalize the first letter after a period, select the Capitalize First Letter of Sentences checkbox.

   - To have AutoCorrect change the lowercase first letter in the name of a day to uppercase, select the Capitalize Names of Days checkbox.

   - To have AutoCorrect change uppercase letters that were typed when Caps Lock was accidentally turned on into lowercase letters, select the Correct Accidental Usage of cAPS LOCK Key checkbox.

3. Choose OK.

To exclude some abbreviations and capitalized text from being corrected automatically, follow these steps:

1. Choose Tools ➤ AutoCorrect to display the AutoCorrect dialog box.

2. Choose Exceptions to display the AutoCorrect Exceptions dialog box.

3. To prevent AutoCorrect from changing a lowercase character into uppercase after a specific AutoCorrect entry has been typed in your documents, type the name of the entry in the Don't Capitalize After text box, and then choose Add.

4. Select the Automatically Add Words to List checkbox to have AutoCorrect automatically add entries to the Don't Capitalize After list box.

5. To prevent AutoCorrect from changing a specified word with two initial caps, select the INitial CAps tab, type the word in the Don't Correct text box, and then choose Add.

6. Select the Automatically Add Words to List checkbox to have AutoCorrect automatically add words with two initial caps to the Don't Correct list box.

7. Choose OK in the AutoCorrect Exceptions dialog box, and then choose OK again in the AutoCorrect dialog box.

When the Automatically Add Words to List checkbox is selected on the First Letter and INitial

CAps tabs, you can add AutoCorrect entries and words with initial caps to the list boxes without displaying the AutoCorrect Exceptions dialog box. When you type an entry or a word with two initial caps that you don't want AutoCorrect to change, press Backspace immediately after the change is made to delete the change, and then retype the entry or word with two initial caps to automatically add it as an exception to the appropriate list box.

To delete an exception you have added to the Don't Capitalize After or Don't Correct list box, highlight the word in the list box and choose Delete.

Creating an AutoCorrect Entry

An AutoCorrect entry consists of two parts—the entry's name, which is usually an abbreviation or a misspelling of the item being replaced, and the replacement item. Each entry must have a unique name. The name you create can contain a maximum of 31 characters, but it cannot contain any spaces. If you use a word as the entry name, add a character or a symbol to the name so that AutoCorrect will not replace a real word in your document with an entry. The replacement item can contain as many as 255 characters, including spaces, punctuation marks, and paragraph marks. Or, you can include a graphic in a selection to which an AutoCorrect entry name is being assigned.

To create an AutoCorrect entry, follow these steps:

1. To create an entry using an item that is already in your document, select the item.

2. Choose Tools ➤ AutoCorrect to display the AutoCorrect tab in the AutoCorrect dialog box.

3. Be sure that the Replace Text As You Type checkbox is selected.

4. Type an abbreviation or a word you often misspell in the Replace text box.

5. Type the text with which to replace the abbreviation or misspelled word in the With text box. (If you selected text in your document as specified in step 1 above, it already appears in the With text box.)

6. If you selected text in your document as the replacement item in step 1 above, select Plain Text or Formatted Text to define how the text will appear each time it replaces the abbreviation or misspelled word.

7. Choose Add to add the entry to the list.

8. Choose OK.

To automatically replace the entry's name with the replacement item, type the name followed by a space.

If you want to temporarily turn off AutoCorrect, clear the Replace Text As You Type checkbox on the AutoCorrect tab, and then choose OK.

Editing an AutoCorrect Entry

To delete an AutoCorrect entry, follow these steps:

1. Choose Tools ➤ AutoCorrect to display the AutoCorrect tab in the AutoCorrect dialog box.

2. Highlight the entry in the Replace Text As You Type list, and then choose Delete.

3. Choose OK to close the AutoCorrect dialog box.

To edit an entry you typed in the Replace Text As You Type list, follow these steps:

1. Choose Tools ➤ AutoCorrect to display the AutoCorrect tab.

2. Be sure the Replace Text As You Type checkbox is selected.

3. Highlight the entry you want to edit in the list. Both the name and the replacement item appear in the Replace and With text boxes.

4. To edit the name, select it in the Replace text box. Type the new name, and then choose Add.

5. To edit the replacement item, select the text in the With text box. Make the changes you want to the selected item, and then choose Replace. Select Yes to redefine an entry for a name that is already in the list.

6. Choose OK.

To edit either the name or replacement item of an item you selected in your document, follow these steps:

1. If necessary, make the changes to the replacement item text in your document, and then select the item.

2. Choose Tools ➤ AutoCorrect to display the AutoCorrect tab.

3. Type a name in the Replace text box. If it is a new name, choose Add. If the abbreviation is currently in use, choose Replace, and then choose Yes to confirm the replacement.

4. Click on OK.

AutoFormat

You can use the AutoFormat feature to automatically apply uniform styles and formatting to a document or a WordMail message and improve its appearance. AutoFormat can automatically make some formatting changes as you type. In addition, AutoFormat can apply consistent formats to selected document text or to an entire document. You can review these changes and either accept or reject them.

Formatting Text Automatically

Word's templates come with many built-in styles, such as headings, bulleted lists, and body text. If you want AutoFormat to apply your own styles, you must redefine the styles that are built into Word. To use AutoFormat, follow these steps:

1. Place the insertion point anywhere in a document to format the entire document, or select the text you want to format automatically.

2. Choose Format ➤ AutoFormat to display the AutoFormat dialog box.

3. Choose one of the following options to specify how you want AutoFormat to format your document:

   • Select AutoFormat Now (the default) to apply formatting without allowing you to accept or reject the changes.

   • Select AutoFormat and Review Each Change to apply formatting and then allow you to accept or reject the changes.

4. Select General Document, Letter, or Email in the Please Select a Document Type to Help Improve the Formatting Process drop-down list to specify the type of formatting for AutoFormat to use.

5. Choose OK to automatically format the document or the selection. The status bar displays the progress of the AutoFormat.

If you chose AutoFormat Now in step 3, the AutoFormat dialog box closes, and Word displays the document with the newly applied format. If you chose AutoFormat and Review Each Change, however, the AutoFormat dialog box reappears when the format is complete, but contains different options.

Reviewing Changes Made by AutoFormat

When you select Review Changes in the AutoFormat dialog box, the Review AutoFormat Changes dialog box appears, and track change marks temporarily appear in your document as follows:

   • Paragraph marks in blue indicate that a style was automatically applied to the paragraph.

   • Paragraph marks in red show that a paragraph mark was deleted.

   • A red strikethrough character appears where text or spaces were deleted.

   • A blue underline character appears under text to which an underline was added.

- Change bars appear in the margin beside any line in which formatting changes occurred.

You can suppress the display of the track change marks by selecting Hide Marks in the Review AutoFormat Changes dialog box.

To review the changes made by AutoFormat, follow these steps:

1. To select a different document template that contains the styles you want AutoFormat to use in your document, choose Style Gallery, select the name of the template in the Template list box, and then choose OK.

2. Choose Review Changes in the AutoFormat dialog box to display the Review AutoFormat Changes dialog box.

3. Choose ← Find to highlight the previous change, or choose → Find to highlight the next change in the document. Alternatively, you can use the scroll bars to scroll through the document and review the changes.

4. To change the style of selected text, click on the Style drop-down list button on the Formatting toolbar and select another style in the list.

5. To reject an AutoFormat suggestion and return the selection to its original format, choose Reject. (If you accidentally reject a suggested formatting change, choose Undo to reverse the rejection.)

6. When you have finished reviewing and revising changes, choose Cancel in the Review AutoFormat Changes dialog box.

7. In the AutoFormat dialog box, choose Accept All to accept all the changes you didn't revise, or choose Reject All to reject all the changes made by AutoFormat.

Setting the AutoFormat Options

You can specify the elements of the document to which AutoFormat applies styles. You can also manage some other changes AutoFormat makes to the text, such as replacing extra paragraph marks and spaces with paragraph formats that include spacing. The elements you specify can be different when using AutoFormat As You Type and when using AutoFormat to apply formatting to a document or selection.

To set AutoFormat options, follow these steps:

1. Choose Tools ➤ AutoCorrect and click on the AutoFormat tab, or choose Format ➤ AutoFormat and choose Options to display the options on the AutoFormat tab in the AutoCorrect dialog box. Alternatively, choose Tools ➤ AutoCorrect and click on the AutoFormat As You Type tab to display its options.

2. Select any of the following options you want AutoFormat to manage:

- In the Apply area on the AutoFormat tab, select Headings to automatically apply heading styles to headings in a document such as an outline; select Lists to automatically change a number preceding a space, tab, or period into a numbered list; select Automatic Bulleted Lists to change a bullet preceding a space or tab into a bulleted list; and select Other Paragraphs to automatically apply formatting, such as the Body Text style, to paragraphs other than headings and lists.

- In the Apply As You Type area on the AutoFormat As You Type tab, select Headings to apply heading styles to text that you manually format as a heading; select Borders to insert a thin-line border above a paragraph when at least three dashes are typed, to insert a thick-line border above a paragraph when at least three underscores are typed, or to insert a double-line border above a paragraph when at least three equals signs are typed; select Automatic Bulleted Lists to change a bullet preceding a space or tab into a bulleted list; and select Automatic Numbered Lists to change a number preceding a space, tab, or period into a numbered list.

- In the Replace area on the AutoFormat tab and the Replace As You Type area on the AutoFormat As You Type tab, select the Straight Quotes with 'Smart Quotes,' Ordinals (1st) with Superscript, Fractions (1/2) with Fraction Character (½), and Symbol Characters (--) with Symbols (—) checkboxes to specify which characters you want to automatically replace during an AutoFormat or as you are typing. Select the *Bold* and _Underline_ with Real Formatting checkbox to apply bold format to characters within asterisks and a single underline to words within underscore characters. Select the Internet and Network Paths with Hyperlinks checkbox to apply hyperlink field formatting to those paths.

- In the Preserve area on the AutoFormat tab, select the Styles checkbox to have AutoFormat keep the styles you have applied in the document instead of replacing applied styles with Word's built-in styles.

- In the Always AutoFormat area on the AutoFormat tab, select the Plain Text WordMail Documents checkbox to automatically format WordMail messages when they are opened.

- In the Automatically As You Type area on the AutoFormat As You Type tab, select the Format Beginning of List Item Like the One Before It checkbox to automatically apply the same formatting to the beginning of a new list item as that applied to the previous list item. Select the Define Styles Based on Your Formatting checkbox to automatically create new styles based on the formatting you applied in your documents.

3. Choose OK in the AutoCorrect dialog box. If the AutoFormat dialog box appears, choose OK to automatically format the document with the selected options, or choose Cancel to return to the document window.

AutoSummarize

Use AutoSummarize to automatically create a summary using the important points in a document. AutoSummarize defines the key points in a document by analyzing the sentences that contain the words used most frequently in a document. AutoSummarize is useful for structured documents such as reports, articles, and scientific papers.

AutoSummarize works best when the Find All Word Forms tool (which is installed by default) is installed. In addition, text that is formatted with the No Proofing option in the Language dialog box and text in a language other than English cannot be automatically summarized.

To AutoSummarize the active document, follow these steps:

1. Choose Tools ➤ AutoSummarize to display the AutoSummarize dialog box.

2. In the Type of Summary area, select one of the following options to specify the appearance of the summary:

   - Choose Highlight Key Points to highlight the key points in the document without hiding any existing text.

   - Choose Create a New Document and Put the Summary There to open a new document and insert a copy of the key points in it.

   - Choose Insert an Executive Summary or Abstract at the Top of the Document to place a copy of the key points at the beginning of the document.

   - Choose Hide Everything but the Summary without Leaving the Original Document to apply hidden text format to all the document text except for the key points.

3. Specify the length of the summary in the Percent of Original drop-down list. A larger percentage covers more key points in the document; a smaller percentage covers fewer.

4. Select the Update Document Statistics checkbox (selected by default) to copy the key words and the sentences that contain the most frequently discussed points to the Keywords and Comments text boxes on the Summary tab in the document's Properties dialog box.

5. Choose OK.

The AutoSummarize toolbar appears. Click on the Highlight/Show Only Summary button to toggle the way the summary appears by either displaying highlighted key points in the document or hiding all the document text except the key points. You can also adjust the length of the summary by changing the percentage in the Percent of Original text box.

AutoText

Use AutoText to quickly insert entries you have saved in a document. You can create named entries for text or graphics that you use often, such as the return address or closing of a letter. Word comes with many built-in AutoText entries, such as salutations and closings for use in letters.

Creating an AutoText Entry

AutoText entry names can contain as many as 32 characters and can include spaces. You can also specify that AutoComplete insert the AutoText entry when the first four letters of the entry's name are typed in a document. When an AutoText entry appears in your document as you are typing, you can either press Enter to accept the insertion or continue typing to refuse it.

To create an AutoText entry, follow these steps:

1. Select the text or item you want to save as an AutoText entry, including any spaces or punctuation you want to insert when you insert the entry in your document. If you want to save the format of selected text, be sure you also select its paragraph mark (¶).

2. Choose Insert ➤ AutoText ➤ AutoText to display the AutoText tab in the AutoCorrect dialog box.

3. Select the Show AutoComplete Tip for AutoText and Dates checkbox (selected by default) to have AutoComplete suggest the AutoText entry when the first four letters of the entry's name are typed.

4. If necessary, type a new name for the entry in the Enter AutoText Entries Here text box.

5. If necessary, select the name of the document template where the entry will be saved in the LookIn drop-down list. By default, entries are saved to the Normal.dot template.

6. Select Add to add the entry to the Enter AutoText Entries Here list box.

You can quickly add a selection to the list of AutoText entries by either clicking on the New button on the AutoText toolbar or choosing Insert ➤ AutoText ➤ New (Alt+F3) to display the Create AutoText dialog box. If necessary, type a different name in the Please Name Your AutoText Entry text box, and then choose OK.

To delete an AutoText entry, choose Insert ➤ AutoText ➤ AutoText, highlight the name of the entry in the Enter AutoText Entries Here list box, and then choose Delete. Choose OK to return to your document.

Displaying the AutoText Toolbar

You can easily display the AutoText tab in the AutoCorrect dialog box, insert an AutoText entry, or create a new AutoText entry using the buttons available on the AutoText toolbar. Use either of the following methods to display the AutoText toolbar:

- Choose Insert ➤ AutoText ➤ AutoText to display the AutoText tab in the AutoCorrect dialog box, and then choose Show Toolbar.

- Right-click on any displayed toolbar, and then choose AutoText.

Inserting an AutoText Entry

To insert an AutoText entry in a document, select it in the list of AutoText entries that appears on the Insert ➤ AutoText ➤ AutoText sub-menu or when you click on the All Entries button on the AutoText toolbar. The AutoText entry list contains only the entries that were created in the same paragraph style as the paragraph that contains the insertion point. To display a list of all AutoText entries, hold down the Shift key while you click on the All Entries button on the Auto-Text toolbar or as you point to AutoText on the Insert ➤ AutoText menu.

In addition, only the AutoText entries stored in the Normal.dot template (or any other template that is loaded for use with all your documents) appear in the list. If you stored AutoText entries in any other template, those entries are available only when a document based on that template is active.

To edit an AutoText entry, insert the entry in your document, and then make the desired changes. Select the entry, including the paragraph mark if you want to save the entry's formatting, and either click on the New button on the AutoText toolbar or choose Insert ➤ Auto-Text ➤ New (Alt+F3). Choose OK in the Create AutoText dialog box, and then choose Yes to redefine the entry you selected.

Background

To make your online documents and Web pages more interesting, you can add a background with a color, gradient, texture, or picture for documents that are displayed in Online Layout view. These backgrounds are specifically used for viewing on your screen and do not print when you print the document.

To display a background for an online document, follow these steps:

1. Click on the Online Layout View button beside the status bar or choose View ➤ Online Layout.

2. To display a background color, choose Format ➤ Background and then either click on the color in the palette that appears or choose More Colors to display the Colors dialog box, click on a color in the graphic that appears on the Standard tab, and then choose OK. Alternatively, you can create a new color by clicking in an area on the Custom tab in the Colors dialog box and then choosing OK.

3. To display a background fill in an online document, choose Format ➤ Background ➤ Fill Effects to display the Fill Effects dialog box, and then choose one of the following options:

   • To display a gradient in the background, click on the Gradient tab, select One Color or Two Colors, and then choose the corresponding color in the Color 1 or Color 2 palette. If you choose One Color, drag the scroll button along the Dark/Light scroll bar to adjust the contrast in the gradient. Alternatively, choose Preset, and then select one of the built-in color combinations in the Preset Colors drop-down list. Select the direction of the shading in the gradient in the Shading Styles area, the pattern used in the gradient in the Variants area, and then choose OK.

   • To display a texture in the background, click on the Texture tab, click on one of the built-in background textures, and then choose OK. Alternatively, choose Other Texture to display the Select Texture dialog box, select the name of the file that contains the background texture you want, and then choose OK.

   • To display a pattern in the background, click on the Pattern tab, select the pattern in the Pattern area, choose a color in both the Foreground and Background palettes, and then choose OK.

- To display a picture in the background, click on the Picture tab, and then choose Select Picture to display the Select Picture dialog box. Select the name of the file that contains the picture, and then choose OK.

4. Choose OK in the Fill Effects dialog box.

Bookmark

Use bookmarks to name a selection or location in your document. You can then move quickly to the location, calculate numbers, mark pages for an index entry, or create cross-references.

Creating a Bookmark

When you create a bookmark, you assign a name to a selection or a location in your document. Bookmark names can contain a maximum of 40 characters, must begin with a letter, and can contain numbers. Although you cannot include spaces in a bookmark name, you can use _ (underline character).

1. Select the text or item, or move the insertion point to the place in your document where you want to insert a bookmark.

2. Choose Insert ➤ Bookmark (Ctrl+Shift+F5) to display the Bookmark dialog box.

3. Type a name for the bookmark in the Bookmark Name text box.

4. Select Add to add the bookmark name to the list box.

You can delete a bookmark that you no longer need. Use any of the following methods to delete a bookmark in your document:

- If you assign a bookmark name that is already in the document to a new bookmark, the original bookmark with that name is deleted.
- Choose Insert ➤ Bookmark, highlight the name of the bookmark you want to delete, and then choose Delete to delete the bookmark but leave its marked text in the document.

- Select the bookmark bracket and its marked text, and then press Backspace or Delete to delete both the bookmark and its marked text.

When you display bookmarks in a document, they appear as square black brackets for selected text or as a large I-beam for a marked location. To display bookmarks in all your documents, choose Tools ➤ Options, and select the View tab. Select the Bookmarks checkbox in the Show area, and then choose OK.

To move to a specific bookmark in your document, follow these steps:

1. Choose Insert ➤ Bookmark.

2. In the Sort By area, select either the Name option button (to display the bookmark names alphabetically in the Bookmark Name list box) or the Location option button (to sort the bookmark names in the order of their locations in the document).

3. If necessary, select the Hidden Bookmarks checkbox to display the names of hidden bookmarks, such as cross-references, in the Bookmark Name list box.

4. Highlight the name of the bookmark in the Bookmark Name list box, and then choose Go To. If the bookmark is a location, the insertion point moves to the location. If the bookmark is selected text, the text is selected when you move to it. Choose Close to return to your document.

Editing a Marked Item

Keep the following points in mind when editing an existing bookmark:

- When you copy a bookmark or part of a bookmark to a location in the same document, only the text or item is copied, not the actual bookmark.
- When you copy a bookmark and paste it in another document, both documents will have the same bookmarks.

- When you cut a bookmark and paste it in a location in the same document or a different document, both the text or item and the bookmark move to the new location.

- If you cut or copy a bookmark to another document and that document already has a bookmark with that assigned name, the bookmark will not be pasted into the document. The original bookmark with the name will keep its name and location.

- If you delete part of a bookmark, the undeleted portion of the item stays marked.

- When you add text between any two characters in a bookmark, it becomes part of the bookmark.

- To add text at the beginning of a bookmark, insert it just before marked text.

- To add text at the end of bookmark text, type the text, and then select all the text and the bookmark brackets. Choose Insert ➤ Bookmark, and then choose Add.

- When you add a new row at the end of marked table, the inserted row is included in the marked table.

Borders and Shading

You can add borders and shading to a paragraph or to an item such as regular document text, text in a cell, a text box, or a frame, the actual cell, text box, or frame, or a table. You can also add a border to the pages in a document.

The borders and shading you apply to a paragraph can either surround only the text (if the paragraph is a short line of text) or extend between the paragraph indents. You can adjust the width of extended paragraph borders or shading paragraphs by adjusting the indentation.

Applying Borders and Shading

Use any of the following methods to specify which item is to receive a border or shading:

- To apply a border or shading to a paragraph, activate only the paragraph, even if it is in a cell or a frame, by selecting it or positioning the insertion point in it.

- To apply a border or shading to a table cell, including its contents, position the insertion point in the cell.

- To apply a border to a table, click in any cell in the table.

- To apply a border to a graphic or frame or to apply shading to a frame, select the graphic or frame.

Display the Tables and Borders toolbar to quickly apply predefined borders or shading to a paragraph, table cell, table, or frame. To display the Tables and Borders toolbar, click on the Tables and Borders button on the Standard toolbar or choose Format ➤ Borders and Shading ➤ Show Toolbar.

Use the following buttons and drop-down lists on the Tables and Borders toolbar to apply the corresponding border and color:

- In the Line Style drop-down list, select a line style for the border.

- In the Line Weight drop-down list, select the thickness of the border.

- In the Border Color palette, select a color for the border.

- To apply a border to the selection, click on the *Type of* Border drop-down list button to display a palette of borders, and then click on the graphic of the border.

- To apply a fill color within the border, select the bordered item, click on the Shading Color drop-down list, and then click on the background color in the palette that appears.

You can customize the borders you apply to an item, apply a shadow border, move the borders in relation to the selection, or apply borders to a page using the options in the Borders and Shading dialog box. To do so, follow these steps:

1. Activate the paragraph or item to which you want to apply a custom border or shading.

2. Choose Format ➤ Borders and Shading to display the Borders and Shading dialog box.

3. Select either the Borders or the Page Borders tab, and then choose any of the following options to customize and apply a border:

- Choose None, Box, Shadow, Three-D, or Custom in the Setting area to define the type of border to place around the item.

- In the Style list box, select the style of line you want for the border.

- In the Color drop-down list, select a color for the border.

- In the Width drop-down list, choose the border's width.

- Click on the position or the corresponding button where you want to add a top, bottom, left, right, inside, or outside border, or to remove the current border in the Preview area.

- In the Apply To drop-down list, select the item, such as Paragraph or Whole Document, to which to apply the border.

- If you are creating a paragraph border, choose Options, adjust the amount of space in points between the borders and the paragraph in the From Text area, and then choose OK.

- If you are creating a page border, choose Options, and then select either Edge of Page or Text in the Measure From drop-down list to define the relative position of the border. In the Margins area, adjust the amount of space in points between each border and each edge of the page or between the text and each border. In the Options area, select Align Paragraph Borders and Table Edges with Page Border to arrange those items along the border of a page in which the border is positioned relative to text. Select the Surround Header and Surround Footer checkboxes to include those items in the border on a page in which the border is positioned relative to text. Select the Always Display in Front checkbox to position a page border on top of any text or other object that is placed in the position of the border. Choose OK.

4. To apply and customize the shading for the object, select the Shading tab, and then choose any of the following options:

- In the Fill area, choose one of the colors in the palette, or choose None to remove all shading from the item.

- In the Patterns area, select a shading density or pattern to apply in the Style drop-down list. If necessary, select a color for the shading or pattern in the Color drop-down list.

- In the Apply To drop-down list, select the item to which to apply the specified shading.

5. Choose OK.

Captions

Use Word's Caption feature to add a caption to a selected item or to all items of the same type in your document. Captions are added as field codes. You can change the format of automatic caption numbers and edit the caption text in your document. All the captions are automatically updated in your document when you add or delete a captioned item.

Inserting Captions Automatically

Use Word's AutoCaption feature when you create a document that will contain items to which you want to add a caption. When AutoCaption is toggled on, captions inserted in the document are uniformly formatted and correctly numbered. Word automatically saves your AutoCaption changes to the Normal.dot template when you exit.

You can add more than one type of caption to your document. For each type of caption you add automatically, select a specific caption label and position.

To insert captions, follow these steps:

1. Position the insertion point in your document where you want to begin adding captions automatically, and then choose Insert ➤ Caption to display the Caption dialog box.

2. Choose AutoCaption to display the Auto-Caption dialog box.

3. Select the checkbox beside an item to which you want to automatically add captions in the Add Caption When Inserting list box. If necessary, scroll through the list to find the item.

4. Select the label for the item in the Use Label drop-down list. Or, select New Label, type the text for the label in the Label text box, and then choose OK in the New Label dialog box.

5. To define the placement of the caption, choose Above Item or Below Item in the Position drop-down list.

6. Repeat steps 3 through 5 for each item to which you want to automatically add a caption in the document.

7. Choose OK in the AutoCaption dialog box.

Inserting Captions Manually

To insert captions manually in your document, follow these steps:

1. Select the item to which you want to add a caption, and then choose Insert ➤ Caption to display the Caption dialog box.

2. The label and caption number for the item appear in the Caption text box. Type the text for the caption in the text box.

3. To change the caption label, choose Equation, Figure, or Table in the Label drop-down list. Or, choose New Label, type a name for the caption label in the Label text box, and then choose OK in the New Label dialog box.

4. Choose OK in the Caption dialog box.

To delete a caption label you have created, select the label in the Label drop-down list, and then choose Delete Label.

Modifying the Caption-Numbering Format

You can change the default format of the caption's numbering. You can also include the chapter number in the caption label if you assign one of Word's built-in heading styles to the chapter titles in your document. The format for all captions of the same type will be changed in your document.

To modify the caption-numbering format, follow these steps:

1. Select a caption of the type whose numbering format you want to change, and then choose Insert ➤ Caption.

2. Select Numbering to display the Caption Numbering dialog box.

3. Select any of the following options, and then choose OK:

   • To change the number format for the type of label, select a different format in the Format drop-down list.

   • To include the chapter number in the caption label, select the Include Chapter Number checkbox, and then select the heading style that you applied to the chapter titles in your document in the Chapter Starts with Style drop-down list. Select the separator character to use between the chapter number and the number of the captioned item in the Use Separator drop-down list.

4. Choose OK again in the Caption dialog box.

Replacing Caption Text and Labels

Once you have added a caption either automatically or manually, you can easily edit the text you added to the caption using Word's regular editing techniques.

You can also edit the caption label for a single label or for all the labels of a specific type. You cannot, however, change the label or number of a caption by typing over it.

To change a single caption's label, follow these steps:

1. Select the caption label you want to change.

2. Delete the label by pressing Backspace or Delete.

3. Choose Insert ➤ Caption to display the Caption dialog box.

4. Select a different label in the Label drop-down list, and then choose OK.

To change the labels of all captions of the same type, follow these steps:

1. Select one of the caption labels you want to change, and then choose Insert ➤ Caption.

2. Select a different label in the Label drop-down list, and then choose OK.

Columns

You can add newspaper columns to a document or part of a document. Newspaper columns are columns that let text flow from the bottom of one column to the top of the next column.

Columns can be of equal or unequal widths. When you insert columns in a document, you can either format the whole document in multiple columns or automatically add a section break to the portion of the document you want to be columnar.

To view columns in your document, you must be in Page Layout view or Print Preview.

Inserting Columns in Your Document

To quickly create equal columns in the current document section, click on the Columns button on the Standard toolbar, drag to highlight the number of columns you want and then click in the columns palette.

To create custom columns, follow these steps:

1. Position the insertion point where you want to create columns.

2. Choose Format ➤ Columns to display the Columns dialog box.

3. In the Presets area, select One, Two, or Three as the number of equal columns, or choose Left or Right as the position of the smaller column for columns of unequal widths.

4. If necessary, choose any of the following options to further define the appearance of the columns:

   • Adjust the value in the Number of Columns text box to specify the number of columns you want.

   • If you selected columns of unequal width in the Presets area, you can adjust the measurement that specifies the width of each column in the Width text box. To specify the amount of space that appears between columns, adjust the measurement in the Spacing text box.

   • Select the Equal Column Width checkbox to quickly format the columns with equal width. Clear the checkbox for columns of unequal width.

   • Choose Selected Text, This Section, This Point Forward, or Whole Document as the portion of the document to be columnar in the Apply To drop-down list.

   • Select the Line Between checkbox to create a line between the columns.

   • Select the Start New Column checkbox (if you selected This Point Forward in the Apply To drop-down list) to add a column break in the position of the insertion point.

5. Choose OK in the Columns dialog box.

You can also edit some column features using the horizontal ruler, shortcut keys, or menu commands:

- Drag the left or right column marker to change the width of the column.

- Drag the indent marker to align it with the column marker to remove indents from the paragraph that contains the insertion point. Or, select an indented paragraph in a column, either right-click on the selection and choose Paragraph or choose Format ➤ Paragraph, and then change its indentation to 0.

- To start a new column, position the insertion point where you want to insert a column break, and then press Ctrl+Shift+↵. Or, position the insertion point, select Insert ➤ Break, select Column Break, and then choose OK.

- To balance the lengths of columns on a page, position the insertion point at the end of the column you want to balance and choose Insert ➤ Break. Select Continuous, and then choose OK.

Comments

You can add text or voice notes and comments to a document. Comment marks are formatted as hidden text, and each comment mark in the document appears with the initials of its author, which are entered by default in the Initials text box on the User Information tab of the Options dialog box during Setup. You must have a sound board, speakers, and a microphone installed on your system to insert voice notes.

Comments appear in your document with a light yellow highlight. Click on the Show/Hide ¶ button on the Standard toolbar to toggle the display of comment marks in your document. Select View ➤ Comments to toggle the display of both the comment marks in your document and the comment pane on your screen.

Inserting a Comment

Text in the comment pane can be edited when the pane is active. Text in the document window can be edited when the window is active. To switch between the comment pane and the document window, press F6 or click in the document window or comment pane. Comment marks are automatically renumbered whenever you insert, copy, or delete a comment.

To insert a text or voice comment, follow these steps:

1. Select the text or position the insertion point where you want to insert a comment.

2. Choose Insert ➤ Comment. A hidden comment mark containing the number of the comment and the initials of its author is inserted in the document, and the comment pane containing the insertion point opens at the bottom of your screen.

3. To insert a text comment, type the text of the comment, and add any formatting you want to the text in the comment pane.

4. To insert a voice comment, follow these steps:

   a. Click on the Insert Sound Object button in the comment pane to display the Sound Object dialog box.

   b. Click on the Record button in the Sound Object dialog box and then speak into your microphone to record your comment. If necessary, check your sound board's documentation for instructions on recording a sound object.

   c. Click on the Stop button in the Sound Object dialog box when you are finished recording your comment.

5. When you are finished inserting or editing the comments, close the comment pane by choosing Close (Alt+Shift+C).

To insert a comment that is both text and voice, insert the text portion of the comment first. Then move the insertion point just after the text and add the voice comment.

To delete a comment, select the comment mark in your document and press the Delete key.

To copy a comment, select the comment mark in the document pane, and then click on the Copy button on the Standard toolbar. Position the insertion point in the document where you want to place a copy of the comment and click on the Paste button.

Listening to or Viewing Comments

To play back a voice comment, double-click on a comment mark in the document or select View ➤ Comments to display the comment pane, and then double-click on the sound symbol of the comment you want to hear.

Follow these steps to display the text of a comment:

1. Double-click on the comment mark you want to view, or select View ➤ Comments to display the comment pane.

2. If necessary, highlight the name of the reviewer whose comments you want to see in the Comments From drop-down list.

3. If necessary, scroll through the list until the comment you want to see is displayed.

Cross-Reference

Cross-references refer the reader to additional or related information in the same document or a different document (if both documents are part of the same master document). You can create cross-references to heading text formatted with a heading style, footnotes and endnotes, captions, and bookmarks.

Cross-references are inserted as field codes and are especially useful in long documents such as a master document. You can insert cross-references as hyperlinks, which allow you to jump to the item being referenced.

Creating Cross-references

To create cross-references, follow these steps:

1. Position the insertion point in your document where you want to create a cross-reference, and then type any introductory text, such as **See Page**. Make sure you type a space after the introductory text.

2. Choose Insert ➤ Cross-reference to display the Cross-reference dialog box.

3. Highlight the type of item you want to cite in the Reference Type list box. You can select Numbered Item, Heading, Bookmark, Footnote, Endnote, Equation, Figure, Table, or a caption label you created as the type of reference.

4. Highlight the portion of the item that is to appear in the cross-reference in the Insert Reference To list box. The options in the list box depend on the type of reference you selected in step 3.

5. Select the Insert As Hyperlink checkbox to attach a hyperlink to the item.

6. Select the specific item that you want to refer to in the For Which *Type of Item* list box.

7. If necessary, select the Include Above/ Below checkbox to insert the word *above* or *below* to the cross-reference.

8. Choose Insert.

9. Click in the document window to activate it, and then insert any optional text or the new introductory text for the next cross-reference. Repeat steps 3 through 8 to create each additional cross-reference.

10. Choose Close to return to your document when you have finished creating cross-references.

Editing Cross-references

You can edit both the text you inserted for a reference and the reference itself.

- To replace the introductory or optional text you typed for a reference, select the text and then type new text.

- To delete a reference, select the reference and press Backspace or Delete. When you delete an item you have cited, an error message appears the next time you update the cross-reference.

- To change a selected reference to a different type of reference, choose Insert ➤ Cross-reference, and then select the portion of the item that is to appear in the reference in the Insert Reference To list box.

Database

You can easily insert an existing database or some other source of data into a Word document. You can select which fields of data you want from the data source, and filter the selection of records to be inserted in a table in your document. You can also format the table to meet your needs and have Word update the table if the data source changes.

Word can insert Excel and Access files and can convert many other types of files. You can also filter and insert records from a Word database, such as a mail merge data source file, into another Word document.

Inserting a Database in a Document

To insert a database into the active document, follow these steps:

1. Position the insertion point where you want the database to appear in your document.

2. Right-click on a displayed toolbar, and then select Database to display the Database toolbar.

3. Click on the Insert Database button on the Database toolbar to display the Database dialog box.

4. Select Get Data to display the Open Data Source dialog box.

5. If necessary, select the name of the folder that contains the database file in the Look In drop-down list.

6. If necessary, select the type of files to display in the Look In list box in the Files of Type drop-down list. Then, highlight the name of the database file to be used as the data source in the list box and choose Open.

7. If necessary, select Query Options to display the Query Options dialog box, select any of the following options on the corresponding tab, and then choose OK to define and sort specific information that is to be inserted from the data source:

- Specify which records to insert in the document on the Filter Records tab. In the Field drop-down list, highlight the data source field you want to use in the comparison. In the Comparison drop-down list, highlight the operator you want to use for alphabetic and numeric data. Type the alphabetic or numeric value you want to compare with the field you selected in the Compare To text box. If you want to include more fields, operators, and comparison values, select the And/Or drop-down list. Choose And if additional criteria must be met in the filter, or choose Or if only one of the criteria should be met. To erase all the selection criteria and insert all the data source records, select Clear All.

- Specify the order in which the records will appear in the table you insert in your document on the Sort Records tab. Highlight the field that contains the data on which to sort the records inserted in your document in the Sort By drop-down list. Select Ascending (a-z) or Descending (z-a) to define the alphabetic or numeric order of the records in the table. If necessary, choose the second and third fields on which to define the sort in the Then By drop-down lists, and then select Ascending or Descending as the sort order for each field. To remove all the sorting criteria, choose Clear All.

- Specify which fields in each record will be included in the table on the Select Fields tab. All the fields are listed in the Fields in Data Source list box. Fields that will be included in the table are listed in the Selected Fields list box. Highlight a field in the Selected Fields list box and choose Remove to prevent the field from appearing in the table. Choose Remove All to prevent all the fields from appearing in the table. If you highlight a field in the Fields in Data Source list box, choose Select to add the field to the Selected Fields list box. Choose Select All to include all the data source fields in the table. Select the Include Field Names checkbox to use the field names as column names in the table. To remove all the field selection criteria, choose Clear All.

8. If necessary, select Table AutoFormat and select the name of the predefined table format you want to use in the Formats list box.

9. Select Insert Data to display the Insert Data dialog box, and then choose any of the following options:

- Choose All to insert all the records that meet the selection criteria. If no selection criterion is specified, all the data source records are inserted.

- Type the number of the first record in the range of records you want to include in the table in the From text box, and type the number of the last record in the range in the To text box.

- Select the Insert Data As Field checkbox to insert the specified source data as a database field. When the table is inserted as a field in your document, you can update changes made to the data source in your Word document.

10. Choose OK to insert the database into your document.

If you insert the database as a field in your document, each time you update the database you will lose any table formatting you have applied to the table. To update a database with a selected table format, you must reinsert the database and the table format in your document. If you edit a table inserted as a Database field, your changes will be lost when you next update the field.

Document Map

Use the Document Map to display your document in a window with two panes. The left pane contains all the text to which a heading style is applied in the document. The right pane contains all the document text. You can quickly move around in the document by clicking on a heading in the heading pane. The heading directly above the paragraph that contains the insertion point is highlighted in the heading pane so that you can monitor your position in the document.

Displaying the Document Map

To display the active document in Document Map view, click on the Document Map button on the Standard toolbar, or choose View ➤ Document Map. The Document Map appears by default in Online Layout view. You can display the Document Map in any view. When you change to a different view, however, the Document Map disappears, and you must redisplay it.

You control the level of detail that appears in the headings pane using any of the following methods:

- Click on the - (minus sign) icon to the left of a heading that contains a subordinate heading to hide the subordinate heading.

- Click on the + (plus sign) icon to the left of a heading to reveal its subordinate heading.

- To hide all subordinate headings below a specific level, right-click on a heading in the heading pane, and then highlight the lowest level you want to display.

Dropped Capital

You can add dropped capital formatting to a paragraph to make selected text at the beginning of the paragraph appear in a large, bold font. The selected text is placed in a frame, and the paragraph text wraps around the frame. For the best results with dropped capitals, use either PostScript fonts or scaleable fonts such as True-Type and ATM.

Creating Dropped Capitals

To create a dropped capital, follow these steps:

1. Position the insertion point in the paragraph where you want a dropped capital letter, or select the first word of the paragraph.

2. Choose Format ➤ Drop Cap to display the Drop Cap dialog box.

3. In the Position area of the dialog box, choose either Dropped to place the selection within the paragraph, or In Margin to place the selection in the margin beside the top of the paragraph. (You cannot place a dropped cap in the margin of a multicolumn document.)

4. Optionally, choose a different font for the selection in the Font drop-down list.

5. To change the height of the dropped capital (or a selected graphic at the beginning of a paragraph), adjust the number in the Lines To Drop text box.

6. To change the distance between the dropped capital and the paragraph text, adjust the measurement in the Distance from Text text box.

7. Choose OK.

To remove the dropped capital format from a paragraph, position the insertion point anywhere in the paragraph and choose Format ➤ Drop Cap. Select None in the Position area of the Drop Cap dialog box, and then choose OK.

E-mail

You can send an online document to other people for their comments and revisions or for them to fill in a form. You can choose how the document is sent—to each person simultaneously or to selected people in a specific order (*routing*). If the document is routed, the revisions and annotations inserted by all the reviewers are collected in the document. You can also insert a text message with the document.

Sending a Document Online

When you send a document online, it appears as a message in the recipient's Inbox folder, located in Microsoft Outlook.

To send the active document, follow these steps:

1. Choose File ➤ Send To ➤ Mail Recipient to display the Message window with the document's icon inserted in the message area. If the Choose Profile dialog box appears, choose OK to select Microsoft Outlook in the Profile Name drop-down list.

2. Choose To to display the Select Names dialog box.

3. If necessary, select a different address book in the Show Names from The drop-down list.

4. Highlight a name in the Type Name or Select From List list box, and then choose To to place the name in the Message Recipients list box.

5. Repeat step 4 for each person to whom the file is to be sent. The names in the Message Recipient list box are separated by semicolons.

6. To send a copy of the message to a person, highlight the name of the person in the Type Name or Select From List list box, and then choose Cc to place it in the corresponding Message Recipients list box.

7. Choose OK to place the names in the Message dialog box's To and Cc text boxes.

8. If necessary, type the subject of the online message in the Subject text box.

9. If necessary, click in the message area, and then type the text of a message you want to include with the file.

10. Click on the Send button on the Outlook SendMail toolbar, or choose File ➤ Send (Ctrl+Enter) to send the message and the document.

If you want others to suggest revisions or add comments to a document, send it online and add a routing slip. To add a routing slip to a document you are sending online, follow these steps:

1. Activate the document you want to send, and then choose File ➤ Send To ➤ Routing Recipient to display the Routing Slip dialog box.

2. Your name appears in the From area in the Routing Slip dialog box. Choose Address, and then select the name of the address book that contains the names of the people to whom you want to send the file in the Show Names from The drop-down list.

3. Select a name to whom you want to send the document in the Type Name or Select From List list box, and then choose To to place the name in the To list box.

4. Repeat step 3 for each person to whom the document is to be sent, and then choose OK to return to the Routing Slip dialog box.

5. If necessary, click on the ↑ or ↓ Move button to arrange the highlighted name in the To list box in the order you want the document to be routed to that recipient.

6. If necessary, type the subject of the document in the Subject text box.

7. Type any messages or instructions to the document's recipients in the Message Text text box.

8. In the Route To Recipients area, choose One After Another to send the document to the people in the order they are listed in the To list box, or choose All at Once to simultaneously send a copy of the document to all the people in the To list box.

9. Select the Return When Done checkbox to have the document returned to you when the last person closes the document.

10. If One After Another is selected, select the Track Status checkbox to receive a message when the document is forwarded to the next person on the list.

11. Select (None), Tracked Changes, Comments, or Forms to define how to protect the document from any changes to its text in the Protect For drop-down list.

12. Select Route to send the document. A message appears in the status bar when the document is being routed.

To return to your document in order to edit it before you send it, choose Add Slip. When you have finished editing the document, select File ➤ Send To ➤Next Routing Recipient, and then choose OK to send the document.

Envelope

Use Word's Envelope feature to quickly print an envelope for a document. Word will automatically insert the return and delivery addresses.

You can also mark the return and delivery addresses in your document with bookmarks recognized by Word's Envelope feature. Use

EnvelopeAddress as the bookmark name for the delivery address, and use EnvelopeReturn to mark the return address in a document that contains several addresses.

Addressing and Printing an Envelope

To address and print an envelope, follow these steps:

1. Select the mailing address if the document contains more than one address, and then choose Tools ➤ Envelopes and Labels to display the Envelopes and Labels dialog box.

2. If necessary, select the Envelopes tab.

3. If necessary, type a different return address in the Return Address text box. Or, select the Omit checkbox to suppress the printing of the return address if your envelopes are preprinted.

4. If necessary, choose Options to display the Envelope Options tab in the Envelope Options dialog box.

5. Choose any of the following options to define the appearance of the envelope, and then choose OK.

    • Highlight the definition of the envelope size you want to use in the Envelope Size drop-down list, or select Custom Size to define an envelope size that does not appear in the list.

    • Select the Delivery Point Bar Code checkbox to have Word automatically print the bar code of the delivery address's zip code. Select the FIM-A Courtesy Reply Mail checkbox to print a facing identification mark on the front of a courtesy reply envelope. Word inserts an FIM-A code when the checkbox is selected. To insert an FIM-C code for bulk mail, insert a BarCode field with the \f "C" switch.

    • In the Delivery Address and Return Address areas, choose Font to change the format of the font in the specified area. If necessary, adjust the measurement in both the corresponding From Left text boxes to indicate the distance from the left edge of the envelope, and in the From Top text boxes to indicate the distance from the top edge of the envelope.

6. Choose Print to print the envelope. Or, choose Add To Document to add a section containing the envelope to the beginning of the document so that the envelope is printed when you print the document.

If you edit an envelope that was added to a document, the Add To Document button changes to Change Document.

Word will automatically select the options on the Printing Options tab in the Envelope Options dialog box as those necessary to print the envelope using the default printer. If you change any of the envelope printing options, choose Reset to return them to Word's original selections.

Including Graphics on an Envelope

To add special text or a graphic to an envelope and use it each time you create an envelope based on the current template, save the text or graphic as an AutoText entry. You can insert two AutoText envelope entries named Envelope-Extra1 and EnvelopeExtra2. You must be in Page Layout view to display graphics on an envelope.

To print a graphic or special text on an envelope, follow these steps:

1. Create the envelope, and then select Add To Document or Change Document.

2. If necessary, choose Insert ➤ Text Box to insert a text box around a selected object or text. You can then adjust the position of the special text or graphic on your envelope.

3. Type any special text, insert a graphic, or create a drawing on the envelope.

4. Select the text or graphic, and choose Insert ➤ AutoText ➤ New (Alt +F3) to display the Create AutoText dialog box.

5. Type EnvelopeExtra1 or EnvelopeExtra2 in the Please Name Your AutoText Entry text box, and then choose OK.

Delete the AutoText entry when you no longer want to use it for every envelope you print based on the template.

Field Codes

Use field codes to have Word automatically enter specific information in your documents. You can use field codes to enter the date and time, individual page numbers, or the total number of pages in a document and to mark entries for indexes, cross-references, and tables of contents. Word supports more than 70 types of fields.

Displaying Field Codes or Results in a Document

When you enter a field code in your document, the results of the field code are displayed rather than the actual code. To toggle the display of all the field codes in the document between field codes and results, right-click on a field code to display its shortcut menu, and then select Toggle Field Codes. Or, press Shift+F9 to toggle the display of a selected field code, or Alt+F9 to toggle the display of all the field codes in the document.

It is easier to see what information has been entered as a field code if you select a shading option for field codes in your documents. You can also change the display to view the field codes instead of their results in your document.

To display field codes and results, follow these steps:

1. Choose Tools ➤ Options and select the View tab in the Options dialog box.

2. In the Show area of the tab, select Always in the Field Shading drop-down list.

3. Select the Field Codes checkbox to display the codes in your documents instead of their results.

4. Choose OK.

To unlink a linked field (change its last results into text), press Ctrl+Shift+F9.

Inserting a Field Code

A field code consists of field characters, which look like braces, a field type, and the instructions you enter. The instructions can be either required or optional and may have optional switches.

Add the appropriate format switch (*) to the field code instructions to automatically format the field code results. If you do, the formatting will remain in the field results when you update the field. You can use case conversion switches, number conversion switches, and character formatting switches in your field code instructions. You can also directly format the results of a field code in your document, although the formatting may be lost when you update the field unless you specify that it is to be preserved.

To insert a field code, follow these steps:

1. Position the insertion point where you want to enter the field code.

2. Choose Insert ➤ Field to display the Field dialog box.

3. Select a field category In the Categories list box.

4. Select the field code in the Field Names list box. The name you select appears in the Field Codes text box.

5. Type the instructions for the field code after the name in the Field Codes text box.

6. Select the Preserve Formatting During Updates checkbox to preserve the formatting you have applied directly to the results of the field code when the field is updated.

7. If necessary, choose Options, choose the formatting switches or specific information, such as an AutoText entry name, choose Add to Field, and then choose OK in the Field Options dialog box.

8. Choose OK in the Field dialog box.

You cannot enter the field characters using the brace keys. Instead, press Ctrl+F9 to enter the field characters if you want to type the field code and instructions in your document.

Press F11 to select the next field in your document, or press Shift+F11 to select the previous field.

To edit a selected field code, use Word's regular editing techniques. If necessary, toggle the results to display the actual field code, make the necessary changes, and then press Shift+F9 to toggle the field code display back to its results.

Updating Fields

You can update fields in your document in one of several ways:

• Select the field and press F9 (Update).

• Choose Edit ➤ Select All (Ctrl+A) to select the entire document, and then press F9 to update all the fields in the document.

• Right-click on a field code to display its shortcut menu, and then select Update Field.

• To update the field codes when you print your document, choose Tools ➤ Options and select the Print tab. Select the Update Fields checkbox in the Printing Options area, and then choose OK.

Press Ctrl+F11 to lock a field that you do not want to update. Press Ctrl+Shift+F11 to unlock a locked field.

Find and Replace

You can search for text, formats, special characters, and other document items. You can also search for and replace a found item with a specified item.

Finding Document Items

1. Choose Edit ➤ Find (Ctrl+F) to display the Find tab in the Find and Replace dialog box.

2. Type the text you want to find in the Find What text box, or select one of the last seven previously entered items in the Find What drop-down list.

3. To narrow the search results, choose More, and then specify any of the following options:

• In the Search drop-down list, choose Down to search from the position of the insertion point to the end of the selection or document; choose Up to search from the position of the insertion point to the beginning of the selection or document; or choose All to search the entire selection or document beginning at the insertion point.

• Select the Match Case checkbox to find document items with the exact uppercase and lowercase letters entered in the Find What text box. If Small Caps or All Caps formatting was applied to a document item, the case is ignored.

• Select the Find Whole Words Only checkbox to find only text that is a whole word. In a search for formatting, only whole words to which the specified formatting was applied are found.

• Select the Use Wildcards checkbox to use advanced search criteria.

• Select the Sounds Like checkbox to find homonyms of the text displayed in the Find What text box.

• Select the Find All Word Forms checkbox to find all occurrences of the characters in the Find What text box, regardless of case, formatting, or whether the characters are a whole word or part of a word.

- Choose No Formatting to remove all specified formatting from the search.

- Choose Format to display a pop-up list of formatting options. Choose Font, Paragraph, Tabs, Language, Frame, or Style to display each command's dialog box, and then choose the formatting for which you want to search in each dialog box. Or, choose Highlight to specify highlighted items as the format for which to search. You can search for formatting only, without searching for any text.

- Choose Special to display a pop-up list of special characters from which to choose to enter in the Find What text box.

4. Choose Find Next to start the search. The first occurrence of the specified item or format appears highlighted in your document.

5. To edit the document while the Find and Replace dialog box is displayed, click in the document window or press Alt+F6 to activate the document window. When you are finished editing the item, click in the Find and Replace dialog box to reactivate it.

6. Repeat steps 4 and 5 as necessary.

7. If necessary, select Yes in the dialog box that appears when Word reaches the beginning or end of the document to continue the search back to the location of the insertion point.

8. When you have finished searching for the document item, choose Cancel.

9. If necessary, choose OK to remove the message box that appears to tell you when the search is complete, and then choose Cancel or press Esc.

To quickly repeat your last search after you have closed the Find dialog box, press Shift+F4. The Find dialog box will not reappear.

Searching for and Replacing Document Items

To find an item and replace it, follow these steps:

1. Choose Edit ➤ Replace (Ctrl+H), or click on the Replace tab in the Find and Replace dialog box.

2. Type the text you want to find in the Find What text box, or select one of the last seven previously entered items in the Find What drop-down list.

3. Type the text with which you want to replace a found document item in the Replace With text box.

4. If necessary, choose More, and then select any of the options described in step 3 of "Finding Document Items," above, to limit the search results.

5. Choose Find Next to start the search. The first occurrence of the specified item appears highlighted in your document.

6. Choose Replace to change the highlighted item to the characters in the Replace With text box. Or, choose Find Next to find the next instance of the document item without replacing the currently highlighted item. Alternatively, choose Replace All to automatically find all occurrences of the search item and replace each one with the characters in the Replace With text box.

7. Repeat steps 5 and 6 as necessary.

8. If necessary, choose Yes in the dialog box that appears when Word reaches the beginning or end of the document to continue the search back to the location of the insertion point. Choose OK to remove the message box that appears to tell you the search is complete.

9. Alternatively, when you have finished replacing items in your document, choose Cancel to close the Replace dialog box and return to your document.

To delete the item you are searching for, remove all the characters from the Replace With text box and all the formatting from the area below the Replace With text box, and then choose Replace.

Footnotes and Endnotes

Use footnotes and endnotes to provide explanations or references to marked items in the text of a document. By default, footnotes appear at the bottom of the page where the marked item appears, and endnotes appear at the end of the chapter, section, or document. Your documents can contain both footnotes and endnotes.

Word automatically updates footnote and endnote numbering when you add or delete a marked item in your document and places the text of either in the correct position in your document. Because Word manages footnotes and endnotes the same way, they are called "notes" in this entry.

Inserting a Note

Notes are made up of two parts—the note reference mark and the note text. By default, footnotes are numbered 1, 2, 3, and so on, and endnotes are numbered i, ii, iii, and so on. To insert a note, follow these steps:

1. Click on the Normal View button by the horizontal scroll bar or choose View ➤ Normal to change to Normal view.

2. Position the insertion point where you want to add a note reference mark in your document, and then choose Insert ➤ Footnote to display the Footnote and Endnote dialog box.

3. Select Footnote or Endnote in the Insert area of the dialog box to indicate the type of note you want to insert.

4. Choose either of the following options in the Numbering area:

   • Select AutoNumber (selected by default) to have Word automatically update the note numbers in your document.

   • Select Custom Mark, choose Symbol to display the Symbol dialog box, select the symbol to use to mark the reference in your document, and then choose OK in the Symbol dialog box.

5. To change the format of notes in your document, select Options to display the Note Options dialog box, choose the All Footnotes or All Endnotes tab, change any of the following options, and then choose OK:

   • In the Place At drop-down list, choose either Bottom of Page to print each footnote just above the bottom margin on the same page as its reference mark, or Beneath Text to print each footnote just below the last line of text on the page. Choose either End of Document to print all the endnotes after the last line of the document text or End of Section to print each endnote just after the last line of the section containing its reference mark.

   • In the Number Format drop-down list, choose arabic numbers, lowercase or uppercase letters or roman numerals, or symbols as the numbering format for notes.

   • Adjust the value in the Start At text box to define the first note number.

   • In the Numbering area, choose either Continuous to number notes throughout the document in sequence, or Restart Each Section to start note numbers in each section with the number in the Start At text box. Or, select Restart Each Page for footnotes, to start numbering on each page with the number in the Start At text box.

   • Choose Convert, select Convert All Footnotes to Endnotes, Convert All Endnotes to Footnotes, or Swap Footnotes and Endnotes to convert both simultaneously, and then choose OK in the Convert Notes dialog box.

6. Choose OK in the Footnote and Endnote dialog box to display the note pane at the bottom of the document window.

7. Press Tab, and then type the note text in the note pane.

8. Choose Close (Alt+Shift+C) in the note pane to close it and return to your document.

The text of a note appears in the note pane in Normal view and in its correct location in Page Layout view. You can directly edit the text of a note in either view. To display the text of notes while you are working in your document:

- Position the mouse pointer over the note reference mark to display the text of the note.

- Double-click on the note mark in your document. In Normal view, the note pane opens, and the insertion point moves to the note's text in the note pane. In Page Layout view, the insertion point moves to the note's text.

- Choose View ➤ Footnotes. In Normal view, the note pane opens to the last viewed note type. You can change the type of note that appears in the pane by selecting All Footnotes or All Endnotes in the Notes dropdown list. In Page Layout view, the insertion point moves directly to the notes area if your document contains only footnotes or only endnotes. If your document contains both types of notes, the View Footnotes dialog box appears. Choose View Footnote Area or View Endnote Area, and then choose OK to move the insertion point to the note text area in the document.

Use either of the following methods to continue editing the document:

- Double-click on a note mark in the note pane or note area of your document to move back to the mark in the document text.

- If necessary, click in the document window to keep the note pane open and continue editing your document.

Use the following methods to insert additional notes or edit existing notes:

- Press Alt+Ctrl+F to add another footnote to the document, or press Alt+Ctrl+E to add another endnote to the document.

- To convert a single footnote or endnote, position the insertion point in the note text within either the note pane or the document, right-click on the note to display its shortcut menu, and then choose Convert to Footnote or Convert to Endnote.

- To move or copy a note, select the note reference mark in your document and then cut or copy and paste the mark or drag and drop it in a different location.

- To delete a selected note in your document, press Backspace or Delete. To delete all footnotes or endnotes in the document, choose Edit ➤ Replace (Ctrl+H), choose More, and then choose Special. Select Footnote Mark or Endnote Mark in the pop-up list, delete the contents of the Replace With text box, and then choose Replace All.

- You can edit the format of the text of individual notes, or you can change the style of the note text to apply the format to all footnotes or endnotes automatically. To make the note style available to all documents based on the current template, add the style to the template.

- To prevent the current section's endnotes from printing at the end of the section, choose File ➤ Page Setup, click on the Layout tab, select the Suppress Endnotes checkbox, and then choose OK. The endnotes will be printed in the next section, just before that section's endnotes.

Modifying Note Separators

By default, a Footnote Separator or Endnote Separator appears as a two-inch horizontal line, called a *note separator*, which separates notes from the document text. If the notes on one page continue on the next, a line spanning from the left to the right margin, called a *continuation separator*, separates the notes from the document text. You can add graphics or borders to note separators or insert informational text above a separator. The note separator will appear in the notes pane.

To modify note separators, follow these steps:

1. If necessary, click on the Normal View button by the horizontal scroll bar or choose View ➤ Normal to change to Normal view.

2. Choose View ➤ Footnotes to display the note pane.

3. Select All Footnotes or All Endnotes in the Notes drop-down list at the top of the note pane to display the note pane whose separator you want to edit.

4. Select the type of notes separator to be modified from the Notes drop-down list.

5. To insert text or a graphic before or after a separator, click in the desired location to position the insertion point, and then insert the text or graphic. Or, to insert text or a graphic above a separator or a continuation separator, insert a paragraph above the separator or continuation separator in the note pane, and then insert the text or graphic in the paragraph.

6. To add informational text before a continuation separator, select Footnote Continuation Notice or Endnote Continuation Notice in the Notes drop-down list, and then type the text you want to appear.

7. Choose Close (Alt+Shift+C) to close the note pane and return to your document.

To delete the separator so that it does not appear in your printed document, select it and then press Backspace or Delete.

To return the note separator to its default appearance, choose Reset.

FTP

If you have an account that allows you access to the Internet or if your company has an Intranet, you can add an FTP (file transfer protocol) site to the list of Internet sites. The list allows you to quickly access a selected file.

File transfer protocol is one convention that allow files to be moved from one location to another over the Internet or an intranet.

To add an FTP site to the list, follow these steps:

1. Click on the Open button on the Standard toolbar, or choose File ➤ Open to display the Open dialog box.

2. Select Add/Modify FTP Locations in the Look In drop-down list to display its dialog box. You can find the Add/Modify FTP Locations icon below the Internet Locations icon when any drive letter is selected in the Look In drop-down list.

3. Type the name of the FTP site in the Name of FTP Site text box.

4. Select either of the following options in the Log On As area:

- Choose Anonymous to log on to a site that allows anyone to visit.
- Choose User and then type your password to log on to a site for which visitors must have been assigned user privileges.

5. Choose Add to add the FTP site to the list displayed in the FTP Sites list box.

6. Choose OK to close the Add/Modify FTP Locations dialog box.

You can also perform the following actions when the Add/Modify FTP Locations dialog box is displayed:

- To edit the address or logon information for an FTP site, highlight the site in the FTP Sites list box, and then choose Modify. Make the necessary changes in the dialog box, and then choose Add.
- To delete an FTP site from the list, highlight its address in the FTP Sites list box, and then choose Remove.

To open one of the FTP sites, double-click on its icon in the Open dialog box [when Internet Locations (FTP) appears in the LookIn list box]. You can then double-click on the folder in which the file is stored to display its contents. Double-click on the name of the file you want to open.

Go To

You can go to a specific document item when you want to move quickly to another location in a document. To do so, follow these steps:

1. Use one of the following methods to display the Go To tab in the Find and Replace dialog box:

   - Double-click on one of the first two sections on the status bar.
   - Click on the Select Browse Object button below the vertical scroll bar and then click on the Go To graphic.
   - Choose Edit ➤ Go To (F5).

2. Highlight the document item to which you want to move the insertion point in the Go To What list box.

3. To go to the next specified document item, choose Next; to go to the previous item, choose Previous. Or, type the number of the item in the Enter *Document Item* text box, then choose Go To to move the insertion point to that item.

4. When you are finished moving to document items, choose Close.

Alternatively, press Shift+F5 to quickly move to the last three positions of the insertion point.

Headers and Footers

Headers are displayed and printed in the top margin, and footers are displayed and printed in the bottom margin of each page of your document.

Creating or Editing a Header and Footer

To create or edit a header or a footer, follow these steps:

1. Choose View ➤ Header and Footer to display the Header and Footer toolbar. The header area of the current page is activated.

2. Type the text for the header of your document, using Word's regular formatting techniques to format your text.

3. Click on the Switch Between Header and Footer button on the Header and Footer toolbar to activate the footer.

4. Type the footer text and apply the appropriate formatting.

5. Choose one of the following options on the Header and Footer toolbar to quickly insert the corresponding item in the position of the insertion in the active header or footer:

   - Click on the Insert AutoText button, and then select one of the AutoText entries in the pop-up list that appears to insert that entry in the header or footer.
   - Click on the Insert Page Number button to insert automatic page numbers in the header or footer.

- Click on the Insert Number of Pages button to insert the total number of pages in the document or section.

- Click on the Format Page Number button to display the Page Number Format dialog box to change the appearance of the current page numbers.

- Click on the Insert Date button to insert the current date.

- Click on the InsertTime button to insert the current time.

6. If necessary, click on the Page Setup button to display the Page Setup dialog box to change any of the page layout options for your document.

7. When you are finished creating or editing the header and footer, click on the Close button (Alt+Shift+C) on the Header and Footer toolbar to remove the toolbar and return to your document.

Click on the Show/Hide Document Text button on the Header and Footer toolbar to display or hide the regular text in your document while you are editing the header or footer.

If you want to edit the text or update a field code in a header or footer, you must activate the header or footer and display the Header and Footer toolbar. Use either of the following methods:

- In Page Layout view, double-click on either the header or footer.

- In Normal view, select View ➤ Header and Footer.

Creating Different Headers and Footers in a Document

To make the first page header and footer different from those in the rest of the document, follow these steps:

1. Choose View ➤ Header and Footer to activate the header and display the Header and Footer toolbar.

2. Click on the Page Setup button on the Header and Footer toolbar to display the Page Setup dialog box, and then choose the Layout tab.

3. Select the Different First Page checkbox in the Headers and Footers area, and then choose OK in the Page Setup dialog box.

4. If necessary, create the header and footer that is to appear on the first page. To omit a header and footer on the first page, leave the areas blank.

5. Click on the Show Next button on the Header and Footer toolbar to move to the next header area, and then create the header for the rest of the document. Click on the Switch Between Header and Footer button to activate the footer area, and then create the footer for the rest of the document.

6. Click on the Close button (Alt+Shift+C) on the Header and Footer toolbar to return to your document.

To make odd and even page headers and footers different, follow these steps:

1. Follow steps 1 and 2 above.

2. Select the Different Odd and Even checkbox in the Headers and Footers area, and then choose OK.

3. If necessary, click on the Show Previous or Show Next button on the Header and Footer toolbar to move to an even page number. Create the header and footer that are to appear on even pages. Click on the Switch Between Header and Footer button as necessary.

4. Click on the Show Previous or Show Next button on the Header and Footer toolbar to move to an odd page number, and then create the header and footer that are to appear on odd pages. Click on the Switch Between Header and Footer button as necessary.

5. Click on the Close button (Alt+Shift+C) on the Header and Footer toolbar to return to your document.

Hidden Text

To hide text in your document, apply the hidden text format to it. By default, hidden text does not appear on your screen or print when you print the document. If you display hidden text, however, it will appear on the screen with a dotted underline.

Creating Hidden Text

Choose either of the following methods to hide selected text in your document:

- Select the text you want to hide, and then press Ctrl+Shift+H.
- Choose Format ➤ Font, select the Hidden checkbox in the Effects area of the Font tab in the Font dialog box, and then choose OK.

Use either of the following methods to display hidden text:

- To display all nonprinting characters, including hidden text, click on the Show/Hide ¶ button on the Standard toolbar.
- To display only hidden text without displaying other nonprinting characters, choose Tools ➤ Options and select the View tab. Clear all the checkboxes in the Nonprinting Characters area except the Hidden Text checkbox, and then choose OK.

To unhide hidden text, you must first display it. Then, select the hidden text and either press Ctrl+Shift+H or clear the Hidden checkbox on the Font tab in the Font dialog box.

Printing Hidden Text

When you print hidden text with your document, the document may not print as it appears on your screen. Display the hidden text so that page and line breaks in the document can be adjusted if necessary. To print hidden text, follow these steps:

1. Choose File ➤ Print (Ctrl+P) to display the Print dialog box, and then choose Options. Alternatively, choose Tools ➤ Options and select the Print tab.

2. Select the Hidden Text checkbox in the Include with Document area.

3. Choose OK in the Options dialog box. If necessary, choose OK again in the Print dialog box.

HTML Document

HyperText Markup Language, also called HTML, is the procedure used to create documents that are published on the World Wide Web. HTML documents include formatting tags and graphics that can be used to link to reference information. You can create HTML documents in Word and view them with a Web browser. You can also convert HTML documents to regular Word documents.

Creating a Web Page

Create a Web page the same way you create any other Word document. You can apply a background format to a Web page and insert hyperlinks to other documents.

1. Click on the New button on the Standard toolbar to open a new document.

2. Type any text and insert any hyperlinks and graphics for the Web page.

3. If necessary, choose Format ➤ Background and click on a color for the background in the palette that appears. Alternatively, choose Fill Effects and then select a gradient, texture, pattern, or picture for the background.

4. Choose File ➤ Save to display the Save As dialog box. Select HTML Document in the Save As Type ddl.

5. Type a name for the Web page in the File Name text box, and then choose Save.

Opening a Web Page in Word

Word contains a file converter that automatically opens a file saved in HTML format as a regular Word document. Once the file is open, you can save it as a regular Word document. To open a Web page in Word, follow these steps:

1. Click on the Open button on the Standard toolbar or choose File ➤ Open (Ctrl+O) to display the Open dialog box.

2. Select HTML Document in the Files of Type drop-down list.

3. Highlight the name of a file with the .HTML extension in the Look In list box.

4. Choose Open.

When you open a document that was saved in HTML format, only the text and placeholders for graphics appear in the document window. To view the Web page as it will appear when published on the Internet or on an Intranet, you must have a Web browser, such as Microsoft Internet Explorer or Netscape Navigator.

To display an open HTML file in your Web browser, choose File ➤ Open, and then double-click on the name of the file.

Hyperlink

A hyperlink is a field code you insert in a Word document or a Web page that allows you to jump to related information in the same or a different file. The item you select to be the hyperlink appears as the result of the field code.

Hyperlinks are often used to jump to multimedia files that contain sounds and videos and to other text documents. The document to which a hyperlink jumps can be on your hard drive, on a network drive, or an address on the Internet or an Intranet.

Inserting a Hyperlink

To insert a hyperlink in a document, follow these steps:

1. Select the text or graphic that is to be the hyperlink.

2. Click on the Insert Hyperlink button on the Standard toolbar or choose Insert ➤ Hyperlink (Ctrl+K) to display the Insert Hyperlink dialog box.

3. Type the path of the file this hyperlink will jump to in the Link to File or URL text box. Alternatively, choose Browse and then select the name of the file to automatically enter its path in the text box.

4. To jump to a specific location within the file, type the name of the location (such as the bookmark or range name) in the Named Location in File text box. If the file to which the hyperlink will jump is a Word document, choose Browse to display a list of names, and then select the name of the bookmark to automatically enter it in the text box.

5. To specify that the location of the file containing the hyperlink may be moved, select the Use Relative Path for Hyperlink checkbox.

6. Choose OK.

The selected text is changed into the hyperlink display text, which appears as blue underlined text in your document. When you position the mouse pointer over the hyperlink display text, the mouse pointer appears as a pointing finger, and the path to the file to which the hyperlink jumps is displayed in a yellow note. Click on the hyperlink text to jump to the specified file. If the file is a Word document, the Web toolbar is automatically displayed.

Indent

Indentation is the distance between the text and the margins in a document. You can change the indentation for an entire paragraph or for the paragraph's first line, and you can indent text from either the left or the right margin.

Indenting One Paragraph

To indent a single paragraph to the next or previous tab stop, move the insertion point into the paragraph or select the paragraph, including the paragraph mark, and then use one of the following methods:

- To create a hanging indent to the next tab stop for each line except the first, press Ctrl+T.
- To decrease a hanging indent with the indent for each line except the first moved to the previous tab stop, press Ctrl+Shift+T.

Alternatively, you can quickly change the indentation of the paragraph where the insertion point is located using one of the following methods:

- Display the horizontal ruler and then drag the First Line Indent, Hanging Indent, Left Indent, or Right Indent marker to reposition that indentation for the paragraph.
- Click on the Increase Indent button on the Formatting toolbar to expand the paragraph's left indentation by one tab stop.
- Click on the Decrease Indent button on the Formatting toolbar to reduce the paragraph's left indentation by one tab stop.

Indenting a Paragraph Using Exact Measurements

If you press the Tab key or Spacebar to indent a paragraph, the text may not be properly aligned. Instead, you can use the following instructions to set exact indentation measurements:

1. Select Format ➤ Paragraph, and then select the Indents and Spacing tab in the Paragraph dialog box.
2. In the Indentation area, adjust the distance to indent the paragraph from the corresponding margin in the Left or Right text box. Enter a negative number in the Left or Right text box to make text appear in either margin.

3. Choose (None), First Line, or Hanging to define the indentation for the first line of the paragraph in the Special drop-down list.
4. In the By text box, adjust the measurement to define the distance to indent the first line or hanging indent in the paragraph.
5. Choose OK.

Index

Creating an index for a document involves two steps. You must first mark index entries, and then you must compile the index in a document.

Index entries can be marked in the main document text and in footnotes and endnotes. You can also create cross-references to other entries or show a topic covered within a range of pages. Only the first occurrence of the entry text in a paragraph is marked.

Creating Manual Index Entries

You can manually mark your index entries in the document that will contain the index. An XE (index entry) field is inserted as hidden text in the location of a marked entry. The field code displays no results in the document. Instead, the results are displayed in the index when it is compiled.

To create manual index entries, follow these steps:

1. Select the text in your document to mark, or move the insertion point to the location where you want to insert an index entry, and then press Alt+Shift+X to open the Mark Index Entry dialog box. Alternatively, select Insert ➤ Index and Tables, choose the Index tab, and then choose Mark Entry to display the Mark Index Entry dialog box.
2. If necessary, edit the text in the Main Entry text box. Or, type the entry you want to insert in your document in the text box.

3. Type the subentry text in the Subentry text box. To create a subentry for a subentry, type a colon after the subentry in the Subentry text box, then type the sub-subentry.

4. Choose one of the following options for the entry:

- Select Cross-reference to add cross-reference text to an index entry. The insertion point moves into the text box after "See." Type the informational text for the cross-reference.

- Select Current Page to list the number of the current page for the index entry.

- Select Page Range, and then select a pre-defined bookmark name in the drop-down list to define the page range for the index entry.

5. Select the Bold or Italic checkboxes to format the entry's page number with either attribute.

6. Choose Mark to mark the entry defined in the Main Entry text box, or choose Mark All to mark the exact text for each occurrence of the text in the document.

7. Repeat steps 1 through 6 as necessary for each index entry you want to mark in your document.

8. Choose Close in the Mark Index Entry dialog box.

You can edit all text in the Main Entry, Subentry, and Cross-reference text boxes and apply formatting to selected text in each text box using the formatting shortcut keys.

To edit a marked entry, click the Show/Hide ¶ button on the Standard toolbar to display all nonprinting characters.

- To edit the text of an index entry, select the characters between the quotation marks.

- To delete the entry, select the entire field code, including the field code characters, and then press Backspace or Delete.

You can use switches with the XE field code to format the entry's page number in bold or italic, redefine the type of entry, include a range of pages in the entry, or enter text instead of page numbers in the entry. Click on the Office Assistant button on the Standard toolbar, then type XE in the text box, and then choose Field Codes: SE (Index Entry) Field in the list of topics and press Enter to display online help for XE field codes.

Inserting an Index in a Document

The index can be inserted in a predefined or customized format in your document. You can also choose a format for the subentry text.

Chapter numbers that are included with page numbers and inserted using Insert ➤ Page Numbers are included in the index.

When you insert an index in a document, you are actually inserting the Index field code. To see the field code, right-click in the index, and then select Toggle Field Codes. Right-click on the Index code and select Toggle Field Codes again to redisplay the results of the Index code.

To insert an index in a document, follow these steps:

1. In a document with marked index entries, position the insertion point where you want the index to appear.

2. Type and format any text that is to appear before the generated index.

3. Choose Insert ➤ Index and Tables and select the Index tab.

4. Choose from the following options to define the format of the index:

- In the Type area, choose either Indented to indent subentries on lines below the main index entry or Run-in to place subentries on the same line as the main entry.

- Select one of the predefined formats in the Formats list box. Or, choose From Template, select Modify to display the Style dialog box, and then change any of the index styles.

- Select the Right Align Page Numbers checkbox to align the main entry and subentry page numbers along the right margin.

- Adjust the number of columns you want in the index in the Columns text box to 1 to 4 columns, or choose Auto to keep the same number of columns in the specified format.

- Select the tab leader that is to be placed before right-aligned page numbers in the index in the Tab Leader drop-down list.

5. Choose OK to insert the Index field code in your document.

If you edit your document or mark any new entries after the index is inserted, use one of the following methods to update the index to make sure it is correct:

- Right-click in the index, and then choose Update Field to update the index.

- Move the insertion point into the index and press F9 (Update) to update the Index field code.

You can also edit the text of an index you have inserted in your document. However, if you edit the marked entries in your document text, you will lose all the edits when the index is updated.

Marking Index Entries Automatically

Create a *concordance file* if you want to automatically mark index entries in your document. A concordance file is a separate document that contains two columns of information—the words and phrases to be indexed in your document, and the actual index entries you want to generate.

To create a concordance, follow these steps:

1. Click on the New button on the Standard toolbar or press Ctrl+N to create a new document for the concordance file.

2. Click on the Insert Table button on the Standard toolbar and then drag, or select Table ➤ Insert Table and then choose OK to insert a two column table in the document.

3. Type or paste the text that you want to mark as an index entry in the first column. The text must be entered exactly as it appears in your document because text in a concordance file is case-sensitive.

4. Type the index entry for the item, exactly as it will appear in the index, in the second column.

5. Repeat steps 3 and 4 as necessary for each item of text you want to mark.

6. Save the concordance file, and then close it.

Once you have created a concordance file, you can automatically mark the index entries in your document. To do so, follow these steps:

1. With the document to be indexed active, choose Insert ➤ Index and Tables to display the Index and Tables dialog box, and then choose the Index tab.

2. Choose AutoMark to display the Open Index AutoMark File dialog box.

3. Highlight the name of the concordance file you want to use in the Look In list box.

4. Choose Open to automatically mark the index entries in your document.

Label

Word allows you to print one label or a page of labels with the same text. You can select one of Word's built-in label definitions, which were created based on many different Avery® label types and sizes, or you can customize a label definition to use with another brand of labels whose dimensions are not among those in the list.

Before you select a type of label, select and set up the printer on which the labels will be printed. The selected printer driver determines how the labels will be set up and printed.

Printing Labels

To print labels, follow these steps:

1. If necessary, select the address you want to print.

2. Choose Tools ➤ Envelopes and Labels to display the Envelopes and Labels dialog box, and then select the Labels tab.

3. Selected text appears in the Address text box. Choose any of the following options to change the address in the Address text box:

- Type the text you want to appear on the label in the Address text box.

- Select the Use Return Address checkbox to print the default return address.

- Select the Delivery Point Bar Code checkbox to include the POSTNET bar code on a mailing label printed on a dot matrix printer.

4. Click on the Label area of the dialog box or select Options to display the Label Options dialog box.

5. Select any of the following options to define the label and printer specifications, and then choose OK:

- In the Printer Information area, select Dot Matrix or Laser and Ink Jet to define the type of printer that is set up. If Laser and Ink Jet is selected as the type of printer, highlight the location in which the labels will be fed to the printer in the Tray drop-down list.

- Highlight the kind of label you are using in the Label Products drop-down list.

- Select the manufacturer's product number for the label in the Product Number list box. A description of the label appears in the Label Information area.

- Choose Details to display the *Type and Number* Information dialog box to customize the selected label. Make any necessary changes, and then choose OK.

- Choose New Label to display the New Custom *Printer* dialog box, specify the measurements for the custom label, and then choose OK.

6. In the Print area of the Labels tab, select Full Page of the Same Label to print the text in the Address text box on each label on the page of labels. Or, select Single Label to print the text on only one label, and then adjust numbers in the Row and Column text boxes to define the position of the label on the page of labels.

7. Choose Print to print the page of labels or the single label. Or, choose New Document to place a full sheet of labels in a table in a new document, and then save the document.

You can also use Mail Merge to print labels if you have created a data file.

Line Numbering

Add line numbers to a document to refer to individual lines in the text. The numbers you insert appear on screen if you are in Page Layout or Print Preview and are printed with the document. The lines of text in tables, footnotes, endnotes, headers, footers, and frames are not numbered.

Adding Line Numbering

To add line numbering to a document, follow these steps:

1. Position the insertion point where you want line numbering to begin in your document.

2. Choose File ➤ Page Setup and then choose the Layout tab in the Page Setup dialog box.

3. Select Line Numbers to display the Line Numbers dialog box.

4. Select the Add Line Numbering checkbox.

5. Choose any of the following options, and then choose OK.

   • In the Start At text box, adjust the value to define the starting line number.

   • In the From Text text box, adjust the measurement to specify the distance from the right edge of line numbers to the left edge of the line of text. The default for one column is 0.25 inch, and for two columns it is 0.13 inch.

   • In the Count By text box, adjust the value to specify the increments in which numbers appear in line numbering.

   • In the Numbering area, choose Restart Each Page to begin with line 1 at the top of each page, Restart Each Section to begin with line 1 at the beginning of each document section, or Continuous to specify consecutive numbers throughout the document.

6. Select This Section, This Point Forward, or Whole Document as the portion of the document to which line numbering is applied in the Apply To drop-down list.

7. Choose OK in the Page Setup dialog box.

Line numbers are printed in the margins or between columns of text unless the margin or space between columns is not wide enough. Display the document in Print Preview before you print it to be sure the line numbers will print. If necessary, change the line number format by modifying the line numbering style.

Clear the Add Line Numbering checkbox in the Line Numbers dialog box to remove line numbers from a document or from a selected section of a document.

To remove numbers from selected paragraphs in a document and resume the numbering for text that is located after the selection, choose Format ➤ Paragraph, select the Line and Page Breaks tab, select the Suppress Line Numbers checkbox, and then choose OK.

Line Spacing

A paragraph's line spacing defines the height of each line in the text. The height of a line depends on the font used in the paragraph. If, for example, you select a 12-point font (a point is 1/72 of an inch), the height of a single-spaced line is just over 12 points so that some white space, called *leading*, can be included above the text and below the baseline of the text above. The height of a 12-point double-spaced line would be just over 24 points. You can set the line spacing to adjust the amount of white space that appears above the text in each line.

If a line contains an oversized character, its line spacing is automatically adjusted to accommodate the character. You can adjust the line spacing so that all the lines are evenly spaced in the paragraph.

By default, line spacing in Word is set for single-spacing. You can set the line spacing to a preset definition, or you can customize the line spacing for your document.

Changing the Line Spacing in a Paragraph

To change the line spacing in a paragraph, follow these steps:

1. Position the insertion point in the paragraph, or select the paragraphs whose spacing is to be changed.

2. Choose Format ➤ Paragraph, and select the Indents and Spacing tab.

3. To add leading above and below the selected paragraphs, adjust the measurement in the Before and After text boxes in the Spacing area.

4. Select one of the following line-spacing options in the Line Spacing drop-down list, and then choose OK.

   - Choose Single (Ctrl+1) to adjust the line height to accomodate the tallest character in the line.

   - Choose 1.5 Lines (Ctrl+5) to adjust the line height to 1.5 times that of single spacing.

   - Select Double (Ctrl+2) to double the line height of single-spacing.

   - Choose At Least and then specify the minimum line height in the At text box so that Word can adjust the line spacing for various types of characters or graphics.

   - Choose Exactly, and then define an exact line height in the At text box that Word cannot adjust.

   - Select Multiple to adjust the line spacing to a specific multiple of single spaced text; then specify the number of lines in the At text box. The default number of lines is 3.

Look Up Reference

You can have Word automatically look up information in Microsoft Bookshelf or Microsoft Bookshelf Basics using the new Look Up Reference feature. To do so, follow these steps:

1. Choose Tools ➤ Look Up Reference to display the Look Up Reference dialog box.

2. Select the reference in which to look up information in the Available Reference Titles list box.

3. Choose one of the following options in the Search area:

   - Choose Keyword, and then type the keywords on which to search for information in the Text text box.

   - Choose Full Text, and then type a specific string of text for which to search in the reference in the Text text box.

   - Choose None to perform the search from within the reference.

4. Choose OK to open the specified reference.

5. If necessary, insert the selected reference's CD in your CD ROM drive, and then choose OK in the message box.

Macro

You can record the commands and keystrokes you use to perform a task in a macro. Macros allow you to to automate a task that you regularly perform. You can assign a macro to a shortcut key sequence or to a toolbar for easy access.

Creating and Running a Macro

While you are recording a macro, the Macro Record toolbar appears on your screen, and the mouse pointer appears with a graphic of a cassette tape. You can use the mouse to select commands or to scroll while you are recording a macro, but not to select text or move the insertion point in the document window.

To create a macro, follow these steps:

1. Double-click on REC on the status bar or select Tools ➤ Macro ➤ Record New Macro to display the Record Macro dialog box.

2. Type a name for the macro in the Macro Name text box, and type a description in the Description text box.

3. If necessary, select All Documents (Normal .dot) or the active template as the location to store the macro in the Store Macro In drop-down list.

4. Select Toolbars or Keyboard as the method of access to use to run the macro in the Assign Macro To area, and then assign the macro to the appropriate toolbar or shortcut key sequence.

5. Choose OK in the Record Macro dialog box.

6. Select the commands and type the keystrokes necessary for the macro.

7. Double-click on REC on the status bar or click on the Stop Recording button on the Stop Recording toolbar to stop recording the macro. Or, choose Tools ➤ Macro ➤ Stop Recording.

To run a macro, follow these steps:

- Click on the toolbar button to run a macro assigned to a toolbar.

- Press the shortcut key sequence to run a macro assigned to the keyboard.

- Choose Tools ➤ Macro ➤ Macros (Alt+F8) to display the Macro dialog box, select the name of the macro to run in the Macro Name list box, and then choose Run.

If you accidentally record something you didn't want to record in a macro, immediately click on the Undo button on the Standard toolbar or choose Edit ➤ Undo. The action you reversed will not play back when you run the macro.

To temporarily stop recording the commands and keystrokes in a macro, click on the Pause Recording button on the Stop Recording toolbar. To resume recording your macro, click on the Resume Recorder button again.

Mail Merge

Use Word's Mail Merge feature to combine a *data source* with a *main document*. The data source can be a Word database file that contains the information that changes for each document, or it can be a database created in another application. The main document contains the text that

stays the same in each document, and merge field codes, which instruct Word where to insert the data source information in the main document text.

Performing a Mail Merge involves three basic steps: (1) specify the file that is the main document, (2) specify the data source, and (3) perform the merge.

Creating a Main Document

To create a main document for a mail merge, follow these steps:

1. Select Tools ➤ Mail Merge to display the Mail Merge Helper dialog box.

2. Choose Create in the Main Document area, and then select Form Letters, Mailing Labels, Envelopes, or Catalog as the type of document.

3. In the dialog box that appears, choose either Active Window to confirm that the currently active document is to be the main document, or choose New Main Document to open a new document as the main document.

Once the main document is created, the Mail Merge Helper dialog box is reactivated.

To change a Mail Merge main document back into a regular Word document by breaking the connection between the main document and the data source, choose Restore to Normal Word Document in the Create drop-down list.

Designating a Data Source

A field name in a Word data source file must begin with a letter and can contain as many as 40 characters, including letters, numbers, and the underline character, but it cannot contain any spaces. To designate a data source, follow these steps:

1. Select Get Data in the Data Source area of the Mail Merge Helper dialog box.

2. Choose one of the following options to define the type and location of the data source file:

- To create a new document as the data source, select Create Data Source to display the Create Data Source dialog box, which contains a list of often-used field names. For each new field you want to create, type the new field name in the Field Name text box, and then select Add Field Name to add the new field name to the end of the Field Names in Header Row list box. To move an existing field name, highlight it in the Field Names in Header Row list box, and then select the ↑ or ↓ Move button to move its position in the list. To delete a highlighted field name, choose Remove Field Name. When you have created the data source, choose OK in the Create Data Source dialog box to display the Save As dialog box, and then save the data source file. In the dialog box that appears, select either Edit Data Source to add records to the data source or Edit Main Document to modify the text in the main document. Alternatively, press Esc to return to the Mail Merge Helper dialog box.

- Choose Open Data Source to display the Open Data Source dialog box. Select the file that contains the data in the Look In list box or type the name of the file in the File Name text box, and then choose Open.

- Choose Use Address Book to display the Use Address Book dialog box. Highlight the name of the address book that contains the data in the Choose Address Book list box, and then choose OK. If necessary, choose Edit Main Document to insert merge fields in the main document.

- Choose Header Options to display the Header Options dialog box to create or open a *header source document*, a document that contains only the merge fields of a data source. You can use the merge fields in the header source in many different merge documents. If you must change a merge field, you can change it in the header source instead of in each of

your data source documents. Choose Create to display the Create Header Source dialog box, add to or remove any field names from the header source, choose OK, and then save the header source as a file. Or, choose Open to display the Open Header Source dialog box, select the name of the header source file in the Look In list box, and then choose Open.

Editing a Data Source File

Once you have created a data source, you must add to it the records you want to include. (You can add records to a data source other than one created in Word from within the source application.) To edit a Word data source file, follow these steps:

1. Choose Edit Data Source in the dialog box that appears after you have saved a newly created data source, or click on the Mail Merge Helper button on the Mail Merge toolbar and then select Edit ➤ *Filename* in the Data Source area to display the Data Form dialog box.

2. Type the appropriate information in the first text box and press Enter to enter that information in the displayed record and move the insertion point to the next field text box.

3. Repeat step 2 until all the data for the fields in the displayed record are completed, and then press Enter to display the next record, or choose Add New to display a new, blank record.

4. Repeat steps 2 and 3 until all the records for the data source have been added, and then choose View Source to display the data source document.

5. Click on the Save button on the Standard toolbar to save the data source.

The data source appears in its own document window, with the Database toolbar displayed above it. The data source document contains all the records in the data source in a table format. Each row is a record, and each column is a field in the table.

To edit an existing record in the data source, change any of the data directly in the table cell that contains it in the data source document. Or, you can display the Data Form dialog box, and then add the new data into each field in the displayed record.

Click on the Data Form button on the Database toolbar to display the current record in the Data Form dialog box, and then use any of the following options while editing the records:

- Type the number of the record you want to display in the Record text box. Or, click on the First Record, Previous Record, Next Record, or Last Record button to display the specified record.

- Choose Delete to remove the record displayed in the Data Form dialog box from the data source.

- Choose Restore to reverse the changes that were just made to the displayed record.

- To quickly locate text in a selected data field, choose Find to display the Find in Field dialog box. Type the characters you want to find in the Find What text box, select the name of the field in which to search for the text in the In Field dropdown list, and then choose Find First or Find Next to find the first occurrence or the next occurrence of those characters. Each time Word finds the specified text, the found record is displayed in the Data Form dialog box. Choose Close when the search is complete.

You can also make changes to the data source document using any of the following buttons on the Database toolbar:

- To add, delete, or rename a field in the data source, click on the Manage Fields button to display the Manage Fields dialog box. To add a new field, type a new field name in the Field Name text box and then choose Add to insert it at the bottom of the Field Names in Header Row list box. To remove an existing field, which also deletes any data entered in the field in each record in the data source, highlight the field in the list box, and then choose Remove. To rename the field that is highlighted in the list box, choose Rename, type a new name in the New Field Name text box, and then choose OK. After you make the changes to the field names, choose OK in the Manage Fields dialog box.

- Click on the Add New Record button to insert a new row at the end of the table in the data source document.

- Click on the Delete Record button to delete the record that contains the insertion point.

- With the insertion point in a cell in the column that contains the data on which to sort, click on the Sort Ascending button to rearrange the order of the records in the table from lowest to highest (A-Z) or on the Sort Descending button to rearrange the order of the records in the table from highest to lowest (Z-A).

- To insert the data from another data source at the end of the active data source, position the insertion point below the table, click on the Insert Database button, and then choose Get Data to display the Open Data Source dialog box.

- To update and display the results of selected fields in the data source, click on the Update Field button.

- To search for each occurrence of specified text in a field, click on the Find Record button to display the Find in Field dialog box.

Editing the Main Document

After you have opened a data source, you can insert the data source field names into the main document as merge fields. To do so, follow these steps:

1. If necessary, click on the Mail Merge Main Document button on the Database toolbar, or choose Edit ➤ *Filename* in the Main Document area in the Mail Merge Helper dialog box to activate the main document.

2. Edit the text and any other document items you want to change in the main document window.

3. Position the insertion point where you want to add a merge field, click on the Insert Merge Field button on the Mail Merge toolbar, and then choose the field to insert.

4. Type any characters or punctuation you want to include with the field.

5. Repeat steps 3 and 4 for each location in your main document that will contain a merge field.

6. Click on the Save button on the Standard toolbar to save the main document.

You can also click on the Insert Word Field button on the Mail Merge toolbar, and then select one of the fields in the drop-down list to insert a Word field in the position of the insertion point. The fields in the drop-down list can be used to help perform the merge.

Merging the Data File and the Main Document

To merge the data file and the main document, follow these steps:

1. In the main document window, click on the View Merged Data button on the Mail Merge toolbar to display the fields from the first record in the data source in the main document merge field locations you assigned.

2. To have Word make certain that no errors will occur during the merge, click on the Check for Errors button on the Mail Merge toolbar.

3. To merge the data source and the main document, use one of the following buttons on the Mail Merge toolbar:

   • Click on the Merge to New Document button to send all the merged documents to a single new document.

   • Click on the Merge to Printer button to print a document for each record in the data source.

• Click on the Mail Merge Helper button to display the Mail Merge Helper dialog box, and then choose Query Options to select a range of records to merge.

To display the main document with the data from a different record in step 1 above, click on the First Record, Previous Record, Next Record, or Last Record button on the Mail Merge toolbar. Or, type a record number in the Go to Record text box on the Mail Merge toolbar, and then press Enter.

Margins

Margins define the distance from the edge of the paper to the beginning of document text. In Word, you can print between the left, right, top, and bottom margins, or you can print some document items, such as headers or footers, in the margins. You can define a different set of margins in each section of a document.

Setting Precise Margins

By default, Word's top and bottom margins are set at 1 inch, and the left and right margins at 1.25 inch. The minimum margins you can set depend on the size of your paper and your printer's capabilities. To set exact margins, follow these steps:

1. Position the insertion point in the section of the document where the margins are to be changed.

2. Choose File ➤ Page Setup to display the Page Setup dialog box, and then choose the Margins tab.

3. Adjust the measurement in the Top, Bottom, Left, and Right text boxes as necessary to change the corresponding margin.

4. Choose any of the following options to further modify the margins, and then choose OK.

   • Adjust the measurement in the Gutter text box to define the amount of additional space to allow for the binding margin of a document. The gutter is added to the value in the Left or Inside text box.

- Select the Mirror Margins checkbox to change the widths of the inside and outside margins for facing pages if printing is to appear on both sides of the paper. In the Inside text box, specify the distance from the left edge of the paper to the left edge of the text on the odd-numbered pages, and the distance between the right edge of the paper and the right edge of the text on the even-numbered pages. In the Outside text box, specify the distance from the right edge of the paper to the right edge of the text on the odd-numbered pages, and the distance between the left edge of the paper and the left edge of the text on the even-numbered pages.

- In the From Edge area, adjust the distance from the edge of the paper for the header and the footer in your document in the Header and Footer text boxes.

- Select Whole Document, Selected Text, This Point Forward, This Sections, or Selected Section in the Apply To dropdown list as the portion of the document for which the margins are being set.

- Select Default to change the default margins in the current template to the settings specified on the Margins tab, and then choose Yes to confirm the change.

You can also drag the margin markers on the horizontal Ruler to set the left and right margins in the current section of the active document, and drag the margin markers on the vertical Ruler to set the top and bottom margins.

If your document contains a large header or footer, the header or footer area on the page is automatically expanded to accommodate the entire header or footer. However, the measurement in the Top or Bottom text box on the Margins tab remains the same.

Master Document

Create a *master document*, a file that contains subdocument files, to manage long documents.

The subdocument files can be opened and edited, renamed, and relocated. When you save the changes in the subdocument file, all the changes will be updated in the master document file.

Master documents can contain a maximum of 80 subdocuments and can be as large as 32MB, not counting graphics. You must be in Master Document view to create a new master document or to turn an existing document file into a master document. Both the Master Document and Outlining toolbars appear when you are in Master Document view. However, when you want to work with the entire master document, click on the Normal View button by the horizontal scroll bar to switch to Normal view.

If you create a template for your master document, it will override a different subdocument template except for special subdocument formatting such as columns, margin settings, and special page number settings. Styles or formatting can be applied to the master document or to any of its subdocuments.

Each subdocument is in a separate section of the master document. You can apply different headers and footers to each section of a master document.

Changing a Document into a Master Document

Each subdocument is assigned its own filename based on the text of its heading. However, if a file in the directory is already named what Word would normally choose, the subdocument is assigned a numbered filename based on the text.

When you display a document in Master Document view, you can turn on the Document Map (if it is not automatically turned on for you) to allow you to easily move around in the master document. In addition, both the Outlining and Master Document toolbars are displayed on top of the Formatting toolbar. Hide the Formatting toolbar so you that can see all the buttons on the Master Document toolbar.

To change a document into a master document, follow these steps:

1. Activate the document to be changed into a master document.

2. Choose View ➤ Master Document.

3. Use the buttons on the Outline toolbar to arrange the headings in the document. By default, Word's built-in heading styles are applied to headings in the document.

4. Select the headings and text to be included in subdocuments, and then click on the Create Subdocument button on the Master Document toolbar. A new subdocument is created each time Word finds the same heading level as the first heading level in the selection.

5. Save the master document. Each subdocument will also be saved as a separate file.

When you create a master document, a hyperlink is inserted in it for each subdocument, and a continuous section break is automatically inserted both before and after it. To remove the hyperlink to change a subdocument back into master document text, click on the Remove Subdocument button on the Master Document toolbar. If you wish, you can also delete the section break before and after the former subdocument's text.

Creating a New Master Document

To create a new master document, follow these steps:

1. Click on the New button on the Standard toolbar, press Ctrl+N, or choose File ➤ New and choose OK to create a new document.

2. Choose View ➤ Master Document.

3. Type the master document's outline. Be sure the outline headings are in Word's built-in heading styles.

4. Select the headings and text in the outline that is to be included in subdocuments, and then click on the Create Subdocument button on the Master Document toolbar.

5. Save the master document. Each subdocument will also be saved as a separate file.

To delete a subdocument from the master document, select the subdocument's icon and then press Backspace or Delete. If you wish, you can also delete the file from your disk.

Editing a Subdocument

Subdocuments can be edited using the same techniques as those used to edit any other documents. Follow these steps:

1. Double-click on the subdocument' icon or its hyperlink in the master document to open the subdocument file in its own window.

2. If necessary, close the master document to allow access to it by others.

3. Edit the subdocument as you would any other document.

4. Save the subdocument.

Inserting a Subdocument into a Master Document

To insert a subdocument into a master document, follow these steps:

1. Open the master document file, and then choose View ➤ Master Document to change to Master Document view.

2. Position the insertion point where you want to insert a new subdocument.

3. Click on the Insert Subdocument button on the Master Document toolbar to display the Insert Subdocument dialog box.

4. Select the name of the file to insert in the Look In list box, and then choose Open.

The document is inserted into the master document with its original filename. If the document is based on a different template or is formatted differently than the master document, the settings in the master document will be used in the subdocument when it is opened in the master document. The template and formatting settings in the subdocument file will be used when the subdocument file is opened with

File ➤ Open (Ctrl+O) or by clicking on the Open button on the Standard toolbar.

To reposition a subdocument within the master document, click on its icon to select the subdocument, and then drag it to the new location in the master document.

To reposition a heading in a subdocument, select the heading in the heading pane of the window, and then click on the Move Up or Move Down button on the Outlining toolbar to position it before or after an adjacent paragraph.

When the insertion point is positioned on the lower Section Break mark in a section, the new subdocument will be inserted in its own section as a separate subdocument. If the insertion point is positioned in an existing subdocument when the master document is in Document Map view, the new subdocument will be a subdocument of the existing subdocument. Split the subdocument to place the new sub-subdocument in the master document. A master document can contain a maximum of eight layers of subdocuments.

Locking a Subdocument

If you share the use of a master document with other people, you can lock the subdocuments you create. A locked subdocument appears with a padlock icon on it and can be opened only as a read-only file by anyone other than the author of the subdocument. The author's identity is taken from the Properties AUTHOR field code. However, anyone can unlock a locked subdocument.

To lock a subdocument, follow these steps:

1. With the master document open and in Master Document view, click on the icon of the subdocument to be locked or unlocked.

2. Click on the Lock Document button on the Master Document toolbar to lock an unlocked subdocument or to unlock a locked subdocument.

If you lock a subdocument that has been changed since you last saved it, choose Yes to save the changes and lock the subdocument.

Merging and Splitting Subdocuments

Merged subdocuments are saved as a single subdocument of the master document. After subdocuments are merged, their original, individual subdocument files can be deleted. To merge subdocuments, follow these steps:

1. If necessary, reposition the subdocuments that are to be merged so that they are next to each other in the master document.

2. Click on the icon of the first subdocument.

3. Hold down the Shift key while you click on the icon of the next and any subsequent subdocuments that are to be merged.

4. Click on the Merge Subdocument button on the Master Document toolbar.

5. Click on the Save button on the Standard toolbar to save the master document.

To split a subdocument, position the insertion point where you want to begin a new subdocument, and then click on the Split Subdocument button on the Master Document toolbar.

Moving or Renaming a Subdocument File

Open a subdocument from within its master document when you want to save the subdocument to a different file name and location without breaking its link to the master document. Follow these steps:

1. With the master document open and displayed in Master Document view, double-click on the icon of the subdocument to be moved or renamed. Leave the master document open.

2. Choose File ➤ Save As to display the Save As dialog box.

3. If necessary, type the new name and path for the subdocument in the File Name text box, and then choose Save in the Save As dialog box.

4. Click on the document Close button, or choose File ➤ Close to close the subdocument.

5. Save the master document.

Object Linking and Embedding

Use Object Linking and Embedding (OLE) to create and edit objects in your documents. You can link or embed graphics, equations, spreadsheets, and drawings in a document and then edit the selected object in the Word document.

A linked object contains information that remains connected to its original file. By default, Word automatically updates the data in your document each time the linked data is changed in its original file. The link in a Word document is stored as a {LINK} field code.

An embedded object becomes part of the document in which it is placed. To edit an embedded object, double-click on it to open the application in which it was created and make any necessary changes. The changes you made appear when you return to your Word document. Embedded objects are the results of the {EMBED...} field code.

Creating and Embedding an Object

To create and embed an object, follow these steps:

1. Position the insertion point where you want to embed a new object, choose Insert ➤ Object to display the Object dialog box, and then choose the Create New tab.

2. Select the kind of object you want to embed in the document in the Object Type list box.

3. Choose from the following options to define how the object is displayed in your document:

   • To display the object in the drawing layer in your document, select the Float Over Text checkbox. Objects in the drawing area can be positioned in front of or behind document text. Clear the checkbox to place the object at the position of the insertion point.

   • To display the object as an icon in your document, select the Display As Icon checkbox.

4. Choose OK to open the application used to create the object.

5. Create the object.

6. To embed the object and return to your Word document, click in the document outside the object.

7. Click on the Save button on the Standard toolbar to save the document with the embedded object.

The method used to embed the object and return to your document will vary slightly from one application to another. For example, if the object is a Word Picture, click on the Close Picture button on the Word Picture toolbar.

Editing an Embedded Object

To edit an embedded object, follow these steps:

1. Double-click on the object in your Word document, or select the object and then choose Edit ➤ *Type of* Object ➤ Open.

2. Make any necessary changes to the object.

3. To update the object and return to your document, click in the Word document outside the object.

Linking or Embedding an Existing File

To link or embed an existing file in your document, follow these steps:

1. Position the insertion point where you want to embed the object in your document.

2. Choose Insert ➤ Object and select the Create from File tab.

3. Type the path and name of the file to be embedded in the File Name text box. Or, select Browse to display the Browse dialog box, select the name of the file in the Look In list box, and then choose OK.

4. Choose from the following options to define how the object is displayed in your document:

   - To link the specified file to the active document, select the Link to File checkbox. Clear the checkbox to embed the file in the active document.

   - To display the object in the drawing layer in your document, select the Float over Text checkbox. Objects in the drawing area can be positioned in front of or behind document text. Clear the checkbox to place the object at the position of the insertion point.

   - To display the object as an icon in your document, select the Display As Icon checkbox.

5. Choose OK to embed the object in your document.

6. Save the active document with the embedded or linked object.

Linking or Embedding Part of a File

The source file must be saved before you can link or embed selected data in it to the active Word document. Follow these steps:

1. Position the insertion point where you want to link or embed the object in your document.

2. Open the source application and file, and then select the data to be linked or embedded.

3. Click on the Copy button or choose Edit ➤ Copy (Ctrl+C) in the source application, and then click on the Microsoft Word button on the Windows 95 taskbar to switch back to your Word document, or choose Window ➤ *Name of Document* to return to the object's destination document.

4. Choose Edit ➤ Paste Special to display the Paste Special dialog box.

5. Choose either of the following options:

   - Choose Paste, and then highlight the first item in the As list box that includes "Object" in its name to embed the object in the active document.

   - Choose Paste Link to insert the selected data into the Word document as a link.

6. Choose one of the following options in the As list box to specify how to link the data in your Word document (different options may be available, depending on the source application):

   - To link the contents of the Clipboard to the document as a graphic, select *Application Name* Object.

   - To link the contents of the Clipboard to the document as text data with its current formatting, select Formatted Text (RTF).

   - To link the contents of the Clipboard to the document with no formatting, select Unformatted Text.

   - To link the Clipboard contents to the document as a graphic, select Picture.

   - To create a hyperlink to the source file, select *Application* Hyperlink.

7. Choose from the following options to define how a linked or embedded object is displayed in your document:

   - To display the object in the drawing layer in your document, select the Float over Text checkbox. Objects in the drawing area can be positioned in front of or behind document text. Clear the checkbox to place the object at the position of the insertion point.

- To display the object as an icon in your document, select the Display As Icon checkbox.

8. Choose OK.

Modifying the File Format of an Embedded Object

If an embedded object is in a file format that you want to change or whose application you do not have, you can convert the file to a format that is available on your system.

An embedded object appears as a picture of the data you have embedded. However, all the data is still in the object. To reduce the size of a file with an embedded object, you can sometimes convert an object into a graphic. If you do, the original data is no longer embedded in the object, and the object can only be edited as a drawing. Follow these steps:

1. Select the object that is in the file format you want to change.

2. Choose Edit ➤ *Type of* Object ➤ Convert to display the Convert dialog box.

3. Select the format you want for the object in the Object Type list box. To convert the selected object into a graphic, highlight Picture in the Object Type list box.

4. Choose either Convert To to permanently convert the file format or Activate As to temporarily convert the file format.

5. If you chose Convert To in step 4, choose from the following options to define how the object is displayed in your document:

- To display the object in the drawing layer in your document, select the Float over Text checkbox. Objects in the drawing area can be positioned in front of or behind document text. Clear the checkbox to place the object at the position of the insertion point.

- To display the object as an icon in your document, select the Display As Icon checkbox.

6. Choose OK.

Modifying a Link

You can break an established link, reconnect a link to a file that has been moved or renamed, store the link as a picture in your document, specify how the link will be updated, update the link yourself, or lock a link in your document. Follow these steps:

1. Activate the Word document that contains the link, and then choose Edit ➤ Links to display the Links dialog box.

2. Choose any of the following options to modify a link, and then choose OK:

- The name and source file, range of the linked item, the name of the source application, and the update option of each link in the document are displayed in the Source File list box. Highlight the link you want to modify. Hold down the Ctrl key as you click on additional links to select more than one.

- In the Update area, choose either Automatic to update the selected link whenever the source is changed or Manual if you want to update the selected link in your document.

- Select the Locked checkbox to prevent the highlighted link from being updated. Clear the Locked checkbox when you want to update the link.

- Select the Save Picture in Document checkbox (selected by default) to save the link as a picture of the linked data in your document rather than the actual information. Clear the checkbox if the link is a graphic and you want to reduce the size of your Word document. However, the link will take longer to display because Word must interpret the data in the source file and then create the picture.

- Choose Update Now to update all the highlighted links in the Source File list box.

- Choose Open Source to open the source document of the selected link to edit its data.

- Choose Change Source to display the Change Source dialog box for links you lost when a source was moved or renamed, and then select the name of the file you want to link in the Look In list box. The name or range of the item that is linked appears in the Item text box. If necessary, type a different name or range for the link, and then choose Open.

- Choose Break Link to break the link between the selected file and your document. The current data remains in your Word document, but it can no longer be updated.

You cannot reconnect a broken link as you can restore a link that was lost when the source file was moved or renamed. Instead, you must reestablish a link that is broken by mistake.

You can also manage links when the Links dialog box is not displayed from within your document using any of the following methods:

- To lock a link, select the link in your document and press Ctrl+F11. Press Ctrl+ Shift+F11 when a link is selected to unlock it if you want to update the link.

- To update a selected link, press F9 (Update).

- To break a selected link, press Ctrl+Shift+F9.

- To have Word update manual links to your documents each time you print, select Tools ➤ Options, choose the Print tab, select the Update Links checkbox in the Printing Options area, and then choose OK.

Office Assistant

Use the new Office Assistant to provide onscreen help and tips about the current action. The Office Assistant is an animated graphic displayed by default in a small window that moves around on the screen to stay out of your way.

Managing the Office Assistant

You can choose how the Office Assistant appears on your screen, or you can hide it so that it doesn't appear at all.

- To hide the Office Assistant, right-click on it and then choose Hide Assistant.

- To redisplay the hidden Office Assistant, click on the Office Assistant button on the Standard toolbar or choose Help ➤ Microsoft Word Help (F1).

- To specify how the Office Assistant works for you, right-click on the Office Assistant and then choose Options to display the Options tab in the Office Assistant dialog box. Select the checkbox of any action you want Office Assistant to perform, or choose Reset My Tips to allow tips you've already seen to be redisplayed, and then choose OK.

- To specify the Office Assistant graphic, right-click on the Office Assistant and then choose Choose Assistant to display the Gallery tab in the Office Assistant dialog box. Choose Next to display each succeeding graphic, or choose Back to return to the previous graphic. When you find a graphic you like, display it, and then choose OK.

- To make the Office Assistant graphic perform, right-click on the Office Assistant and then choose Animate.

Using the Office Assistant

Use any of the following methods to obtain online help with the Office Assistant:

- When the Office Assistant has tips available for the current activity, a yellow light bulb appears in its window. To display the tip in a small message balloon, click on the light bulb or right-click on the Office Assistant, and then choose See Tips. Choose OK or Close in the Tip to remove it.

- To ask for information about a command or feature, click on the Office Assistant or on the Office Assistant button on the Standard toolbar. Then type your question in the balloon's text box, and choose Search.

Outline

Switch to Outline view when you want to display an existing document as an outline or create a new outline. To switch to Outline view, click on the Outline View button by the horizontal scroll bar or choose View ➤ Outline. In Outline view, the Outline toolbar appears just above the document window. Use the buttons on the toolbar to help create or edit an outline. In addition, you can display the document in Document Map view, with the text to which a built-in heading style was applied in the left pane and the document text in the right pane.

By default, the headings in an outline are formatted with one of Word's nine built-in heading styles. Click on the Show Formatting button on the Outline toolbar to suppress the display of character formatting in your outline.

Creating an Outline

To create an outline, follow these steps:

1. In an existing document, position the insertion point in the paragraph to which you want to apply a heading or paragraph style. To create a new outline, type the text for the first heading and press Enter.

2. If necessary, choose one of the following buttons on the Outline toolbar to change the heading level or paragraph style applied to the paragraph:

   - Click on the Promote button (Alt+ Shift+←) to apply Heading 1 style to the active paragraph in an existing document or to move the selected outline text to the left and apply the heading style for that level.

   - Click on the Demote button (Alt+ Shift+→) to apply Heading 2 style to the active paragraph in an existing document or to move the selected outline text to the right and apply the heading style for that level.

   - Click on the Demote to Body Text button (Ctrl+Shift+N) to change selected text from an outline level to which a heading style is applied into regular paragraph text.

3. Repeat steps 1 and 2 for each heading or paragraph in your outline.

The plus icon next to a heading indicates that the heading has subtext, and a minus icon indicates that the heading does not have subtext. A small square icon indicates text in a paragraph (subtext). Click on a heading's plus icon to select the heading and its subtext. Click on the small square icon to select only the subtext. Click between the icon and the heading to select only the heading.

You can also use any of the following methods to promote, demote, or move headings in an outline:

- Drag the plus or minus icon to the left to promote or to the right to demote the heading and its subtext.

- Drag the paragraph icon to the left to promote or to the right to demote the subtext.

- When you drag the plus, minus, or paragraph icon to promote or demote the heading and/or body text, a vertical line appears on your screen. Release the mouse button when the line is in the location where you want the outline item.

- Click on the Move Up (Alt+Shift+↑) or Move Down (Alt+Shift+↓) button to move the selected heading (in both the heading pane and the document pane while you are in Document Map View) or body text up or down one paragraph.

- Drag the plus or minus icon up or down to move the heading and subtext up or down.

- Drag the paragraph icon up or down to move the selected subtext paragraph up or down.

- When you drag the plus, minus, or paragraph icon to move the heading and or body text up or down, a horizontal line appears on your screen. Release the mouse button when the line is in the location where you want the outline item.

Expanding or Collapsing an Outline

Expand or collapse the headings and paragraphs in an outline so that the text you want to print is displayed on your screen, and then print the document as usual. The plus, minus, and paragraph icons will not print.

Collapse the text in an outline if you want to move the headings to a different location in the document or quickly scroll through the outline. To collapse or expand the text in an outline, toggle the following Outline toolbar buttons:

- Position the insertion point in an outline heading and click on the Expand button (Alt+Shift++) to expand one level of the heading's text, or click on the Collapse button (Alt+Shift+-) to collapse one level.

- Double-click on the plus icon or click on the Expand button to expand all the text under a heading. Double-click on the plus icon or click on the Collapse button to collapse all the heading text.

- Click on the All button (Alt+Shift+A) to expand all the outline's heading and paragraph text. Click on the All button (Alt+Shift+A) again to collapse the outline.

- Click on one of the heading number buttons or press Alt+Shift+n (where n is a number from 1 – 8 to display all the level headings in the outline up to that number.

- Click on the Show First Line Only button (Alt+Shift+L) to collapse each paragraph to display only the first line of text. Click on it again to expand the first line into the entire paragraph.

Page Break

Word automatically inserts a soft page break when a page is full and then begins a new page in the document. Soft page breaks are automatically adjusted when you edit the document.

You can insert a *manual* or *hard* page break to start a new page in your document. The hard page break will not be adjusted automatically when you edit the document. However, you can adjust the location of a hard page break by deleting it and inserting one in a different location.

Inserting a Hard Page Break

To insert a hard page break, follow these steps:

1. Position the insertion point where you want to start a new page.

2. Press Ctrl+Enter. Or, choose Insert ➤ Break to display the Break dialog box, choose Page Break, and then choose OK.

To delete a hard page break, click on the Normal View button by the horizontal scroll bar, or select View ➤ Normal. (In Normal view, a hard page break appears as a horizontal line with "Page Break" on it.) Select the hard page break, and then press Backspace or Delete.

Another way to delete hard page breaks is to choose Edit ➤ Replace (Ctrl+H) to display the Replace tab in the Find and Replace dialog box, choose More, select Manual Page Break in the Special pop-up list as the item to find, and replace each hard page break with "nothing."

Keeping Text on a Page

Word adjusts the pagination of your document according to the absence or presence of several document items. For example, soft page breaks are affected by hyphenation, displaying hidden text, footnotes, and graphics. Graphics cannot be broken—each must appear as a whole item. If a graphic will not fit on a page, Word adjusts the page break to occur before the graphic. However, you can keep some specified text together on a page. Follow these steps:

1. Remove any manual page breaks you have placed between paragraphs whose text you want to keep together.

2. Position the insertion point in the document or in the paragraph, or select multiple paragraphs whose text you want to control.

3. Choose Format ➤ Paragraph, and then choose the Line and Page Breaks tab in the Paragraph dialog box.

4. Select any of the following checkboxes in the Pagination area of the dialog box, and then choose OK.

   • Widow/Orphan Control, which is selected by default, prevents a single line of text from appearing as the first line at the top of a page or as the last line at the bottom of a page and prevents a single word from appearing as the last line of a paragraph. Widow/orphan control applies to the entire document.

   • When selected, Keep Lines Together prevents a page break from occurring within the paragraph that contains the insertion point.

   • When selected, Keep With Next keeps two or more paragraphs together on the same page. Move the insertion point into the first paragraph of two you want to keep together, or select each paragraph except the last one that you want to keep together.

   • When selected, Page Break Before places the page break before the paragraph that contains the insertion point.

In Normal and Page Layout views, a small, black square appears next to paragraphs for which Keep Lines Together, Keep With Next, or Page Break Before is selected.

Page Numbering

You can add automatic page numbers to a document. The page numbers are placed in a frame in the header or footer. You can drag the frame containing the page number to any position in the document.

Creating Page Numbers

To insert page numbers in a document, follow these steps:

1. Position the insertion point in the document section where you want to add page numbering, and then choose Insert ➤ Page Numbers to display the Page Numbers dialog box.

2. Choose any of the following options to insert page numbers:

   • Select Top of Page (Header) or Bottom of Page (Footer) in the Position drop-down list to define the location of the page numbers.

   • Choose Left, Center, Right, Inside, or Outside in the Alignment drop-down list as the position where the page number will appear in the header or footer.

   • Select the Show Number on First Page checkbox to begin numbering on the first page of the document or section.

3. If necessary, choose Format to display the Page Number Format dialog box.

4. Choose any of the following options to define the format of the page numbers, and then choose OK.

   • Choose arabic numerals, roman numerals, or letters in the drop-down list as the method of page numbering in the Number Format drop-down list.

   • Select the Include Chapter Number checkbox to insert the chapter number just before the page number. Select the heading style that you applied to each chapter number in the Chapter Starts with Style drop-down list, and choose the separator between the chapter heading text and the page numbers in the Use Separator drop-down list.

- In the Page Numbering area, select Continue from Previous Section to maintain consecutive numbers in adjacent document sections, or adjust the number at which to begin the section's page numbering in the Start At text box.

5. Choose OK in the Page Numbers dialog box.

You can also apply character formatting to a selected page number in a header or footer. Or, you can apply a style to the page number if you want page numbers in all your documents based on the template to have the same format.

To delete page numbers from the section that contains the insertion point, choose View ➤ Header and Footer. If necessary, click on the Switch between Header and Footer button on the Header and Footer toolbar, select the page number, and then press Backspace or Delete.

Picture

Enhance your documents by inserting pictures (graphics), including clip art, photographs, sounds, or videos in them. Word comes with many files you can use in your documents.

Word can interpret many different graphics file formats, even those created in other applications, so you can import pictures into your documents. You can also paste a graphic from the Clipboard or draw a picture using Word's Drawing tools in your document.

Inserting a Graphic

By default, Word stores an interpretation of the inserted graphic rather than the actual graphic file in your document. To insert a graphic in a document, follow these steps:

1. Position the insertion point where you want the graphic to appear.

2. Choose Insert ➤ Picture, and then choose any of the following options:

- Select Clip Art to display the Microsoft Clip Gallery 3.0 dialog box, choose a clip art, photograph, sound, or video file, and then choose Insert.

- Select From File to display the Insert Picture dialog box. Highlight the name of the file to insert in the Look In list box. If necessary, select the Link To File checkbox to link the graphic file to the document rather than inserting it, and select the Float over Text checkbox to insert the file in the drawing layer so that it can be positioned in front of or behind text. Then choose Insert.

- Select AutoShapes to display the AutoShapes toolbar, and then click on the button that contains the shape you want to insert to display a palette of shapes. Click on the shape in the palette, and then draw the shape in your document.

- Choose WordArt to display the WordArt Gallery dialog box. Select the style for the text and then choose OK to display the Edit WordArt Text dialog box. Edit the text as necessary, and then choose OK to insert it in the document and display the WordArt toolbar.

- Select Chart to display a datasheet window, a chart in the document, and the Chart toolbar. Edit both the datasheet and the chart as necessary, and then click in the document.

A linked graphic saves disk space, because the link is stored in the document rather than the entire graphics file. If you select the Link to File checkbox in the Insert Picture dialog box, clear the Save with Document checkbox.

You can move an inserted graphic or change the formatting applied to a selected graphic using the options on the Picture toolbar or on the various tabs in the Format Picture dialog box. Click on a graphic to select it. When a graphic is selected, eight handles appear around it.

If the Picture toolbar does not appear automatically, right-click on the picture and then choose Show Picture Toolbar. You can use any of the following options to format a picture.

- To quickly move a graphic, position the mouse pointer over it until it appears as a four-headed arrow. Then drag the graphic to a different position on the page. Alternatively, adjust the options on the Position tab in the Format Object dialog box.

- To resize a selected graphic, move the pointer to one of its handles until it appears as a two-headed arrow, and then drag a corner handle to resize the graphic but retain its original proportions. Or, drag one of its middle handles to resize the graphic without retaining its original proportions. Alternatively, adjust the options on the Size tab in the Format Picture dialog box.

- Click on the Insert Picture button on the Picture toolbar to display the Insert Picture dialog box to select another picture for your document.

- Click on the Image Control button on the Picture toolbar, and then select Automatic to display the picture in its original colors; select Grayscale to display the picture in black and white with each color in its grayscale equivalent; select Black & White to display the picture in only black and white; or select Watermark to change the picture into a light gray picture. Alternatively, select any of the above options in the Color dropdown list on the Picture tab in the Format Picture dialog box.

- Click on the More Contrast or Less Contrast button on the Picture toolbar to adjust the intensity of the picture's color. Alternatively, adjust the Contrast option on the Picture tab in the Format Picture dialog box.

- Click on the More Brightness or Less Brightness button on the Picture toolbar to adjust the amount of black or white in the picture. Alternatively, adjust the Brightness option on the Picture tab in the Format Picture dialog box.

- Click on the Crop button on the Picture toolbar, and then position the mouse pointer over a handle of the picture to crop the picture. Alternatively, adjust the values in the Crop From area on the Picture tab in the Format Picture dialog box.

- Click on the Line Style button on the Picture toolbar and then select the line to place around the borders of the picture in the pop-up list. Alternatively, adjust the options on the Colors and Lines tab in the Format Picture dialog box.

- Click on the Text Wrapping button on the Picture toolbar, and then select the way text will wrap around the graphic in your document. Alternatively, adjust the options on the Wrapping tab in the Format Picture dialog box.

- Click on the Format Picture button on the Picture toolbar to display the Format Picture dialog box.

- Click on the Set Transparent Color button on the Picture toolbar to and then click on the color in a bitmap image to make it transparent.

- Click on the Reset Picture Button on the Picture toolbar or choose Reset on the Size or Picture tab in the Format Picture dialog box to return the picture to its original color, brightness, and contrast and to remove any cropping.

To use the Drawing tools to extensively edit an inserted graphic, double-click on it. The graphic appears in a separate window, and the Drawing toolbar is displayed above the status bar.

To change the application window used to edit an imported graphic, choose Tools ➤ Options, select the Edit tab, choose Microsoft Word or Microsoft Drawing in the Picture Editor drop-down list, and then choose OK.

Properties

You can display information and statistics about the active file, and you can add or change the summary information for each file you create. Summary information can be used to search for the file.

Creating Custom Properties

Although Word comes with many properties already defined for your files, you can create custom properties, if necessary, to further define a search or to link to specific data (which is marked as a bookmark) in a file. To create custom properties, follow these steps:

1. Activate the file for which you want to create a custom property, choose File ➤ Properties to display the *FileName* Properties dialog box, and then select the Custom tab.

2. Type the name for the custom property in the Name text box. To force the property to appear exclusively in Word instead of other applications, type an _ (underline character) as the first character in the property's name.

3. Select Text, Date, Number, or Yes or No as the type of property in the Type drop-down list.

4. To link the data in a bookmark to the custom property, select the Link to Content checkbox.

5. Type a value for the property in the Value text box. If the value is a bookmark in your document, choose one of the bookmarks in the Source drop-down list.

6. Choose Add to add the custom property to the Properties list box.

7. Choose OK in the *FileName* Properties dialog box.

Displaying Document Information and Statistics

Word automatically maintains information and statistics for each document you create, which are updated each time you save the file.

To display the name, type, location, size, DOS filename, date created, last date modified and accessed, and the attributes of the active file, choose File ➤ Properties to display the *FileName* Properties dialog box, and then choose the General tab.

Select the Statistics tab to display the date and time the file was created and last modified, the date the file was last accessed and printed, the name of the person who last saved the file, the number of revisions made to the file, and the total amount of time spent editing the file. The Statistics area contains detailed file information, such as the number of pages, paragraphs, lines, words, and characters in the document and the number of bytes in the file.

To display the first line of the active file, select the contents tab. The first line appears in the Document Contents list box.

Protect Document

Assign a password to protect specific text in a document from being changed by others. Passwords are case sensitive. They can contain as many as 15 characters and can include numbers, letters, symbols, and spaces.

Protecting the Text of a Document

If you don't want others to revise your document, protect the text of the document or a section of the document with a password. Only a person who knows the password can change the text of a protected document. Others can, however, add comments or track change marks to a protected document, and they can fill in fields in a protected form.

To password protect a document, follow these steps:

1. Choose Tools ➤ Protect Document to display the Protect Document dialog box.

2. Choose one of the following options:

   • Select Tracked Changes to mark any changes made as revisions while the document is protected. Revisions cannot be accepted or rejected, and reviewers cannot turn off revision marking.

- Select Comments to allow reviewers to insert comments, but not change any of the contents of the document.

- Select Forms to allow users to fill in the form fields, but not change any of the form's text. Then, if necessary, select Sections to display the Section Protection dialog box. Select the checkbox beside each section in the Protected Sections list box (all are selected by default) that is to be protected from changes, and then choose OK.

3. Type the password in the Password text box. An asterisk appears for each character you type.

4. Choose OK to display the Confirm Password dialog box.

5. Type the password again in the Reenter Password to Open text box, and then choose OK.

To turn off the text protection of a document, choose Tools ➤ Unprotect Document to display the Unprotect Document dialog box. Type the protection password in the Password text box, and then choose OK.

Repaginate

By default, Word adjusts soft page breaks while you are editing your document. Word always repaginates when you switch to Page Layout view or Print Preview and when you print the document. You can speed your editing in other views by turning off background repagination.

Controlling Background Repagination

To control when Word repaginates, follow these steps:

1. Click on the Normal View button by the horizontal scroll bar, or choose View ➤ Normal to switch to Normal view.

2. Choose Tools ➤ Options to display the Options dialog box, and then choose the General tab.

3. Select the Background Repagination checkbox (selected by default) to have Word adjust the pagination each time you pause during editing a document. Clear the checkbox to speed up the editing process.

4. Choose OK in the Options dialog box.

Repeat

Characters you type and formatting changes you make to text are stored in Word until you perform any action except moving the insertion point. You can then insert the characters you just typed in the position of the insertion point anywhere in your document by repeating your last action.

Repeating Your Last Edit

To repeat your last editing, follow these steps:

1. Position the insertion point where you want to insert the last text you typed or attribute you applied.

2. Choose Edit ➤ Repeat *Edit* (F4).

Ruler

The horizontal ruler is displayed by default under the toolbars in Normal view. In Page Layout view and Print Preview, both the horizontal and vertical rulers are displayed.

Using the Ruler

Use the horizontal ruler to adjust the indentation of a paragraph, to set the left and right margins, to add or remove tab stops in a paragraph, and to adjust the widths of columns. Use the vertical ruler to set top and bottom margins in your document.

To display or hide the rulers, choose View ➤ Ruler.

To change the margins, indentation, or tab stops in a document, click on the Page Layout View button or choose View ➤ Page Layout to change to Page Layout view. You then have the following options:

- To set the first line indentation of the paragraph that contains the insertion point, drag the First Line Indent marker.

- To adjust the indentation of all lines except the first in the current paragraph, drag the Hanging Indent marker.

- To adjust the indentation of all the lines in the paragraph relative to the First Line Indent and Hanging Indent markers, drag the Left Indent marker.

- To adjust the right indentation of all lines in the current paragraph, drag the Right Indent marker.

- To adjust the left and right document margins, drag the Left Margin and Right Margin markers on the horizontal ruler.

- To adjust the top and bottom document margins, drag the Top Margin and Bottom Margin markers on the vertical ruler.

- To add tab stops to the current paragraph, click on the *TypeOf* Tab button until the type of tab you want to set appears on the button. Then click in the position for the tab on the horizontal ruler.

- To remove an existing tab stop from the current paragraph, drag its *TypeOf* Tab marker off the ruler.

- To adjust the widths of columns, drag the Column Margin markers.

You can also change the tabs and indentation of the paragraph that contains the insertion point when you are in Normal view. To change to Normal view, click on the Normal View button by the horizontal scroll bar, or choose View ➤ Normal.

Section Layout

You can divide a document into sections. For example, if your document consists of several chapters, each chapter can be in a separate section.

Each section in a document can contain its own formatting, which is saved in the section mark. Apply any formatting you want to use in all sections of the document before you divide it into sections. Each section will contain the formatting that is applied to the entire document.

Adding a Section Break

When you add a section break, a section mark is inserted in your document. When nonprinting characters are displayed, the section mark appears in either Page Layout or Normal view as a double-dotted line with "Section Break (*Type*)" on it. Click on the Show/Hide ¶ button on the Standard toolbar to toggle on the display of nonprinting characters. Neither the line nor the text will be printed when you print the document.

The last paragraph mark in the document contains the formatting for the last section in the document.

To insert a section break in a document, follow these steps:

1. Position the insertion point where you want to insert a section break, and choose Insert ➤ Break to display the Break dialog box.

2. Choose one of the following options in the Section Breaks area, and then choose OK:

- Select Next Page to insert a section break mark and begin the new section at the top of the next page.

- Select Continuous to insert a section break mark and begin the new section on the same page, just below the previous section.

- Select Even Page to insert a section break mark and begin a new section on an even-numbered page. The next odd-numbered page is blank if the section break is inserted on an even-numbered page.

- Select Odd Page to insert a section break mark and begin a new section on an odd-numbered page. The next even-numbered page is blank if the section break is inserted on an odd-numbered page.

To delete a section break, select the section mark, and press Backspace or Delete. Both the section break mark and formatting for the text above the section break are deleted, and the text takes on the formatting of the following section. Alternatively, use Word's Replace feature to find a section break by selecting Section Break in the Special pop-up list. You can replace it with "nothing" to delete it.

Sort

You can sort selected text to rearrange it numerically, alphabetically, or by date. Paragraphs, lists separated by commas or spaces, and table rows can be sorted. Items are sorted in ascending (smallest to largest or A-Z) or descending (largest to smallest or Z-A) order.

Word sorts items according to a specific order of precedence. List items that start with punctuation marks or other symbols such as !, %, <, >, or $ are sorted first, followed by items that start with numbers, then items that start with letters. Uppercase letters precede lowercase

letters in the list. Subsequent characters decide the sort order if items begin with the same character, and subsequent fields decide the sort order if list items contain the same data in a field.

Performing a Sort

To sort a list of items, follow these steps:

1. Select the items you want to sort, and then choose Table ➤ Sort to display the Sort Text dialog box.

2. Choose any of the following options, and then choose OK.

- Select Field N, Column N, or Paragraphs, depending on the selection in your document, as the first items on which to sort text in the Sort By drop-down list. Choose Text, Number, or Date as the kind of data to be sorted in the Type drop-down list, and then choose Ascending or Descending as the sort order.

- Select the second, and if necessary, the third type of data on which to sort in the corresponding Then By drop-down lists. You can choose fields, columns, and paragraphs, depending on the selection in your document, as the items on which to perform the sort. In the corresponding Type drop-down list, choose Text, Number, or Date as the kind of data to be sorted. Select Ascending or Descending as the sort order in the corresponding Then By area.

- In the My List Has area, select Header Row to disregard the first row of data while sorting a table so that all heading rows are ignored in the sort. Or, select No Header Row to sort all rows of data.

- Select Options to display the Sort Options dialog box. In the Separate Fields At area, choose Tabs or Commas as the separator character, or choose Other, and then type the separator character in the text box to sort text outside a table. In the Sort Options area, choose Sort Column Only (selected by default) to sort only the selected column of table data or text, and select Case Sensitive to sort uppercase text before lowercase text. Select the name of the language whose sorting rules you want to use in the Sorting Language drop-down list. Choose OK in the Sort Options dialog box.

If no text is selected in step 1, Word automatically selects all the text in the document when you choose Table ➤ Sort. If the insertion point is in a table, the entire table is selected when you choose Table ➤ Sort.

Spelling and Grammar

Use Word's Spelling tool to catch typographical errors, grammatical errors, or misspelled words in your documents. You can create *custom dictionaries* to prevent special words that are not in the main dictionary from being questioned, and you can create *exclude dictionaries* to question the spelling of words in the main dictionary.

Checking the Spelling in the Active Document

Word automatically checks the spelling of each word as you type and places a wavy red line under every word that is not in any of the open dictionaries.

To check the spelling of a word underlined with a wavy red line, right-click on the word to display its Spelling shortcut menu, and then select one of the words that appear in bold at the top of the menu. Or, choose any of the following options:

- Select Ignore All to ignore each word spelled the same way in the document.
- Select Add to add the word to the custom dictionary.
- Select AutoCorrect, and then select the word to insert each time you type the underlined word.
- Select Spelling to display the Spelling dialog box.

Double-click on the Spelling and Grammar Status button on the status bar to select the next word underlined with a wavy red line and to display its shortcut menu.

When you display the Spelling dialog box, each word in the document that is not in the main or custom dictionaries or that is in the exclude dictionary is highlighted in succession in your document.

To spell-check a document, follow these steps:

1. Click on the Spelling button on the Standard toolbar or select Tools ➤ Spelling and Grammar (F7) to highlight the first misspelled word after the position of the insertion point and to display the Spelling and Grammar dialog box.

2. Clear the Check Grammar checkbox to have Word highlight only spelling errors in the document.

3. The word that is highlighted in the document appears with bold red characters in context in the Not in Dictionary text box. Choose any of the following options:

   - Select the spelling that you want to use in the list of suggested spellings in the Suggestions list box for the highlighted word, or directly edit any of the text in the Not in Dictionary text box.

   - Choose Change to change the text that appears in the Not in Dictionary text box in your document.

   - Choose Change All to change the spelling of each occurrence of the word highlighted in your document to the spelling that appears in the Not in Dictionary text box.

   - Choose Ignore to disregard the spelling of the word that is highlighted in your document.

   - Choose Ignore All to disregard the spelling of each occurrence of the word that is highlighted in your document.

   - Choose Add to place the word that appears in bold red characters in the Not in Dictionary text box in the selected custom dictionary.

- Choose AutoCorrect to automatically add the word highlighted in your document to the list of AutoCorrect entries. Then, each time you type the word followed by a space or punctuation mark, it will be replaced with the spelling selected in the Suggestions list box.

- Choose Undo to restore the change you made to the last word that was highlighted in your document.

4. Choose Cancel or Close to close the Spelling dialog box and return to your document. To check the spelling of a single word, select the word and then click on the Spelling and Grammar button on the Standard toolbar to display the Spelling and Grammar dialog box (or a message box if the word is in one of the open dictionaries).

Creating a Dictionary of Excluded Words

By default, any words that are in the main dictionary are not questioned during a spelling check. To question correctly spelled words because you prefer a different spelling, create an exclude dictionary to be used with the main dictionary.

The exclude dictionary has the same filename as the main dictionary, but it has the .EXC extension. For example, if you are using the US English dictionary, the main dictionary filename is MSSP2_EN.LEX. The exclude dictionary associated with it is named MSSP2_EN.EXC.

To create a dictionary of excluded words, follow these steps:

1. Click on the New button on the Standard toolbar or press Ctrl+N to open a new document based on the Normal.dot template.

2. Type a word you want to exclude and press Enter to start a new paragraph.

3. Repeat step 2 for each word in the exclude dictionary.

4. Choose Table ➤ Sort to display the Sort Text dialog box, and then choose OK to arrange the words in alphabetic order.

5. Click on the Save button on the Standard toolbar or choose File ➤ Save (Ctrl+S) to display the Save As dialog box.

6. Choose the c:\windows\msapps\proof folder or the c:\program files\common files\ microsoft shared\proof folder in the Save In drop-down list as the location in which to store the exclude dictionary file.

7. Choose Text Only (*.txt) in the Save As Type drop-down list.

8. Type a name for the exclude dictionary (usually MSSP2_EN.EXC) in the File Name text box.

9. Choose Save in the Save As dialog box, and then choose Yes in the message box that appears to save the file in Text Only format.

The next time you type a word that is in the exclude dictionary, Spelling places a wavy red line under it. If you check the spelling in a document, the words in the exclude dictionary will be highlighted in your document.

Creating and Using a Custom Dictionary

If you often use technical terms or other words that are questioned by Spelling, create a custom dictionary that contains words that are not in the main dictionary. Words in a custom dictionary will be questioned only when they are not spelled the way they are in the custom dictionary.

Word comes with a custom dictionary, and you can create additional custom dictionaries to use. The custom dictionaries are Word documents and can be edited using the same techniques you use in regular documents.

To create a custom dictionary, follow these steps:

1. In a document with at least one misspelled word, click on the Spelling and Grammar button on the Standard toolbar or choose Tools ➤ Spelling and Grammar (F7), and then choose Options to display the Spelling & Grammar tab in the Options dialog box. Or, choose Tools ➤ Options and select the Spelling & Grammar tab.

2. Choose Dictionaries to display the Custom Dictionaries dialog box.

3. Choose New to display the Create Custom Dictionary dialog box, with the contents of the Proof folder displayed in the Save In list box. Type a name in the File Name text box, and then choose Save to create a new custom dictionary file.

4. If necessary, choose any of the following options to manage your custom dictionaries:

   • Highlight a dictionary in the Custom Dictionaries list box, choose Edit, and then choose OK to open the custom dictionary as a document. Edit the dictionary as necessary, and then click on the Save button on the Standard toolbar to save the dictionary. Click on the Document Close button to close the custom dictionary file.

   • Choose Add to display the Add Custom Dictionary dialog box to add a custom dictionary file that is stored in a different path to the Proof folder.

   • Choose Remove to delete the highlighted custom dictionary from the list in the Custom Dictionaries list box. The dictionary file is not deleted from your hard disk.

   • If you have created a custom dictionary to check the spelling of words in another language, select the language in the Language drop-down list.

5. In the Custom Dictionaries list box, select the checkbox of each custom dictionary you want Word to open and use during a spelling check.

6. Choose OK in the Custom Dictionaries dialog box.

7. Choose OK in the Options dialog box. If necessary, choose Cancel in the Spelling and Grammar dialog box to return to your document.

Word's automatic spell-checking feature is turned off each time you edit a custom dictionary. To turn it back on, select the Check Spelling As You Type checkbox on the Spelling & Grammar tab in the Options dialog box, and then choose OK.

Setting the Spelling Check and Grammar Options

1. In the Spelling and Grammar dialog box, choose Options to display the Spelling & Grammar tab in the Options dialog box. Or, choose Tools ➤ Options and select the Spelling & Grammar tab.

2. Choose any of the following options to use when checking the spelling in a document:

   • Select the Check Spelling As You Type check box to turn on automatic spell checking.

   • Select the Hide Spelling Errors in Current Document checkbox to suppress the display of the wavy red line that appears under misspelled words while you are creating or adding text to a document.

   • Select the Always Suggest Corrections checkbox (selected by default) to have Word display suggestions for the correct spelling of the word highlighted in the document in the Spelling dialog box's Suggestions list box.

   • Select From Main Dictionary Only to display suggestions from the main dictionary rather than any open custom dictionaries.

   • Select the Ignore Words in UPPERCASE checkbox to have Word disregard words typed in uppercase letters during the spelling check.

- Select the Ignore Words with Numbers checkbox to have Word omit words that have numbers during the spelling check.

- Select the Ignore Internet and File Addresses checkbox to have Word omit them during a spelling check.

- Click on the Custom Dictionary drop-down list to make sure that all the custom dictionaries you want to use appear in the list.

3. Choose any of the following options to use when checking the grammar in a document:

- Select the Check Grammar As You Type checkbox to turn on automatic grammar checking.

- Select the Hide Grammatical Errors in This Document checkbox to suppress the wavy green line that appears below potential grammatical errors.

- Select the Check Grammar with Spelling checkbox to have Word check both spelling and grammar.

- Select the Show Readability Statistics checkbox to have Word display the readability statistics after Grammar Checker is run.

- Select the style of writing that is used in this document in the Writing Style drop-down list so that the correct grammatical rules will be applied during a grammar check.

- To change the style and grammar rules for the selected writing style, choose Settings, and then change any necessary option.

4. Select Recheck Document to check both the spelling and grammar again and to remove all the words from the current session list for which you chose Ignore All in the Spelling dialog box.

5. Choose OK in the Options dialog box. If necessary, choose Cancel in the Spelling dialog box to return to your document.

Style

To present your documents with consistent formatting, apply *styles*, named groups of formatting commands, to the text. When you apply a style, each format in the style is applied simultaneously to selected text. Word comes with many built-in styles already created for you.

The two types of styles are paragraph styles and character styles. Paragraph styles manage all the formatting in a paragraph, including the font and size, line spacing, alignment, tab stops, and the borders and shading. Character styles are created using the options in the Font dialog box.

Applying a Style

To apply a style to selected text or to the paragraph that contains the insertion point:

- Select the style you want to apply in the Style drop-down list on the Formatting toolbar.

- Choose Format ➤ Style to display the Style dialog box, select the style to be applied in the Styles list box, and then choose Apply.

To display the names of paragraph styles on the left side of the window, click on the Normal View or Outline View button by the horizontal scroll bar, or choose View ➤ Normal or View ➤ Outline to switch to the corresponding view. Then choose Tools ➤ Options, select the View tab, adjust the measurement in the Style Area Width text box to a number greater than 0, and choose OK.

To see a list of the styles in the active document and the description of the highlighted style, select Format ➤ Style to display the Style dialog box and glance at the Styles list box. You can change the list of styles by selecting Styles in Use, All Styles, or User-Defined Styles in the List drop-down list. Choose Cancel to return to your document.

To print a list of all the styles in the active document and their descriptions, choose Styles in the Print What drop-down list in the Print dialog box.

To display a message box with information about the formatting and styles applied to text, choose Help ➤ What's This (Shift+F1) and then click on the text. Click outside any text to remove the message box.

Copying Styles

You can copy the styles in a document or template to a different document or template to save time and to make sure the styles in each are the same. To do so, follow these steps:

1. Choose Format ➤ Style, select Organizer to display the Organizer dialog box, and then choose the Styles tab.

2. Highlight the name of the style to be copied in the In *Document Name* list box. Press Ctrl as you click on each name to highlight multiple names in the list box.

3. Select Copy to copy the selected style to the To *Template Name* list box.

4. Choose any of the following options to manage the styles, and then choose Close in the Organizer dialog box.

   - Select the name of the document or template that contains the style you want to copy in the appropriate Styles Available In drop-down list. If necessary, click on the appropriate Close File button to either close the current document and its attached template and remove the list of styles in it from the In *Document Name* list box or to close the active template. Then click on the appropriate Open File button to display the Open dialog box, and select the file that contains the styles you want to copy or the template file in which to place the copied styles.

   - Choose Delete to remove the style selected in the In *Document Name* or To *Template Name* list box from the corresponding document or template, and then choose Yes to confirm the deletion.

   - Select the style in either the In *Document Name* or To *Template Name* list box that you want to rename, and then select Rename to display the Rename dialog box. Type a name for the style in the New Name text box, and then choose OK.

Word's built-in styles cannot be renamed or deleted. If you want to change the name of one of the built-in styles, give it an *alias*, an alternate name. To assign an alias to the selected built-in style, type a comma and the alternate name in the New Name text box, and then choose OK in the Rename dialog box.

Creating or Modifying a Style

You can create your own named style to use in documents created with the template in which the style is stored. A document cannot contain two styles that have the same name, but you can assign more than one name to the same style. Style names are case-sensitive and can contain as many as 253 characters. Do not place \, {, }, or ; in a style name. A new or modified style that is based on an existing style will be updated when you change the style on which it is based.

To create or modify a style using the formatting applied to selected text or to the paragraph that contains the insertion point, click in the Style text box on the Formatting toolbar to highlight the name of the current style, and then press Enter to modify the highlighted style or type a different name and then press Enter to create a new style.

You can redefine Word's Normal style. However, all new documents are based by default on the Normal.dot template, and many existing styles in other templates are based on Normal style.

To create an entirely new style or modify an existing style, follow these steps:

1. Choose Format ➤ Style, and then select New or Modify to display the New Style or Modify Style dialog box.

2. Type a name for the new or modified style in the Name text box.

3. To create a new style, select Paragraph or Character in the Style Type drop-down list.

4. In the Based On drop-down list, select a style that is similar to the style you want to create.

5. In the Style for Following Paragraph drop-down list, select the style that is to be applied automatically to a new paragraph started after the style is applied.

6. Optionally, select Shortcut Key to display the Customize Keyboard dialog box, and then assign a key sequence to the new style.

7. Choose Format, and then select the formatting you want to assign to the style.

8. Select the Add to Template checkbox to make the style available for any document you create based on the same template.

9. Select the Automatically Update checkbox to have Word automatically redefine the specified (existing) style when you manually apply different formatting to text to which the style is applied.

10. Choose OK in the New Style or Modify Style dialog box, and then choose Apply in the Style dialog box to apply the new style to the selection or to apply the modified style to all the characters or paragraphs to which the unmodified style was applied.

You can also remove an existing user-defined style from a document. If the style is a paragraph style, any paragraph to which the style was applied is formatted with Normal style. If the style is a character style, the style is removed from any characters to which it was applied. To delete a style, choose Format ➤ Style, select the name of the style in the Styles list box, choose Delete, and then choose Yes to confirm the deletion. Choose Close in the Style dialog box to return to your document.

Style Gallery

Use Word's Style Gallery to add styles from a different template to an existing document.

You can see a preview of the way the document will appear when the new styles are applied.

Changing the Document Template

When you use the Style Gallery, the styles in the selected template are copied to the document. The template's style takes precedence over the same style in the document. Any style in the template that is not already in the document is added to the document. Styles that are not in the template stay the same in the document.

To change a document template, follow these steps:

1. Activate the document whose template you want to change, and then select Format ➤ Style Gallery to display the Style Gallery dialog box.

2. Select the template that contains the styles you want to copy to the document in the Template list box. By default, a sample of the document's appearance using the styles in the template is displayed in the Preview Of list box.

3. If necessary, select Example in the Preview area to display a sample document that contains the styles in the template, or, select Style Samples to display a list of the styles in the template and samples of text formatted with the styles.

4. Choose OK in the Style Gallery dialog box.

You can also double-click on the name of the template in the Template list box to immediately apply the styles in the selected template to the active document.

To return to the document's original template, click on the Undo button on the Standard toolbar or choose Edit ➤ Undo Style Gallery.

TABLE | 1021

Table

Use tables instead of tabs in documents that contain columns of data, for text that is positioned in side-by-side paragraphs, or to present graphics beside text.

Tables are made up of rows and columns of data entered into cells. The cells' contents are individual paragraphs and can be formatted with the same methods as those used to format any paragraph.

Press Tab to move the insertion point to the next cell in the table. To insert a tab character in a cell, press Ctrl+Tab. Set tab stops in a table cell with the Ruler or with Format ➤ Tabs. The measurements entered in the Tabs dialog box are relative to the margin of the cell, not to the margin of the page.

Calculating Numeric Data in a Table

You can create simple spreadsheets in a Word table and then perform calculations on the table data by entering formulas. For example, click on the AutoSum button on the Tables and Borders toolbar to have Word calculate as a sum all the values above or to the left of the cell into which you enter the formula.

You can use the same types of cell references as those in an electronic spreadsheet (such as Excel) to specify the cells whose values you want to calculate. In a spreadsheet or a Word table, the columns are lettered and the rows are numbered.

Cell references in a Word table are always absolute and must be enclosed within parentheses in the formula. Use cell references to specify values in cells other than those above or to the left of the cell that contains the formula.

To calculate numeric data in a table, follow these steps:

1. Position the insertion point in the cell where the calculation's results will appear, and then choose Table ➤ Formula to display the Formula dialog box.

2. Type the formula in the Formula text box, preceded by an equal sign. Alternatively, either select one of Word's built-in functions in the Paste Function drop-down list and then add the necessary arguments in the function's parentheses, or select the name of a defined bookmark to use in the formula in the Paste Bookmark drop-down list.

3. Select a format for the calculation's result in the Number Format drop-down list.

4. Choose OK in the Formula dialog box.

Creating a Table

By default, table borders are inserted when you insert a table in your document. Table borders are printed when you print the document.

If you remove the default table borders, the table's gridlines are displayed. Gridlines are nonprinting characters. Select Table ➤ Hide Gridlines or Table ➤ Show Gridlines to toggle the display of gridlines in a table on your screen.

Click on the Show/Hide ¶ button on the Standard toolbar to toggle the display of the end-of-cell mark, which indicates the end of each cell's contents, and the end-of-row mark, which indicates the end of each row.

To create a simple table, follow these steps:

1. Position the insertion point where you want to place the table, click on the Insert Table button on the Standard toolbar, and then drag the mouse over the palette to create a table with the highlighted number of rows and columns. Or, choose Table ➤ Insert Table to display the Insert Table dialog box.

2. In the Insert Table dialog box, choose any of the following options to define the appearance of the table, and then choose OK:

- Adjust the value in the Number of Columns text box to define the number of columns you want in the table.

- Adjust the value in the Number of Rows text box to define the number of rows you want in the table.

- Adjust the measurement in the Column Width text box to define the width of each column in the table. If you select Auto, the table columns are evenly adjusted between the left and right margins.

- Choose AutoFormat to display the Table AutoFormat dialog box. Select the format for the new table, and then choose OK. The name of the format applied to the table appears in the Table Format area.

To create a complex table, choose Table ➤ Draw Table or click on the Tables and Borders button on the Standard toolbar to display the Table and Borders toolbar, and then draw a table, one cell at a time.

You can also convert the data in a table into regular text in the document. To change tabular data into regular document text, follow these steps:

1. Select the table rows that contain the text you want to change into paragraphs, and then choose Table ➤ Convert Table to Text to display the Convert Table to Text dialog box.

2. Select Paragraph Marks, Tabs, or Commas, or choose Other and type a character in the text box to separate the text that is in each cell.

3. Choose OK in the Convert Table to Text dialog box.

To create a table using existing document text, add paragraph marks, tabs, or commas in the text as separators, and then select the text that is to be changed into table text. Choose Table ➤ Convert Text to Table to display the Convert

Text to Table dialog box, which is similar to the Insert Table dialog box. Select the separator you inserted in the text and then choose OK. The separated text will be placed in individual cells in the table.

Creating Table Headings

Table headings are the data that you want as the "title" of the table. The headings consist of data that is entered in the first row of the table (the *header row*) unless a manual page break is inserted in the table.

Merge two or more cells to place a table heading in one cell that spans several columns in the first row of a table. When cells are merged, their contents are converted to paragraphs within a single cell.

Or, you can split a selected cell to divide its contents according to the number of paragraph marks in the cell. If the cell contains only one paragraph mark, the text is placed in the left cell and empty cells are added to its right.

To merge or split cells, follow these steps:

1. Select at least two cells to merge or one cell to split.

2. Choose either of the following options:

- Choose Table ➤ Merge Cells or click on the Merge Cells button on the Tables and Borders toolbar to merge the cells.

- Choose Table ➤ Split Cells or click on the Split Cells button on the Tables and Borders toolbar, specify the number of columns and rows, select the Merge-Cells before Split checkbox to reconfigure the selected cells before splitting them into the specified number of columns and rows, and then choose OK to split cells.

The data in the heading row in a table is not automatically repeated across hard page breaks. However, you can have Word repeat the heading row in tables that contain soft page breaks and automatically update heading text that is edited.

TABLE | **1023**

T

To create a table heading, follow these steps:

1. Select the row or rows, starting with the first table row, that contains the text to be used as headings.

2. Choose Table ➤ Headings.

To remove the heading text that was updated across soft page breaks, select the original row or rows you selected as the table headings, and then choose Table ➤ Headings to toggle off the headings.

Editing a Table

The table's appearance can be changed to fit your data.

To delete cells, rows, or columns, follow these steps:

1. Select the cells to be deleted or select a cell in each row or column to be deleted, and then choose Table ➤ Delete Cells to display the Delete Cells dialog box.

2. Choose one of the following options, and then choose OK:

   - Select Shift Cells Left to move the remaining cells in the row to the left after the deletion.

   - Select Shift Cells Up to move the remaining cells in the column up after the deletion.

   - Select Delete Entire Row to delete the row that contains the selected cell.

   - Select Delete Entire Column to delete the column that contains the selected cell.

Select an entire row or column, and then choose Table ➤ Delete Rows or Table ➤ Delete Columns to delete the selection.

To insert cells, rows, or columns in the table, follow these steps:

1. Select the number of cells, rows, or columns in the position in which new ones are to be inserted in the table.

2. Click on the Insert Cells, Insert Rows, or Insert Columns button on the Standard toolbar, or choose Table ➤ Insert Cells. The Insert Cells dialog box appears.

3. Choose one of the following options, and then choose OK:

   - Select Shift Cells Right to insert cells in the position of the selection and move the originally selected cells to the right.

   - Select Shift Cells Down to insert cells in the position of the selection and move the originally selected cells down.

   - Select Insert Entire Row to insert a row(s) and move the original selection down.

   - Select Insert Entire Column to insert a column(s) and move the original selection to the right.

If you selected rows, the rows are moved down to make room for the inserted rows. If you selected columns, the columns are moved to the right so that the new columns can be inserted.

You can also use either of the following methods to add a row or column:

- With the insertion point in the last cell, press Tab to add another row at the end of a table.

- To add a column on the right edge of the table, select the end-of-row marks and then click on the Insert Cells button on the Standard toolbar choose InsertEntire-Column in the Insert Cells dialog box, and then choose OK.

To quickly change the width of a column, position the mouse pointer on the column's boundary (the border or gridline), and then drag it to the left to decrease the width or to the right to increase the width. As you drag, the mouse pointer appears as two vertical lines with horizontal arrows attached.

To change the column width with the mouse, use one of the following methods:

- Drag the column boundary to change the width of the column to the right of the column in proportion so that the overall width of the table is not changed.

- Hold down the Shift key while you drag to change the widths of the column and the table.

- Hold down the Ctrl key while you drag the column boundary to change its size and simultaneously change all columns to the right to the same width without changing the width of the table.

- Choose Table ➤ Distribute Columns Evenly or click on the Distribute Columns Evenly button on the Tables and Borders toolbar to change the width of selected columns or cells so they are equal.

To change the width of a column or a cell to exact specifications, follow these steps:

1. Select the cells or columns whose widths are to be changed.

2. Choose Table ➤ Cell Height and Width, and then choose the Column tab.

3. Select any of the following options, and then choose OK:

   - Specify the width of the selected cell or column in the Width of Column *No.* text box.

   - Specify the amount of blank space between the column boundaries and the cell contents in the Space between Columns text box.

   - Choose Previous Column to select the previous column in the table.

   - Choose Next Column to select the next column in the table.

   - Choose AutoFit to automatically adjust the widths of selected columns to their minimum widths.

To quickly change the height of a row, display the table in Page Layout view, and then drag the row marker at the lower edge of the row on the vertical ruler. The size of the table changes proportionally.

To quickly change the height of several rows so that they are of equal height, select a cell in each row, and then choose Table ➤ Distribute

Rows Evenly or click on the Distribute Rows Evenly button on the Tables and Borders toolbar.

To specify the exact row height and set other row formatting options, follow these steps:

1. Select the row to be changed.

2. Choose Table ➤ Cell Height and Width, and then choose the Row tab.

3. Change any of the following options, and then choose OK:

   - In the Height of Row *No.* drop-down list, select Auto to allow Word to adjust the height automatically; or select At Least, and then specify a minimum row height or Exactly, and then specify an exact row height in the At text box.

   - Specify the distance from the left margin to the left edge of the row in the Indent from Left text box.

   - Select the Allow Row to Break Across Pages checkbox (selected by default) to split a table across a page break at the selected row.

   - In the Alignment area, choose Left to align the row along the left margin, Center to align the row between the left and right margins, or Right to align the row along the right margin.

   - Choose Previous Row to select the previous table row.

   - Choose Next Row to select the next table row.

Formatting a Table

Use Table AutoFormat to apply predefined styles to a new or existing table and to size the table automatically. To format a table with Table AutoFormat, follow these steps:

1. Position the insertion point in the table, and then click on the Table AutoFormat button on the Tables and Borders toolbar, or choose Table ➤ Table AutoFormat to display its dialog box.

2. Highlight the predefined border and shading format for the table in the Formats list box.

3. Choose any of the following options to define the format for the table, and then choose OK:

   • In the Formats to Apply area, select the corresponding checkbox to apply the Borders, Shading, Font, or Color specified in the format. To automatically adjust the size of the table to fit its contents, select the AutoFit checkbox.

   • In the Apply Special Formats To area, select the corresponding checkbox to apply special formats to Heading Rows, the First Column, Last Row, and Last Column, depending on the selected format.

To place text or a graphic between table rows, position the insertion point in a cell in the row at which the table is to be divided, and then choose Table ➤ Split Table. A paragraph mark is inserted above the row where the table is split. Delete the paragraph mark to reunite the table.

You can also align the contents of selected cells. To do so, click on the Align Top, Center Vertically, or Align Bottom button on the Tables and Borders toolbar to align the contents within those cells.

To number selected cells, click on the Numbering button on the Formatting toolbar. The cells are numbered from left to right across the rows, row by row.

Selecting Cells, Rows, Columns, or Data

You can select items in a table in several ways:

• Drag over text in a cell to select the text.

• Click in the *cell selection bar* (the left margin of the cell) to select the cell.

• Click in the *row selection bar* (the left page margin beside the row) to select a row. Or, choose Table ➤ Select Row to select the entire row that contains the cell in which the insertion point is positioned.

• Position the mouse pointer on the column's top gridline until it appears as a heavy, black downward-pointing arrow, and then click to select the column. Or, choose Table ➤ Select Column to select the column that contains the cell in which the insertion point is positioned.

• Hold down the Shift key while you click another cell, row, or column to extend the selection.

• Hold down the Shift key while pressing any of the arrow keys to extend a selection.

• Choose Table ➤ Select Table to select the entire table.

• Press Tab to select the contents of the next cell, or press Shift+Tab to select the contents of the previous cell.

Table of Contents

In Word, a table of contents is a list of document headings and the pages on which they appear. You can have a maximum of nine levels of table of contents headings in your document.

You can create entries in your document for the table of contents in two basic ways—by applying Word's built-in heading styles to the headings in your document, or by inserting TC (table of contents) field codes in the document. When you compile the table of contents, a TOC field is inserted in your document. To quickly go to a page in your document, double-click on its page number in the table of contents.

Creating a Table of Contents Using Heading Styles

To create a table of contents using Word's built-in heading styles, follow these steps:

1. Apply one of Word's built-in heading styles to each heading in your document that will appear in the table of contents.

2. Position the insertion point where you want to place the table of contents.

3. Choose Insert ➤ Index and Tables, and then choose the Table of Contents tab.

4. Choose any of the following options, and then choose OK:

- Select one of Word's six predefined table formats in the Formats list box. Or, to create your own style, choose From Template and then click on Modify to display the Style dialog box.

- Select the Show Page Numbers checkbox to display page numbers in the table of contents.

- Select the Right Align Page Numbers checkbox to align the page numbers in the table of contents along the right margin.

- Adjust the number in the Show Levels text box to show how many heading levels you want to appear in the table of contents.

- Select the character in the Tab Leader drop-down list that is to appear before the page numbers in the table of contents.

Creating a Table of Contents Using Other Styles

To create a table of contents using other styles, follow these steps:

1. Position the insertion point where you want to place the table of contents, choose Insert ➤ Index and Tables, and then choose the Table of Contents tab.

2. Select the format for the table of contents in the Formats list box.

3. Choose Options to display the Table of Contents Options dialog box.

4. Choose either of the following options:

- Select the Styles checkbox (selected by default). In the Available Styles area, find each style in your document that you want to use for a table of contents level, and then type the number of the level for that style in the corresponding TOC Level text box. Highlight a level number for a style you do not want in the table of contents in the corresponding TOC

Level text box, and then press Backspace or Delete to remove its level number.

- If you marked selected text in a document by inserting TC field codes along with any formatting switches, select the Table Entry Fields checkbox.

5. Choose OK in the Table of Contents Options dialog box, and then choose OK in the Index and Tables dialog box to create the table of contents.

To restore the table of contents settings to Word's defaults, including the original heading levels and clearing the Table Entry Fields checkbox, choose Reset in the Table of Contents Options dialog box.

Editing the Table of Contents

To edit the text that appears in a table of contents, edit the text in the heading in your document. Or, you can edit your document, and then update the TOC field to change the page numbers that it contains.

To edit a table of contents, follow these steps:

1. Position the insertion point in the table of contents and then press F9. Or, right-click on the field to display its shortcut menu and then select Update Field. The Update Table of Contents dialog box appears.

2. Choose Update Page Numbers Only to change only the page numbers of the headings in the table of contents, or choose Update Entire Table to change both the headings and the corresponding page numbers.

3. Choose OK.

Table of Figures

Use a table of figures to list figures, illustrations, charts, slides, or photographs in the sequence in which they appear in your document. You can create the entries for the table of figures using the captions inserted with Insert ➤ Caption, by applying the same unique style to all the captions in the document, or by marking each caption as an entry with the TC (table of contents) field code.

Creating a Table of Figures Using Automatic Captions

To create a table of figures using automatic captions, follow these steps:

1. Position the insertion point where you want to place the table of figures, choose Insert ➤ Index and Tables, and then choose the Table of Figures tab.

2. In the Caption Label list box, select the label assigned to the captions in your document that you want to appear in the table of figures.

3. Select one of Word's five predefined formats for the table of figures in the Formats list box. Alternatively, choose From Template in the Formats list box, and then choose Modify to display the Style dialog box to create a custom format for the table of figures.

4. Choose any of the following options, and then choose OK.

   • Select the Show Page Numbers checkbox to display page numbers in the table.

   • Select the Right Align Page Numbers checkbox to align page numbers in the table of figures along the right margin.

   • Select the Include Label and Number checkbox to include the caption labels in the table of figures along with the text that you added to the caption.

   • Select the character in the Tab Leader drop-down list that is to appear before the page numbers in the table of figures.

Creating a Table of Figures Using Styles or TC Entries

To create a table of figures using styles or TC entries, follow these steps:

1. Apply the same unique style to each caption that you want to appear in the table of figures or insert the TC field code for each caption.

2. Position the insertion point where you want to place the table of figures, select Insert ➤ Index and Tables, and then choose the Table of Figures tab.

3. Choose Options to display the Table of Figures Options dialog box.

4. Choose from the following options:

   • Select the Style checkbox, and then select the style you applied to the captions in the corresponding drop-down list.

   • To compile the table of figures if you marked the captions as entries with the TC (table of contents) field code, select the Table Entry Fields checkbox, and then select the first letter of the caption labels in the Table Identifier drop-down list.

5. Choose OK in the Table of Figures Options dialog box, and then choose OK in the Index and Tables dialog box.

Tabs

By default, tab stops are set at a distance of 0.5 inches between the left and right margins. To move to the next tab stop, press Tab to insert a tab character.

Click on the Show/Hide ¶ button on the Standard toolbar to toggle on the display of tab characters on your screen.

Setting Tab Stops

To set tab stops for a paragraph, follow these steps:

1. Position the insertion point in the paragraph whose tab stops you want to change.

2. Select Format ➤ Tabs to display the Tabs dialog box.

3. Choose any of the following options, and then choose OK:

   • Type a location for a new tab stop in the Tab Stop Position text box, or select an existing tab stop in the list box.

- Adjust the measurement in the Default Tab Stops text box to reset the distance between the default tab stops in the paragraph.

- In the Alignment area, choose Left to align the text to the right of the tab stop, Center to align the text at the center, Right to align the text to the left of the tab stop, Decimal to align the decimals within text at the tab stop, or Bar to place a vertical bar at the tab stop.

- In the Leader area, select None, Dots, Dashes, or Underline as the repeating character you want to appear before the tab stop.

- Choose Set to set the tab stop that appears in the Tab Stop Position text box.

- Choose Clear to remove the tab stop that appears in the Tab Stop Position text box.

- Choose Clear All to remove all tab stops in the active paragraph except the tab stops set in the Default Tab Stops text box.

To quickly set tab stops in the paragraph that contains the insertion point, click on the *Typeof* Tab button on the left side of the horizontal ruler until the type of tab you want to set is displayed on the button, and then click in the position for the tab on the ruler.

Template

You can use a template file to save the styles, formatting, and text that you use in Word documents that are similar to one another. You can also place AutoText entries and macros used for similar documents in the template. To create a document using the styles, formatting, text, AutoText entries, and macros that are saved in the template file, open a new document based on the template.

Creating a Document Based on a Template

Word's template files are stored in various folders in the c:\msoffice\templates folder. By default, all new documents are created with the Normal .dot template.

To create a document based on a different template, follow these steps:

1. Choose File ➤ New to display the New dialog box.

2. Select the tab that describes the type of document you want to create.

3. Click on the icon of the template you want to use to display its contents in the Preview area.

4. If necessary, select Document (selected by default) in the Create New area.

5. Choose OK.

By default, the templates appear as captioned icons in the list box that appears on the tab that is displayed in the New dialog box. Click on the List button to display the templates' icons and captions in a list; click on the Details button to display the templates' icons with details such as the size and type of each template file, and the date each was last modified; or click on the Large Icons button to return the list box display to the default captioned icons.

Creating a New Template

To create a new template, follow these steps:

1. Choose File ➤ New to display the New dialog box.

2. If necessary, select the tab that describes the type of document template you want to create, and then select the icon of the template on which to base the new template.

3. Choose Template in the Create New area, and then choose OK.

4. Make the necessary changes to the template. For example, type any text, create any macros or AutoText entries, define the page setup, customize the toolbars, and create any styles necessary for the documents that will be created based on the template.

5. Click on the Save button on the Standard toolbar, or choose File ➤ Save (Ctrl+S) to display the Save As dialog box. Word automatically selects the Templates folder in which to store the file, and adds the .DOT extension to the name you enter in the File Name text box.

6. If necessary, double-click on the folder in which to store the new template file in the Save In list box. Alternatively, place the template file in the Templates folder so that it will appear on the General tab in the New dialog box.

7. Type a name for the template in the File Name text box.

8. Choose Save in the Save As dialog box.

9. Click on the Document Close button or choose File ➤ Close to close the new template file.

To edit a template, open the .DOT file that contains the template, and then make the necessary changes as you would in a regular document file, following these steps:

1. Click on the Open button on the Standard toolbar, or choose File ➤ Open (Ctrl+O) to display the Open dialog box.

2. Select Document Templates (*.dot) in the Files of Type drop-down list.

3. If necessary, select the `c:program files\ msoffice\templates` folder in the Look In drop-down list, and then double-click on the folder in the Look In list box that contains the template you want to edit.

4. Highlight the template file to be edited in the Look In list box.

5. Choose Open in the Open dialog box.

6. Make the necessary changes to the template.

7. Click on the Save button on the Standard toolbar to save the template to the same filename.

8. Click on the Document Close button, double-click on the Document Control icon, or choose File ➤ Close to close the new template file.

Managing Templates

You can attach a different template to the active document, copy template items to other templates, or customize template items. Here are the steps:

1. Choose Tools ➤ Templates and Add-Ins to display the Templates and Add-ins dialog box.

2. Choose any of the following options:

   - Type the path and name of the template to attach to the current document in the Document Template text box. Or, select Attach to display the Attach Template dialog box, double-click on the folder that contains the template you want to attach to the current document, highlight the name of the template in the Look In list box, and then choose Open. Select the Automatically Update Document Styles checkbox to replace the styles in the current document with those of the same name in the attached template.

   - In the Global Templates and Add-ins list box, select the checkbox of any template that you want to be available whenever you start Word. To add another template to the Global Templates and Add-ins list box, choose Add to display the Add Template dialog box, select the name of a template file in the Look In list box, and then choose OK. To remove a template from the Global Templates and Add-ins list box, highlight the name of the template, and then choose Remove.

- Choose Organizer to display the Organizer dialog box when you want to copy styles, macros, AutoText, and toolbars to other documents or templates.

3. Choose OK.

Toolbars

You can customize Word's built-in toolbars or create entirely new toolbars to use. Toolbar buttons can be assigned to commands, macros, AutoText entries, fonts, menus, and styles for easy access.

You can drag a toolbar anywhere on your screen. If you drag it into the document window, it becomes a floating toolbar. You can drag the edge of a floating toolbar to change its shape, or you can click on its Close button to hide the toolbar. You can also dock toolbars vertically along the left or right edge of the window or horizontally above Word's status bar.

Creating or Editing Toolbars

To create or edit a toolbar, follow these steps:

1. Choose Tools ➤ Customize, or choose View ➤ Toolbars ➤ Customize to display the Customize dialog box.

2. Choose any of the following options on the Toolbars tab:

- Select the checkbox of any toolbar you want to display in the Toolbars list box.

- Choose New to display the New Toolbar dialog box. Type a name for the toolbar in the Toolbar Name text box, select the template in which to store the toolbar in the Make Toolbar Available To drop-down list, and then choose OK to add the new toolbar to the bottom of the Toolbars list box. The new toolbar appears on your screen.

- Choose Rename to display the Rename Toolbar dialog box, type a different name for the highlighted toolbar in the Toolbar Name text box, and then choose OK.

- Choose Delete to delete the custom toolbar selected in the Toolbars list box. Choose OK to confirm that the toolbar is to be deleted.

- Choose Reset to display the Reset Toolbar dialog box for the built-in toolbar selected in the Toolbars list box. Select the template in which the defaults for the toolbar are to be returned, and then choose OK to reset the toolbar.

3. Choose any of the following options on the Commands tab to customize an existing toolbar:

- Select the template in which you want the changes made to the toolbar to appear in the Save In drop-down list.

- To add a button, select an item in the Categories list box. The item's built-in buttons are displayed in the Commands area. Drag the button to its new location on a displayed toolbar.

- Choose Description to see a description of the selected command.

- To delete a button from a displayed toolbar, drag the button off the toolbar.

- To move a toolbar button on a displayed toolbar, drag the button to a different location or to a different displayed toolbar.

- To copy a button, press Ctrl while dragging the button to a different location or toolbar.

4. Choose any of the following options on the Options tab to customize the selected toolbar:

- Select the Large Icons checkbox to increase the size of the buttons on each toolbar that is displayed.

- Select the Show ScreenTips on Toolbars checkbox (selected by default) to display the name and a short description of a button's function when the mouse points to it.

- Select the Show Shortcut Keys in ScreenTips checkbox to display the shortcut keys that are assigned to a button in the ScreenTip that appears when the mouse points to it.

5. Choose Close in the Customize dialog box.

You can also copy a button on a displayed toolbar to another toolbar, or delete a button on a displayed toolbar without displaying the Customize dialog box. Here's how:

- To copy another button to a displayed toolbar, hold down Ctrl+Alt while you drag the button.

- To remove a button from a displayed toolbar, hold down the Alt key while you drag the button off the toolbar.

Track Changes

You can track the changes made by others to a document. The changes appear both on screen and in the printed document in the form of underline and strikethrough characters. If more than one person revises a document for which you are tracking changes, their track change marks appear in different colors. The name of the reviser and the date and time of the change is displayed when track changes are reviewed.

Comparing Versions of a Document

If you have two documents with different filenames or that are in different directories, you can compare the original document to the edited version and add track change marks to the edited document. To do so, follow these steps:

1. With the edited document active, choose Tools ➤ Track Changes ➤ Compare Documents.

2. Select the name of the original version of the document in the Look In list box, and then choose Open. The changes made in the edited version appear as track change marks in the edited document.

You can accept or reject the tracked changes that appear in the edited document the same way you do in a revised document.

Marking Changes

When track change marking is turned on in a document, you can display or hide track change marks and modify the format of the marks. Word keeps track of changes even if they are not displayed in the document.

To quickly turn on track change marking in the active document, double-click on TRK on the status bar.

To specify the track change marking options, follow these steps:

1. Choose Tools ➤ Track Changes ➤ Highlight Changes to display the Highlight Changes dialog box.

2. Select the Track Changes While Editing checkbox to turn on track change marking in the document.

3. If you want to suppress the display of track change marks on your screen, clear the Highlight Changes on Screen checkbox.

4. To suppress the printing of the track change marks, clear the Highlight Changes in Printed Document checkbox.

5. To change the format of the track change marks in the document, choose Options to display the Track Changes tab, choose any of the following options, and then choose OK:

- In the corresponding Mark drop-down list, select the character or attribute with which to mark inserted and deleted text, changed formatting, and to indicate which lines of text were revised.

- In the corresponding Color drop-down list, select the color to apply to inserted and deleted text, changed formatting, and for revision lines.

6. Choose OK in the Highlight Changes dialog box.

To turn off track change marking in the document, clear the Track Changes While Editing checkbox and then choose OK in the Highlight Changes dialog box.

You can also choose Tools ➤ Options and then select the Track Changes tab to change the format of the track change marks.

Merging Tracked Changes

When others have added comments or track change marks to your document, you can insert their marked comments and changes in the original document. By default, Word assigns one of eight colors to the comments and track change marks. If more than eight reviewers revise the document, the same colors are used again.

To merge the tracked changes made by others to your document, follow these steps:

1. Activate the revised document.

2. Choose Tools ➤ Merge Documents to display the Select File to Merge into Current Document dialog box.

3. Select the name of the original document in the Look In list box, and then choose Open to merge the tracked changes into the original document.

If you sent a document to all reviewers simultaneously by electronic mail, double-click on the document's icon when the mail is returned. Choose OK to confirm that you want to merge the tracked changes, and then choose OK again to merge the tracked changes into the original document. Repeat this process for each reviewer's document.

Reviewing Tracked Change Marks

You can review each tracked change and either accept or reject its inclusion in the document. Here are the steps:

1. With the revised document active on your screen, choose Tools ➤ Track Changes ➤ Accept or Reject Changes.

2. Select one of the following options in the View area to specify which changes are to be reviewed:

   - Choose Changes with Highlighting to display the document with all the track change marks in it.

   - Choose Changes without Highlighting to display the document as it would appear if all the changes were accepted.

   - Choose Original to display the document as it would appear if all the changes were rejected.

3. Choose → Find to highlight the next marked change, or choose ← Find to highlight the previous marked change.

4. To include the proposed change in your document, choose Accept. To remove the marked change, choose Reject.

5. To change the acceptance or rejection of the last marked change, choose Undo.

6. When you are finished reviewing the marked changes, select Cancel or Close to return to the document.

To accept or reject all the tracked changes without reviewing them first, choose Accept All or Reject All in the Accept or Reject Changes dialog box, and then choose Yes to confirm the acceptance or rejection of the tracked changes.

Undo/Redo

Word tracks your last few editing changes. You can use Undo to reverse the last several actions you performed, and you can use Redo to reverse the last action or the last several actions you canceled.

- To reverse your last action, click on the Undo button on the Standard toolbar or choose Edit ➤ Undo (Ctrl+Z).

- To reverse your last several actions, select the Undo drop-down list on the Standard toolbar, and then select the action you want to undo.

- To immediately reverse the last undone action, click on the Redo button on the Standard toolbar or select Edit ➤ Redo (Ctrl+Y).

- To reverse the last several actions, click on the Redo drop-down list on the Standard toolbar, and then select the action you want to reverse.

User Information

Information about the person who uses Word appears on the User Information tab in the Options dialog box. The items displayed are inserted as the return address for envelopes and labels, the author of a file, when reviewing revision marks, and as the initials used when creating comments.

Editing the User Information

To revise the user information, follow these steps:

1. Choose Tools ➤ Options and select the User Information tab.

2. In the Name text box, type the name you want to appear in the AUTHOR field of a file's summary information and when reviewing revision marks.

3. Type the initials you want to use for your comments in the Initials text box.

4. If necessary, type the name and address you want to use as the return address on envelopes or labels in the Mailing Address text box.

5. Choose OK in the Options dialog box.

If you have used Tools ➤ Envelopes and Labels to create an envelope with a return address and saved the return address as the default, the correct return address is already entered in the Mailing Address text box.

Versions

You can save multiple versions of a document in a single file instead of saving each version in a separate file. When you use the new Versioning feature, Word saves snapshots of the changes made instead of saving the entire version of the document.

Managing Document Versions

The versions of the active document can be opened for review, editing, and printing, or you can delete a version you no longer need. Follow these steps:

1. Choose File ➤ Versions to display the Versions In *Filename* dialog box.

2. Highlight the version of the document to be managed in the Existing Versions list box.

3. Select any of the following options for the selected version:

   - Choose Open to open the highlighted version of the document. Both the originally opened version and the highlighted version appear in tiled windows on your screen, and the highlighted version is active.

   - Choose Delete, and then choose Yes to delete the highlighted version.

   - Choose View Comments to display the View Comments dialog box with the full text of the comments that were entered by the highlighted version's author, and then choose Close to return to the Versions In *Filename* dialog box.

4. If necessary, choose Close to return to your document.

Saving a Version of a Document

To save a version of a document, follow these steps:

1. Choose File ➤ Versions to display the Versions In *Filename* dialog box.

2. Choose Save Now, type your comments in the Comments on Version text box, and then choose OK in the Save Version dialog box.

3. Click on the Save button on the Standard toolbar to save your document.

Each new version you save appears at the top of the Existing Versions list box in the Versions In *Filename* dialog box. Multiple versions of a document increase the size of its file.

To have Word automatically save a new version of the document each time it is closed, select the Automatically Save a Version on Close checkbox, and then choose Close to return to your document. Click on the Save button on the Standard toolbar to save the document.

You can also save the a version of the active document by choosing File ➤ Save As and then choosing Save Version to display the Save Version dialog box. Type your comments in the Comments on Version text box, and then choose OK.

Saving a Version as a Separate File

You can save an open version of a document in a separate file. Do so when you want to compare two versions of a document or when sending a version for review by other editors so that they cannot open other versions of the document.

Each time you open a highlighted version of the document, its name appears along with the date and time the version was created and "version"

on its title bar. When you save the version, you can either specify a different filename or accept the filename assigned to the version.

To save a version as a separate file, follow these steps:

1. Choose File ➤ Versions to display the Versions In *Filename* dialog box.

2. Highlight the version of the document to be saved as a separate file in the Existing Versions list box, and then choose Open.

3. Click on the Save button on the Standard toolbar.

4. If necessary, type a different name for the file in the File Name text box.

5. Choose Save to save the version to the specified filename.

View

Change the way your document appears on screen and the way you work with the text in it by changing the view. Each view is designed for a specific task.

Changing the View

To change to another view, select from the following options:

- Click on the Normal View button by the horizontal scroll bar or choose View ➤ Normal to work more quickly as you create, edit, and format your documents. In Normal view, the formatting applied to text appears on screen, but the page layout does not. To work even faster while in Normal view, limit the number of font sizes and the alignments and spacing available. To do so, select the Draft Font checkbox on the View tab in the Options dialog box.

- Click on the Online Layout View button by the horizontal scroll bar, or choose View ➤ Online Layout to make it easier to read a document on your screen. Online Layout view is useful when reading or editing the text of a document.

- Click on the Page Layout View button by the horizontal scroll bar, or choose View ➤ Page Layout to display and edit a document just as it will appear when printed. Use Page Layout view to make any necessary formatting changes to the document's appearance.

- To control how much of the document is displayed, click on the Outline View button on the horizontal scroll bar, or choose View ➤ Outline. In Outline view, you can easily change the arrangement of text in the document or the structure of the document.

- Click on the Master Document View button on the Outlining toolbar or choose View ➤ Master Document to control the arrangement of subdocuments in a long document.

- Click on the Print Preview button on the Standard toolbar or select File ➤ Print Preview to display the document at a smaller magnification to see its overall appearance before it is printed.

- To display more of the worksheet or document on screen, choose View ➤ Full Screen. All toolbars, menus, scroll bars, rulers, and the status bar and Windows taskbar are removed. Click on the Close Full Screen button that appears in its own toolbar while you are in Full Screen view or press Esc to redisplay the screen items.

Word Count

You can display the number of words, characters, pages, paragraphs, and lines in the current document. The character count includes punctuation

marks, numbers, and letters. The line count includes blank lines added after paragraphs. However, the statistics displayed for the active document do not include its headers and footers.

Displaying Document Statistics

To display statistics for a document, follow these steps:

1. Choose Tools ➤ Word Count to display the Word Count dialog box with the number of pages, words, characters, paragraphs, and lines in the active document displayed in the Statistics area.

2. If necessary, select the Include Footnotes and Endnotes checkbox to include the pages, words, characters, paragraphs, and lines in the footnotes or endnotes of a document in the statistics.

3. Choose Close to return to your document.

You can add any of the word count statistics to a document using the corresponding field code for the statistic.

Zoom

You can adjust the magnification of the characters displayed on your screen. Enlarge the magnification to make the characters easier to read, or reduce it to display the overall effect of an entire page.

Adjusting the Magnification

The percentage of magnification is the amount the data is reduced or enlarged on your screen in relation to its normal size. The magnification appears only on your screen, not on a page printed while the magnification is in effect.

To enlarge or reduce the magnification of the data displayed on your screen, select a different

INDEX

Note to the Reader: First level entries are in **bold**. Page numbers in **bold** indicate the principal discussion of a topic or the definition of a term. Page numbers in *italic* indicate illustrations.

— **E** —

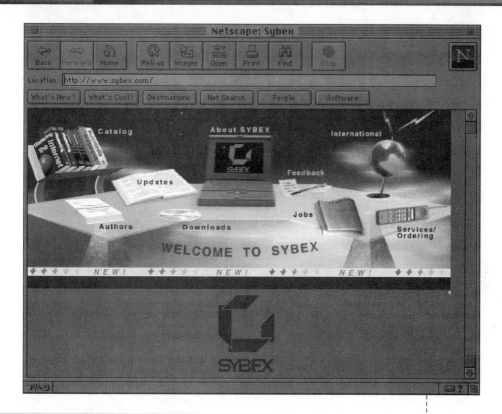